Handbook Series in Occupational Health Sciences

Series Editors

Kevin Daniels, University of East Anglia, Norwich Business School, Norwich, UK

Johannes Siegrist, Centre for Health and Society, Faculty of Medicine, Heinrich-Heine-Universität Düsseldorf, Düsseldorf, Nordrhein-Westfalen, Germany

The Handbook Series in Occupational Health Sciences offers a unique opportunity to get acquainted with robust updated evidence on specific topics of key interest in occupational health research and practice. The series provides a venue for the large amount of significant recent scientific advances in research on occupational health due to the overriding importance of work and employment in developed and rapidly developing countries. The series is interdisciplinary, encompassing insights from: occupational medicine, epidemiology, ergonomics, economics, occupational health psychology, health and medical sociology, amongst others. Volumes in the series will cover topics such as socioeconomic determinants of occupational health; disability, work and health; management, leadership and occupational health; and health implications of new technologies at work and of new employment-related global threats. With a broad scope of chapters dealing with in-depth aspects of the volume's themes, this handbook series complements more traditional publication formats in the field (e.g. textbooks; proceedings), using a new system of online updating and providing explanatory figures and tables. Written by an international panel of eminent experts, the volumes will be useful to academics, policy researchers, advanced students and high-level practitioners (e.g. consultants, government policy advisors).

Morten Wahrendorf • Tarani Chandola •
Alexis Descatha
Editors

Handbook of Life Course Occupational Health

With 66 Figures and 7 Tables

🐴 Springer

Editors
Morten Wahrendorf
Medical Faculty
Heinrich-Heine-University Düsseldorf
Düsseldorf, Nordrhein-Westfalen
Germany

Tarani Chandola
Faculty of Social Sciences
University of Hong Kong
Hong Kong SAR, China

Alexis Descatha
Univ Angers, CHU Angers, Univ
Rennes, Inserm, EHESP, Irset (Institut de
recherche en santé, environnement et travail)
UMR_S 1085, SFR ICAT, Ester Team
Angers, France

CHU Angers
Poisoning Control Center-Clinical Data Center
Angers, France

Epidemiology and Prevention, Donald and
Barbara Zucker School of Medicine
Hofstra University Northwell Health
New York, NY, USA

ISSN 2730-7409 ISSN 2730-7417 (electronic)
Handbook Series in Occupational Health Sciences
ISBN 978-3-031-30491-0 ISBN 978-3-031-30492-7 (eBook)
https://doi.org/10.1007/978-3-031-30492-7

© Springer Nature Switzerland AG 2023

This work is subject to copyright. All rights are reserved by the Publisher, whether the whole or part of the material is concerned, specifically the rights of translation, reprinting, reuse of illustrations, recitation, broadcasting, reproduction on microfilms or in any other physical way, and transmission or information storage and retrieval, electronic adaptation, computer software, or by similar or dissimilar methodology now known or hereafter developed.
The use of general descriptive names, registered names, trademarks, service marks, etc. in this publication does not imply, even in the absence of a specific statement, that such names are exempt from the relevant protective laws and regulations and therefore free for general use.
The publisher, the authors, and the editors are safe to assume that the advice and information in this book are believed to be true and accurate at the date of publication. Neither the publisher nor the authors or the editors give a warranty, expressed or implied, with respect to the material contained herein or for any errors or omissions that may have been made. The publisher remains neutral with regard to jurisdictional claims in published maps and institutional affiliations.

This Springer imprint is published by the registered company Springer Nature Switzerland AG.
The registered company address is: Gewerbestrasse 11, 6330 Cham, Switzerland

Paper in this product is recyclable.

Series Preface

The Handbook Series in Occupational Health Sciences offers a unique opportunity to get acquainted with robust updated evidence on specific topics of key interest in occupational health research and practice. The series provides a venue for the large amount of significant recent scientific advances in research on occupational health due to the overriding importance of work and employment in developed and rapidly developing countries. The series is interdisciplinary, encompassing insights from: occupational medicine, epidemiology, ergonomics, economics, occupational health psychology, health and medical sociology, among others. Volumes in the series will cover topics such as socioeconomic determinants of occupational health; disability, work, and health; management, leadership, and occupational health; and health implications of new technologies at work and of new employment-related global threats. With a broad scope of chapters dealing with in-depth aspects of the volume's themes, this handbook series complements more traditional publication formats in the field (e.g., textbooks; proceedings), using a new system of online updating and providing explanatory figures and tables. Written by an international panel of eminent experts, the volumes will be useful to academics, policy researchers, advanced students, and high-level practitioners (e.g., consultants, government policy advisors).

Volume Preface

Occupational conditions have strong positive and negative effects on health and well-being. As occupational careers become more fragmented and precarious as a result of the profound changes in modern work, these health effects need to be studied from a life course perspective, analyzing discontinuities, interruptions, and the burden of cumulative exposures. This perspective complements and extends the mainstream approach in occupational health research, which deals with stable, static rather than dynamic, changing occupational conditions. This book is the first to provide a comprehensive overview of recent research developments along these lines. Among other things, it demonstrates the impact of early life on later occupational health and the long-lasting effects of mid-life occupational exposures on health in old age. These findings guide intervention approaches to promote healthy work.

The volume covers conceptual and methodological developments as well as reviews of recent research on the associations between occupational careers and health. It includes more traditional approaches, but places particular emphasis on the analysis of modern working and employment conditions, which are often characterized by flexibility, interruption, discontinuity, and marked mobility patterns. At the same time, cumulative disadvantage is emphasized in a life course perspective. A life course approach is becoming a leading perspective in many fields of social and behavioral research, including epidemiology. With this volume, we aim to produce the first comprehensive volume representing this new perspective.

After a brief introduction and background on pathways, the next set of chapters discuss the transformation of modern work with new technologies, with key methodological challenges presented. Topics covered in the subsequent chapters range from early-life effects using the example of mental health and genetic and epigenetic factors, to mid-life with exposure to chronic hazards at work (chemical, biomechanical, long working and shift work, psychosocial), to exposure to irregular and psychosocial hazards at work such as adverse employment histories, precarious and gig work, including a focus on gender. Occupational trajectories in the context of disability in general, or in relation to specific health conditions, are also analyzed, with a particular focus on pathways to retirement. Interventions and policy implications and future perspectives are presented in the final section.

We, the editors, are grateful to the authors who have given their time and expertise to contribute to this volume in the series.

We hope that readers will enjoy reading this book on the life course in occupational epidemiology, with very original insights contributed from each author.

We are grateful to Johannes Siegrist for inviting us on this adventure, and for the constructive and fruitful collaboration with John Jebaraj and the Springer Nature team involved in the production of the book.

Düsseldorf, Germany	Morten Wahrendorf
Hong Kong SAR, China	Tarani Chandola
Angers, France/New York, USA	Alexis Descatha
September 2023	Editors

Contents

1 **Introduction** 1
   Tarani Chandola, Morten Wahrendorf, and Alexis Descatha

Part I Background 15

2 **Two Pathways Between Occupation and Health** 17
   Melanie Bartley and David Blane

3 **Transformation of Modern Work, Rise of Atypical Employment, and Health** 27
   Werner Eichhorst and Arne L. Kalleberg

4 **The Impact of New Technologies on the Quality of Work** 41
   Karen Van Aerden, Christophe Vanroelen, and Jessie Gevaert

Part II Methodological Challenges 57

5 **Sequence Analysis and Its Potential for Occupational Health Studies** 59
   Matthias Studer and Nicola Cianferoni

6 **Job-Exposure Matrices: Design, Validation, and Limitations** 77
   Alexis Descatha, Bradley A. Evanoff, and Annette Leclerc

7 **Challenges of Large Cohort and Massive Data in Occupational Health** 95
   Ingrid Sivesind Mehlum and Michelle C. Turner

8 **Integration of Occupational Exposure into the Exposome** 121
   Jean-François Viel, Nathalie Bonvallot, and William Dab

9 **Methods in Modeling Life Course** 137
   Adrien Le Guillou and Pascal Wild

Part III Early Life Impact on Work and Health **155**

10 Genetics, Epigenetics, and Mental Health at Work 157
Jelena Bakusic, Olivia Lavreysen, and Lode Godderis

11 A Life Course Perspective on Work and Mental Health:
The Working Lives of Young Adults 175
Karin Veldman, Sander K. R. van Zon, Iris Arends,
Benjamin C. Amick III, and Ute Bültmann

Part IV Occupational Trajectories and Midlife Health: *Exposure
to Chronic Hazards at Work* **193**

12 Chemical Hazards at Work and Occupational Diseases Using
Job-Exposure Matrices 195
Irina Guseva Canu

13 Biomechanical Hazards at Work and Adverse Health Using
Job-Exposure Matrices 213
Johan H. Andersen, Bradley A. Evanoff, and Alexis Descatha

14 Long Working Hours and Health Effects 227
Marc Fadel, Jian Li, and Grace Sembajwe

15 Health Effects of Shift Work and Night Shift Work 245
Pascal Guénel and Damien Léger

16 Psychosocial Work Environment and Health: Applying
Job-Exposure Matrices and Work Organization and
Management Practice 267
S. Solovieva and Y. Roquelaure

17 Occupational Differences in Work-Related Mental Health:
A Life Course Analysis of Recent Trends in the European
Context 283
Tarani Chandola

Part V Occupational Trajectories and Midlife Health: *Exposure
to Irregular and Discontinued Hazards at Work* **301**

18 Adverse Employment Histories: Conceptual Considerations
and Selected Health Effects 303
Morten Wahrendorf and Johannes Siegrist

19	**Precarious Work and Health**	319
	Gillian Weston and Anne McMunn	
20	**Gig Work and Health**	343
	Hua Wei and Martie van Tongeren	
21	**Gender Differences in Work Participation over the Life Course and Consequences for Socioeconomic and Health Outcomes**	357
	Anne McMunn	

Part VI Occupational Trajectories in the Context of Disability and Ageing **375**

22	**Changing Experiences, Needs, and Supports Across the Life Course for Workers Living with Disabilities**	377
	Arif Jetha and Monique A. M. Gignac	
23	**Working Careers with Common Mental Disorders**	399
	Gunnel Hensing	
24	**Adverse Effect of Psychosocial Stressors at Work and Long Working Hours Along the Cardiovascular Continuum**	419
	Xavier Trudel, Mahée-Gilbert Ouimet, Alain Milot, and Chantal Brisson	
25	**Pathways to Retirement and Health Effects**	443
	Jenny Head, Maria Fleischmann, and Baowen Xue	

Part VII Interventions and Policy Implications **467**

26	**Worksite Health Promotion: Evidence on Effects and Challenges**	469
	Paula Franklin	
27	**Falling Sick While Working: An Overview of the EU-Level Policy Framework on Returning to Work Following Chronic Disease(s)**	493
	Mehtap Akgüç	
28	**The Role of Social and Labor Policies in Shaping Working Conditions Throughout the Life Course**	511
	Mariann Rigó and Thorsten Lunau	

Part VIII Future Perspectives 525

29 Occupational Trajectories and Health Inequalities in a Global Perspective 527
Johannes Siegrist and Michael Marmot

30 Conceptual and Methodological Directions of Occupational Life Course Research 545
Alexis Descatha, Tarani Chandola, and Morten Wahrendorf

Index 559

About the Series Editors

Kevin Daniels is a professor of Organizational Behavior at the University of East Anglia, United Kingdom. He has a Ph.D. in Applied Psychology (1992) and is a fellow of the British Psychological Society, the Academy of Social Sciences, and the Royal Society of Arts. His research covers approaches to health, safety, and well-being, originally with particular focus on the psychology of job design and more latterly an interest in multidisciplinary approaches to well-being. He has authored or coauthored over 90 peer-reviewed journal articles, 30 book chapters, and 20 books or major reports. From 2015 to 2021, he was lead investigator for an evidence program on work and well-being, one of the foundational research programs of the UK's What Works Centre for Wellbeing. From 2015 to 2019, he served as editor of the *European Journal of Work and Organizational Psychology* and also in associate editor positions at the *British Journal of Management, Human Relations*, and the *Journal of Occupational and Organizational Psychology*.

Johannes Siegrist is currently a senior professor of Work Stress Research at the Heinrich Heine University Duesseldorf in Germany. He received his Ph.D. in Sociology from the University of Freiburg i. Br. in 1969, and he held professorships for medical sociology at the Universities of Marburg and Duesseldorf from 1973 to 2012. He was a visiting professor at the Johns Hopkins University (USA) (1981) and at Utrecht University (NE) (1994). With his long-standing research on health-adverse psychosocial work environments and social inequalities in health, he has published more than 500 papers and book chapters and has written or edited several international books. In addition to his collaboration in distinct European research networks, he served as a consultant to the World Health Organization, and he chaired several national and international academic societies. Among other distinctions, he is a member of Academia Europaea (London) and a corresponding member of the Heidelberg Academy of Sciences.

About the Volume Editors

Morten Wahrendorf works at the Institute for Medical Sociology of the University Düsseldorf, Germany, where he leads the working group on "Work & Health." He has previously worked at the International Centre for Life-course Studies in Society and Health (ICLS) at the University College London. His main research areas are work stress, health inequalities, life course epidemiology, aging, and the comparative analyses of longitudinal cohort studies. He leads several projects that investigates both individual and national predictors of working conditions across the life course and their long-term effects on health at older ages. His research expertise spans different disciplines – including public health, epidemiology, statistics, and sociology.

Tarani Chandola is a professor of Medical Sociology. He is the head of the Department of Sociology and the director of the Methods Hub in the Faculty of the Social Sciences at the University of Hong Kong. He joined the University of Hong Kong in August 2021 and was formerly the head of the Department of Social Statistics at the University of Manchester. His research is primarily on the social determinants of health, focusing on health inequalities and psychosocial factors, social-biological research, and the analysis of longitudinal cohort studies.

Alexis Descatha is a professor of Occupational Health in Paris then in Angers (Western of France), at University of Angers/Inserm Irster/Ester, and leads the Clinical Toxicological Unit – Poison Control Center, in university hospital of Angers.

His research focuses on the epidemiology of work disorders, musculoskeletal, and other chronic diseases. He has interest on exposure assessment using a job exposure matrix and on performing systematic reviews.

As emergency physician, he also conducts research on emergencies in occupational settings and created the ICOH's scientific committee on Emergency Preparedness and Response, and involved in ICOH as board member in 2022–2024. He is the Editor-in-Chief of *Les Archives des Maladies Professionnelles et de l'Environnement*. Recently, he was appointed clinical professor of Occupational Medicine, Epidemiology, and Prevention at Hofstra School of Medicine, USA.

In 2021, he received the *Légion d'Honneur*. To promote transfer research to practitioners in occupational health in a Translational Epidemiology Center on Occupational Health, Toxicology, and Preparedness, he is presenting a *YouTube channel* (with University of Angers support). He is working also in promoting research in occupational health for different national and international agencies.

Contributors

Mehtap Akgüç European Trade Union Institute, Brussels, Belgium

IZA (Institute of Labor Economics), Bonn, Germany

Benjamin C. Amick III Department of Epidemiology, Fay W. Boozman College of Public Health, University of Arkansas for Medical Sciences, Little Rock, AR, USA

Winthrop P Rockefeller Cancer Institute, University of Arkansas for Medical Sciences, Little Rock, AR, USA

Johan H. Andersen Danish Ramazzini Centre, Department of Occupational Medicine – University Research Clinic, Goedstrup Hospital, Herning, Denmark

Iris Arends University of Groningen, University Medical Center Groningen, Department of Health Sciences, Community and Occupational Medicine, Groningen, The Netherlands

Arbo Unie, Utrecht, The Netherlands

Jelena Bakusic KU Leuven, Centre for Environment and Health, Leuven, Belgium

KU Leuven, University Psychiatric Centre KU Leuven (UPC KU Leuven), Kortenberg, Belgium

Melanie Bartley UCL, Institute of Epidemiology & Health Care, London, UK

David Blane Imperial College, London, UK

Nathalie Bonvallot Univ Rennes, EHESP, Inserm, Irset (Institut de recherche en santé, environnement et travail), Rennes, France

Chantal Brisson Social and Preventive Medicine Department, Université Laval, Québec City, QC, Canada

Population Health and Optimal Health Practices, CHU de Québec Research Center, Québec City, QC, Canada

Ute Bültmann University of Groningen, University Medical Center Groningen, Department of Health Sciences, Community and Occupational Medicine, Groningen, The Netherlands

Tarani Chandola Faculty of Social Sciences, University of Hong Kong, Hong Kong SAR, China

Nicola Cianferoni SECO State Secretariat for Economic Affairs and Institute for Sociological Research, Faculty of Social Sciences, University of Geneva, Geneva, Switzerland

William Dab Laboratoire MESuRS, Conservatoire national des Arts et Métiers, Paris, France

Catholic University of Paris, Paris, France

Alexis Descatha Univ Angers, CHU Angers, Univ Rennes, Inserm, EHESP, Irset (Institut de recherche en santé, environnement et travail), UMR_S 1085, SFR ICAT, Ester Team, Angers, France

CHU Angers, Poisoning Control Center-Clinical Data Center, Angers, France

Epidemiology and Prevention, Donald and Barbara Zucker School of Medicine, Hofstra University Northwell Health, New York, NY, USA

Werner Eichhorst IZA and University of Bremen, Bremen, Germany

Bradley A. Evanoff Division of General Medical Sciences, Washington University School of Medicine, St. Louis, MO, USA

Marc Fadel Research Institute for Environmental and Occupational Health (IRSET), UMR_S1085, University of Angers, Angers, France

Maria Fleischmann Rotterdam University of Applied Sciences, Research Center for Innovations in Care, Rotterdam, the Netherlands

Paula Franklin European Trade Union Institute (ETUI), Brussels, Belgium

Jessie Gevaert Interface Demography, Department of Sociology, Vrije Universiteit Brussel, Brussels, Belgium

Monique A. M. Gignac Institute for Work & Health, Toronto, ON, Canada

Dalla Lana School of Public Health, University of Toronto, Toronto, ON, Canada

Lode Godderis KU Leuven, Centre for Environment and Health, Leuven, Belgium

IDEWE, External Service for Prevention and Protection at Work, Heverlee, Belgium

Pascal Guénel Paris-Saclay University, UVSQ, Gustave Roussy, Inserm, CESP, Team Exposome and Heredity, Inserm, Villejuif, France

Irina Guseva Canu Department of Occupational and Environmental Health; Center for Primary Care and Public Health (Unisanté), University of Lausanne, Lausanne, Switzerland

Jenny Head Department of Epidemiology and Public Health, University College London, London, UK

Gunnel Hensing School of Public Health and Community Medicine, Institute of Medicine, The Sahlgrenska Academy at University of Gothenburg, Gothenburg, Sweden

Arif Jetha Institute for Work & Health, Toronto, ON, Canada

Dalla Lana School of Public Health, University of Toronto, Toronto, ON, Canada

Arne L. Kalleberg Department of Sociology, University of North Carolina, Chapel Hill, NC, USA

Olivia Lavreysen KU Leuven, Centre for Environment and Health, Leuven, Belgium

Adrien Le Guillou Department of Epidemiology, Emory University, Atlanta, GA, USA

Annette Leclerc Inserm UMS 011, Cohort in Population Unit, Villejuif, France

Damien Léger VIFASOM (ERC 7330 Vigilance Fatigue Sommeil et Santé Publique), Université Paris Cité, Paris, France

APHP, Hôtel-Dieu, Centre du Sommeil et de la Vigilance, Centre de ressources en pathologie professionnelle Sommeil Vigilance et Travail, Paris, France

Jian Li Department of Environmental Health Sciences, Fielding School of Public Health, School of Nursing, University of California, Los Angeles, CA, USA

Thorsten Lunau Institut für Sozialforschung und Sozialwirtschaft (iso) e.V., Saarbrücken, Germany

Michael Marmot Institute of Health Equity; University College London, London, UK

Anne McMunn Research Department of Epidemiology and Public Health, University College London, London, UK

Ingrid Sivesind Mehlum National Institute of Occupational Health (STAMI), Oslo, Norway

Institute of Health and Society, University of Oslo, Oslo, Norway

Department of Occupational and Environmental Medicine, Bispebjerg and Frederiksberg Hospitals, Copenhagen, Denmark

Department of Public Health, University of Copenhagen, Copenhagen, Denmark

Alain Milot Population Health and Optimal Health Practices, CHU de Québec Research Center, Québec City, QC, Canada

Medicine Department, Université Laval, Québec City, QC, Canada

Mahée-Gilbert Ouimet Social and Preventive Medicine Department, Université Laval, Québec City, QC, Canada

Department of Health Science, Université du Québec à Rimouski, Rimouski, QC, Canada

Mariann Rigó Institute of Medical Sociology, Centre for Health and Society, Medical Faculty and University Hospital Düsseldorf, Heinrich-Heine-University, Düsseldorf, Germany

Y. Roquelaure INSERM, EHESP, IRSET (Institut de Recherche en Santé, Environnement et Travail), UMR_S 1085, University of Angers, CHU Angers, Angers, France

University of Rennes, Rennes, France

Grace Sembajwe Department of Occupational Medicine, Epidemiology and Prevention, Donald and Barbara Zucker School of Medicine, Hosftra University Northwell Health, New York, NY, USA

Johannes Siegrist Centre for Health and Society, Institute of Medical Sociology, Medical Faculty, Heinrich Heine University of Düsseldorf, Düsseldorf, Germany

S. Solovieva Finnish Institute of Occupational Health, Helsinki, Finland

Matthias Studer LIVES Centre and Institute of Demography and Socioeconomics, Faculty of Social Sciences, University of Geneva, Geneva, Switzerland

Xavier Trudel Social and Preventive Medicine Department, Université Laval, Québec City, QC, Canada

Population Health and Optimal Health Practices, CHU de Québec Research Center, Québec City, QC, Canada

Michelle C. Turner Barcelona Institute for Global Health (ISGlobal), Barcelona, Spain

Universitat Pompeu Fabra (UPF), Barcelona, Spain

CIBER Epidemiología y Salud Pública (CIBERESP), Madrid, Spain

Karen Van Aerden Interface Demography, Department of Sociology, Vrije Universiteit Brussel, Brussels, Belgium

Martie van Tongeren Division of Population Health, Health Services Research & Primary Care, School of Health Sciences, University of Manchester, Manchester, UK

Sander K. R. van Zon University of Groningen, University Medical Center Groningen, Department of Health Sciences, Community and Occupational Medicine, Groningen, The Netherlands

Christophe Vanroelen Interface Demography, Department of Sociology, Vrije Universiteit Brussel, Brussels, Belgium

Karin Veldman University of Groningen, University Medical Center Groningen, Department of Health Sciences, Community and Occupational Medicine, Groningen, The Netherlands

Jean-François Viel Univ Rennes, CHU Rennes, Inserm, EHESP, Irset (Institut de recherche en santé, environnement et travail), Rennes, France

Morten Wahrendorf Centre for Health and Society, Institute of Medical Sociology, Medical Faculty, Heinrich Heine University of Düsseldorf, Düsseldorf, Germany

Hua Wei Division of Population Health, Health Services Research & Primary Care, School of Health Sciences, University of Manchester, Manchester, UK

Gillian Weston Research Department of Epidemiology & Public Health, University College London, London, UK

Pascal Wild PW Statistical Consulting, Laxou, France

Baowen Xue Department of Epidemiology and Public Health, University College London, London, UK

Introduction

Tarani Chandola, Morten Wahrendorf, and Alexis Descatha

Contents

Introduction	2
Concepts of the Life Course	2
Emerging Themes	11
Occupational Health in the Context of the COVID-19 Pandemic	11
Lack of Data from the Developing World	11
Lack of Relevant Data	12
Conclusion	12
Cross-References	12
References	13

Abstract

Occupational health is implicitly about the life course, even if the term has not been explicitly used in a lot of occupational health research. The chapter describes the contributions made by the chapters within this book in terms of key concepts of life course research – trajectories, transitions, turning points, culture and contextual influences, the timing of life events, linked lives, and adaptive strategies. The authors of the chapters demonstrate how life course occupational health is a

---

T. Chandola (✉)
Faculty of Social Sciences, University of Hong Kong, Hong Kong SAR, China
e-mail: chandola@hku.hk

M. Wahrendorf
Centre for Health and Society, Institute of Medical Sociology, Medical Faculty, Heinrich Heine University of Düsseldorf, Düsseldorf, Germany

A. Descatha
Univ Angers, CHU Angers, Univ Rennes, Inserm, EHESP, Irset (Institut de recherche en santé, environnement et travail), UMR_S 1085, SFR ICAT, Ester Team, Angers, France

CHU Angers, Poisoning Control Center-Clinical Data Center, Angers, France

Epidemiology and Prevention, Donald and Barbara Zucker School of Medicine, Hofstra University Northwell Health, New York, NY, USA

© Springer Nature Switzerland AG 2023
M. Wahrendorf et al. (eds.), *Handbook of Life Course Occupational Health*, Handbook Series in Occupational Health Sciences, https://doi.org/10.1007/978-3-031-30492-7_8

much broader topic than a standard list of occupational health risk factors, restricted to the working life course. They reveal a complexity of life course processes and concepts that are relevant to occupational health, encompassing occupational histories of exposure to toxic elements, the accumulation of these toxic elements over an occupational life history, the importance of taking into account the life course context of workers, such as gender and power relationships, the differentiation between aging, period, and cohort effects, and the recent changes in working life and related exposures to occupational risks in some industries and occupations. However, key gaps in our understanding of life course processes in occupational health remain, which are highlighted throughout the book.

Keywords

Trajectories · Transitions · Turning points · Timing · Sequence · Context · Linked Lives

Introduction

Occupational conditions exert powerful positive as well as negative effects on individual health and well-being. As occupational careers become more fragmented and insecure, resulting from far-reaching transformations of modern work, these health effects need to be studied in a life course perspective, analyzing discontinuities, interruptions, and the burden of cumulative exposure. The life course perspective complements and extends the mainstream approach in occupational health research that often deals with stable, static rather than dynamic, changing occupational conditions.

Occupational health is implicitly about the life course, even if the term "life course" has not been explicitly used in a lot of occupational health research. Exposures to hazardous working conditions have typically been analyzed in relation to long-term health outcomes, with research study designs following up workers' health even after they have left the specific workplace unit or have left the workforce. Some elements of time, such as changes through time from birth to death, are always implicit in any reference to the life course. However, the analysis of occupational health with an explicit reference to time is often missing. The chapters in this book are an attempt to explicitly refer to theories and concepts of the life course in relation to occupational health. Some authors in this book have explicitly used life course models, concepts, and frameworks to structure their chapters, while other authors touch upon concepts related to the life course. In this chapter, we discuss some of the concepts related to the life course and how they are used in the different chapters.

Concepts of the Life Course

The term "life course" is increasingly used in social and behavioral research. The popularity of life course theories in epidemiological research is partly because of the potential to integrate different explanations for individual or group differences in health, by including themes such as personality factors, life history, as well as current and previous social conditions and contextual effects that have often been researched in silos. However, there are considerable differences in the concepts and theories related to the life course, and the ways in which they have been applied in research. For example, the concept of "life course" is often conflated with the concepts of "life cycle" and "life span." Alwin distinguishes between different concepts of the term "life course" in research (Alwin 2012). It is commonly used to describe a progression through time, with the phrase "over the life course" being used to refer to events or processes that occur to people in chronological time, as they age or get older. A second use is in terms of stages of the life cycle, which has origins in biological processes such as a sequence of developmental changes by an organism from a primary form. Life cycles can also refer to the socially defined, age-related sequence of stages individuals pass through beginning with birth and ending with death. The life course often refers to events, transitions, and trajectories, a "study of a sequence of events," or life trajectories marked by a sequence of life events and transitions, with some changes in a person's status being more sudden, while other changes are not so abrupt, continuing the path of a preexisting trajectory. Concepts related to human development are also often inherent in life course research. In contrast to a life span perspective on human development, which an emphasis on growth, fertility, and reproduction, elder identified the social timetable of the life course, such as entry into the labor market, marriage, or retirement (Elder 1975). Epidemiological concepts of the life course often refer to early life experiences as risk factors for adult chronic diseases (Kuh and Ben-Shlomo 2004).

Wethington distinguishes between seven key concepts that are widely used by researchers using the life course perspective (Wethington 2005). This chapter uses her conceptual framework to highlight the life course concepts that are explicitly or implicitly discussed by the chapters within this book. It is important to note that while the occupational life course represents only a part of an individual's life span, many of the chapters extend their analysis of the life course beyond the working lifetime, to describe and analyze early life course influences on occupational health, as well as the health of individuals after they have left the labor force.

1. **Trajectories** are stable patterns of behavior or health that persist across time. They often have inertia and it is often not easy to change trajectories once they are set in motion. Trajectories that accumulate occupational health risk factors over the life course are an underlying concept for methodological tools like job-exposure matrices (JEMs) and concepts like the occupational exposome or the "worksome."

Descatha et al.'s ▶ Chap. 6, "Job-Exposure Matrices: Design, Validation, and Limitations," describes how JEMs are a powerful tool for exposure assessment in epidemiological studies, especially in population-level studies with limited occupational information. It is often difficult and complex to estimate occupational exposures over a working life course. Job-exposure matrices enable the estimation of life course occupational exposures based on job title and industry data, allowing researchers to assess the role of workplace factors on chronic and acute diseases beyond traditional occupational diseases.

Andersen et al.'s ▶ Chap. 13, "Biomechanical Hazards at Work and Adverse Health Using Job-Exposure Matrices," argues that the estimation of the occupational health risks of workplace biomechanical exposures is limited by the time and cost of detailed direct observational assessments of working conditions that include biomechanical exposures such as repeated, forceful hand motions, whole-body vibration, carrying or lifting heavy loads, and working in awkward postures. JEMs provide unbiased estimates of past biomechanical exposures across different jobs, thus enabling estimates of exposures across the life course and their association with chronic health conditions such as musculoskeletal disorders.

Guseva Canu's ▶ Chap. 12, "Chemical Hazards at Work and Occupational Diseases Using Job-Exposure Matrices," describes the developments in JEMs specific to chemical hazards at work. The chapter describes the evolution of chemical hazards JEMs from inhalation exposure at the workplace to other forms of exposure contact such as through dermal and ingested routes of contact and internalization of chemicals. These JEMs are particularly suitable for estimating the effects of emerging occupational health risk factors such as nanoparticles and nanomaterials, where individual-level worker exposure is hard to measure and quantify. This is another example of the use of JEMs in occupational life course risk estimation, which enables researchers to go beyond individual worker's work history and to draw potential causal links between occupational-level exposures over the working life course and later life ill-health and disease outcomes.

Roquelaure and Solovieva's ▶ Chap. 16, "Psychosocial Work Environment and Health: Applying Job-Exposure Matrices and Work Organization and Management Practice," describes the use of JEMs in relation to psychosocial risk factors at work. The use of JEMs to measure psychosocial exposures is perhaps more controversial than chemical or biomechanical hazards at work, because of the subjective nature of work-related psychosocial risk factors. The chapter highlights some key considerations for researchers using such JEMs to measure work-related psychosocial risk factors.

Mehlum and Turner's ▶ Chap. 7, "Challenges of Large Cohort and Massive Data in Occupational Health," describes the concept of the occupational exposome. The concept of the exposome, which was originally developed to better characterize environmental exposures over the life course, has tended to neglect work-related exposures. The collection of life course data on working life exposome (including occupational exposures as well as their interaction with nonoccupational factors) is now being made possible through the large cohort data collections in occupational health risks, as well as methodological advances in job coding algorithms from free-text job descriptions.

Viel et al.'s ▶ Chap. 8, "Integration of Occupational Exposure into the Exposome," further develops the concept of the occupational exposome by using the term "worksome" to describe cumulative occupational exposures over the life course. The chapter highlights several of the difficulties in the estimation of the worksome, but also some novel methodological tools to measure lifelong occupational exposures.

Wahrendorf and Siegrist's ▶ Chap. 18, "Adverse Employment Histories: Conceptual Considerations and Selected Health Effects," argues for the need to analyze dynamic work arrangements to understand occupational health risks, and in particular to consider the trajectories of employment conditions over an extended period of the life course. The authors use an accumulation model of psychosocial work stressors over the working life course to argue that workers employed in atypical employment are more often exposed to cumulative load of psychosocial adversity for longer periods of the life course, leading to chronic stress such as exhaustion and breakdown.

2. **Transitions** can be understood as changes in social roles or responsibilities, usually characterized as significant changes in the responsibilities of an existing role, such as a transformation in job or family responsibilities. Some transitions are gradual or incremental and are often accommodated within a person's ongoing trajectory. Other transitions are unexpected and stressful, which can lead to larger than expected changes in a person's trajectory. Within occupational health research, transitions often refer to stages of the life course when workers take on new roles (such as when they enter the labor market) or leave existing roles (such as when they retire). These stages of the life course can be characterized as sensitive periods during which changes that occur can get amplified in later life by setting people on different trajectories.

Siegrist and Marmot's ▶ Chap. 29, "Occupational Trajectories and Health Inequalities in a Global Perspective," highlights two stages of occupational careers which are crucial in generating occupation-related health inequalities: young adulthood when workers enter the labor market and during midlife when large parts of workers have achieved their main occupational position. Young adults who experience a disruption in entering the labor market, such as during recessions, have much higher risks of poor health compared to their age-peers who did not experience such disruptions. During midlife, there is consistent evidence of several highly prevalent chronic diseases and disorders due to exposure to a stressful psychosocial work environment. They argue that analyses that combine the occupational health risks across these different stages of the occupational life course are more powerful and revealing of occupational health risks than analysis of a single life course period.

Veldman et al.'s ▶ Chap. 11, "A Life Course Perspective on Work and Mental Health: The Working Lives of Young Adults," identifies young adulthood as a key life course stage for occupational health risks. The timing of early entry into the labor market puts young adult workers at a more disadvantaged position. De Groot and colleagues examined whether the timing and duration of mental health problems from childhood and young adulthood were associated with labor market participation in young adulthood (de Groot et al. 2021). Young adults with a long duration of internalizing and externalizing problems (i.e., accumulation of risk over three or more measurement waves) showed an increased risk of having no paid job. Young adults with an early onset and a short duration of internalizing and externalizing problems were not affected indicating a potential sensitive period. The chapter highlights studies that not only show the long-term impact of early life mental health problems on labor market participation, but also that the timing and duration of mental health problems matters.

Hensing's ▶ Chap. 23, "Working Careers with Common Mental Disorders," identifies two sensitive periods of the life course that are particularly important for occupational risks of poor mental health. They are the period of entering into the labor market and the period when reduced capacity to work develops. The timing of adverse experiences during entry into the first job can set in motion chains of risk that increase health problems later on in life. The other sensitive period when a worker's capacity to work reduces is an important stage for early interventions to reduce sickness absence later on in life.

3. **Turning points** are major transitions that are associated with major life changes or breaks in ongoing trajectories. Within occupational health, the onset of chronic illness or disability is often a key turning point in an occupational trajectory that can change workers' trajectories. Similarly, the period of retirement or leaving the labor market is another turning point which has the potential to disrupt pre-existing trajectories.

Jetha and Gignac's ▶ Chap. 22, "Changing Experiences, Needs, and Supports Across the Life Course for Workers Living with Disabilities," demonstrates the importance of a life course perspective in understanding the occupational health challenges faced by workers with disabilities which differ according to their life phase and career stage. Young adults with disabilities have limited access to high-quality employment, career progression, and workplace support. Older workers with disabilities face additional barriers at work and outside work that may limit their ability to participate meaningfully at work.

Akgüç's ▶ Chap. 27, "Falling Sick While Working: An Overview of the EU-Level Policy Framework on Returning to Work Following Chronic Disease(s)," highlights how life course changes in working lives has resulted in an increase in workers with long-term health conditions or disability. Her analysis of European Union–level policy initiatives in the context of return to work reveals "a lack of a comprehensive framework or a tailored approach to the work reintegration following chronic diseases during the occupational life course." Despite the recognition that chronic illness and the onset of disability represents a key turning point for many workers, there is often a lack of comprehensive policies at the national and international levels that address this period of the working life course.

Head, Fleischmann, and Xue in ▶ Chap. 25, "Pathways to Retirement and Health Effects," demonstrate how the life course perspective enables the integration of different theoretical frameworks on the effect of retirement on health such as role theory, continuity theory, and social capital theory. By defining retirement as a life course transition, the authors suggest that the retirement transition can lead to different health trajectories depending on the worker's current and past personal and environmental conditions, the timing and choice of their retirement process, and their postretirement environment and activities.

4. **Culture and contextual** influences refer to the wider social and cultural factors that not only affect the health of workers but influence their ability to adapt and change to external shocks and events. The socioeconomic background of workers, both in terms of their early childhood, as well as their current living and working conditions, have important contextual influences on workers' health. Access to high-quality occupational health services enable workers who experience an illness episode to return to work more quickly. Moreover, traumatic events that occur in specific historical periods could also have long-lasting effects on the health of workers that extend well beyond the period of trauma.

Bartley and Blane's ▶ Chap. 2, "Two Pathways Between Occupation and Health," refers to classic texts in occupational health such as Donald Hunter's *Diseases of Occupations*, but also to the importance of environmental risk factors such as asbestos fibers for people who lived near but had never worked in the asbestos factories of East London. A life course approach to occupational health does not mean a sole focus on occupational risk factors, but also includes other life course risk factors that arise from the environments and contexts those occupations are located.

They delineate two pathways between occupations and health. The first focuses on occupation-specific hazards, that not just arise from the occupations that workers find themselves in, but also from the toxic polluting environments that are created by certain industries. They develop the concept of "technical fragmentation" to characterize how occupational health physicians and epidemiologists process different types of knowledge and evidence to characterize these occupational hazards. The second pathway emphasizes the importance of social class in the accumulation of social advantage or disadvantage over the occupational life course. Worker's health in early old age and retirement "is influenced by both social conditions during the biological phase of childhood & adolescent growth and development and by social conditions during adulthood when biological functioning can be worn down either faster or more slowly than usual."

Eichhorst and Kalleber's ▶ Chap. 3, "Transformation of Modern Work, Rise of Atypical Employment, and Health," describes the growth of atypical or nonstandard work in many postindustrial labor markets. While atypical work might facilitate access to paid employment for some workers, they are also characterized by inequality, competition, insecurity, and lack of access to training and social protections, which in turn increases occupational health risks.

Weston and McMunn's ▶ Chap. 19, "Precarious Work and Health," describes the two main forms of precarious work, temporary work and self-employment and their associations with mental health and sleep. In the first part of the twenty-first century in Europe, temporary work increased among younger adults, while self-employment increased among older adults. Although job insecurity is associated with poorer health, there is no evidence that temporary workers experience poor or insufficient sleep, and only a little evidence that the self-employed experience poor sleep quality and longer sleep durations than working employees. However, the evidence is mainly cross-sectional, with little research conducted on the occupational life course of workers engaged in these precarious forms of work over their working life course. As temporary workers tend to be younger than workers in permanent jobs, their risks of ill-health may only become apparent with longitudinal follow-up data.

Van Aerden et al.'s ▶ Chap. 4, "The Impact of New Technologies on the Quality of Work," uses a life course perspective on employment and new technologies, to review the evidence on the risks and opportunities for workers and their health. They emphasize the importance of broadening out the concept of job quality to "the quality of working life," which explicitly considers the fit between job characteristics and a worker's circumstances at a particular stage of their life course. New technologies bring potentially positive outcomes for workers, such as place and working hours flexibility, but the same technological tools can also lead to negative work experiences.

Wei and van Tongeren ▶ Chap. 20, "Gig Work and Health," highlights the rapid growth of the online digital platform ("gig") economy in recent years and the occupational health risks of the fastest growing occupational group within this sector – location-based tasks such as delivery or taxi services. They argue that some practices of these digital labor platforms have made workers vulnerable to exploitation from "algorithmic management, efficiency optimisation and employment precarity." The occupational health and safety protections (such as sick leave) that are part of traditional work and business organizations are not always available to many gig workers, who also face traditional occupational health risks (such as work-related stressors) and emergent risks (arising from the organization of work through digital platforms). While digital platform–based delivery and transport workers tend to be younger and male, the rapid expansion of such gig work across other occupational groups and industry sectors could result in an expansion of occupational health risks across all stages of the life course.

Chandola's ▶ Chap. 17, "Occupational Differences in Work-Related Mental Health: A Life Course Analysis of Recent Trends in the European Context," examines aging and period differences in the mental health of workers in Europe. In particular, he asks whether the aging of European workers can explain some of the deteriorating trends in work-related stress, depression, or anxiety, and whether some occupations are at risk of worsening mental health. While workers in occupations that have a high proportion of public contact have consistently higher rates of work-related poor mental health, there was no difference in the trends for these occupations compared to the overall worsening trend in work-related mental health. Although the period of the coronavirus pandemic exacerbated this deterioration in work-related mental health, the worsening trend in work-related mental health was evident even prior to the pandemic.

5. The **timing of life events** specifies that events or exposures that occur at a particular or more sensitive periods of early life may have long-lasting effects on how a person develops. Typically, sequence analysis and growth trajectory models are often used in life course research to highlight the role of timing and sequencing of life events.

Wild and Le Guillou's ▶ Chap. 9, "Methods in Modeling Life Course," describes methodological developments in life course analysis and estimation. However, the chapter also highlights that the time dimension is often neglected within occupational life course analysis. In particular, the life course timing of occupational exposure risks and the consequence for ill-health are probably limited because of the limited data availability on longitudinal occupational exposures lined to health outcomes.

Studer and Cianferoni's ▶ Chap. 5, "Sequence Analysis and Its Potential for Occupational Health Studies," identifies sequence analysis as a key methodological tool for life course analysis. Sequence analysis methods in occupational health are typically used to characterize occupational health risk trajectories over the life course and to describe how previous trajectories are linked to a later-life health outcome. These methods are able to take into account the three key aspects of a previous trajectory according to the life course paradigm, namely its timing, duration, and sequencing, and to link them to later life outcomes. As mentioned in other chapters in this book, the time dimension of occupational health risk factors is often neglected in most occupational health research, and sequence analysis allows researchers to better characterize how the timing of exposures to occupational risk factors over the life course have long-lasting adverse effects on health.

Bakusic et al.'s ▶ Chap. 10, "Genetics, Epigenetics, and Mental Health at Work," describes how stress in early childhood can lead to epigenetic changes in the way genes involved in biological responses to stress are expressed later on in life. These epigenetic changes can persist to adulthood, shaping the way the workers will respond to stress later in life and increasing their risk of psychopathology including burnout.

One dimension of time that is often analyzed in the context of occupational health is the duration of working hours. Fadel et al.'s ▶ Chap. 14, "Long Working Hours and Health Effects," emphasizes how long working hours have become a leading cause of death attributed to work due to the high prevalence of long working hours globally. Moreover, they suggest that while long working hours may act as an acute trigger for cardiovascular diseases for some workers, the effect of long working hours on a range of other diseases suggests a persistent burden of disease beyond the exposure during the working lifetime.

Trudel et al's ▶ Chap. 24, "Adverse Effect of Psychosocial Stressors at Work and Long Working Hours Along the Cardiovascular Continuum," summarizes the evidence that psychosocial stressors at work leads to cardiovascular disease and related outcomes. They argue that since most adults spend over half their awake time at work and around 20–25% of them are exposed to psychosocial stressors at work, psychosocial factors are potentially important intervention points to prevent cardiovascular disease. They also highlight how cumulative and chronic experiences of adverse psychosocial working conditions lead to increased cardiovascular risks.

The importance of the time dimension in exposure to potential occupational harms is also highlighted in Guénel and Léger's ▶ Chap. 15, "Health Effects of Shift Work and Night Shift Work." The evidence that disruption to diurnal circadian rhythms by shift work (and night shift work in particular) is harmful to workers' health is reviewed in this chapter. Additionally, these harmful effects of the nocturnal timing of the occupational health risk appear to have accumulative effects with greater duration of exposure (e.g., years of night shift work) having more harmful health effects, with some evidence of a reduction in risk when workers quit shift work.

6. The concept of "**linked lives**" highlights the dependence of the development of one person on others, such as their coworkers and family members. The family, community, or organizational contexts of workers are a key component of linked lives, but there is often a lack of occupational health data collected on the different members of these groups of linked lives.

In Mcmunn's ► Chap. 21, "Gender Differences in Work Participation over the Life Course and Consequences for Socioeconomic and Health Outcomes," she argues that entry to parenthood is part of a gendered life course transition where gender differences in employment are not so much driven by gender as by the interaction between gender and parenthood. Similar to Head, Fleischmann, and Xue, she argues that differences between early theories on gender differences in occupational health can be integrated within "a life course approach to the study of employment and health which characterises the timing and nature of transitions alongside the duration of states such as employment and partnership." The occupational life course of women continues to be disadvantaged in terms of labor market participation and working conditions and this disadvantage is linked with poor health across a range of outcomes and across the life course.

7. **Adaptive strategies** have usually been understood in the context of the individual making choices and decisions to adapt to changes in their circumstances. However, in relation to occupational health, adaptive strategies can also be considered to be at the organizational or national policy level that promote healthy work environments.

Rigó and Lunau's ► Chap. 28, "The Role of Social and Labor Policies in Shaping Working Conditions Throughout the Life Course," describes the role of national labor policies, and in particular, active and passive labor market policies, in contributing toward a healthier workforce. Job training is a key characteristic of active labor market policies which enable workers to expand and refresh their skills and improve their knowledge over the life course. Psychosocial working conditions tend to be better in countries with well-developed labor policies indicated by higher investments into active and passive labor market programs. Furthermore, investing in labor market policy measures was found to be effective not only in terms of decreasing the average level of work stress, but also in decreasing socioeconomic inequalities in work stress.

In Franklin's ► Chap. 26, "Worksite Health Promotion: Evidence on Effects and Challenges" she discusses how even though ideas of the occupational life course are implicit in the concept of workplace health promotion, there remain many policy and organizational challenges to achieving health promotion across the occupational life course. Ideas on workplace health promotion initially had little explicit conceptualization of the life course, with a narrow focus on risk prevention and on single individual behavior interventions. Incorporating life course perspectives from the health inequalities literature, she highlights that no single, individual-level health interventions can enable workplace health promotion, and emphasizes the need for the combination of individual worker level and organizational policies to enable workplace health promotion.

Emerging Themes

A number of common themes have emerged from the descriptions of the life course concepts within the chapters of this book which we discuss below.

Occupational Health in the Context of the COVID-19 Pandemic

Many of the chapters in the handbook highlight how occupational health risks have been affected during the COVID-19 pandemic and this is a theme we explore in our concluding chapter (▶ Chaps. 6, "Job-Exposure Matrices: Design, Validation, and Limitations" and ▶ 30, "Conceptual and Methodological Directions of Occupational Life Course Research"). Wei and van Tongeren examined evidence from the UK logistics sector during the COVID-19 pandemic and found that the occupations which were at increased risk of COVID-19 mortality involved contact with patients or the public, such as bus and taxi drivers (▶ Chap. 20, "Gig Work and Health"). While some COVID-19 risk mitigation measures were put in place (such as contact-free delivery), other occupational groups such as the majority of parcel and food couriers were self-employed and had no access to sick leave pay. Lack of access to sick leave pay is a risk factor for presenteeism. Bartley and Blane remark that there is a remarkable overlap in the occupations most adversely affected by COVID-19 and those that had been identified as key or essential workers by the government, arguing that socioeconomic disadvantage is the key to understanding the continued occupational health risks many workers face before and during the pandemic (▶ Chap. 2, "Two Pathways Between Occupation and Health"). Head, Fleischmann, and Xue observed how the pandemic interrupted the trend of yearly increases in employment rate among people aged 55–64 years, exacerbating preexisting inequalities in employment conditions and outcomes (▶ Chap. 25, "Pathways to Retirement and Health Effects"). Mcmunn provides further evidence of the exacerbation of inequalities documenting the gendered effect of the closure of schools and childcare facilities during periods of the pandemic (▶ Chap. 21, "Gender Differences in Work Participation over the Life Course and Consequences for Socioeconomic and Health Outcomes").

Lack of Data from the Developing World

Another theme that emerges from the chapters is the lack of data and analyses of life course occupational risks from developing countries. This is particularly worrying as demographic aging is occurring rapidly in the developing world. In many of these countries, a large proportion of workers do not have access to occupational pensions or social security benefits.

Lack of Relevant Data

Longitudinal data are the bedrock of life course analysis, but all too often there is a paucity of longitudinal data that is repeatedly collected across the entirety of a person's life course, let alone the entirety of their working life course. Moreover, even when longitudinal data on a person's health are collected, similar longitudinal data on the occupational exposome are limited, making it hard to develop more sophisticated inferences around the timing and sequencing of exposures to occupational risk factors for ill-health. In addition, longitudinal data on national-level and organizational-level policies that are relevant for occupational health should be more easily integrated into life course occupational health analysis, but often such data are not available or difficult to access.

Conclusion

The chapters in this handbook reveal a complexity of life course processes and concepts that are relevant to occupational health. These include occupational histories of exposure to toxic elements, the accumulation of these toxic elements over an occupational life history, the importance of taking into account the life course context of workers, such as gender and power relationships, the differentiation between aging, period, and cohort effects, the recent changes in working life, and related exposures to occupational risks in some industries and occupations.

One of the limitations of much of existing life course occupational health research is that many studies do not go beyond an accumulation of occupational health risk factors approach. Ill-health related to occupational exposures are thus viewed as an aggregation of cumulative exposure to risk factors, with relatively little consideration of the timing and sequencing of those risk factors. With newer sources of occupational data, methods, and tools becoming increasingly available, new insights into occupational health from life course research may soon be a possibility.

Cross-References

- ▶ A Life Course Perspective on Work and Mental Health: The Working Lives of Young Adults
- ▶ Adverse Effect of Psychosocial Stressors at Work and Long Working Hours Along the Cardiovascular Continuum
- ▶ Adverse Employment Histories: Conceptual Considerations and Selected Health Effects
- ▶ Biomechanical Hazards at Work and Adverse Health Using Job-Exposure Matrices
- ▶ Challenges of Large Cohort and Massive Data in Occupational Health
- ▶ Changing Experiences, Needs, and Supports Across the Life Course for Workers Living with Disabilities

- Chemical Hazards at Work and Occupational Diseases Using Job-Exposure Matrices
- Conceptual and Methodological Directions of Occupational Life Course Research
- Falling Sick While Working: An Overview of the EU-Level Policy Framework on Returning to Work Following Chronic Disease(s)
- Gender Differences in Work Participation over the Life Course and Consequences for Socioeconomic and Health Outcomes
- Genetics, Epigenetics, and Mental Health at Work
- Gig Work and Health
- Health Effects of Shift Work and Night Shift Work
- Integration of Occupational Exposure into the Exposome
- Job-Exposure Matrices: Design, Validation, and Limitations
- Long Working Hours and Health Effects
- Methods in Modeling Life Course
- Occupational Differences in Work-Related Mental Health: A Life Course Analysis of Recent Trends in the European Context
- Occupational Trajectories and Health Inequalities in a Global Perspective
- Pathways to Retirement and Health Effects
- Precarious Work and Health
- Psychosocial Work Environment and Health: Applying Job-Exposure Matrices and Work Organization and Management Practice
- Sequence Analysis and Its Potential for Occupational Health Studies
- The Impact of New Technologies on the Quality of Work
- The Role of Social and Labor Policies in Shaping Working Conditions Throughout the Life Course
- Transformation of Modern Work, Rise of Atypical Employment, and Health
- Two Pathways Between Occupation and Health
- Working Careers with Common Mental Disorders
- Worksite Health Promotion: Evidence on Effects and Challenges

References

Alwin DF (2012) Integrating varieties of life course concepts. J Gerontol Ser B Psychol Sci Soc Sci 67B(2):206–220. https://doi.org/10.1093/geronb/gbr146

de Groot S, Veldman K, Amick BC III et al (2021) Does the timing and duration of mental health problems during childhood and adolescence matter for labour market participation of young adults? J Epidemiol Community Health 75(9):896–902. https://doi.org/10.1136/jech-2020-215994

Elder GH (1975) Age differentiation and the life course. Annu Rev Sociol 1(1):165–190. https://doi.org/10.1146/annurev.so.01.080175.001121

Kuh D, Ben-Shlomo Y (eds) (2004) A life course approach to chronic disease epidemiology, Oxford medical publications, 2nd edn. Oxford University Press, New York

Wethington E (2005) An overview of the life course perspective: implications for health and nutrition. J Nutr Educ Behav 37(3):115–120. https://doi.org/10.1016/S1499-4046(06)60265-0

Part I
Background

Two Pathways Between Occupation and Health

Melanie Bartley and David Blane

Contents

Introduction	18
First Pathway: Technical Fragmentation	18
Second Pathway: Social Class	21
Covid-19 Pandemic	22
Practical Exercise	23
Cross-References	24
Appendix	24
Immediate Producers of the Cotton T-Shirt	24
Inputs to the Immediate Producers	25
References	25

Abstract

The chapter starts by celebrating a classic text in occupational health, to which it adds socioeconomic context and some new terms (technical fragmentation, three levels of knowledge, Neison defense, and remit blur). It then points out that an occupation also influences the wider social advantages or disadvantages of those employed within it, and that these cumulate across the life course. Finally, these observations are illustrated by the Covid-19 pandemic, which started in late 2019/ early 2020, and enacted via a student practical exercise.

M. Bartley (✉)
UCL, Institute of Epidemiology & Health Care, London, UK
e-mail: m.bartley@ucl.ac.uk

D. Blane
Imperial College, London, UK
e-mail: d.blane@imperial.ac.uk

© Springer Nature Switzerland AG 2023
M. Wahrendorf et al. (eds.), *Handbook of Life Course Occupational Health*, Handbook Series in Occupational Health Sciences, https://doi.org/10.1007/978-3-031-30492-7_11

| Keywords |

Technical fragmentation · Neison defense · Gender · Social class · Status · Accumulation · Covid-19 pandemic

Introduction

This chapter reflects some key ideas of life course occupational health through the life course of two key researchers on this topic – David Blane (DB) and Melanie Bartley (MB).

In pursuit of the idea that prevention is better than cure, DB largely abandoned clinical medicine for public health and, assuming this involved the importance of the social, studied postgraduate sociology, where, among other things, he was introduced to the concept of *victim-blaming* (where the oppressor blames the oppressed for their own misfortune); the history of eugenics (particularly, Mackenzie's 1981 study); and the distinction between class, status, and power (of which more later); followed by a half-century of teaching and researching in London's medical schools, and lifelong membership of what became one of the UK's largest trade unions.

While studying for an MSc in medical sociology, MB was deeply influenced by the official data on social class differences in mortality. A determination to understand this inequity eventually led to spending several years as a clerical and skilled manual worker, first in the NHS and then in a printing factory belonging to a revolutionary organization. After a while, her comrades pointed out she was never going to be a very good typesetter and encouraged her to go back to research on how our work affects our health. One of her first research efforts was to oppose the idea that manual workers have higher mortality because their health was not good in the first place. Despite graduating PhD in 1988 and publishing quite a few papers, Mel was obliged to self-fund her whole subsequent research career. This of course was a great source of insight into the effects of unemployment and stress.

First Pathway: Technical Fragmentation

As far as I (DB) can remember, occupational health was ignored by the mid-1960s' undergraduate medical curriculum I studied in London.[1] But even at that age, I realized that the best hours of most days of the best years of most lives are spent at

---

[1] It is perhaps relevant to note that occupational medicine is not part of the UK's National Health Service, and that, according to the President of the UK Faculty of Occupational Medicine, less than 1% of General Medical Council-registered doctors are accredited specialist Occupational Physicians and that less than 1% of Nursing and Midwifery Council-registered nurses are suitably qualified occupational health nurses. And that their scarcity is amplified by a geographical mismatch between the location of occupational nurses and physicians, concentrated in large companies in southern England, and the large number of low-paid employees with insecure jobs in small and medium-sized companies in northern England (De Bono A. Quoted in: Thakrar S. *Promoting Work as a Health Outcome – Summary of the Conference "Good Work is Good for You."* Academy of the Royal Medical Colleges, May 2019:5).

work, with possible implications for health, so I was most happy to discover Donald Hunter's *Diseases of Occupations*, the first edition of which had been published a decade earlier. This classic volume started with bone fractures among Neanderthals from hunting large, dangerous mammals and went on to describe, among other things: Paracelsus' early sixteenth century interest in the toxicology and medicinal effects of chemicals; Andreas Vesalius' mid-sixteenth century description of lead poisoning among plumbers; late nineteenth century diagnosis of anthrax among leather workers; and ending with two pages of the names of all the radiographers who died of leukemia before the carcinogenic properties of radium were recognized.

Later I came to understand that the application of such information can involve legal and financial considerations. Sometimes these are employee claims for compensation; sometimes threats to employer profits and the organization of their production processes; and sometimes negotiations over health and safety between these two sides of industry. Bartley coined the term "*technical fragmentation*" to describe what can happen in such negotiations when a distinction is made between the undeniably hazardous, which subsequently are banned, and the contentious which are declared either safe or not work-related. The former happened when one type of asbestos (*blue*) was banned and the other type (*white*) was declared safe; as a result of which, for another 30 or 40 years, building workers broke up white asbestos sheets and hand-mixed the fibers with cement to lag power station pipes – a tragedy that ended only when the laggers' Trade Union branch secretary in Glasgow asked an investigative journalist why he found himself attending so many of his members' funerals.[2] The latter (*not work-related*) happened with miners' lung disease when silicosis and pneumoconiosis were legally recognized as caused by specific types of coal dust, while chronic obstructive pulmonary disease, the most prevalent respiratory disease among miners, was supposedly caused by their leisure-time tobacco smoking – a situation rectified only after the UK State took financial responsibility for COPD compensation claims when privatizing the rump of its mining industry.

Technical fragmentation requires the knowledge and ingenuity of occupational health physicians and epidemiologists to reach what, at the time, may seem like a compromise which allows both sides to come away with a partial victory; something which I think of as the three types of knowledge. The first type is what the lay citizens exposed to a potential hazard think about, say, the fumes from a local incinerator or cotton dust clogging a mill's extractor fans. The second type is expert opinion that the potential hazard may be a nuisance but there is no evidence that it is harmful to health (something I call *the Neison defense* (Neison 1844), after the statistician who said this in response to Edwin Chadwick's 1842 *Report on The Sanitary Conditions of the Labouring Population of Gt Britain*). The third type is

---

[2] Alan Dalton (*Hazards Newsletter*) was also active at this time, as was the Workers' Educational Association (Le Serve A, Vose C, Wigley C, Bennett D. *Chemicals, Work and Cancer*. Walton-on-Thames, Thomas Nelson 1980), the Politics of Health (Doyal L, Green K, Irwin A, Russell D, Steward F, Williams R, Gee D, Epstein S. *Cancer in Britain: The Politics of Prevention*. London, Pluto Press 1983), and the Society for the Social History of Medicine (Weindling P, ed. *The Social History of Occupational Health*. London, Croom Helm 1985).

deduced from the experts' behavior: if incinerator fumes, for example, are merely a nuisance, why do experts not use this insider knowledge to buy local property at knockdown bargain-basement prices, and why has the State never found it necessary to prohibit such insider trading?

What is the limit of the remit of occupational health? In one sense, the answer is straightforward: at the factory gate or the office security desk. But considerable leakage is possible in situations where the boundaries are less clear-cut.[3] Are air or water pollution caused by industry included? Are road accidents involving commercial vehicles? Dermot Hourihane's autopsy series long ago showed that asbestos fibers were widespread in the lungs of people who lived near but had never worked in the asbestos factories of East London. Sewage plants continue to discharge untreated feces into rivers. Chemical plants discharge many harmful substances including the carcinogenic synthetic white pigment dioxin now present in all forms of life worldwide. Neither type of pollution is considered occupational, despite their commercial origins and employees and managers' involvement in their discharge. The health effects of such unregulated mingling of the commercial and the domestic are most acute on the roads, where motor vehicles cause a significant number of deaths and disabling injuries, mostly to pedestrians, cyclists, and motor cyclists. Many of these are industrial accidents, in the sense that the vehicles are commercially owned and were being driven by paid employees as part of their job: road haulage trucks, vans, and company motor cars, with the latter the most difficult to identify. When I used to read financial newspapers, a significant proportion of new motor cars sales went to commercial organizations for hire or fleet purposes, although neither the police nor the department for transport record their involvement in serious or fatal accidents. Such acute effects are additional to the chronic health effects of these vehicles' exhaust fumes, which are also inadequately controlled by the present regulatory arrangements.

Our editor quite rightly has described what I have written so far as a male version of events and has suggested an explicit consideration of the occupational health of women. Doing so, I make three points, all based on my experience as either a hospital trade unionist or an attached visiting scholar general practitioner. First, both women and men hospital workers share exposure to many hazards: chemical and microbial contamination in pathology laboratories; X-rays in radiology departments; heavy lifting of patients on the wards; and the hard physical graft of keeping a complex building clean and hygienic. Second, women hospital workers more often than their men colleagues carry the double burden of domestic responsibilities in addition to paid employment and bring demands for parental leave, workplace nurseries, meal breaks long enough to food shop for the evening meal, flexitime to cope with fluctuation in the health of those for whom they provide informal, unpaid

---

[3] A series of disasters demonstrated that these issues have become global, as hazardous production processes are moved offshore: the Seveso dioxin explosion in 1976; the Bhopal chemical explosion in 1984; the Piper Alpha oil platform explosion in 1988; the Exxon Valdez oil spill in 1989; the Gulf of Mexico oil spill in 2010; the Niger Delta oil pollution in 2011; and the Volkswagen exhaust fume scandal in 2015.

care. Such domestic labor can be performed by men but, by and large, it is women who do it (such issues may become more salient if post-Covid *working from home* becomes widespread). Third, my experience in general practice, epidemiology, and social policy has made me suspect that much occupationally derived health damage is belittled because it is mostly women who are affected. I started work in an old *Florence Nightingale* hospital whose long central ground floor corridor was scrubbed and polished for hours on end by women on their knees. This activity produced a predictable occupationally induced pathology, for which the rather disparaging medical shorthand was *Housemaid's Knee*. A more contemporary equivalent would be musculoskeletal pain in the back of the neck and the shoulder girdle and the forearm tendon trauma from long hours spent computer typing, which often are accompanied by chronic, severe headaches, self-medicated with *over-the-counter* analgesics. Women predominate among professional cleaners and typists but, tellingly, men working in these occupations suffer from the same health problems. Nevertheless, I suspect it is the predominance of women that allows social policy to victim-blame early retirees by saying mostly their health problems are nonfatal musculoskeletal and mental health issues, so those suffering them need to be subject to *Workfare*'s fitness for work testing (*conditionality*) and benefit cuts (*sanctioning*).

Second Pathway: Social Class

So far, the present chapter has addressed only the pathway between occupation-specific threats and health, but there is also a second pathway: occupations have a more general effect based on the levels of economic and social advantage or disadvantage experienced by those employed to work in them. This more general effect is well illustrated by the UK's official National Statistics Socio-Economic Classification (NS-SEC) (Rose and Pevalin 2003), which classifies all occupations according to seven criteria:

1. The timing of payment for work (monthly versus weekly, daily or hourly)
2. The presence of regular increments
3. Job security (over or under 1 month)
4. How much autonomy the worker has in deciding when to start and leave work
5. Promotion opportunities
6. Degree of influence over planning of work
7. Level of influence over designing their own work tasks

Questions covering each of the seven criteria were asked of some 60,000 employees in the UK Labour Force Survey of 1997 (Rose and Harrison 2010). Occupations could then be allocated into social classes according to the typical answers of members of each occupation to these questions.

The NS-SEC is clearly based on the fact that social classes are made up of occupations, not individuals, and individual characteristics such as physical strength, intelligence, kindness, and the number of languages spoken are irrelevant. Conceptually, social classes could exist even if the whole population consisted of clones of the same person.

Occupational advantages and disadvantages tend to cluster cross-sectionally (Bartley 1992); for example, those employed in occupations where employment is paid by the hour or day and supervision is close, with little autonomy over the content or order of tasks, are also likely to be low paid. This means they tend to be more limited in terms of where they live (perhaps in crowded residences in more polluted areas), the nutritional quality of their diet, and their opportunities for fulfilling and healthy leisure activity. Conversely, those employed in occupations where employment is secure and supervision is light, with considerable autonomy over the content and organization of their work, are likely to be well paid, allowing wider choice over nutrition, home, and leisure.

Such advantages or disadvantages also tend to accumulate longitudinally. Children brought up in an impoverished family are disadvantaged at school, more likely to leave at the minimum school leaving age and find employment in a disadvantaged occupation without an occupational pension scheme, meaning, in the UK, reliance after labor market exit on the state old-age pension, perhaps supplemented by the means-tested pension guarantee. Conversely, children brought up in an affluent family tend to do well at school and continue their education to graduate or postgraduate level, after which they find employment in an advantaged occupation with a defined benefit, final salary pension scheme that funds a comfortable retirement. Occupation also casts a long shadow forward via its strong influence on the types of second pension schemes available and the amount of money, surplus to immediate requirements, that can be saved, thereby shaping living standards during the whole of postretirement life (Glickman et al. 2018).

A range of biological aspects of later life are associated with these life course social differences, as illustrated by the projects within Stephane Cullati's LIFETRAIL research program of health in early old age (Sieber 2022), which investigated cognitive function (Aartsen et al 2019), respiratory function (Cheval et al. 2019), muscle strength (Cheval et al. 2018), disability (Landoes et al. 2018), and frailty (Van der Linden et al. 2019). Associations were found between childhood circumstances and these various measures of health at older ages; associations which were attenuated but not abolished when adult circumstances were taken into account. These findings are consistent with the idea that health in early old age is influenced by both social conditions during the biological phase of childhood and adolescent growth and development and by social conditions during adulthood when biological functioning can be worn down either faster or more slowly than usual (Blane et al. 2016).

Covid-19 Pandemic

The SARS-CoV-2 viral pandemic that started in early 2020 illustrates well the clinical relevance to health of this longitudinal life course aspect of an occupation.

In rich countries, poor health before the pandemic started proved to be one of the main predictors of the need for intensive care and, where that failed, premature death; while in less affluent countries, as Gindo Tampubolon (personal communication) found in Indonesia, the pandemic uncovered a large clinical iceberg of medically undiagnosed pre-Covid morbidity. In UK, for some reason, the Office for National Statistics has never published NS-SEC social class differences in Covid deaths, but it did publish something similar for the period March 9–December 28, 2020, which showed that male and female age-standardized Covid-19 mortality rates for people aged 20–64 were very similar to those for all-cause mortality; in Spieghalter and Masters' (Spiegelhalter & Masters 2021) words ... *professionals have much lower risk and manual workers higher risk* ... Similar things may explain why it is the most disadvantaged ethnic groups that have the highest rates of Covid mortality, due plausibly to a combination of factors, some of which are cross-sectional (little control at work over proximity to others; inadequate or nonexistent workplace ventilation; last in line for access to personal protective equipment) and others longitudinal (employment in disadvantaged occupations; residential crowding; preexisting limiting long-standing illnesses).

A sociologically challenging aspect of this phenomenon is the sizeable overlap between the disadvantaged occupations and those identified by the UK government as *key, essential,* or *critical* (the terms were used interchangeably) during its Covid lockdown. How is it possible that many of the most important occupations are also the most disadvantaged? Two strands of thought within the sociological tradition may throw some light on this puzzle. First, the social division of labor which may be one of humanity's greatest achievements, driving complexity, differentiation, diversity, creativity, quality, and productivity, topics that preoccupied nineteenth century social thought from Adam Smith (Smith 1976) to Emile Durkheim (Durkheim 1997). Second, Max Weber's (Weber 1966) early twentieth century distinction between social class and social status which he implied could vary independently; he instanced the respect given to penniless aristocrats and ascetic priests, to which we could add its converse, the scorn directed at rich war criminals and fraudsters. As class and status have a degree of independence of each other, status hierarchy could be disconnected from the social division of labor, as illustrated by the T-shirt exercise below.

Practical Exercise

As a practical exercise, I ask my students to imagine they are going to a clothing store to buy a cotton T-shirt and challenge them to list all of the occupations that have made possible this unremarkable action. In an appendix to the present chapter, I list my answer to the challenge, broken down into the immediate producers of the cotton T-shirt and the inputs to these producers – reassuringly, my students come up with much the same list. It would seem that even the simplest of objects contains traces of the innumerable occupations which have contributed its existence.

Interestingly, my students also find themselves unable to rank the occupations according to their importance, saying the interdependence of occupations means they are all equally dependent on each other. Which poses the question: why were many of the Covid lockdown's *key/essential/critical* occupations previously and subsequently disadvantaged? Here, the distinction between social class and social status could be useful. A good population-representative survey measure of social class needs to be nonhierarchical because societies contain the remains of their predecessors and the seeds of their successors alongside their dominant socioeconomic formation; in the contemporary UK, subsistence farmers (Hebrides crofters) and multi-jobbed self-employed live alongside the dominant organizational structure of owner-executives, professionals, clericals, artisans, foremen, and laborers. Being nonhierarchical (no "*Up*" and no "*Down*") is one of the strengths of the NS-SEC measure of social class. And the solution to the puzzle might be that the social division of labor's potential for equality between occupations is undermined by its contamination with social status.

Cross-References

▶ Integration of Occupational Exposure into the Exposome
▶ The Role of Social and Labor Policies in Shaping Working Conditions Throughout the Life Course
▶ Transformation of Modern Work, Rise of Atypical Employment, and Health

Appendix

Immediate Producers of the Cotton T-Shirt

Farmers to plough, grow, and harvest the cotton.
    Biologists to match seed types to climate and terrain.
    Agricultural chemists to produce fertilizers.
    Biochemists to produce pesticides.
    Truck drivers to move the raw cotton to a factory and the finished product to, first, the docks, then a warehouse at the destination port, and then the retail store.
    Cotton cleaners and spinners in the factory.
    Artists to design the garment and its packaging.
    Chemists to produce aniline dyes.
    Telecommunication satellite technicians to link the designers, in say, Germany, to a factory, perhaps in Bangladesh.
    Quality testers and packers in the factory.
    Dockers to crane load and off-load the freight containers.
    Seafarers to crew the container ship.
    Satellite satnav technicians to keep the ship on course.
    Store retail staff and security staff to deter theft and enforce payment.
    Mint staff to print currency notes and mold coins.
    Bank staff to enable debit and credit card transactions.
And now the T-shirt is in your possession.

Inputs to the Immediate Producers

Schoolteachers to produce numerate and literate employees.
Farmers to grow and drivers to deliver food to the producers.
Building workers, electricians, and plumbers to house the producers.
Miners to dig ore, metallurgists to refine metals, engineers to design machines, and foundry workers to mold component parts.
Geologists to find oil, drillers to extract it, and refiners to separate its components into gasoline for trucks, trains, ships, and aeroplanes, and the base chemicals for plastics.
And these are just some of the occupations within the social division of labor.

References

Asterisk indicates a LIFETRAIL project
*Aartsen M, et al (2019) Adverse socio-economic conditions in childhood are associated with cognitive function and cognitive decline in older age. Proceedings of the National Academy of Sciences of the United States of America (published electronically 25th February 2019)
Bartley M (1992) Authorities and partisans: the debate on unemployment and health. Edinburgh University Press, Edinburgh
Blane D, Akinwale B, Landy R, Matthews K, Wahrendorf M (2016) Comment and debate: what can the life course approach contribute to an understanding of longevity risk? Longitud Life Course Stud 7:165–196
Chadwick E (1965) Report on the sanitary condition of the labouring population of Gt Britain, Flinn M (ed). Re-printed Edinburgh University Press, Edinburgh
*Cheval B, et al (2018) Association of early and adult life socio-economic circumstances with muscle strength in older age. Age Ageing 47:398–407
*Cheval B, Chabert C, Orsholits D, Sieber S, Guessous I, Blane D, Kliegel M, Janssens JP, Burton-Jeangros C, Pison C, Courvoisier DS, Boisgontier MP, Cullati S (2019) Disadvantaged early-life socioeconomic circumstances are associated with low respiratory function in older age. J Gerontol A Biol Sci Med Sci 74(7):1134–1140. https://doi.org/10.1093/gerona/gly177. PMID: 31211384; PMCID: PMC7330463
Durkheim E (1997) The division of labour in society. The Free Press, New York
Glickman M, Bartley M, Blane D (2018) Occupational pensions: a bridge between social class before and after labour market exit? International Centre for Life Course Studies in Society and Health working paper 2, March 2018. ISBN 978-0-9527377-4-2 (link here: ICLS-Publications-Working papers)
Hourihane D (1964) The pathology of mesothelioma and an analysis of their association with asbestos exposure. Thorax 19:277–283
Hunter D (1955) Diseases of occupations, 1st edn. The London Hospital, London
*Landoes A, et al (2018) Childhood socio-economic circumstances and disability trajectories in older men and women: a European cohort study. Eur J Pub Health 29:1–9
Mackenzie D (1981) Statistics in Britain, 1865–1930: the social construction of scientific knowledge. Edinburgh University Press, Edinburgh
Neison F (1844) On a method recently proposed for conducting enquiries into the comparative sanitary conditions of various districts, with illustrations, derived from numerous places in Great Britain at the period of the last census. J Stat Soc Lond 7:4668
Rose D, Pevalin D (eds) (2003) A Researcher's guide to the national statistics socio-economic classification. Sage Publications, London

Rose D, Harrison E (2010) Social class in Europe: an introduction to the European socio-economic classification. Routledge, London

Sieber S (2022) Life-long impact of disadvantaged socioeconomic conditions in childhood on health in old age: what difference does the welfare state make to improve healthy ageing? LIVES Impact 13/2022. www.centre-lives.ch

Smith A (1976) An inquiry into the nature and causes of the wealth of nations, vol 1, authorised reprint edn. Oxford University Press, Oxford

Spiegelhalter D, Masters A (2021) Covid by numbers: making sense of the pandemic with data. Penguin Books, London. (Figure 13–2 pp124–127)

*Van der Linden et al (2019) Life course circumstances and frailty in old age within different European welfare regimes: a longitudinal study with SHARE. J Gerontol

Weber M (1966) *The theory of social and economic organization* (edited with an introduction by Talcott Parsons). The Free Press, New York

ND
Transformation of Modern Work, Rise of Atypical Employment, and Health

3

Werner Eichhorst and Arne L. Kalleberg

Contents

Introduction	28
From Standard to Nonstandard Employment Relationships	28
Part-Time Work	30
Temporary Agency Work and Fixed-Term Contracts	31
Self-Employment and the "Gig" Economy	33
Atypical Work and Health	34
Conclusions	37
References	38

Abstract

Nonstandard or atypical work has grown in many countries over the last decades. It takes many different forms, ranging from fixed-term contracts and temporary agency work to solo self-employment, platform-based work, on-call work, work at low or unpredictable working hours, and informal work (especially in non-Northern countries). Nonstandard work has major implications for job quality and employment trajectories over the life course. The chapter will discuss the main driving forces behind the rise of atypical work, such as the shift toward the service sector and labor market reforms. It will also show major trends and patterns of nonstandard work in OECD countries. Furthermore, in line with the volume, we discuss the consequences of atypical work with respect to its health and safety implications. We refer to core findings from existing research as it has emerged as nonstandard employment has gained prominence in postindustrial labor markets.

W. Eichhorst (✉)
IZA and University of Bremen, Bremen, Germany
e-mail: eichhorst@iza.org

A. L. Kalleberg
Department of Sociology, University of North Carolina, Chapel Hill, NC, USA

Keywords

Nonstandard work · Atypical employment · Health

Introduction

Employment relations provide the link between individuals and their employing organizations. They specify the reciprocal expectations and obligations connecting employers and employees and can be either implicit or explicit contractual arrangements that describe how work is organized, governed, evaluated, and rewarded. Employment relations differ in their scope, ranging from broadly defined relational exchanges that are often open ended in duration and provide training and welfare supports for employees to narrowly defined transactional relations that are more instrumental, entailing little commitment and often for work performed within a fixed time frame (see Kalleberg and Marsden 2015).

Employment relations differ in more developed, industrialized countries from those in developing countries. Relatively rich countries are characterized by a formal economy in which employment relations are regulated in varying degrees, depending on a country's political and labor market institutions. Developing countries, by contrast, are dominated by an "informal" economy (in the Global North also referred to as the "black," "grey," "underground," or "shadow" economy) in which enterprises, employment relationships, and work are partially or fully outside of government regulation and taxation and is not covered by labor laws or social protection. While developed countries also have informal economies to some degree, in developing countries the informal economy *is* most of the economy.

From Standard to Nonstandard Employment Relationships

A useful starting point for assessing changes in employment relations is the standard employment relationship, the SER, which involves long-term relational exchanges between employers and employees. The SER was the employment norm in industrial nations for the middle of the twentieth century and was a central part of the social contract that accompanied the spread of Fordist mass production and the ascendancy of large organizations. Nevertheless, the SER was far from universal and characterized only a minority of employment relations; it was found mainly in larger organizations and was concentrated among white-collar employees (usually men) in managerial occupations and among blue-collar workers in certain highly organized industries.

The SER was generally typified by the performance of work on a preset schedule at the employer's place of business and under the employer's control and direction. It often, but not always, involved full-time employment and a shared expectation of continued employment assuming satisfactory employee performance. SERs were associated with a psychological contract in which employees exchanged their commitment to employers in exchange for earnings and often the possibility of careers within firm internal labor markets having job ladders, with entry restricted to the bottom rungs and upward movements associated with the progressive development of skills and knowledge. SERs were also the normative foundation in industrial countries of a variety of labor laws and regulations such as protections against unsafe working conditions and the right to bargain collectively, as well as welfare benefits such as social insurance and pensions (Stone and Arthurs 2013). The institutions supporting the SER presumed models of employment relations and the family having a full-time, primary-breadwinner husband, and a wife who cared for children and the home.

Changing political, social, technological, and economic conditions in the last quarter of the twentieth century in all developed countries prompted governments and employers to seek greater flexibility in their employment systems than what was available through the SER (Cappelli 1999; Kalleberg 2011). Growing price competition and more fluid capital markets put pressure on firms to maximize profitability and respond to rapidly changing consumer tastes and preferences. Slow economic growth triggered high unemployment and made it difficult for economies to generate enough jobs to assure all workers of full-time wage employment. Rapidly proliferating computer-based technologies and communication and information systems made quick adaptation to changing market opportunities both possible and necessary. Corporations outsourced many of their functions, leading to the "fissuring" of organizations and the proliferation of subcontracting relationships (Weil 2014). The expansion of the service sector made it necessary for some employers to staff their organizations on a 24/7 basis. New legal regimes also contributed to the growth in nonstandard work in virtually all rich countries by allowing employers to avoid the mandates and costs associated with labor laws that provide protection for permanent employees. So too did demographic shifts in labor force composition involving growth in worker groups – such as married women and older people – who sometimes prefer the flexibility that nonstandard arrangements offer, though not necessarily the associated insecurity.

Together, these changes made the fixed costs and overhead obligations associated with the SER less viable for employers and led to the rise of a new normative form of employment relations often referred to as *nonstandard employment relations* (Kalleberg 2000); other labels – with diverse connotations – include alternative work arrangements, market-mediated arrangements, nontraditional employment relations, flexible staffing arrangements, atypical employment, precarious employment, disposable work, and contingent work.

While atypical employment relations take several distinct forms, they generally differ from the SER in one or more ways (see also ILO 2016). In particular, they tend to involve more transactional exchanges and provide less employment security than the SER. Some nonstandard work arrangements, including self-employment and independent contracting, collapse the employer-employee distinction. In these situations, workers administer and direct their own activities and are paid by clients for services performed or goods provided. By hiring independent contractors, employers avoid many of the regulations (such as the requirement to pay taxes and benefits of various kinds) associated with the employment and so the issue of misclassifying employees as independent contractors has become a matter of considerable dispute.

Atypical employment relations are not new in developed countries. Unstable jobs, temporary work and peripheral labor force attachment, and many employment relations that do not involve full-time work or open-ended employer-employee commitments have dominated industrial societies historically (see Jacoby 1985). For instance, under the "inside contracting" system in nineteenth-century US manufacturing, management engaged contractors, provided them with machinery and factory space, supplied raw material and capital, and sold products, while the contractors were responsible for organizing production and for hiring, paying, and directing the actual workers. Indeed, the efficiencies associated with SERs and internal labor markets in the post-World War II period are the historical anomaly, not the use of nonstandard employment relations. Nonetheless, the latest incarnation of nonstandard employment relations does have novel features that distinguish it from earlier ones: for example, contemporary nonstandard employment relations increasingly involve labor market intermediaries, and advances in technology and communication enable employees to be spatially very distant from their employers.

Since the 1980s, a large and growing proportion of all employment across the developed OECD countries was in nonstandard employment relations (i.e., self-employed, full-time temporaries, part-time temporaries, and part-time permanent). The share of atypical work arrangements continues to vary considerably across countries, but one can clearly see a general trend toward an increasing role of different nonstandard work arrangements over time. However, there are important differences across groups of workers, sectors, and occupations – but also across countries – reflecting different institutional arrangements and labor supply and demand conditions as well sectoral specialization (Eichhorst and Marx 2015).

The types of nonstandard or atypical arrangements are not homogenous: for example, permanent part-time workers have different employment relations and contracts from temporary workers. The characteristics of particular nonstandard arrangements also differ among countries: in the Netherlands, for example, part-time work is regulated and relatively well rewarded, as compared to the more precarious position of part-timers in the USA and UK. Thus, the relative attractiveness of nonstandard work depends on how such employment relations are protected, regulated, and rewarded. In some countries, working in temporary or part-time work (or even being unemployed) may constitute an appealing alternative to regular, full-time employment.

Part-Time Work

OECD figures for 2021 show that about 17% of the OECD countries' workforce work less than 30 hours per week (the generally accepted cutoff for defining part-time work), and that in most countries the number of part-time jobs has grown faster than full-time jobs over the last decades. Women are far more likely to work part-time in the OECD world than men (25% vs. 10%; ILO 2016). While part-time work has expanded in general, it reaches record levels for both sexes in the Netherlands with 57% for women and 19% for men (OECD 2022, part-time employment rate doi: 10.1787/f2ad596c-en) (Accessed on 13 July 2022).

The quality and nature of part-time work varies considerably among countries (see Fagan et al. 2014). Indeed, there is some debate as to whether all part-time work should be considered nonstandard work, because in some countries many less-than-full-time jobs incorporate all other features of the SER (such as part-time work in the Netherlands, for example). In addition, some part-time arrangements represent employer accommodations to employee preferences for reduced hours and more flexible schedules. Many other part-time jobs, however, are highly insecure, lacking enhancements such as benefits, training opportunities, and the expectation of continuity. Part-timers are more likely than full-timers to hold two or more jobs in order to make a living. Countries differ considerably in their regulation of part-time work, though the ILO reports that there have been increases in protections regarding equal treatment and equal dismissal rights in both OECD and emerging countries (but not in developing countries) since the early 1990s.

Workers' preferences and needs must also be considered when evaluating the desirability of part-time work. Some women work part-time because their time is constrained by childcare or eldercare responsibilities; other men and women work part-time while they are students, approaching retirement, or because of chronic ill-health. Much of the part-time work in developing and transition countries is involuntary part-time, in which workers would prefer full-time work in order to obtain an adequate income. The proportion of involuntary part-time has increased since the recent economic crisis due to the relative scarcity of full-time jobs (Fagan et al. 2014), but declined in the second half of the 2010s. Involuntary part-time employment accounted for 3.4% of total employment within the OECD in 2021, and 17% of total part-time employment.

Temporary Agency Work and Fixed-Term Contracts

Temporary work includes both persons hired on a fixed-term temporary basis and workers procured via labor intermediary organizations such as contract companies and temporary help agencies. Fixed-term contracts have become particularly important in countries where employment protections make it difficult for employers to terminate open-ended contracts, mostly in Continental European and Mediterranean countries such as the Netherlands, France, Italy, and Spain, but also in such diverse settings as Sweden, Germany, and Poland. Latest OECD figures show rates as high as 27% in the Netherlands and 25% in Spain. Of course, not all temporary jobs are precarious. If they are associated with vocational training, they typically lead to permanent employment, e.g., in Germany, while in France or Spain transitions to open-ended contracts are more unlikely.

Temporary agency work (TAW), in particular, illustrates a major shift in employment relations, which is here mediated via a third party rather than being a bilateral relation. TAW is characterized by a distinct triangular employment structure where workers are typically employed and dispatched by private employment agencies while working at the facilities, and under the authority, of user firms on limited-term contracts, normally ranging from 1 day to a few months. The shift from a bilateral to trilateral arrangement has fundamentally changed the nature of the employment relationship: the worker's *de jure* employer is an intermediary organization rather than the *de facto* employer that pays for and directs the use of the worker's labor.

Over the past two decades, TAW has not only registered exponential growth but also become a globalizing service industry with considerable geographic expansion and industrial diversification; leading agencies have taken up some functions of human resource management and extended their services to new areas including search and placement, recruitment process outsourcing, outplacement, and online recruitment. Still, the share of TAWs in total employment is around 1–2% in most OECD countries. The latest data from the OECD (2021) indicate that total employment organized via TAW reached 3–4% in 2019 only in some countries such as the Netherlands, Spain, Slovakia, and Slovenia. Despite the low percentages of total employment, the expansion of TAW indicates that the industry has gained considerable political acceptability among the social partners – governments, businesses, and labor unions – that create new regulatory conditions favorable for employment agencies and businesses. Much has been said about how public policies are geared toward a reregulation, rather than a deregulation, of employment relations in the interests of capital. The corollary is that many of the protective coverings that postwar "embedded liberalism" allowed and occasionally nurtured are stripped away; as Harvey (2005:168) avers, "the individualised and relatively powerless worker then confronts a labour market in which only short-term contracts are offered on a customized basis."

A large body of empirical research shows that agency workers are subject to precarious work and unequal treatment (e.g., Kalleberg 2000). Except for a handful of high-status and affluent knowledge workers, a great many are excluded from – or differentially included in – the same array of pay and benefits that are available to full-time workers in some countries including job security, bonus payments, social security and protection, childcare, sick leave, and paid holidays. To a great extent, the contemporary "temp revolution" reflects a shift toward labor precarity and inequality. Although often characterized by promises of flexibility, individuality, and freedom, TAW constitutes an important element of social division, intersecting with other axes of inequality such as gender, age, region, ethnicity, and race.

It is noteworthy that employment relations involving TAWs are prone to legal ambiguities, making it difficult for the law to tackle exploitation and manipulation on the part of agencies and user firms. The situation is especially grave in emerging TAW markets that generally lack broad regulatory support and effective enforcement measures. For example, in China, in addition to tens of millions of migrants from rural villages who account for the vast majority of agency workers, vocational student interns have also become constrained labor, being subject to double control of teachers and schools, who act as labor-dispatching agencies, and factory managers (Smith and Chan 2015).

Besides temporary agency work, fixed-term contracts are another form of temporary employment. By definition, the continuation of such jobs is less secure and contingent upon firm, individual, and economic conditions. Fixed-term contracts can create entry positions for people seeking access to paid work, allowing employers to screen such entrants, in particular after leaving school or graduating or after phases of unemployment or inactivity, in strongly regulated and segmented labor markets with strict dismissal protection for permanent jobs. However, this often leads to longer chains of temporary jobs with low probabilities to move to a permanent job. The situation looks more favorable in more flexible labor markets. Empirical evidence further suggests that vocational training, based on temporary contracts with an employer providing training, helps overcome the barrier between fixed-term and permanent contracts, making a temporary job more of a "stepping stone" than a "dead end" (Eichhorst 2014; ILO 2016).

Self-Employment and the "Gig" Economy

The so-called "gig" economy – consisting of self-employed persons such as independent contractors or freelancers who often work on discrete projects that are managed by online platforms that mediate between employers and workers and often customers – has attracted much recent attention. The term originated in the USA to refer to short-term, "on-demand" work arrangements between persons or between a person and an organization and has since been used to describe the situation in industrial countries more generally. The rise of the gig economy recalls the small-scale entrepreneurship of the eighteenth century. The gig economy also takes a number of forms, including transportation platforms such as Uber and Lyft that connect drivers with riders, "crowdsourcing" arrangements in which people group their efforts to achieve particular outcomes, and freelance platforms (such as Upwork.com) that match skilled workers to jobs. Technological advances in communication and information systems have made it easier for organizations to specialize their production, assemble temporary workers quickly for projects, and rely more on outside suppliers. "Gigs" are also becoming more common offline, as in short-term engagements in which persons contract with other persons or organizations for specific activities.

Estimates of the size of the "gig" economy vary between countries, but also differ widely across studies due to diverse definitions and measurement issues. In the USA, for example, some earlier estimates ranged from 600,000 workers (or 0.4% of total US employment) who work with an online intermediary to one-third of the workforce (Harris and Krueger 2015). More recent data for Europe shows shares of gig work activity in the labor force between 1% and 3% (Schwellnus et al. 2019). Statistics on the size of the gig economy in industrial countries are hampered by the difficulty in distinguishing independent contractors, for example, from employees. Employers receive financial advantages from hiring independent contractors (such as not needing to pay them benefits or assume liability for their actions) and so are often motivated to avoid counting them as employees, thus creating a form of "hidden employment" (e.g., De Stefano 2016) that circumvents labor laws and other obligations. In the USA, there is a lively and still unsettled legal battle over whether Uber drivers should be considered employees of the company – since Uber exerts considerable control over their actions and remuneration – or as independent contractors. In the UK, courts recently ruled that Uber drivers are workers and thus covered by some aspects of labor law.

Work in the gig economy is heterogeneous, with considerable differences in the quality of jobs. Certain high-skilled workers can garner higher economic rewards as independent contractors or consultants than they might as employees in SERs, for example. In these instances, nonstandard arrangements allow workers to capitalize on abundant market opportunities and demands for their skills, despite the insecurity and instability associated with any particular "gig." Workers with fewer marketable skills, on the other hand, do not benefit as much from the flexibility afforded by the gig economy.

Atypical Work and Health

It is well established that work is an important determinant of health. This is not surprising, given the importance of work to the lives of most people. The Whitehall studies of male civil servants in England, for example, showed that socioeconomic status and other work-related factors affect health, leading to greater interest in how work is related to occupational health and safety (Gorman 2012; Howard 2017). Empirical studies of how work – especially atypical and precarious work – affects physical health and psychological well-being have increased, due to the changes in work and employment relations that we have discussed above (Benach et al. 2014) as well as the greater availability of new datasets that measure these things.

The fundamental cause theory provides a theoretical foundation for understanding how aspects of work affect health (Link and Phelan 1995). This theory hypotheses that individuals' personal resources – such as their money, knowledge, power, prestige, and social connections – facilitate their ability to amass health advantages over time. Inequalities in health are linked to differences in these personal resources. Atypical work is generally assumed to be negatively related to health because such work is associated with job insecurity and relative lack of social and legal protections; therefore, atypical workers have fewer resources to promote their health.

Despite the importance of work for health, how and why atypical work affects health is still understudied: Julià et al. (2017: p. 391) summarize the evidence on atypical work and health, most of which comes from research on job insecurity or temporary employment as having

> ...demonstrated consistent associations between these approximations of precariousness and various health outcomes, especially poor mental health (De Witte et al. 2016; Virtanen et al. 2005). However, these approaches have important conceptual limitations because they provide an incomplete picture of the multidimensional phenomenon of employment precariousness...

Kim et al. (2012: 100) argue that inconsistent results in empirical studies and thus the lack of precise conclusions on how precarious employment affects health is due to:

...the lack of a sound interpretative framework that is capable of facilitating an understanding of different social and employment realities; and limited contextual and labour market-related variables that interact with individual employment situations (Virtanen et al. 2005 ...).

In this section, we provide a brief overview of research on atypical work and health. We first discuss how atypical work is measured in this literature, from categories of work arrangements to broader aspects of employment relations and conditions. We then argue that country differences in the use and consequences of alternative work arrangements differ due to institutional and cultural forces.

Job Insecurity and Health Early studies of the effects of atypical work on health focused on the single concept of job insecurity. This emphasis was often promoted by fears over the consequences of the threat of job loss due to organizational restructuring. Studies of the effects of insecurity increased in the epidemiological literature during the 1990s as business restructuring and downsizing accelerated (Benach et al. 2014). A key assumption of these studies was that atypical work was more insecure than standard employment relations, and so would be associated with higher stress. Temporary workers especially tended to report experiencing poorer working conditions than permanent employees (Benach et al. 2014). Agency and contract workers were twice as likely as standard workers to report work-related injuries than standard workers (Benavides et al. 2006). Moreover, over half of the international studies reviewed by Virtanen et al. (2005) showed an increased risk of work-related injuries among contingent workers (see also Howard 2017; Quinlan et al. 2001). However, results were often ambiguous and contradictory, though they showed a greater impact on mental than physical health (Scott-Marshall and Tompa 2011).

Precarious Work, Employment Quality, and Health Other scholars have expanded the notion of atypical work to include the quality of employment relations more generally and broader conceptions of precarious employment beyond insecurity. People often work in precarious jobs because they lack alternative employment opportunities and so must cope with low wages and low social protections. These social and material aspects of work are also important for health and may constrain workers' ability to achieve personal and family obligations and goals.

Some studies examine the effects of atypical work through the framework of precarious work. For example, Tompa et al. (2007) refer to precarious work as being unstable and insecure, as well as socially and economically vulnerable, rather than identifying specific work classifications and categories such as atypical or nonstandard work. This recognizes that much of the work that is generally regarded as "standard" work has also become insecure and negatively impacts health. Hence, the nature of the labor arrangement or labor contract is only one factor associated with precarious work that may lead to insecurity and negatively affect health.

Julià et al. (2017) review recent work on precarious employment and job quality on workers' health and well-being in European Union countries. Their broad perspective on employment precariousness and quality is reflected in their Employment Precariousness Scale (EPRES), which includes measures of employment conditions and relations such as stability of employment as well as economic rewards, control over scheduling and working time, workers' rights and social protections, opportunities for training, collective representation, and power relations. They find that temporary workers had higher employment precariousness than permanent workers. While having a permanent contract seems to buffer the exposure to employment precariousness, however, it does not guarantee protection against precarity.

Pirani (2017) looks at the relationship between atypical work and mental health in Italy. She argues that atypical jobs are heterogeneous (temporary, casual, and varieties of chosen and not chosen part-time jobs). While the idea of precariousness emphasizes negative aspects of work, such as in temporariness and insecurity, low wages, fewer rights, and protections, some atypical work is not necessarily precarious. We discussed above how some gig workers with skills that are in high demand may thrive in this form of atypical work. Morever, a worker may choose to work part-time or on a temporary basis, to be able to spend time in other activities, such as family. Temporary work by itself is not strongly and negatively related to mental health. Rather, casual work has the strongest negative effects on mental health.

Lewchuk et al. (2008) show that in Canada there is a complex association between less permanent employment and health. For example, the effects of certain aspects of the employment relationship and nonpermanent employment were negatively associated with self-reported health, mental health, and stress. Other aspects, however, were not. Thus, poorer health was linked to scheduling uncertainty but not to employment fragility or earnings uncertainty. Workers who perceived their received higher individual support reported better health, while those who were constantly evaluated had poorer health outcomes.

Scott-Marshall and Tompa (2011), also in a study of Canada, found that while part-time or fixed-term work was not related to adverse self-reported health measures, other aspects of precarious work were, such as low earnings, lack of earnings growth, substantial unpaid overtime hours, and an absence of pension coverage.

Pathways There has been more progress in documenting the relationship between atypical and precarious work and health than in uncovering the mechanisms by which this relationship exists. Insecurity is a source of stress, which is the main way that atypical work affects health. But there are other pathways too: Julià et al. (2017: 401; see also Benach et al. 2014) argue that precarious work affects health through three main pathways:

> (1) through direct psychological effects related to uncertainty, feelings of unfairness, and powerlessness in instable and suboptimal employment conditions; (2) through the experience of higher exposure to detrimental physical and psychosocial working conditions, weaker occupational health and safety measures, and low-quality social relations at the work floor; and finally, (3) through material deprivation and its associated health consequences that may result from low income and under-protection from social risks such as unemployment, disability, and, later in life, retirement.

Peckham et al.'s (2019) study of the US operationalized personal resources as operating through three similar pathways that link employment quality and health: material deprivation; stressors rooted in employment conditions (e.g., job insecurity and pay equity); and occupational risk factors (nonstandard workers generally receive less training than those in standard employment relations and so are more likely to be exposed to injuries at work) (Julià et al. 2017; Tompa et al. 2007). They found that aspects of low employment quality – such as high workplace harassment and low opportunity to develop skills, control over schedule, and employee involvement – had lower levels of self-reported general and mental health as well as higher rates of occupational injury.

While we have assumed that work affects health, some research suggests that the association between them may be bidirectional (Pirani 2017). The pathways we described are ways in which work impacts various aspects of health. While we believe that these mechanisms are mainly responsible for the association between work and health, poor health may also hamper or prevent access to less precarious employment. The reciprocal relations between the two are important questions to answer in the future with more systematic longitudinal panel data. In view of the weak empirical evidence for causality at the moment, more prospective cohort studies are needed.

Country Differences
How atypical work affects health is likely to differ among countries due to differences in their institutions (such as their labor laws and social protection systems) and cultures (Benach et al. 2014; Kim et al. 2012; Kalleberg 2018).

Kim et al.'s (2012) review of the literature` concludes that welfare regimes affect the degree to which atypical work has adverse health outcomes such as poor self-rated health, musculoskeletal disorders, and mental health problems. Some types of atypical jobs are negatively related to health regardless of welfare regime, such as workers (especially females) who are on-call, substitute, apprenticeship, or involuntary temporary workers. Compared to permanent workers, workers in these nonstandard categories are more likely to suffer from poor self-rated health, back/neck pain, chronic diseases, and/or psychological distress.

However, while job insecurity is generally negatively related to health, Kim et al. (2012: 101–102) also conclude that approximately a third of studies on job insecurity and downsizing in Scandinavian countries (Denmark, Finland, Norway, and Sweden) report no or only partial associations between experiences of job insecurity and adverse health outcomes. In contrast to Scandinavian countries, almost all studies from Bismarckian (Belgium, Germany, the Netherlands, and Switzerland) and Southern (Italy and Spain) welfare states report a significant association between job insecurity and adverse health outcomes.

Conclusions

The growth of atypical or nonstandard work has transformed both the structure and the functioning of postindustrial labor markets. Different forms of atypical work might facilitate access to paid employment, but they also bring in a new dimension of inequality and competition into the labor market for those in temporary, part-time, agency work, or self-employed work arrangements. In addition to differences in wages or access to training and social protections, nonstandard contracts also affect health risk profiles. From a policy perspective, differences across countries in the incidence of nonstandard work and – even more important – inequalities in job quality, in transitions to regular employment, or in health risks point to a prominent role of institutions in governing the labor market and in mitigating the impacts of precarious work and inequality within employment systems.

References

Benach J, Vives A, Amable M, Vanroelen C, Tarafa G, Muntaner C (2014) Precarious employment: understanding an emergent social determinant of health. Annu Rev Public Health 35:229–253

Benavides FG, Benach J, Muntaner C, Delclos GL, Catot N, Amable M (2006) Associations between temporary employment and occupational injury: what are the mechanisms? Occup Environ Med 63(6):416–421

Cappelli P (1999) The new deal at work: managing the market-driven workforce. Harvard Business School Press, Boston

De Stefano V (2016) The rise of the 'just-in-time workforce': on-demand work, crowdwork and labour protection in the 'gig-economy', Conditions of work and employment series no 71. International Labour Organization, Geneva

De Witte H, Pienaar J, De Cuyper N (2016) Review of 30 years of longitudinal studies on the association between job insecurity and health and well-being: is there causal evidence? Aust Psychol 51(1):18–31

Eichhorst W (2014) Fixed-term contracts. IZA World of Labor

Eichhorst W, Marx P (eds) (2015) Non-standard employment in post-industrial labour markets. An occupational perspective. Edward Elgar, Cheltenham

Fagan C, Norman H, Smith M, González Menéndez M (2014) In search of good quality part-time employment. International Labour Office, Geneva. http://www.ilo.org/travail/whatwedo/publications/WCMS_237781/lang%2D%2Den/index.htm

Gorman S (2012) Inequality, stress and health: the Whitehall studies

Harris SD, Krueger AB (2015) A proposal for modernizing labor laws for twenty-first-century work: the independent worker, The Hamilton Project discussion paper 2015–10

Harvey D (2005) A brief history of neoliberalism. Oxford University Press, New York

Howard J (2017) Nonstandard work arrangements and worker health and safety. Am J Ind Med 60: 1–10

International Labour Organization (2016) Non-standard employment around the world. ILO, Geneva

Jacoby SM (1985) Employing bureaucracy: managers, unions, and the transformation of work in the 20th century. Columbia University Press, New York

Julià M, Vanroelen C, Bosmans K, Van Aerden K, Benach J (2017) Precarious employment and quality of employment in relation to health and well-being in Europe. Int J Health Serv 47(3): 389–409

Kalleberg AL (2000) Nonstandard employment relations: part-time, temporary, and contract work. Annu Rev Sociol 26:341–365

Kalleberg AL (2011) Good jobs, bad jobs: the growth of polarized and precarious employment systems in the United States, 1970s to 2000s. Russell Sage Foundation, New York

Kalleberg AL (2018) Precarious lives: job insecurity and well-being in rich democracies. Polity, Cambridge

Kalleberg AL, Marsden PV (2015) Transformation of the employment relationship. In: Scott R, Kosslyn S (eds) Emerging trends in the social and Behavioral sciences. John Wiley and Sons, Hoboken

Kim I-H, Muntaner C, Vahid Shahidi F, Vives A, Vanroelen C, Benach J (2012) Welfare states, flexible employment, and health: a critical review. Health Policy 104:99–127

Lewchuk W, Clarke M, de Wolff A (2008) Working without commitments: precarious employment and health. Work Employ Soc 22(3):387–406

Link BG, Phelan J (1995) Social conditionsm as fundamental causes of disease. J Health Soc Behav 35:80–94

OECD (2021) OECD employment outlook. OECD, Paris

Peckham T, Fujishiro K, Hajat A, Flaherty BP, Seixas N (2019) Evaluating employment quality as a determinant of health in a changing labor market. RSF J Soc Sci 5(4):258–281

Pirani E (2017) On the relationship between Aytpical work(s) and mental health: new insights from the Italian case. Soc Indic Res 130:233–252

Quinlan M, Mayhew C, Bohle P (2001) The global expansion of precarious employment, work disorganization, and consequences for occupational health. Int J Health Serv 31(2):335–414

Schwellnus C, Geva A, Pak M, Veiel R (2019) Gig economy platforms: boon or bane? OECD Economics Department working paper 1550

Scott-Marshall H, Tompa E (2011) The health consequences of precarious employment experiences. Work 38:369–382

Smith C, Chan J (2015) Working for two bosses: student interns as constrained labour in China. Hum Relat 68:305–326

Stone KVW, Arthurs H (eds) (2013) Rethinking employment regulation: after the standard contract of employment. Russell Sage Foundation Press, New York

Tompa E, Scott-Marshall H, Dolinschi R, Trevithick S, Bhattacharyya S (2007) Precarious employment experiences and their health consequences: towards a theoretical framework. Work 28: 209–224

Virtanen M, Kivimaki M, Joensuu M, Virtanen P, Elovainio M, Vahtera J (2005) Temporary employment and health: a review. Int J Epidemiol 34:610–622

Weil D (2014) The fissured workplace: why work became so bad for so many. Harvard University Press, Camridge

The Impact of New Technologies on the Quality of Work

4

Karen Van Aerden, Christophe Vanroelen, and Jessie Gevaert

Contents

Introduction	42
Digitalization and Advanced Digital Technologies	44
The Impact of New Technologies on Job Quality	46
Intrinsic Quality of Work	46
Employment Quality	48
Discussion: A Contextual, Life Course Perspective on Work and Technology	51
Cross-References	53
References	53

Abstract

Given the importance of digitalization in shaping individual life courses and working lives, this chapter focuses on the transformation of work related to the introduction of new technologies. The chapter starts with a short description and historical account of the digitalization process and with a brief overview of the most recent technologies that are incorporated by organizations. Considering the impact of these new technologies on work and employment, rather than concentrating on the debate of job destruction versus job creation, this chapter highlights the qualitative changes for jobs and workers associated with the introduction of new technologies. Both the potentially beneficial and detrimental impact of technology on several aspects of job quality will be discussed: health and safety, intrinsic characteristics of work, pay and other rewards, terms of employment, work-life balance, representation, and voice. This job quality overview will be complemented by a life course perspective on employment and technology, focusing on the risks and opportunities for careers and the quality of working life in general. The chapter concludes with an overall assessment of the role of

---

K. Van Aerden · C. Vanroelen (✉) · J. Gevaert
Interface Demography, Department of Sociology, Vrije Universiteit Brussel, Brussels, Belgium
e-mail: christophe.vanroelen@vub.be

technology in shaping the world of work and with some insights on how to include the topic of technological innovation in job quality research.

Keywords

Quality of work · Quality of working life · Technology · Digital labor platforms · ICT · Occupational health and safety

Introduction

Processes of digitalization and the introduction of new advanced technologies have a profound impact on individual life courses and working lives. From a historical perspective, concerns about the disruptive nature of technological innovations on work and employment are certainly not new (Deschacht 2021) and even date back to antiquity. The recent development and introduction of advanced digital technologies has again led to the expression of fears that these technologies pose a threat for many jobs and occupations (Frey and Osborne 2017), leading to disruptive and discontinuous employment histories. Even though predictions about "the end of work" due to technological innovation do not appear to come true, the introduction of digital technologies does have substantial effects on the allocation, the continuity, the nature, and the quality of jobs (Deschacht 2021). However, although technology is a powerful factor of change in societies, it is not a deus ex machina: The impact of technology on the quality of workers' jobs is strongly mediated by the political economy of countries, the priorities of management, and the work organizational models applied by management (Munos de Bustillo et al. 2022).

Job quality can be defined as the extent to which a set of job attributes fosters beneficial outcomes regarding psychological and physical well-being and positive job attitudes of workers (Holman 2013). Munos de Bustillo et al. (2022) mention three main ways in which technological innovation can impact the overall level of job quality in a labor market. First, technological change is the main factor explaining increased productivity. Increased productivity, in turn, has always been a crucial enabling factor for rising wages and reductions in working time, which are two important dimensions of job quality (Munos de Bustillo et al. 2022). Second, technological innovation has an important effect on the structure of the economy because the adoption of new technology by organizations can result in "product innovation," i.e., the emergence of new products and related occupations and relative decline of others (Munos de Bustillo et al. 2022). Product innovation affects overall job quality, since job features and job quality levels vary between different segments of the economy. For example, the emergence of entirely new niches in the service sector – e.g., digital entertainment – is supposed to create many new highly skilled, creative, and well-rewarded jobs. Third, technological innovation is also an important driver behind "process innovation," i.e., it causes changes in the way existing products are produced (Munos de Bustillo et al. 2022). Process innovation leads to changes in the share of human labor that is substituted by machines and in the task composition of the remaining jobs. As a consequence, new occupations emerge, others diminish, and certain occupations change in terms of their task content.

Changes in aggregate job quality due to technological innovation have been heavily debated in labor economics (Autor 2015). This also holds for the dominant direction of change in the skills content and quality of jobs, i.e., upskilling, deskilling, or polarization (Warhurst and Hunt 2019). Two competing hypotheses have been debated in the literature (Warhurst and Hunt 2019). The "skills biased technological change hypothesis" asserts that new technology predominantly tends to substitute unskilled labor in routine tasks and complements workers with higher-level skills (e.g., problem-solving and analytical skills), resulting in higher aggregate levels of job quality, or "upskilling" (Autor et al. 2003). In contrast, the "routine biased technological change hypothesis" assumes that technology replaces workers with codifiable routine tasks and enables the offshoring of semiskilled jobs (Warhurst and Hunt 2019). This leads to reduced demand for these semiskilled jobs relative to low- and high-skilled jobs, resulting in a pattern of polarization with both growth in "lousy" (deskilling) and "lovely" (upskilling) jobs in terms of earnings, stability, and other features (Goos and Manning 2007). These macro analyses, however, do not give a lot of information about the impact on day-to-day work experiences of individual workers. In this chapter, the focus lies exactly there.

In order to be clear on what we are aiming for, it is important to further unpack the concept of job quality. Job quality is usually conceived as consisting of two main dimensions: "quality of work," i.e., features that are strongly related to the performance of work tasks (job content and different types of exposures and demands); and "quality of employment," i.e., employment conditions and relations "surrounding" the actual work task (Warhurst et al. 2017). Underneath that basic distinction, a variety of subdimensions have been determined. For example, Warhurst et al. (2017) distinguish six dimensions after an extensive literature review: health and safety, intrinsic characteristics of work, pay and other rewards, terms of employment, work-life balance, representation, and voice. We will loosely follow this subdivision to structure the overview of evidence further on in this chapter.

However, it needs to be clear that these "objective job characteristics" (Warhurst et al. 2017) have a differential impact on workers' life and career. This is what Eurofound labeled the "quality of working life." It refers to a broader and more subjective set of individual worker outcomes such as social protection, job satisfaction, turnover intentions, opportunities for personal growth, well-being, and the compatibility of work with other life spheres (Eiffe 2021). In other words, while job quality attempts to objectify concrete job characteristics, the quality of working life-concept relates more to the fit between job characteristics and individual circumstances and needs throughout their life course (Eiffe 2021). A good quality of working life leads to sustainable work, i.e., work that allows for workers to age in their job/career, which aligns with the scope of this handbook.

The remainder of this chapter is organized following this logic: First, we will discuss the process of digitalization and the introduction of advanced digital technologies in the world of work. Then, we will proceed with an overview of the impact of new technologies on different job quality dimensions. We conclude this chapter with attention toward the contextuality and life course perspective, by highlighting the impact of digitalization and the adoption of new technologies on the quality of working life. Moreover, we stress the room for agency of all stakeholders involved when it comes to optimizing the link between technology and job quality.

Digitalization and Advanced Digital Technologies

Digitalization has been described as an evolution in which digital processes have made it possible to enhance the processing, storing, and communication of information. Examples can be not only digitally enabled machines with artificial intelligence (AI), but also digital networks coordinating economic transactions through platforms with algorithms (Warhurst and Hunt 2019). According to Warhurst and Hunt (2019), digitalization involves two transformations: the *digitalization of production* and the *digitalization of work*. The first relates to the way that new digital technologies have dramatically reconfigured how goods and services are produced (i.e., referring to the potential of technological innovations to undertake both physical and cognitive tasks that have hitherto been undertaken by humans). The second transformation refers almost exclusively to the emergence of platform companies, and the migration of work to these platforms where "standard labour contracts" are expected to be supplemented or replaced by "on-demand labour" (Warhurst and Hunt 2019).

Historically, technological innovations – similar to the ones described above – have had a huge impact on employment (Frey and Osborne 2017). For example, inventions like steam engines (first Industrial Revolution), electricity and railroads (second Industrial Revolution), and computers and communication technologies (third Industrial Revolution) all have in common that they fundamentally changed industrial processes and the world of work (Schwab 2016). The new wave of technologies in computing, information networks, robotics, and artificial intelligence, emerging from the end of the twentieth century onward, has been described as the fourth Industrial Revolution (Schwab 2016) or "2nd machine age" (Brynjolfsson and McAfee 2014). While such writings imply a sudden and discontinuous, qualitative leap over a relatively short time span, others point at the historical continuity implying that the economic restructuring related to technological change is much more gradual (Deschacht 2021). Digitalization can thus be described as an impactful process involving the generalization, amplification, and intensification of many types of digital technologies.

Technologies that can be conceived as key factors of change in the current world of work are the following:

Information and Communication Technologies (ICT) refer to a collection of different technologies that surged around the 1970s and mostly characterized the third industrial revolution. The emergence of ICT occurred with *chips, hardware,* and new materials, followed by *software and telecommunication equipment*, and e-services, such as e-mail, the Internet, and other new forms of electronic communication (Korunka and Vartiainen 2017).

Internet of Things (IoT). The "Internet," as a term, emerged in 1974, was defined as "an internetworking between multiple computers," and became "the world wide web" in 1991, which was a user interface providing the organization and access to distributed data across computer networks (Curran et al. 2012). While the Internet seems most important for the service industry, many different industries like manufacturing, telecommunications, and other backbone services were affected by being able to decentralize certain operations, and linking knowledge exchange (Castells and Aoyama 1994). The Internet of Things involves a next step, describing the integration of the cyber world and the physical world enabling data flows and communication between physical objects, software applications, measuring devices, databases, etc. (Čolaković and Hadžialić 2018). It is crucial technology to sustain automatic processes of production, to generate "intelligent services" or to coordinate global communication networks in an autonomous way (Čolaković and Hadžialić 2018). Probably the best-known application of IoT is the so-called "Industry 4.0" concept referring to the networking of industrial machines and processes supported by ICT (Schwab 2016).

Robots and Robotic Process Automation (RPA). "Robots" are defined as: "programmed actuated mechanisms, with a degree of autonomy (to perform intended tasks without human intervention), to perform locomotion, manipulation or positioning" (ISO 2021). They can be fixed in place (which is the case for most industrial robots) or mobile platforms (ISO 2021). The largest sectors to make use of robots are by far the automotive, and electrical and electronics, sectors (Upchurch 2018). But while they are indeed primarily useful in the manufacturing industry (e.g., for mass production and/or specialized repetitive tasks), robotic process automation (RPA) (i.e., when robots are used to automate a business process through software, capable of following a graphical representation of said process (Moreau 2018)) is also increasingly used in service industries to automate time-consuming tasks with low added value (e.g., data entry, data consolidation, information extraction, and compliance verification) (Moreau 2018). There is an obvious link with IoT – discussed above.

Artificial Intelligence (AI). Whereas RPAs tend to mimic human actions and aim to *act*, "artificial intelligence" (AI) concerns the actual simulation of human intelligence by machines and thus aims to *think* (Simmons and Chappell 2018). AI involves numerous applications and techniques ranging from neural networks to speech-pattern recognition, to deep learning, but generally also involves common elements of natural language processing (i.e., algorithms that enable systems to learn and recognize language patterns), or machine vision (i.e., algorithmic inspection and analyses of images) (Jarrahi 2018). The use of AI systems has been accelerated in sectors and occupations (e.g., white-collar workers) that were originally viewed as immune to automation (Jarrahi 2018). More specifically, AI technologies and machine learning applications can be found in management tasks (algorithmic management), human resources (screening software), the financial sector (investment risk assessments), or even in medical occupations (diagnosis from medical imaging).

Big data is not a digital technology, but rather a by-product of the use of technology. Big data generally concern large volumes of extremely varied data that are generated, collected, processed, and stored at high speed. These data are created through data production, as well as secondary data generation from sources like the Internet, social networks, digital surveillance, cookies, and IP addresses (Menger and Paye 2017). In the world of work, the use of big data is increasing in sectors like "research and development" (R&D) or "customer service work" with the goal of improving business intelligence and strategic planning (Jantti and Hyvarinen 2018).

In sum, we might assume that jobs effectively change due to these new technologies, either through chances in production or through chances in the organization of work itself. In the next part of this chapter, relations between digitalization and dimensions of job quality are described.

The Impact of New Technologies on Job Quality

Aggregate changes in job quality do not say much about how the working life of concrete workers is affected by technological change. Some job characteristics may improve due the complex interplay of technology and work organization, others might deteriorate, and side effects on other aspects of job quality can arise (Munos de Bustillo et al. 2022). In this section, we have a look at a series of important job quality characteristics and provide an overview of how the adoption of abovementioned technologies might affect them for better or for worse.

Intrinsic Quality of Work

Warhurst et al. (2017) make a distinction between the dimensions of "health and safety," including physical and psychosocial risks, and "intrinsic characteristics of work," including physical, ergonomic, and psychological demands as well as the skill content of tasks.

Health and Safety at Work: Physical, Ergonomic, and Psychological Demands Historically, one of the most important rationales to substitute human labor by technological solutions is to eradicate repetitive, harsh, and dangerous work. This has been the case when steam-driven machinery was introduced in mining, transport, and agriculture or when car manufacturing saw the introduction of the early robotics systems in the 1960s. Industrial robots continue to fulfill the same function in assembly plants, up to the extreme of "lights-out factories," where human labor is limited to routine controls and problem-solving in plants where all assembly work is taken over by robots (Cooke 2021). Also in logistic warehouses, robotization leads to reduced physical demands for workers (Berkers et al. 2022). Another application are exoskeletons, which are used in industry and construction to support and strengthen the movements of human workers – and thus reduce the physical harshness of their work (Bär et al. 2021).

Automation of routine processes and efficiency gains in work organization have dramatically reduced the time allocated to waiting, checking, and communicating with colleagues. While the reduction of monotonous and plainly boring work has been a positive consequence, it has also led to work intensification (Moore 2019). Examples of this tendency can be found in hospitality, order picking, and industry. The massive and radical turn toward home-based and hybrid work – supported by enabling ICT-applications – has also created new and often underestimated ergonomic risks for office workers. Where office environments have established ergonomic standards and control practices, the home and other remote environments largely escape OHS-controls (Davis et al. 2020).

Also recent ICT applications have been designated as causes of increasing psychological demands, including time pressure and work intensification. Diagnostic processes and office tools aided by ICT-applications have taken out much of the routine work of knowledge workers, leading to work intensification (Pérez-Zapata et al. 2016). Specific concerns have been raised for the role played regarding work intensification by de-humanized forms of "algorithmic management" (Aloisi and De Stefano 2022). However, virtual assistants and other "smart" office applications also allow freeing up professionals' time to carry out more satisfying tasks and to alleviate their workload and help them in improving their services (Warhurst and Hunt 2019). In other sectors, automation of processes creates new elementary jobs solely consisting of "left-over tasks" that cannot be handled by machines, leading to simple, repetitive, and intense work. This has been documented, for instance, among order pickers and packers in warehouses (Berkers et al. 2022).

Skill Requirements A dominant theme considering the impact of digitalization is the assumed enrichment of the task content of occupations and related changes in skill requirements. So far, researchers have observed a few different trends: (1) New jobs are being created with their own specific skill sets; (2) old jobs are destroyed because certain skills are being taken over by new technologies; and (3) there is an overall demand for more digital skills even in industries outside of the technology industry (Berger and Frey 2016).

Another consequence is the increased complexity and "richness" of tasks due to "simple" or "physical tasks" being taken over by technological tools, while analytical, problem-solving, and other intellectual tasks become more prominent in all kinds of occupations (see supra). Such processes have been documented for professions as diverse as assembly line workers (Rosini 2018), nonmanual professionals, and managers, who "switched from executive positions to strategic decision planners and information and knowledge sharing facilitators inside an organization" (Lavtar 2013: 881). However, as discussed earlier, other authors do point out that robotization and the creation of jobs consisting of "left-over tasks" can also give rise to reduced autonomy for the workers involved (Berkers et al. 2022).

Employment Quality

In line with Warhurst et al.'s (2017) typology, four separate topics are discussed: work, pay, and other rewards; terms of employment (e.g., contractual stability, opportunities for training and career progression); work-life balance (e.g., working time arrangements and scheduling flexibility); and representation and voice (e.g., employee consultation and involvement in decision-making).

Work, Pay, and Other Rewards (See Also ▶ Chap. 26, "Worksite Health Promotion: Evidence on Effects and Challenges") Overall, the adoption of new digital technologies is assumed to lead to productivity gains and thus to increase incomes, purchasing power and consumer welfare (Caselli and Manning 2019). Income levels in society can also be expected to rise because jobs that disappear due to automatization are usually low-skilled and low-income jobs. At the same time, growing income inequality is one of the most prominent outflows of job polarization related to technological innovation (Goos and Manning 2007), with new technologies as the driver behind very high incomes for the most talented who reach extremely large markets due to digital technologies.

The relationship between digitally mediated work (i.e., platform work and freelance work), on the one hand, and economic sustainability, on the other hand, remains unclear. Overall, income levels derived from digital platform work appear to be very low compared with the median earnings of nonplatform full-time workers (ETUI 2022). This is related to the observation that activities on digital labor platforms can be a primary source of income, but for most workers they are rather a small additional source of income. Often, platform work is characterized by fragmented work tasks (gigs), highly variable earnings, and income levels that are economically unsustainable if not supplemented by other sources of income in the household (Elmer et al. 2019). In other words, information about the wider economical dependency of platform workers is crucial to assess the financial implications of their digitally mediated work (Elmer et al. 2019).

Terms of Employment (See Also ▶ Chap. 23, "Working Careers with Common Mental Disorders") When it comes to the stability of employment, concerns have been voiced that the availability of advanced digital technologies decreases coordination costs (Weil 2014) and therefore further enables the proliferation of instable employment contracts. Moreover, companies might prefer a more substantial temporary workforce as part of a strategy to be able to answer to rapidly changing circumstances because of fast-moving digital technologies (Rosini 2018). In contrast, flexible manpower strategies, in the peripheral labor force, can lead to greater employment stability of the permanently employed core workers as well (Rosini 2018). However, also for what used to be the strategical core of the labor force (e.g., managers, highly skilled professionals), evidence shows increasing popularity of freelancing, facilitated by the availability of advanced ICT (McKeown 2015). Digital technologies also made competition between workers in certain types of professional occupations to become literally "global." Due to much easier communication and exchange of information worldwide, companies have more opportunities to offshore. This is the case for high- (IT, accounting) and medium-skilled (customer support) occupations. The evidence on the wage effects of offshoring is inconclusive, although it clearly presents a breach with standard full-time employment (Cardoso et al. 2021).

The breach with any traditional notion of standard employment becomes complete when considering Internet-based and digital platform work (Lenaerts and Smits 2019). Different authors have questioned the ambiguity of the employment status of platform workers, and the fact that they might work as de-facto employees under the de-jure status of self-employed or even informally employed (Warhurst and Hunt 2019). An important issue in that regard is the limited level of control over their activities, working times, and wages on behalf of the platform (Aloisi and De Stefano 2022). Another issue – fairly contrasting with the overall promise of upskilling related to the application of new technologies – are the poor opportunities for training for digital platform workers, while they are a requirement for further career progression (Kilhoffer et al. 2020). Moreover, also for jobs requiring digital skills on the traditional waged labor market, studies have reported that workers tend to feel they are not given the adequate resources and necessary time to learn about new technologies (Jantti and Hyvarinen 2018).

In sum, the evidence suggests that the introduction of new technologies has an overall negative impact on employment stability. Moreover, even when a job is not objectively threatened, perceived job insecurity might arise because of assumptions that technology might replace a part of the workforce, facilitate outsourcing, or make employment inherently less stable (Jantti and Hyvarinen 2018).

Working Times and Work-Life Balance Munos de Bustillo et al. (2022) state that technological innovation leads to productivity growth and in doing so creates the possibility to combine a reduction in working time with an increase in labor income. At the same time, the use of new digital technologies and mobile devices has brought new opportunities for a globally dispersed (across time borders), fast-paced, 24/7, online economy. This increases the possibilities for "place- and time-independent work" (Nierling and Krings 2022), a trend that inevitably influences how much (see ▶ Chap. 16, "Psychosocial Work Environment and Health: Applying Job-Exposure Matrices and Work Organization and Management Practice") and when (see ▶ Chap. 27, "Falling Sick While Working: An Overview of the EU-Level Policy Framework on Returning to Work Following Chronic Disease(s)") people work. The COVID19-crisis evidently saw a brutal increase of technologies facilitating "place- and time-independent work."

From a positive perspective, place- and time-independent work enables working hours flexibility, helps to better reconcile work and private life throughout the life course, and leads to more autonomy in the arrangement of one's working hours (Daniels et al. 2001). However, on a negative note, possibilities for remote working may also lead to a blurring of boundaries between work and nonwork time, working during free time, problems to (mentally) disconnect from work, and working at nonstandard hours such as evenings and weekends (Daniels et al. 2001). How remote work applications impact the working hours and work schedules of employees and whether this leads to better or worse outcomes for workers depend for a large part on how the organization approaches said technology (Tagliaro and Migliore 2022).

Digital platform work is characterized by a variety of working time arrangements. Drahokoupil and Piasna (2019) find that, overall, platform work is characterized by unsocial and irregular working times. But while for a majority working hours are usually short and fragmented (mostly for on-location platform labor*)*, for others working hours might be very long (characteristic for online platform labor) and might include – in the case of delivery jobs – long unpaid waiting times (Pulignano et al. 2021).

Representation and Voice New technologies and digitalization tend to raise new questions regarding the protection of workers' rights, representation, and voice (see also ► Chap. 30, "Conceptual and Methodological Directions of Occupational Life Course Research").

Regarding workers' rights, new information technologies may offer opportunities for social emancipation and trade union movements (Degryse 2016). After all, new technologies may act as additional tools for the exchange of information, cooperation, mobilization, new ways of organizing, and increased international synchronization of labor union strategies (Degryse 2016). On top of this, new technologies may help set up new collective tools for the evaluation of employers, the creation of data cooperatives, as well as for the creation of incubators aimed at a cooperative, social, and solidaristic economy (Degryse 2016). Nevertheless, digitalization also poses a lot of challenges to workers' rights and social protection, including challenges for established labor regulations, social dialogue structures, social rights, and social protection schemes (Degryse 2016). Digital labor platforms in particular cause fundamental challenges related to workers' rights and social protection (Nierling and Krings 2022). Many platform companies tend to avoid the issue of workers' rights based on employment status grounds (Vallas and Schor 2020). One's employment status, however, is important because it can provide or limit access to social and OHS-protection systems (Elmer et al. 2019). In addition, more fundamental (human) rights are also being challenged, for example, the workers' right to privacy (i.e., the difficult balance between workers' privacy and employers' need to monitor and control their workers using ICT tools) (Aloisi and De Stefano 2022) and the right to disconnect from work (Vargas-Llave et al. 2020).

Worker empowerment, however, also comes from informal employment relations. First, in a context of technological change, the involvement of employees is crucial for a successful implementation of new technologies, since they are the ones who will use the technology and are most familiar with the current work processes (Kadir and Broberg 2020). A second important issue to address is the potentially difficult social relations associated with full-time online work such as home-based telework or online platform work (Kilhoffer et al. 2020). The absence of support from or even contact with colleagues and managers could lead to the isolation of workers. In contrast, there are also positive side effects associated with the digitalization of work. Digital technologies can facilitate (geographically dispersed) teamwork and more cooperative types of work design, including increased information sharing (Rosini 2018).

The formal aspects of employee empowerment are mainly related to collective bargaining, social dialogue, and union representation. In recent years, social partners' attention for the topic of digitalization and its impact on workers has grown. Established frameworks for collective bargaining are challenged by certain technology-induced developments, such as the emergence of the platform economy and the highly transnational character of contemporary labor markets (Willems 2019).

Discussion: A Contextual, Life Course Perspective on Work and Technology

This chapter has provided an overview of how digitalization and the adoption of new (advanced) technologies impacts the world of work. We have specifically aimed to move beyond the debates on job creation versus job destruction or changing skill requirements on the labor market by focusing on job quality and its consequences for sustainable employment. In doing so, we were able to shed light on the more qualitative changes associated with digitalization and on the ways in which the impact of technology can be both beneficial and detrimental for workers, depending on the broader context of its implementation and the specific situation of the employees involved.

The main conclusion is that technological innovation comes with great opportunities to improve job quality and the work situation of employees, but at the same time possess serious threats to several aspects of job quality and to individual worker outcomes. A large part of the unclarity in the relationship between digitalization and job quality and the different outcomes that are observed can be explained by the enormous complexity of both concepts (Warhurst et al. 2018). Processes of digitalization and innovation encompass a very wide variety of tools and technologies that can be used in different ways. On top of this, both job quality and sustainable employment are multidimensional concepts that refer to different aspects related to the work situation of employees. This also means that technological change can have a beneficial impact on a certain job quality dimension, while causing problems for another component.

How workers experience the quality of their working life results from the job characteristics employees are confronted with in their work. However, it is important to keep in mind that a similar work situation or job feature can yield different results for workers, depending on how it fits with their needs and preferences during that particular phase of their life course.

For example, regarding musculoskeletal health problems, we can observe that the digitalization of work has partly reduced the risks where workers are confronted with, by aiding their work tasks via automation of processes, remote diagnostics, etc. However, digitalization also implies some risks for the physical health of workers. Since more and more workers are spending a large amount of time in a sedentary position, behind their computers or working on mobile devices, the risk of musculoskeletal disorders and of visual fatigue due to screen time increases (Garben 2017). This is certainly the case for home-based telework because the home offices of workers are usually less well-equipped and no control on the ergonomic quality of the work situation is present (Davis et al. 2020). This is only a demonstration on how context, personal factors, and career stage of a worker might result in different OHS-outcomes based on the same types of technology.

A second example concerns the work-life balance of workers. Here the effect of digitalization processes can go in two directions as well. Digitalization opens a whole range of possibilities for more flexible working hours and more worker-autonomy in adapting work schedules, thus leading to a better work-life balance. However, digitalization also blurs boundaries between professional and private life and could make it harder for workers to disconnect from work during their free time, which would result in a poorer work-life balance (Daniels et al. 2001).

The takeaway message from this overview is that the impact of digitalization on job quality and the sustainability of employment is ambiguous and largely depends on factors lying outside a strict notion of technology. A lot depends on how organizations, managers, workers, and worker representatives approach the introduction of new technologies and on the specific context of the worker. Many of the important mediating factors are still understudied (Warhurst et al. 2018). However, it is clear that a number of factors are destined to determine the outcome of digitalization: (1) the extent to which workers are involved in the implementation process of a new technology; (2) the motivation underlying the decision to adopt the technology in the organization (i.e., to facilitate control over and monitoring of employees or to strengthen the autonomy and control of workers); (3) the extent to which both the job design and organizational context are adapted to the new technologies and provide the necessary training and support to use them; and (4) the fit between job features, on the one hand, and the needs and characteristics of the worker during that particular moment in their life course, on the other hand. Also, it is important to keep in mind that workers with different socioeconomic background characteristics are likely confronted with different realities when it comes to the impact of technological innovation on their jobs. Whereas high-educated workers in high-quality job are more likely to experience the empowering and enabling effects of digitalization, workers in more vulnerable situation might be exposed to the more detrimental side effects associated with this evolution.

An issue that comes to the fore when studying the role of technology in shaping the world of work is how to better include (the impact of) technological innovation in employment quality and precarious employment research (Vanroelen et al. 2021). Related to this, but from the perspective of policymaking, Warhurst et al. (2018) state that although the European Commission recognizes the importance of both innovation and job quality, they tend to position both topics separately within their current policy-agenda.

Finally, we have conceived this chapter implicitly assuming a causal relationship running from technology to job quality. However, Munos de Bustillo et al. (2022) point out that job quality can also be a driver of technological development. Aforementioned authors see two mechanisms at play: (1) A highly committed and empowered labor force is likely to be more willing to uptake technological innovation and more creative in its application; (2) moreover, increasing job quality inevitably also implies higher wages, in turn pushing companies to increase their productivity via the adoption of new technologies (Munos de Bustillo et al. 2022). This final remark – again – demonstrates that there is no need for defeatism when considering the relation between technology and job quality. Instead, there is much more room for policy and agency of the relevant stakeholders as is often assumed in common thought about the issue.

Cross-References

- ▶ Conceptual and Methodological Directions of Occupational Life Course Research
- ▶ Falling Sick While Working: An Overview of the EU-Level Policy Framework on Returning to Work Following Chronic Disease(s)
- ▶ Psychosocial Work Environment and Health: Applying Job-Exposure Matrices and Work Organization and Management Practice
- ▶ Working Careers with Common Mental Disorders
- ▶ Worksite Health Promotion: Evidence on Effects and Challenges

References

Aloisi A, De Stefano V (2022) Your boss is an algorithm: artificial intelligence, platform work and labour. Bloomsbury Publishing, London

Autor DH (2015) Why are there still so many jobs? The history and future of workplace automation. J Econ Perspect 29:3–30. https://doi.org/10.1257/jep.29.3.3

Autor DH, Levy F, Murnane RJ (2003) The skill content of recent technological change: an empirical exploration. Q J Econ 118:1279–1333. https://doi.org/10.1162/003355303322552801

Bär M, Steinhilber B, Rieger MA, Luger T (2021) The influence of using exoskeletons during occupational tasks on acute physical stress and strain compared to no exoskeleton – a systematic review and meta-analysis. Appl Ergon 94:103385. https://doi.org/10.1016/j.apergo.2021.103385

Berger T, Frey CB (2016) Did the computer revolution shift the fortunes of U.S. cities? technology shocks and the geography of new jobs. Reg Sci Urban Econ 57:38–45. https://doi.org/10.1016/j.regsciurbeco.2015.11.003

Berkers HA, Rispens S, Le Blanc PM (2022) The role of robotization in work design: a comparative case study among logistic warehouses. Int J Hum Resour Manag:1–24. https://doi.org/10.1080/09585192.2022.2043925

Brynjolfsson E, McAfee A (2014) The second machine age: work, progress, and prosperity in a time of brilliant technologies. W. W. Norton & Company

Cardoso M, Neves PC, Afonso O, Sochirca E (2021) The effects of offshoring on wages: a meta-analysis. Rev World Econ 157:149–179. https://doi.org/10.1007/s10290-020-00385-z

Caselli F, Manning A (2019) Robot arithmetic: new technology and wages. Am Econ Rev Insights 1:1–12. https://doi.org/10.1257/aeri.20170036

Castells M, Aoyama Y (1994) Paths towards the informational society – employment structure in G-7 countries, 1920–90. Int Labour Rev 133:5–33

Čolaković A, Hadžialić M (2018) Internet of Things (IoT): a review of enabling technologies, challenges, and open research issues. Comput Netw 144:17–39. https://doi.org/10.1016/j.comnet.2018.07.017

Cooke P (2021) Image and reality: 'digital twins' in smart factory automotive process innovation – critical issues. Reg Stud 55:1630–1641. https://doi.org/10.1080/00343404.2021.1959544

Curran J, Fenton N, Freedman D (2012) Misunderstanding the Internet. Routledge, London

Daniels K, Lamond D, Standen P (2001) Teleworking: frameworks for organizational research. J Manag Stud 38:1151–1185. https://doi.org/10.1111/1467-6486.00276

Davis KG, Kotowski SE, Daniel D et al (2020) The Home Office: ergonomic lessons from the "new normal". Ergon Des Q Hum Factors Appl 28:4–10. https://doi.org/10.1177/1064804620937907

Degryse C (2016) Digitalisation of the economy and its impact on labour markets, Working paper 2016.02. Brussels

Deschacht N (2021) The digital revolution and the labour economics of automation: a review. ROBONOMICS J Autom Econ 1

Drahokoupil J, Piasna A (2019) Work in the platform economy: deliveroo riders in Belgium and the SMart arrangement, Working paper 2019.01

Eiffe F (2021) Eurofound's reference framework: sustainable work over the life course in the EU. Eur J Work Innov 6:67–83. https://doi.org/10.46364/ejwi.v6i1.805

Elmer M, Herr B, Klaus D, Gegenhuber T (2019) Platform workers centre stage! Taking stock of current debates and approaches for improving the conditions of platform work in Europe. Hans-Böckler-Stiftung, Düsseldorf

Frey CB, Osborne MA (2017) The future of employment: how susceptible are jobs to computerisation? Technol Forecast Soc Change 114:254–280. https://doi.org/10.1016/j.techfore.2016.08.019

Garben S (2017) Protecting workers in the online platform economy: an overview of regulatory and policy developments in the EU European Agency for Safety and Health at Work-EU-OSHA 1. EU-OSHA, Bilbao

Goos M, Manning A (2007) Lousy and lovely jobs: the rising polarization of work in britain. Rev Econ Stat 89:118–133

Holman D (2013) Job types and job quality in Europe. Indus Relat 66:475–502

ISO – International Organization for Standardization (2021) Robotics vocabulary

Jantti M, Hyvarinen S (2018) Exploring digital transformation and digital culture in service organizations. In: 15th international conference on service systems and service management (ICSSSM). IEEE, Hangzhou, pp 1–6

Jarrahi MH (2018) Artificial intelligence and the future of work: human-AI symbiosis in organizational decision making. Bus Horiz 61:577–586. https://doi.org/10.1016/j.bushor.2018.03.007

Kadir BA, Broberg O (2020) Human well-being and system performance in the transition to industry 4.0. Int J Ind Ergon 76:102936

Kilhoffer Z, De Groen WP, Lenaerts K et al (2020) Study to gather evidence on the working conditions of platform workers

Korunka C, Vartiainen M (2017) Digital technologies at work are great, aren't they? The development of information and communication technologies (ICT) and their relevance in the world of work. In: Chmiel N, Fraccaroli F, Sverke M (eds) An introduction to work and organizational psychology: an international perspective, third edit. John Wiley & Sons, Hoboken, pp 102–120

Lavtar R (2013) Ways and side ways of using the information and communication technology (ICT) in knowledge sharing in organizations. Lex Localis 11:871–882. https://doi.org/10.4335/11.4.871-882(2013)

Lenaerts K, Smits I (2019) A structured mapping of the challenges related to the job quality of platform work: identifying drivers and potential responses

McKeown T (2015) What's in a name? The value of 'entrepreneurs' compared to 'self-employed'... but what about 'freelancing' or 'IPro'? In: The handbook of research on freelancing and self- employment. Senate Hall Academic Publishing, Dublin, pp 121–134

Menger P-M, Paye S (2017) Big Data et Traçabilité Numérique: Les sciences sociales face à la quantification massive des individus. OpenEdition Books, Paris

Moore PV (2019) OSH and the future of work: benefits and risks of artificial intelligence tools in workplaces. In: Digital Hu (ed) HCII2019, Orlando, FL, pp 292–315

Moreau I (2018) RPA: Quand l'automatisation investit l'économie. J du Net

Munos de Bustillo R, Grande R, Fernandez-Macias E (2022) Innovation and job quality. In: Warhurst C, Mathieu C, Dwyer RE (eds) The Oxford handbook of job quality. Oxford Univerity Press, Oxford, pp 37–72

Nierling L, Krings BJ (2022) Digitalisation and concepts of extended work. In: Post-growth work: employment and meaningful activities within planetary boundaries. Routledge Earthscan, London, pp 134–146

Pérez-Zapata O, Pascual AS, Álvarez-Hernández G, Collado CC (2016) Knowledge work intensification and self-management: the autonomy paradox. Work Organ Labour Glob 10. https://doi.org/10.13169/workorgalaboglob.10.2.0027

Pulignano V, Piasna A, Domecka M et al (2021) Does it pay to work? Unpaid labour in the platform economy

Rosini S (2018) Future of manufacturing car assemblers: occupational report, Luxembourg

Schwab K (2016) The fourth industrial revolution. World Economic Forum, Cologny/Geneva

Simmons AB, Chappell SG (2018) Artificial intelligence definition and meaning. IEEE J Ocean Eng 13:14–42

Tagliaro C, Migliore A (2022) "Covid-working": what to keep and what to leave? Evidence from an Italian company. J Corp Real Estate 24:76–92. https://doi.org/10.1108/JCRE-10-2020-0053

Upchurch M (2018) Robots and AI at work: the prospects for singularity. New Technol Work Employ 33:205–218. https://doi.org/10.1111/ntwe.12124

Vallas S, Schor JB (2020) What do platforms do? Understanding the gig economy. Annu Rev Sociol 46:273–294. https://doi.org/10.1146/annurev-soc-121919-054857

Vanroelen C, Julià M, Van Aerden K (2021) Precarious employment: an overlooked determinant of workers' health and Well-being? In: Flexible working practices and approaches. Springer International Publishing, Cham, pp 231–255

Vargas-Llave O, Weber T, Avogaro M (2020) Right to disconnect in the 27 EU Member States

Warhurst C, Hunt W (2019) The digitalisation of future work and employment. Possible impact and policy responses. Seville

Warhurst C, Wright S, Lyonette C (2017) Understanding and measuring job quality, London

Warhurst C, Mathieu C, Keune M et al (2018) Linking innovation and job quality: challenges and opportunities for policy and research, QuInnE Work 1–43

Weil D (2014) The fissured workplace. Why work became so bad for so many and what can be done to improve it? Harvard University Press, Cambridge

Willems M (2019) Le virage numérique rend-il le syndicalisme obsolète? Expérience syndicale avec les coursiers de Deliveroo. Rev Nouv 2

Part II
Methodological Challenges

Sequence Analysis and Its Potential for Occupational Health Studies

5

Matthias Studer and Nicola Cianferoni

Contents

Introduction	60
Work-Related Stress Trajectories Following Corporate Restructuring	61
Holistic Methods for Life Course Research	63
Sequence Analysis	64
Coding Trajectories	65
Describing Trajectories	66
Creating Typology of Trajectories	67
Linking Trajectories to Covariates	72
Software	73
Sequence Analysis Potential for the Study of Occupational Health Across the Life Course	74
Cross-References	75
References	75

Abstract

This chapter introduces the sequence analysis methodological framework to study trajectories in a life course perspective and discusses its potential for occupational health research. Aside from a conceptual presentation of the main concepts, it also aims to provide general and practical recommendations on the main decisions to be made when using sequence analysis.

Regularly identified as one of the key approaches for life course analysis, sequence analysis aims to analyze trajectories described as a sequence of categorical states using a holistic perspective. It regroups methods ranging from

---

M. Studer (✉)
LIVES Centre and Institute of Demography and Socioeconomics, Faculty of Social Sciences, University of Geneva, Geneva, Switzerland
e-mail: matthias.studer@unige.ch

N. Cianferoni
SECO State Secretariat for Economic Affairs and Institute for Sociological Research, Faculty of Social Sciences, University of Geneva, Geneva, Switzerland

© Springer Nature Switzerland AG 2023
M. Wahrendorf et al. (eds.), *Handbook of Life Course Occupational Health*, Handbook Series in Occupational Health Sciences, https://doi.org/10.1007/978-3-031-30492-7_18

visualization to explanatory methods and provides a comprehensive overview of the observed trajectories taken as a whole. This overview can then be used for various purposes, such as describing a set of entire trajectories, identifying relevant or atypical regularities, or contrasting these trajectories according to other key aspects such as gender or education level. This general introduction to sequence analysis is based on a simple illustrative study of work-related stress trajectories following a corporate restructuring in Switzerland.

Keywords

Sequence analysis · Cluster analysis · Longitudinal methods · Occupational health · Stress trajectory · Corporate restructuring · Optimal matching · Visualization · Typology · Validation

Introduction

Occupational epidemiology aims to study workers' health considering their exposure to a variety of chemical, biological, physical, and organizational constraints. Its aim is to determine if the exposures result in adverse health outcomes. It provides key insight to inform public health policy and reduce health risks among workers by issuing preventive measures. While studies on working conditions commonly use cross-sectional analyses, the potential association between working conditions and health outcomes can benefit from a longitudinal perspective, because the effects on health unfold over the long term. Such perspective offers key insights not only on the patterns leading to health deterioration, and how working conditions accumulate to affect health, but also on how workers might recover in the middle to the long run from disease or accidents (Checkoway et al. 2004). Occupational epidemiology is therefore increasingly interested in the study of working or recovery trajectories and how these trajectories are related to various health outcomes.

The life course paradigm offers a key theoretical approach to study such trajectories and has gained an increasing importance over the last decades in numerous disciplines ranging from sociology to epidemiology, and medicine to psychology (Elder et al. 2003; Bernardi et al. 2019). This paradigm emphasizes the need to take a holistic, or global, perspective on trajectories, taking into account the plurality of the situation occurring along the trajectories, and their unfolding in the medium or the long run (Elder et al. 2003). More precisely, three aspects of trajectories can be of key importance, for instance, to understand later life outcomes (Studer and Ritschard 2016). First, the critical period model states that the consequences of a situation or an event depend on its timing, i.e., when it occurs within the trajectory (Kuh et al. 2003). The same working conditions experienced in youth, middle, or old age might have different health consequences. Second, the sequencing of the situations within trajectories is of key importance to capture its dynamic, or the idea that the path taken should be considered (Kuh et al. 2003). For instance, ascending or descending professional career might have very different mental health consequences.

The precariousness of a professional trajectory is also defined by a peculiar sequencing, made of several back and forth movements between employment and unemployment. Finally, the time spent in a given situation is also of key interest as it captures the exposure to a situation, sometimes also referred to as the accumulation model (Kuh et al. 2003). This is generally the most studied aspect of trajectories.

This chapter aims to introduce the sequence analysis methodological framework to study trajectories in a life course perspective, and to discuss its potential for occupational health research. We also aim to issue general recommendations on the main decisions to be made. Regularly identified as one of the key approaches for life-course analysis (Shanahan 2000; Mayer 2009; Buchmann and Kriesi 2011; Liefbroer 2019), SA aims to analyze trajectories described as a sequence of categorical states using a holistic perspective. It regroups methods ranging from visualization to explanatory methods and provides a comprehensive overview of the observed trajectories taken as a whole. This overview can then be used for various purposes, such as describing a set of entire trajectories, identifying relevant or atypical regularities, or contrasting these trajectories according to other key aspects such as gender or education level. This general introduction to sequence analysis is based on a simple illustrative study of work-related stress trajectories following a corporate restructuring in Switzerland.

The chapter is organized as follows. We start by presenting our sample application before moving to a general presentation of the different methodological approaches available to study trajectories and processes. We then go through a standard application of sequence analysis using our sample study highlighting the key decisions and steps to be taken. We conclude by discussing the potential of sequence analysis for occupational health research and presenting some of its recent extensions.

Work-Related Stress Trajectories Following Corporate Restructuring

In this chapter, we illustrate the use of sequence analysis with a study on work-related stress trajectories following corporate restructuring in Switzerland. Corporate restructurings are common events, occurring when a corporate entity decides to change its internal organization. There are different types of corporate restructuring which can include closures, outsourcing, merging, delocalization, internal job mobility, business expansion, or internal reorganizations. Some of them imply job cutting and can lead to industrial disputes.

Previous longitudinal studies have shown that restructuring events have negative consequences on employees' well-being, with or without staff reductions – and regardless of the latter (see de Jong et al. 2016 for a systematic review). These negative consequences are related to increasing job insecurity, but not only. Corporate restructurings can trigger long periods of stress and increase health troubles such as poor sleep quality and emotional exhaustion (Kieselbach et al. 2010). According to the *Job-Demand Control Model* (Karasek 1979), the stress level experienced by employees depends on working environment and more precisely job demands (workload, psychological involvement, etc.) and job control (autonomy, decision-making over the organization of work, etc.). Karasek argues that workers dealing with high job demands experience lower stress levels if job control is high. Thus, in assessing the consequences of a corporate restructuring on stress, we have to take into account both the workload and the resources to cope with it.

According to the vulnerability framework (Spini et al. 2017), we should not only look at the immediate impact of an event, but also at its medium-term consequences. The vulnerability to an event such as a corporate restructuring is then defined as "a lack of resources, which in a specific context places individuals or groups at a major risk of experiencing (1) negative consequences related to sources of stress; (2) the inability to cope effectively with stressors; and (3) the inability to recover from the stressor or to take advantage of opportunities by a given deadline" (Spini et al. 2017). The vulnerability therefore refers not only to the direct consequences of the event, but also to the ability of individuals to cope with it. For instance, some workers might be strongly affected but might then have the condition to overcome it. Thus, aside from an immediate impact, corporate restructuring might also affect workers in the medium term.

Orsholits (2020, 60–64) then identifies five ideal-typical trajectories following a stressful event, which are schematically represented in Fig. 1. First, some people might not be vulnerable and therefore do not experience any negative consequences, nor immediately nor in the medium term (trajectories 1 and 2 in Fig. 1). In our example, it could be a worker not experiencing any work-related stress following corporate restructuring. Second, some workers might follow a resilient trajectory,

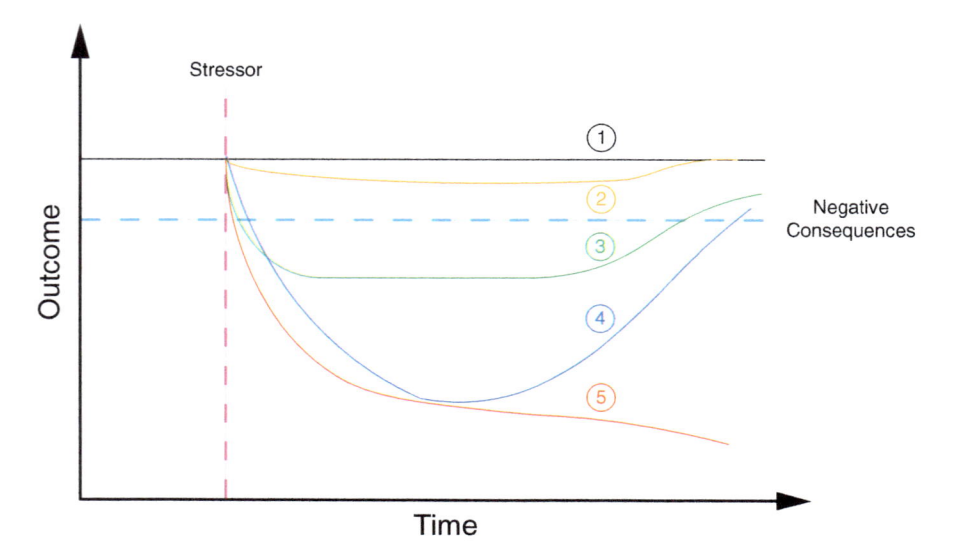

Fig. 1 Typical trajectories according to the vulnerability framework. (Reproduced from Orsholits 2020, p. 61, https://doi.org/10.13097/archive-ouverte/unige:149511)

marked by negative direct consequences followed by a fast recovery (trajectory 3 and 4 in Fig. 1) for instance, a worker might only briefly experience stress following a corporate restructuring. Third, some individuals might be affected for a longer period, but still recover from it (trajectory 5 in Fig. 1). For instance, a worker might experience higher work-related stress level for a short period. Fourth, some workers might experience strong and intense negative consequences in the long-run, but still recover from it. Finally, some workers might not recover from the stressful event even in the medium term.

The vulnerability framework also emphasizes several key factors that should be taken into account. Their resources, taken in a broad sense including their biological, psychological, and socioeconomic resources, might help them to avoid and/or cope with the negative consequences associated with the event. As a result, the vulnerability process might increase inequalities among individuals. These resources might be individual but also be made available in the collective context. Thus, the context itself might help individuals to avoid, cope, or overcome the negative consequences of the event. This includes, for instance, measures taken by the corporation or the state, as well as working culture.

Following this approach, we aim to understand the evolution of work-related stress of workers following corporate restructuring. We distinguish between three situations over time: working in a stressful environment, not experiencing work-related stress, and not working. We expect the type of trajectories followed by an individual to be related to his own characteristics (gender, age, etc.), as well as his individual (education level, etc.) and collective (workload, autonomy, etc.) resources.

Our illustrative application is based on data from the Swiss Household Panel. This panel includes questions on both restructuring and work-related stress over time. We kept the trajectories of 1348 individuals who have experienced a corporate restructuring between 2004 and 2019. For sake of simplicity, we only kept the first restructuring event. Although the corporate can occur several times in one's life or even every year during a period, we consider here that the first one is the most stressful.

Holistic Methods for Life Course Research

The methods to study trajectories or processes can be divided in two broad families. First, some research is interested in a specific state occupied at each point in time. For instance, one might focus on the probability of being stressed at work. Similarly, one might center on a specific transition or event in these trajectories, such as a transition between stressed and not stressed. In both cases, the typical questions are related to how the timing of an event or a state occurrence, how exposure to a situation (duration), and/or how previous events (sequencing) affect the outcome of interest. If this outcome can be described as by a single event or state, the main methods of interest are survival analysis to study events (see Blossfeld and Rohwer 2002) and panel data analysis to study occupied states (see Wooldridge 2002).

However, a trajectory can often not be fully described by a single state or event. A transition should be situated in the whole trajectory to be understood. This is particularly true when there are many possible transitions as in our sample application. For instance, a transition between stress and nonstress is typically interpreted differently depending on the time spent afterward in nonstress. One typically would like to avoid considering such transition as a recovery if people are stressed again just the year after.

Second, holistic methods aim to study the trajectory taken as whole by simultaneously considering all possible situations and/or transitions over a predefined period. For instance, such perspective allows studying at once several possible states, including stressed at work, nonstressed at work, or not having a job. At the same time, such approaches aim to study a whole period of interest to uncover the medium term consequences instead of focusing on a specific time point. Several holistic methods have been developed; see Piccarreta and Studer 2019 for a review. Briefly, growth curve models provide a holistic view on trajectories described with numerical values, while sequence analysis focuses on trajectories of categorical states. The present chapter focuses on the latter approach.

Sequence Analysis

The sequence analysis (SA) standard use revolves around a "core program" involving four typical steps (Gauthier et al. 2014), which typically involves choices to be made and important points to take care of. In this chapter, we go through them and discuss the most common decisions and issues using our sample application.

First, the trajectories – or narratives in Abbott (1990) terms – are coded as states' sequences. This implies specifying the situation occupied by an observation at each time point to describe its trajectory over time. This coding is of key importance and has large consequences on the results. It therefore deserves a great attention.

Second, the trajectories are described and visualized using several methods. Each of these methods focuses on a different aspect of the trajectories. They typically aim to describe difference in timing, duration, or sequencing.

Third, a typology of the trajectories is created. This analysis implies two steps. The trajectories are first compared to one another using a so-called distance measure. Then these distances are used to create the typology itself using cluster analysis. This typology describes the various kinds of patterns observed in the data without making any assumptions on the data generation mechanisms. This exploratory approach can capture complex and potentially unexpected dynamics in trajectories, which is particularly well suited to understanding the many interdependencies of the life course (Bernardi et al. 2019; Piccarreta and Studer 2019). Depending on the issue, such typology might highlight regularities in the timing of situations, ordering of states, or time spent in each state.

Finally, the typology is used in subsequent analyses (Gauthier et al. 2014). Technically, it can be included in any statistical methods handling categorical data.

Two main uses can be distinguished. First, the typology might be used as a dependent variable in a multinomial (or similar) regression model. The aim is then to understand how the type of trajectory is associated with variables of key interest. In our sample application, we are interested to understand how the type of work-stress trajectory followed by an individual after a corporate restructuring is related to its working conditions, such as job intensity. Second, the typology might be used as an explanatory variable in a subsequent regression. In this case, the aim is to understand how a previous trajectory is linked with a later-life outcome. For instance, Giudici and Morselli (2019) looked at how previous employment trajectories are linked with indicators of depression in later age, showing that precarious career can strongly affect individuals.

In the following subsection, we go through these different steps taking our sample application as an example.

Coding Trajectories

The first step of any SA studies is to code the trajectories as state sequences, which involves the specification of two key aspects: the so-called alphabet and the time alignment of the trajectories. First, the alphabet, i.e., the list of possible situations, needs to be defined. As with any categorical variable, the alphabet should be exhaustive – all observations should be classified in a state – and mutually exclusive – observation should be classified in only one state. Generally, this list should be as parsimonious as possible. One should therefore only keep key distinctions and avoid infrequent states unless they are central for the research question. To keep things simple, we consider here only three states: stressed at work, nonstressed at work, and not working. However, it should be noted that more categories can be used if the information is available, for instance, to detail the work-related stress level.

Second, we need to define the time alignment, i.e., how the time is measured. One generally distinguishes between calendar and process time. With calendar time, time is measured relative to a common date, for instance, the start of a survey or a specific year. From our experience, calendar time often leads to poor results as it often has a very different meaning for each observation.

Process time refers to the time elapsed since an event triggering the start of the process. It should be preferred when the aim is to understand the unfolding of a process or its consequences. It is often useful to start analyzing the start of the process a few time units before the triggering event. This strategy allows taking into account the previous situation.

In our example, we focus on work-related stress trajectories *following* (or *starting with*) the event corporate reorganization. In other words, "corporate restructuring" acts as the triggering event. The timing of the process is then defined relative to this triggering event, i.e., $t = 1$ is therefore the first time point following the event. In our sample application, we started the sequences 2 years before the corporate restructuring to account for the previous work-related stress level.

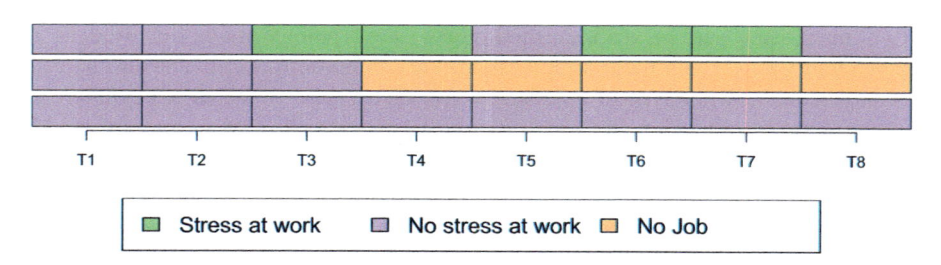

Fig. 2 Coding of trajectories

Finally, the process is sometimes defined according to an end event or time, as the trajectory leading to a given situation. For instance, one might be interested in how a professional trajectory over the last 10 years is related with current health status.

Once the alphabet and time alignment are defined, the sequences can be coded. Practically, this is done by creating one variable for each time point following the start of the process. Figure 2 presents three observed trajectories illustrating the required coding. The bottom sequence shows the trajectory of an individual never experiencing stress at work. At each time point, their situation is coded using the same state and the state is repeated for each observed time point. On the contrary, the top trajectory shows stress occurring at the time points 3 and 4, i.e., just following corporate restructuring. The trajectory represented in the middle shows an individual losing their job at time point 4.

Once the trajectory of every individual has been coded as a sequence, the trajectories can be described using several visualization methods.

Describing Trajectories

According to the life course paradigm, there are three main aspects of trajectories and processes of interest: the timing of a situation; the time spent in (or exposure to) each state; and the sequencing of the states, which captures the dynamic of the trajectory. One therefore generally aims to understand and describe each of these three aspects. SA provides several tools for this purpose.

Figure 3 presents four types of graphics to represent a set of trajectories, each focusing on different characteristics. *Index plots* represent each individual trajectory using a thin horizontal line (Scherer 2001). To improve its readability, the sequences are ordered according to the first state in the sequences, and the subsequent states in case of ties. Our index plot reveals stable stress or nonstress trajectories, but also some sequences with transitions at the beginning. However, it should be noted that the ordering of the sequences makes it more difficult to identify changes in the end. More generally speaking, since the sequences are fully represented, information about timing, duration, or sequencing is reproduced and can be interpreted. However, the information might be overwhelming with a large number of cases or when studying complex trajectories, particularly for the sequencing of the states. Fasang and Liao (2014) propose an extension to simplify the plot and overcome these issues.

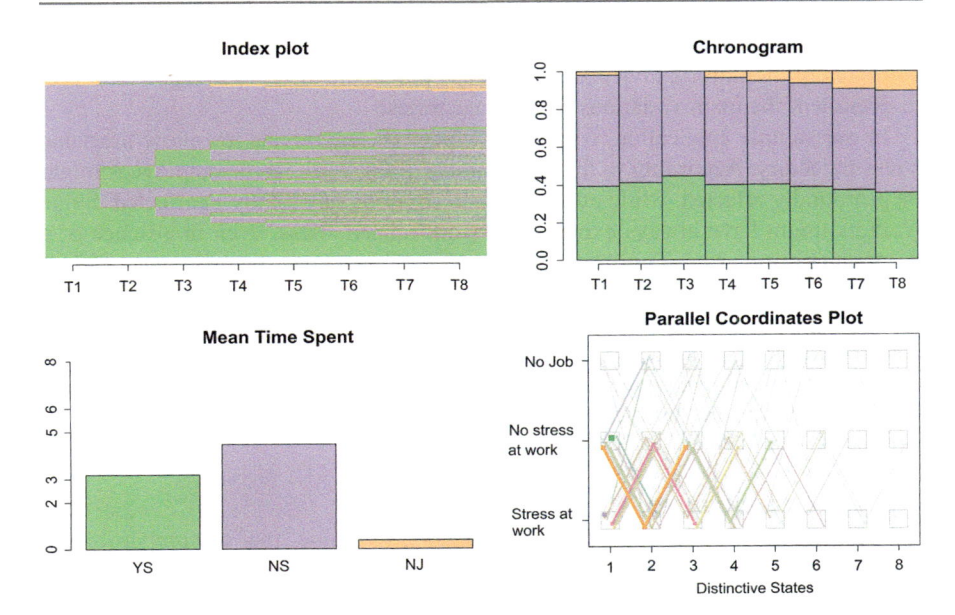

Fig. 3 Visualization methods of trajectories using sequence analysis

The *Chronogram* presents the distribution of the states at each time point. As such, it concentrates on the timing by showing which states are frequent at which time points. However, by doing so, any longitudinal information, such as sequencing or duration, is lost. In our case, we can identify an increase in the stress around the time of the corporate restructuring. The *Mean Time Spent* plot represents the average time spent in each state and therefore focuses on the duration. Finally, the decorated *Parallel Coordinates Plot* emphasizes common ordering of the states, and therefore the dynamics of the trajectories (Bürgin and Ritschard 2014). This graphic shows the ordering position of the states on the x-axis. Common sequencing of states are then highlighted using colored lines, while gray lines show infrequent orderings. For instance, the brown line shows that the ordering "No stress – Stress – No stress" is frequent, while the green square represents individuals staying in the "No stress" states for the whole trajectory.

Summarizing, several graphical representations of state sequences are available, each focusing on a different aspect of the trajectories. They can be used to understand the most common states, timing, and sequencing of the data.

Creating Typology of Trajectories

The aim of the standard application of SA is to identify recurrent patterns or ideal-typical trajectories in the sequences (Abbott and Forrest 1986). Individual sequences can show many small variations and differences. By building a typology, one aims to regroup similar sequences into a same type. Such procedure allows ignoring small and (ideally) noninformative differences. The procedure also offers a powerful tool to document the main variations of the trajectories.

In our sample application, we do not expect all individuals to follow the same stress trajectory. According to the vulnerability framework, some employees might be profoundly affected, while others might recover or stay totally unaffected. Some workers might have always experienced work-related stress, even in absence of a corporate restructuring. The aim of the typology is to uncover the main type of stress trajectories *found* in the data.

The typology is created using cluster analysis, involving two steps. First, a distance measure is used to identify which sequences are similar and which are different. Then, similar sequences are grouped together in types using the information provided by the distance measures. Let us describe these two steps in more detail.

Comparing Sequences

In order to regroup similar sequences, we need to define how to compare them. Figure 4 presents three toy sequences to illustrate this process.

To compare these three sequences, one typically relies on a criterion. As already stated, the life course perspective emphasizes the importance of three aspects of trajectories: timing, duration, and sequencing (Studer and Ritschard 2016). According to the timing aspect, the bottom and middle sequences are the most similar: They are in the same states at the same time for most of the trajectory. For the same reason, they are also similar according to the duration aspect. However, these two sequences show opposite ordering of the states and therefore opposite dynamics. They are thus completely dissimilar according to the sequencing criteria. Therefore, depending on the chosen criterion, one reaches different conclusions about the similarity of the sequences. A similar reasoning can be made when comparing top and middle sequences. As a result, there are no definitive answers about which sequences are similar or not. It depends on the chosen criterion. Therefore, a choice needs to be made about the criterion to be used to compare the sequences.

Each of the three aspects might be of interest depending on the research question. For instance, in our sample issue, focusing on timing could highlight the states occupied around corporate restructuring. The duration aspect might emphasize exposure to work-related stress. Finally, the sequencing of the states might reveal

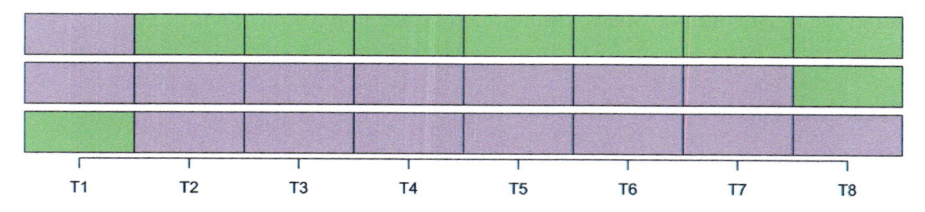

Fig. 4 Three illustrative sequences

recovery dynamics. We therefore need to make a choice about the main aspect(s) of interest. This is a sociological question, not a statistical one. In our sample application, we focus on the duration and sequencing aspects.

Technically, in SA, this comparison is achieved using a distance measure, also called dissimilarity measure. Several of them are available (see Studer and Ritschard 2016 for a review). Let us briefly present the most used one before discussing how to make a choice among them.

The *Hamming distance* is the simplest one (Hamming 1950). The distance between two sequences is computed by counting the number of positions with different states. For instance, the distance between the top and middle sequences equals six, while the distance between the middle and bottom ones equals two. As the Hamming distance is only based on the state occupied at each time point, it mainly focuses on the timing of the sequences.

The *optimal matching distance* is the most used one since its introduction in the social sciences by Abbott and Forrest (1986). Built upon the Levenshtein (1966) distance, it aims to overcome two core limitations of the Hamming distance. First, in Hamming distance, all states are considered as equally different, which is the standard treatment of categorical variables. However, in some applications, it might be useful to consider that some states are closer than others. For instance, when analyzing trajectories of ordinal values, it is natural to account for the ordering of the states when measuring differences between trajectories. This can be achieved by weighting the mismatches between states differently according to the states involved. Technically, this *can* be specified using the *substitution cost* matrix, which set the weights of each possible mismatch. There is, however, no requirement to specify such matrix, and in most applications, we can follow the standard treatment of categorical data by weighting each mismatch equally.

Second, optimal matching aims to better take into account the sequencing of the states. The Hamming distance typically fails to account for time lags in the comparison of sequences. This can be simply illustrated using the two sequences of Fig. 5. Since the occupied states are different at many time points, the Hamming distance is large, even if the two sequences show the same pattern.

The optimal matching distance overcomes this limitation by allowing time shifts in the comparison of sequences. The weight of these time shifts is controlled through the *insertion-deletion* (indel) parameter. A high *indel* value penalizes time shifts in sequences comparison. If this parameter is set to half of the constant substitution cost, then the computed distances can be linked to the length of the longest common

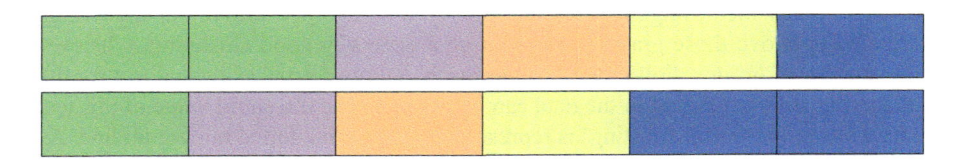

Fig. 5 Two illustrative sequences

subsequences between the two sequences. This is the strategy adopted for our sample application.

Following the criticisms made to optimal matching (see Aisenbrey and Fasang 2010), many new distances measures were developed, each with their own strengths and weaknesses. Studer and Ritschard (2016) ran an extensive simulation study to measure the sensitivity of most SA distance measures to the three key life course aspects of timing, duration, and sequencing. They further propose recommendations depending on the main aspect(s) of interest. If one wants to focus on timing, then the *Hamming distance* should be used. If the focus is given on duration, then *Optimal matching* is a good option as it also accounts for (some) sequencing. Finally, for sequencing, the *SVRspell* measure (Elzinga and Studer 2015), *optimal matching of spells*, or *optimal matching of transitions* (Studer and Ritschard 2016) provide the best options. The latter two distances measures can also be parameterized to offer an intermediary position between these three aspects. Details about each of these methods can be found in Studer and Ritschard (2016).

Cluster Analysis

Once all the sequences have been compared with the chosen distance measure, one can create a typology of the sequences using cluster analysis. As a recall, this typology aims to describe the main types of trajectories *found* in the data. Several clustering algorithms are available, but *Ward* and *K-Medoids* are the most used ones.

In this process, one needs to decide on how many types of trajectories are required to describe the trajectories found in the data. We want our typology to be parsimonious (i.e., have only few types) while still describing the different types of trajectories found in the data. There is therefore a trade-off to be made.

The choice among clustering algorithms or among different number of types can be made using a *cluster quality index* (CQI) (see Studer 2013 for a review), such as the *average silhouette width* (ASW). According to the ASW, a good typology is found when the types are homogeneous (i.e., regroup only similar sequences) and well separated from one another (i.e., sequences in different types are very dissimilar). The left-hand side plot of Fig. 6 presents the value of the ASW for different number of groups using the K-Medoids algorithm with a black line. According to this analysis, the best clustering solutions are found for two or five groups.

However, all CQIs lack clear interpretation thresholds. To overcome this issue, Studer (2021) proposes to compare the obtained CQI to the ones obtained by clustering similar but nonclustered data, i.e., the CQI values obtained when we should not cluster the data. These CQI values obtained by clustering nonclustered data are represented using thin gray lines in Fig. 6. The CQI values of our clusterings are always above those gray lines indicating a generally good clustering, whatever the number of groups. Following this approach, a more formal statistical test for the clustering structure found in the data can be derived. The threshold value of this test (accounting for multiple testing) is represented using a red dotted horizontal line. As the CQI values for 2 and 5 groups are above this line, one can conclude that we found a "significant" structure in the data.

5 Sequence Analysis and Its Potential for Occupational Health Studies

Raw ASW   **Standardized ASW**

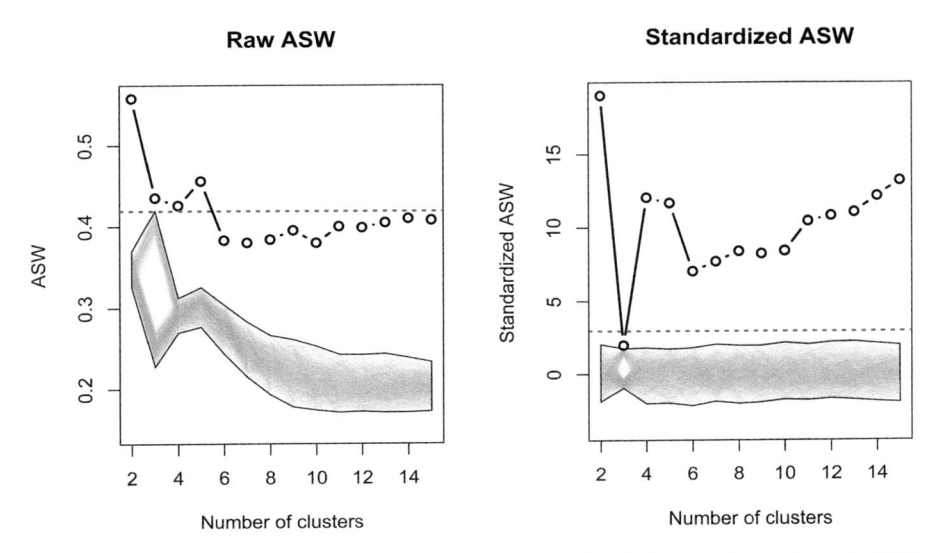

Fig. 6 Observed Average Silhouette Width (ASW) values (black lines) and bootstrapped ASW null values according to combined null model (gray lines)

This analysis also allows standardizing the CQI values to make them more comparable across different number of groups. The standardized values should therefore be preferred to decide on the number of groups. These values are represented in the right-hand plot of Fig. 6. According to this analysis, two, four, or five groups are all found to be "significant." In this case, the choice among them should be based on the substantive interpretation of the typology. Since we are interested in describing the diversity of the trajectories followed by individuals, we use the five-group typology.

The typology in five groups is presented in Fig. 7, where a label was assigned to each type of trajectory identified by the cluster analysis. The "Constant low stress" type of trajectories regroups workers not experiencing stress at work during the observation period. This is a nonvulnerable trajectory. On the opposite, the "Constant high stress" type highlights workers always stressed at work. This is a highly vulnerable trajectory, but it should be noted that the work-related stress might have preexisted corporate restructuring. The workers regrouped in the "Vulnerable" type show a pattern of increasing stress at work, which remains at a high level. The workers in the "Recovery" type experienced work stress around corporate restructuring, but not afterward. Finally, some workers "Stop working," either following a job loss or retirement. Our typology therefore describes work-related stress patterns and employment dynamics.

These five types of trajectories reflect most of the ideal-type trajectories highlighted by Orsholits (2020). According to the vulnerability framework, we expect the type of trajectory followed by an individual to depend on their resources and contexts. These research questions can be answered by studying the statistical association between our typology and covariates of interest. This is the topic of the next subsection.

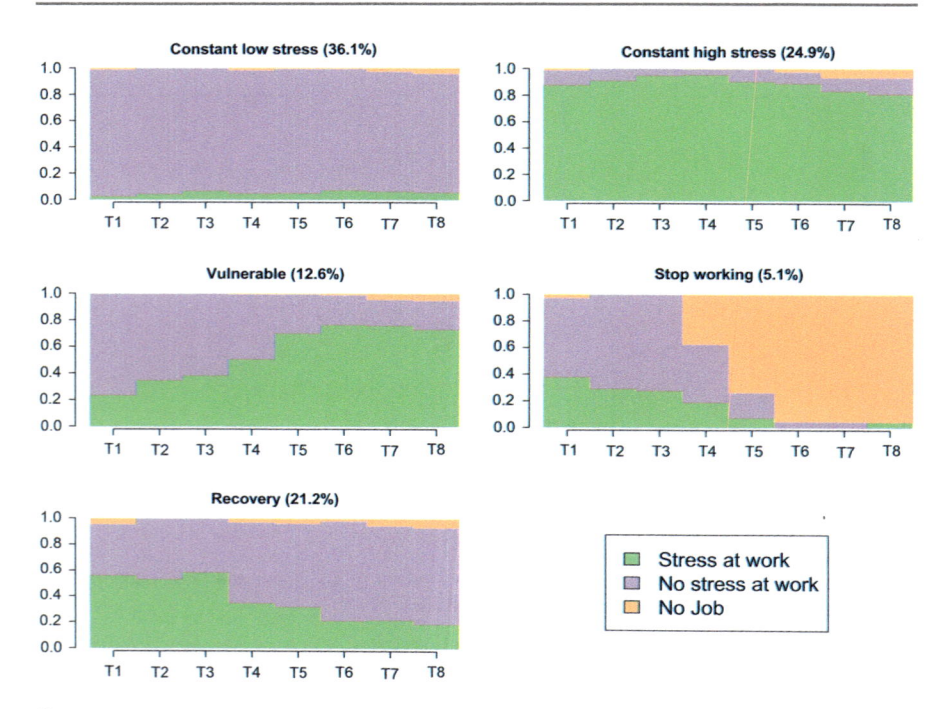

Fig. 7 Typology of work-related stress trajectories following a corporate restructuring

Linking Trajectories to Covariates

Once the typology has been created, the relationships between covariates and the type followed by an observation can be studied using multinomial regression. For instance, in our sample application, we expect the type of trajectories followed by an individual to be related to its own resources including education level. Indeed, qualified workers generally earn a higher wage and can expect to find another job more easily if needed. According to the *Job-Demand Control Model*, we also expect workers to better cope with a corporate restructuring if they have higher job control. At the same time, higher workload might exhaust their psychosocial resources. These aspects are measured using the two variables: work intensity (as an indicator of the workload) and supervision tasks (as a proxy for a worker that has both autonomy and responsibility in his job). Finally, we are also interested in possible age effects as older workers might have more difficulties to find a job, and the opportunity to retire.

Table 1 presents the results of a multinomial regression model, where the "Constant low stress" is taken has the reference category. The coefficients of a multinomial model are on the log-odds scale, as in logistic regression. They measure the relationships between covariates and each type contrasted with the reference category. They are therefore suitable to study the relationships between covariates and the kind of trajectories followed by an individual.

The "Constant high stress" is positively associated with secondary ($\beta = 0.705^{**}$) or tertiary ($\beta = 0.557^{***}$) education level, job intensity ($\beta = 0.282^{***}$), and

5 Sequence Analysis and Its Potential for Occupational Health Studies

Table 1 Multinomial regression of the type of work-related stress trajectories

	Constant high stress	Vulnerable	Stop working	Recovery
Scaled age	−0.060	−0.258*	9.370***	−0.022
	(0.097)	(0.117)	(1.870)	(0.087)
Scaled age squared	−0.069	−0.084	−2.538***	0.112
	(0.079)	(0.086)	(0.626)	(0.064)
Woman	−0.136	−0.255	0.114	−0.169
	(0.173)	(0.201)	(0.338)	(0.174)
Secondary education	0.705***	0.153	0.010	0.185
	(0.208)	(0.242)	(0.401)	(0.215)
Tertiary education	0.557**	−0.145	0.260	0.189
	(0.205)	(0.249)	(0.395)	(0.207)
Job intensity	0.282***	0.115**	0.089	0.123***
	(0.038)	(0.041)	(0.065)	(0.036)
Supervisory tasks	0.509**	0.129	0.443	0.661***
	(0.177)	(0.205)	(0.348)	(0.181)
Constant	−2.604***	−1.525***	−8.865***	−1.729***
	(0.312)	(0.316)	(1.416)	(0.285)

Note: *p < 0.05; **p < 0.01; ***p < 0.001

supervisory tasks ($\beta = 0.509^{**}$), both measured before restructuring. This suggests that the high constant stress level mainly affects qualified workers with a great workload and responsibilities in the firm. The "Vulnerable" regroups young workers (scaled age, $\beta = 0.557^{***}$) with high job intensity ($\beta = 0.115^{***}$). The "Stop working" regroups older workers (scaled age $\beta = 9.370^{***}$, scaled age-squared $\beta = -2.538^{***}$). This reflects the difficulty for old workers to remain in the labor market. Finally, the "Recovery" group is also composed of workers with high job intensity ($\beta = 0.123^{***}$) and supervisory tasks ($\beta = 0.661^{***}$). However, these workers had the opportunity to cope with or be less affected by the restructuring in the medium term.

Summarizing, job intensity is associated with medium-term work-related stress trajectories. Supervisory tasks are associated not only with constant high stress, but also with the recovery pattern, supporting the idea that job control is a valuable resource to overcome corporate restructuring. Education level mainly distinguishes the "Constant high stress" pattern, and, interestingly, gender does not seem to play a role in explaining these patterns. Finally, younger individuals are more likely to be in the "Vulnerable" pattern of medium-term work-related stress, while older ones are more likely to "Stop working."

Software

At the time of writing this chapter, several SA software are available for sequence visualization and the creation of typologies. In Stata, one can rely on the SQ-Ados (Brzinsky-Fay et al. 2006) or the SADI (Halpin 2017) packages. In R, the TraMineR and WeightedCluster packages are available (Gabadinho et al. 2011; Studer 2013).

The R packages offer more advanced methods, including advanced visualization, typology validation, and more distance measures.

Sequence Analysis Potential for the Study of Occupational Health Across the Life Course

In this chapter, we illustrated the use of sequence analysis with a simple study of work-related stress following a corporate restructuring. However, the domain of applications of SA is much broader. It can be used to study trajectories following any key events for occupational epidemiology, including professional accident, promotion, unemployment, and giving birth, to name a few. It can further be used to study trajectories characterized, for instance, by their employment status, exposure to risk factors, or health status, which could be measured using self-assessment, symptoms, or diagnostics. For instance, McLeod et al. (2018) used a similar approach to understand return-to-work patterns among workers with work-related musculoskeletal disorders. They showed that sickness absences and recovery trajectories vary according to the type of musculoskeletal disorders.

SA is also a key method to describe how a previous trajectory is linked with a later-life outcome. In this context, SA typologies can be used to describe a previous trajectory, such as the professional career. The typology can then be used to study a later-life outcome such as health status. Giudici and Morselli (2019) and Eisenberg-Guyot et al. (2020) used such approach to study the consequences of unstable work trajectories. Among others, they showed that unstable paths as well as long exposure to work insecurity and poor employment quality are associated with adverse health outcomes. More generally, such perspective allows taking into account the three key aspects of a previous trajectory according to the life course paradigm, namely, its timing, duration, and sequencing, and to link them to later life outcomes.

Each of these aspects can be linked to an epidemiological model, which can be thought to have long-term consequences. The *accumulation model* emphasizes exposure to a given situation and can be linked with the duration aspect. The *pathway model* highlights the potential consequences of the paths taken by individuals which can be linked to the sequencing aspect. Finally, the *critical/sensitive period model* considers the different potential consequences of a situation depending on when it occurred in a previous trajectory. This perspective can be linked to the timing aspect of a previous trajectory.

The SA framework takes these three key aspects into account by considering the previous trajectory as a whole unit of analysis. It offers tools not only to describe and visualize these trajectories, but also to summarize the information by building a typology of the trajectories. As such, it is a valuable tool for occupational health research.

Cross-References

▶ A Life Course Perspective on Work and Mental Health: The Working Lives of Young Adults
▶ Adverse Employment Histories: Conceptual Considerations and Selected Health Effects
▶ Gender Differences in Work Participation over the Life Course and Consequences for Socioeconomic and Health Outcomes

Acknowledgment Matthias Studer gratefully acknowledges the support of the Swiss National Science Foundation (project "Strengthening Sequence Analysis," grant number: 10001A_204740).

References

Abbott A (1990) Conception of time and events in social science methods: causal and narrative approaches. Hist Methods 23(4):140–150
Abbott A, Forrest J (1986) Optimal matching methods for historical sequences. J Interdiscip Hist 16:471–494
Aisenbrey S, Fasang AE (2010) New life for old ideas: the 'second wave' of sequence analysis bringing the 'course' back into the life course. Sociol Methods Res 38(3):430–462
Bernardi L, Huinink J, Settersten RA (2019) The life course cube: a tool for studying lives. Adv Life Course Res 41:100258. https://doi.org/10.1016/j.alcr.2018.11.004
Blossfeld H-P, Rohwer G (2002) Techniques of event history modeling, new approaches to causal analysis, 2nd edn. Lawrence Erlbaum, Mahwah
Brzinsky-Fay C, Kohler U, Luniak M (2006) Sequence analysis with Stata. Stata J 6(4):435–460
Buchmann MC, Kriesi I (2011) Transition to adulthood in Europe. Annu Rev Sociol 37(1):481–503. https://doi.org/10.1146/annurev-soc-081309-150212
Bürgin R, Ritschard G (2014) A decorated parallel coordinate plot for categorical longitudinal data. Am Stat 68(2):98–103. https://doi.org/10.1080/00031305.2014.887591
Checkoway H, Pearce NE, Kriebel D (2004) Research methods in occupational epidemiology. Oxford University Press. https://doi.org/10.1093/acprof:oso/9780195092424.001.0001
de Jong T, Wiezer N, de Weerd M, Nielsen K, Mattila-Holappa P, Mockałło Z (2016) The impact of restructuring on employee Well-being: a systematic review of longitudinal studies. Work & Stress 30(1):91–114. https://doi.org/10.1080/02678373.2015.1136710
Eisenberg-Guyot J, Peckham T, Andrea SB, Oddo V, Seixas N, Hajat A (2020) Life-course trajectories of employment quality and health in the U.S.: a multichannel sequence analysis. Soc Sci Med 264(November):113327. https://doi.org/10.1016/j.socscimed.2020.113327
Elder GH, Johnson MK, Crosnoe R (2003) The emergence and development of life course theory. In: Mortimer JT, Shanahan MJ (eds) Handbook of the life course, Handbooks of Sociology and Social Research. Springer U.S., pp 3–19. https://doi.org/10.1007/978-0-306-48247-2_1
Elzinga CH, Studer M (2015) Spell sequences, state proximities and distance metrics. Sociol Methods Res 44(1):3–47. https://doi.org/10.1177/0049124114540707
Fasang AE, Liao TF (2014) Visualizing sequences in the social sciences. Sociol Methods Res 43(4): 643–676. https://doi.org/10.1177/0049124113506563
Gabadinho A, Ritschard G, Müller NS, Studer M (2011) Analyzing and visualizing state sequences in R with TraMineR. J Stat Softw 40(4):1–37. http://www.jstatsoft.org/v40/i04
Gauthier J-A, Bühlmann F, Blanchard P (2014) Introduction: sequence analysis in 2014. In: Blanchard P, Bühlmann F, Gauthier J-A (eds) *Advances in sequence analysis: theory, method, applications*, Life Course Research and Social Policies, vol 2. Springer, Heidelberg

Giudici F, Morselli D (2019) 20 years in the world of work: a study of (nonstandard) occupational trajectories and health. Soc Sci Med 224(March):138–148. https://doi.org/10.1016/j.socscimed.2019.02.002

Halpin B (2017) SADI: sequence analysis tools for Stata. Stata J 17(3):546–572(27). https://www.stata-journal.com/article.html?article=st0486

Hamming RW (1950) Error detecting and error correcting codes. Bell Syst Tech J 26(2):147–160

Karasek RA (1979) Job demands, job decision latitude, and mental strain: implications for job redesign. Adm Sci Q 24(2):285. https://doi.org/10.2307/2392498

Kieselbach T, Nielsen K, Triomphe CE (2010) Psychosocial risks and health effects of restructuring. Brussels: Investing in well-being at work: Addressing psychosocial risks in times of change

Kuh D, Ben-Shlomo Y, Lynch J, Hallqvist J, Power C (2003) Life course epidemiology. J Epidemiol Community Health 57(10):778–783. https://doi.org/10.1136/jech.57.10.778

Levenshtein V (1966) Binary codes capable of correcting deletions, insertions, and reversals. Soviet Phys Doklady 10:707–710

Liefbroer AC (2019) Methodological diversity in life course research: blessing or curse? Adv Life Course Res 41(September):100276. https://doi.org/10.1016/j.alcr.2019.04.006

Mayer KU (2009) New directions in life course research. Annu Rev Sociol 35:413–433. https://doi.org/10.1146/annurev.soc.34.040507.134619

McLeod CB, Reiff E, Maas E, Bültmann U (2018) Identifying return-to-work trajectories using sequence analysis in a cohort of workers with work-related musculoskeletal disorders. Scand J Work Environ Health 44(2):147–155. https://doi.org/10.5271/sjweh.3701

Orsholits D (2020) Modelling the dynamics of vulnerability with latent variable methods. PhD Thesis, University of Geneva

Piccarreta R, Studer M (2019) Holistic analysis of the life course: methodological challenges and new perspectives. Adv Life Course Res 41:100251. https://doi.org/10.1016/j.alcr.2018.10.004

Scherer S (2001) Early career patterns: a comparison of Great Britain and West Germany. Eur Sociol Rev 17(2):119–144

Shanahan MJ (2000) Pathways to adulthood in changing societies: variability and mechanisms in life course perspective. Annu Rev Sociol 26:667–692. http://www.jstor.org/stable/223461

Spini D, Bernardi L, Oris M (2017) Toward a life course framework for studying vulnerability. Res Hum Dev 14(1):5–25. https://doi.org/10.1080/15427609.2016.1268892

Studer M (2013) WeightedCluster Library manual: a practical guide to creating typologies of trajectories in the social sciences with R, LIVES working papers 24. NCCR LIVES, Switzerland. https://doi.org/10.12682/lives.2296-1658.2013.24

Studer M (2021) Validating sequence analysis typologies using parametric bootstrap. Sociol Methodol 51(2):290–318. https://doi.org/10.1177/00811750211014232

Studer M, Ritschard G (2016) What matters in differences between life trajectories: a comparative review of sequence dissimilarity measures. J R Stat Soc Ser A 179(2):481–511. https://doi.org/10.1111/rssa.12125

Wooldridge J (2002) Econometric analysis of cross section and panel data. MIT Press

Job-Exposure Matrices: Design, Validation, and Limitations

6

Alexis Descatha, Bradley A. Evanoff, and Annette Leclerc

Contents

Introduction	78
Definition	79
Literature Review	80
Design of Job-Exposure Matrices	81
Will the Job-Exposure Matrix Be Based on Measured Exposure Data, Worker Self-Reports, or Expert Ratings of Exposures?	82
What Type of Job Classifications Should Be Used?	82
What Exposure Components Should Be Considered: Level (Intensity), Duration, Frequency, or Probability?	82
Should Time and/or Location Be Considered (Date/Year, Region)?	83
Other Variables	83
Development	84
Development of a JEM Based on Expert Assessments	84
Development of JEMs Based on Existing Exposure Data	84
Mixed Approaches	84
Validation	85

A. Descatha (✉)
Univ Angers, CHU Angers, Univ Rennes, Inserm, EHESP, Irset (Institut de recherche en santé, environnement et travail), UMR_S 1085, SFR ICAT, Ester Team, Angers, France

CHU Angers, Poisoning Control Center-Clinical Data Center, Angers, France

Epidemiology and Prevention, Donald and Barbara Zucker School of Medicine, Hofstra University Northwell Health, New York, NY, USA
e-mail: alexis.descatha@inserm.fr

B. A. Evanoff
Division of General Medical Sciences, Washington University School of Medicine, St. Louis, MO, USA

A. Leclerc
Inserm UMS 011, Cohort in Population Unit, Villejuif, France

© Springer Nature Switzerland AG 2023
M. Wahrendorf et al. (eds.), *Handbook of Life Course Occupational Health*, Handbook Series in Occupational Health Sciences, https://doi.org/10.1007/978-3-031-30492-7_9

Some Examples of JEM 85
    SYNJEM 85
    O*NET 86
    Matgéné 86
    DOC*X 87
    JEM Constances 87
    Mat-O-Covid 87
Limitations 88
Why Use JEMs in Public Health Research and Practice? 89
Conclusion 90
References 91

Abstract

In the context of the need to evaluate past occupational exposures, job-exposure matrices or JEMs are a common method used in occupational epidemiology research to estimate workers' exposure based on job titles, industry information, and population exposure data. This chapter discusses major steps of JEM design (including source of the exposure data and job classification systems) and the processes of developing and validating JEMs for reliability and validity. Examples of JEMs available in North America or Europe are also given. This chapter also discusses limitations that should be known by users, including the lack of individual variation in exposure estimates within a job category, potential bias related to the source of the JEM, and the potential error of job coding schemes. The chapter also discusses merging JEMs from different sources, and their use in the broader public health area.

Keywords

Job-exposure matrix · Public health · Occupational · Work

Introduction

The large burden of disease caused by specific workplace exposures has been recognized for centuries. A growing body of work shows that workplace exposures including chemical exposures, biomechanical exposures, sedentary work, long work hours, and psychosocial exposures are important risk factors for many chronic diseases (GBD 2017 Risk Factor Collaborators 2018; Vos et al. 2020; Pega et al. 2021). Obtaining valid, unbiased estimates of relevant exposures is often difficult and complex, but is necessary for conducting epidemiological studies of occupational hazards. Several methods of exposure assessment exist, each with its own strengths and limitations (Kauppinen 1994). Direct measurements of exposure are often used to measure levels of chemicals, biological agents, noise, or radiation in the work environment, using either individual dosimetry or measures of an area where multiple workers are exposed. These methods are accurate but are sometimes expensive and time consuming, and capture exposures during a defined sampling period that may or may not be representative of work that is highly variable. Direct observation of workers for movement and posture has similar strengths and limitations (van der Beek and Frings-Dresen 1998). Biological measures such as blood or urine levels of a chemical offer an accurate measure of exposure over a recent time period of varying length depending on the substance sampled. Exposure questionnaires are easier to administer to large populations, but worker-reported exposures are generally less precise than measured exposures, and responses may be subject to recall bias or altered perceptions of exposures among symptomatic workers. One advantage of exposure questionnaires (or interviews) is that workers can summarize their exposures over time in jobs with varying exposure (Stock et al. 2005). Although individual-level data are considered the best estimates of exposure, these methods are difficult to gather in large cohort studies, and cannot be added to studies of existing data. The ability to add exposure information to the health outcomes contained in large population datasets would greatly improve our knowledge of the health effects of workplace exposures, particularly for chronic diseases such as cancer and osteoarthritis, where the relevant exposures may be cumulative or have occurred years before disease recognition. Job-exposure matrices offer researchers the ability to estimate recent and past exposures based on job title and industry information.

Definition

Since the 1980s, job-exposure matrices (JEMs) have been suggested for estimating exposure to work hazards, primarily chemicals, particularly for estimating past exposures and for populations without individual-level exposure measures (Hoar et al. 1980; Hoar 1983; Pannett et al. 1985). The use of JEMs became an accepted method to estimate workers' exposure to chemical and other physical risk factors based on job titles, industry information, and population exposure data (Coggon et al. 1984; Bouyer and Hémon 1994). Job-exposure matrices enable an individual's exposure to be estimated for epidemiological studies using coded job titles, which are converted into mean exposure estimates during different time windows. While JEM exposure estimates do not account for individual variation in the same job, they can estimate the average exposures for workers in different jobs, providing an inexpensive and useful exposure assessment method for general population studies or other populations where there is sufficient contrast in exposure levels between different jobs.

Simply put, a JEM is a matrix, or table, that links job titles (generally defined by a combination of an occupation and an industry sector) and indices of exposure to one or more work exposures. From the relatively simple collection of worker's job titles, JEMs make it possible to infer more complex information, converting coded job titles into exposure estimates for epidemiological studies. This technique has frequently been used in studies of occupational cancers and respiratory disease, where long disease latencies make it necessary to estimate past exposures to workplace chemicals. JEMs are being used more frequently to assign exposures such as workplace physical activities relevant to health outcomes including vascular disease, pregnancy outcomes, and musculoskeletal disorders (Dembe et al. 2014; Mocevic et al. 2014; Torén et al. 2015; Kjellberg et al. 2016; Dale et al. 2018; Kwegyir-Afful et al. 2018; Consonni et al. 2019; Hall et al. 2020). In addition to their relatively low cost, JEMs have additional advantages: They can decrease information bias between cases and noncases, and they allow the estimation of exposure data when no such data are otherwise available, including the estimation of historical exposures (Descatha et al. 2018b).

While the objective of most JEMs is to evaluate occupational exposure at the population level, the same approach can be relevant for specific populations, leading to the development of matrices relevant for segments of the population. A first example is industry-specific JEM, developed for the surveillance of occupational risks in a company or industrial sector. In this case, the job titles are specific of the company or the industrial sector (Descatha et al. 2022). A second example is task-exposure matrices, developed for workers employed in a specific industrial sector (Fevotte et al. 2006). This category includes also crop-exposure matrices, aiming at linking specific types of agricultural work to potentially hazardous substances, such as pesticides (Ohlander et al. 2020).

Literature Review

Using PubMed and Scopus databases we found job-exposure matrix included in the title, abstract, or keywords, of 1208 papers published before September 2021 (Fig. 1).

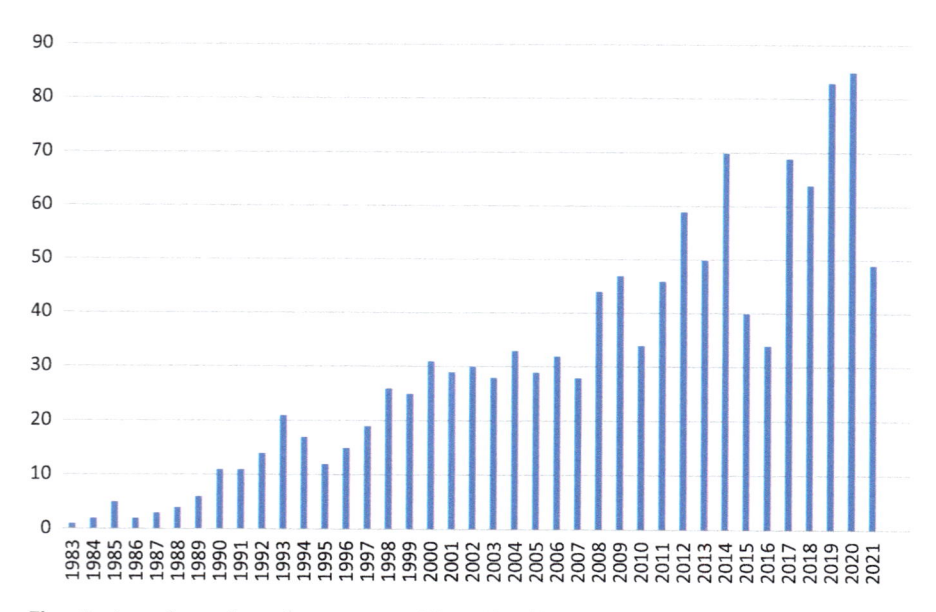

Fig. 1 Annual number of papers on JEMs identified via PubMed and Scopus through September 2021

Fig. 2 Countries reported in the papers on JEMs identified via PubMed and Scopus until September 2021

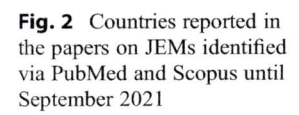

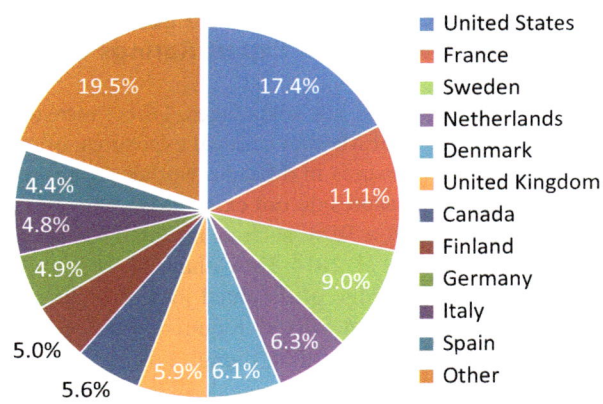

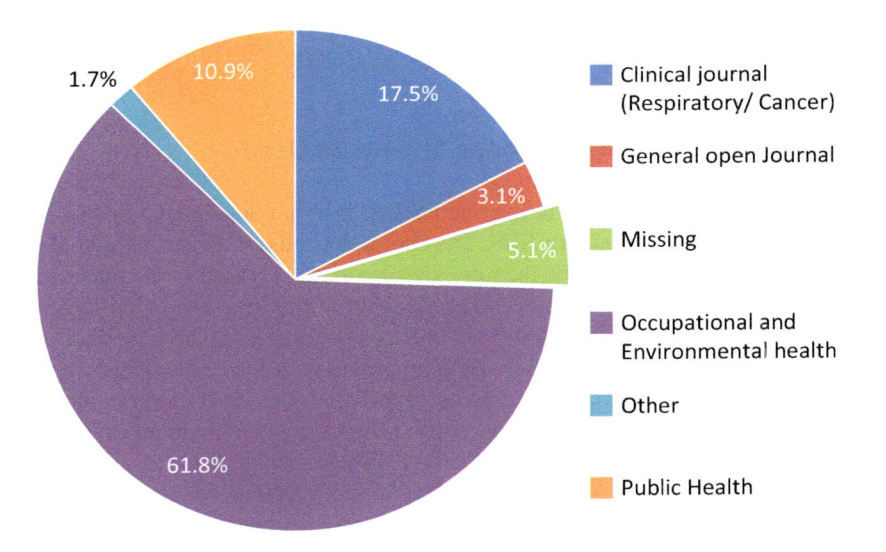

Fig. 3 Type of journals of the papers on JEMs identified via PubMed and Scopus until September 2021

Publications mostly came from countries in North America and Europe (Fig. 2), and were primarily published in occupational health journals (Fig. 3).

Design of Job-Exposure Matrices

Before building a job-exposure matrix, some questions should be answered:

Will the Job-Exposure Matrix Be Based on Measured Exposure Data, Worker Self-Reports, or Expert Ratings of Exposures?

Each of these methods has advantages. Direct measures of airborne chemicals are often used to create JEMs for chemical exposures, often supplemented with experts' assessments of exposures in different worker groups at different time points. When sufficient direct measures do not exist, a common situation, expert assessment may be used to construct a JEM, such as recent JEMs for physical activities (Svendsen et al. 2013; Rubak et al. 2014; Descatha et al. 2018a). These JEMs rely on assessors with accurate knowledge of the rated jobs. For general population studies, knowledge of many different jobs is required. Use of self-reported exposures is less common in constructing JEMs, though this method offers some advantages. JEMs based on self-reported exposures make use of workers' knowledge of their usual job exposures. By pooling information and assigning exposures based on group-level rather than individual-level responses, JEMs reduce information biases due to individual variation in reporting. A number of JEMs use a mixed approach such as expert assessment supplemented by direct measures, or use of both worker-reported and expert-rated exposures (Févotte et al. 2011; Dalbøge et al. 2016).

What Type of Job Classifications Should Be Used?

The relevant version of either an International or National Standard Classification of Occupations is usually used in a JEM. The choice depends on the availability of data, either for building or validating the job-exposure matrix, as well as the intended use and the format of the job classification data that are linked to the health outcomes under study. For example, the 1968 and 1988 International Standard Classification of Occupations (*ISCO*) were used for assessing previous exposures within the context of delayed diseases such as cancer across different countries (Olsson et al. 2011), whereas a study in one country looked at the risks associated with an occupational classification unique to that country (Kerbrat and Descatha 2018).

In addition to job titles, it may also be important to include further differentiation based on industry sector. Such differentiation may be mandatory for a chemical job-exposure matrix (Févotte et al. 2011) yet unnecessary for a biomechanical job-exposure matrix (Evanoff et al. 2019b).

What Exposure Components Should Be Considered: Level (Intensity), Duration, Frequency, or Probability?

Choice of exposure measure is often dependent on the source data (past exposure records, or an exposure questionnaire), and may also be influenced by the hypotheses that are being tested. Measurements of chemical or noise exposure may have multiple exposure elements, including peak exposure, time-weighted average, and duration in the working day. Some biomechanical JEM data consists primarily of duration of exposure at a given intensity level (Kauppinen et al. 1998; Evanoff et al. 2019b), while other JEMs provide data on intensity of exposure as well as frequency and duration (O*NET) (Cifuentes et al. 2010). Other JEMs have described the probability that a worker would have been exposed in each job. Probability, intensity, duration, and frequency of exposure may all be useful for assessing cumulative exposures if data are sufficiently precise (Févotte et al. 2011; Peters et al. 2016; Siemiatycki and Lavoué 2018).

Should Time and/or Location Be Considered (Date/Year, Region)?

When exposure is thought to be different between periods of time, or in different geographic regions, extra cells should be added to the JEM. For example, a JEM estimating past asbestos exposure took into account the time course of government regulations that reduced and eventually banned asbestos use (Févotte et al. 2011). When job histories are known over many years, use of a JEM may allow examination of risks of disease resulting from exposure during different time windows. For example, a Danish study examined risks of acute myocardial infarction (AMI) related to lifting and standing/walking at work, and found that AMI in men was not related to recent lifting at work (past 0–2 years), but was related to past cumulative lifting over the life course (Bonde et al. 2020). Most JEMs are specific of the country in which they have been developed. Using them for assessing exposure in other countries is an interesting possibility, particularly if a country-specific JEM is not available in the country of interest. Such transnational use is feasible, and is expected to be more frequent in the future, despite two difficulties: first, each country has country-specific classification systems for occupations and activity sectors. Unless the International Standard Classification of Occupations has been used, then transcoding of the job an industry codes in the JEM to those of the population under study is needed. Other difficulties or limitations are inherent to the fact that, for the same job, exposure could differ between countries. This is very obvious in some situations: working outside implies exposure to cold or to heat, depending on the country. Government legislations could differ too. For those reasons, efforts to create and use cross-national or international JEMs must consider differences in exposures between countries as well as different job classification schemes (Lavoué et al. 2012; Descatha et al. 2019). Such uses exist, for example, the American O*NET JEM has been linked to job titles in the UK through transcoding the two job coding systems, and has since been used to estimate work exposures relevant to SARS-CoV-2 and rotator cuff disorders in the large UK Biobank cohort (Yanik et al. 2022).

Other Variables

Other elements may be considered if they have a significant contribution to the development or the generalizability of the JEM. For example, specification of gender may be important, as exposures within the same job title may differ between men and women, prompting some recent JEMs to give separate values by sex, as well as size of the employer (Falkstedt et al. 2021; Niedhammer et al. 2021). Prevention through attenuation of exposure levels is sometime important to consider, like wearing mask or vaccination proportion for COVID-19 (Descatha et al. 2021).

Development

The methods of developing a JEM are driven by the methods used to estimate exposures.

Development of a JEM Based on Expert Assessments

An expert assessment–based JEM is generally constructed by a group of experts following a Delphi method (Bouyer and Hémon 1994). A group of experts familiar with coding issues and with the jobs and exposures considered are asked to perform individual, blinded assessments of the exposures for each job. Differences in exposure estimates between experts are then identified and compared, with assessment of inter-rater agreement and the magnitude of differences between raters (Goldberg et al. 1986; Descatha et al. 2018a). Jobs with unacceptable agreement between raters are recoded in subsequent rounds to reach an agreed level of consensus on mean or median exposures at the job level.

Development of JEMs Based on Existing Exposure Data

Existing exposure data may consist of direct measures of airborne chemicals or physical exposures such as noise or radiation, collected in individual workers or in an area with multiple workers. Self-reported exposures can also be used. JEMs may be constructed at the level of an individual factory or industry, or at the level of the general population. Large datasets are required for general population JEMs, because a minimum number of measures for each risk factor is needed within each job category (Choi 2019). Different statistical methods are possible for creating the JEM. When reporting JEM-assigned exposure values, studies have used different exposure metrics, typically arithmetic means and medians of exposure levels. Other studies have reported bias-corrected means created using empirical quantile mapping (Evanoff et al. 2019b). Other methods have used a segmentation method (Classification and Regression Tree "CART") to incorporate industrial activity sectors and other important variables that may influence exposure (Siemiatycki and Lavoué 2018; Niedhammer et al. 2019).

Mixed Approaches

Mixed approaches are often used to create or improve JEMs. To optimize the accuracy of the expert results, available exposure data may be given as examples before the beginning of the JEM construction, or between the Delphi rounds. Indeed, where JEM originally assigned exposures at a qualitative or semiquantitative level based on expert ratings, quantitative exposure estimates can also be derived when measurements are used to calibrate these ratings (Peters et al. 2011; Friesen et al. 2012; Peters et al. 2016). In JEMs generated through existing exposure data where the number of available measures is low in some job categories, expert opinion can be used to group similar job codes to create adequately sized groupings. Directly measured exposures can also be used to supplement JEMs created by expert opinion (Dalbøge et al. 2016).

Validation

Assessment of both reliability and validity is important for evaluation of the accuracy of the exposure estimates provided by a JEM. Intraclass correlation coefficients (ICC) and other agreement scores such as weighted kappas are often calculated among the blinded experts to assess the agreement between expert assessors. For data-driven JEMs, the reliability is usually based on the comparison of the within-job and between-job exposure variance for exposures (Evanoff et al. 2019b; Choi 2020). The goal of a JEM is to create homogenous exposure groupings that distinguish between different jobs such that between-job variance is higher than within-job variance. A number of techniques are available to evaluate between-job and within-job variances for each exposure variable.

In some cases, validity can be assessed by comparing JEM-estimated exposures to a gold standard of exposure, following the methodology of diagnostic accuracy studies. Often, no gold standard is available. Other methods of testing validity include replicating known exposure-outcome associations, and measuring agreement of exposure estimations with different JEMs (Yung et al. 2020a, b). External validation can also be done with datasets from different time points and environment.

Some Examples of JEM

SYNJEM

Data come from SYNERGY, a large pooled analysis of case-control studies on the joint effects of occupational carcinogens and smoking in the development of lung cancer. The quantitative JEM (SYN-JEM) was developed to assign exposures to five major lung carcinogens (asbestos, chromium, nickel, polycyclic aromatic hydrocarbons (PAH), and respirable crystalline silica [RCS]) (Peters et al. 2013, 2016). This quantitative exposure assessment was based on an exposure database that included 356,551 measurements from 19 countries. In total, 140,666 personal and 215,885 stationary data points were available. Measurements were distributed over the five agents as follows: RCS (42%), asbestos (20%), chromium (16%), nickel (15%), and

PAH (7%). The measurement data cover the time period from 1951 to present. However, only a small portion of measurements (1.4%) were performed prior to 1975. The major contributing countries for personal measurements were Germany (32%), the UK (22%), France (14%), and Norway and Canada (both 11%). Empirical linear models were developed using personal occupational exposure measurements (n = 102,306) from Europe and Canada, as well as auxiliary information like job (industry), year of sampling, region, an a priori exposure rating of each job (none, low, and high exposed), sampling and analytical methods, and sampling duration. The model outcomes were used to create a JEM with a quantitative estimate of the level of exposure by job, year, and region (Consonni et al. 2019; Hall et al. 2020).

O*NET

O*NET is a large, publicly available American database that provides information on the physical and mental job demands of more than 800 occupations identified by the US Standard Occupational Classification (SOC) codes (www.onetonline. org). Estimates of job demands in O*NET were provided by expert job analysts and by surveys of workers in different jobs (Cifuentes et al. 2010). O*NET has most commonly been used to estimate workplace activities and requirements such as handling and moving objects, kneeling, standing, use of static and dynamic force, and bending and twisting. Physical exposures in O*NET are scored on five-point or eight-point ordinal scales with exposure-specific descriptive anchors. Scale ratings pertain to the frequency (five-point ordinal scale) or intensity (eight-point ordinal scale) of different job demands. O*NET data provide the mean ratings for each demand for each job title. O*NET has also been used to estimate psychological job strain, and exposure to respiratory hazards (Cifuentes et al. 2007).

Matgéné

Matgéné is a program to develop 18 JEMs concerning a variety of chemical agents, including organic and mineral dust, mineral fibers, and solvents, relevant to the general population in France for the period from 1950–2006 (Févotte et al. 2011). JEMs were drawn up by a team of six industrial hygienists who based their assessments on available occupational measurements, economic and statistical data, and several thousand job descriptions from epidemiological studies performed in France since 1984. Each JEM is specific to one agent, assessing exposure for a set of homogeneous combinations (occupation × activity × period) according to two occupational classifications (ISCO 1968 and PCS 1994) and one economic activities classification (NAF 2000). The cells of the JEM carry an estimate of the probability and level of exposure. Level is estimated by the duration and intensity of exposure-linked tasks or by description of the tasks when exposure measurement data are lacking for the agent in question. The JEMs were applied to a representative sample of the French population in 2007, and prevalence for each exposure was estimated in various population groups.

DOC*X

The Danish Occupational Cohort with eXposure data (DOC*X) contains estimates of a wide variety of occupational exposures provided by JEMs (Flachs et al. 2019). To enable linkage between the Danish Occupation and Industry Register and the JEMs, all exposure estimates are classified according to Danish national job coding systems DISCO-88 and DB-07. Additionally, the included JEMs have found use in combination with other databases with similar coding of occupation and industry. The psychosocial JEM includes six psychosocial exposures based on data from a questionnaire survey of a random sample of 15,207 Danish employees in the Work Environment and Health in Denmark cohort study; the biomechanical JEMs include 18 exposures and have been constructed based on expert ratings. Also included are chemical and particulate airborne exposure JEMs, as well as lifestyle JEMs that cover some factors associated with both job/industry and health/disability. Lifestyle factors covered include smoking, alcohol consumption, body mass index, leisure-time physical activity, and intake of fruit and vegetables, which vary by occupational category.

JEM Constances

JEM Constances is based on 27 different biomechanical factors and physical activities reported by ~35,000 active workers participating in a large French prospective cohort study representative of the general population. These self-reported exposures, which are based on four or five category ordinal scales describing the usual duration of different exposures, were pooled at the level of the job using the French Classification of Occupations (*Profession et Catégories Socioprofessionnelles* PCS 2003), and subsequently transcoded to the International Standard Classification of Occupations 2008 (*ISCO-08*) and to the American SOC codes (Evanoff et al. 2019a). For each exposure the JEM gives the distribution of exposures reported in >400 different jobs. This JEM has been used to examine associations between cumulative work exposures and the risk of several outcomes, including Dupuytren's contractures and decreased physical abilities in later life (Fadel et al. 2019; Ngabirano et al. 2020).

Mat-O-Covid

A group of French experts of infectious disease and occupational health developed a SARS- CoV-2 JEM workplace exposure using the 2003 Occupation and

Socioprofessional Categories (with a transcoding gateway to the 2008 International Standard Classification of Occupations), with a focus on the health and care sector (Descatha et al. 2021; Fadel et al. 2021). The average of the experts' coding was used to estimate exposures to other workers, to the public, and patients, as well as the probability of prevention for each (wearing mask, vaccination, ventilation, etc.).

Limitations

Users should be aware of the limitations that exist for the development and use of JEMs. By assigning the same exposure to all workers in a job, JEMs reflect an "average" level of exposures, and cannot account for exposure heterogeneity of individual workers within the same job. This creates nondifferential misclassification of estimated individual exposures, which differ within a job due to individual behaviors and other factors (Peters 2020). JEMs work best when there is large variability between the exposures in different jobs, such as in a general population study, and are less able to discriminate between groups of workers with very similar exposures. In other words, a JEM can efficiently estimate differences in average exposures between different jobs, but cannot account for exposure heterogeneity between workers in the same job. Researchers must not forget that occupational classification systems have been developed primarily from a socioeconomic perspective, and may not accurately reflect exposure categories. Users must critically evaluate if the exposures of interest can be reasonably assessed at the job group level. Some exposure heterogeneity may be accounted for by adding more detail, by expanding the number of variables in the JEM. For example, a sex- and age-specific exposure estimates may help explain some exposure heterogeneity within jobs. As previously described, this type of information needs to be available in the large studies where JEMs are being applied. In addition to within-job variability between workers, exposures may have large temporal variability among tasks. Since levels can vary from day to day and in the work day, this variability may not be captured in a JEM. Indeed, assessing exposure through a JEM implies that the variability of exposure within jobs is relatively small, or that an estimate of average exposures is relevant to the outcomes of interest. This can be a limitation, for example, for psychosocial work exposures. For some work organization exposures, estimates at the job level could be relevant. For other exposures such as social support, exposure information at the individual level may be preferred (Solovieva et al. 2014). Another example is JEMs addressing lifestyle factors, with the objective of controlling for potential confounding factors such as smoking or drinking. With this approach, variability in exposures that occur within each job is not taken into account, whereas it is expected to be large for smoking and drinking habits (Friesen 2018). For some health conditions, the effects of short-term high exposures may be more relevant than average levels over time. For a recent COVID JEM, the authors have observed that exposures are strongly influenced by factors not accounted for in the JEM, including fluctuations in viral circulation over time and workplace prevention measures (Oude Hengel et al. 2022; Descatha et al. 2021).

JEMs must also be used with caution given the limitations of their construction, based either on expert assessments or on data collected at the individual and aggregate level. The expertise and opinions of the experts influence the exposures assigned in the JEM and could create biases or nondifferential misclassification. JEM construction should take into account efforts to identify and avoid potential biases. For instance, a JEM for biomechanical exposure based on self-reported exposures may wish to exclude subjects with musculoskeletal pain who might overestimate their level of work exposure (Evanoff et al. 2019b).

Coding of occupations from job titles and industry can be time intensive, and can influence the exposures assigned to individual workers. Coding by trained professionals blinded to disease status, or use of automatic coding algorithms is often suggested. However, professional manual coding of each individual's job category is a very time-consuming and costly task. Systems that automatically translate free text into occupational codes can increase the efficiency, feasibility, and reproducibility of investigating occupational risk factors using JEMs in large-scale epidemiological studies. Automated job coding systems exist for several national job coding systems, though such automated coding may need to be supplemented by manual coding (Buckner-Petty et al. 2019). Agreement of automatic coding with manual coding is fair to good, and is an area of ongoing research (Davis et al. 2021).

Several items need to be considered by researchers wishing to apply a JEM to their data (Descatha et al. 2022). First, is there an existing JEM on the exposure of interest? Is the JEM available? Does the JEM contain relevant exposure metric(s)? Is the job coding system compatible with that of the target population? Next, is the selected JEM appropriate for the research question? Be aware of a JEM's general limitations (and strengths). Are the methods of JEM development and validation reported appropriate? Researchers should also consider additional validation in the context of the proposed study.

Why Use JEMs in Public Health Research and Practice?

In addition to the use of JEMs for studies specifically assessing associations between workplace exposure and related disorders, it is increasingly clear that public health risk factor models should include all relevant factors in the "exposome," including workplace factors (Rappaport 2011). Indeed, given the large amount of time that people spend at work, exposures and behaviors at the workplace should be considered when describing risk factors for future disease. There is increasing interest in assessing the role of workplace factors on chronic and acute diseases that have not been traditionally considered to be "occupational diseases." For instance, a JEM was used to study the influence of workplace physical exposures on aging in the Copenhagen Aging and Midlife Biobank (Møller et al. 2015). In addition to the known risk factors of age, smoking, body mass index, hypertension, diabetes, and socioeconomic status, atrial fibrillation was also independently associated with exposure to occupational psychosocial stress (assessed with a JEM), in a large study of the Swedish population. Another study used a JEM to assess lifting during pregnancy and found an increased risk of stillbirth among women with a prior fetal death who lifted over 200 kg/day at work (Mocevic et al. 2014). In the COVID crisis, the risk of becoming infected with SARS-CoV-2 and the occupational conditions related with this have led develop workplace exposure JEMs (Fadel et al. 2021; Descatha et al. 2021; van Veldhoven et al. 2021). These examples illustrate the importance of considering occupational exposures in combined risk factor studies, and JEMs offer efficient opportunities to public health researchers to incorporate workplace exposures into analyses.

In addition to research applications, JEMs may play a role in risk factor surveillance and other public health activities, and in clinical management (Fadel et al. 2020). JEM could assist in the clinical care of workers, in return to work assessments, and in the workers' compensation or other social benefits process, by providing a basic assessment of relevant exposures within different jobs. Because occupational diseases are often under-recognized, another practical application is using a JEM to screen for occupational exposures as part of health surveillance. By summarizing multiple exposures at a job level, JEM may also assist policymakers in setting priorities for hazards and controls at work, and assist occupational practitioners to target prevention efforts and direct the conduct of more precise exposure measures to particular jobs.

Several research initiatives are also working on improvements in the use of JEM: for instance, the Exposome Project for Health and Occupational Research (EPHOR, www.ephor-project.eu) and JEMINI (for Job-Exposure Matrix InterNatIonal) initiative (Descatha et al. 2019) aim to explore the possibility of developing international JEMs that could be used across countries.

Finally, JEM can also help *occupational practitioner*. One example was constructed from data from the medical surveillance survey of employees' exposure to risk (Guéguen et al. 2004). It provided a tool for occupational physicians on certain work organization and other occupational exposures to target prevention efforts. Such use of a JEM may help occupational health professionals to reserve their efforts and expertise for complex situations. It also might be used when occupational practitioners are scarce or nonexistent.

Conclusion

Given the many hours people spend at work and the risk of common diseases attributable to occupational factors, including physical activity and workplace psychosocial factors, there are clear opportunities for improving risk factor models by incorporating workplace exposures. JEMs can be a powerful tool for exposure assessment in epidemiology studies, particularly in large-scale studies with limited occupational information. This useful tool should be more widely used outside of the field of occupational disease epidemiology.

References

Bonde JPE, Flachs EM, Madsen IE, Petersen SB, Andersen JH, Hansen J et al (2020) Acute myocardial infarction in relation to physical activities at work: a nationwide follow-up study based on job-exposure matrices. Scand J Work Environ Health 46(3):268–277

Bouyer J, Hémon D (1994) Job exposure matrices. Rev Epidemiol Sante Publique 42(3):235–245

Buckner-Petty S, Dale AM, Evanoff BA (2019) Efficiency of autocoding programs for converting job descriptors into standard occupational classification (SOC) codes. Am J Ind Med 62(1):59–68

Choi B (2019) Determining an optimal minimum number of subjects in each occupation for a job exposure matrix (JEM) using self-reported data: a missing test. Scand J Work Environ Health 45(4):421–422

Choi B (2020) Developing a job exposure matrix of work organization hazards in the United States: a review on methodological issues and research protocol. Saf Health Work 11(4):397–404

Cifuentes M, Boyer J, Gore R, d'Errico A, Tessler J, Scollin P et al (2007) Inter-method agreement between O*NET and survey measures of psychosocial exposure among healthcare industry employees. Am J Ind Med 50(7):545–553

Cifuentes M, Boyer J, Lombardi DA, Punnett L (2010) Use of O*NET as a job exposure matrix: a literature review. Am J Ind Med 53(9):898–914

Coggon D, Pannett B, Acheson ED (1984) Use of job-exposure matrix in an occupational analysis of lung and bladder cancers on the basis of death certificates. J Natl Cancer Inst 72(1):61–65

Consonni D, Calvi C, De Matteis S, Mirabelli D, Landi MT, Caporaso NE et al (2019) Peritoneal mesothelioma and asbestos exposure: a population-based case-control study in Lombardy, Italy. Occup Environ Med 76(8):545–553

Dalbøge A, Hansson GÅ, Frost P, Andersen JH, Heilskov-Hansen T, Svendsen SW (2016) Upper arm elevation and repetitive shoulder movements: a general population job exposure matrix based on expert ratings and technical measurements. Occup Environ Med 73(8):553–560

Dale AM, Ekenga CC, Buckner-Petty S, Merlino L, Thiese MS, Bao S et al (2018) Incident CTS in a large pooled cohort study: associations obtained by a job exposure matrix versus associations obtained from observed exposures. Occup Environ Med 75(7):501–506

Davis J, Peek-Asa C, Dale AM, Zhang L, Casteel C, Hamann C et al (2021) Determining occupation for National Violent Death Reporting System records: an evaluation of autocoding programs. Am J Ind Med 64(12):1018–1027

Dembe AE, Yao X, Wickizer TM, Shoben AB, Dong XS (2014) A novel method for estimating the effects of job conditions on asthma and chronic lung disease. J Asthma 51(8):799–807

Descatha A, Despréaux T, Petit A, Bodin J, Andersen JH, Dale AM et al (2018a) Development of "MADE", a French job exposure matrix for evaluation of biomechanical exposure. Sante Publique 30(3):333–337

Descatha A, Leclerc A, Goldberg M (25 juill 2018b) Job exposure matrix: from research to public health. Rev Epidemiol Sante Publique

Descatha A, Evanoff BA, Andersen JH, Fadel M, Ngabirano L, Leclerc A et al (2019) JEMINI (job exposure matrix InterNatIonal) initiative: a utopian possibility for helping occupational exposure assessment all around the world? J Occup Environ Med 61(7):e320–e321

Descatha A, Fadel M, Pitet S, Verdun-Esquer C, Esquirol Y, Legeay C et al (30 juill 2021) SARS-CoV-2 (COVID-19) job exposure matrix: "Mat-O-Covid" creation (COVID-Mate in French), accuracy study, and perspectives. Archives des Maladies Professionnelles et de l'Environnement [Internet]. [cité 20 août 2021]; Disponible sur: https://www.ncbi.nlm.nih.gov/pmc/articles/PMC8321772/

Descatha A, Fadel M, Sembajwe G, Peters S, Evanoff BA (2022) Job-exposure matrix: a useful tool for incorporating workplace exposure data into population health research and practice. Front Epidemiol [Internet]. [cité 21 mai 2022];2. Disponible sur: https://www.frontiersin.org/article/10.3389/fepid.2022.857316

Evanoff B, Yung M, Buckner-Petty S, Baca M, Andersen JH, Roquelaure Y et al (2019a) Cross-national comparison of two general population job exposure matrices for physical work exposures. Occup Environ Med 76(8):567–572

Evanoff BA, Yung M, Buckner-Petty S, Andersen JH, Roquelaure Y, Descatha A et al (31 janv 2019b) The CONSTANCES job exposure matrix based on self-reported exposure to physical risk factors: development and evaluation. Occup Environ Med

Fadel M, Leclerc A, Evanoff B, Dale AM, Ngabirano L, Roquelaure Y et al (2019) Association between occupational exposure and Dupuytren's contracture using a job-exposure matrix and self-reported exposure in the CONSTANCES cohort. Occup Environ Med 76(11):845–848

Fadel M, Evanoff BA, Andersen JH, d'Errico A, Dale AM, Leclerc A et al (2020) Not just a research method: if used with caution, can job-exposure matrices be a useful tool in the practice of occupational medicine and public health? Scand J Work Environ Health 46(5):552–553

Fadel M, Salomon J, Descatha A (2021) COVID-19 job exposure matrix: from the Mat-O-Covid design to its execution. J Occup Environ Med 63(3):e168

Falkstedt D, Hemmingsson T, Albin M, Bodin T, Ahlbom A, Selander J et al (2021) Disability pensions related to heavy physical workload: a cohort study of middle-aged and older workers in Sweden. Int Arch Occup Environ Health 94(8):1851–1861

Fevotte J, Charbotel B, Muller-Beauté P, Martin JL, Hours M, Bergeret A (2006) Case-control study on renal cell cancer and occupational exposure to trichloroethylene. Part I: exposure assessment. Ann Occup Hyg 50(8):765–775

Févotte J, Dananché B, Delabre L, Ducamp S, Garras L, Houot M et al (2011) Matgéné: a program to develop job-exposure matrices in the general population in France. Ann Occup Hyg 55(8):865–878

Flachs EM, Petersen SEB, Kolstad HA, Schlünssen V, Svendsen SW, Hansen J et al (2019) Cohort profile: DOC*X: a nationwide Danish occupational cohort with eXposure data – an open research resource. Int J Epidemiol 48(5):1413–1413k

Friesen MC (2018) Job-exposure matrices addressing lifestyle factors. Occup Environ Med 75(12):847

Friesen MC, Coble JB, Lu W, Shu XO, Ji BT, Xue S et al (2012) Combining a job-exposure matrix with exposure measurements to assess occupational exposure to benzene in a population cohort in shanghai, China. Ann Occup Hyg 56(1):80–91

GBD 2017 Risk Factor Collaborators (2018) Global, regional, and national comparative risk assessment of 84 behavioural, environmental and occupational, and metabolic risks or clusters of risks for 195 countries and territories, 1990–2017: a systematic analysis for the Global Burden of Disease Study 2017. Lancet 392(10159):1923–1994

Goldberg M, Leclerc A, Chastang JF, Goldberg P, Brodeur JM, Fuhrer R et al (1986) Retrospective evaluation of occupational exposure in epidemiologic studies. Use of the Delphi method. Rev Epidemiol Sante Publique 34(4–5):245–251

Guéguen A, Goldberg M, Bonenfant S, Martin JC (2004) Using a representative sample of workers for constructing the SUMEX French general population based job-exposure matrix. Occup Environ Med 61(7):586–593

Hall AL, Kromhout H, Schüz J, Peters S, Portengen L, Vermeulen R et al (2020) Laryngeal cancer risks in workers exposed to lung carcinogens: exposure-effect analyses using a quantitative job exposure matrix. Epidemiology 31(1):145–154

Hoar S (1983) Job exposure matrix methodology. Clin Toxicol 21(1–2):9–26

Hoar SK, Morrison AS, Cole P, Silverman DT (1980) An occupation and exposure linkage system for the study of occupational carcinogenesis. J Occup Med 22(11):722–726

Kauppinen TP (1994) Assessment of exposure in occupational epidemiology. Scand J Work Environ Health 20(Spec No):19–29

Kauppinen T, Toikkanen J, Pukkala E (1998) From cross-tabulations to multipurpose exposure information systems: a new job-exposure matrix. Am J Ind Med 33(4):409–417

Kerbrat J, Descatha A (2018) The recognition of health consequences of difficult working conditions in France and its evaluation with the use of a job-exposure matrix. Archives des Maladies Professionnelles et de l'Environnement 79(4):493–500

Kjellberg K, Lundin A, Falkstedt D, Allebeck P, Hemmingsson T (2016) Long-term physical workload in middle age and disability pension in men and women: a follow-up study of Swedish cohorts. Int Arch Occup Environ Health 89(8):1239–1250

Kwegyir-Afful E, Lamminpää R, Selander T, Gissler M, Vehviläinen-Julkunen K, Heinonen S et al (2018) Manual handling of burdens as a predictor of birth outcome-a Finnish Birth Register Study. Eur J Pub Health 28(6):1122–1126

Lavoué J, Pintos J, Van Tongeren M, Kincl L, Richardson L, Kauppinen T et al (2012) Comparison of exposure estimates in the Finnish job-exposure matrix FINJEM with a JEM derived from expert assessments performed in Montreal. Occup Environ Med 69(7):465–471

Mocevic E, Svendsen SW, Jørgensen KT, Frost P, Bonde JP (2014) Occupational lifting, fetal death and preterm birth: findings from the Danish National Birth Cohort using a job exposure matrix. PLoS One 9(3):e90550

Møller A, Reventlow S, Hansen ÅM, Andersen LL, Siersma V, Lund R et al (2015) Does physical exposure throughout working life influence chair-rise performance in midlife? A retrospective cohort study of associations between work and physical function in Denmark. BMJ Open 5(11): e009873

Ngabirano L, Fadel M, Leclerc A, Evanoff BA, Dale AM, d'Errico A et al (2020) Association between physical limitations and working life exposure to carrying heavy loads assessed using a job-exposure matrix: CONSTANCES cohort. Arch Environ Occup Health 16:1–5

Niedhammer I, Milner A, Geoffroy-Perez B, Coutrot T, Lamontagne AD, Chastang JF (2019) Prospective associations of psychosocial work exposures with mortality in France: STRESSJEM study protocol. BMJ Open [Internet] 9(10). Disponible sur: https://www.scopus. com/inward/record.uri?eid=2-s2.0-85074550954&doi=10.1136%2fbmjopen-2019-031352& partnerID=40&md5=7bca4005cb3f019573af22b4bbfea538

Niedhammer I, Milner A, Coutrot T, Geoffroy-Perez B, LaMontagne AD, Chastang JF (2021) Psychosocial work factors of the job strain model and all-cause mortality: the STRESSJEM prospective cohort study. Psychosom Med 83(1):62–70

Ohlander J, Fuhrimann S, Basinas I, Cherrie JW, Galea KS, Povey AC et al (2020) Systematic review of methods used to assess exposure to pesticides in occupational epidemiology studies, 1993–2017. Occup Environ Med 77(6):357–367

Olsson AC, Gustavsson P, Kromhout H, Peters S, Vermeulen R, Brüske I et al (2011) Exposure to diesel motor exhaust and lung cancer risk in a pooled analysis from case-control studies in Europe and Canada. Am J Respir Crit Care Med 183(7):941–948

Oude Hengel KM, Burdorf A, Pronk A, Schlünssen V, Stokholm ZA, Kolstad HA et al (2022) Exposure to a SARS-CoV-2 infection at work: development of an international job exposure matrix (COVID-19-JEM). Scand J Work Environ Health 48(1):61–70

Pannett B, Coggon D, Acheson ED (1985) A job-exposure matrix for use in population based studies in England and Wales. Br J Ind Med 42(11):777–783

Pega F, Náfrádi B, Momen NC, Ujita Y, Streicher KN, Prüss-Üstün AM et al (2021) Global, regional, and national burdens of ischemic heart disease and stroke attributable to exposure to long working hours for 194 countries, 2000-2016: a systematic analysis from the WHO/ILO joint estimates of the work-related burden of disease and injury. Environ Int 154:106595

Peters S (2020) Although a valuable method in occupational epidemiology, job-exposure matrices are no magic fix. Scand J Work Environ Health 46(3):231–234

Peters S, Vermeulen R, Portengen L, Olsson A, Kendzia B, Vincent R et al (2011) Modelling of occupational respirable crystalline silica exposure for quantitative exposure assessment in community-based case-control studies. J Environ Monit 13(11):3262–3268

Peters S, Kromhout H, Portengen L, Olsson A, Kendzia B, Vincent R et al (2013) Sensitivity analyses of exposure estimates from a quantitative job-exposure matrix (SYN-JEM) for use in community-based studies. Ann Occup Hyg 57(1):98–106

Peters S, Vermeulen R, Portengen L, Olsson A, Kendzia B, Vincent R et al (2016) SYN-JEM: a quantitative job-exposure matrix for five lung carcinogens. Ann Occup Hyg 60(7):795–811

Rappaport SM (2011) Implications of the exposome for exposure science. J Expo Sci Environ Epidemiol 21(1):5–9

Rubak TS, Svendsen SW, Andersen JH, Haahr JPL, Kryger A, Jensen LD et al (2014) An expert-based job exposure matrix for large scale epidemiologic studies of primary hip and knee osteoarthritis: the lower body JEM. BMC Musculoskelet Disord 15:204

Siemiatycki J, Lavoué J (2018) Availability of a new job-exposure matrix (CANJEM) for epidemiologic and occupational medicine purposes. J Occup Environ Med 60(7):e324–e328

Solovieva S, Pensola T, Kausto J, Shiri R, Heliövaara M, Burdorf A et al (2014) Evaluation of the validity of job exposure matrix for psychosocial factors at work. PLoS One 9(9):e108987

Stock SR, Fernandes R, Delisle A, Vezina N (2005) Reproducibility and validity of workers' self-reports of physical work demands. Scand J Work Environ Health 31(6):409–437

Svendsen SW, Dalbøge A, Andersen JH, Thomsen JF, Frost P (2013) Risk of surgery for subacromial impingement syndrome in relation to neck-shoulder complaints and occupational biomechanical exposures: a longitudinal study. Scand J Work Environ Health 39(6):568–577

Torén K, Schiöler L, Söderberg M, Giang KW, Rosengren A (2015) The association between job strain and atrial fibrillation in Swedish men. Occup Environ Med 72(3):177–180

van der Beek AJ, Frings-Dresen MH (1998) Assessment of mechanical exposure in ergonomic epidemiology. Occup Environ Med 55(5):291–299

van Veldhoven K, Basinas I, Hengel KO, Burdorf A, Pronk A, Peters S et al (1 Sept 2021) Development and validation of a job exposure matrix for work related risk factors for COVID-19. Int J Epidemiol [Internet]. [cité 10 nov 2021] 50(Supplement_1). Disponible sur: https://doi.org/10.1093/ije/dyab168.678

Vos T, Lim SS, Abbafati C, Abbas KM, Abbasi M, Abbasifard M et al (2020) Global burden of 369 diseases and injuries in 204 countries and territories, 1990–2019: a systematic analysis for the Global Burden of Disease Study 2019. Lancet 396(10258):1204–1222

Yanik EL, Stevens MJ, Harris EC, Walker-Bone KE, Dale AM, Ma Y et al (2022) Physical work exposure matrix for use in the UK Biobank. Occup Med (Lond) 72(2):132–141

Yung M, Dale AM, Buckner-Petty S, Roquelaure Y, Descatha A, Evanoff BA (2020a) Musculoskeletal symptoms associated with workplace physical exposures estimated by a job exposure matrix and by self-report. Am J Ind Med 63(1):51–59

Yung M, Evanoff BA, Buckner-Petty S, Roquelaure Y, Descatha A, Dale AM (2020b) Applying two general population job exposure matrices to predict incident carpal tunnel syndrome: a cross-national approach to improve estimation of workplace physical exposures. Scand J Work Environ Health 46(3):248–258

Challenges of Large Cohort and Massive Data in Occupational Health

Ingrid Sivesind Mehlum and Michelle C. Turner

Contents

Introduction	96
Studies of Large-Scale Registry Data	97
Data to Define or Describe the Population	97
Occupational Exposure Data	98
Outcome Data	100
Data on Potential Confounders and Other Covariates	101
Business or Enterprise Data	101
Access to Registry Data	102
Strengths and Limitations of Registry-Based Studies	102
Consortia of Cohort Studies	103
The Individual-Participant Data Meta-analysis in Working Populations (IPD-Work) Consortium	103
The International Nuclear Workers Study (INWORKS)	104
The Pooled Uranium Miner Analysis (PUMA) Cohorts	104
The International Consortium of Agricultural Cohort Studies (AGRICOH)	105
Multicenter Worker Cohorts	106
Birth Cohort Studies in Occupational Health Research	106

I. S. Mehlum (✉)
National Institute of Occupational Health (STAMI), Oslo, Norway

Institute of Health and Society, University of Oslo, Oslo, Norway

Department of Occupational and Environmental Medicine, Bispebjerg and Frederiksberg Hospitals, Copenhagen, Denmark

Department of Public Health, University of Copenhagen, Copenhagen, Denmark
e-mail: ingrid.s.mehlum@stami.no

M. C. Turner
Barcelona Institute for Global Health (ISGlobal), Barcelona, Spain

Universitat Pompeu Fabra (UPF), Barcelona, Spain

CIBER Epidemiología y Salud Pública (CIBERESP), Madrid, Spain
e-mail: michelle.turner@isglobal.org

© Springer Nature Switzerland AG 2023
M. Wahrendorf et al. (eds.), *Handbook of Life Course Occupational Health*, Handbook Series in Occupational Health Sciences, https://doi.org/10.1007/978-3-031-30492-7_3

Recent Initiatives in Integrating European Occupational Cohorts 107
  Inventory of Occupational Cohort Studies 108
  Inventory of Occupational Exposure Assessment Tools 109
  Theoretical Frameworks, Consensus Definitions, and Recommendations for Future
    Research 110
Exposome Research in Occupation and Health 111
  The Exposome 111
  The Occupational Exposome 112
Conclusion 114
Cross-References 115
References 115

Abstract

There is increasing emphasis in research in occupation and health using large-scale massive cohort data. There are studies based on individual population or patient registries at the national or regional level as well as combined analysis of data from registries across several countries. There are also consortia of cohort studies to combine data from multiple cohorts on specific topics. Recent efforts in Europe have sought to inventory numerous existing occupational cohort studies and to integrate their data to ultimately lead to more definitive research. Advancements in theoretical frameworks to study occupation and health, consensus definitions, and recommendations for future research have been described. Exposome research concepts have also recently been extended to the field of occupation and health. An overview of recent efforts in large cohort and massive data in occupational health is presented along with a description of associated strengths and limitations. Challenges in integrating cohort data for research in occupation and health are described.

Keywords

Data harmonization · Exposome research · Occupational cohorts · Registry-based studies · Research consortia · Research networks

Introduction

There is increasing emphasis on using large-scale massive cohort data in occupational health research. This chapter focuses on different types of large cohort studies. Large registry-based studies are covered in section "Studies of Large-Scale Registry Data," including how to identify data on relevant occupational exposures, outcomes, potential confounders, and other covariates, as well as data at the business or enterprise level. How to obtain registry data and strengths and limitations of registry-based research data are described. Multinational consortia of cohort studies have also been formed to harmonize and pool data from multiple studies on specific topics in occupational health. Section "Consortia of Cohort Studies" provides an overview of consortia of cohort studies, including multinational consortia in Europe and worldwide. Recent initiatives in the coordination and harmonization of

European occupational cohort studies are described in section "Recent Initiatives in Integrating European Occupational Cohorts," in particular the recent Network on the Coordination and Harmonisation of European Occupational Cohorts (OMEGA-NET), which has developed an inventory of occupational cohorts and initiated work to integrate occupational exposure and outcome information as well as recommendations for future research. Finally, the emergence of exposome research in occupation and health and challenges in large-scale data harmonization are introduced in section "Exposome Research in Occupation and Health."

Studies of Large-Scale Registry Data

The largest occupational health studies that are conducted are typically based on large databases or registers from national or regional administrative data sources, which are linked together and may include millions of people. A register is a systematic and complete collection of data (e.g., on all residents of a country), organized in such a way that updating is possible, and requires that all individuals in the register can always be uniquely identified (United Nations Economic Commission of Europe 2007). In the Nordic countries, since the 1960s, everyone is given a unique personal identification number, making reliable individual-level linkage of registers possible. During the last decades, there have been an increasing number of registry-based studies, particularly from the Nordic countries, including studies on occupation and health. The main focus in this section will therefore be on Nordic studies.

For registry-based occupational health research, certain types of data will be needed: (1) data to define or describe the population, (2) occupational exposure data, (3) outcome data, (4) data on potential confounders and other covariates, and possibly (5) data to identify businesses or enterprises (Fig. 1). Often, all the data that ideally would be needed for a study do not exist in registers, and it may be necessary to use methods to impute or approximate needed data, for example, by using proxies for data that are not available, or by specifying assumptions in analysis to overcome this limitation. However, registry-based studies are valuable, supplementing other studies with different strengths and limitations, and potential sources of bias (Lawlor et al. 2016).

Data to Define or Describe the Population

National population registers contain data on sex and dates (or month and year) of birth, death, marriage, emigration, and immigration, often including country of birth and reason for immigration (work, education, refugee, and family reunion), as well as marital status. In order to define the population at risk, it is necessary to know *who* are alive and residing in the geographic region of interest, and therefore available for registration in the registers, and the *time* they are available or at risk. For instance, people who emigrate will be lost to follow-up, and people who immigrate may lack data on relevant exposures and outcomes before immigration.

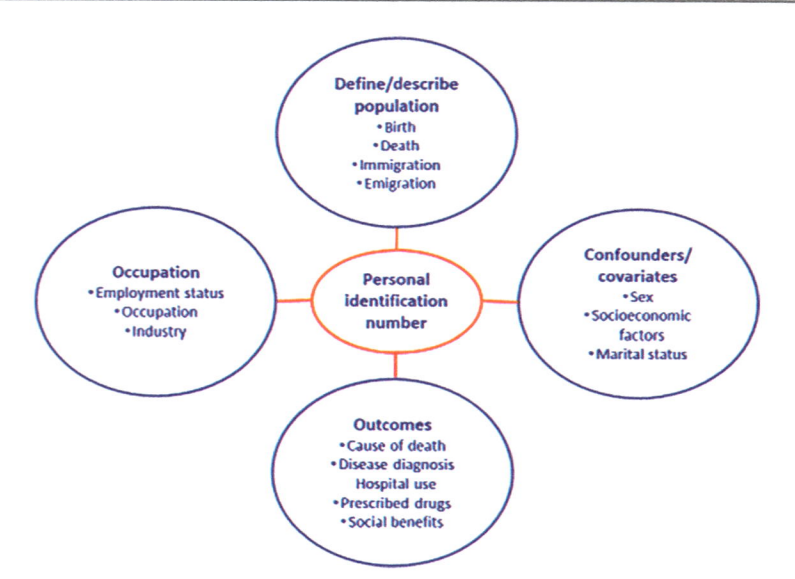

Fig. 1 In the Nordic countries, data from different registers are linked together via the unique personal identification number

Occupational Exposure Data

Registers usually lack data on specific occupational exposures, but some data related to employment and occupation are often available. Employment registers may have data on employment status (employed, nonemployed, full-time/part-time work and possibly percentage, and being a worker/employee or self-employed), as well as the time (day, month, and/or year) of entering and leaving employment in a specific job. Combined with data on occupation and industry for each job, from registers or censuses, it is possible to create work histories.

Occupations and industries are often coded using national or international coding systems. The International Standard Classification of Occupations (ISCO) (International Labour Organization 2010), prepared by the International Labour Organization (ILO), is used in many countries for coding occupations. The standard was developed in 1958 and has been revised several times, resulting in different versions (ISCO-58, ISCO-68, ISCO-88, ISCO-08). Moreover, each of these versions may exist in different national and regional versions (called variants), for instance, the EU has developed a variant of ISCO-88, called ISCO-88(COM), which is the basis for national standards in different European countries. These standards may differ somewhat from each other, although they are based on the same underlying international and European standard. The many available versions and variants may complicate comparisons between countries and over time, but correspondence tables, e.g., between ISCO-08 and ISCO-88 (International Labour Organization 2016), or crosswalks between versions have been developed (t'Mannetje and Kromhout 2003; Peters et al. 2022). However, specific expertise is often needed to apply them, as it may not be possible to convert occupational codes one-to-one. Some codes may have been split up (one-to-many) or combined (many-to-one) from one version to another.

ISCO-88 and ISCO-08 both have a four-level hierarchical structure, divided into ten major groups (first digit of the code), which again are divided into submajor groups (second digit), minor groups (third digit), and unit groups (fourth digit). ISCO-88 is classified into 390 unit groups (occupations), while ISCO-08 has 436 unit groups. However, national classifications may be adjusted to match the national labor market. As an example, occupations which are typical of developing countries are removed in the Norwegian version of ISCO-08 (Statistics Norway 2011). Some country-specific occupations may also be added, e.g., oil- and gas-processing-plant operator and taxidermist (stuffing and mounting animals) are specific occupations in Norway, but do not exist in the more generic ISCO-88(COM). The number of unit groups may therefore differ between countries, e.g., the Norwegian version of ISCO-88 has 356 unit groups (Statistics Norway 1998), and not 390.

Occupation may be used as a proxy for occupational exposure, as for cancer in the Nordic Occupational Cancer Study (NOCCA) (Andersen et al. 1999; Pukkala et al. 2009). However, occupational classification standards were created for statistical purposes, not to group occupations with similar working conditions or exposures. Adding industry may help dividing large diverse occupational groups into smaller groups with more homogenous work exposures. Moreover, occupation has often not been recorded every year, particularly back in time, maybe only in censuses every 5 or 10 years. It is therefore usually assumed that occupation has been stable, which may not have been the case, and sometimes only the first recorded occupation is used in the analysis.

Occupational codes may also be linked with Job-Exposure Matrices (JEMs), which assign similar exposure characteristics (type of exposure, level of exposure, proportion of workers exposed, etc.) to all workers with the same occupational code (or job title). JEMs are described in detail elsewhere in this book, both in general (▶ Chap. 5, "Sequence Analysis and Its Potential for Occupational Health Studies") and for specific occupational exposures: chemical (▶ Chap. 11, "A Life Course Perspective on Work and Mental Health: The Working Lives of Young Adults"), biomechanical (▶ Chap. 12, "Chemical Hazards at Work and Occupational Diseases Using Job-Exposure Matrices"), and psychosocial work exposures (▶ Chap. 15, "Health Effects of Shift Work and Night Shift Work"). JEMs have been specifically constructed for the NOCCA Study (Kauppinen et al. 2009), these are described as three-dimensional (over 300 occupations, over 20 agents, four time-periods covering from 1945 to 1994), and some are also country-specific. These JEMs have been used in studies of specific occupational exposures and risk of certain cancer types, e.g., solvents and acute myeloid leukemia (Talibov et al. 2014), wood dust and nasal and nasopharyngeal cancer (Siew et al. 2017), and benzene exposure and colorectal cancer (Talibov et al. 2018).

Outcome Data

Health outcomes and other outcomes (e.g., related to work participation) may also be retrieved from different registers. The Nordic countries have several national health registers, with mandatory registration of all cases, e.g., of cancers, births, causes of death, etc., in Denmark (Danish Health Data Authority 2022), Finland (FinnGen 2022), Iceland (Directorate of Health 2019), Norway (Norwegian Institute of Public Health 2016), and Sweden (National Board of Health and Welfare 2019). In addition, there are health data registers focused around specific diagnoses or conditions (EIT Health Scandinavia 2022a), which are also available in other countries, such as Belgium, Estonia, and the Netherlands, as well as registers aiming to improve health care quality (Hoque et al. 2017).

National *Cause of Death Registries*, based on data from death certificates, are available in many countries, and death diagnoses and time of death are commonly used as outcomes. These registers are important for health authorities, as well as in research, but the data quality may differ between countries (Phillips et al. 2014). Developed countries generally have higher quality registers on mortality and causes of death than developing countries, but there are differences within both groups, and more heterogeneity in the latter, with some countries having high-quality registers, such as Cuba, Costa Rica, Mexico, and Venezuela (Phillips et al. 2014). The Norwegian Cause of Death Registry has near-complete coverage (about 98% of deaths among Norwegian residents) and high quality, although some unspecific codes (Pedersen and Ellingsen 2015), but was not among the highest ranked in the study by Phillips et al. (2014).

Incident cancer diagnoses, as mentioned in examples above, may be available from nationwide *Cancer Registries*, as in the Nordic countries, where they date back as far as 1943 in Denmark and the 1950s in the other Nordic countries (Pukkala et al. 2009). Regional cancer registries may also exist in some countries. Cancer registration in the Nordic countries has been of high quality for many years (Pukkala et al. 2009), and data from these registers have been used in numbers of publications, separately in each of the countries, as well as combined in the NOCCA Study.

Patient or hospital discharge registries are available in several countries but often only cover specific diseases (European Medicines Agency 2022), as mentioned above for health data registers in general. Health records from certain healthcare providers may also be available. Denmark, Sweden, and Norway have the most comprehensive national patient registries, covering somatic and psychiatric in- and out-patients in all hospitals, as well as emergency room contacts and, to some degree, also patient contacts in private specialist healthcare (Schmidt et al. 2015; Ludvigsson et al. 2011; Bakken et al. 2020). As these registers mainly cover specialist healthcare, recorded diagnoses will usually represent severe diseases. Denmark and Norway also have registries for Primary Health Care (Andersen et al. 2011; Bakken et al. 2020), which cover less severe illnesses, but diagnoses may be less precise and include many symptom diagnoses (i.e., not diagnosed disease), and the validity of diagnoses may be more questionable than for specialist healthcare registers.

Data from national *prescribed drug registries* may also be used as outcomes, often as a proxy for diagnoses, if other data are not available, or to supplement other data. For instance, reliable data on asthma or depression diagnoses may be difficult to find in registers. The patient registries only include the more severe cases which are admitted to a hospital or treated in an out-patient clinic or emergency room, and data from primary health care may not be available, and if they are, the data quality may be uncertain. Prescribed asthma medication and antidepressants may be used as proxies for asthma and depression, respectively; these medicines are usually relatively disease specific.

Social benefits registers may include data on, for instance, sickness absence, disability, or unemployment, and may be used for outcomes in registry-based studies, either the selected benefits themselves, or the diagnosis that is the reason for receiving benefits for sickness absence or disability. The data may also be combined into reasons for leaving paid employment, to estimate Working Life Expectancy and Working Years Lost due to different benefits or work exposures (Pedersen et al. 2020; Schram et al. 2021). However, as employment is a prerequisite for being eligible for some benefits, the population at risk will be restricted to employed people for some outcomes.

Data on Potential Confounders and Other Covariates

Some potential confounders may be available from registers, such as education and income, and will usually be more complete and often of better quality than self-reported data (Kristensen et al. 2018). Variables mentioned in section "Data to Define or Describe the Population" above may also be relevant here. However, some other important confounders will not be available, such as lifestyle or personal factors. A Danish JEM on lifestyle factors has been developed (Bondo Petersen et al. 2018) but might not be valid for other populations, as lifestyle based on occupational grouping may differ more between countries than traditional occupational exposures. Other approaches have also been proposed to account for missing lifestyle covariate data, including estimating the extent of unmeasured confounding and likely impact on study findings (Steenland et al. 2020) or using confirmatory factor analysis models (Haldorsen et al. 2017) or other indirect adjustment methods (Shin et al. 2014) among others.

Business or Enterprise Data

Data may be available at the enterprise level, for instance, whether the enterprise is public or private, which does not necessarily follow from the industry (e.g., the healthcare industry may include both public and private clinics), or the geographical location of the enterprise, which may differ from employees' place of residence. It may also be possible to include the enterprise as a separate level in multilevel analyses.

Access to Registry Data

Although data already exist, the process of accessing them may be long and complicated, with many steps, as described for getting access to registers in Sweden (EIT Health Scandinavia 2022b), including approval from ethics committees and registry owners, dispensation from confidentiality, developing a Data Protection Impact Assessment (DPIA), and selection of relevant variables from long lists of available variables, and may be expensive, depending on the country. Transfer of registry data to other countries is usually not allowed.

Strengths and Limitations of Registry-Based Studies

Strengths and limitations of registry-based research have been well described by Thygesen and Ersbøll (2014) and Aktas et al. (2022). Important strengths are that data already exist and are complete for a large population, with little or no selection bias or attrition bias (loss to follow-up). Due to the large sample size, it is possible to study rare exposures and outcomes and population subgroups. Data are collected prospectively and independently of the research questions, with no differential misclassification. Many registers have a long history, e.g., the Nordic cancer registries that started in the 1940s and 1950s, making it possible to have long follow-up and study diseases with long latency, as well as transgenerational effects.

However, there are also limitations. Data are precollected by others than researchers and limited to what is available in the registers. Necessary information may be unavailable or misclassified (nondifferentially), and coding of variables may be crude and may vary between persons and institutions who record the data. It is often not known exactly how data are generated; therefore, data quality may be uncertain and difficult to validate, and missingness may be difficult to interpret if you do not know whether the event did not happen or was just not recorded. Lack of, or crude, data of important confounders may lead to residual confounding, and potential over- or underestimation of associations observed, while nondifferential misclassification of exposure or outcome data will tend to underestimate true associations. Data from registers are truncated at start of registration (left truncation), persons who had the studied outcome, before start of follow-up, may wrongly be classified as healthy, and it is difficult to differentiate between prevalent and incident cases. Due to large sample size in registry studies, small differences become statistically significant. It is, therefore, important to consider the size of the risk estimates and public health relevance of the results and avoid data dredging ("fishing") and post hoc analysis, which may give misleading results.

Registry-based studies are important in occupational epidemiology, due to large and complete study populations, with data that already exist and are independently collected, and valuable follow-up time has already passed when the study is conducted. However, not all necessary information may be available; in particular, data on work exposures may be crude, and confounder information may be lacking. Different study types often have different strengths and weaknesses and may supplement each other (Aktas et al. 2022). Findings from studies using different methods may be triangulated, to inform decision-making regarding evidence of a causal association (Lawlor et al. 2016).

Consortia of Cohort Studies

Multinational consortia of cohort studies have been formed to combine data from different studies in occupational health. Such initiatives require long-term and sustained coordination. They are valuable to provide improved statistical power compared to analysis conducted in single studies and to examine potential adverse health effects that may be weaker in their magnitude or experienced at low levels of exposure over the working life. There may also be rare occupational exposures or related health effects, where pooling of data from multiple studies is needed for meaningful analysis, as well as between-country differences in findings that may be informative for understanding of factors underlying occupation and health relationships. Results from consortia of cohort studies usually provide more definitive findings, useful to inform evidence-based efforts to improve worker protection. However, careful consideration of potential methodological sources of bias and confounding is needed when pooling data from multiple studies (Basagaña et al. 2018). Harmonizing exposure and outcome information over follow-up time also often require major efforts (also below).

The Individual-Participant Data Meta-analysis in Working Populations (IPD-Work) Consortium

The Individual-Participant Data Meta-Analysis in Working Populations (IPD-Work) consortium is one example of a large consortium of researchers and studies. The IPD-Work consortium conducts predefined meta-analyses of data from cohort studies in European and non-European countries on work-related psychosocial factors and health (Kivimäki et al. 2015). A primary motivation was to address outstanding methodological issues in individual studies, including potential confounding, effect modification, and reverse causation bias, as well as multiple testing and selective reporting. Information on exposures and outcomes is harmonized across all cohorts including in both published and unpublished studies.

Analysis has examined the psychosocial work environment and a range of cardiovascular disease and other health end points, as well as associations with other cardiovascular disease risk factors. Findings have supported the hypothesis that job strain, defined as the combination of high job demands and low job control, is an important risk factor for coronary heart disease, ischemic stroke, diabetes, depression, and mortality among men with cardiometabolic disease, more so than the effects of either high job demands or low job control individually (Kivimäki et al. 2015, 2019). Findings also revealed some suggestion of publication bias, with stronger findings observed among previously published, compared with unpublished findings (Kivimäki et al. 2015). Other work has examined job insecurity, effort-reward imbalance, and long working hours with multiple health outcomes (Ervasti et al. 2021).

New studies to further address potential alternative explanations for findings observed have been suggested (Kivimäki et al. 2015; Madsen and Rugulies 2021). Studies using experimental methods, as well as within-individual comparisons over time, were proposed to complement and further strengthen the evidence base in the field, as were new studies using non-self-reported exposure measures, including using JEMs, to better understand potential reporting bias. Further work to better understand potential residual confounding due to non-workplace factors was also suggested.

The International Nuclear Workers Study (INWORKS)

The International Nuclear Workers Study (INWORKS) is another example and is formed of studies including over 308,000 workers in the nuclear industry in three countries (France, the United Kingdom, and the United States). It was formed to allow for improved assessment of the health risks associated with chronic, low-level ionizing radiation exposure (rather than deriving them from studies of populations exposed to acute, high radiation doses) (Laurier et al. 2017). The three cohort studies were selected from a previous 15-country collaborative study, as being the most informative (Hamra et al. 2016). Extended follow-up of the cohorts allowed for the investigation of a range of specific cancer types, non-cancer end points, and effects of age and time since exposure (Gillies et al. 2017; Laurier et al. 2017). Personal monitoring data of external radiation exposure (largely gamma rays) were captured for cohort participants using individual dosimeters and standardized red bone marrow and colon doses calculated.

There were significant adverse associations observed with risk of leukemia (excluding chronic lymphocytic leukemia) and solid cancers, respectively. The large consolidated multi-country study provided more definitive information on the adverse health effects of low-level ionizing radiation exposure in nuclear industry workers. Some potential limitations included a lack of data on other relevant occupational exposures (neutron exposure, internal contamination), tobacco smoking, or medical radiation exposures. There were also concerns regarding uncertainties in dose estimates, and differences in dosimeters over time. Further integration of such types of cohort consortia into larger-scale multidisciplinary integrative investigations was also suggested (see also Laurent et al. 2016).

The Pooled Uranium Miner Analysis (PUMA) Cohorts

Another recent consortium of cohort studies investigating low-level ionizing radiation exposure is the Pooled Uranium Miner Analysis (PUMA) cohorts, a consortium consisting of seven of the most informative cohorts with personal estimates of exposure to low levels of radon decay products conducted in five countries (Rage et al. 2020). The diversity of included cohorts will allow for examination of new research questions among workers with differing exposure histories. Data on other occupational agents (such as external radiation exposure, diesel, silica, and arsenic) are available in some cohorts. Findings to date have indicated elevated standardized mortality ratios (SMRs) for miners, in comparison with national mortality rates, for several causes of death, including lung cancer, other specific cancers, and non-malignant respiratory diseases (Richardson et al. 2021). Particular attention in future work will be paid to potential sources of bias, exposure measurement error, and sources of heterogeneity in findings between cohorts.

The International Consortium of Agricultural Cohort Studies (AGRICOH)

The AGRICOH consortium of agricultural cohort studies, which also includes general population cohorts with large agricultural populations, is another example of a multinational consortium of studies to support data pooling (Leon et al. 2011). AGRICOH has a focus on examining rare exposures and rare health outcomes, which are often not possible to examine in single cohorts. AGRICOH currently includes 29 cohorts with the USA and France representing countries with the largest number of participating cohorts (n = 7 and 6, respectively), with studies in Africa, Asia and Western Pacific, other European countries, and South and Central America representing a smaller fraction of participating cohort studies (International Agency for Research on Cancer 2022). AGRICOH also seeks to support new agricultural cohorts in lower- and middle-income countries, where exposures are likely higher, and few data exist (Leon et al. 2011; IARC 2017).

Assessment of a range of specific agricultural exposures is captured by questionnaires in the individual studies, with biological specimens also captured in some studies. Assessment of the impact of self-reported pesticide use, compared to country-specific crop-exposure matrices, for 14 chemical groups and 33 active ingredients in three cohorts, observed only poor levels of agreement (Brouwer et al. 2016). Analyses of associations of pesticide use and risk of non-Hodgkin lymphoid (NHL) malignancies noted a range of subtype- and chemical-specific findings; however, caution due to exposure misclassification was suggested (Leon et al. 2019). In analysis of eight cohorts, there were reduced standardized incidence ratios (SIRs) for agricultural workers for all cancers combined, and for a range of specific cancers, likely due to lower rates of cigarette smoking and more physical activity than the general population, though there were some elevated SIRs for prostate cancer among men and for multiple myeloma and skin cancer among women (Togawa et al. 2021). Further analysis examining specific agricultural exposures is needed, as is of protective factors in agricultural populations.

Multicenter Worker Cohorts

There are also examples of multicenter cohorts of workers, with workers recruited from different study sites following the same study design protocol from initiation. An international multicountry cohort of workers exposed to styrene in the reinforced plastics industry was formed. The study included workers from >600 plants in eight study centers in six European countries, initiated in 1988 to examine lymphatic and hematopoietic malignancy risk (Loomis et al. 2019). The study was recently reanalyzed, and although there was no additional follow-up data added, outcome information was regrouped to the approximate modern WHO classification, and more detailed examination of exposure-response relations using quantitative measures of exposure was performed. Data from one country (Norway) were excluded due to new national privacy legislation. Findings were generally similar to previous analyses, with positive associations of NHL mortality observed with mean styrene exposure. There was some evidence of adverse associations with pancreatic cancer and esophageal cancer mortality, supporting the need for further studies. Limitations included not being able to update follow-up of the cohorts due to retirement of key personnel and loss of data due to the long time since cohort initiation, as well as potential exposure measurement error, particularly for more historical exposures.

There are also multicenter general population cohorts with occupational information, such as the European Community Respiratory Health Survey (ECRHS) conducted in 55 centers in 23 countries, beginning in 1990. In one recent work, there were positive findings of occupational exposure to biological dust, gases and fumes, and pesticides, based on a JEM, and increased COPD incidence (Lytras et al. 2018). Recently, the Respiratory Health in Northern Europe, Spain, and Australia (RHINESSA) cohort was established including the offspring of ECRHS participants, to examine respiratory health across multiple generations (Svanes et al. 2022).

The Cultural and Psychosocial Influences on Disability (CUPID) study examined associations of culture and health beliefs on musculoskeletal symptoms and disability, using a baseline and follow-up questionnaire in 12,426 workers in 47 occupational groups across 18 countries (Coggon et al. 2012). Challenges included questionnaire translation into local languages, differences in questionnaire administration, and for some occupations low participation rates.

Birth Cohort Studies in Occupational Health Research

Multinational consortia of birth cohort studies have been formed in the past decade in Europe, to harmonize and pool data from multiple studies on specific topics (Jaddoe et al. 2020; Vrijheid et al. 2012). Though they have typically focused on other exposure topics, such as environmental contaminants, lifestyle, or nutritional factors, it was recently pointed out that birth cohorts also contain a range of often underutilized parental occupational information which can be used to study complex interactions of work and health of parents and families (Fig. 2) (Ubalde-Lopez et al. 2021).

Cohort	General variables				Occupational exposures variables				
	Education	Income	Single parenthood	Employment status	Job title	Occupational exposures	Heavy lifts	Work hours	Work address
ABC	x	x				x			
ABCD	x	x		x	x	x	x	x	
ALSPAC	x					x	x		
BaBi	x	x	x	x	x	x	x		
BABIP	x	x	x	x	x				
Babycarecohort	x	x	x			x	x		
BAMSE	x			x	x				
BASIC	x	x	x	x					
BIB	x	x	x			x			
CELSPAC: TNG	x	x	x	x	x	x	x	x	x
CHOP	x		x	x	x			x	
COLLAGE	x	x				x			
Co.N.ER						x			
CRIBS	x	x	x	x	x	x	x		x
Czech Early Childhood Health						x			
DNBC	x					x	x		
ECLIPSES	x	x	x	x	x				
EDEN	x	x	x	x		x			
ELFE	x					x	x		
ELSPAC	x			x		x	x		
FCOU	x					x	x		
FLEHS 1 RefNb	x	x		x	x	x			
FLEHS 2 Ref Nb	x	x	x	x	x	x			
FLEHS III	x	x	x	x	x	x			
GASPII	x		x			x			
GECKO	x	x	x		x				
Generation R	x					x	x		
GISA	x	x		x	x	x	x		x
HbgBC	x		x	x					
HELMi	x		x	x					
HUMIS	x	x	x			x			
INMA	x			x		x	x		
INUENDO	x					x			
KANC	x		x			x			
KOALA	x						x		
Krakow	x		x			x			
KuBiCo	x		x	x	x				
Lifelines NEXT	x	x	x	x	x	x	x	x	
Lifeways	x	x	x				x		
LiNA	x	x	x	x				x	
LoewenKIDS	x				x				
LucKi	x			x	x	x		x	
Mamma & Bambino	x		x	x	x				
MoBa	x		x			x	x		
MUBICOS						x			
NEHO	x	x	x	x	x	x	x	x	x
NINFEA	x			x	x	x		x	
Odense	x		x			x			
PCB cohort	x		x			x			
PÉLAGIE	x	x	x			x	x		
Piccolipiù	x		x			x	x		
PLASTICITY			x			x	x		
Predict	x		x	x		x			
PRIDE	x	x	x	x	x	x	x	x	
REPRO_PL	x	x	x	x	x	x	x	x	
RHEA	x		x			x			
SWS	x		x	x	x		x	x	
Trieste						x			
WHISTLER	x	x	x			x	x		

Fig. 2 Selected available information related to mothers´ work and socioeconomic status in 59 European birth cohorts (as reported in www.birthcohorts.net catalogue, accessed on 5 Feb 2021). (Source: Ubalde-Lopez et al. 2021. Reprinted under the Creative Commons Attribution 4.0 International License (CC BY 4.0))

Recent Initiatives in Integrating European Occupational Cohorts

There have been recent coordination and harmonization networking initiatives in Europe on occupation and health, due to the recognized need to bring together multidisciplinary research communities to strengthen research capacity in the field.

Europe has a range of valuable occupational, industrial, and population cohorts with occupational information. There is a need for better and ongoing integration of these cohorts to facilitate their exploitation to inform evidence-based policy. In one example, the Network on the Coordination and Harmonisation of European Occupational Cohorts (OMEGA-NET, https://omeganetcohorts.eu) was created to advance collaboration of European occupational cohort studies (Turner and Mehlum 2018). It involved over 300 occupational health researchers in 40 countries. The overarching goal of OMEGA-NET was to advance (i) collaboration of cohorts with information on employment and occupational exposures, (ii) coordination and harmonization of occupational exposure assessments, and (iii) facilitation of an integrated European research strategy. Online inventories of cohorts and occupational exposure assessment tools were created (Kogevinas et al. 2020; Peters et al. 2022), as were position papers on specific topics (see below). There have also been other recent European network initiatives in coordination related to prevention of occupational skin diseases (John and Kezic 2017), as well as trends in occupational diseases (Stocks et al. 2015), for example.

Inventory of Occupational Cohort Studies

In order to facilitate collaboration of cohorts to explore occupation, work-related exposures, and health relationships, an online inventory of cohort studies with occupational information in Europe was created (Kogevinas et al. 2020, https://occupationalcohorts.net). As an essential component toward creating a FAIR (findable, accessible, interoperable, and reusable) research infrastructure (also below), the inventory and online interactive search tool seek to provide findable metadata information on these cohorts. Online cohort inventories on other specific topics, including birth cohort studies, have also been created (above, Vrijheid et al. 2012; Jaddoe et al. 2020; Ubalde-Lopez et al. 2021).

The inventory includes prospective or retrospective cohorts, case-control studies nested within cohorts, and intervention studies that (i) are active or potentially accessible; (ii) collect data on occupation and/or industry or at least one occupational exposure; and (iii) have at least one follow-up, either already conducted or planned. Researchers enter information regarding their cohort using a web-based inventory questionnaire. The published version of the inventory is stored in a searchable web database.

To date (August 2022), over 150 cohorts in more than 20 countries have been registered in the inventory. Information is collected on: (i) identification and basic description; (ii) follow-up; (iii) occupational exposures (dusts and fibers, solvents, pesticides, metals and metal oxides, other chemicals, engineered nanoparticles, biological factors, physical agents, ergonomics, physical workload and injury, psychosocial domains, organization of work, and working time); (iv) outcomes evaluated; (v) biological samples and analysis; and (vi) other information. Although industry or occupational-based studies represent a large proportion of cohorts included in the inventory, there are also general population studies with relevant occupational information (Fig. 3). As in previous consortia of birth cohort studies

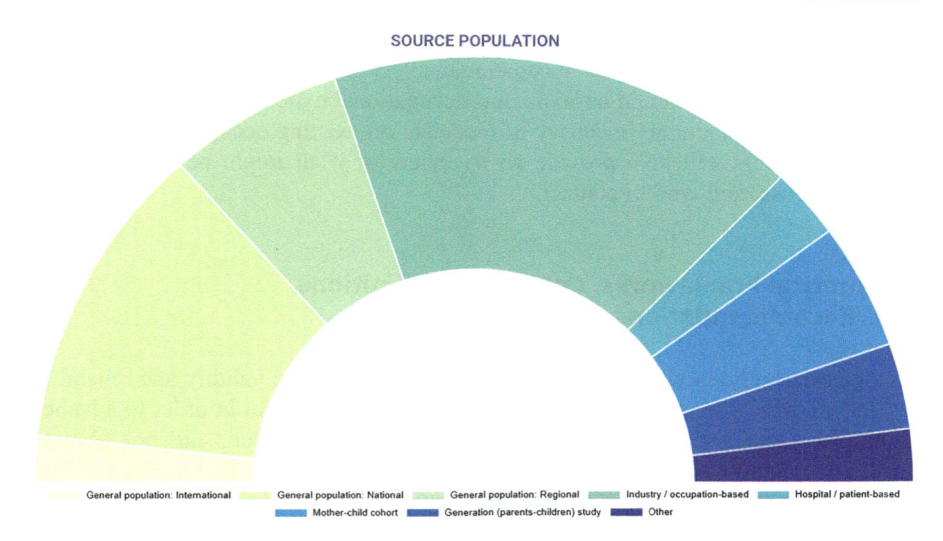

Fig. 3 Source population distribution of cohorts registered in OccupationalCohorts.net. Date Accessed July 14, 2022

(above), cohort registration in the inventory is an important prerequisite for participation in cohort pooling efforts (below), providing important metadata of cohort characteristics, including available occupational information (Jaddoe et al. 2020).

Challenges include recruitment of cohorts into the inventory, completeness, and quality of information about included cohorts, as well as sustained efforts in the maintenance and updating of cohort information over time (Kogevinas et al. 2020). For more detailed information about specific aspects of the cohort, not captured by the inventory, contact with cohort investigators will be needed. Efforts to expand globally may also assist in the long-term viability of the inventory.

Inventory of Occupational Exposure Assessment Tools

To optimize the use of occupational cohorts and advance etiologic research, harmonized, high-quality exposure and outcome information is crucial. OMEGA-NET also initiated work to collect metadata and set up an online inventory on exposure assessment tools, including JEMs, exposure databases, and occupational coding systems and their associated crosswalks (Peters et al. 2022). To date (August 2022), metadata on 39 JEMs and 11 exposure databases have been collected (https://occupationalexposuretools.net). Many different exposures are registered in the inventory. The most common JEM exposures are dusts and fibers, while other JEMs cover biological, physical, mechanical/ergonomic, or psychosocial exposures. The exposure databases include dusts and fibers, as well as solvents and pesticides. Furthermore, the inventory includes information on 30 coding systems from more than ten countries, in addition to crosswalks between coding systems and automated coding from free text. These occupational exposure assessment tools can help researchers in assessing and harmonizing occupational exposures in cohort studies, and the searchable online inventory of metadata on existing occupational exposure assessment tools will help provide an overview of what might be available and relevant to use, and who to contact.

Theoretical Frameworks, Consensus Definitions, and Recommendations for Future Research

The theoretical framework, concepts and definitions, and the validity and reliability of the exposure and outcome measures used are also important in order to advance etiologic research. If different definitions are used, the results are not easy to compare or compile, and if the measures used are not robust, the results may not be reliable. OMEGA-NET, therefore, also initiated work on different topics to meet some of these challenges, mostly published as systematic or scoping reviews, and position or discussion papers. Topics included the following: occupational burnout, musculoskeletal disorders, allergies, and skin diseases, as well as healthy aging and work participation, precarious employment, migrant workers, and working life, health, and well-being of working parents, in addition to COVID-19 and the workplace, among others.

For example, consensus is lacking on the definition and measurement of occupational burnout, leading to inconsistent findings regarding its prevalence, etiology, treatment, and prevention. Guseva Canu et al. (2021) aimed to elaborate a consensual definition of occupational burnout as a health outcome. A systematic review identified 88 unique definitions of burnout, based on 11 original definitions (Fig. 4). Through a semantic analysis of available definitions and a Delphi process, including

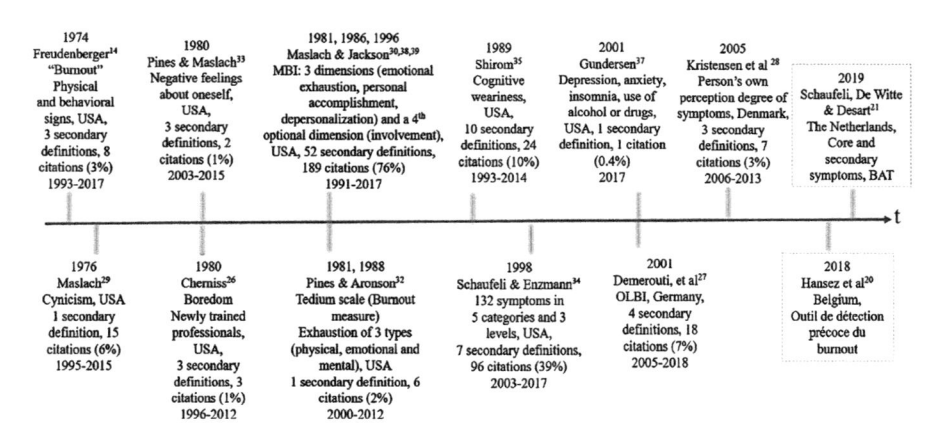

Fig. 4 Chronology of original definitions of occupational burnout. (Source: Guseva Canu et al. 2019. Reprinted under the Creative Commons Attribution 4.0 International License (CC BY 4.0))

50 experts from 29 countries, the following harmonized definition was formulated in accordance with the Systematized Nomenclature of Medicine Clinical Terms (SNOMED-CT) and reached consensus (82% agreement) at the second Delphi round: "In a worker, occupational burnout or occupational physical AND emotional exhaustion state is an exhaustion due to prolonged exposure to work-related problems." A systematic review study by Shoman et al. (2021a) assessed the psychometric validity of the most used inventories of occupational burnout, measured through Patient-Reported Outcome Measures (PROMs), and found that only two of the five most used tools had moderate evidence of psychometric validity, the OLdenburg Burnout Inventory (OLBI), and the Copenhagen Burnout Inventory (CBI). Another systematic review study identified occupational burnout risk and protective factors (Shoman et al. 2021b), and a fourth study assessed whether occupational burnout is acknowledged in Europe as an occupational disease (Guseva Canu et al. 2019). Results showed variability in the burnout diagnosis, assessment of its work-relatedness, and conditions allowing compensation of patients.

In other topics, case definitions of specific work-related musculoskeletal disorders were defined for use in occupational health research in two steps, including an international multidisciplinary Delphi process (van der Molen et al. 2021; Tamminga et al. 2021). A position paper on healthy aging and work participation developed a conceptual framework addressing the complex labor market dynamics of the work-to-retirement process (Leinonen et al. 2022), while another identified the differentiated roles of health in the work–retirement transition, discussed conceptual and methodological challenges in research, and provided recommendations for future research (Hasselhorn et al. 2022). A discussion paper on precarious employment in occupational health summarized research, developed a theoretical framework, and identified key methodological challenges and directions for future research (Bodin et al. 2020). A position paper on occupational health research in migrant workers clarified the definitions of "migrant," summarized characteristics of migrant workers, including work and employment conditions and work-related health problems, identified methodological challenges, and recommended improvements (Aktas et al. 2022).

Exposome Research in Occupation and Health

The Exposome

The concept of the exposome was proposed originally in 2005 and was intended to stimulate large investments into research to better characterize environmental exposures that a person may experience throughout their life course, using novel technologies (Wild 2005), more recently extended to include associated biological response (Zhang et al. 2021). Distinct, yet interrelated internal (such as biomarkers, omics), specific external (such as contaminants, lifestyle), and general external domains (such as socioeconomic and political environment) of the exposome have been described (Wild 2005). Initial multidisciplinary exposome consortia were formed in Europe, as first proof of concept approach (Vineis et al. 2017; Vrijheid et al. 2014). Scientific and policy challenges in exposome research were described, as were priorities for future work (further development and standardization of methods to assess internal and external exposures, data sharing, and demonstration of the value of exposome approaches in answering policy-relevant questions) (Turner et al. 2018).

Despite the explicit focus of the exposome on detailed characterization of environmental exposures experienced throughout the life course, exposome research has typically neglected work-related exposures, and only conceptualized specific aspects of the exposome, such as the early life exposome (Vrijheid et al. 2014, 2021), specific exposures (environmental air pollution and water contaminants, Vineis et al. 2017), or determinants of specific end points (immune mediated diseases, https://www.hedimed.eu/about-hedimed), for example. Occupational risk factors, however, have been estimated to account for a substantial amount of deaths and disability worldwide (WHO/ILO 2021). Further research is needed to improve understanding of a range of occupational health associations, including complex occupational exposure patterns and mixtures in relation to noncommunicable disease risk, including new occupational risks to health and associated biological pathways.

The Occupational Exposome

Exposome concepts offer a more holistic approach for studying working life exposures, including use of both agnostic and hypothesis-driven approaches, detailed internal and external characterization of exposures, and consideration of multiple often correlated exposures in disease risk (see also ▶ Chap. 8, "Integration of Occupational Exposure into the Exposome"). For example, in analysis in a cohort of French uranium miners using extended Bayesian profile regression mixture (PRM) models, chronic exposure to multiple correlated sources of ionizing radiation exposures were examined (radon, external γ-rays, and uranium dust) in relation to lung cancer risk (Belloni et al. 2020). Here, groups of uranium miners were characterized in terms of their lung cancer risk according to specific profiles of correlated ionizing radiation exposures, including modulation by age at first exposure and duration of exposure. Another previous study examining multiple correlated occupational solvent exposures did not observe any associations with lung cancer risk, though clusters of occupations at high risk of lung cancer were identified (Mattei et al. 2016). In an exposome-wide association study (EWAS) conducted in the European Prospective Investigation into Cancer and nutrition study (EPIC), 84 anthropometric, lifestyle, and occupational factors (here occupational physical activity), captured by questionnaire, were examined in relation to B-cell lymphoma incidence. Results confirmed previously reported risk and protective factors and suggested some novel associations, supporting the use of comprehensive, exposome-type approaches in etiological research of occupational and non-occupational factors (Saberi Hosnijeh et al. 2021) (Fig. 5).

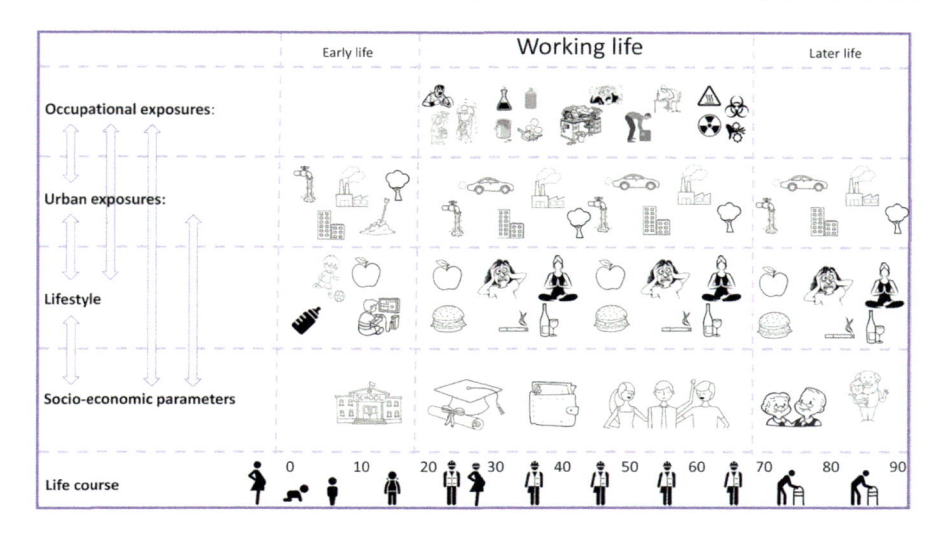

Fig. 5 Working life exposures in the exposome context. (Source: Pronk et al. 2022. Reprinted under the Creative Commons Attribution 4.0 International License (CC BY 4.0))

Recently, the second generation of European exposome studies were launched, as well as the coordinating European Human Exposome Network (EHEN, https://www.humanexposome.eu) that seeks to advance coordination of such studies. The Exposome Project for Health and Occupational Research (EPHOR, https://www.ephor-project.eu) is the first exposome study with a distinct focus on characterizing the working life exposome (including occupational exposures as well as their interaction with nonoccupational factors) and seeks to advance occupational health knowledge by considering interrelated exposures, biological pathways, and health outcomes (Pronk et al. 2022). An emphasis of EPHOR is large-scale harmonization and pooling of European cohort studies, as well as on capturing high-resolution internal and external exposure data in case-studies on specific topics (night shift work, occupational respiratory disease). In EPHOR, work is ongoing to establish a mega cohort of several European cohorts, including general population cohorts with occupational information, industrial cohorts, and registry-based cohorts (above), registered in an online inventory (above), to conduct pooled systematic and agnostic exposome analysis on noncommunicable disease risk (Turner et al. 2022). A harmonized European JEM is being specifically developed for this purpose.

Challenges in large-scale pooling of (occupational) cohort studies have, however, been described. To be able to combine data from different cohorts, e.g., in pooled analysis or meta-analysis, or fully compare results between cohorts, it is not sufficient that the exposure and outcome data are high-quality; they also need to be harmonized as much as possible, regarding measurements and classifications. This applies not only to the exposure and outcome data, but also to potential confounders (covariates). Often different versions or variants of the same classification instrument have been used, e.g., different versions of the International Standard Classification of

Occupations (ISCO) or of the International Classification of Diseases (ICD) over time, or different variants of the same version have been used in different countries (above). In such cases, it is helpful to use or develop crosswalks between the different versions or variants. Recategorization of single variables, from the original categories to other categories, may also be necessary in the harmonization process. To assist with large-scale job coding and recoding, job-coding algorithms, automatically coding free-text job description information (Bao et al. 2020; Buckner-Petty et al. 2019; Russ et al. 2016), as well as computer-assisted tools facilitating job recoding into other classification systems are being developed (Rémen et al. 2018) and may represent useful research tools that are increasingly used in the future.

Other challenges in retrospective cohort data harmonization include timely access to data, restrictions in data access, mobilizing sufficient resources and guidance on procedures, sufficient understanding of study-specific data, recognition of contributing investigators, and long-term maintenance of harmonized data infrastructure (Fortier et al. 2017). Ensuring thorough and transparent documentation of harmonization protocols, procedures, and algorithmic transformations has been emphasized, as has ensuring the quality and validity of the resultant harmonized datasets (Wey et al. 2021). Missing variables and heterogeneity of cohort data are also of concern. In one study, the global harmonization potential across all included variables in all cohorts was moderate (62.8%) (Wey et al. 2021). Understanding sources of variability in harmonized cohort data and the relevance of the harmonized data to the research needs is also of primary importance when conducting large-scale pooling projects.

Tools to facilitate documentation and harmonization of cohort variables in open and accessible formats have been developed and are increasingly being used (Jaddoe et al. 2020). Consortia have also conducted decentralized pooled epidemiological analyses across cohorts, using DataSHIELD (Data Aggregation Through Anonymous Summary-statistics from Harmonised Individual-levEL Databases) technology, originally developed to address ethical and legal constraints of sharing of individual-level research data between countries (Wolfson et al. 2010). Recent extensions and a new architecture have recently been developed to address previous limitations associated with Opal storage formats and analysis capabilities in available DataSHIELD R packages to allow for large and complex datasets to be analyzed (Marcon et al. 2021).

Conclusion

Using large-scale massive cohort data in occupational health research has both advantages and challenges. Large populations enable studying associations with rare exposures and outcomes, as well as population subgroups, e.g., according to gender, age, socioeconomic position, occupation, region, time period, etc. Registry-based studies may be large but may have certain limitations due to the nature of the data and lack of important variables, as described in this chapter. For consortium studies, which combine data from different cohorts, harmonization of data may be challenging. The combination of different study types, with different strengths and limitations, and collaboration between research groups across countries, certainly contributes to increase knowledge in occupation and health. Recent efforts in Europe have sought to develop new theoretical frameworks, concepts, and definitions in occupational health and to inventory numerous existing cohort studies and combine their data, to ultimately lead to more definitive studies in disease etiology.

Cross-References

- Biomechanical Hazards at Work and Adverse Health Using Job-Exposure Matrices
- Chemical Hazards at Work and Occupational Diseases Using Job-Exposure Matrices
- Integration of Occupational Exposure into the Exposome
- Job-Exposure Matrices: Design, Validation, and Limitations
- Precarious Work and Health
- Psychosocial Work Environment and Health: Applying Job-Exposure Matrices and Work Organization and Management Practice

Acknowledgments MCT is funded by a Ramón y Cajal fellowship (RYC-2017-01892) from the Spanish Ministry of Science, Innovation and Universities and cofunded by the European Social Fund. ISGlobal acknowledges support from the Spanish Ministry of Science and Innovation through the "Centro de Excelencia Severo Ochoa 2019-2023" Program (CEX2018-000806-S), and support from the Generalitat de Catalunya through the CERCA Program. COST Action CA16216 (OMEGA-NET) was supported by COST (European Cooperation in Science and Technology). EPHOR is funded by the European Union's Horizon 2020 research and innovation program under grant agreement No 874703.

References

Aktas E, Bergbom B, Godderis L et al (2022) Migrant workers occupational health research: an OMEGA-NET working group position paper. Int Arch Occup Environ Health 95(4):765–777. https://doi.org/10.1007/s00420-021-01803-x

Andersen A, Barlow L, Engeland A et al (1999) Work-related cancer in the Nordic countries. Scand J Work Environ Health 25(Suppl 2):1–116

Andersen JS, Olivarius Nde F, Krasnik A (2011) The Danish National Health Service register. Scand J Public Health 39(7 Suppl):34–37. https://doi.org/10.1177/1403494810394718

Bakken IJ, Ariansen AMS, Knudsen GP et al (2020) The Norwegian patient registry and the Norwegian registry for primary health care: research potential of two nationwide health-care registries. Scand J Public Health 48(1):49–55. https://doi.org/10.1177/1403494819859737

Bao H, Baker CJO, Adisesh A (2020) Occupation coding of job titles: iterative development of an Automated Coding Algorithm for the Canadian National Occupation Classification (ACA-NOC). JMIR Form Res 4(8):e16422

Basagaña X, Pedersen M, Barrera-Gómez J, ESCAPE Birth Outcomes Working Group et al (2018) Analysis of multicentre epidemiological studies: contrasting fixed or random effects modelling and meta-analysis. Int J Epidemiol 47(4):1343–1354. https://doi.org/10.1093/ije/dyy117

Belloni M, Laurent O, Guihenneuc C et al (2020) Bayesian profile regression to deal with multiple highly correlated exposures and a censored survival outcome. First application in ionizing radiation epidemiology. Front Public Health 8:557006. https://doi.org/10.3389/fpubh.2020.557006

Bodin T, Çağlayan Ç, Garde AH et al (2020) Precarious employment in occupational health – an OMEGA-NET working group position paper. Scand J Work Environ Health 46(3):321–329. https://doi.org/10.5271/sjweh.3860

Bondo Petersen S, Flachs EM, Prescott EIB et al (2018) Job-exposure matrices addressing lifestyle to be applied in register-based occupational health studies. Occup Environ Med 75(12):890–897. https://doi.org/10.1136/oemed-2018-104991

Brouwer M, Schinasi L, Beane Freeman LE et al (2016) Assessment of occupational exposure to pesticides in a pooled analysis of agricultural cohorts within the AGRICOH consortium. Occup Environ Med 73(6):359–367. https://doi.org/10.1136/oemed-2015-103319

Buckner-Petty S, Dale AM, Evanoff BA (2019) Efficiency of autocoding programs for converting job descriptors into standard occupational classification (SOC) codes. Am J Ind Med 62(1):59–68. https://doi.org/10.1002/ajim.22928

Coggon D, Ntani G, Palmer KT et al (2012) The CUPID (Cultural and Psychosocial Influences on Disability) study: methods of data collection and characteristics of study sample. PLoS One 7(7):e39820

Danish Health Data Authority (Sundhedsdatastyrelsen) (2022) National health registers. https://sundhedsdatastyrelsen.dk/da/english/health_data_and_registers/national_health_registers. Accessed 12 Aug 2022

Directorate of Health (2019) Registers and health information. https://www.landlaeknir.is/english/registersandhealthinformation. Accessed 12 Aug 2022

EIT Health Scandinavia (2022a) Health data registers. https://www.eithealth-scandinavia.eu/biobanksregisters/registers. Accessed 12 Aug 2022

EIT Health Scandinavia (2022b) Overview of access rules on Health Data Registers in Sweden. https://www.eithealth-scandinavia.eu/biobanksregisters/access/registers-sweden. Accessed 12 Aug 2022

Ervasti J, Pentti J, Nyberg ST et al (2021) Long working hours and risk of 50 health conditions and mortality outcomes: a multicohort study in four European countries. Lancet Reg Health Eur 11:100212

European Medicines Agency (2022) Patient registries. https://www.ema.europa.eu/en/human-regulatory/post-authorisation/patient-registries. Accessed 12 Aug 2022

FinnGen (2022) Health registries. https://www.finngen.fi/en/health-registries. Accessed 12 Aug 2022

Fortier I, Raina P, Van den Heuvel ER et al (2017) Maelstrom research guidelines for rigorous retrospective data harmonization. Int J Epidemiol 46(1):103–105. https://doi.org/10.1093/ije/dyw075

Gillies M, Richardson DB, Cardis E et al (2017) Mortality from circulatory diseases and other non-cancer outcomes among nuclear workers in France, the United Kingdom and the United States (INWORKS). Radiat Res 188(3):276–290. https://doi.org/10.1667/RR14608.1

Guseva Canu I, Mesot O, Györkös C et al (2019) Burnout syndrome in Europe: towards a harmonized approach in occupational health practice and research. Ind Health 57(6):745–752. https://doi.org/10.2486/indhealth.2018-0159

Guseva Canu I, Marca SC, Dell'Oro F et al (2021) Harmonized definition of occupational burnout: a systematic review, semantic analysis, and Delphi consensus in 29 countries. Scand J Work Environ Health 47(2):95–107. https://doi.org/10.5271/sjweh.3935

Hamra GB, Richardson DB, Cardis E et al (2016) Cohort profile: the International Nuclear Workers study (INWORKS). Int J Epidemiol 45(3):693–699. https://doi.org/10.1093/ije/dyv122

Hasselhorn HM, Leinonen T, Bültmann U et al (2022) The differentiated roles of health in the transition from work to retirement – conceptual and methodological challenges and avenues for future research. Scand J Work Environ Health 48(4):312–321. https://doi.org/10.5271/sjweh.4017

Hoque DME, Kumari V, Hoque M et al (2017) Impact of clinical registries on quality of patient care and clinical outcomes: a systematic review. PLoS One 12(9):e0183667. https://doi.org/10.1371/journal.pone.0183667

International Agency for Research on Cancer (2017) IARC monographs on the evaluation of carcinogenic risks to humans; volume 112. Some organophosphate insecticides and herbicides. IARC, Lyon. Available from: https://monographs.iarc.who.int/wp-content/uploads/2018/07/mono112.pdf

International Agency for Research on Cancer (2022) AGRICOH: A consortium of agricultural cohort studies. https://agricoh.iarc.fr/about/about-agricoh. Accessed 12 Aug 2022

International Labour Organization (2010) International Standard Classification of Occupations (ISCO). https://www.ilo.org/public/english/bureau/stat/isco. Accessed 9 Aug 2022

International Labour Organization (2016) ISCO-08 Structure, index correspondence with ISCO-88. ISCO-08 Part 4: Correspondence tables. http://www.ilo.org/public/english/bureau/stat/isco/docs/correspondence08.docx. Accessed 12 Aug 2022

Jaddoe VWV, Felix JF, Andersen AN, LifeCycle Project Group et al (2020) The LifeCycle project-EU child cohort network: a federated analysis infrastructure and harmonized data of more than 250,000 children and parents. Eur J Epidemiol 35(7):709–724. https://doi.org/10.1007/s10654-020-00662-z

John SM, Kezic S (eds) (2017) Occupational skin diseases in Europe: In need of standards for patient care and preventive measures. Diseases. J Eur Acad Dermatol Venereol 31(Suppl S4):1–46. https://doi.org/10.1111/jdv.14321

Kauppinen T, Heikkilä P, Plato N et al (2009) Construction of job-exposure matrices for the Nordic occupational cancer study (NOCCA). Acta Oncol 48(5):791–800. https://doi.org/10.1080/02841860902718747

Kivimäki M, Singh-Manoux A, Virtanen M et al (2015) IPD-work consortium: pre-defined meta-analyses of individual-participant data strengthen evidence base for a link between psychosocial factors and health. Scand J Work Environ Health 41(3):312–321

Kivimäki M, Nyberg ST, Pentti J, On behalf of the IPD-Work consortium et al (2019) Individual and combined effects of job strain components on subsequent morbidity and MORTALITY. Epidemiology 30(4):e27–e29

Kogevinas M, Schlünssen V, Mehlum IS et al (2020) The OMEGA-NET international inventory of occupational cohorts. Ann Work Expo Health 64(6):565–568. https://doi.org/10.1093/annweh/wxaa039

Kristensen P, Corbett K, Mohn FA et al (2018) Information bias of social gradients in sickness absence: a comparison of self-report data in the Norwegian Mother and Child Cohort Study (MoBa) and data in national registries. BMC Public Health 18(1):1275. https://doi.org/10.1186/s12889-018-6208-9

Laurent O, Gomolka M, Haylock R et al (2016) Concerted uranium research in Europe (CURE): toward a collaborative project integrating dosimetry, epidemiology and radiobiology to study the effects of occupational uranium exposure. J Radiol Prot 36(2):319–345. https://doi.org/10.1088/0952-4746/36/2/319

Laurier D, Richardson DB, Cardis E et al (2017) The international nuclear workers study (Inworks): a collaborative epidemiological study to improve knowledge about health effects of protracted low-dose exposure. Radiat Prot Dosim 173(1–3):21–25. https://doi.org/10.1093/rpd/ncw314

Lawlor DA, Tilling K, Davey Smith G (2016) Triangulation in aetiological epidemiology. Int J Epidemiol 45(6):1866–1886. https://doi.org/10.1093/ije/dyw314

Leinonen T, Boets I, Pletea E et al (2022) A conceptual framework addressing the complex labour market dynamics of the work-to-retirement process. Eur J Ageing 1–7. https://doi.org/10.1007/s10433-022-00704-3

Leon ME, Beane Freeman LE, Douwes J, Hoppin JA, Kromhout H, Lebailly P, Nordby KC, Schenker M, Schüz J, Waring SC, Alavanja MC, Annesi-Maesano I, Baldi I, Dalvie MA, Ferro G, Fervers B, Langseth H, London L, Lynch CF, McLaughlin J, Merchant JA, Pahwa P,

Sigsgaard T, Stayner L, Wesseling C, Yoo KY, Zahm SH, Straif K, Blair A (2011) AGRICOH: a consortium of agricultural cohorts. Int J Environ Res Public Health 8(5):1341–1357

Leon ME, Schinasi LH, Lebailly P et al (2019) Pesticide use and risk of non-Hodgkin lymphoid malignancies in agricultural cohorts from France, Norway and the USA: a pooled analysis from the AGRICOH consortium. Int J Epidemiol 48(5):1519–1535. https://doi.org/10.1093/ije/dyz017

Loomis D, Guha N, Kogevinas M et al (2019) Cancer mortality in an international cohort of reinforced plastics workers exposed to styrene: a reanalysis. Occup Environ Med 76:157–162

Ludvigsson JF, Andersson E, Ekbom A et al (2011) External review and validation of the Swedish national inpatient register. BMC Public Health 11:450. https://doi.org/10.1186/1471-2458-11-450

Lytras T, Kogevinas M, Kromhout H et al (2018) Occupational exposures and 20-year incidence of COPD: the European Community respiratory health survey. Thorax 73(11):1008–1015

Madsen IE, Rugulies R (2021) Understanding the impact of psychosocial working conditions on workers' health: we have come a long way, but are we there yet? Scand J Work Environ Health 47(7):483–487

Marcon Y, Bishop T, Avraam D et al (2021) Orchestrating privacy-protected big data analyses of data from different resources with R and DataSHIELD. PLoS Comput Biol 17(3):e1008880

Mattei F, Liverani S, Guida F et al (2016) Multidimensional analysis of the effect of occupational exposure to organic solvents on lung cancer risk: the ICARE study. Occup Environ Med 73(6): 368–377. https://doi.org/10.1136/oemed-2015-103177

National Board of Health and Welfare (2019) Registers. https://www.socialstyrelsen.se/en/statistics-and-data/registers. Accessed 12 Aug 2022

Norwegian Institute of Public Health (2016) Overview of the national health registries. https://www.fhi.no/en/more/access-to-data/about-the-national-health-registries2. Accessed 12 Aug 2022

Pedersen AG, Ellingsen CL (2015) Data quality in the causes of death registry. Tidsskr Nor Laegeforen 135(8):768–770. https://doi.org/10.4045/tidsskr.14.1065. (English, Norwegian)

Pedersen J, Schultz BB, Madsen IEH et al (2020) High physical work demands and working life expectancy in Denmark. Occup Environ Med 77(8):576–582. https://doi.org/10.1136/oemed-2019-106359

Peters S, Vienneau D, Sampri A et al (2022) Occupational exposure assessment tools in Europe: a comprehensive inventory overview. Ann Work Expo Health 66(5):671–686. https://doi.org/10.1093/annweh/wxab110

Phillips DE, Lozano R, Naghavi M et al (2014) A composite metric for assessing data on mortality and causes of death: the vital statistics performance index. Popul Health Metrics 12:14. https://doi.org/10.1186/1478-7954-12-14

Pronk A, Loh M, Kuijpers E, Albin M, Selander J, Godderis L, Ghosh M, Vermeulen R, Peters S, Mehlum I S, Turner MC, Schlünssen V, Goldberg M, Kogevinas M, Harding BN, Solovieva S, Garani-Papadatos T, van Tongeren M, Stierum R (2022) Applying the exposome concept to working life health. Environ Epidemiol 6(2):e185. https://doi.org/10.1097/EE9.0000000000000185

Pukkala E, Martinsen JI, Lynge E et al (2009) Occupation and cancer – follow-up of 15 million people in five Nordic countries. Acta Oncol 48(5):646–790. https://doi.org/10.1080/02841860902913546

Rage E, Richardson DB, Demers P et al (2020) PUMA – pooled uranium miners analysis: cohort profile. Occup Environ Med 77(3):194–200. https://doi.org/10.1136/oemed-2019-105981

Rémen T, Richardson L, Pilorget C et al (2018) Development of a coding and crosswalk tool for occupations and industries. Ann Work Expo Health 62(7):796–807

Richardson DB, Rage E, Demers PA et al (2021) Mortality among uranium miners in North America and Europe: the Pooled Uranium Miners Analysis (PUMA). Int J Epidemiol 50(2): 633–643. https://doi.org/10.1093/ije/dyaa195

Russ DE, Ho KY, Colt JS et al (2016) Computer-based coding of free-text job descriptions to efficiently identify occupations in epidemiological studies. Occup Environ Med 73(6):417–424

Saberi Hosnijeh F, Casabonne D, Nieters A et al (2021) Association between anthropometry and lifestyle factors and risk of B-cell lymphoma: an exposome-wide analysis. Int J Cancer 148(9): 2115–2128

Schmidt M, Schmidt SA, Sandegaard JL et al (2015) The Danish National Patient Registry: a review of content, data quality, and research potential. Clin Epidemiol 7:449–490. https://doi.org/10.2147/CLEP.S91125

Schram JL, Solovieva S, Leinonen T et al (2021) The influence of occupational class and physical workload on working life expectancy among older employees. Scand J Work Environ Health 47(1):5–14. https://doi.org/10.5271/sjweh.3919

Shin HH, Cakmak S, Brion O et al (2014) Indirect adjustment for multiple missing variables applicable to environmental epidemiology. Environ Res 134:482–487. https://doi.org/10.1016/j.envres.2014.05.016

Shoman Y, Marca SC, Bianchi R et al (2021a) Psychometric properties of burnout measures: a systematic review. Epidemiol Psychiatr Sci 30:e8. https://doi.org/10.1017/S2045796020001134

Shoman Y, El May E, Marca SC (2021b) Predictors of occupational burnout: a systematic review. Int J Environ Res Public Health 18(17):9188. https://doi.org/10.3390/ijerph18179188

Siew SS, Martinsen JI, Kjaerheim K et al (2017) Occupational exposure to wood dust and risk of nasal and nasopharyngeal cancer: a case-control study among men in four Nordic countries-with an emphasis on nasal adenocarcinoma. Int J Cancer 141(12):2430–2436. https://doi.org/10.1002/ijc.31015

Statistics Norway (1998) Norwegian Standard Classification of Occupations (STYRK-98). Official Statistics of Norway (NOS C 521). Oslo–Kongsvinger, Norway. Available from: https://www.ssb.no/a/publikasjoner/pdf/nos_c521/nos_c521.pdf

Statistics Norway (2011) Standard Classification of Occupations (STYRK-08). Official Statistics of Norway (Notater 17/2011). Oslo– Kongsvinger, Norway. Available from: https://www.ssb.no/a/publikasjoner/pdf/notat_201117/notat_201117.pdf

Steenland K, Schubauer-Berigan MK, Vermeulen R et al (2020) Risk of bias assessments and evidence syntheses for observational epidemiologic studies of environmental and occupational exposures: strengths and limitations. Environ Health Perspect 9:95002. https://doi.org/10.1289/EHP6980

Stocks SJ, McNamee R, van der Molen HF et al (2015) Working group 2; Cost action IS1002—monitoring trends in occupational diseases and tracing new and emerging risks in a NETwork (MODERNET). Trends in incidence of occupational asthma, contact dermatitis, noise-induced hearing loss, carpal tunnel syndrome and upper limb musculoskeletal disorders in European countries from 2000 to 2012. Occup Environ Med 72(4):294–303. https://doi.org/10.1136/oemed-2014-102534

Svanes C, Johannessen A, Bertelsen RJ, On behalf of the RHINESSA International Collaboration et al (2022) Cohort profile: the multigeneration Respiratory Health in Northern Europe, Spain and Australia (RHINESSA) cohort. BMJ Open 12:e059434. https://doi.org/10.1136/bmjopen-2021-059434

t'Mannetje A, Kromhout H (2003) The use of occupation and industry classifications in general population studies. Int J Epidemiol 32(3):419–428. https://doi.org/10.1093/ije/dyg080

Talibov M, Lehtinen-Jacks S, Martinsen JI et al (2014) Occupational exposure to solvents and acute myeloid leukemia: a population-based, case-control study in four Nordic countries. Scand J Work Environ Health 40(5):511–517. https://doi.org/10.5271/sjweh.3436

Talibov M, Sormunen J, Hansen J et al (2018) Benzene exposure at workplace and risk of colorectal cancer in four Nordic countries. Cancer Epidemiol 55:156–161. https://doi.org/10.1016/j.canep.2018.06.011

Tamminga SJ, Kuijer PPFM, Badarin K, Alfonso JH, Amaro J, Curti S, Canu IG, Mattioli S, Mehlum IS, Rempel D, Roquelaure Y, Visser S, van der Molen HF (2021) Towards harmonisation of case definitions for eight work-related musculoskeletal disorders – an international multi-disciplinary Delphi study. BMC Musculoskelet Disord 22(1):1018. https://doi.org/10.1186/s12891-021-04871-9

Thygesen LC, Ersbøll AK (2014) When the entire population is the sample: strengths and limitations in register-based epidemiology. Eur J Epidemiol 29(8):551–558. https://doi.org/10.1007/s10654-013-9873-0. Epub 2014 Jan 10

Togawa K, Leon ME, Lebailly P et al (2021) Cancer incidence in agricultural workers: findings from an international consortium of agricultural cohort studies (AGRICOH). Environ Int 157:106825

Turner MC, Mehlum IS (2018) Greater coordination and harmonisation of European occupational cohorts is needed. Occup Environ Med 75(7):475–476. https://doi.org/10.1136/oemed-2017-104955

Turner MC, Vineis P, Seleiro E, On behalf of the EXPOsOMICS Consortium et al (2018) EXPOsOMICS: final policy workshop and stakeholder consultation. BMC Public Health 18(1):260. https://doi.org/10.1186/s12889-018-5160-z

Turner MC, Albin M, Boon J et al (2022) Towards the Exposome Project for Health and Occupational Research (EPHOR) mega cohort. ISEE conference abstracts. Environ Health Perspect 2022(1)

Ubalde-Lopez M, Garani-Papadatos T, Scelo G et al (2021) Working life, health and well-being of parents: a joint effort to uncover hidden treasures in European birth cohorts. Scand J Work Environ Health 47(7):550–560. https://doi.org/10.5271/sjweh.3980

United Nations Economic Commission of Europe (2007) Register-based statistics in the Nordic countries. New York. Available from: https://digitallibrary.un.org/record/609979?ln=en

van der Molen HF, Visser S, Alfonso JH et al (2021) Diagnostic criteria for musculoskeletal disorders for use in occupational healthcare or research: a scoping review of consensus- and synthesised-based case definitions. BMC Musculoskelet Disord 22(1):169. https://doi.org/10.1186/s12891-021-04031-z

Vineis P, Chadeau-Hyam M, Gmuender H et al (2017) The exposome in practice: design of the EXPOsOMICS project. Int J Hyg Environ Health 220(2 Pt A):142–151

Vrijheid M, Casas M, Bergström A et al (2012) European birth cohorts for environmental health research. Environ Health Perspect 120(1):29–37. https://doi.org/10.1289/ehp.1103823

Vrijheid M, Slama R, Robinson O et al (2014) The human early-life exposome (HELIX): project rationale and design. Environ Health Perspect 122(6):535–544. https://doi.org/10.1289/ehp.1307204

Vrijheid M, Basagaña X, Gonzalez JR et al (2021) Advancing tools for human early lifecourse exposome research and translation (ATHLETE): project overview. Environ Epidemiol 5(5):e166

Wey TW, Doiron D, Wissa R et al (2021) Overview of retrospective data harmonisation in the MINDMAP project: process and results. J Epidemiol Community Health 75(5):433–441. https://doi.org/10.1136/jech-2020-214259

WHO/ILO (2021) WHO/ILO joint estimates of the work-related burden of disease and injury, 2000–2016: global monitoring report. World Health Organization and the International Labour Organization, Geneva

Wild CP (2005) Complementing the genome with an "exposome": the outstanding challenge of environmental exposure measurement in molecular epidemiology. Cancer Epidemiol Biomark Prev 14(8):1847–1850. https://doi.org/10.1158/1055-9965.EPI-05-0456

Wolfson M, Wallace SE, Masca N et al (2010) DataSHIELD: resolving a conflict in contemporary bioscience–performing a pooled analysis of individual-level data without sharing the data. Int J Epidemiol 39:1372–1382

Zhang P, Carlsten C, Chaleckis R et al (2021) Defining the scope of exposome studies and research needs from a multidisciplinary perspective. Environ Sci Technol Lett 8(10):839–852

Integration of Occupational Exposure into the Exposome

8

Jean-François Viel, Nathalie Bonvallot, and William Dab

Contents

Introduction	122
The Exposome: An Evolving Concept	123
The Origins of the Exposome	123
The Development of "Xeno-Metabolomics" to Decipher Chemical Exposome	123
The Emergence of the Eco-Exposome to Consider Both Ecological and Human Receptors	124
Application to Occupational Health: The "Worksome"	125
"Operationalizing" the Exposome Concept	126
The Main Remaining Challenges	131
Conclusion	132
Cross-References	133
References	133

J.-F. Viel (✉)
Univ Rennes, CHU Rennes, Inserm, EHESP, Irset (Institut de recherche en santé, environnement et travail), Rennes, France
e-mail: jean-francois.viel@univ-rennes1.fr

N. Bonvallot
Univ Rennes, EHESP, Inserm, Irset (Institut de recherche en santé, environnement et travail), Rennes, France
e-mail: nathalie.bonvallot@ehesp.fr

W. Dab
Laboratoire MESuRS, Conservatoire national des Arts et Métiers, Paris, France

Catholic University of Paris, Paris, France
e-mail: william.dab@lecnam.net

© Springer Nature Switzerland AG 2023
M. Wahrendorf et al. (eds.), *Handbook of Life Course Occupational Health*, Handbook Series in Occupational Health Sciences, https://doi.org/10.1007/978-3-031-30492-7_7

Abstract

The exposome concept was proposed to improve the reliability of exposure data for a better understanding of the etiology of chronic diseases. Designed to tackle three issues, namely the multiplicity, temporality, and variability of environmental exposure, the exposome concept is operationalized through a broad array of methodologies and tools. In this chapter, we first address the internal chemical exposome from the point of view of the intense development of bioanalytical technologies, which are briefly reviewed. Despite major advances in this field, the measurement of internal chemical exposure is still unable to provide an overall view of human exposure. Then, we describe how the eco-exposome complements the internal chemical exposome by considering physical exposure and social determinants. We show how new tools and methods deployed for exposome measurement can be applied in the field of occupational health (worksome). Finally, we present the main challenges to the better operationalization of the worksome concept.

Keywords

Occupational health · Eco-exposome · Internal exposome · Risk assessment · Temporality · Vulnerabilities · Epidemiology · Worksome

Introduction

Exposure science has evolved in recent decades as a distinct field, drawing from many disciplines to shed light on the effects that environmental exposure has on a broad range of diseases in an attempt to identify the underlying mechanisms and biological pathways. However, traditional exposure science models have typically examined the impact of the environment on disease through a reductionist approach, supported by discipline-driven theories that have led to narrowly focused assessments, models, and analytical tools (Juarez et al. 2014).

More recently, researchers have increasingly combined exposure science and ecological models to obtain further insights into the underlying causal mechanisms through which environmental exposure affects personal health, potentially leading to population-level disparities. Building on this momentum, the exposome has been proposed as an emerging exposure science paradigm for conceptualizing the cumulative effects of environmental exposure and examining the dynamic multi-dimensional interrelationships between environment and health.

In this chapter, we first address the internal chemical exposome from the point of view of the intense development of bioanalytical technologies. Then, we describe how the eco-exposome complements the internal chemical exposome by considering physical exposure and social determinants. Finally, we show how the tools developed in these approaches can be applied to the field of occupational health to decipher the worksome.

The Exposome: An Evolving Concept

The Origins of the Exposome

Given that genome-wide association studies have yielded only a modicum of success and that the environment has been less precisely measured than genes, Wild (2005) called for an "exposome to match the genome." He proposed the following definition: "at its most complete, the exposome encompasses life course environmental exposure (including lifestyle factors), from the prenatal period onwards." In this original statement, Wild focused on the development of transcriptomics, proteomics, and metabolomics for more complete environmental exposure assessment to improve our understanding of disease etiology.

Intended to organize various ideas and approaches for environmental epidemiology similarly to the genome for genetic research, the exposome is not a discipline but rather a concept. It can be seen as an opportunity or a need to associate epidemiologists, biologists, and bioinformaticians to meet the abovementioned challenges. By answering the questions of multiplicity, temporality, and variability, this approach should improve the reliability of exposure data. As the exposome is a potentially revolutionary concept, many researchers have pushed the exposome concept further (see below).

The Development of "Xeno-Metabolomics" to Decipher Chemical Exposome

Metabolomics technologies provide extensive information about the phenotypic features of populations by integrating upstream information provided by transcriptomics and proteomics approaches. Their most important advantage in environmental health is their ability to detect early biological modifications prior to more obvious signs of toxicity and adverse effects. Thus, they may represent a reliable means of identifying new biomarkers linked to various types of exposure and proposing hypotheses for a better understanding of the mechanistic pathways that associate metabolic changes and diseases. Large-scale studies, such as metabolome-wide association studies, offer the possibility to study both phenotypic and cultural/environmental factors (especially diet). At this scale, it is possible to associate metabolic profiling with the presence of risk factors or diseases, such as diet and cardiovascular diseases (Holmes et al. 2008). The same issues could be considered for environmental epidemiology on a smaller scale, but with special attention to the recruitment of individuals, definition of exposure groups, sampling strategies, analytical and statistical techniques, etc. (Bonvallot et al. 2014). A growing body of literature over the last five years has demonstrated that metabolic fingerprints can efficiently discriminate subpopulations characterized by distinctive exposure modalities using extremely robust and valid multivariate statistical models. Discriminant metabolites provide valuable clues on the mechanisms involved. It is worth mentioning that certain metabolites identified in available studies cannot be considered as specific biomarkers. In addition, the disruption of cellular signaling pathways associated with oxidative stress appears to be among the primary drivers for the further alteration of metabolic pathways, including those for lipids, bile acids, and amino acids, for example. These observations do not provide sufficient data for public health use, and highlight the need to simultaneously provide more quantitative exposure information (Bonvallot et al. 2018). In this context, new high-resolution mass spectrometry techniques have been developed to ensure a high level of sensitivity to capture exposure as accurately as possible, as many xenobiotics are present at only trace levels in human biological fluids. These new approaches of suspect screening or untargeted analyses provide valuable information for the discovery of new biomarkers of exposure and the metabolic effects associated with many chronic diseases, in other words, the "xeno-metabolome." Although progress has been made in recent years (Chaker et al. 2021), these approaches still suffer from limitations related to the diversity of chemical structures, the low-dose characteristics of human exposure, and the difficulty of signal identification.

The Emergence of the Eco-Exposome to Consider Both Ecological and Human Receptors

Although the original framers of the exposome concept considered a broad array of biomarkers (Wild 2005), many subsequent applications of the exposome have been less apt to address individual behaviors and social determinants and have instead focused primarily on chemical exposure and their related "omics" technologies (Senier et al. 2017). Rappaport and Smith (2010) have been influential in this respect, as they found it "reasonable" to consider the "environment" as the body's internal chemical environment and "exposure" as the amounts of biologically active chemicals in this internal environment. They distinguished two opposing approaches to measure the exposome: a bottom-up approach, looking for internal changes starting from external measurements, and a top-down approach, looking for external sources on the basis of internal signals. They expressed, however, a strong preference for the latter, arguing that "this would require *only a single blood specimen* at each time point" compared to the "enormous effort" to measure "all chemicals in each external source" (Rappaport and Smith 2010). Although softened in 2011 (Lioy and Rappaport 2011), this omics-centered approach excluded both complex real-world environmental exposure and the social, political, and economic forces that create vulnerabilities to exposure from scientific discourse (Juarez et al. 2014; Senier et al. 2017).

A broader definition of environmental exposure was therefore needed, and Wild (2012) expanded his original proposal, describing three categories of nongenetic exposure: internal, specific external, and general external. The first category is essentially biology oriented, comprising processes internal to the body "such as metabolism, endogenous circulating hormones, body morphology, physical activity, gut microflora, inflammation, lipid peroxidation, oxidative stress, and ageing." The second is more epidemiology oriented, including "radiation, infectious agents, chemical contaminants and environmental pollutants, diet, lifestyle factors (e.g., tobacco, alcohol), occupation, and medical interventions." Under an umbrella term ("general external"), the third category encompasses "the wider social, economic, and psychological influences on the individual, for example: social capital, education, financial status, psychological and mental stress, urban–rural environment, and climate."

However, the true breakthrough came from the US National Research Council of the National Academies, which issued a report entitled "Exposure Science in the 21st Century: A Vision and Strategy" in 2012 (National Research Council 2012). The exposome concept was broadened to the "eco-exposome," "that is, the extension of exposure science from the point of contact between stressor and receptor inward into the organism and outward to the general environment, including the ecosphere." Broadening the view of receptors to consider both ecological and human receptors improves our knowledge of how environmental exposure affects human health.

Although omics technologies have demonstrated a potential for identifying environmental health associations, internal exposure is not universally more useful than external exposure for epidemiological purposes (National Academies of Sciences, Engineering, and Medicine 2017). External measures are needed to identify sources, consider routes by which environmental stressors reach humans and ecosystems, and address the spatial and temporal variability of exposure. Moreover, there are no biomarkers of current or past exposure for most types of external exposure (Turner et al. 2017). This approach is of utmost importance for the development of targeted mitigation strategies (e.g., at the workplace) or to initiate regulatory actions.

Application to Occupational Health: The "Worksome"

Qualitative and quantitative knowledge of occupational exposure is clearly necessary to study its impact on health. This is particularly important in the context in which low-dose repeated exposure can cause chronic diseases with a latency period of up to several decades. The concept of the exposome opens new perspectives but its operational translation is not straightforward.

Generally speaking, the estimation of lifelong cumulative professional exposure over the life course raises many difficulties. Some are general: the number of pollutants (chemical, physical, or biological), creating thousands of complex mixtures; multiple longitudinal data of various quality and time scale; the diversity of the genetic and epigenetic characteristics that modify the biochemical actions of such pollutants; large spatiotemporal variation; limitations in terms of validity, sensitivity, and specificity of the available analytical tools for measuring external or internal doses and biological effects; and the high cost of these tools, which limits their routine use.

Other difficulties, in addition to the physicochemical factors, are specific to the occupational situation: working conditions are evolving very quickly; professional histories are becoming increasingly complex; certain modes of management can

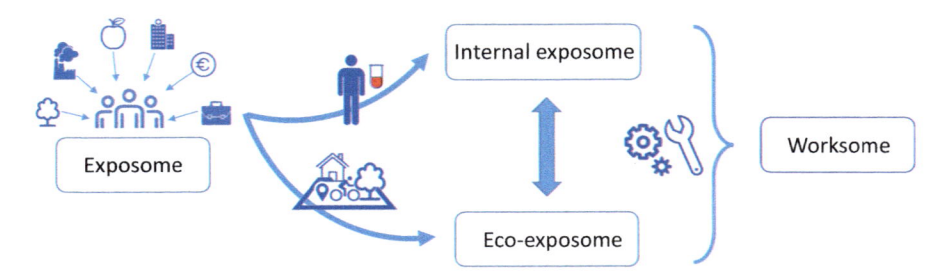

Fig. 1 Conceptual framework of the worksome

create stress, a phenomenon that could modify the biochemical effects of pollutants; and prescribed tasks are not necessarily performed in the field. As a result, the simple knowledge of job titles or tasks may not accurately reflect true occupational exposure.

The important contribution of occupational exposure to the global exposome, sometimes called the "worksome" (Eyles et al. 2019), merits consideration in the exposome building process (Fig. 1). Few studies have been published on this topic, although various types of technological tools have been used to analyze the life course of environmental and occupational exposure (Holland 2017; Kuijpers et al. 2021).

"Operationalizing" the Exposome Concept

As with the genome, an understanding of human exposure, even incomplete and targeted, may allow significant progress and render the research operational. Numerous tools and methodologies have been developed to capture the three crucial issues behind the exposome concept, namely "multiplicity," "dynamics," and "temporality." They are briefly described below and, where they exist, potential applications to occupational health are mentioned.

Occupational Cohorts

Classically, epidemiological studies can start from the exposure and assess the risk of diseases (cohort studies) or begin by selecting one or several diseases and then reconstituting the past exposure (case/control studies). Until now, etiological studies have addressed the potential effects of one type or class of exposure, making the exposome concept promising for environmental/occupational epidemiology. Prospective cohorts are most insightful because they ensure longitudinal follow-up of worker populations, addressing the critical issue of rapidly evolving working conditions.

Temporality can also be addressed through job-exposure matrices (Fevotte et al. 2011; Houot et al. 2021). They are useful for reconstituting the worksome, avoiding the cumbersome task of assessing a given type of exposure related to successive jobs on an individual basis (▶ Chap. 6, "Job-Exposure Matrices: Design, Validation, and Limitations"). These matrices can also be developed from prospective cohort data, as recently reported (Evanoff et al. 2019).

Estimating lifetime occupational exposure is a difficult but inescapable challenge (Houot et al. 2021). The capacity to analyze lifelong exposure clearly offers great potential to identify causal agents (Stingone et al. 2017) and improve the surveillance of work-related diseases (Faisandier et al. 2011). However, as continuous measurement of exposure is not achievable, the life course may be envisioned through specific time points, the choice of which being of utmost importance (Santos et al. 2020).

Owing to repeated sampling over time, different tools for exposure assessment can be used on the same individual: biomarker measurements associated, for example, with detailed questionnaires and geolocation. If biological samples are collected at different times throughout the life course, they can be aliquoted for immediate use and then frozen and stored in a biobank for later studies, when new analytical technologies become available or when new biomarkers are discovered (Vineis et al. 2020; Vrijheid et al. 2021). Such prospective cohorts are now ongoing in the occupational health field (Goldberg et al. 2017; Reedijk et al. 2018).

At the population level, the periods of greatest vulnerability are most often chosen, with special attention to early life, adolescence, or specific life periods during adulthood that include occupational contexts. In particular, numerous mother/child cohort studies have been launched, providing unique opportunities to capture the exposome.

Matching Exposure Biomarkers with Biological Matrices and Analytical Methodologies

In epidemiology, internal exposure measurements by biomonitoring can be used to assess chemical exposure, as it integrates all sources and routes, even if they are not precisely known. This can be especially useful for ubiquitous compounds. In this context, the choice of the most suitable biomarkers, human matrices, and analytical methods has to be considered. The first question addresses the availability of relevant biomarkers, which depends on the physical chemical characteristics and the toxicokinetics of the contaminants of interest. A suitable biomarker is studied through its measurability, its ability to predict exposure, and its specificity. The second question addresses the choice of the matrix in which compounds have to be measured. Although biological fluids, such as urine and blood, have been traditionally used for this purpose, there is increasing interest in hair analysis, especially because it provides information more highly related to chronic exposure, hair is easy to collect, it is noninvasive, and does not require complex transport and storage conditions (Hardy et al. 2021). Finally, the third question addresses analytical techniques, which must be sufficiently robust, sensitive, and selective to produce reliable data. These three issues have to be considered simultaneously because of their tight association: for example, whether the parent compound or a stable metabolite is the most suitable biomarker and what is the best matrix in which it should be determined using what technique. As an illustration, we can cite the recent

European HBM4EU project, in which the most suitable biomarkers, human matrices, and analytical methods were selected for a panel of chemicals considered to be a priority for risk assessment (Vorkamp et al. 2021).

Online Questionnaire via Smartphones

Questionnaires are a critical tool to help capture self-reported personal characteristics, past and present exposure, and environmental risk perception, given their low cost and ease of administration. Technical improvements concerning their administration have updated the utility of this traditional way of collecting data. Smartphone surveys can make survey deployment easier, improve the quality of participants' reported data, offer the ability to collect "enhanced" data (e.g., GPS details about the location of the survey, images of the landscape, as well as the barcode or QR code of a food product), and allow investigators to quickly integrate questionnaire responses into analytical datasets (Turner et al. 2017).

Personal Sensing Technologies

Recent rapid technological advancement in personal sensors offer increased spatial and temporal resolution and real-time data availability to both researchers and citizens, especially workers (Vineis et al. 2020). A broad range of environmental and occupational exposure can be recorded with these devices: noise, temperature, air pollution, radio frequencies, etc. Wristband sensors can also measure basic health data, such as heart and respiratory rates and activity levels. The trend toward increasing precision in various environmental contexts and decreasing prices will yield more reliable exposure estimates both at the individual and population levels.

Geographic Information Technologies

Efforts to characterize exposure have focused on ambient conditions, and an individual was typically assigned to a home address or a worker to a task in an epidemiological health study. Although such exposure assignments have revealed important health risks, they suffer from large measurement errors. Major technological advances in geographic information technologies now offer the possibility to characterize sources and concentrations and to improve our understanding of stressors and receptors when used together with modeling methods and other data.

Global positioning systems (GPSs), which are now embedded in cellular telephones and vehicle navigation systems, provide the accurate location of an individual in time and space. Geocoded data have been used extensively in exposure assessment studies, linking the location of an individual with environmental measurements (e.g., air or water quality). Geolocation technologies are increasingly combined with cellular telephones equipped with location, motion, and pollution sensors, providing more detailed estimates of individual exposure. At the community level, the combination of GPS and sensor technologies with geographic information systems (GISs) provide temporally and spatially resolved data for understanding patterns of exposure (e.g., high-exposure locations leading to source identification). Crowdsourcing methods, customized smartphones, and interactive mapping websites are increasingly being used for specific pollutants and exposure routes (e.g., air pollution), both to assess personal exposure and to visualize environmental and occupational conditions at a local level.

Remote sensing (i.e., the acquisition and processing of satellite data) can measure multiple dimensions of the environment (earth's surface, water, and atmosphere) across time and space more broadly and frequently than traditional technologies (such as ground-based monitoring systems). Enhancing the capacity to assess human and ecological exposure, satellite imagery has been used to estimate an expanding list of types of exposure: concentrations of air pollutants (NO_2, O_3, and $PM_{2.5}$), surface temperature, the built-up environment, land cover classification, water quality, outdoor light at night, etc. Moreover, remote sensing can identify high-exposure locations and source locations on a population scale or at the workplace by mapping pollutant concentrations and identifying exposure patterns that might be related to sources.

Exposure Modeling

External exposure modeling can be deterministic or stochastic. Where the concentration of (or exposure to) pollutants of interest is little monitored, modeling becomes important to elucidate the value of measured data to address data gaps and enhance the application of monitored data to exposure and risk assessment.

Geostatistical methods, such as kernel density estimation or kriging, can predict environmental intensities at unsampled locations, provided the sample points (monitoring stations) are densely and evenly spread. Moreover, kriging not only provides a modeled surface but also yields estimates of its standard deviation at each location. The reliability of the pollution surface can thus be examined and exposure estimates weighted accordingly.

Dispersion models consist of mathematical representations of the processes that generate pollutants and control their movement, dilution, and fate in the environment. They provide realistic estimations of exposure so long as the processes are sufficiently well understood and can be simulated by the available data. Such propagation models have been successfully applied to various forms of pollution: air pollutants, road traffic or industrial noise, radio frequencies emitted by base stations, chlorination by-products in drinking water systems, biological exposure (viruses), etc.

Multimedia models are used to simulate the fate, transport, transformation, and ultimate concentration of chemicals through a range of environmental compartments (such as ambient air, soil, groundwater, indoor air, dust, and consumer products). Such models are widely used to characterize and predict exposure, as well as in regulation concerning chemicals to assist decision making, especially if there is a lack of monitoring data. Recent advances in exposure models and frameworks that couple the far field (outdoors) and near field (indoors) are promising.

Hybrid models use source-based information, monitoring data, geographical or physical modeling, job types, and covariates of pollution to improve exposure data. For example, such an approach combining remote sensing technologies, ground-based monitoring, meteorological data, and land use variables provides concentration estimates of ambient air pollutants on a relatively fine spatial scale.

Concerning chemicals, in addition to modeling external exposure, physiologically based pharmacokinetic (PBPK) modeling allows the prediction of kinetics (i.e., absorption, distribution, metabolism, and excretion) to assess the internal dose of xenobiotics in humans. PBPK modeling may also be used, in combination with computational systems biology, to explore the toxicity of occupational mixtures (Ruiz et al. 2020) or to predict lifelong exposure to persistent organic chemicals (Verner et al. 2008).

Omics and Bioinformatics Tools

Omics and bioinformatics tools use high-throughput technologies to detect and interpret exposure-related changes in genes (genomics, adductomics), mRNA (transcriptomics), proteins (proteomics), and metabolites (metabolomics). Emerging high-throughput exposure models of external exposure will provide exposure estimates that complement those made through expanded biomonitoring programs for more refined individual-level exposure assessments on large human populations. Similar to environmental health, the successful implementation of omics in occupation health requires appropriate study designs, thorough the validation of markers, and careful interpretation of study results (Vlaanderen et al. 2010). For this purpose, metabolomics tools show promise, as they can explore the early biological changes associated with exposure (Bonvallot et al. 2018). Applications to worker populations are already available (Kuo et al. 2012; Jeanneret et al. 2014).

Occupational Databases

Several approaches based on matching data from various sources may be used to estimate the worksome. Lifetime occupational exposure could be estimated by linking job histories collected in a population sample and job exposure matrices using international standards for the classification of occupations, industry classification codes, and occupational periods (Houot et al. 2021). Statistical frameworks have been developed to process occupational disease surveillance data collected by medical experts in the form of an evolving network of relationships between diseases and multiple occupational exposure (Faisandier et al. 2011). The exposome of a specific disease may thus be described with different embedded exposure groups, some of which are more highly represented than others. Other approaches have used multiple factor analyses and hierarchical classification on data from medical monitoring of employee exposure to identify homogeneous profiles of multiple exposure considering chemical, physical, and biological risk factors, as well as organizational and psychosocial hazards (Fourneau et al. 2021).

Multidisciplinary Consortia

Given the complexity and costs of exposome studies, there is an obvious need to promote data sharing and cross-discipline collaboration (Stingone et al. 2017) and to create large interdisciplinary consortia. The European Human Exposome Network, which involves more than 100 research groups in nine large-scale projects, will allow the development of a new toolbox, in particular in the field of prevention to improve health at work (EPHOR project, https://www.humanexposome.eu/). Other relevant examples are HBM4EU (for advancing human biomonitoring in Europe), delivering better evidence on the chemical exposure of citizens (Santonen et al. 2019; Jeddi et al. 2021), and HHEAR, providing a resource for implementing life-stage exposure studies within existing study populations (Viet et al. 2021).

The Main Remaining Challenges

Further developments are needed to improve our knowledge of the worksome.

Conceptual and Societal Challenges

According to Wild (2012), the exposome is unlikely to be characterized for a given individual. Thus, the goal of exposome studies is to better understand disease etiology and environmental risk factors at the population level rather than at the individual level. Therefore, for the time being, benefits are expected in the public health domain (rather than in personalized medicine). To fully address this challenge, the exposome framework should be expanded to better account for the social and political forces that produce hazards and distribute them inequitably, at the workplace and in the general environment (Senier et al. 2017).

Citizens or workers can contribute to exposome studies not only as subjects wearing sensors (crowdsourcing), but as fully informed partners in the research process (Land-Zandstra et al. 2016). More broadly, researchers should engage stakeholders (community members, industry representatives, trade unions, policymakers, research funders, etc.) in formulating research questions, collecting and interpreting data, and disseminating research findings to each audience. Stakeholder engagement has matured globally and has reached the evolutionary point whereby it could represent a standard component of any public health (including the exposome) study.

Despite impressive technological breakthroughs for measurement of the internal and external environment of individuals (analytical chemistry, personal sensing, data mining, etc.), it is crucial to restore or adapt the balance between technology-driven and conceptually driven approaches to avoid fishing expeditions and spurious results. Moreover, as more detailed space-time and personal data (including social contacts and individual behavior) can be captured using these new technologies, careful consideration concerning privacy concerns is required.

Technical Challenges

Technical challenges concern the measurement, integration, and interpretation of data, as well as the development of innovative bioinformatics tools (David et al. 2021). It is not possible to identify and quantify the numerous environmental agents and their analytes that exist at low levels. Aside from analytical measurement errors, quality insurance is at stake. Consequently, reference values are still missing for numerous xenobiotics and biomarkers that are considered in the exposome, even more so for exposure mixtures.

In addition, exposure measurements come from multiple data sources that are heterogeneous in terms of syntax, semantics, spatial and temporal scales, and data domains. Furthermore, most information is fragmented, incompletely organized, and not readily available. Despite this variety and the huge amount of data, a high-velocity process is expected for optimal use. First, powerful and robust statistical techniques are needed to account for the specific characteristics of exposome data: complex correlations, repeated longitudinal data, hierarchical structure, measurement error, variability over time and between subjects, etc. Multiple hypothesis testing brings additional statistical challenges. Several statistical methods are already available to assess exposome-health associations and differ in terms of the balance between sensitivity and the proportion of false discovery and between computational complexity and parsimony (Santos et al. 2020). Concerning multiomics data, several approaches may lead to improved results in this field (Rappoport and Shamir 2018). Second, informatics must provide a coherent framework for dealing with massive multiscale population data, requiring innovative research on data management, analysis, and visualization (▶ Chap. 7, "Challenges of Large Cohort and Massive Data in Occupational Health"). New frameworks to interpret multiscale omics data are emerging, with the goal of performing a comprehensive analysis of the exposome and its relationship with health outcomes and molecular signatures (Hernandez-Ferrer et al. 2019). Finally, the combination of qualitative and quantitative data could help to increase the validity of exposure estimations. This may require the development of mixed methods to better address the complexity of the exposome, as encountered in other areas of public health (evaluation of health care intervention, programs, or public policies, for example) (Palinkas et al. 2019).

Causality Challenges
In the exposome context, the issue of causality, central to observational research, is even more complex because, among other aspects, various environmental agents can be highly correlated. Reverse causality bias is also of particular concern. Does a given biomarker precede the deficiency or is it a consequence of an early physiological disturbance? The "meet-in-the-middle" approach, which proposes to measure intermediate biomarkers in relation to external exposure, could help to explore the biological plausibility of such associations (Vineis et al. 2013).

The selection of pollutants that share the same modes of action to include mechanistic considerations in the risk assessment process can provide a more detailed understanding of the biological plausibility of effect biomarkers, an important criterion for the causality discussion (Jeddi et al. 2021). More classical toxicological methods may also be used to account for multiple aspects of the exposome in experimental models, as recently proposed by combining occupational factors and dietary habits with the collection of biological samples during critical life stages (Antonini et al. 2020).

Conclusion

The history of the exposome concept shows that the measurement of internal exposure (qualified as biomarkers and largely described by Wild [2005, 2012]) has most often been associated with research on the etiology of human diseases.

However, in the area of public health (including occupational health), association of the measurement of "internal" exposure with "external" exposure (i.e., environmental measurements, physical living environment) is still necessary to better prevent diseases by reducing exposure sources.

Our scientific understanding of how exogenous environmental exposure is internalized by an organism and how such exposure is related to endogenous exposure of target organs is in its formative stages. Environmental exposure can leave molecular fingerprints that are detectable for application in epidemiological studies. Omics tools could possibly identify biomarkers on the causal pathway (eventually linked to biomarkers of exposure), increasing the possibility for a better understanding of how various agents of external exposure interact with internal molecules, as conceptualized in the "meet-in-the-middle approach" (Vineis et al. 2013). This approach involves a prospective search for intermediate (omics) biomarkers that are linked to the health outcome under consideration and a retrospective search that links the intermediate biomarkers to past exposure of the environmental agent of concern. If a potential pathway to a disease is found, further exploration is needed.

Environmental and occupational health scientists should remain committed to the broad scope of the original exposome concept and continue to refine tools and methods to capture the broadest possible array of environmental exposure and analyze it as a multilevel phenomenon. There can be no skepticism or over-enthusiasm: the road will still be long to operationalize the notion of occupational exposome, but this is the way to follow while still respecting ethical principles.

Cross-References

▶ Challenges of Large Cohort and Massive Data in Occupational Health
▶ Job-Exposure Matrices: Design, Validation, and Limitations

References

Antonini JM, Kodali V, Shoeb M, Kashon M, Roach KA, Boyce G et al (2020) Effect of a high-fat diet and occupational exposure in different rat strains on lung and systemic responses: examination of the exposome in an animal model. Toxicol Sci 174:100–111. https://doi.org/10.1093/toxsci/kfz247

Bonvallot N, David A, Chalmel F, Chevrier C, Cordier S, Cravedi JP et al (2018) Metabolomics as a powerful tool to decipher the biological effects of environmental contaminants in humans. Curr Opin Toxicol 8:48–56. https://doi.org/10.1016/j.cotox.2017.12.007

Bonvallot N, Tremblay-Franco M, Chevrier C, Canlet C, Debrauwer L, Cravedi JP et al (2014) Potential input from metabolomics for exploring and understanding the links between environment and health. J Toxicol Environ Health-Part B-Crit Rev 17:21–44. https://doi.org/10.1080/10937404.2013.860318

Chaker J, Gilles E, Léger T, Jégou B, David A (2021) From metabolomics to HRMS-based exposomics: adapting peak picking and developing scoring for MS1 suspect screening. Anal Chem 93:1792–1800. https://doi.org/10.1021/acs.analchem.0c04660

David A, Chaker J, Price EJ, Bessonneau V, Chetwynd AJ, Vitale CM et al (2021) Towards a comprehensive characterisation of the human internal chemical exposome: challenges and perspectives. Environ Int 156:106630. https://doi.org/10.1016/j.envint.2021.106630

Evanoff B, Yung M, Buckner-Petty S, Hviid Andersen J, Roquelaure Y, Descatha A et al (2019) The CONSTANCES job exposure matrix based on self-reported exposure to physical risk factors: development and evaluation. Occup Environ Med 76:398–406. https://doi.org/10.1136/oemed-2018-105287

Eyles E, Manley D, Jones K (2019) Occupied with classification: which occupational classification scheme better predicts health outcomes? Soc Sci Med 227:56–62. https://doi.org/10.1016/j.socscimed.2018.09.020

Faisandier L, Bonneterre V, De Gaudemaris R, Bicout DJ (2011) Occupational exposome: a network-based approach for characterizing occupational health problems. J Biomed Inform 44:545–552. https://doi.org/10.1016/j.jbi.2011.02.010

Fevotte J, Dananché B, Delabre L, Ducamp S, Garras L, Houot M et al (2011) Matgéné: a program to develop job-exposure matrices in the general population in France. Ann Occup Hyg 55:865–878. https://doi.org/10.1093/annhyg/mer067

Fourneau C, Sanchez M, Perouel G, Fréry N, Coutrot T, Boulanger G et al (2021) The French 2016-2020 National Occupational Health Plan: a better understanding of multiple exposures. Environ Risque Sante 20:377–382. https://doi.org/10.1684/ers.2021.1570

Goldberg M, Carton M, Descatha A, Leclerc A, Roquelaure Y, Santin G et al (2017) CONSTANCES: a general prospective population-based cohort for occupational and environmental epidemiology: cohort profile. Occup Environ Med 74:66–71. https://doi.org/10.1136/oemed-2016-103678

Hardy EM, Dereumeaux C, Guldner L, Briand O, Vandentorren S, Oleko A et al (2021) Hair versus urine for the biomonitoring of pesticide exposure: results from a pilot cohort study on pregnant women. Environ Int 152:106481. https://doi.org/10.1016/j.envint.2021.106481

Hernandez-Ferrer C, Wellenius GA, Tamayo I, Basagaña X, Sunyer J, Vrijheid M et al (2019) Comprehensive study of the exposome and omic data using rexposome Bioconductor packages. Bioinformatics 35:5344–5345. https://doi.org/10.1093/bioinformatics/btz526

Holland N (2017) Future of environmental research in the age of epigenomics and exposomics. Rev Environ Health 32:45–54. https://doi.org/10.1515/reveh-2016-0032

Holmes E, Loo RL, Stamler J, Bictash M, Yap IK, Chan Q et al (2008) Human metabolic phenotype diversity and its association with diet and blood pressure. Nature 453:396–400. https://doi.org/10.1038/nature06882

Houot M-T, Homère J, Goulard H, Garras L, Delabre L, Pilorget C (2021) Lifetime occupational exposure proportion estimation methods: a sensitivity analysis in the general population. Int Arch Occup Environ Health 94:1537–1547. https://doi.org/10.1007/s00420-021-01691-1

Jeanneret F, Boccard J, Badoud F, Sorg O, Tonoli D, Pelclova D et al (2014) Human urinary biomarkers of dioxin exposure: analysis by metabolomics and biologically driven data dimensionality reduction. Toxicol Lett 230:234–243. https://doi.org/10.1016/j.toxlet.2013.10.031

Jeddi ZM, Hopf NB, Viegas S, Price AB, Paini A, van Thriel C et al (2021) Towards a systematic use of effect biomarkers in population and occupational biomonitoring. Environ Int 146:106257. https://doi.org/10.1016/j.envint.2020.106257

Juarez P, Matthews-Juarez P, Hood D, Im W, Levine R, Kilbourne B et al (2014) The public health exposome: a population-based, exposure science approach to health disparities research. Int J Environ Res Public Health 11:12866–12895. https://doi.org/10.3390/ijerph111212866

Kuijpers E, van Wel L, Loh M, Galea KS, Makris KC, Stierum R et al (2021) A scoping review of technologies and their applicability for exposome-based risk assessment in the oil and gas industry. Ann Work Expo Health 65:1011–1028. https://doi.org/10.1093/annweh/wxab039

Kuo CH, Wang KC, Tian TF, Tsai MH, Chiung YM, Hsiech CM et al (2012) Metabolomic characterization of laborers exposed to welding fumes. Chem Res Toxicol 25:676–686. https://doi.org/10.1021/tx200465e

Land-Zandstra AM, Devilee JLA, Snik F, Buurmeijer F, van den Broek J (2016) Citizen science on a smartphone: participants' motivations and learning. Public Underst Sci 25:45–60. https://doi.org/10.1177/0963662515602406

Lioy PJ, Rappaport SM (2011) Exposure science and the exposome: an opportunity for coherence in the environmental health sciences. Environ Health Perspect 119:A466–A467. https://doi.org/10.1289/ehp.1104387

National Academies of Sciences, Engineering, and Medicine (2017) Using 21st century science to improve risk-related evaluations. National Academy Press, Washington D.C. https://doi.org/10.17226/24635

National Research Council (2012) Exposure science in the 21st century: a vision and a strategy. National Academies Press, Washington, D.C. https://doi.org/10.17226/13507

Palinkas LA, Mendon SJ, Hamilton AB (2019) Innovations in mixed methods evaluations. Annu Rev Public Health 40:423–442. https://doi.org/10.1146/annurev-publhealth-040218-044215

Rappaport SM, Smith MT (2010) Environment and disease risks. Science 330:460–461. https://doi.org/10.1126/science.1192603

Rappoport N, Shamir R (2018) Multi-omic and multi-view clustering algorithms: review and cancer benchmark. Nucleic Acids Res 46:10546–10562. https://doi.org/10.1093/nar/gky889

Reedijk M, Lenters V, Slottje P, Pijpe A, Peeters H, Korevaar JC et al (2018) Cohort profile: LIFEWORK, a prospective cohort study on occupational and environmental risk factors and health in The Netherlands. BMJ Open 8:e018504. https://doi.org/10.1136/bmjopen-2017-018504

Ruiz P, Emond C, McLanahan ED, Joshi-Barr S, Mumtaz M (2020) Exploring mechanistic toxicity of mixtures using PBPK modeling and computational systems biology. Toxicol Sci 174:38–50. https://doi.org/10.1093/toxsci/kfz243

Santonen T, Alimonti A, Bocca B, Duca RC, Galea KS, Godderis L et al (2019) Setting up a collaborative European human biological monitoring study on occupational exposure to hexavalent chromium. Environ Res 177:108583. https://doi.org/10.1016/j.envres.2019.108583

Santos S, Maitre L, Warembourg C, Agier L, Richiardi L, Basagaña X et al (2020) Applying the exposome concept in birth cohort research: a review of statistical approaches. Eur J Epidemiol 35:193–204. https://doi.org/10.1007/s10654-020-00625-4

Senier L, Brown P, Shostak S, Hanna B (2017) The socio-exposome: advancing exposure science and environmental justice in a postgenomic era. Environ Sociol 3:107–121. https://doi.org/10.1080/23251042.2016.1220848

Stingone JA, Buck Louis GM, Nakayama SF, Vermeulen RCH, Kwok RK, Cui Y et al (2017) Toward greater implementation of the exposome research paradigm within environmental epidemiology. Annu Rev Public Health 38:315–327. https://doi.org/10.1146/annurev-publhealth-082516-012750

Turner MC, Nieuwenhuijsen M, Anderson K, Balshaw D, Cui Y, Dunton G et al (2017) Assessing the exposome with external measures: commentary on the state of the science and research recommendations. Annu Rev Public Health 38:215–239. https://doi.org/10.1146/annurev-publhealth-082516-012802

Verner MA, Charbonneau M, López-Carrillo L, Haddad S (2008) Physiologically based pharmacokinetic modeling of persistent organic pollutants for lifetime exposure assessment: a new tool in breast cancer epidemiologic studies. Environ Health Perspect 116:886–892. https://doi.org/10.1289/ehp.10917

Viet SM, Falman JC, Merrill LS, Faustman EM, Savitz DA, Mervish N et al (2021) Human health exposure analysis resource (HHEAR): a model for incorporating the exposome into health studies. Int J Hyg Environ Health 235:113768. https://doi.org/10.1016/j.ijheh.2021.113768

Vineis P, Robinson O, Chadeau-Hyam M, Dehghan A, Mudway I, Dagnino S (2020) What is new in the exposome? Environ Int 143:105887. https://doi.org/10.1016/j.envint.2020.105887

Vineis P, van Veldhoven K, Chadeau-Hyam M, Athersuch TJ (2013) Advancing the application of omics-based biomarkers in environmental epidemiology. Environ Mol Mutagen 54:461–467. https://doi.org/10.1002/em.21764

Vlaanderen J, Moore LE, Smith MT, Lan Q, Zhang L, Skibola CF et al (2010) Application of OMICS technologies in occupational and environmental health research; current status and projections. Occup Environ Med 67:136–143. https://doi.org/10.1136/oem.2008.042788

Vorkamp K, Castaño A, Antignac J-P, Boada LD, Cequier E, Covaci A et al (2021) Biomarkers, matrices and analytical methods targeting human exposure to chemicals selected for a European human biomonitoring initiative. Environ Int 146:106082. https://doi.org/10.1016/j.envint.2020.106082

Vrijheid M, Basagaña X, Gonzalez JR, Jaddoe WV, Genon J, Keun HC et al (2021) Advancing tools for human early lifecourse exposome research and translation (ATHLETE). Environ Epidemiol 5:e166. https://doi.org/10.1097/EE9.0000000000000166

Wild CP (2005) Complementing the genome with an "exposome": the outstanding challenge of environmental exposure measurement in molecular epidemiology. Cancer Epidemiol Biomark Prev 14:1847–1850. https://doi.org/10.1158/1055-9965.EPI-05-0456

Wild CP (2012) The exposome: from concept to utility. Int J Epidemiol 41:24–32. https://doi.org/10.1093/ije/dyr236

Methods in Modeling Life Course

9

Adrien Le Guillou and Pascal Wild

Contents

Introduction	138
Sequence Analysis	139
Analysis of Growth Trajectories	141
Tracing the Average Z-scores	141
The Life Course Plot and Path Analysis	142
Conditional Models for Independent Variables	142
Regression Models with Change Scores	143
Multilevel Models	143
Latent Growth Curve Models	144
Growth Mixture Models	144
Hierarchy of Life Course Hypotheses: A Bayesian Approach	145
Causal Inference in Life Course Epidemiology	147
Discussion	151
References	152

Abstract

Life course epidemiology (LCE) is a subfield of epidemiology that emphasizes the timing of events over and above cumulative exposure. This implies that the data at hand are mostly observational, longitudinal, and with repeated measures. Describing the data, formulating life course hypotheses and testing them requires specific conceptual and statistical tools. In this chapter, we provide an overview of some statistical methods based on four LCE papers both methodological and subject matter based. Although not exhaustive, this selection covers both sides of

---

A. Le Guillou (✉)
Department of Epidemiology, Emory University, Atlanta, GA, USA
e-mail: contact@aleguillou.org

P. Wild
PW Statistical Consulting, Laxou, France
e-mail: pascal@pw-statistical-consulting.eu

© Springer Nature Switzerland AG 2023
M. Wahrendorf et al. (eds.), *Handbook of Life Course Occupational Health*, Handbook Series in Occupational Health Sciences, https://doi.org/10.1007/978-3-031-30492-7_13

the theory building process. First, purely descriptive methods requiring few or no hypotheses are presented. At the other end, we describe the framework to formally formulate life course hypotheses. With them come several statistical methods to measure how well they hold up against real-life data. Along the way, many difficulties such as missing data, heterogeneous data sources, and hypothesis hierarchy are discussed with tools and approaches available to handle them.

Keywords

Life course epidemiology · Methodology · Statistical methods · Modeling · Sequence analysis · Growth curves · Trajectories · Bayesian statistics · Causal inference

Introduction

Life course epidemiology is, according to Kuh and Ben-Shlomo (Kuh 2003), the study of long-term processes that link adult health or socioeconomic states (our addition) to physical or social exposures acting previously in life or even across generations. It could be argued that in this sense, there is nothing specific with life course epidemiology as most of the chronic disease epidemiology uses some function of the past exposure as independent variables, e.g., duration of exposure, cumulative exposure, or exposure in specific time windows (see, e.g., Colin et al.). However, what could be seen as a simple difference in scale quickly becomes a difference in kind as specific questions arise and new difficulties are to be tackled. Indeed, one tends to reserve the term life course epidemiology to situations in which repeated longitudinal data (panel data) are available over long periods.

In 2016, Ben-Shlomo et al. (2016) gave a revised view of their earlier models (Kuh 2003) in light of two decades of life course epidemiology research. As mentioned in this paper, the main specificity of LCE is the emphasis on the timing of events over and above cumulative exposure. The way they describe the main framework is as an accumulation model over time where different periods can have different importance as predictors of the outcome. Within this framework, they distinguish sensitive and critical periods where the latter is a period where the exposure must occur, i.e., the exposure has no effect if it does not occur in this period, whereas the former only increases the risk. These periods can also interact with one another to create chains of risk. An example cited in this paper related to smoking as a risk factor of breast cancer. Cumulative smoking as measured in pack-years on its own does not capture the whole picture. Adding puberty as a sensitive period shows that for constant pack-years, those who smoked during puberty are at higher risk. Starting from this framework, a host of statistical models were used to explicitly model trajectories. This in turn stimulated the development of methods to differentiate between competing models.

However, these models and the expansion of the scope of study to the full life of an individual makes the issue of mediation, confounders, and time-varying intermediaries even more complex as many more exposures are now included in the study period. To help with this aspect, LCE greatly benefited from the growing literature on directed acyclic graph and their uses in causal inference (De Stavola and Daniel 2016; Pearl 2000). This equips the researcher with a tool that serves two purposes. On the first hand, DAGs are a communication device to present the reader with an explicit account of the theoretical models and the hypothesis that it implies (Pearl et al. 2016).

Such clarity is a necessity for the explicit formulation of hypotheses on which the analyses are based but also for the peer review process to work as expected. Indeed, reviewers cannot criticize what is not fully understood. On the other hand, DAGs can also inform the researcher on the minimal set of covariates to include in its statistical model to have it show the desired unconfounded effect according to the theoretical model chosen. This is particularly important as the relevant data is hard to come by. In Chap. 40 of the Handbook of Epidemiology, Ben-Shlomo et al. described LCE as being a speculation-rich data-sparse environment (Ahrens and Pigeot 2014).

In addition to the theoretical complexity added by looking at the whole life of individuals, this also exacerbates the logistical difficulties of working with longitudinal data. These issues are numerous and include missing data, disparities in the measurements over time and over different sources, and how to manage repeated measurements.

As is always the case in research, there is no single way to tackle these issues. In this chapter, we provide an overview of some statistical methods based on four LCE papers both methodological and subject matter based. Although this overview does not pretend to be exhaustive, it covers a relatively large spectrum of methods from mostly data-based methods (sequence analysis) to an explicit theory-based paper.

Sequence Analysis

Sequence analysis refers to an approach to longitudinal data that focuses on sequences (e.g., work histories) as a whole. As such it is different from the framework described by Ben-Shlomo and coworkers who identify or hypothesize periods to be either sensitive or critical as predictors of later mostly health-related events. Such is not the purpose of sequence analysis which originated in the work in sociology of Abbott (1983, p. 83).

Sequence analysis is often exploratory and descriptive in intention, typically oriented to generating data-driven typologies. It does not focus, contrary to other approaches we will present in this chapter, on modeling the processes generating the sequences. For example, in the paper by Eisenberg-Guyot et al. (2020), the authors consider life course trajectories of what they term employment quality based on a large US panel study conducted among respondents followed up from ages 29–31 to 48–51. They identified five clusters among women and seven clusters among men based on yearly sequences of a series of indicators (e.g., union membership) characterizing, respectively, employment stability, material rewards, and working time arrangements.

The way these typologies of sequences are obtained is by performing cluster analyses on the individual sequences (trajectories). A prerequisite for any clustering algorithm is the existence of a measure of the distance (or dissimilarity) between the sequences which allow to regroup the "closest" trajectories in order to form clusters. Several measures of dissimilarity between sequences have been proposed starting with the so-called optimal matching (OM) which has been proposed in the early applications of sequence analysis in sociology (see Abbott and Forrest 1986) and has since then been successfully applied in bioinformatics for (among others) comparing DNA sequences. An OM distance between two sequences is basically the number of substitutions one has to make in one sequence before it is identical to the other. Other dissimilarity measures include the longest common subsequence (LCS), the Hamming distance (HD), and dynamic Hamming distance (DHD).

Studer and Ritschard (2016) compare the different measures and conclude that there is no universally optimal distance index and that the choice depends on which aspect one wants to focus on. They nevertheless provide some guidelines as to which measure to choose. Once a relevant dissimilarity metric has been chosen, basically all clustering algorithms can be applied but hierarchical clustering (HC) is by far the most commonly used. HC starts by agglomerating the closest sequences and sequentially regroups the closest groups of sequences until all sequences have been merged in one group. There are still several options (the so-called linkage options) on how to implement HC in the way one computes the dissimilarity between groups. The most common options are single linkage (the proximity between two groups is the proximity between the closest pairs in the two groups), complete linkage (the proximity between two groups is the proximity between the furthest pairs in the two groups), and average linkage (the proximity between two groups is the average of the proximities between all the pairs in the two groups). The final choice to be made is the number of clusters to be interpreted. This number is usually taken on the basis of substantive considerations but can also rely on the silhouette method (Rousseeuw 1987). The silhouette method computes silhouette coefficients of each point that measure how much a point is similar to its own cluster compared to other clusters.

Coming back to our motivating example (Eisenberg-Guyot et al. 2020), the authors used the DHD for each channel (dimension of EQ) and summed these distances to get a summary dissimilarity matrix. The already mentioned five clusters among women were chosen based both on substantive considerations and silhouette widths. The average silhouette width (ASW) was highest for four clusters, but as written by the authors "this four-cluster solution lacked typologies found in prior research (e.g., a precariously-employed cluster), while six-to-ten cluster solutions had low ASWs and clusters with small sizes." Up to now, we concentrated on the typology identification part, but in most applications of sequence analyses in life course analyses, there is the consideration of how the identified clusters are related to health. When assessing differences in health within the sequence analysis, standard (longitudinal) regression models are generally applied. In our motivating example, prevalence ratios for self-rated (poor) health and moderated mental illness were presented among each cluster relative to the prevalence among their reference cluster (standard employment relationships like nonunion workers). These prevalence ratios were obtained using Poisson generalized estimated equations with family-clan-level exchangeable correlations structure and cluster-robust standard errors.

However, sequence analyses have their drawbacks. Even when individual longitudinal life course data are available, sequence analyses are not always applicable. Indeed, in order to apply these methods, in particular to be able to compute the distances between trajectories, one must have the same numbers of items available at the same times, i.e., all sequences have the same lengths and can be aligned. Thus, any missing item means that it must be either imputed or the entire sequence must be dropped. In our motivating example, "when respondents missed a wave or had missing values invariables of interest, we carried their forwards from the prior wave," but in this paper variables had less than 4% missingness, which seems acceptable.

Finally, there are two packages we know of that implement sequence analysis: first the R-package TraMineR (Gabadinho et al. 2011) and second the series of stata tools SADI (Halpin 2017). The latter acknowledges that it provides similar functionality to the R package but claims to be substantially faster than the latter.

Analysis of Growth Trajectories

The present section is based on a comparison of statistical approaches of a life course dataset considering the developmental origins of health and disease hypotheses published by Tu et al. (Tu et al. 2013). The dataset consisted of the body weights of 960 boys measured immediately after birth and at ages 1, 2, 8, 15, and 19 years as well as systolic blood pressure (SBP) measured at age 19. The dataset is a subset of a larger set so that in the considered dataset none of the listed data was missing. However, at ages 8, 15, and 19 years the body weights were measured at only roughly the same ages. The hypothesis to be tested is "that small birth size in conjunction with rapid compensatory childhood growth might yield a greater risk of developing ... coronary heart disease (CHD)." The methods presented in this section actually model parametrically the effect of the independent variables and their evolution on the health outcome but their primary goal is not to focus on specific periods.

The different statistical approaches we present following this paper go from the simplest to more sophisticated methods.

Tracing the Average Z-scores

The first mentioned method is computing and graphing z-scores, that is by subtracting at each age, the sample average weights from individual weights and dividing by the sample standard deviations. It is then used by computing averaged z-scores in groups defined by the health outcomes. While this method has the advantage of being simple and is straightforward to implement, it can only be used in absence of any missing data. Moreover, it is just a connection of a series of cross-sectional associations at different ages and their interpretation can easily be subject to statistical artifacts. Indeed "substantial upward or downward slopes reflect ages during which the magnitude of the association of body size with health outcomes is changing rapidly, rather than average growth trajectories."

The Life Course Plot and Path Analysis

The life course plot belongs to the approaches based on conditioning, i.e., which estimate the relation between the outcome and the body weight at a given age adjusting for the body weights at other ages in the same model. The life course model uses a multiple regression model including the different age-specific weights (or their z-scores). The age-specific regression coefficients are then plotted against the corresponding ages. A change in the direction is then interpreted as indicating a critical phase of the relationship between growth and later CHD.

A major difficulty in the interpretation arises from the collinearity among the body weight measurements at different ages. It may well be (and this was the case in the dataset considered) that regression coefficients have different signs at different ages which may be entirely due to this collinearity. Collinearity causes unstable regression coefficients and wide confidence intervals which might preclude the identification of critical periods. Another issue with this method is that one conditions on measures that were taken later in time. The path analysis is very similar to the life course plot but tries to estimate direct and indirect (causal) paths in one model. Path analyses were developed as far back than the 1930s in the context of psychometry as a way to explicitly deal with causal types of relationships. Correspondingly, specific software (e.g., LISREL or MPLus) was developed very early on. In recent years, however, path analysis has been considered as a subclass of structural equation modeling which is available within many packages (SAS, Stata) or as stand-alone packages (e.g., AMOS).

Conditional Models for Independent Variables

Conditional body weight (in our example) is defined as the difference between observed and predicted body weight. The predicted body weight at a given age is obtained by regressing the observed weight on all precedingly recorded weights since birth and potentially other variables. This residual error is thus uncorrelated to the covariates measured previously and all preceding conditional body weights. In the conditional body weight approach, the health outcome in later life is regressed on all conditional body weights plus the initial (birth) weight. Thus, the two issues of collinearity and adjusting on future events are to some extent taken into account. The interpretation of the results of this model is therefore straightforward: the expected change in SBP given the conditional body weights, conditional on all previous weights. Thus, if a given period has a specific impact, this will theoretically allow detection of such an impact. It must be noted that statistically this method is completely equivalent to a series of multiple regression models with raw body size measures included one by one. As noted by the authors, "this method may not completely resolve the collinearity and associated issues.(...) the size of the standard error is likely to increase with age, since the number of other weight measures included in the model increases."

Regression Models with Change Scores

Oftentimes, the kinetics of the trajectories are what interests us more than the values themselves. In these situations, regression with change scores allows us to examine the effect of the speed of growth. In the dataset considered, the SBP would be regressed on either the birth weight or the last weight and the five differences in weights. Compared to the life course plot, this method reduces the collinearity between measurement but changes the meaning of the regression coefficients as they now correspond to changes in weights and not to the weights themselves. However, these models are re-parameterizations of the life course plot model and therefore share its disadvantages.

All models considered as yet in this section can be fitted with any basic software which performs multiple linear regressions. The next three models require more specific software although most of these methods can be fitted using standard professional software like SAS, Stata, or R.

Multilevel Models

Multilevel models (also called mixed models or random effect models) can be considered as the standard model for the statistical analysis of longitudinal data (see, e.g., Singer and Willett 2003) of which growth curve data are just a specific example. Mixed models for longitudinal data consist in the specification of two levels. Multilevel models consist in specifying two (or more in other contexts) levels: a first level consists of variables specified at the subject level and nested within subjects the repeated variables (in our case the measurements of weight at different ages. These models describe the process of development or growth in a random coefficient framework, by assuming that individual observations deviate around a single underlying population trajectory. These models are very flexible and have nonlinear growth (using either polynomials or splines) and complex specifications of variance and covariances within subjects can be included. Many people find this approach to longitudinal data attractive because it allows to explicitly model the shape of trajectories of individual subjects over time and how these trajectories vary both systematically, because of time or subject-specific covariates and randomly. In order to fit such models, the longitudinal data are in the long format, i.e., stacked in one column. This goes with the major advantage of these models in that they do not require that the modeled outcome, i.e., the body weight to be measured at the same ages, neither must the number of ages at which weight is measured be the same, so that subjects with missing observations for some ages can be included. Chapter 7 of Rabe-Hesketh and Skrondal illustrates how these models can be fitted and interpreted for the analysis of growth curves using Stata. There is, however, a drawback in that a second analysis step may be required to test the association between growth and the health outcome in later life.

Latent Growth Curve Models

The latent growth curve model (LGCM) is a special kind of structural equation model (SEM) for longitudinal data (see, e.g., [Everitt and Howell 2005]), redefining certain random coefficients defined in multilevel models as latent factors, but are thus basically equivalent to multilevel models. Its interpretation may, however, be slightly different.

In order to apply SEM, the data must be in wide shape, i.e., the body weights at ages 0–19 are treated as six different variables. In LGCM, the baseline body weight and change in weight are estimated by two latent variables obtained in the measurement part (factor analysis) of the structural equation model. The factor loadings for the first factor are always constrained to 1 so that the first factor is the estimated birth weight. The factor age is incorporated explicitly in the model by constraining the factor loadings of the second factor (the latent variable representing growth velocity) explicitly to its known values to represent the ages at which the weights were measured. This is, however, not a necessary restriction; it is possible to estimate a more general, i.e., nonlinear, model in which the factor loadings are estimated. Thus, instead of constraining the loadings to (0, 1, 2, 8, 15, and 19), some elements are left free to be estimated, providing information on the shape of the growth curve. For the purposes of identification, at least two elements of these need to be fixed. When fixing the first loading to 0 and the last to 19, the four factor loadings estimated by this nonlinear model are 2.0, 2.7, 6.6, and 16.6 for weight at ages 1, 2, 8, and 15 years. This shows, e.g., that the growth between birth and age 1 is about twice than the overall average.

Within SEM, it is straightforward to include the effect of birthweight (first factor) and growth velocity (second factor) on SBP. These associations may, however, be difficult to interpret as these associations are mutually adjusted so that the association between birthweight and later SBP is conditioned on subsequent growth. If the aim is to estimate the effect of growth in different periods on later SBP, more than two latent variables can be specified representing the growth velocities at different age periods.

Growth Mixture Models

The growth mixture model (GMM) is a relatively recent development of LGCMs (see, e.g., Nagin 2005). Repealing the assumption that the entire population is statistically homogeneous, which is intrinsic in the preceding growth curve models, it assumes that there are two or more latent subgroups of the population whose member trajectories appear to be more similar to each other than to the remaining individuals in a given dataset. Each individual is assigned a probability of belonging to a finite number of subgroups, each of which represents a component of a mixture distribution. Assuming homogeneity conditional on trajectory group membership, this model requires, however, that the trajectories are given a parametric shape.

Thus, while this method has some similarities with the sequence analysis presented in the beginning of the chapter in which it is grouping the trajectories, the present method is set within a likelihood framework so that likelihood-based statistics like the Akaike information criterion (AIC) or the Bayesian information criterion (BIC) can be applied to check the fit of this model. Another difference is that for each subgroup one gets an estimated mean trajectory around which the individuals deviate. Packages fitting these models include PROC TRAJ within SAS (Jones et al. 2001) or the lcmm package within R (Proust-Lima et al. 2017).

One major drawback of the GMM is its sensitivity to assumptions regarding the number of latent groups and shape of the trajectories within each group. The usual strategy is to estimate many models differing across these two dimensions and to select the model which maximizes some measure of model fit such as AIC or BIC. In practice, however, these indices may have limited usefulness. In the motivating example presented by the authors, they used a quartic curve for each group and found that both AIC and BIC values reduced with the number of classes. However, when the number increases the interpretation of each class becomes complex and the authors settled finally for a three class model which they viewed as "best" in terms of the balance between model interpretability and complexity. Several papers tackled the issue of numbers of classes, e.g., (Klijn et al. 2017). A recent paper provided a Bayesian model averaging method with respect to the choice of the functional form of the trajectory (Zang and Max 2020).

Hierarchy of Life Course Hypotheses: A Bayesian Approach

In this section, we focus on identifying life periods in which the effect of exposures has the major effects. In order to do so we refer to the typology of life course models proposed by Ben-Schlomo and Kuh (Kuh 2003) that we described in the introduction. Knowing whether the health outcome is affected by the exposure only in a critical period or accumulates over time with multiple sensitive periods is usually the main question.

To answer this question, the different periods and the impact the exposure have in each of them can be formulated as the sum of exposures weighted differently on each period. In a critical model, the critical period is weighted 1 and all other periods are weighted 0. In a sensitive model, the weights are spread across multiple periods and add up to 1. The periods with higher weights are the sensitive periods (Ben-Shlomo et al. 2016). With this formulation, the different models are nested, allowing model comparison (Mishra et al. 2009; Smith et al. 2016).

In their paper, Madathil et al. (2018), propose the so-called Bayesian relevant life course exposure model (RLM) (Madathil et al. 2018) and use it for evaluating the risk of oral cancer due to life course betel quid chewing (HeNCe Life Study (Madathil et al. 2016)). They considered the exposure to betel chewing in three periods (T = 3): up to age 20 years, between 21 and 40 years, and older than 40. Their results show evidence for a sensitive period model with exposures in earlier life having a greater relevance.

To get these contributions, the relevant life course exposure l_{xi} must be as the weighted sum of all exposures in all time periods:

$$l_{xi} = \sum_{t=1}^{T} W_t * x_{ti} \qquad (1)$$

where $t = 1, 2, \ldots, T$ is the temporal ordering of the repeated measurements of the exposure, x_{ti} is the amount of betel chewed on period t for the $i^{th}(i = 1, 2, \ldots, N)$ participant, and W_t is the weight which is to be estimated for exposure at time t. The RLM assumes that each weight takes a value between 0 and 1 and that the sum of all weights is equal to 1.

The outcome y_i is modeled as a generalized linear model $g\{E(y_i)\} = \mu_i$ where $g\{.\}$ is link function, in this case the Logit function for a logistic model:

$$\mu_i = \beta_0 + \delta * l_{xi} + \lambda * C_i \qquad (2)$$

where δ is the lifetime effect for the exposure and $\lambda * C_i$ denotes the other covariates C and their coefficients λ.

As with all Bayesian models, to fit the Bayesian RLM, one has to set priors on the weights. These can be used to express the level of uncertainty about the life course hypotheses. The authors chose a noninformative Dirichlet distribution (Dir(1, 1, 1)) as the goal here is to identify the life course hypothesis supported by the data alone. The Dirichlet distribution is a multivariate distribution where output values are in (0, 1) and add up to 1. It is the multivariate generalization of the Beta distribution.

By taking the median of the posterior distribution of weights the author could express the contribution of each period to the *relevant life course exposure*. These contributions were 70.2%, 23.6%, and 6.1%, respectively; these values show evidence for a sensitive period model with exposures in earlier life having a greater relevance. As is customary with Bayesian analysis, the full posterior was plotted as well as the marginal posterior over each period. Another way of presenting the result is to say that "Among betel quid users, there was 85.3% posterior probability for the hypothesis that 20 years and younger is a sensitive period for betel quid exposure compared with later life periods for the risk of oral cancer. In addition, there was 74.3% posterior probability that betel quid exposure earlier compared with later in life results in higher odds of developing oral cancer."

In this paper, the authors also demonstrated Bayesian RLM on simulation data to prove that it was able to recover the "true" probability of each hypothesis and performed at least as well as other methods for hypotheses selection, namely Mishra et al.'s structural method (Mishra et al. 2009). They further demonstrated the use of informative priors for the weights distribution. This can be useful if the sample size is small, if prior information is available on the subject, or simply as a means to evaluate the robustness of the model. If there is enough data available, as in the example, the choice of prior has little impact as the posterior distribution will be mainly driven by the data.

In this motivating example, Bayesian RLM directly estimated the probabilities that different life course hypotheses were true, conditioned on the observed data and prior beliefs as the use of a Bayesian framework permits to simultaneously estimate the weights and the lifetime effect in a unified model. This framework also offers additional advantages such as the ability to handle measurement error, missing data, or incorporate further hierarchy in the data and parameters.

Bayesian RLM nevertheless has some drawbacks. Given that the *relevant life course exposure* is captured as a single variable and the weights are always positive or 0, the effect of the exposure over time is necessarily one-directional. This means that an exposure cannot increase the risk in one period and reduce it in another. However, such an assumption is likely to be valid for most exposures. Also, and similarly to other strategies proposed for the investigation of life course hypotheses, RLM assumes that there is no time-dependent confounding or effect measure modification. This type of measure modification could occur through the mediation effect of previous periods. Structural models and more complex causal modeling techniques can estimate such effects but they usually address different questions (De Stavola and Daniel 2012).

Finally, Bayesian RLM can be fitted with any Bayesian statistical inference software such as Stan (Stan Development Team 2021), with R, stata, and other, or SAS using PROC MCMC. Madathil et al. provided the code for their model in Stan with RStan and SAS in the supplementary data of their paper. For readers willing to learn Bayesian inference in a more comprehensive course, we recommend "Statistical Rethinking" by Richard McElreath (McElreath 2020) and the recording of the classes by Pr McElreath on YouTube.

Causal Inference in Life Course Epidemiology

Since the beginning of this chapter, we have considered methods that are more or less data driven. The last section corresponds to the other end of the spectrum where the goal is to uncover the mechanisms underlying the effect we observe. Contrary to experimental settings where the researcher isolates the impact of an exposure through random assignment, the causality problem in observational data and in particular life course epidemiology has to be tackled differently. From the 1970s on, Donald Rubin and after him Judea Pearl developed tools to express causal relationships through testable models (Pearl 2000; Rubin 1974, p. 74) in observational data.

In this section, we focus on a study by Carmeli et al. (2020) exploring the multiple causal mechanisms linking early-life socioeconomic position (SEP) to adulthood-heightened inflammation. In this paper, the authors show in detail how they dealt with many of the struggles pertaining to observational research in general and to life course epidemiology in particular.

Because the link between early-life SEP and adulthood-heightened inflammation had been previously studied (Berger et al. 2019), the focus of this paper is on the mediating role of other variables such as educational attainment, occupational position, or financial hardships. The authors thereby explored multiple causal mechanisms linking early-life SEP to adult-heightened inflammation. For this, they used longitudinal data from two Swiss population studies (5152 participants) and applied path-specific mediation based on a counterfactual framework. The first aspect to notice is the use of two different cohorts, SKIPOGH (Alwan et al. 2014) and CoLaus/PsyCoLaus (Firmann et al. 2008). Such pooling is a good way to increase the sample size but comes with a set of difficulties which need to be taken into account. Both cohorts must be similar enough with respect to the elements required by the study at hand (date, population, data gathered, etc.). Here, both studies took place in Switzerland and started in the year 2000. The participants were 18–90 years old in the former and 35–75 years in the later. To fit the question of the study and to be made comparable, some measurements from both cohorts have to be adapted.

The next difficulty to handle with respect to these cohorts is the question of missing data. Often, entries containing missing data are simply removed from the analysis. However, doing so presumes that the data are missing completely at random (MCAR), that is: the probability of an observation being missing does not depend on observed or unobserved measurements. Without this strong hypothesis, the analysis would be biased by this removal. In the present paper, Carmeli et al. hypothesized missingness at random (MAR) which means that given the observed data, the missingness mechanism does not depend on the unobserved data. This hypothesis is less stringent than MCAR and appears more reasonable in practice although it cannot be formally tested. Unlike the missing not at random (MNAR) hypothesis which assumes that missingness depends on unobserved data, it allows the analysis to be performed (Little and Rubin 2019). Under the MAR hypothesis, multiple imputation by chained equations can be performed (Carpenter and Kenward 2013). This method results in the production of multiple datasets (here 20) where the missing data are replaced by imputed values with different initial conditions. The rest of the analysis is then performed on all 20 datasets with their results pooled. Multiple imputation is available in many statistical packages, e.g., the MICE package in R (van Buuren and Groothuis-Oudshoorn 2011), the set of mi programs in Stata or PROC MI, and PROC MIANALYZE in SAS.

To represent the causal structures underlying the study, the authors used the directed acyclic graphs (DAGs) displayed in Fig. 1. When using DAGs, a cause is defined as follows: "A variable X is a direct cause of a variable Y if X appears in the function that assigns Y's value. X is a cause of Y if it is a direct cause of Y, or of any cause of Y" (Pearl et al. 2016). This definition is only about the presence or absence of a variable in a model. It does not make any assumption on the functions themselves. DAGs are a great tool to easily communicate the structural assumptions made by researchers.

9 Methods in Modeling Life Course

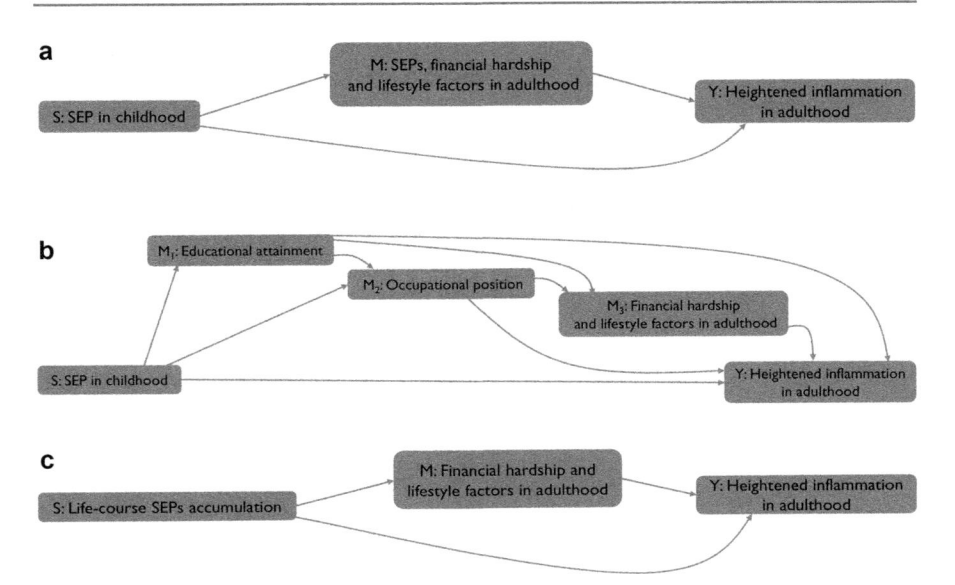

Fig. 1 Causal models posited in the study *Courtesy of Cristian CARMELI.* (**a**) DAG1 of the effect of socioeconomic position (SEP) in childhood (S) on adulthood-heightened inflammation (Y). SEPs (individual's educational attainment and occupational position), financial hardship, and lifestyle factors (BMI, alcohol intake, smoking status, and physical inactivity) in adulthood are considered en bloc mediators M. (**b**) DAG2 of the effect of childhood SEP on adulthood-heightened inflammation through an individual's educational attainment (M1), occupational position (M2), and lifestyle behaviors and financial hardship in adulthood (M3). (**c**) DAG3 of the effect of accumulation of life course SEPs () on adulthood-heightened inflammation. Financial hardship and lifestyle factors in adulthood are considered en bloc mediators

The first two DAGs (Fig. 1a, b) describe how the outcome (Y: heightened inflammation in adulthood) is impacted by the exposure (S: SEP in childhood) directly and indirectly through intermediate mechanisms. In Fig. 1a, the indirect effect represents the joint mediated effect by adulthood SEPs, financial hardship, and lifestyle factors en bloc. No assumption is made on the causal order of these mediators. Figure 1b on the other hand posits that education attainment (M1) causes the occupational position (M2) and that they both impact financial hardship and lifestyle factors in adulthood (M3). Carmeli et al. then describe that in the model based on Fig. 1a, a null indirect effect would be in favor of an early critical period. The DAG from Fig. 1b will help understand if financial hardship and lifestyle behavior in adulthood provide additional mediation compared to socioeconomic positions only. And if so, the paths themselves can be investigated as well. The third DAG (Fig. 1c) is similar to the first one with the exposure being the life course SEPs accumulation. This measure is constructed using a social mobility model, where the SEP trajectory from childhood to adulthood is encoded into a five-level variable: stable high, stable intermediate, stable low, upward, and downward. One can note that contrary to the sequence analysis or the latent class growth curves, these classes were predetermined based on subject knowledge.

To disentangle the direct and indirect effect of the exposure on the outcome via multiple mediators, the authors adopted the counterfactual mediation framework and fitted marginal natural effect models (Lange et al. 2012). To make their methods explicit, the authors define $Y(s, M(s^*))$ as the counterfactual heightened inflammation that would have been observed with low SEP (s) and mediators M to the value it would have taken if exposure were set to high SEPs (s^*). And, with C the set of confounders, the following natural effect model can be written as follows:

$$logit[E\{Y(s, M(s^*))\}|C] = \beta_0 + \beta_1 s + \beta_2 s^* + \beta_3 C \qquad (3)$$

From this equation, one can simultaneously estimate the natural direct effect odd ratio as

$$\frac{odds\{Y(s, M(s^*)) = 1|C\}}{odds\{Y(s^*, M(s^*)) = 1|C\}} = exp\{\beta_1(s - s^*)\}$$

and the natural indirect effect as

$$\frac{odds\{Y(s, M(s)) = 1|C\}}{odds\{Y(s, M(s^*)) = 1|C\}} = exp\{\beta_2(s - s^*)\} \qquad (4)$$

Their product measures the total effect:

$$\frac{odds\{Y(s) = 1|C\}}{odds\{Y(s^*) = 1|C\}} \qquad (5)$$

Fitting natural effect models can be performed with any statistical software. Lange et al. provided examples in SAS and R. Furthermore, the "medflex" package for R (Steen et al. 2017) has been proposed to fit such models.

The model from Fig. 1a showed that individuals with low SEP in childhood had an OR of 1.5 [1.3, 1.8] for heightened inflammation in adulthood and that 59[34, 93]% of it was mediated by adulthood SEPs, financial hardship, and lifestyle factors en bloc. In thepath-specific mediation model (Fig. 1b), the joint indirect effect (through M3) contributed to 33 [14, 69]%, partial mediation through educational attainment to 30 [11, 64]%, and through occupational position to only 3 [−4, 13]%. In the life course occupational positions trajectories model (Fig. 1c), all trajectories had an increased OR of heightened inflammation compared to the stable high one. A 63 [44, 97]% of this effect was mediated through the joint mediation path (M).

These results were interpreted by the authors as in favor of the direct and indirect impact of low SEP in childhood on heightened adulthood inflammation. Furthermore, the results from the path-specific mediation model (Fig. 1b) was in favor of a chain of risk additive model.

The natural effects model allows a relative simplicity in the implementation of the counterfactual framework to estimate direct and indirect effects. However, this comes at the price of relying on correct specification of models for the distribution of mediators (Lange et al. 2012). Indeed, the odd ratios estimated are using observed data as well as their counterfactual counterparts. Therefore, misspecification of the models could lead to biased estimates. Other methods for mediation analysis can circumvent this limitation at the cost of more complicated expressions for the definition of mediators and confounders (VanderWeele 2014, 2014).

Discussion

With this brief overview of several methods that are employed in life course epidemiology, we want to insist on the necessity to put the researchers' question first and only then to choose the methodology to best answer it. When researchers find themselves at the beginning of the theory building process, they will be more inclined to use data-driven approaches to shed new light on their data-set to formulate new hypotheses. Sequence analysis and growth trajectories offer some good tools in this regard. The former would be used with categorical data and the later with quantitative values. They both allow the definition of subgroups which can be used later for inference. On the other hand, when the goal is to formally test causal hypotheses, DAGs are almost a necessity as they allow the precise description of the models to be tested. Then, several frameworks, such as Bayesian, structural equations, natural effect models, etc. exist. They each come with trade-offs in terms of complexity, resilience to unaligned data, ability to work around missing data, etc. Overall, designing a life course analysis plan involves choosing the tools to meet the set of challenges unique to a study. We outlined several of such challenges but were obviously far from exhaustivity. One element often absent in epidemiological study is the question of measurement error. Multiple approaches exist to address it and this question can become central when working with data from many places and periods.

In order to assess which statistical models are most employed in the occupational epidemiology field, we identified all papers mentioned in the symposium of the (online) 2021 EPICOH conference on life course methods as well as all papers mentioning the term "life course" in either the title or the abstract in the *Occupational and Environmental Medicine* journal. It is striking to observe that most, if not all, of the abovementioned, although probably not representative, entries concentrated on obtaining clusters of trajectories using either sequence analysis or mixture growth analyses. Thus, very few of these studies are set in the formal framework of life course as set up by Ben-Shlomo et al. (Ben-Shlomo et al. 2016). Exploring whether certain periods of time have different importance as predictors of the outcome is therefore only rarely central in these papers. This can to a certain extent be explained by the fact that occupational epidemiology has always been "time course epidemiology" in that lifetime job histories have always been taken into account and identifying critical "time windows" has been a lasting concern at least since the 1990s (Finkelstein 1991)and is still a topic of recent research (Wagner et al. 2021).

However, the treatment of time has usually been based on exposure estimation through job-exposure matrices and has only rarely taken into account individual trajectories. This may be due to the fact that only a limited number of prospective longitudinal occupational exposure datasets exist. This might, however, soon change. Peters et al. (2020) estimated that "approximately 30 million individuals in Europe are represented in existing cohorts with extensive occupational and employment information," which are now organized within the OMEGA-NET network. Within these cohorts, several prospective cohorts with detailed occupational information each comprising over 100,000 members have been launched in the last 10 years (France, Germany, UK, and the Netherlands...). One can, therefore, hope that within these cohorts, the life course methods presented in the present chapter, notably similar to Matadil (Madathil et al. 2018) and Carmeli (Carmeli et al. 2020), will be applied and enable new discoveries in the interaction between time and occupational exposures.

References

Abbott A (1983) Sequences of social events: concepts and methods for the analysis of order in social processes. Hist Methods 16(4):129–147. https://doi.org/10.1080/01615440.1983.10594107

Abbott A, Forrest J (1986) Optimal matching methods for historical sequences. J Interdiscip Hist 16(3):471. https://doi.org/10.2307/204500

Ahrens W, Pigeot I (eds) (2014) Handbook of epidemiology, 2nd edn. Springer Reference

Alwan H, Pruijm M, Ponte B, Ackermann D, Guessous I, Ehret G, Staessen JA, Asayama K, Vuistiner P, Younes SE, Paccaud F, Wuerzner G, Pechere-Bertschi A, Mohaupt M, Vogt B, Martin P-Y, Burnier M, Bochud M (2014) Epidemiology of masked and white-coat hypertension: the family-based SKIPOGH study. PLoS One 9(3):e92522. https://doi.org/10.1371/journal.pone.0092522

Ben-Shlomo Y, Cooper R, Kuh D (2016) The last two decades of life course epidemiology, and its relevance for research on ageing. Int J Epidemiol 45(4):973–988. https://doi.org/10.1093/ije/dyw096

Berger E, Castagné R, Chadeau-Hyam M, Bochud M, d'Errico A, Gandini M, Karimi M, Kivimäki M, Krogh V, Marmot M, Panico S, Preisig M, Ricceri F, Sacerdote C, Steptoe A, Stringhini S, Tumino R, Vineis P, Delpierre C, Kelly-Irving M (2019) Multi-cohort study identifies social determinants of systemic inflammation over the life course. Nat Commun 10(1):773. https://doi.org/10.1038/s41467-019-08732-x

Carmeli C, Steen J, Petrovic D, Lepage B, Delpierre C, Kelly-Irving M, Bochud M, Kivimäki M, Vineis P, Stringhini S (2020) Mechanisms of life-course socioeconomic inequalities in adult systemic inflammation: findings from two cohort studies. Soc Sci Med 245:112685. https://doi.org/10.1016/j.socscimed.2019.112685

Carpenter JR, Kenward MG (2013) Multiple imputation and its application: carpenter/multiple imputation and its application. John Wiley & Sons. https://doi.org/10.1002/9781119942283

De Stavola BL, Daniel RM (2012) Commentary: marginal structural models the way forward for life-course epidemiology? Epidemiology 23(2):233–237. https://doi.org/10.1097/EDE.0b013e318245847e

De Stavola BL, Daniel RM (2016) Commentary: incorporating concepts and methods from causal inference into life course epidemiology. Int J Epidemiol 45(4):1006–1010. https://doi.org/10.1093/ije/dyw103

Eisenberg-Guyot J, Peckham T, Andrea SB, Oddo V, Seixas N, Hajat A (2020) Life-course trajectories of employment quality and health in the U.S.: a multichannel sequence analysis. Soc Sci Med 264:113327. https://doi.org/10.1016/j.socscimed.2020.113327

Everitt B, Howell DC (eds) (2005) Encyclopedia of statistics in behavioral science. John Wiley & Sons

Finkelstein MM (1991) Use of "time windows" to investigate lung cancer latency intervals at an Ontario steel plant. Am J Ind Med 19(2):229–235. https://doi.org/10.1002/ajim.4700190210

Firmann M, Mayor V, Vidal PM, Bochud M, Pécoud A, Hayoz D, Paccaud F, Preisig M, Song KS, Yuan X, Danoff TM, Stirnadel HA, Waterworth D, Mooser V, Waeber G, Vollenweider P (2008) The CoLaus study: a population-based study to investigate the epidemiology and genetic determinants of cardiovascular risk factors and metabolic syndrome. BMC Cardiovasc Disord 8(1):6. https://doi.org/10.1186/1471-2261-8-6

Gabadinho A, Ritschard G, Müller NS, Studer M (2011) Analyzing and Visualizing State Sequences in *R* with TraMineR. J Stat Softw 40(4). https://doi.org/10.18637/jss.v040.i04

Halpin B (2017) SADI: sequence analysis tools for Stata. Stata J 17(3):546–572

Jones BL, Nagin DS, Roeder K (2001) A SAS procedure based on mixture models for estimating developmental trajectories. Sociol Methods Res 29(3):374–393. https://doi.org/10.1177/0049124101029003005

Klijn SL, Weijenberg MP, Lemmens P, van den Brandt PA, Lima Passos V (2017) Introducing the fit-criteria assessment plot – a visualisation tool to assist class enumeration in group-based trajectory modelling. Stat Methods Med Res 26(5):2424–2436. https://doi.org/10.1177/0962280215598665

Kuh D (2003) Life course epidemiology. J Epidemiol Community Health 57(10):778–783. https://doi.org/10.1136/jech.57.10.778

Lange T, Vansteelandt S, Bekaert M (2012) A simple unified approach for estimating natural direct and indirect effects. Am J Epidemiol 176(3):190–195

Little RJ, Rubin DB (2019) Statistical analysis with missing data, vol 793. John Wiley & Sons

Madathil SA, Rousseau M-C, Wynant W, Schlecht NF, Netuveli G, Franco EL, Nicolau B (2016) Nonlinear association between betel quid chewing and oral cancer: implications for prevention. Oral Oncol 60:25–31. https://doi.org/10.1016/j.oraloncology.2016.06.011

Madathil S, Joseph L, Hardy R, Rousseau M-C, Nicolau B (2018) A Bayesian approach to investigate life course hypotheses involving continuous exposures. Int J Epidemiol 47(5):1623–1635. https://doi.org/10.1093/ije/dyy107

McElreath R (2020) Statistical rethinking: a Bayesian course with examples in R and Stan, 2nd edn. Taylor and Francis, CRC Press

Mishra G, Nitsch D, Black S, De Stavola B, Kuh D, Hardy R (2009) A structured approach to modelling the effects of binary exposure variables over the life course. Int J Epidemiol 38(2):528–537. https://doi.org/10.1093/ije/dyn229

Nagin DS (2005) Group-based modeling of development. Harvard University Press

Pearl J (2000) Causality: models, reasoning, and inference. Cambridge University Press

Pearl J, Glymour M, Jewell NP (2016) Causal inference in statistics: a primer. Wiley

Peters S, Turner MC, Bugge MD, Vienneau D, Vermeulen R (2020) International inventory of occupational exposure information: OMEGA-NET. Ann Work Expos Health 64(5):465–467. https://doi.org/10.1093/annweh/wxaa021

Proust-Lima C, Philipps V, Liquet B (2017) Estimation of extended mixed models using latent classes and latent processes: the *R* Package lcmm. J Stat Softw 78(2):10.18637/jss.v078.i02

Rousseeuw PJ (1987) Silhouettes: a graphical aid to the interpretation and validation of cluster analysis. J Comput Appl Math 20:53–65. https://doi.org/10.1016/0377-0427(87)90125-7

Rubin DB (1974) Estimating causal effects of treatments in randomized and nonrandomized studies. J Educ Psychol 66(5):688–701. https://doi.org/10.1037/h0037350

Singer JD, Willett JB (2003) Applied longitudinal data analysis. Oxford University Press. https://doi.org/10.1093/acprof:oso/9780195152968.001.0001

Smith ADAC, Hardy R, Heron J, Joinson CJ, Lawlor DA, Macdonald-Wallis C, Tilling K (2016) A structured approach to hypotheses involving continuous exposures over the life course. Int J Epidemiol:dyw164. https://doi.org/10.1093/ije/dyw164

Stan Development Team (2021) Stan modeling language users guide and reference manual 2.16. https://mc-stan.org/users/documentation/

Steen J, Loeys T, Moerkerke B, Vansteelandt S (2017) medflex: an *R* Package for Flexible Mediation Analysis using Natural Effect Models. J Stat Softw 76(11). https://doi.org/10.18637/jss.v076.i11

Studer M, Ritschard G (2016) What matters in differences between life trajectories: a comparative review of sequence dissimilarity measures. J R Stat Soc A Stat Soc 179(2):481–511. https://doi.org/10.1111/rssa.12125

Tu Y-K, Tilling K, Sterne JA, Gilthorpe MS (2013) A critical evaluation of statistical approaches to examining the role of growth trajectories in the developmental origins of health and disease. Int J Epidemiol 42(5):1327–1339. https://doi.org/10.1093/ije/dyt157

van Buuren S, Groothuis-Oudshoorn K (2011) Mice: multivariate imputation by chained equations in R. J Stat Softw 45(3):1–67. https://doi.org/10.18637/jss.v045.i03

VanderWeele TJ (2014) Commentary: resolutions of the birthweight paradox: competing explanations and analytical insights. Int J Epidemiol 43(5):1368–1373. https://doi.org/10.1093/ije/dyu162

Wagner M, Grodstein F, Leffondre K, Samieri C, Proust-Lima C (2021) Time-varying associations between an exposure history and a subsequent health outcome: a landmark approach to identify critical windows. BMC Med Res Methodol 21(1):266. https://doi.org/10.1186/s12874-021-01403-w

Zang E, Max JT (2020) Bayesian estimation and model selection in group-based trajectory models. Psychol Methods. https://doi.org/10.1037/met0000359

Part III

Early Life Impact on Work and Health

Genetics, Epigenetics, and Mental Health at Work

10

Jelena Bakusic, Olivia Lavreysen, and Lode Godderis

Contents

Introduction	158
Relevance of Biological Research in Work-Related Stress and Burnout	158
Neurobiology of Stress	159
Genetics	161
Epigenetics	162
Relevance of (Epi)genetics for Work-Related Stress and Burnout	164
Overview of the (Epi)genetic Mechanisms Linked to Work-Related Stress and Burnout	165
(Epi)genetic Regulation of the HPA Axis	165
(Epi)genetic Regulation of BDNF	167
Other (Epi)genetic Mechanisms	168
Implications for Clinical Practice and Future Perspectives	169
References	171

Abstract

Despite an increasing amount of research on work-related stress and burnout, our knowledge on the underlying biological mechanisms remains scarce. So far, biomarkers of work-related stress and burnout have been used to identify the biological stress response. Recently, epigenetics has emerged as the key mechanism by which environment and genetics interact, making it an appealing target

---

J. Bakusic
KU Leuven, Centre for Environment and Health, Leuven, Belgium

KU Leuven, University Psychiatric Centre KU Leuven (UPC KU Leuven), Kortenberg, Belgium

O. Lavreysen
KU Leuven, Centre for Environment and Health, Leuven, Belgium

L. Godderis (✉)
KU Leuven, Centre for Environment and Health, Leuven, Belgium

IDEWE, External Service for Prevention and Protection at Work, Heverlee, Belgium
e-mail: lode.godderis@idewe.be

© Springer Nature Switzerland AG 2023
M. Wahrendorf et al. (eds.), *Handbook of Life Course Occupational Health*, Handbook Series in Occupational Health Sciences, https://doi.org/10.1007/978-3-031-30492-7_27

biomarker for stress-related phenotypes such as burnout. In the present chapter, we provide an **overview of current knowledge on (epi)genetic mechanisms linked to work-related stress and burnout** and we discuss their **potential contribution to our understanding** of these phenomena. Moreover, we try to elucidate the potential translational contribution of (epi)genetics and its significance for clinical practice.

Keywords

Genetics · Epigenetics · Biomarker · Work-related stress · Burnout

Introduction

Over the recent years, work-related stress and burnout have become an object of ever-increasing interest in industrialized countries. Major changes in the working environment, technological advances, increasing time pressure, work pace and complexity, job insecurity, etc. are just some of the challenges workers in Western countries are facing (Weber and Jaekel-Reinhard 2000). Moreover, the capitalistic imperatives of achievement, performance, productivity, and individualism are putting additional pressure on the modern workforce (Butler 2019). Witnessing the COVID-19 pandemic has increased awareness of the importance of mental well-being and burnout risk (Godderis et al. 2020).

Numerous studies have shown that job stress and long-term exposure to stressful environments are positively and highly related to job burnout (Abarghouei et al. 2016; Cao et al. 2018; Chirico 2016; Chou et al. 2014). The differential diagnosis with other psychological conditions is not always clear as there exists overlap between stress, burnout, and depression symptoms (Ahola et al. 2014). Hence, it is important to investigate the differences to support the clinical assessment of burnout. However, literature still lacks in-depth knowledge on burnout diagnosis and mechanisms. Despite the increasing amount of research on work-related stress and burnout, insight on biological mechanisms remains scarce. Recently, epigenetics has emerged as the key mechanism by which environment and genetics interact. Bakusic et al. investigated the epigenetic changes thoroughly in burnout (Bakusic et al. 2021a, b). However, an integrated overview of the genetic and epigenetic mechanisms and changes over time in work-related stress and burnout is still lacking in literature.

Relevance of Biological Research in Work-Related Stress and Burnout

Biological research on phenomena where chronic stress plays an important role, such as work-related stress and burnout, are important for several reasons. First, it helps us to gain more insight into the understanding of development of these outcomes, which have a fundamental value but can also lead to potential translational and clinical applications (Holtzheimer 3rd and Nemeroff 2006). For example, by providing a better understanding of the phenomenon itself, which might in the long run shed light on the vagueness and controversy around burnout. In addition, it could provide more insight into the differences with other psychological diseases, as well as the vulnerability factors and early biological warning signals, which could in turn help develop timely preventive strategies for employees (Kerr et al. 2020).

Neurobiology of Stress

In general, our stress response system is supposed to react to acute stressors, or at least stressors of limited duration (Chrousos and Gold 1992). In order to achieve homeostasis, our body will react with a "fight or flight" response, which mobilizes a range of molecular, cellular, and behavioral mechanisms in order to ensure survival, e.g., running away from a predator. Even though this acute stress reaction is necessary and adaptive in life-threatening situations, accumulating long-term chronic stress in the form of psychological stressors can result in inability of our body to recover properly and even permanent reprogramming of the whole stress response system (Schneiderman et al. 2005). It seems that our stress response system has not evolved over the past several thousands of years, meaning that exposure to any kind of psychosocial stressor we are commonly facing today, such as work pressure, will trigger almost the same biological response as when our ancestors were facing a predator (Chrousos and Gold 1992). Many scientists working in the field of stress evolution are speculating that our stress response system was never meant to deal with chronic, psychosocial stressors and is therefore "outdated," which causes its maladaptive response to chronic stress (Chrousos and Gold 1992; McEwen 1998; McEwen and Stellar 1993). To better describe the effect of chronic stress on our body, Bruce McEwen introduced the term "allostasis," which he defined as reprograming of the stress response system according to expected demands (McEwen 1998). This can cause the stress system to become permanently hyperactive or hypoactive, both of which are maladaptive and present a risk for mental health. When we are exposed to a stressor, two main response systems will be activated: the autonomic nervous system (**ANS**) and the hypothalamic pituitary adrenal (**HPA**) axis (Fig. 1) (Bakusic et al. 2021a, b). The sympathetic part of the ANS is in charge of sending the information from the central nervous system to the periphery rapidly and immediately triggering the "fight or flight response." The main mediators of ANS are adrenalin and noradrenaline, which trigger a number of physiological changes, such as increase in blood pressure and heart rate, pupil dilatation, increased blood flow into muscles, etc. all of which prepare our body to react (Goldstein 2010). The HPA axis on the other hand is a neuroendocrine system and therefore acts somewhat slower but its effects can persist longer. HPA axis response involves a cascade of events, starting with activation of the hypothalamus, which releases corticotrophin-releasing hormone (CRH) to the anterior pituitary gland. In response to this, the anterior pituitary

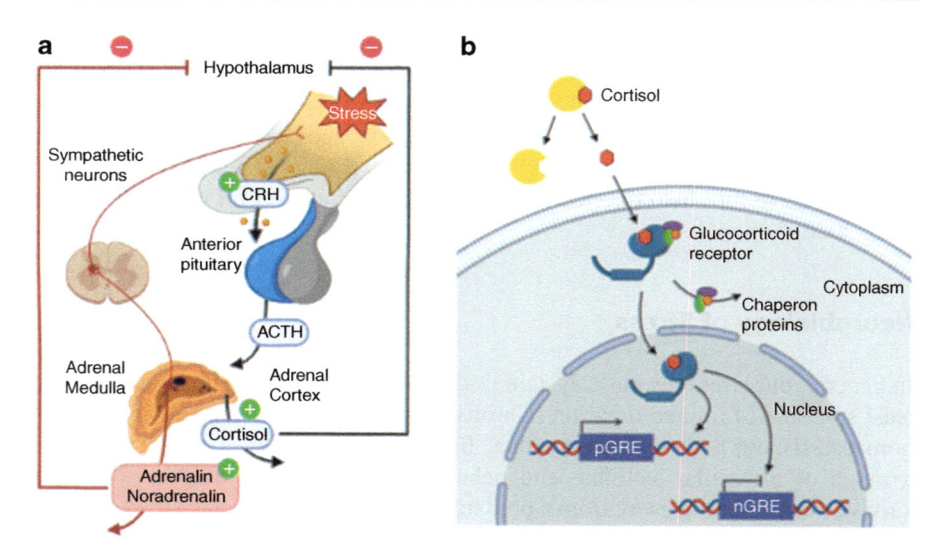

Fig. 1 (**a**) Stress can either activate the sympathetic adrenal medullary (SAM) axis of the autonomic nervous system (ANS) (shown left in red), which triggers the release of adrenalin and noradrenaline; adrenalin and noradrenaline exert a negative feedback or stress can activate the hypothalamic pituitary adrenal (HPA) axis (shown right in blue), which triggers the release of cortisol; cortisol exerts a negative feedback mediated by the glucocorticoid receptors (GRs) in the hypothalamus and anterior pituitary. (**b**) GR signaling on a cellular level. CRH: corticotropin-releasing hormone, ACTH: adrenocorticotropic hormone, pGRE: positive glucocorticoid response elements (enhance transcription), nGRE: negative glucocorticoid response elements (repress transcription). Adjusted in BioRender from epigenetic changes in burnout and depression by J. Bakusic, 2021. (Reprinted with permission)

further releases adrenocorticotropic hormone (**ACTH**) into the blood stream, which finally reaches the adrenal cortex and stimulates production and release of cortisol (Smith and Vale 2006). Cortisol induces a range of reactions in different organic systems, including increase in blood pressure, immunosuppression, elevation in blood glucose levels to provide more energy, etc. In addition, it provides a negative feedback mechanism, by which it shuts down the HPA axis stress response and prevents its excessive continuation.

On a cellular level, cortisol achieves its effects by binding to two different types of receptors – the mineralocorticoid receptor (**MR**) and the glucocorticoid receptor (**GR**). The MR has high affinity for endogenous glucocorticoids and plays a role in circadian fluctuations in these hormones. In contrast, the GR has lower affinity for endogenous glucocorticoids and therefore plays a crucial role in the states of increased cortisol, such as in chronic stress. As a steroid receptor, the GR is located in the cytoplasm. In response to ligand (cortisol) binding, the GR-cortisol homodimer translocates to the cell nucleus, where it can activate or suppress the activity of certain genes, by binding to specific hormone response elements in the promoter regions of the target genes (Oakley and Cidlowski 2013). In this way, cortisol can also regulate the expression of the HPA axis–related genes, such as the CRH and GR genes.

In addition, the transcriptional effects of cortisol extend beyond the HPA axis itself. One of the examples is the effect of glucocorticoids on adult **hippocampal neurogenesis**, which entails the formation of new neurons and synapses. Namely, the hippocampus is the area of the limbic brain particularly important for cognition and memory formation. As such, the hippocampus is particularly rich with GRs and is therefore very sensitive to elevated cortisol levels (Saaltink and Vreugdenhil 2014). In recent years, a growing body of literature emerged showing that chronic stress and increased cortisol levels inhibit adult hippocampal neurogenesis, which is in turn associated with cognitive impairment, such as those occurring in burnout. In this regard, the interplay between the HPA axis and the brain-derived neurotrophic factor (**BDNF**) seems to play an essential role, since BDNF is one of the key neurotrophins stimulating neural proliferation (Schaaf et al. 2000). However, the exact molecular mechanisms by which this interaction takes place remain largely unknown. Another system interacting with the HPA axis in the states of chronic stress is the serotonergic system. **Serotonin (5-hydroxytryptamine or 5-HT)** is a neurotransmitter mainly known for its function in the mood regulation. Moreover, additional functions of this neurotransmitter keep on being discovered, one of them being the regulation of the HPA axis (Duval et al. 2002). Moreover, the neuropeptide **oxytocin** can also influence the HPA axis, resulting in an ameliorating effect on the stress response. Oxytocin is being released from the neurohypophysis during or immediately after stress. This can (in)directly affect the CRH-induced ACTH secretion, which enhances the negative feedback mechanism (Winter and Jurek 2019).

The exact way these systems interact and in which direction is still not completely elucidated. However, alterations in the expression of regulatory genes, such as those encoding for the 5-HT receptors and transporters, have been implicated as potential mediators. As the effects of chronic stress via cortisol involve alterations in different genes involved in the HPA axis itself but also other systems, such as BDNF, 5-HT, and oxytocin. One of the key-suggested mediating mechanisms of those effects is (epi)genetics (Bakusic et al. 2021a, b).

Genetics

Genetics play a significant role in both physical and psychological characteristics. Genetic polymorphisms could explain the differences between risk groups of burnout and other diseases. A DNA polymorphism is an alternate form (allele) of a chromosomal locus in the genome. A difference in one base pair at a particular site within (non)coding regions at the genome is called a single-nucleotide polymorphism (SNP) (Russell 2014). A growing body of research emphasizes the significance of the interplay between genetic vulnerability, reflected in the existence of SNPs and epigenetic regulation in psychopathology. For example, many polymorphisms in the *BDNF* gene and their interaction with epigenetics were found to be associated with stress-related disorders (He et al. 2020).

Epigenetics

The term epigenetics emerged in 1940s and literally means "above" or "on top of" genetics (Jablonka and Lamb 2002). As such, epigenetics refers to external modifications to DNA that turn genes "on" or "off" or determine which genes will be activated or silenced. In other words, epigenetics is known as the study of heritable changes in gene expression that do not involve a change in the DNA sequence itself. Simply put, if we imagine the DNA sequence or our genetic code as letters of a sentence, epigenetics would present all the additional information necessary to read this sentence properly, such as the formatting, spacing, and punctuation marks. During ontogenesis, epigenetic modifications are necessary for proper formation and differentiation of different cell types from one single cell – the zygote. In other words, epigenetic changes will orchestrate the process in which two different cells containing identical genetic sequences will differentiate in two cells with completely different function and set of expressed genes – such as for instance a neural and a muscle cell (Fraser and Lin 2016). There are three types of epigenetic modifications involved in gene regulation: DNA methylation, histone modifications, and microRNAs (Fig. 2) (Bakusic et al. 2021a, b).

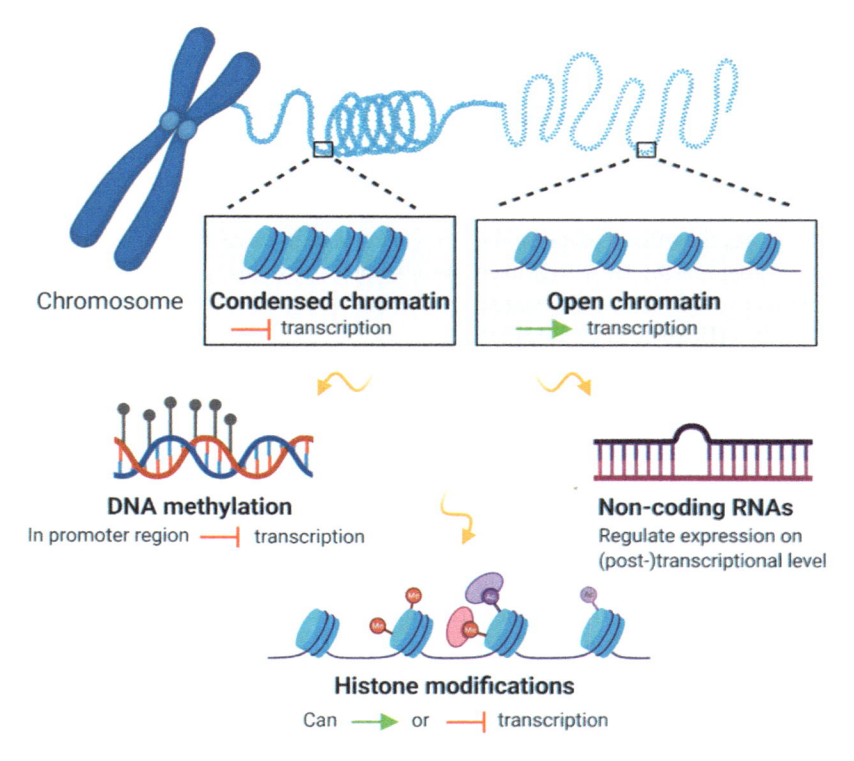

Fig. 2 Overview of epigenetic mechanisms. From epigenetic changes in burnout and depression by J. Bakusic, 2021. (Reprinted with permission)

DNA Methylation

Methylation of the DNA occurs when a methyl group (CH3) is covalently added to position 5 of the cytosine pyrimidine ring. This reaction is catalyzed by the enzymes DNA methyltransferases (DNMTs), whereby a methyl-group is transferred from the methyl donor S-adenosylmethionine to cytosine. De novo DNA methylation is catalyzed by DNMT3a and DNMT3b whereas further maintenance of DNA methylation throughout DNA replication cycles is catalyzed by DNMT1. DNA methylation predominantly occurs in the context of CpG dinucleotides (a location within the DNA where a cytosine nucleotide is followed by a guanine nucleotide). CpG dinucleotides predominantly cluster in CpG islands (regions enriched with densely packed CpG dinucleotides), which are most often located in promoter regions of genes, often near transcription start sites. CpG islands are predominantly unmethylated, allowing the binding of regulatory transcription factors, which activate gene transcription and consequently enhance gene expression (turning genes on). In contrast, CpG sites residing elsewhere such as in gene bodies and repetitive elements are often highly methylated (Smith and Meissner 2013).

Demethylation on the other hand can either take place passively – through loss of DNA methylation marks during successive rounds of replication, or can be an active process. In case of active demethylation, an enzymatic process takes place, whereby methyl groups are modified or removed from methylated cytosines (5-mC). This process occurs in several steps, in which 10–11 translocation (TET1, 2 and 3) enzymes catalyze the oxidation of 5-mC to 5-hydroxymethylcytosine (5-hmC) and the oxidation of 5-hmC to 5-formylcytosine (5-fC) and 5-carboxycytosine (5-caC), the final products of the reaction (Kohli and Zhang 2013).

Histone Modifications

In the nucleus, the DNA strand is wrapped around proteins called histones, together forming the known *beads-on-a-string* structure of chromatin. There are two different forms of chromatin: heterochromatin and euchromatin. Heterochromatin is a condensed form in which the DNA strand is more tightly wound around the histones, which decreases the accessibility of DNA for the transcription machinery and resulting in decreased gene expression. Conversely, euchromatin is a decondensed form, in which DNA is accessible for transcription and therefore gene expression is increased in this area. These changes in chromatin packing are mediated by different types of posttranslational covalent modifications of histones, mainly occurring in the tail domains. There are at least eight different types of histone modifications including acetylation and methylation of lysines and arginines, phosphorylation of serines and threonines, ubiquitinylation and sumoylation of lysines, ADP ribosylation, deamination, and proline isomerization (Kouzarides 2007; Peterson and Laniel 2004).

MicroRNAs

The third type of epigenetic changes are the so-called noncoding RNAs. Regulatory noncoding RNAs can be classified into microRNAs (miRNAs), short-interfering

RNAs, long noncoding RNA, etc. Unlike messenger RNAs (mRNA), these noncoding RNAs are not translated into functional proteins. On the contrary, they regulate gene expression at the (post-)transcriptional level, binding to and degrading those RNA molecules that would normally translate into proteins (Holoch and Moazed 2015).

Relevance of (Epi)genetics for Work-Related Stress and Burnout

It is important to mention that the three epigenetic processes (DNA methylation, histone modifications, and miRNAs) are highly interconnected. For instance, DNA methylation can silence the expression of a miRNA, which would have silenced a certain gene. In this way, DNA methylation would indirectly lead to enhanced expression rather than silencing (Han et al. 2007). Similarly, a miRNA can directly target DNA methyltransferases (Fabbri et al. 2007) or enzymes involved in histone modifications (Bianchi et al. 2017) and thus inhibit DNA methylation or chromatin arrangement. Such modifications can pose a persisting impact on the gene functioning (Lee and Sawa 2014). The epigenetic effect on work-related stress or burnout can be explained by disruption of two types of stress-associated genes. On the one hand, genes modulating the intracellular glucocorticoid signaling and sensitivity, and therefore directly influencing the HPA-axis; for example, GR itself or CRH. And on the other hand, genes like *BDNF* causing long-term dysregulation of neural processes involved in mood, emotions, and cognition (Lee and Sawa 2014).

Knowing that epigenetics is the key mechanism by which the environment and genetics interact, it is beyond doubt that its relevance and implications for stress-related mental health problems are huge (Mahgoub and Monteggia 2013). The interplay between genetic vulnerability and adverse environmental factors are known to play a key role in the development of psychopathology. Not surprisingly, the environment-genetics interplay is not so clear in burnout due to insufficient research and contradictory findings. Namely, whereas one study suggested that familial clustering in burnout was entirely due to common environmental factors (Middeldorp et al. 2005), another study reported a modest contribution of genetics (30% in men and 13% in women) (Middeldorp et al. 2006). The genetic contribution was confirmed by a large Swedish study reporting a heritability of 33% equal for men and women (Blom et al. 2012). However, the variance attributed to individual and common environmental factors still explain the largest part in burnout which could pose opportunities for prevention efforts.

Another reason why epigenetics is appealing for stress-related research is the fact that epigenetic changes, DNA methylation in particular, are relatively stable alterations, which are more likely to reflect chronic exposure, such as that to psychosocial stress. In this view, a large body of longitudinal research on the epigenetic effects of early life stress has shown that prenatal and early life adverse environment can lead to epigenetic changes in the genes involved in the HPA axis regulation (Janusek et al. 2019).

These changes can persist to adulthood, shaping the way the child will respond to stress later in life and increasing the risk of psychopathology. In addition, DNA methylation changes were associated with adult psychosocial stress (Matosin et al. 2017) as well as range of psychiatric disorders (Kuehner et al. 2019), mainly through cross-sectional and case-control studies. On the other hand, epigenetic changes are also potentially reversible, and can therefore potentially present biological correlates of treatment progression and recovery (Kular and Kular 2018). Indeed, several longitudinal studies demonstrated that both psychotropic treatment and psychotherapy can contribute to the reversal of DNA methylation patterns in stress-related genes (Roberts et al. 2019; Thomas et al. 2018; Vinkers et al. 2021). Therefore, investigating epigenetic patterns can help us overcome the limitations of purely measuring circulating proteins and hormones (such as cortisol), which undergo daily fluctuations, are much less stable and are affected by a large number of confounding factors, all of which limit their utility in stress research (Kular and Kular 2018).

Overview of the (Epi)genetic Mechanisms Linked to Work-Related Stress and Burnout

Although several studies already explored the genetic interplay in work-related stress and burnout, no systematic review has been done on the topic. The most studied genetic polymorphisms were related to cortisol, serotonin, and BDNF.

Regarding epigenetics, limited studies exist on the role in work-related stress and burnout. Only one systematic review has been conducted to provide any kind of insight into potential DNA methylation mechanisms in burnout (Bakusic et al. 2017). From this review, only three clinical studies were identified that investigated work-related stress, burnout, and DNA methylation (Alasaari et al. 2012; Miyaki et al. 2015; Song et al. 2014). More recently, two additional studies by Bakusic et al. (Bakusic et al. 2020a, 2021a, b) published thereafter provided further insights into epigenetic mechanisms in burnout.

Here we summarize the current state-of-art knowledge on the genetic and epigenetic mechanisms linked to work-related stress and burnout.

(Epi)genetic Regulation of the HPA Axis

Research on genetic regulation of the HPA axis mainly focused on cortisone and serotonin. However, these results were not significant and therefore not confirmative. He et al. did not find a significant independent effect of the corticotrophin-releasing hormone receptor 1 (CRHR1) rs110402 polymorphism on burnout, instead CRHR1 rs110402 interacted with work-related stress to increase the emotional exhaustion dimension and depersonalization of burnout. This indicates that individuals with the AA genotype display a higher susceptibility to work-related stress than those with one or two G alleles (He et al. 2019). When investigating the serotonin-transporter-linked promoter region (5-HTTLPR) genotype, no correlation was found between 5-HTTLPR polymorphism and work-related stress or burnout (Alasaari et al. 2012). In addition, the 5-HTT rs6354 polymorphism showed no association with burnout (Cao et al. 2018). However, when looking into the 5-HTT rs6354 genotypes, higher susceptibility to changes in environmental stress was observed in TT homozygotes, but not in those with one or two G alleles (Cao et al. 2018).

With regard to epigenetic research, Bakusic et al. observed altered DNA methylation in the *Nuclear Receptor Subfamily 3 Group C Member 1 (NR3C1)*, a gene encoding GR, in the comparison between the burnout and control group. More specifically, increased methylation of CpG21 in amplicon 1 and decreased methylation of CpG30 in amplicon 3 was found in the burnout group. Both of these CpGs overlap with the nerve growth factor–inducible protein A (NGFI-A) binding site, which plays an important role in the regulation of gene expression (Bakusic et al. 2021a, b). These findings further complicate the interpretation and conclusiveness on the potential effect of these changes on mRNA expression and GR receptor sensitivity. However, overall, a bigger region of this gene was hypomethylated in burnout and therefore it could be assumed that the potential functional effect of these changes could be increased expression of the GR and the consequent increased sensitivity of the HPA axis (Bakusic et al. 2021a, b). What could additionally support this hypothesis is the fact that a negative association between salivary cortisone levels and the average *NR3C1* methylation, and a clear increase in cortisone levels have been observed in the burnout group (Bakusic et al. 2021a, b). As this is the first study to provide any data on *NR3C1* regulation in burnout, further studies simultaneously assessing *NR3C1* methylation, GR sensitivity (for instance, by performing in vitro lysozyme suppression test or cortisol response to a psychological or pharmacological stressor [Yehuda et al. 2015]), and potentially other endpoints such as inflammatory markers (Ratman et al. 2013) could complement these findings.

In case of the epigenetic regulation of serotonin, Alasaari and colleagues (Alasaari et al. 2012) examined DNA methylation in five CpG sites in the promoter region of the *Solute Carrier Family 6 Member 4 (SLC6A4)* gene, encoding the serotonin transporter (SERT or 5-HTT). In all five CpG sites individually, high work-related stress was associated with lower levels of DNA methylation. When adjusting for work stress environment, burnout contributed to higher methylation levels (Alasaari et al. 2012). In contrast, Bakusic et al. (Bakusic et al. 2021a, b) did not observe any differences in the average level of *SLC6A4* methylation in burnout compared to a control group. They did, however, notice an increased methylation in one specific CpG region, namely CpG8, which was associated with all three burnout dimensions, job stress as well as increased salivary cortisol and cortisone (Bakusic et al. 2021a, b). In previous research, increased methylation in the same CpG already has been associated with major depression (Bakusic et al. 2020b; Li et al. 2019). This could indicate that disruption of serotonin follows the same mechanism in burnout and depression.

However, these studies were conducted cross-sectional and are therefore unable to conclude any causality.

(Epi)genetic Regulation of BDNF

Another important hypothesized pathway involved in burnout is the regulation of BDNF. The expression of the BDNF protein is regulated during transcription and translation, and also by post-translational modifications in the *BDNF* gene. The *BDNF* gene has a complex structure, containing 11 exons and 9 have functional promoters that are brain region and tissue specific (Pruunsild et al. 2011). Val66Met polymorphism (rs6265) in the *BDNF* gene ultimately alters the intracellular trafficking and secretion of BDNF (Egan et al. 2003). However, no role of the common Val66Met BDNF polymorphism in association with serum BDNF was observed. In addition, He et al. found no significant association between burnout and serum BDNF or BDNF rs2049046 (He et al. 2020). This indicates the absence of genetic vulnerability at this specific locus, and emphasizes the environmental component in BDNF regulation in burnout.

Regarding the different dimensions, individuals with a BDNF rs6265 TT genotype reported a higher degree of emotional exhaustion and cynicism (Jia et al. 2021). Whereas carriers with a C-allele for rs6265 had lower job burnout under high job stress, especially on cynicism (Jia et al. 2021). Regarding the rs16917237 polymorphism, Li et al. found a significant interaction with work-related stress on burnout. Again, individuals with a TT genotype had slightly higher job burnout dimension scores, making them more likely to suffer from emotional exhaustion and cynicism than the GG/GT genotype subgroup (Li et al. 2022).

In the study by Bakusic et al., methylation of the *BDNF* promoter of exon I and IV was increased in subjects with burnout compared to healthy controls, which was also associated with downregulation of the serum BDNF protein levels (Bakusic et al. 2020a). Apart from the group differences in DNA methylation patterns, BDNF methylation was also associated with burnout symptoms dimensionally, in the expected direction in line with the underlying mechanisms.

In another study, DNA methylation of the *BDNF* gene has been compared between work-related stress and depressive symptoms. The methylation assessment was done in the entire *BDNF* gene which included all 97 CpG sites. Work-related stress was associated with decreased average methylation of the gene, whereas, in contrast, depressive symptoms contributed to hypermethylation of the promoter region as well as the whole gene (Song et al. 2014). This distinction could identify biomarkers that set apart the diagnosis of depression from work-related stress.

It is generally considered that changes in BDNF signaling induced by chronic stress contribute to the development of symptoms via their deteriorating effect on hippocampal neurogenesis (Duman 2004). This could also be supported by the evidence showing cognitive decline in burnout patients (Deligkaris et al. 2014);

however, this was not directly assessed and therefore more research is needed to further explore this hypothesis.

Other (Epi)genetic Mechanisms

Tyrosine hydroxylase (TH) is an enzyme involved in catecholamines (dopamine, norepinephrine, and epinephrine) biosynthesis (Bear et al. 2015). Even though catecholamines are neurotransmitters implicated in various physiological processes associated with mental health, there is still little evidence about epigenetic changes of the *TH* gene in response to stress. Miyaki et al. explored the role of TH in work-related stress (Miyaki et al. 2015). They assessed DNA methylation in all CpG sites located throughout the *TH* gene and the 5′ flanking region using DNA extracted from saliva samples. The average methylation level of all CpG sites was significantly increased in the highest job strain group compared to the one of the lowest job strain group. In addition, hypermethylation associated with job strain was observed in the promoter region of the gene as well as in the majority of the individual CpG sites located throughout the whole gene sequence (64%) (Miyaki et al. 2015). However, there are no other studies examining TH methylation in the context of work-related stress or burnout. Therefore, no additional conclusions can be made on the work-related stress or burnout biomarker potential of this gene. Additional studies are needed to further explore TH methylation patterns in this context.

Recently, the investigation of epigenomic changes in burnout after acupuncture shed light on the underlying pathways involved in burnout (Petitpierre et al. 2022). They conducted a genome-wide trial to assess the DNA methylation pattern during a burnout episode. Genes corresponding to the most differentially methylated CpGs after acupuncture showed enrichment in the brain dopaminergic signaling, steroid hormone synthesis, and in the insulin signaling pathways (Petitpierre et al. 2022).

The DNA methylation levels at the different CpG sites in the genome can be scored as epigenetic clocks. The epigenetic age acceleration (EAA), difference between epigenetic clocks and chronological age, has been investigated in different epigenetic aging biomarkers (Freni-Sterrantino et al. 2022). PhenoAgeAA was associated with job strain, active work compared to reference low strain. Overall, few statistically significant results were identified once adjusted for covariates. The inconsistent patterns of associations of job stress compared with the current literature highlight the need for additional studies on this topic.

Another epigenetic biomarker that has been explored recently is the telomere length (Wei et al. 2022). Telomeres are DNA-protein complexes at the end of chromosomes, and they cap chromosomal ends to promote chromosomal stability and protect the regions from degradation. As accelerated telomere shortenings are associated with chronic stress, it poses a candidate biomarker for stress-related disorders. Nurse's telomere lengths were assessed pre- and during the COVID-19 pandemic. Regardless of the age group, telomere lengths were significantly shorter during the pandemic compared to before. However, no significant bivariate relationship was found between the absolute telomere length and nurse's burnout symptoms. As this study was conducted cross-sectionally, to further explore this area, there is a need for long-term longitudinal observation of telomere length in burnout.

Implications for Clinical Practice and Future Perspectives

A common question coming from general audience is whether it is possible to identify burnout by analyzing persons' DNA. The current answer is obviously "no," but it is important to discuss potential translational aspects of this research.

In the context of burnout, biomarkers could help better characterize this phenomenon. Unfortunately, due to vagueness of the burnout phenomenon, we often hear in clinical practice or in the media that some people including employers "do not believe" in burnout. Research on the genetic and epigenetic mechanisms can have an important contribution in acclaiming this phenomenon (without necessarily calling it a disease) by showing that it is reflected in disruption of biological (epigenetic) processes occurring in our body. In addition, some of the findings presented in this chapter are an interesting starting point for identifying biological mechanisms differing in work-related stress and burnout. Finally, epigenetic markers could have an implication for screening of workers with high risk of developing burnout. However, bearing in mind the costs of epigenetic analysis, in order for this to be cost-efficient and reasonable, these biomarkers would be expected to provide more information than the existing self-reported screening tools, which are far more simple and less expensive to use. Nevertheless, this might not be so unrealistic. It is known that burnout develops over a long period of time, which means that employees often push themselves far beyond their limits and ignore early warning signs and symptoms. Therefore, perhaps feedback in the form of biological warning signals would be more effective in making people aware (both employees and employers) that it is time to take the necessary action before falling into a severe burnout. In order for any of this applications to become more realistic, first more data from longitudinal studies are necessary, which would give insight into stability and reversibility of the epigenetic patterns. More specifically, studies following workers exposed to high stress and those following workers with burnout during recovery would be of particular interest and added value. Moreover, these studies would provide more insight into the within-person evaluation of DNA methylation patters, which could have additional translational potential in predicting evolution of symptoms.

Discussion on translation implication of epigenetic biomarkers cannot go without mentioning development of epigenetic pharmacotherapy (Karsli-Ceppioglu 2016). DNA methyltransferase inhibitors targeting the whole epigenome have already been recognized in the context of cancer treatment; however, targeted gene-specific approaches are more likely to be of relevance for mental health. Interestingly, one such approach (CRISPR-dCas9) has recently been proposed and was shown to induce long-lasting targeted changes in DNA methylation (including BDNF) in vitro and in vivo in rodents (Choudhury et al. 2016; Liu et al. 2016;

Vojta et al. 2016). This approach relies on its long-lasting, albeit reversible, action, thus possibly limiting chronic or repeated administration in patients. In addition, novel approaches using natural or synthetic carrier nanoparticles are aimed at overcoming the tissue-specificity limitation, by delivering the epimodifier to the central nervous system (Lu et al. 2014). No matter how promising and appealing, this research is still in its initial stage and time will show whether the enthusiasm around it was justified.

Despite all the enthusiasm around the possible translational relevance of epigenetic biomarkers, there are still numerous technical and methodological considerations and limitation that need to be dealt with before this gets closer to reality. The first one is related to technical challenges concerning pyrosequencing analyses (the most common method to assess gene-specific methylation changes), including reproducibility and sensitivity. Most of the identified changes in DNA methylation are small differences in methylation % − below 5%, which therefore require very high sensitivity and reproducibility in order to be sure that it is not a variability artifact (Moore and Kobor 2020). Pyrosequencing is currently the most sensitive technique and is therefore considered the method of choice to detect these small differences in DNA methylation, however epigenetics is a fast evolving field and it is possible that we will dispose of improved techniques in the near future that will allow even more sensitive detection of such DNA methylation patterns. However, the variability can also differ between the target genes and therefore there is certainly still room for improvement, which will hopefully be achieved by introducing novel techniques.

Finally, even though these results point out the relevance of gene-specific DNA methylation changes for phenotypes such as burnout, the observed size effects are mostly small, indicating that they explain small portion of variability of the analyzed outcomes. Even though these small changes were previously shown to significantly affect gene expression and we also demonstrated their importance for different functional outcomes, it is certain that these processes are not isolated and that they most likely act in synergy with other epigenetic and biological changes. Therefore, the future perhaps lies in simultaneous assessment of different epigenetic markers − including DNA methylation in multiple genes but also other epigenetic marks such as histone modifications and microRNAs in combination with different proteins (such as serum BDNF, inflammatory markers, etc.), which could allow to obtain bigger effect sizes and a more comprehensive set of biomarkers. The genetic-epigenetic interaction adds on another layer of complexity as these two can in an additive manner, in synergy, or through mediation process. Therefore, taking into account the genetic-epigenetic interplay when assessing target genes (such as *BDNF* Val66Met and *BDNF* methylation of different exons) should be a mandatory step. Application of more sophisticated statistical methods and artificial intelligence in future studies might provide novel approaches toward assessing more complex sets of biomarkers in work-related stress and burnout in an integrative way, which is certainly necessary to further understand these complex phenotypes and eventually reduce their medical and socioeconomic burden.

References

Abarghouei MR, Sorbi MH, Abarghouei M, Bidaki R, Yazdanpoor S (2016) A study of job stress and burnout and related factors in the hospital personnel of Iran. Electron Physician 8(7): 2625–2632. https://doi.org/10.19082/2625

Ahola K, Hakanen J, Perhoniemi R, Mutanen P (2014) Relationship between burnout and depressive symptoms: a study using the person-centred approach. Burn Res 1(1):29–37

Alasaari JS, Lagus M, Ollila HM, Toivola A, Kivimaki M, Vahtera J, Kronholm E, Harma M, Puttonen S, Paunio T (2012) Environmental stress affects DNA methylation of a CpG rich promoter region of serotonin transporter gene in a nurse cohort. PLoS One 7(9):e45813. https://doi.org/10.1371/journal.pone.0045813

Bakusic J, Schaufeli W, Claes S, Godderis L (2017) Stress, burnout and depression: a systematic review on DNA methylation mechanisms. J Psychosom Res 92:34–44. https://doi.org/10.1016/j.jpsychores.2016.11.005

Bakusic J, Ghosh M, Polli A, Bekaert B, Schaufeli W, Claes S, Godderis L (2020a) Epigenetic perspective on the role of brain-derived neurotrophic factor in burnout. Transl Psychiatry 10(1): 354. https://doi.org/10.1038/s41398-020-01037-4

Bakusic J, Vrieze E, Ghosh M, Bekaert B, Claes S, Godderis L (2020b) Increased methylation of NR3C1 and SLC6A4 is associated with blunted cortisol reactivity to stress in major depression. Neurobiol Stress 13:100272. https://doi.org/10.1016/j.ynstr.2020.100272

Bakusic J, Ghosh M, Polli A, Bekaert B, Schaufeli W, Claes S, Godderis L (2021a) Role of NR3C1 and SLC6A4 methylation in the HPA axis regulation in burnout. J Affect Disord 295:505–512. https://doi.org/10.1016/j.jad.2021.08.081

Bakusic J, Godderis L, Claes M, Schaufeli W (2021b). Epigenetic changes in burnout and depression

Bear MF, Connors BW, Paradiso MA (2015) Neuroscience : exploring the brain, 4th edn. Jones and Bartlett Publishers, Inc

Bianchi M, Renzini A, Adamo S, Moresi V (2017) Coordinated actions of MicroRNAs with other epigenetic factors regulate skeletal muscle development and adaptation. Int J Mol Sci 18(4). https://doi.org/10.3390/ijms18040840

Blom V, Bergstrom G, Hallsten L, Bodin L, Svedberg P (2012) Genetic susceptibility to burnout in a Swedish twin cohort. Eur J Epidemiol 27(3):225–231. https://doi.org/10.1007/s10654-012-9661-2

Butler S (2019) The impact of advanced capitalism on well-being: an evidence-informed model. Human Arenas 2:200–227

Cao Z, Wu S, Wang C, Wang L, Soares JC, He SC, Zhang XY (2018) Serotonin transporter gene (5-HTT) rs6354 polymorphism, job-related stress, and their interaction in burnout in healthcare workers in a Chinese hospital. Psychopharmacology 235(11):3125–3135. https://doi.org/10.1007/s00213-018-5009-2

Chirico F (2016) Job stress models for predicting burnout syndrome: a review. Ann Ist Super Sanita 52(3):443–456. https://doi.org/10.4415/ANN_16_03_17

Chou LP, Li CY, Hu SC (2014) Job stress and burnout in hospital employees: comparisons of different medical professions in a regional hospital in Taiwan. BMJ Open 4(2):e004185. https://doi.org/10.1136/bmjopen-2013-004185

Choudhury SR, Cui Y, Lubecka K, Stefanska B, Irudayaraj J (2016) CRISPR-dCas9 mediated TET1 targeting for selective DNA demethylation at BRCA1 promoter. Oncotarget 7(29): 46545–46556. https://doi.org/10.18632/oncotarget.10234

Chrousos GP, Gold PW (1992) The concepts of stress and stress system disorders. Overview of physical and behavioral homeostasis. JAMA 267(9):1244–1252

Deligkaris P, Panagopoulou E, Montgomery AJ, Masoura E (2014) Job burnout and cognitive functioning: a systematic review. Work Stress 28(2):107–123. https://doi.org/10.1080/02678373.2014.909545

Duman RS (2004) Depression: a case of neuronal life and death? Biol Psychiatry 56(3):140–145. https://doi.org/10.1016/j.biopsych.2004.02.033

Duval F, Mokrani MC, Monreal J, Weiss T, Fattah S, Hamel B, Macher JP (2002) Interaction between the serotonergic system and HPA and HPT axes in patients with major depression: implications for pathogenesis of suicidal behavior. Dialogues Clin Neurosci 4(4):417. https://www.ncbi.nlm.nih.gov/pubmed/22033833

Egan MF, Kojima M, Callicott JH, Goldberg TE, Kolachana BS, Bertolino A, Zaitsev E, Gold B, Goldman D, Dean M, Lu B, Weinberger DR (2003) The BDNF val66met polymorphism affects activity-dependent secretion of BDNF and human memory and hippocampal function. Cell 112(2):257–269. https://doi.org/10.1016/s0092-8674(03)00035-7

Fabbri M, Garzon R, Cimmino A, Liu Z, Zanesi N, Callegari E, Liu S, Alder H, Costinean S, Fernandez-Cymering C, Volinia S, Guler G, Morrison CD, Chan KK, Marcucci G, Calin GA, Huebner K, Croce CM (2007) MicroRNA-29 family reverts aberrant methylation in lung cancer by targeting DNA methyltransferases 3A and 3B. Proc Natl Acad Sci U S A 104(40):15805–15810. https://doi.org/10.1073/pnas.0707628104

Fraser R, Lin CJ (2016) Epigenetic reprogramming of the zygote in mice and men: on your marks, get set, go! Reproduction 152(6):R211–R222. https://doi.org/10.1530/REP-16-0376

Freni-Sterrantino A, Fiorito G, D'Errico A, Robinson O, Virtanen M, Ala-Mursula L, Jarvelin MR, Ronkainen J, Vineis P (2022) Work-related stress and well-being in association with epigenetic age acceleration: a Northern Finland birth cohort 1966 study. Aging (Albany NY) 14(3):1128–1156. https://doi.org/10.18632/aging.203872

Godderis L, Boone A, Bakusic J (2020) COVID-19: a new work-related disease threatening healthcare workers. Occup Med (Lond) 70(5):315–316. https://doi.org/10.1093/occmed/kqaa056

Goldstein DS (2010) Adrenal responses to stress. Cell Mol Neurobiol 30(8):1433–1440. https://doi.org/10.1007/s10571-010-9606-9

Han L, Witmer PD, Casey E, Valle D, Sukumar S (2007) DNA methylation regulates MicroRNA expression. Cancer Biol Ther 6(8):1284–1288. https://doi.org/10.4161/cbt.6.8.4486

He SC, Wu S, Du XD, Jia Q, Wang C, Wu F, Ning Y, Wang D, Wang L, Zhang XY (2019) Interactive effects of corticotropin-releasing hormone receptor 1 gene and work stress on burnout in medical professionals in a Chinese Han population. J Affect Disord 252:1–8. https://doi.org/10.1016/j.jad.2019.03.084

He SC, Wu S, Wang C, Wang DM, Wang J, Xu H, Wang L, Zhang XY (2020) Interaction between job stress, serum BDNF level and the BDNF rs2049046 polymorphism in job burnout. J Affect Disord 266:671–677. https://doi.org/10.1016/j.jad.2020.01.181

Holoch D, Moazed D (2015) RNA-mediated epigenetic regulation of gene expression. Nat Rev Genet 16(2):71–84. https://doi.org/10.1038/nrg3863

Holtzheimer PE 3rd, Nemeroff CB (2006) Future prospects in depression research. Dialogues Clin Neurosci 8(2):175–189. https://www.ncbi.nlm.nih.gov/pubmed/16889104

Jablonka E, Lamb MJ (2002) The changing concept of epigenetics. Ann N Y Acad Sci 981:82–96. https://doi.org/10.1111/j.1749-6632.2002.tb04913.x

Janusek LW, Tell D, Mathews HL (2019) Epigenetic perpetuation of the impact of early life stress on behavior. Curr Opin Behav Sci 28:1–7. https://doi.org/10.1016/j.cobeha.2019.01.004

Jia H, He M, Zhang X, Li Y, He SC, Zhang XY (2021) The relationship between job stress and job burnout moderated by BDNF rs6265 polymorphism. Psychopharmacology 238(10):2963–2971. https://doi.org/10.1007/s00213-021-05911-x

Karsli-Ceppioglu S (2016) Epigenetic mechanisms in psychiatric diseases and epigenetic therapy. Drug Dev Res 77(7):407–413. https://doi.org/10.1002/ddr.21340

Kerr JI, Naegelin M, Weibel RP, Ferrario A, La Marca R, von Wangenheim F, Hoelscher C, Schinazi VR (2020) The effects of acute work stress and appraisal on psychobiological stress responses in a group office environment. Psychoneuroendocrinology 121:104837. https://doi.org/10.1016/j.psyneuen.2020.104837

Kohli RM, Zhang Y (2013) TET enzymes, TDG and the dynamics of DNA demethylation. Nature 502(7472):472–479. https://doi.org/10.1038/nature12750

Kouzarides T (2007) Chromatin modifications and their function. Cell 128(4):693–705. https://doi.org/10.1016/j.cell.2007.02.005

Kuehner JN, Bruggeman EC, Wen Z, Yao B (2019) Epigenetic regulations in neuropsychiatric disorders. Front Genet 10:268. https://doi.org/10.3389/fgene.2019.00268

Kular L, Kular S (2018) Epigenetics applied to psychiatry: clinical opportunities and future challenges. Psychiatry Clin Neurosci 72(4):195–211. https://doi.org/10.1111/pcn.12634

Lee RS, Sawa A (2014) Environmental stressors and epigenetic control of the hypothalamic-pituitary-adrenal axis. Neuroendocrinology 100(4):278–287. https://doi.org/10.1159/000369585

Li M, D'Arcy C, Li X, Zhang T, Joober R, Meng X (2019) What do DNA methylation studies tell us about depression? A systematic review. Transl Psychiatry 9(1):68. https://doi.org/10.1038/s41398-019-0412-y

Li Y, Xue T, Jin J, Wu HE, Dong Y, Zhen S, He SC, Zhang XY (2022) Interaction between the BDNF gene rs16917237 polymorphism and job stress on job burnout of Chinese university teachers. J Affect Disord 309:282–288. https://doi.org/10.1016/j.jad.2022.04.135

Liu XS, Wu H, Ji X, Stelzer Y, Wu X, Czauderna S, Shu J, Dadon D, Young RA, Jaenisch R (2016) Editing DNA methylation in the mammalian genome. Cell 167(1):233–247 e217. https://doi.org/10.1016/j.cell.2016.08.056

Lu CT, Zhao YZ, Wong HL, Cai J, Peng L, Tian XQ (2014) Current approaches to enhance CNS delivery of drugs across the brain barriers. Int J Nanomedicine 9:2241–2257. https://doi.org/10.2147/IJN.S61288

Mahgoub M, Monteggia LM (2013) Epigenetics and psychiatry. Neurotherapeutics 10(4):734–741. https://doi.org/10.1007/s13311-013-0213-6

Matosin N, Cruceanu C, Binder EB (2017) Preclinical and clinical evidence of DNA methylation changes in response to trauma and chronic stress. Chronic Stress (Thousand Oaks) 1. https://doi.org/10.1177/2470547017710764

McEwen BS (1998) Protective and damaging effects of stress mediators. N Engl J Med 338(3):171–179. https://doi.org/10.1056/NEJM199801153380307

McEwen BS, Stellar E (1993) Stress and the individual: mechanisms leading to disease. Arch Intern Med 153(18):2093–2101. https://doi.org/10.1001/archinte.1993.00410180039004

Middeldorp CM, Stubbe JH, Cath DC, Boomsma DI (2005) Familial clustering in burnout: a twin-family study. Psychol Med 35(1):113–120. https://doi.org/10.1017/s0033291704002983

Middeldorp CM, Cath DC, Boomsma DI (2006) A twin-family study of the association between employment, burnout and anxious depression. J Affect Disord 90(2–3):163–169. https://doi.org/10.1016/j.jad.2005.11.004

Miyaki K, Suzuki T, Song Y, Tsutsumi A, Kawakami N, Takahashi M, Shimazu A, Inoue A, Kurioka S, Kan C, Sasaki Y, Shimbo T (2015) Epigenetic changes caused by occupational stress in humans revealed through noninvasive assessment of DNA methylation of the tyrosine hydroxylase gene. J Neurol Neurol Disord 2(2). https://doi.org/10.15744/2454-4981.2.201

Moore SR, Kobor MS (2020) Variability in DNA methylation at the serotonin transporter gene promoter: epigenetic mechanism or cell-type artifact? Mol Psychiatry 25(9):1906–1909. https://doi.org/10.1038/s41380-018-0121-6

Oakley RH, Cidlowski JA (2013) The biology of the glucocorticoid receptor: new signaling mechanisms in health and disease. J Allergy Clin Immunol 132(5):1033–1044. https://doi.org/10.1016/j.jaci.2013.09.007

Peterson CL, Laniel MA (2004) Histones and histone modifications. Curr Biol 14(14):R546–R551. https://doi.org/10.1016/j.cub.2004.07.007

Petitpierre M, Stenz L, Paoloni-Giacobino A (2022) Epigenomic changes after acupuncture treatment in patients suffering from burnout. Complement Med Res 29(2):109–119. https://doi.org/10.1159/000521347

Pruunsild P, Sepp M, Orav E, Koppel I, Timmusk T (2011) Identification of cis-elements and transcription factors regulating neuronal activity-dependent transcription of human BDNF gene. J Neurosci 31(9):3295–3308. https://doi.org/10.1523/JNEUROSCI.4540-10.2011

Ratman D, Vanden Berghe W, Dejager L, Libert C, Tavernier J, Beck IM, De Bosscher K (2013) How glucocorticoid receptors modulate the activity of other transcription factors: a scope beyond tethering. Mol Cell Endocrinol 380(1–2):41–54. https://doi.org/10.1016/j.mce.2012.12.014

Roberts S, Keers R, Breen G, Coleman JRI, Johren P, Kepa A, Lester KJ, Margraf J, Scheider S, Teismann T, Wannemuller A, Eley TC, Wong CCY (2019) DNA methylation of FKBP5 and response to exposure-based psychological therapy. Am J Med Genet B Neuropsychiatr Genet 180(2):150–158. https://doi.org/10.1002/ajmg.b.32650

Russell PJ (2014) iGenetics, 3rd edn. Pearson

Saaltink DJ, Vreugdenhil E (2014) Stress, glucocorticoid receptors, and adult neurogenesis: a balance between excitation and inhibition? Cell Mol Life Sci 71(13):2499–2515. https://doi.org/10.1007/s00018-014-1568-5

Schaaf MJ, De Kloet ER, Vreugdenhil E (2000) Corticosterone effects on BDNF expression in the hippocampus. Implications for memory formation. Stress 3(3):201–208. https://doi.org/10.3109/10253890009001124

Schneiderman N, Ironson G, Siegel SD (2005) Stress and health: psychological, behavioral, and biological determinants. Annu Rev Clin Psychol 1:607–628. https://doi.org/10.1146/annurev.clinpsy.1.102803.144141

Smith ZD, Meissner A (2013) DNA methylation: roles in mammalian development. Nat Rev Genet 14(3):204–220. https://doi.org/10.1038/nrg3354

Smith SM, Vale WW (2006) The role of the hypothalamic-pituitary-adrenal axis in neuroendocrine responses to stress. Dialogues Clin Neurosci 8(4):383–395. https://www.ncbi.nlm.nih.gov/pubmed/17290797

Song Y, Miyaki K, Suzuki T, Sasaki Y, Tsutsumi A, Kawakami N, Shimazu A, Takahashi M, Inoue A, Kan C, Kurioka S, Shimbo T (2014) Altered DNA methylation status of human brain derived neurotrophis factor gene could be useful as biomarker of depression. Am J Med Genet B Neuropsychiatr Genet 165B(4):357–364. https://doi.org/10.1002/ajmg.b.32238

Thomas M, Knoblich N, Wallisch A, Glowacz K, Becker-Sadzio J, Gundel F, Bruckmann C, Nieratschker V (2018) Increased BDNF methylation in saliva, but not blood, of patients with borderline personality disorder. Clin Epigenetics 10(1):109. https://doi.org/10.1186/s13148-018-0544-6

Vinkers CH, Geuze E, van Rooij SJH, Kennis M, Schur RR, Nispeling DM, Smith AK, Nievergelt CM, Uddin M, Rutten BPF, Vermetten E, Boks MP (2021) Successful treatment of post-traumatic stress disorder reverses DNA methylation marks. Mol Psychiatry 26(4):1264–1271. https://doi.org/10.1038/s41380-019-0549-3

Vojta A, Dobrinic P, Tadic V, Bockor L, Korac P, Julg B, Klasic M, Zoldos V (2016) Repurposing the CRISPR-Cas9 system for targeted DNA methylation. Nucleic Acids Res 44(12):5615–5628. https://doi.org/10.1093/nar/gkw159

Weber A, Jaekel-Reinhard A (2000) Burnout syndrome: a disease of modern societies? Occup Med (Lond) 50(7):512–517. https://doi.org/10.1093/occmed/50.7.512

Wei H, Aucoin J, Kuntapay GR, Justice A, Jones A, Zhang C, Santos HP Jr, Hall LA (2022) The prevalence of nurse burnout and its association with telomere length pre and during the COVID-19 pandemic. PLoS One 17(3):e0263603. https://doi.org/10.1371/journal.pone.0263603

Winter J, Jurek B (2019) The interplay between oxytocin and the CRF system: regulation of the stress response. Cell Tissue Res 375(1):85–91. https://doi.org/10.1007/s00441-018-2866-2

Yehuda R, Flory JD, Bierer LM, Henn-Haase C, Lehrner A, Desarnaud F, Makotkine I, Daskalakis NP, Marmar CR, Meaney MJ (2015) Lower methylation of glucocorticoid receptor gene promoter 1F in peripheral blood of veterans with posttraumatic stress disorder. Biol Psychiatry 77(4):356–364. https://doi.org/10.1016/j.biopsych.2014.02.006

A Life Course Perspective on Work and Mental Health: The Working Lives of Young Adults

11

Karin Veldman, Sander K. R. van Zon, Iris Arends, Benjamin C. Amick III, and Ute Bültmann

Contents

Introduction	176
Emerging Adulthood: Five Challenging Transitions	177
Young Adults Entering the Labor Market in a Challenging and Changing World of Work	178
Labor Markets and Life Course Challenges: The Link with Mental Health	180
Integrating a Life Course Perspective to Work and Mental Health Research	181
Life Course Principles	181
Life Course Concepts	182
Benefits for Policy and Practice to Integrating a Life Course Perspective When Looking at Work and Mental Health Among Young Adults	183
Applying a Life Course Perspective to Young Adults' Working Lives: Early Life Mental Health and Adverse Experiences	184
Does the *Timing and Duration* of Mental Health Problems in Childhood and Adolescence Affect the Working Life of Young Adults?	184
Do *Trajectories* of Mental Health Problems in Childhood and Adolescence Affect Young Adults' Educational Attainment, Labor Market Participation, and Functioning at Work?	185

K. Veldman · S. K. R. van Zon · U. Bültmann (✉)
University of Groningen, University Medical Center Groningen, Department of Health Sciences, Community and Occupational Medicine, Groningen, The Netherlands
e-mail: u.bultmann@umcg.nl

I. Arends
University of Groningen, University Medical Center Groningen, Department of Health Sciences, Community and Occupational Medicine, Groningen, The Netherlands

Arbo Unie, Utrecht, The Netherlands

B. C. Amick III
Department of Epidemiology, Fay W. Boozman College of Public Health, University of Arkansas for Medical Sciences, Little Rock, AR, USA

Winthrop P Rockefeller Cancer Institute, University of Arkansas for Medical Sciences, Little Rock, AR, USA

© Springer Nature Switzerland AG 2023
M. Wahrendorf et al. (eds.), *Handbook of Life Course Occupational Health*, Handbook Series in Occupational Health Sciences, https://doi.org/10.1007/978-3-031-30492-7_1

How Do *Labor Market Trajectories* of Today's Young Adults Look Like and How Are They Affected by Early Life Circumstances? 186
Looking Forward: Today's Youth Is Tomorrow's Workforce 187
References 189

Abstract

Young adulthood is a challenging life phase including major life transitions like leaving the parental home, finishing education, starting a first job, starting romantic relationships, and parenthood. These transitions are interrelated, and are likely to be influenced by earlier life experiences, such as childhood adversities and poor mental health. At the same time, young adults have to earn a living in a new world of work characterized by temporary employment, self-employment, and a 24/7 work cycle in a global economy. To promote sustainable employment throughout the working lives of young adults, a life course perspective must be integrated into work and mental health research, policy, and practice. A life course perspective highlights the importance of prior life experiences, such as where individuals grew up, who they grew up with, and their education and health status prior to working. This chapter explains and emphasizes the importance of applying a life course perspective to the working lives of young adults.

Keywords

Young adults · Mental health · Work · Labor markets · Transition · Trajectories · Life course

Introduction

Getting a job and maintaining a healthy working life is fundamental for individuals and society. Today, the changing nature of work and labor markets creates opportunities and challenges for the current generation of young adults, i.e., people who were born in the 1990s and are currently at the end of their 20s. Young adults have to earn a living in a new world of work partially characterized by more temporary employment and self-employment as well as less job security and a 24/7 work cycle in a global economy (see ▶ Chap. 3, "Transformation of Modern Work, Rise of Atypical Employment, and Health"). At the same time, young adults, as they enter working life, experience other major life transitions, such as leaving the parental home and starting parenthood. These transitions are affected by earlier life experiences, such as childhood adversities and prior mental health problems, which in turn may affect future mental health and later life labor market and work outcomes. Mental health problems constitute a major challenge for youth entering the labor market and for young adults in the labor market. Across many countries of the Organization for Economic Cooperation and Development (OECD) between 30% and 50% of all new disability benefit claims are due to mental health problems; among young adults the percentage goes up to 50–80% (OECD 2012).

To date, there is very little understanding of how young adults transition into the labor market, and how to positively support their working life trajectories. It is not known to what extent their working life trajectories are shaped by, for example, mental health, adverse experiences, and family life during childhood, adolescence, and young adulthood. The available evidence on young adults' work and mental health is fragmented. Research has not connected earlier life to later life and lacks an understanding of the underlying mechanisms accounting for differences in different groups and lacks a fundamental understanding of the role of social context in shaping experiences. By adopting a life course perspective, a better understanding of the complex and dynamic interplay between work, mental health, and family life in the early work career can be provided.

A life course perspective on young adults' working lives highlights the importance of prior life experiences such as where individuals grew up, who they grew up with, and their education as well as their mental and physical health status prior to working. Life course research has been applied to develop more robust causal models (Shanahan 2000), for example, to understand (developmental) health trajectories and socioeconomic inequalities in health (Pavalko and Caputo 2013; Corna 2013; Kuh et al. 2003; Halfon and Hochstein 2002; Ben-Shlomo and Kuh 2002). But, few studies have focused on work and health (Amick III et al. 2016; Amick III and Lavis 2000; Bültmann et al. 2020).

Integrating a life course perspective into work and health research involves two steps. The first step is to elaborate how timing, duration, intensity, and place of past and present exposures (i.e., pre-working, working, and nonworking exposures) are related to health and work outcomes. The second step is to describe how the exposure-outcome relationship is formed in a particular social, historical, and cultural context (Amick III et al. 2016). A life course perspective demands work and health researchers to expand their attention toward what happens earlier in life, preemployment, and how that period of time contributes to working and the work-health relationship. It also requires expanding our focus to understand what is happening in a person's life contemporaneously outside of work and how these experiences contribute to work and the work-health relationship in the working lives of young adults. This historical and contemporaneous expansion is not only important for research, but also for policy and practice.

The chapter starts with a presentation of the five challenging transitions in emerging adulthood, followed by a description of the changing world of work and labor markets, with challenges for young adults entering the labor market that affect their mental health. Life course principles and life course concepts are introduced, translated to work and mental health research, and benefits for policy and practice are presented. Selected applications of a life course perspective to research on young adults' early working lives are presented. The chapter ends with avenues for future research.

Emerging Adulthood: Five Challenging Transitions

The period of young adulthood is characterized by five major life transitions including leaving the parental home, finishing education, starting a first job, starting romantic relationships, and parenthood (Settersten et al. 2015). In a relatively short period, there are potential transitions to be made covering different aspects of life, and resulting in a great heterogeneity of life courses. As the five transitions are intertwined, the consequences of transitions are likely to accumulate. Although there is no prescribed or single normative pathway for emerging adulthood, early transitions tend to move into a more disadvantageous chain than later transitions (Elder Jr et al. 2003). For example, an early transition into motherhood is associated with low educational attainment, poor labor market participation, and mental health (Boden et al. 2008; Räikkönen et al. 2011).

Whether transitions are early, on time, or late is largely dependent on social expectations, i.e., on normative timetables. These social expectations are shaped by time and place, e.g., in 1975 young adults were likely to have made all transitions by the age of 22, while for young adults living in the 2020s many transitions are yet to come. Also, contextual factors impact the timing of transitions. For example, young adults tend to study longer when unemployment rates are high (Barr and Turner 2015). The higher the educational level young adults attain, the later transitions into work and parenthood take place (Mills et al. 2011). Large differences between countries have been observed, as social policies play an important role for the timing of transitions. For example, more liberal welfare states tend to have more generous compensation for maternity and paternity leave, which is suggested to lead to earlier parenthood (Mills et al. 2011; Zabel 2008).

The transitional period may be challenging for all, but some young adults may struggle more. For example, mental health problems in childhood and adolescence can influence the transitions, their timing, and their impact. Previous studies have shown that the 12-months prevalence of mental health problems among youth is around 30% (Ormel et al. 2015). Recent OECD data show mental health problems have increased since the start of the COVID-19 pandemic (OECD 2021). The majority of these early life mental health problems track into adulthood (Ravens-Sieberer et al. 2014; Kessler et al. 2012). Several studies have shown that mental health problems in childhood and adolescence increase the risk of school dropout, poor labor market participation, and early parenthood (e.g., McLeod and Fettes 2007; de Groot et al. 2021; Evensen and Lyngstad 2020). Young adults not engaged in education, employment, or jobs training (NEET) are most at risk of adverse labor market outcomes and eventually social exclusion later in life (Bardak et al. 2015; Carcillo et al. 2015; EECEA Eurodice 2015).

The transitional period during young adulthood may also have a positive impact on someone's life. Having multiple roles, for example, as an employee and as a parent, and thus having more responsibilities, may result in a breakup of old patterns, e.g., a reversed day-night rhythm often cannot be combined with a job or care for children. However, research into the positive consequences of transitions made during young adulthood for later life is still scarce.

Young Adults Entering the Labor Market in a Challenging and Changing World of Work

The world of work has transformed for all workers with increased nonstandard work arrangements (e.g., temporary, part-time or on-call work, (solo) self-employment, and platform work), digitalization, artificial intelligence, and automation (see ▶ Chaps. 3,"Transformation of Modern Work, Rise of Atypical Employment, and Health," ▶ 4, "The Impact of New Technologies on the Quality of Work," ▶ 18, "Adverse Employment Histories: Conceptual Considerations and Selected Health Effects," ▶ 19, "Precarious Work and Health," and ▶ 20, "Gig Work and Health"). Nevertheless, some challenges specifically relate to young adults' anno 2020.

First, compared with older age groups, young adults are most often confronted with nonstandard work arrangements (Chung et al. 2012; Canivet et al. 2017; Thorley and Cook 2017). Such work arrangements increase employment precariousness through job insecurity and reduced rights and protection compared with permanent and full-time work (Chung et al. 2012; Canivet et al. 2017; Thorley and Cook 2017).

Second, young adults today are experiencing a weakening nexus between education and employment, i.e., a higher diploma does not necessarily pay off in terms of stable employment. Across the globe, education policies are implemented to encourage young people to engage in post-compulsory, tertiary education to improve their chances of finding and maintaining employment (OECD 2018). However, data show that increased employment opportunities do not necessary follow from higher educational attainment. For example, among young adults with a high educational level, there was an average 3.5% increase in the share of low-paid jobs and an average 6.5% decrease in the share of high-paid jobs between 2006 and 2016, across OECD countries. As comparison, for young adults with a medium educational level the increase in low-paid jobs was 2.6% and the decrease in high-paid jobs was 1.5%. For some countries, like Spain, the numbers were much more discouraging, going up to a 20% increase in the share of low-paid jobs and a 10% decrease in the share of high-paid jobs for highly educated young adults (OECD 2019). Also, 20 years of research on two longitudinal cohorts of young Australians born in the 1970s and the 1990s showed that young adults with tertiary education struggled with finding secure jobs until in their 30s (Cuervo and Wyn 2016).

Third, and related to the previous point, rates of overeducation have been rising in the past decades and especially young adults report being overeducated in their work. Overeducation (also called overqualification) implies that a person has more years of education or higher qualifications than needed for their work (International Labor Office 2013; Thorley and Cook 2017). Based on data from the European Social Survey between 2002 and 2014, Sparreboom and Tarvid (2017) showed that the average incidence of overeducation rose from 7.6–11.0%. Also, young adults aged 15–30 years had higher levels of overeducation compared to adults aged 31 and over, although differences exist between European countries (Sparreboom and Tarvid 2017). Similarly, Thorley and Cook (2017) showed that the chance of being overeducated has increased over time for young adults in the UK: the share of young graduates in a nonprofessional or managerial job (compared to a professional or managerial job) increased from 10% in 2004 to 20% in 2014 (Thorley and Cook 2017).

To conclude, young adults need to navigate their working lives in a landscape of more differentiated, nonstandard employment arrangements compared with the

40-h, permanent employment contracts of older generations. Also, work may become more varied and labor markets less integrated with education and training. Hence, more flexibility and continuous learning may be needed throughout their working lives in adjusting knowledge and skills to be able to match the competencies needed for new forms of work created by digitalization, artificial intelligence, automation, and other technological innovations.

Labor Markets and Life Course Challenges: The Link with Mental Health

Nonstandard work, the weakening nexus between education and employment, and overeducation have been linked to worse mental health outcomes among young adults (Quesnel-Vallée et al. 2010; Canivet et al. 2017; Thorley and Cook 2017; Winefield et al. 2017; Dudal and Bracke 2019). For example, Canivet et al. (2017) showed that being in a nondesired occupation or precarious employment was more common among young adults aged 18–34 years, compared with adults aged 35–54 years, and that both were associated with poor mental health. Furthermore, monitoring reports from the UK and the Netherlands have shown that today's young adults more frequently report mental health problems compared to older age groups (Thorley and Cook 2017; Houtman et al. 2019). Besides these studies and reports, there is limited knowledge on how young adults' working lives affect their mental health and more longitudinal research is needed to unravel the underlying mechanisms and direction of effects.

When studying the relationship between work and mental health, it is important to also take mental health before the start of the working life into account. Various studies have shown that early life conditions such as the family context and (mental) health affect later life employment (e.g., Hale et al. 2015; Veldman et al. 2017; Clayborne et al. 2019; Christiansen et al. 2021; Hansen et al. 2021). For example, Clayborne et al. (2019) systematically reviewed longitudinal studies investigating associations between adolescent depression and psychosocial outcomes, including employment, in early adulthood (ages at outcome assessment ranged between 18 and 35 years with the average unweighted age being approximately 24 years). They found that adolescents with depression were over 1.5 times more likely to experience current or recent unemployment as well as long-term or multiple unemployment spells compared to controls (Clayborne et al. 2019). Similarly, research has shown that adolescents with many adverse childhood experiences (e.g., maltreatment, parental mental illness, and parental unemployment) are significantly more likely to be inactive (i.e., not in education, training, or employment) in young adulthood compared to adolescents with fewer adverse childhood experiences (Lund et al. 2013; Hansen et al. 2021). Thus, to improve the understanding of the relationship between young adults' working lives and their mental health, pre-working life factors need to be incorporated when investigating later life mental health and work; i.e., a life course perspective on work and mental health has to be adopted.

Integrating a Life Course Perspective to Work and Mental Health Research

A longitudinal, life course perspective offers a research framework for guiding research on health, human development, and aging (Kuh et al. 2003) from aggregate institutionalized pathways to the lived experience of people working out their life course (Elder Jr et al. 2003). In sociology and neighboring fields, life courses are studied as developmental processes, as culturally and normatively constructed life stages and age roles, as biographical meanings, as aging processes, as outcomes of institutional regulation and policies, as demographic accounts, or as mere empirical connectivity across the life course (Mayer 2009). Life course epidemiology is defined as the study of long-term effects of physical or social exposures during gestation, childhood, adolescence, young adulthood, and later adult life on chronic disease risk (Ben-Shlomo and Kuh 2002). The aim is to elucidate biological, behavioral, and psychosocial pathways that operate across an individual's life course, as well as across generations, to influence the development of chronic diseases (Ben-Shlomo and Kuh 2002). Below, we briefly present the key life course principles and main life course concepts and reflect on the benefits for policy and practice to integrating a life course perspective when looking at work and mental health among young adults.

Life Course Principles

Five key principles emerge from the conceptual life course literature (Elder Jr et al. 2003). First, human development and aging are lifelong processes, also referred to as the *principle of life span development*. When we translate this principle to research on how mental health of young adults influences their schooling and early working life, it is important to realize that mental health changes within a continuum over time and that poor mental health in young adulthood may be the result of accumulation over time (Veldman et al. 2017). Second, individuals construct their own life course through the choices and actions they take within opportunities and constraints of history and social circumstance, known as the *principle of agency*. In the Netherlands, young adults can move through the educational system through various pathways (Veldman et al. 2014). Moreover, they can switch between vocation-oriented and academic-oriented education. Through these options, young adults have agency regarding their educational trajectory. Third, the life course of individuals is embedded and shaped by the historical times and places they experience over their lifetime, called the *principle of time and place*. For example, it matters whether young adults enter the workforce during an economic boom or an economic recession (Elder Jr 1974; Haaland 2016). Studies have shown that young adults entering the labor market during an economic recession experience long-lasting scarring effects regarding earnings, employment, and disability pension (Haaland 2016). Furthermore, it matters in which country, or even in which part of the country, they try to enter the workforce. As an example, in 2020, the youth unemployment rate in Greece was, with 31.8%, 2.8 times higher than in the Netherlands, where the youth unemployment rate was 11.4% (OECD 2022). Entering the workforce as a young adult in Greece would therefore have been more difficult than it would have been for a young adult in the Netherlands. Fourth, the developmental antecedents and consequences of the life transitions, events, and behavioral patterns vary according to their timing in a person's life, referred to as the *principle of timing*. For example, young women who continue longer in education are more likely to have children at a later age (Mills et al. 2011). Fifth and last, lives are lived interdependently and sociohistorical influences are expressed through this network of shared relationships, known as the *principle of linked lives*. An example of the principle of linked lives is the intergenerational transmission of work values. A meta-analytic review showed that parents significantly affect their children's work values through both their own work values and parenting behavior (Cemalcilar et al. 2018). In other words, the work values of parents and their offspring are linked.

All in all, the school-to-work transition and the early working life of young adults is not only an exciting period for the young adults themselves, it is also an interesting period for life course researchers due to its multitude of potentially social and economic life altering transitions. Life course concepts (mechanisms) have been developed in life course sociology and life course epidemiology, but have been largely ignored and never been applied to understand the transition into work and the subsequent working life trajectories of young adults. The application of life course concepts may help researchers understand and disentangle the relationships between (early) life experiences, mental health, education, and work experiences of young adults.

Life Course Concepts

While many life course concepts exist (see Kuh et al. 2003 for an extensive overview), important concepts include accumulation of risk, critical and/or sensitive period(s), chain of risk, transitions, and trajectories. *Accumulation of risk (i.e., [health] disadvantages and advantages)* refers to the notion that (adverse or protective) exposures accumulate over time during the life course, like episodes of illness, poor health behavior, and environmental, work, and nonwork influences. In young adults, multiple episodes of poor mental health, or the accumulation of poor mental health over time, may affect their level of schooling, labor market participation, and work functioning in young adulthood (Veldman et al. 2017; de Groot et al. 2021; de Groot et al. 2022). *Critical and sensitive periods* refer to time windows when a particular exposure has an adverse or protective effect on a particular outcome (Kuh et al. 2003). While a *critical period* refers to a limited time period in which an exposure can have adverse or protective effects on a certain outcome (period of exclusive risk), a *sensitive period* is a time period when an exposure has a stronger effect on a certain outcome than it would have at other times (period of heightened risk). For example, Duncan et al. compared the effects of income in early life (ages 0–5 years), mid-childhood (ages 6–10 years), and early adolescence (ages

11–15 years) and showed that poverty experienced during early life was a sensitive period for the relationship between poverty and poorer academic achievement (Duncan et al. 1998). *Chain of risk* refers to a sequence of linked exposures that raise health risk (Kuh et al. 2003). Understanding chains of risk (or protective chains), e.g., from preemployment to employment, is dependent on how social and labor market contexts cluster exposures into specific sequences. *Transitions* are short-term events marking changes in physiological, psychological, or social states (Kuh et al. 2003). Important transitions in adolescents' or young adults' lives are, for example, the transition from secondary school to vocational education/university or the "school-to-work" transition toward entering the labor market (Bryzinski-Fay 2015). *Trajectories* are a sequence of transitions over a longer time period. In young adults, educational transitions (e.g., primary school to secondary school) and employment transitions (e.g., apprenticeship to full-time contract) together form a "school-to-working-life trajectory."

Benefits for Policy and Practice to Integrating a Life Course Perspective When Looking at Work and Mental Health Among Young Adults

An important aspect of mental and physical health is that it is a determinant and a resource or capability, which shapes working life trajectories. Adopting a life course perspective in work and mental health research involves understanding the key life course principles and concepts related to timing, duration, sequencing of exposure, and place (context). Researchers, policymakers, and practitioners need to acknowledge that past and present exposures and experiences that have been or are shaped in a particular social, historical, and/or cultural context influence future health and labor market outcomes (Amick III et al. 2016).

Moving from research to policy and practice requires life course research to: (1) elucidate the *critical* and *sensitive periods* in the life course; (2) describe *accumulation of risk* across time and within work and nonwork contexts; and (3) describe *chains of risk* from preemployment to employment. These three important life course concepts are described above and can help identify the most effective points, periods, and/or places to intervene, i.e., they offer policymakers and practitioners a window through which to exercise institutional agency and to define policies or practices. To illustrate, an example drawn from Amick III et al. (2016): depression in high school affects school achievement and thus educational outcomes and consequently employment outcomes. One may suggest depression or more broadly anxiety and mood disorders among high school students is a period of great sensitivity for later life work outcomes. Identifying this sensitive period supports employment and health practitioners to ensure they are identifying and managing mental health problems with the appropriate tools. It further may demand local and national changes to school policy integrating mental health care into the school system and connecting school health care with occupational health care. A second example from current day would be the accumulation of risk from young refugees experiencing the traumas of war, then the traumas of relocation. These traumas accumulate over time and policymakers and practitioners alike need to stop the accumulation providing off-ramps for individuals. For example, when young refugees are provided easy access to education, training, or work (depending on their age), they can develop their competences, increase autonomy, and experience relatedness (by taking part in classes or being part of the workforce), which are essential, basic human needs (Ryan and Deci 2017). On the short term, participation in education, training, or work could thus improve young refugees' well-being and offset (some of) the negative consequences of the accumulated trauma. On the long term, their education, training, and/or work experiences could facilitate integration into the host country's or home country's labor market.

Applying a Life Course Perspective to Young Adults' Working Lives: Early Life Mental Health and Adverse Experiences

A few illustrative examples are presented of studies that applied life course principles related to life span development, timing, duration, sequencing of exposure, and place (context) to better understand the effect of early life mental health and adverse experiences on employment and work outcomes in young adulthood. These life course studies addressed life course concepts, such as sensitive periods, accumulation, chain of risk and trajectories, and answered research questions like: "Does the *timing and duration* of mental health problems in childhood and adolescence affect the working life of young adults?"; "Do *trajectories* of mental health problems in childhood and adolescence affect young adults' educational attainment, labor market participation, and functioning at work?; and "How do *labor market trajectories* of today's young adults look like and how are they affected by early life circumstances?". These study results may inspire future life course research on this topic (see also section "Looking Forward: Today's Youth Is Tomorrow's Workforce") and can stimulate policy and practice debate and action as suggested below based on the illustrative examples.

Does the *Timing and Duration* of Mental Health Problems in Childhood and Adolescence Affect the Working Life of Young Adults?

The life course concepts of sensitive periods, accumulation of risk(s), and chain of risk are illustrated in a Dutch and a Danish cohort study, tracking children and adolescents into young adult life. De Groot and colleagues examined whether *the timing and duration of* mental health problems from childhood and young adulthood were associated with labor market participation in young adulthood (De Groot et al. 2021). Data from the Tracking Adolescents' Individual Lives Survey (TRAILS), a Dutch prospective cohort study with a 15-year follow-up, were used. Internalizing and externalizing mental health problems were measured at ages 11, 13.5, 16, 19, and 22. Labor market participation, operationalized as having a paid job (yes/no), was assessed at age 26. Internalizing problems at all ages and externalizing problems at ages 13, 19, and 22 were associated with an increased risk of not having a paid job. Young adults with a long duration of internalizing and externalizing problems (i.e., accumulation of risk over three or more measurement waves) showed an increased risk of having no paid job. Young adults with an early onset and a short duration of internalizing and externalizing problems were not affected.

In the second study, Veldman et al. (2022) investigated the effects of *timing and duration* of depressive symptoms in adolescence on NEET (Neither in Employment, Education, nor Training) in young adulthood. Additionally, the mediating or moderating role of educational attainment on the depressive symptoms-NEET status relationship was examined (i.e., direct, mediation, and interaction effects were identified) among girls and boys, reflecting the chain of risk concept in a gendered social context. Data were used from the Vestliv Study. Depressive symptoms were measured at ages 14, 18, and 21. Information on educational attainment at age 21 and the NEET outcome at age 23 were derived from Danish national registers. Among boys, depressive symptoms at ages 14 and 21 increased the risk of NEET, while depressive symptoms at ages 18 and 21 increased the risk of NEET in girls. For the duration of depressive symptoms, among girls, only persistent depressive symptoms (at two or three time points) increased the risk of NEET. Among boys, single and persistent exposure to depressive symptoms increased the risk of NEET. No mediation or moderation of educational attainment in the association between depressive symptoms and NEET was found.

The results of these studies not only show the long-term impact of early life mental health problems on labor market participation, but also that the timing and duration of mental health problems matters. As such both studies may indicate potential sensitive periods. Furthermore, both studies provide important information about entrees for both policy and practice to get early mental health monitoring and/or mental health surveillance systems in place, to develop mental health care to shorten the duration of mental health problems and to initiate the (early) provision of school and employment support to improve young adult's school-to-work transition and labor market participation.

Do *Trajectories* of Mental Health Problems in Childhood and Adolescence Affect Young Adults' Educational Attainment, Labor Market Participation, and Functioning at Work?

The following two studies illustrate the life course concept of trajectories, how trajectories can be shaped by the context and how they can affect later life outcomes. In a cross-country comparative study, Minh and colleagues investigated the impact of trajectories *of depressive symptoms during adolescence and young adulthood*, as compared with a single time point or a lifetime measure, on early adult education and labor market participation in Canada and the USA (Minh et al. 2021). The study compared data from two National Longitudinal Surveys on Child and Youth in

Canada and the USA. Four depressive symptom trajectories from ages 16–25 years were identified and linked with five educational and employment outcomes at age 25. In both country samples, increasing, decreasing, and mid-peak depressive symptom trajectories were associated with higher odds of working with low educational credentials, and/or NEET (Neither in Employment, Education, nor Training) relative to low-stable depressive symptom trajectories. The Canadian sample, however, was more likely to have better education and employment outcomes.

De Groot and colleagues linked trajectories *of mental health problems during childhood and adolescence* with work functioning among young adults (de Groot et al. 2022). In this study, work functioning reflected the experience of difficulties in meeting the job demands during the workday given a health state. With 18-year follow-up data from the Dutch TRacking Adolescents' Individual Lives Survey, the authors identified mental health problem trajectories, including 11, 13.5, 16, 19, 22, and 26 as age points. Work functioning was assessed at age 29. The authors showed that young adults with trajectories of persistent high or elevated levels of mental health problems from childhood to young adulthood reported lower work functioning scores compared with their peers with trajectories of persistent low levels of mental health problems. More specific, young adults with trajectories of persistent high mental health problems experienced difficulties in meeting their work demands for approximately 1 day a week given a full-time work week.

The findings of Minh et al. (2021) and de Groot et al. (2022) point to the importance of developing interventions (1) for the prevention, or at least reduction, of mental health problems in adolescence and (2) for educational, employment, and work functioning support in early adulthood. Given the institutional differences between Canada and the USA, but in the Netherlands alike, researchers and policymakers are recommended to further investigate how specific changes to mental health, education, and labor market policy in each country may improve the (working) life chances of young people with histories of poor mental health as they transition into adulthood.

How Do *Labor Market Trajectories* of Today's Young Adults Look Like and How Are They Affected by Early Life Circumstances?

A Danish cohort and data record linkage study on adverse childhood experiences and labor market trajectories illustrates the life course concepts accumulation of risk and life course trajectories and how these concepts can be connected as predictor and outcome, respectively. In this research, Hansen and colleagues investigated the extent to which adverse childhood experiences are associated with differences in *labor market trajectories* of young adults (Hansen et al. 2021). Monthly information on labor market participation, educational events, and public transfer records was analyzed between ages 16 and 32 for a cohort of Danish adolescents born in 1983. "In employment" was the state in which the young adults spent most time during their early life courses. Three clusters of labor market trajectories were identified. The most distinct cluster was characterized by a mean time of 149 months (73% of the follow-up time) spent "outside the labor market" and only 17 months (8%) spent "in employment." Cumulative adverse childhood experiences (i.e., accumulation) increased the probability of being included in this "outside the labor market" cluster compared with adolescents who had experienced fewer childhood adversities. In particular, experiencing parental divorce, witnessing a violent event, and being abused were strongly associated with the "outside the labor market" cluster.

This study clearly moved beyond the simple dichotomy of labor market participation "yes/no" by constructing different labor market trajectories built on sequences of monthly data and showed the effect of cumulated exposure to adverse childhood experiences on "disadvantaged" labor market trajectories. More life course research is needed on *how* early life circumstances affect labor market trajectories and *how* these vary by jurisdiction. This new information on the long-lasting consequences of early life exposures and experiences provides key input for the design of welfare policies and action directed toward "healthy" labor market trajectories.

Looking Forward: Today's Youth Is Tomorrow's Workforce

While publications on mental health and work among young adults with a life course lens are growing, this body of evidence is still in its infancy. To better build the body of evidence requires a common nomenclature about the life course. We have presented a set of key life course principles and concepts from sociology, psychology, and epidemiology to enrich work and health research. A better theory- and evidence-based understanding of the life course mechanisms that put young individuals at risk for poor labor market outcomes or put them on a positive more resilient trajectory is required. More research must focus on the role of the social context to better inform policymakers and practitioners at the intersections of youth health, mental health, and occupational health.

To further advance science on how early life influences later life work outcomes, a more rigorous investigation of life course mechanisms is needed. Relevant questions to better understand the transition into work and the subsequent working life trajectories of young adults' concern: "*which* life course mechanisms matter (e.g., sensitive periods, accumulation of disadvantage/advantage, and chain of risk), *when* do they matter (i.e., in which life phase), and *how* do they matter (e.g., whether they work in a complementary or competitive way)." A comprehensive example from psychopathology is the study by Dunn et al. (2018), who examined three life course theoretical models (i.e., sensitive periods, accumulation, and recency) to explain the relationship between exposure to childhood adversity and psychopathology symptoms. By using existing birth cohorts with long-term follow-up and/or matured longitudinal youth cohorts, researchers have opportunities to examine these life course mechanisms when constructing the educational and early working life trajectories of young adults.

Future life course research should further elaborate on transitions in building young adults' mental health and early working life trajectories, considering varying views for subgroups of society (Bültmann et al. 2020). More explicitly, intersectional research, which acknowledges the interconnected nature of social categorizations, such as gender, class, and race, which may create systems of disadvantage or discrimination that affect transitions and track into adult working life, is deeply needed. Also, transition research should focus on the positive impact of transitions during young adulthood on a person's life. Having multiple roles, for example, as an employee and as a parent, and thus having more responsibilities, may result in a breakup of old patterns, e.g., a reversed day-night rhythm often cannot be combined with a job or care for children or both.

When investigating both life course mechanisms and transitions in the context of young adults' working lives and mental health, more attention should be paid to the contextual factors that shape these mechanisms and transitions. A prominent contextual factor is the Covid-19 pandemic. In their paper "Understanding the Effects of Covid-19 Through a Life Course Lens" Settersten and colleagues argue *"one thing is sure: there is a time before Covid-19 and a time after it. This watershed moment is marking the psyches and lives of individuals, families, and cohorts in ways both known and unknown. A life course perspective is necessary to bring these effects, and the mechanisms that create them, into focus for investigation and intervention"* (Settersten et al. 2020). In line with the seminal life course research in the past century of Glen Elder Jr (1974) on "Children of the Great Depression," rigorous life course research in this century is needed on the long-term impact of Covid-19 on today's youth. For example, the first OECD data show that the prevalence of symptoms of depression and anxiety increased in particular among young people compared with pre-crisis levels and other generations (OECD 2021). The increase of mental health problems may be attributed to disruptions in access to mental health services, the wide-ranging impacts of school closures, and a labor market crisis that disproportionally affected young people. Not only the effects of Covid-19 should be addressed in further life course research, but also other contextual factors that may shape the lives of youth and young adults, such as, e.g., access to mental health services across the life course, the availability and affordability of childcare and living spaces, the provision of informal care, and the rapidly changing worlds of education, training, work, and labor markets.

Further life course research and evidence will provide policymakers and practitioners with a better understanding of the potential long-term, negative and positive, impact of early life exposures and transitions on later life employment outcomes. The identification of sensitive periods ("when") and chains of risk ("how") will offer policymakers and practitioners insights for the most effective entrees for intervention, i.e., points, periods, and and/or places. Further, the knowledge on how the social, historical, and/or cultural context has shaped past and shapes present exposures and experiences and how these experiences induce, exacerbate, or ameliorate future health and labor market outcomes will help to define policies and practices to support the young individuals early in life during education and training as well as the young adults at work.

To conclude, as *today's youth is tomorrow's workforce* and as *a person's mental health does not start when work begins*, further research with both a life course lens and action is needed from all people with a stake in the support of today's youth and the generations to come to build their careers and to respond to the challenge of healthy working lives.

Acknowledgments KV and IA were funded as part of a Netherlands Organization for Scientific Research (NWO) Vici project ("Today's youth is tomorrow's workforce: Generation Y at work"; NWO Vici 453-16-007/2735) that was granted to UB.

References

Amick BC III, Lavis JN (2000) Labor markets and health. A framework and set of applications. In: Tarlov AR, St Peter RF (eds) The society and population health reader: a state and community perspective. The New Press, New York

Amick BC III, McLeod C, Bültmann U (2016) Labor markets and health: an integrated life course perspective. Scand J Work Environ Health 42:346–353. https://doi.org/10.5271/sjweh.3567

Bardak U, Maseda MR, Rosso F (2015) Young people Not in Employment, Education or Training (NEET): an overview in ETF partner countries. European Training Foundation, Turin

Barr A, Turner S (2015) Out of work and into school: labor market policies and college enrollment during the great recession. J Public Econ 124:63–73. https://doi.org/10.1016/j.jpubeco.2014.12.009

Ben-Shlomo Y, Kuh D (2002) A life course approach to chronic disease epidemiology: conceptual models, empirical challenges and interdisciplinary perspectives. Int J Epidemiol 31:285–293. https://doi.org/10.1093/ije/31.2.285

Boden J, Fergusson D, John Horwood L (2008) Early motherhood and subsequent life outcomes. J Child Psychol Psychiatry 49:151–160. https://doi.org/10.1111/j.1469-7610.2007.01830.x

Bryzinski-Fay C (2015) Gendered school-to-work transitions? A sequence approach on how women and men enter the labour market in Europe. In: Blossfeld HP, Skopek J, Triventi M et al (eds) Gender differences at labor market entry – the effect of changing educational pathways and institutional structures. Edward Elgar, Cheltenham

Bültmann U, Arends I, Veldman K et al (2020) Investigating young adults' mental health and early working life trajectories from a life course perspective: the role of transitions. J Epidemiol Community Health 74:179–181. https://doi.org/10.1136/jech-2019-213245

Canivet C, Aronsson G, Bernhard-Oettel C et al (2017) The negative effects on mental health of being in a non-desired occupation in an increasingly precarious labour market. SSM – Popul Health 3:516–524. https://doi.org/10.1016/j.ssmph.2017.05.009

Carcillo S, Fernández R, Königs S et al (2015) NEET youth in the aftermath of the crisis: challenges and policies. OECD social, employment and migration working papers no 164. OECD Publishing, Paris. https://doi.org/10.1787/5js6363503f6-en

Cemalcilar Z, Secinti E, Sumer N (2018) Intergenerational transmission of work values: a meta-analytic review. J Youth Adolesc 47:1559–1579. https://doi.org/10.1007/s10964-018-0858-x

Christiansen M, Labriola M, Kirkeskov L et al (2021) The impact of childhood diagnosed ADHD versus controls without ADHD diagnoses on later labour market attachment – a systematic review of longitudinal studies. Child Adolesc Psychiatry Ment Health. https://doi.org/10.1186/s13034-021-00386-2

Chung H, Bekker S, Houwing H (2012) Young people and the post-recession labour market in the context of Europe 2020. Transfers Eur Rev Labour Res 18:301–317. https://doi.org/10.1177/1024258912448590

Clayborne Z, Varin M, Colman I (2019) Systematic review and meta-analysis: adolescent depression and long-term psychosocial outcomes. J Am Acad Child Adolesc Psychiatry 58:72–79. https://doi.org/10.1016/j.jaac.2018.07.896

Corna L (2013) A life course perspective on socioeconomic inequalities in health: a critical review of conceptual frameworks. Adv Life Course Res 18:150–159. https://doi.org/10.1016/j.alcr.2013.01.002

Cuervo H, Wyn J (2016) An unspoken crisis: the 'scarring effects' of the complex nexus between education and work on two generations of young Australians. Int J Lifelong Educ 35:122–135. https://doi.org/10.1080/02601370.2016.1164467

de Groot S, Veldman K, Amick B III et al (2021) Does the timing and duration of mental health problems during childhood and adolescence matter for labour market participation of young adults? J Epidemiol Community Health 75:896–902. https://doi.org/10.1136/jech-2020-215994

de Groot S, Veldman K, Amick B III et al (2022) Work functioning among young adults: the role of mental health problems from childhood to young adulthood. Occup Environ Med 79:217–223. https://doi.org/10.1136/oemed-2021-107819

Dudal P, Bracke P (2019) On the moderation of the relation between overeducation and depressive symptoms through labor market and macro-economic factors. Health Place 56:135–146. https://doi.org/10.1016/j.healthplace.2018.12.009

Duncan G, Yeung W, Brooks-Gunn J, Smith J (1998) How much does childhood poverty affect the life chances of children? Am Sociol Rev 63:406–423. https://doi.org/10.2307/2657556

Dunn E, Soare T, Raffeld M et al (2018) What life course theoretical models best explain the relationship between exposure to childhood adversity and psychopathology symptoms: recency, accumulation, or sensitive periods? Psychol Med 48:2562–2572. https://doi.org/10.1017/s0033291718000181

Elder GH Jr, Kirkpatrick JM, Crosnoe R (2003) The emergence and development of life course theory. In: Mortimer JT, Shanahan MJ (eds) Handbook of the life course. Kluwer Academic/Plenum Publishers, New York

Elder GH Jr (1974) Children of the great depression: social change in life experience. University of Chicago Press, Chicago

European Education and Culture Executive Agency, Eurydice (2015) Tackling early leaving from education and training in Europe: strategies, policies and measures. Publications Office of the European Union, Luxembourg. https://doi.org/10.2797/33979

Evensen M, Lyngstad T (2020) Mental health problems in adolescence, first births, and union formation: evidence from the young HUNT study. Adv Life Course Res 43:100324. https://doi.org/10.1016/j.alcr.2020.100324

Haaland VF (2016) The lost generation: effects of youth labor market opportunities on long-term labor market outcomes. Statistics Norway, Research Department, discussion papers no 835

Hale D, Bevilacqua L, Viner R (2015) Adolescent health and adult education and employment: a systematic review. Pediatrics 136:128–140. https://doi.org/10.1542/peds.2014-2105

Halfon N, Hochstein M (2002) Life course health development: an integrated framework for developing health, policy, and research. Milbank Q 80:433–479. https://doi.org/10.1111/1468-0009.00019

Hansen C, Kirkeby M, Kjelmann K et al (2021) The importance of adverse childhood experiences for labour market trajectories over the life course: a longitudinal study. BMC Public Health. https://doi.org/10.1186/s12889-021-12060-5

Houtman I, Kraan, K, Venema A (2019) Oorzaken, gevolgen en risicogroepen van burn-out [Causes and consequences of and risk groups for burn-out]. TNO, Leiden. Available at: https://www.rijksoverheid.nl/documenten/rapporten/2019/12/13/oorzaken-gevolgen-en-risicogroepen-van-burn-out

ILO (2013) Global employment trends for youth 2013: a generation at risk. International Labour Office, Geneva

Kessler RC, Avenevoli S, Costello EJ et al (2012) Prevalence, persistence, and sociodemographic correlates of DSM-IV disorders in the national comorbidity survey replication adolescent supplement. Arch Gen Psychiatry 69:372. https://doi.org/10.1001/archgenpsychiatry.2011.160

Kuh D, Ben-Shlomo Y, Lynch J et al (2003) Life course epidemiology. J Epidemiol Community Health 57:778–783. https://doi.org/10.1136/jech.57.10.778

Lund T, Andersen J, Winding T et al (2013) Negative life events in childhood as risk indicators of labour market participation in young adulthood: a prospective birth cohort study. PLoS One 8: e75860. https://doi.org/10.1371/journal.pone.0075860

Mayer K (2009) New directions in life course research. Annu Rev Sociol 35:413–433. https://doi.org/10.1146/annurev.soc.34.040507.134619

McLeod J, Fettes D (2007) Trajectories of failure: the educational careers of children with mental health problems. Am J Sociol 113:653–701. https://doi.org/10.1086/521849

Mills M, Rindfuss R, McDonald P et al (2011) Why do people postpone parenthood? Reasons and social policy incentives. Hum Reprod Update 17:848–860. https://doi.org/10.1093/humupd/dmr026

Minh A, Bültmann U, Reijneveld S et al (2021) Depressive symptom trajectories and early adult education and employment: comparing longitudinal cohorts in Canada and the United States. Int J Environ Res Public Health 18:4279. https://doi.org/10.3390/ijerph18084279

OECD (2012) Sick on the job? Myths and realities about mental health and work. OECD Publishing, Paris. https://doi.org/10.1787/9789264124523-en

OECD (2018) Education policy outlook 2018: putting student learning at the centre. OECD Publishing, Paris. https://doi.org/10.1787/9789264301528-en

OECD (2019) OECD employment outlook 2019: the future of work. OECD Publishing, Paris. https://doi.org/10.1787/9ee00155-en

OECD (2021) Supporting young people's mental health through the COVID-19 crisis. OECD Publishing, Paris. https://www.oecd.org/coronavirus/policy-responses/supporting-young-people-s-mental-health-through-the-covid-19-crisis-84e143e5/#section-d1e868

OECD (2022) Youth unemployment rate. https://data.oecd.org/unemp/youth-unemployment-rate.htm. Accessed 13 July 2022

Ormel J, Raven D, van Oort F et al (2015) Mental health in Dutch adolescents: a TRAILS report on prevalence, severity, age of onset, continuity and co-morbidity of DSM disorders. Psychol Med 45:345–360. https://doi.org/10.1017/s0033291714001469

Pavalko E, Caputo J (2013) Social inequality and health across the life course. Am Behav Sci 57: 1040–1056. https://doi.org/10.1177/0002764213487344

Quesnel-Vallée A, DeHaney S, Ciampi A (2010) Temporary work and depressive symptoms: a propensity score analysis. Soc Sci Med 70:1982–1987. https://doi.org/10.1016/j.socscimed.2010.02.008

Räikkönen E, Kokko K, Rantanen J (2011) Timing of adult transitions: antecedents and implications for psychological functioning. Eur Psychol 16:314–323. https://doi.org/10.1027/1016-9040/a000050

Ravens-Sieberer U, Otto C, Kriston L et al (2014) The longitudinal BELLA study: design, methods and first results on the course of mental health problems. Eur Child Adolesc Psychiatry 24:651–663. https://doi.org/10.1007/s00787-014-0638-4

Ryan RM, Deci EL (2017) Self-determination theory: basic psychological needs in motivation, development, and wellness. Guilford, New York

Settersten RA, Ottusch TM, Schneider B (2015) Becoming adult: meanings of markers to adulthood. In: Scott RA, Buchmann MC, Kosslyn S (eds) Emerging trends in the social and behavioral sciences. John Wiley & Sons, Inc, New York

Settersten R, Bernardi L, Härkönen J et al (2020) Understanding the effects of Covid-19 through a life course lens. Adv Life Course Res 45:100360. https://doi.org/10.1016/j.alcr.2020.100360

Shanahan M (2000) Pathways to adulthood in changing societies: variability and mechanisms in life course perspective. Annu Rev Sociol 26:667–692. https://doi.org/10.1146/annurev.soc.26.1.667

Sparreboom T, Tarvid A (2017) Skills mismatch of natives and immigrants in Europe. International Labour Office, Conditions of Work and Equality Department, Geneva

Thorley C, Cook W (2017) Flexibility for who? Millennials and mental health in the modern labour market. IPPR, London. http://www.ippr.org/publications/flexibility-for-who

Veldman K, Bültmann U, Stewart R et al (2014) Mental health problems and educational attainment in adolescence: 9-year follow-up of the TRAILS study. PLoS One 9:e101751. https://doi.org/10.1371/journal.pone.0101751

Veldman K, Reijneveld S, Verhulst F et al (2017) A life course perspective on mental health problems, employment, and work outcomes. Scand J Work Environ Health 43:316–325. https://doi.org/10.5271/sjweh.3651

Veldman K, Reijneveld S, Andersen JH et al (2022) The timing and duration of depressive symptoms from adolescence to young adulthood and young adults' NEET status: the role of educational attainment. Soc Psychiatry Psychiatr Epidemiol 57:83–93. https://doi.org/10.1007/s00127-021-02142-5

Winefield A, Delfabbro P, Winefield H et al (2017) The psychological effects of unemployment and unsatisfactory employment on young adults: findings from a 10-year longitudinal study. J Genet Psychol 178:246–251. https://doi.org/10.1080/00221325.2017.1342594

Zabel C (2008) Eligibility for maternity leave and first birth timing in Great Britain. Popul Res Policy Rev 28:251–270. https://doi.org/10.1007/s11113-008-9098-1

Part IV

Occupational Trajectories and Midlife Health: *Exposure to Chronic Hazards at Work*

Chemical Hazards at Work and Occupational Diseases Using Job-Exposure Matrices

12

Irina Guseva Canu

Contents

Introduction	196
Main Strategies of Occupational Exposure Assessment to Chemicals	198
Brief Overview of JEM Development for Chemical Hazards	200
Type of Chemicals Considered in the Generic JEMs	200
Example of a Company-Specific JEM for Radioactive Chemicals	202
JEMs and Emerging Risks	204
JEMs and New Exposure Settings	206
Future Perspectives in Chemical Exposure Assessment and Conclusive Remarks	206
Cross-References	207
References	207

Abstract

Occupational health is shaped by a complex set of occupational exposures and their determinants occurring throughout the life course. The assessment of occupational exposure to a chemical hazard is a complex process, which ideally results in an estimate of internal dose integrated over the exposure duration throughout the individual's professional carrier. However, in practice, existing data rarely allow such an assessment. Job-exposure matrices – or JEMs – established for one or several chemical hazards present a valid alternative, enabling assessment of chemical exposure per job, or homogeneous group of workers at company, or industry, or on the population level.

This chapter presents the principles and main constrains in exposure assessment for chemical hazards and summarizes the most common strategies and methods. JEM approach is presented in more details, to emphasize the methodological improvement achieved over the last four decades and chemicals for

---

I. Guseva Canu (✉)
Department of Occupational and Environmental Health, Center for Primary Care and Public Health (Unisanté), University of Lausanne, Lausanne, Switzerland
e-mail: irina.guseva-canu@unisante.ch

which the exposure has been assessed using JEMs. An illustrative example of a plant-specific JEM constructed for the nuclear industry emphasizes the JEMs' usefulness in occupational health research, and particularly in the estimation of the dose-response relationship with health outcomes. Finally, the use of JEMs for emergent exposures is discussed, along with potential extension of JEM approach to improve the exposure assessment to chemicals in the constantly changing world.

Keywords

External exposure · Biologically effective dose · Dose-response relationship · Exposure assessment

Introduction

Exposure is generally defined as a contact of an individual with a chemical agent through any medium or environment. Human population is exposed to a large number of hazardous chemicals, with around 140,000 and 86,000 chemicals registered for use in Europe and the United States, respectively (ECHA 2017). However, currently available chemical exposure assessment studies cover only a small fraction of these chemicals. Of the approximately 30,000 chemicals most used commercially in the United States, the risk assessment reports have been registered for less than 5% of substances (Hernández-Mesa et al. 2021). For many chemicals, exposure can occur occupationally, environmentally, and through consumer use of products containing the substance of interest. However, because the chemicals are first produced in the primary chemical manufacturing facilities, then used in the secondary manufacturing, and finally commercially distributed and subsequently released in the environment, there is an advantage to focus on occupational exposures in chemical risk assessment. Moreover, occupational exposures tend to be greater than those experienced from the wider environment (Nieuwenhuijsen et al. 2006) and benefit from the long history of occupational safety and health and the development of a wide range of techniques and methods for their assessment (Lioy and Weisel 2014).

Accurate exposure assessment is paramount in risk assessment and occupational epidemiology. Yet, it remains challenging, particularly in the case of new exposure patterns and pathways. Today's challenges in epidemiology are to demonstrate small increases in risk, to deal with mixture of exposures while trying to disentangle the causal risk factors of a disease, and, particularly, to provide exposure-response association for decision and policy makers. Moreover, from a life course perspective, it is important to causally link exposures across the life course to long-term health outcomes via longitudinal studies.

In the era of big data, numerous sensors easily installed to capture exposure close to its sources, in the worker's personal breathing zone (PBZ) or even in his body, send information measured continuously in real time in different locations directly to a centralized server. The "omics revolution" enables comprehensive screening of the genome, transcriptome, proteome, metabolome, and fluxome, and the discovery of biomarkers for risk assessment of chemicals (Karczewski and Snyder 2018; Hernández-Mesa et al. 2021). However, although this technological process is very promising, the realm of occupational epidemiology and chemical risk assessment is still highly dependent of exposure assessment success.

Exposure assessment is the process aiming to produce a valid and efficient classification of subjects with respect to the exposure. The ultimate goal of exposure assessment is to measure the biologically effective dose. In epidemiology, the latter is usually called the *internal dose*, a rather ambiguous term that deserves clarification.

When investigating the exposure-response relationship or dose-response relationship, it is important to distinguishes between *external dose* (i.e., the concentration of the chemical compound present in the environment), *intake dose* (i.e., the concentration of the chemical compound brought into contact with the body's barriers such as intestinal walls, pulmonary alveoli, and skin), *absorbed dose* (i.e., the concentration of agent absorbed in the body or at the level of a particular target organ), *uptake dose* (i.e., the concentration of agent or of its metabolized product(s) remaining in the body or in a particular target organ after its metabolization and excretion), and *biologically effective dose* (i.e., the concentration of agent or of its metabolized product(s) causing biological or physiopathological changes which contribute to the etiologic process of the studied disease). The measurement of the latter is often challenging, because the biological mechanisms by which a chemical agent might cause disease are often not clearly identified and the operational marker of these mechanisms are unavailable.

In such a context, the exposure assessment can be defined as a process of using available (and often imperfect) exposure measurement data in order to approach the relevant dose.

Individual biological measurements during the relevant time window (accounting for exposure regimen and the biological half-life of the chemical agent concerned) is considered the gold standard to approximate the biologically relevant dose (Table 1).

The accurate qualitative information and quantitative measurements of external exposure recorded at the time of exposure are less ideal but are still very useful. As chronic diseases such as cancers often result from the lifetime exposure, cumulative exposure can be assessed retrospectively using historical records of objective exposure measurements. Self-reported exposure information by means of diaries or questionnaires used in case-control studies would be the next best, followed by proxy-reported information. However, these two types of information are prone to information and recall bias, due to workers' unawareness of the chemical substances that they handle or encounter in their jobs and the fading memory of the substance brand names as they change jobs and as the time elapses.

Table 1 Data typically available for occupational exposure assessment and quality of exposure estimate

Type of data	Quality of dose approximation
Individual measurement of body or organ-specific burden/dose for all workers	Perfect
Individual measurement of the external concentration in PBZ[a] for all workers	↓
Measurement of external concentration at workstations or in specific industrial areas	
Ordinal/relative classification of jobs or tasks by exposure level	
Duration of employment in industry or job	
Binary ranking (yes/no) by industry job	Mediocre

[a]Personal breathing zone

Main Strategies of Occupational Exposure Assessment to Chemicals

The complexity of the exposure assessment process depends on the goal of the study (e.g., hypothesis test, hypothesis generation, or surveillance), the resources available, the level of detail, and the accuracy of the exposure data. Surrogates of exposure usually warrant less intensive effort in exposure assessment than processing of historical measurement records with detailed contextual data.

In occupational epidemiology, exposure assessors usually use a combination of multiple pieces of exposure information to produce exposure estimates. The earliest exposure estimates were based on the job titles and industry, with a poor documentation on how these estimates were obtained, and considering only current (i.e., recent) exposure. Then, this strategy evolved towards a more sophisticated classification, allowing grading the exposure level as an ordinal qualitative variable or a categorized quantitative variable based on historical exposure measurements records. Another significant improvement was a possibility to assess work histories and to link them to historical exposure records and exposure classification schemes, provided by the panels of experts or job-exposure matrices (JEMs). A JEM is a cross-section tabulation of jobs (or combination of industry and job) and chemical agents by time that automatically assigns the same exposure level to all individual having the same job (Goldberg et al. 1993). Linked to a complete subject's work history, JEM or expert classification provides an individual score of exposure to a given chemical. This score could be estimated yearly or cumulated over the exposure duration or employment period. In the case of chronic exposure to chemicals, which are common in industry and change mostly with changes in production processes, these exposure estimates brought a significant progress in hazard identification and risk assessment of many chemicals. A more detailed consideration of specific tasks while grouping subjects with respect to exposure offered a further refinement of this strategy (Benke et al. 2001). The documentation of subject's work history is an important endeavor from the life course perspective, considering the dynamic of exposures at different periods of life and at various levels (social, environmental, behavioral, and biological). Thus, the work history should be assessed as thoroughly as possible to enable coding the jobs and industries using standardized classifications with at least four digits (Plys et al. 2022).

With investigation of exposure determinants such as the presence of exposure control measures (e.g., ventilation or local exhaust boots), the use of personal protective equipment and, particularly, the quantity of the chemical in the workplace, a more elaborated classification schemes and algorithms became available. As inhalation is the most common route of exposure to airborne chemical, external concentration of chemical has been typically measured by drawing a volume of workplace air using a personal sampling pump and measuring the material that has deposited on an attached filter or sorbent, which is often placed in the breathing zone of the worker. The total mass collected reported to the volume of air sampled corresponds to the concentration of chemical, expressed as mg/m^3, ppm, or fibers/ml. For many chemicals, such as benzene and trichloroethylene, there are validated sampling and analytical methods, while for others, such as carbon nanotubes or glycol ethers, there are still no validated methods (Guseva Canu et al. 2020a; Bergamaschi et al. 2021; Borgatta et al. 2021).

Modeling exposure as a quantitative exposure score or exposure distributions by using measured chemical concentrations, knowledge on the physical-chemical features of the chemical (e.g., dustiness, particle size, or surface charge) (van de Ven et al. 2010; Savic et al. 2017; Savic et al. 2020), and contextual information on exposure regimen has considerably increased in occupational epidemiology in the last decade (Lesmes-Fabian 2015; Ribalta et al. 2019; Gao et al. 2021).

Finally, biomonitoring of exposure (i.e., measurement of chemicals, their metabolites, or reaction products in biological matrices), which entered in use in occupational exposure assessment since the late 1800s, has slowly gained in importance (Zare Jeddi et al. 2021). Although this strategy is the closest to the biologically effective dose assessment, it is still underused in occupational exposure assessment (Viegas et al. 2020). Exposure biomonitoring is invasive and costly, requiring a heavy logistics related to the biological sample collection, transport, storage and analysis, as well as an intensive data processing. For biomarkers of exposure, a thorough knowledge of "biomarkers kinetics" (i.e., absorption, distribution, metabolism, and excretion) is pivotal for identification of an appropriate sampling scheme. For instance, an exposure biomarker that has a very short half-life (plasma, blood) requires precise sampling times or can be better sampled through excretion into the urine. Moreover, there are legal concerns about the use and consequences of implementing occupational biomonitoring (Jones 2020). Nevertheless, several exposure biomarkers have been identified and validated. For instance, micronuclei assay seems to correctly reflect exposure to chromium and several other occupational carcinogens (Hopf et al. 2019).

In this context, despite growing technological possibilities in individual exposure assessment, some traditional strategies of classifying individuals in homogeneous exposure groups by jobs or tasks are still a common practice, particularly in the retrospective exposure assessment of prolonged exposure to chemicals. JEM is by far the most used example of such a strategy.

Brief Overview of JEM Development for Chemical Hazards

The first JEM description can be found in a textbook of occupational medicine published in 1941 (Reed and Harcourt 1941). Yet, the development and use of JEMs in occupational health research became increasingly common only in the 1970s. In 1980, Hoar et al. presented the concept as a quick and systematic mean of converting coded occupational data (job titles) into a matrix of possible exposures, circumventing the need to assess each individual's exposure in detail. As the latter requires more time and expertise, JEMs development is cheaper, although it could be less accurate. Historically, there were three main ways of methodological improvements in JEM development. One direction was a more precise grouping of subjects by considering distinctive features in their occupational activity more specifically. In this direction, the shift from generic JEMs to the industry- and company-specific JEMs (Goldberg et al. 1993), and from these JEMs to the task-exposure matrices in the early 2000s (Benke et al. 2001) were important milestones. Secondly, JEM developers progressively incorporated additional dimensions to account for temporal and spatial variations in exposure levels, for instance, by adding calendar period (Kauppinen and Partanen 1988), region (Peters et al. 2016), or gender (Kauppinen et al. 2014) to the JEMs. Finally, a third direction was in a more precise consideration of the nature of the chemical components assessed, from large families of chemical agents (e.g., solvents) towards individual chemicals, and event towards their subdivision with respect to their physical-chemical properties (Guseva Canu et al. 2008; Guseva Canu et al. 2013; Zhivin et al. 2014). Of course, the more and more precise quantification of the exposure levels through all these dimensions, based on consistent measurement data from important national and international databases (Kauppinen et al. 2000; Gabriel et al. 2010; Peters et al. 2012; Fonseca et al. 2022), contributed to the methodological improvement in JEM development.

Type of Chemicals Considered in the Generic JEMs

Theoretically, there is no limitation with respect to which chemical agent or a family of agents should be included in a JEM. As presented in the general JEM ▶ Chap. 8, "Integration of Occupational Exposure into the Exposome," all types of agents, including chemical, but also biological, organizational, and ergonomic, can be assessed per homogeneous exposure group in a JEM. What decides the JEM developers regarding the chemicals to include is the goal of their work: exploratory (i.e., aimed to generate hypothesis), surveillance-oriented, etiological (i.e., aimed to test the hypothesis), or methodological (e-g., aimed at assessing confounding factors or addressing sensitivity/sensibility and exposure misclassification issues). The earliest JEMs included a large range of chemicals, while the most recent ones encompass only a few chemical agents for which etiological hypothesis could be tested. For instance, in the first US JEM, an exposure score was assigned to 334 chemical hazards, including primarily known or suspected chemical carcinogens but also chemicals with other chronic or acute effects (Hoar et al. 1980). The first British JEM included 49 chemical agents, mostly agents suspected to cause occupational diseases, namely cancer, commonly encountered in different jobs or industries, but also several known industrial carcinogens (Coggon et al. 1984). The inclusion of the latter aimed at controlling for their potential confounding in the associations with other occupational exposures and evaluating the sensitivity of the matrix method (Pannett et al. 1985). In the first Canadian JEM (CANJEM), there were about 300 chemicals (Siemiatycki et al. 1981), while its updated version includes 258 agents to support exposure assessment efforts in epidemiology and prevention of occupational diseases (Sauvé et al. 2018). In the FINJEM developed in Finland in 1998, 48 chemical agents were originally included. In 2009, FINJEM was extended to eight new agents (six individual solvents, sulfur dioxide, and welding fumes) for use in the Nordic Occupational Cancer study (NOCCA) jointly conducted in Denmark, Finland, Iceland, Norway, and Sweden (Kauppinen et al. 2009). Besides these countries, FINJEM has been used in the Netherlands, Germany, Spain, France, Italy, and Australia (Kauppinen et al. 2014). As exposure levels are updated every 3 years, FINJEM also serves as a tool for epidemiological surveillance of occupational exposures. It provides an overview of the extent and level of exposure to chemical and physical agents but also data on exposure trends over time and exposure profiles by occupation and agent. The estimated levels of exposure are compared with the occupational exposure limits, which enables the identification of possibly hazardous exposures by agent and occupation for preventive purposes (Kauppinen et al. 2014). The success and so extensive use of the FINJEM is due to the accuracy of its quantitative exposure estimates, which have been compared for validation purpose with other national and international measurement data. This is not the case of the French JEMs constructed within MATGENE program (Févotte et al. 2011). In these JEMs, exposure level estimates are semi-quantitative (none, low, medium, and high) and are based on the published data and national exposure surveys, which does not preclude their successful use for all abovementioned purposes in France (Houot et al. 2021; Marant Micallef et al. 2021; Letellier et al. 2022).

A recent inventory conducted by the Network on the Coordination and Harmonization of European Occupational Cohorts, https://occupationalexposuretools.net/inventory/, identified 36 generic JEMs covering a wide variety of chemicals (Peters et al. 2021). This inventory focused on the recent and currently active JEMs, which could be used today in the exposure assessment of general population cohorts. Fourteen of these JEMs assessed the exposure to dusts and fibers, among which asbestos was the most assessed exposure (10 JEMs), followed by quartz and wood dust (both in 7 JEMs). JEMs that were specific for one type of occupation, one study population, or one company using its internal job classification were beyond this inventory, as these JEMs are deemed not applicable to other settings. Nevertheless, company-specific JEMs could be extremely valuable, namely for identifying new chemical hazards and assessing their risk for human health. The next part will illustrate such JEMs.

Example of a Company-Specific JEM for Radioactive Chemicals

In nuclear industry, particularly in developed countries, workers have usually benefited from a routine health and exposure surveillance, encompassing annual medical checkups, biomonitoring using urine and fecal analyses (reported as mass (in µg/L) or radioactivity (in Bq/L) measurements) along with a direct lung counting measurements (in Bq), and individual external dose measurements (in Sv) to assess the compliance with radioprotection measures. Unlike many other industries, nuclear workers have extremely precise individual exposure estimates for external radiation exposure. In some situations (e.g., accident or incident), internal absorbed doses to the whole body, lung, or another target organ are estimated by expert dosimetrists using appropriate pharmacokinetic and dosimetry models. However, because it is a time-consuming and costly process, internal absorbed doses are rarely available. This explains why, for decades, radiation epidemiology mostly focused on external radiation effects. This also explains why uranium, the most used natural radioelement, has remained in IARC Group C, impossible to classify with respect to its carcinogenicity, although ionizing radiation, including alpha radiation, was classified as a human carcinogen.

Depending on the degree of its enrichment in 235-Uranium isotope, uranium compounds could be more or less radioactive (e.g., military-degree enriched uranium versus natural or depleted uranium). However, as uranium mostly emits alpha radiation, which has a very short pathway in the air, uranium health damage are mostly expected after its intake, primarily through inhalation. In fact, uranium potentially exhibits a triple toxicity: radiological (as alpha emitter), chemical (being a heavy metal), and particulate (being in the form of fine and ultrafine particles when nongaseous). Indeed, cumulative external dose measured individually is not an appropriate exposure metric for assessing uranium toxicity. Unsurprisingly, in a cohort of 2897 Areva-NC-Pierrelatte plant workers at risk of uranium exposure, no dose-response relationship with the cumulative external dose was observed for any of the outcome studied (Guseva Canu et al. 2014).

The construction of a plant-specific JEM helped circumventing the problem of unavailable internal dosimetry data, but also data on other exposures, which might confound the exposure-response relationship. In this JEM covering the period 1960–2006, different uranium compounds were distinguished and categorized according to their solubility (highly, moderately, and slowly soluble) and purity (natural versus reprocessed/recycled uranium) in six categories. Moreover, 16 other categories of pollutants: chemicals, fibers, vapors, dust, and heat were included. For 73 jobs and for each pollutant, the amount and frequency of exposure were assessed on a four-level scale by different times using the panel of expert and the Delphi method of expert consensus (Guseva Canu et al. 2008). Compared with available exposure measurement data, this JEM showed 73% sensitivity and 83% specificity overall (Guseva Canu et al. 2009). Although exposure assessment was semiquantitative, it was possible to calculate the individual cumulative exposure score for each chemical across workers' carriers.

To assess the relevance of the cumulative exposure score to different categories of uranium compounds, a comparison with the retrospective estimates of internal doses based on bioassay data (the benchmark method) was performed for 30 workers randomly selected from the cohort. A moderate to strong correlation observed between the two types of estimators enabled validating the JEM for epidemiological use (Guseva Canu et al. 2010). Moreover, this study showed that the JEM is a valuable complement to the interpretation of bioassay results, in providing information on exposure periods, on physical and chemical form of the radionuclides, and on exposure in the years with missing records.

The use of this JEM for exposure-response analyses of cancer mortality showed that exposure to reprocessed uranium entails increasing risks of mortality from lung cancer and lymphatic and hematopoietic malignancies (with hazard ratios (HR) being respectively 1.14 (95% CI: 1.00–1.31) and 1.20 (95% CI: 1.01–1.43) per unit of a time-lagged log-transformed continuous exposure scores) (Guseva Canu et al. 2011). The analysis also showed that the HRs tend to increase with decreasing solubility of the uranium compounds. It is noteworthy that this study was the first to suggest that uranium carcinogenicity may depend on isotopic composition and solubility of uranium compounds. This study was also the first to identify the slowly soluble reprocessed uranium as having carcinogenic effect on two uranium target organs, controlled for potential co-exposures. Independently of uranium exposure, exposure to aromatic solvents was associated with increased risk of brain and central nervous system malignancies after adjustment for other chemicals (HR = 6.53, 95% CI:1.14–37.41). Furthermore, some types of lympho-hematopoietic cancers were found associated with solvent exposure (Zhivin et al. 2013).

With respect to cardiovascular outcomes, the dose-response relationship was the most evident and confirmed the importance of the solubility in uranium-associated health risks. Compared to unexposed workers, mortality from cardiovascular diseases was increased among workers exposed to slowly soluble reprocessed (HR = 2.13, 95% CI: 0.96–4.70) and natural uranium (HR = 1.73, 95%:1.11–2.69). The risk increased with cumulative exposure and with exposure duration. Moreover, in the subgroup of smokers, the risk estimates were higher (Guseva Canu et al. 2012).

These findings were unprecedented to suggest that uranium can be also toxic for circulatory system. To confirm this discovery, a nested case-control study was launched to reassess the dose-response relationship using cumulative internal absorbed doses to the lung and heart (in mGy) and adjusting for potential confounding factors. Historical monitoring records were retrieved from medical archives and computerized. The database contained 13,864 bioassay records for 350 workers, including 89 death from cardiovascular diseases. On average, each worker had two bioassays per year (minimum 1, maximum 31). Workers without any bioassay data were assumed unexposed. This study showed a positive dose-response relationship (excess OR per mGy = 0.2, 95% CI: 0.004–0.5), which was imprecise because of very low internal dose estimates (1 mGy to the lung and 0.01 mGy to the heart). Nevertheless, this study confirmed that uranium exposure can be a risk factor of cardiovascular diseases independently of attained age, sex, birth cohort, socio-professional status, smoking, BMI, hypertension, total cholesterol and glycemia, and external gamma radiation (Zhivin et al. 2018).

It is noteworthy that the realization of the latter study took more than 13 years and 7 years longer than the study based on JEM. Although the former confirmed that uranium can be an independent risk factor of cardiovascular diseases, by adjusting for important confounders, which have not been documented for the entire cohort, this study does not bring as much information as the study based on JEM. Although internal absorbed dose to the heart and lung could be assessed, which corresponds to the gold standard in epidemiology, it brought no information on the nature of exposure and did not allow identification of new hazards, such as slowly soluble reprocessed uranium. Indeed, the cost of the JEM construction was much lower than the dose estimation. Given the interest of JEMs for assessing radiological and especially non-radiological exposures in different nuclear plants, the construction of similar JEMs has been mandated by the French nuclear industry for other nuclear plants (Guseva Canu et al. 2013). The structure and methodology of this plant-specific JEM was also transposed to the nuclear plants in the United Kingdom (de Vocht et al. 2019; Riddell et al. 2019) and the United States (Hahn 2005; Figgs 2013). Finally, an international consortium concluded that these JEMs are also a valuable exposure assessment methodology for imputation of missing exposure data for nuclear worker cohorts with data not missing at random (Liu et al. 2016). This is just one example of a success story in occupational health research, which was made possible by the use of JEMs outside of chemical industry. In fact, JEMs could find applications in a large variety of settings, with different types of exposures. The next part will illustrate it.

JEMs and Emerging Risks

According to the definition, emerging risk arises "when the background knowledge is weak but contains indications or justified beliefs that a new type of event could occur in the future and potentially have severe consequences to something humans value" (Flage and Aven 2015). The weak background knowledge can result in difficulty specifying consequences and/or in fully specifying the event itself (risk scenarios). Engineered nanomaterials perfectly meet these criteria and are recognized as emerging risk. By extension, this is also the case of non-manufactured nano-sized particles, incidentally produced by widespread technological processes such as diesel engines and welding.

For some chemicals, like titanium dioxide (TiO_2), which have been produced for decades as noncarcinogenic for humans in bulk form, the switch to the nano-size TiO_2 exhibiting new physical-chemical properties suited for new applications (e.g., UV-catalysis) was associated with new biological effects and risk reassessment. As a result, TiO_2 in all its forms was classified suspected carcinogen to humans after inhalation (Guseva Canu et al. 2020b). While existent occupational cohorts of TiO_2 production workers have no information on physical-chemical properties of titanium dioxide handled at different plants (e.g., particle size distribution or crystalline phase), such information can be added using a JEM and combined with historical records of exposure measurements. This would enable stratification of exposure according to specific properties of TiO_2 compounds and a more specific risk assessment, as it was done for uranium with the AREVA-Pierrelatte JEM.

JEM could be also an approach to assess the exposure to other nanoparticles and nanomaterials (Guseva Canu et al. 2017), in particular the carbon nanotubes and nanofibers, for which there is already a database with exposure measurements from 15 US facilities (Dahm et al. 2019). The authors tried to model individual exposure according to different exposure determinants considering commonly performed tasks, material forms used, mass quantities handled, and engineering controls used by the various US industries that produce or use carbon nanotubes/nanofibers. However, they concluded that the model alone would not adequately predict workplace exposures and needs to be supplemented with other methods and additional exposure measurement collection. A JEM could be an alternative approach after appropriate standardization in job tasks or job titles across companies and industries (Guseva Canu et al. 2018). A harmonization in measuring exposure to carbon nanotubes/nanofibers and reporting exposure levels per job and task within each job, while documenting contextual information would help designing a JEM at least for this type of nanomaterials (Guseva Canu et al. 2020a).

Regarding the incidental ultrafine particle, a JEM has been recently created in France (Audignon-Durand et al. 2021). In this JEM, 57 work processes were identified as well as the chemical composition of incidental ultrafine particle emitted, based on a literature review and expert assessment. These work processes were linked to occupational codes defined according to the ISCO 1968 classification. The probability and frequency of exposure were assessed for each combination of occupational code and process. Summarized probabilities and frequencies were then calculated for all occupational codes associated with several processes. Moreover, the authors accounted for variations in exposure over time or across industrial sectors (Audignon-Durand et al. 2021). This JEM has already allowed demonstrating that maternal occupational exposure to unintentionally emitted carbonaceous nanoparticles was associated with a small birth weight for gestational age in the ELFE cohort (OR = 1.80, 95% CI: 1.29, 2.46) (Manangama et al. 2020a), and this outcome can be explained by placental hypoplasia associated with maternal occupational exposure to ultrafine particles during pregnancy (Pasquiou et al. 2021). In the reanalysis of two independent case-control studies, significant associations between occupational exposure to ultrafine particles and lung cancer (OR = 1.51; 95% CI: 1.22–1.86 and brain tumors (OR = 1.69; 95% CI: 1.17–2.44) were observed (Manangama et al. 2020b). Furthermore, the presence of ultrafine particles in bronchoalveolar lavage of patients with interstitial lung diseases was associated with occupational exposure to incidental ultrafine particles (Forest et al. 2021). These findings suggested a role of titanium nanoparticles in idiopathic pulmonary fibrosis and a contribution of silica submicron particles to sarcoidosis and strengthen the array of presumptions on the contribution of some inhaled particles (from nano to submicron size) to some idiopathic lung diseases (Forest et al. 2021).

JEMs and New Exposure Settings

In the context of globalization, some well-known but also some completely new occupation hazards migrate to new places, typically the low- and medium-income countries (LMIC), where they can generate emergent risks. This might be due to new ways of handling hazardous chemicals, insufficient personal hygiene, or exposure control. This could also be due to the relocation of activities at risk, for instance, the recycling of electronic wastes. As biological monitoring and exposure measurements are usually difficult to implement in the LMICs because of lacking infrastructure and financial and logistical resources, JEM approach represents a good alternative to initiate an exposure assessment. For example, to tackle the pesticide exposure, which is widespread in Africa and in the LMICs more generally, it should be possible to generate a JEM or a CEM (crop exposure matrix), as it was done in some developed countries (Brouwer et al. 2016; Carles et al. 2018). JEMs from pesticide exposure were recognized a relevant approach (Carles et al. 2017) and applied successfully to investigate the relationship of ever use of 14 selected pesticide chemical groups and 33 individual active chemical ingredients with non-Hodgkin lymphoid malignancies overall or major subtype in pooled analysis of US, French, and Norwegian agricultural worker cohorts (Leon et al. 2019).

Another example of JEM method extension could be the assessment of professional bus driver exposures, by constructing bus exposure matrix (BEM). Such a BEM is currently under development in Switzerland and encompasses 374 bus models, which constitute the Swiss bus fleet aver the last 60 years (Remy 2022). As many of buses included in this BEM were constructed and used in other countries (e.g., the Netherlands, Sweden, Belgium, Poland, and Germany), this BEM could be used beyond Switzerland. Moreover, as many old buses could be sent in the LMICs, the BEM could also inform the exposures of bus drivers in those countries.

Future Perspectives in Chemical Exposure Assessment and Conclusive Remarks

Besides the extension of the JEM to the emerging hazards and new occupational settings, the future JEMs for chemical exposure should better consider all possible exposure routes. In fact, inhalation exposure has been the traditional focus for most epidemiological investigations, but there is now growing awareness of the importance of the dermal and ingested routes of contact and internalization of chemicals (Niemeier et al. 2020), consistent with the exposome paradigm (see "Integration of Occupational Exposure into Exposome"). Gender-specific exposure estimates are also warranted in chemical exposure assessment, as it is already the case in JEMs for psychosocial and mechanical risk factors (see "Job-Exposure Matrices: Design, Validation, and Limitations" and "Psychosocial Work Environment and Health: Applying Job-Exposure Matrices"). New applications of JEMs, in combination with other exposure-related data, are suggested, as some JEMs could solve issues of missing exposure data, lacunar information on the physical-chemical properties of a chemical, and other similar concerns. Despite the belief that occupational exposure measurement data enable estimating exposure levels for all types of jobs and time periods by statistical modeling (Peters et al. 2021), in many situations and settings, modeling is still not possible. The use of occupational exposure measurement data could be limited because these data are not easily findable, accessible, interoperable, and reusable. Moreover, these data can be insufficient to produce adequate model and exposure predictions. The increasing use of exposure biomonitoring and biomarker discovery and validation thanks to the omics approaches and in silico studies are certainly a future in chemical exposure and risk assessment. In this perspective, JEM is not "an old vine in a new bottle," but rather a pragmatic alternative, which has demonstrated its validity and usefulness in chemical exposure and risk assessment.

Cross-References

▶ Integration of Occupational Exposure into the Exposome
▶ Job-Exposure Matrices: Design, Validation, and Limitations
▶ Psychosocial Work Environment and Health: Applying Job-Exposure Matrices and Work Organization and Management Practice

References

Audignon-Durand S, Gramond C, Ducamp S, Manangama G, Garrigou A, Delva F, Brochard P, Lacourt A (2021) Development of a job-exposure matrix for ultrafine particle exposure: the MatPUF JEM. Ann Work Expo Health 65:516–527

Benke G, Sim M, Fritschi L, Aldred G, Forbes A, Kauppinen T (2001) Comparison of occupational exposure using three different methods: hygiene panel, job exposure matrix (JEM), and self reports. Appl Occup Environ Hyg 16:84–91

Bergamaschi E, Garzaro G, Wilson Jones G, Buglisi M, Caniglia M, Godono A, Bosio D, Fenoglio I, Guseva Canu I (2021) Occupational exposure to carbon nanotubes and carbon Nanofibres: more than a cobweb. Nanomaterials (Basel) 11:745

Borgatta M, Hechon J, Wild P, Hopf NB (2021) Influence of collection and storage materials on glycol ether concentrations in urine and blood. Sci Total Environ 792:148196

Brouwer M, Schinasi L, Beane Freeman LE, Baldi I, Lebailly P, Ferro G, Nordby KC, Schüz J, Leon ME, Kromhout H (2016) Assessment of occupational exposure to pesticides in a pooled analysis of agricultural cohorts within the AGRICOH consortium. Occup Environ Med 73:359–367

Carles C, Bouvier G, Lebailly P, Baldi I (2017) Use of job-exposure matrices to estimate occupational exposure to pesticides: a review. J Expo Sci Environ Epidemiol 27:125–140

Carles C, Bouvier G, Esquirol Y, Pouchieu C, Migault L, Piel C, Fabbro-Peray P, Tual S, Lebailly P, Baldi I (2018) Occupational exposure to pesticides: development of a job-exposure matrix for use in population-based studies (PESTIPOP). J Expo Sci Environ Epidemiol 28:281–288

Coggon D, Pannett B, Acheson ED (1984) Use of job-exposure matrix in an occupational analysis of lung and bladder cancers on the basis of death certificates. J Natl Cancer Inst 72:61–65

Dahm MM, Bertke S, Schubauer-Berigan MK (2019) Predicting occupational exposures to carbon nanotubes and nanofibers based on workplace determinants modeling. Ann Work Expo Health 63:158–172 de Vocht F, Riddell A, Wakeford R, Liu H, MacGregor D, Wilson C, Peace M, O'Hagan J, Agius R (2019) Construction, validation and sensitivity analyses of a job exposure matrix for early plutonium Workers at the Sellafield Nuclear Site, United Kingdom. Radiat Res 191:60–66

ECHA (2017) Guidance for the identification and naming of the substances under REACH and CLP. European Chemicals Agency, Helsinki, Finland

Févotte J, Dananché B, Delabre L, Ducamp S, Garras L, Houot M, Luce D, Orlowski E, Pilorget C, Lacourt A, Brochard P, Goldberg M, Imbernon E (2011) Matgéné: a program to develop job-exposure matrices in the general population in France. Ann Occup Hyg 55:865–878

Figgs LW (2013) Lung cancer mortality among uranium gaseous diffusion plant workers: a cohort study 1952-2004. Int J Occup Environ Med 4:128–140

Flage R, Aven T (2015) Emerging risk – conceptual definition and a relation to black swan type of events. Reliab Eng Syst Saf 144:61–67

Fonseca AS, Jørgensen AK, Larsen BX, Moser-Johansen M, Flachs EM, Ebbehøj NE, Bønløkke JH, Østergaard TO, Bælum J, Sherson DL, Schlünssen V, Meyer HW, Jensen KA (2022) Historical Asbestos measurements in Denmark-A National Database. Int J Environ Res Public Health 19

Forest V, Pourchez J, Pélissier C, Audignon Durand S, Vergnon JM, Fontana L (2021) Relationship between occupational exposure to airborne nanoparticles, Nanoparticle Lung Burden and Lung Diseases. Toxics 9(9):204

Gabriel S, Koppisch D, Range D (2010) The MGU – a monitoring system for the collection and documentation of valid workplace exposure data. Gefahrst Reinhalt L 70:43–79

Gao X, Zhou X, Zou H, Wang Q, Zhou Z, Chen R, Yuan W, Luan Y, Quan C, Zhang M (2021) Exposure characterization and risk assessment of ultrafine particles from the blast furnace process in a steelmaking plant. J Occup Health 63:e12257

Goldberg M, Kromhout H, Guenel P, Fletcher AC, Gerin M, Glass DC, Heederik D, Kauppinen T, Ponti A (1993) Job exposure matrices in industry. Int J Epidemiol 22:S10–S15

Guseva Canu I, Molina G, Goldberg M, Collomb P, David JC, Perez P, Paquet F, Tirmarche M (2008) Development of a job exposure matrix for the epidemiological follow-up of workers in the French nuclear industry. Rev Epidemiol Sante Publique 56:21–29

Guseva Canu I, Paquet F, Goldberg M, Auriol B, Bérard P, Collomb P, David JC, Molina G, Perez P, Tirmarche M (2009) Comparative assessing for radiological, chemical, and physical exposures at the French uranium conversion plant: is uranium the only stressor? Int J Hyg Environ Health 212:398–413

Guseva Canu I, Laurier D, Caër-Lorho S, Samson E, Timarche M, Auriol B, Bérard P, Collomb P, Quesne B, Blanchardon E (2010) Characterisation of protracted low-level exposure to uranium in the workplace: A comparison of two approaches. Int J Hyg Environ Health 213:270–277

Guseva Canu I, Jacob S, Cardis E, Wild P, Caër S, Auriol B, Garsi JP, Tirmarche M, Laurier D (2011) Uranium carcinogenicity in humans might depend on the physical and chemical nature of uranium and its isotopic composition: results from pilot epidemiological study of French nuclear workers. Cancer Causes Control 22:1563–1573

Guseva Canu I, Garsi JP, Caër-Lorho S, Jacob S, Collomb P, Acker A, Laurier D (2012) Does uranium induce circulatory diseases? First results from a French cohort of uranium workers. *Occup Environ Med* 69:404–409

Guseva Canu I, Faust S, Knieczak E, Carles M, Samson E, Laurier D (2013) Estimating historic exposures at the European gaseous diffusion plants. Int J Hyg Environ Health 216:499–507

Guseva Canu I, Zhivin S, Garsi JP, Caër-Lorho S, Samson E, Collomb P, Acker A, Laurier D (2014) Effects of chronic uranium internal exposure on mortality: results of a pilot study among French nuclear workers. Rev Epidemiol Sante Publique 62:339–350

Guseva Canu I, Jezewski-Serra D, Delabre L, Ducamp S, Iwatsubo Y, Audignon-Durand S, Ducros C, Radauceanu A, Durand C, Witschger O, Flahaut E (2017) Qualitative and Semi-quantitative assessment of exposure to engineered nanomaterials within the French EpiNano program: inter- and Intramethod reliability study. Ann Work Expo Health 61:87–97

Guseva Canu I, Schulte PA, Riediker M, Fatkhutdinova L, Bergamaschi E (2018) Methodological, political and legal issues in the assessment of the effects of nanotechnology on human health. J Epidemiol Community Health 72:148–153

Guseva Canu I, Fraize-Frontier S, Michel C, Charles S (2020a) Weight of epidemiological evidence for titanium dioxide risk assessment: current state and further needs. J Expo Sci Environ Epidemiol 30:430–435

Guseva Canu I, Batsungnoen K, Maynard A, Hopf NB (2020b) State of knowledge on the occupational exposure to carbon nanotubes. Int J Hyg Environ Health 225:113472

Hahn KM (2005) Estimating historic exposure to arsenic, beryllium, hexavalent chromium, nickel, and uranium at a uranium enrichment, gaseous diffusion plant. University of Cincinnati, Cincinnati, OH

Hernández-Mesa M, Le Bizec B, Dervilly G (2021) Metabolomics in chemical risk analysis – a review. Anal Chim Acta 1154:338298

Hoar SK, Morrison AS, Cole P, Silverman DT (1980) An occupation and exposure linkage system for the study of occupational carcinogenesis. J Occup Med 22:722–726

Hopf NB, Bolognesi C, Danuser B, Wild P (2019) Biological monitoring of workers exposed to carcinogens using the buccal micronucleus approach: A systematic review and meta-analysis. Mutat Res Rev Mutat Res 781:11–29

Houot MT, Homère J, Goulard H, Garras L, Delabre L, Pilorget C (2021) Lifetime occupational exposure proportion estimation methods: a sensitivity analysis in the general population. Int Arch Occup Environ Health 94:1537–1547

Jones K (2020) Occupational biological monitoring-is now the time? Ind Health 58:489–491

Karczewski KJ, Snyder MP (2018) Integrative omics for health and disease. Nat Rev Genet 19: 299–310

Kauppinen T, Partanen T (1988) Use of plant- and period-specific job-exposure matrices in studies on occupational cancer. Scand J Work Environ Health 14:161–167

Kauppinen T, Toikkanen J, Pedersen D, Young R, Ahrens W, Boffetta P, Hansen J, Kromhout H, Maqueda Blasco J, Mirabelli D, de la Orden-Rivera V, Pannett B, Plato N, Savela A, Vincent R, Kogevinas M (2000) Occupational exposure to carcinogens in the European Union. Occup Environ Med 57:10–18

Kauppinen T, Heikkilä P, Plato N, Woldbæk T, Lenvik K, Hansen J, Kristjansson V, Pukkala E (2009) Construction of job-exposure matrices for the Nordic occupational cancer study (NOCCA). Acta Oncol 48:791–800

Kauppinen T, Uuksulainen S, Saalo A, Mäkinen I, Pukkala E (2014) Use of the Finnish information system on occupational exposure (FINJEM) in epidemiologic, surveillance, and other applications. Ann Occup Hyg 58:380–396

Leon ME, Schinasi LH, Lebailly P, Beane Freeman LE, Nordby KC, Ferro G, Monnereau A, Brouwer M, Tual S, Baldi I, Kjaerheim K, Hofmann JN, Kristensen P, Koutros S, Straif K, Kromhout H, Schüz J (2019) Pesticide use and risk of non-Hodgkin lymphoid malignancies in agricultural cohorts from France, Norway and the USA: a pooled analysis from the AGRICOH consortium. *Int J Epidemiol* 48:1519–1535

Lesmes-Fabian C (2015) Dermal exposure assessment to pesticides in farming systems in developing countries: comparison of models. Int J Environ Res Public Health 12:4670–4696

Letellier N, Gutierrez LA, Pilorget C, Artaud F, Descatha A, Ozguler A, Goldberg M, Zins M, Elbaz A, Berr C (2022) Association between occupational exposure to formaldehyde and cognitive impairment. Neurology 98:e633–ee40

Lioy P, Weisel C (2014) Chapter 1 – history and foundations of exposure science. In: Lioy P, Weisel C (eds) Exposure Science. Oxford, Academic Press

Liu H, Wakeford R, Riddell A, O'Hagan J, MacGregor D, Agius R, Wilson C, Peace M, de Vocht F (2016) A review of job-exposure matrix methodology for application to workers exposed to radiation from internally deposited plutonium or other radioactive materials. J Radiol Prot 36: R1–R22

Manangama G, Audignon-Durand S, Migault L, Gramond C, Zaros C, Teysseire R, Sentilhes L, Brochard P, Lacourt A, Delva F (2020a) Maternal occupational exposure to carbonaceous nanoscale particles and small for gestational age and the evolution of head circumference in the French longitudinal study of children – Elfe study. Environ Res 185:109394

Manangama G, Gramond C, Audignon-Durand S, Baldi I, Fabro-Peray P, Ilg AGS, Guénel P, Lebailly P, Luce D, Stücker I, Brochard P, Lacourt A (2020b) Occupational exposure to unintentionally emitted nanoscale particles and risk of cancer: from lung to central nervous system – results from three French case-control studies. Environ Res 191:110024

Marant Micallef C, Charvat H, Houot MT, Vignat J, Straif K, Paul A, El Yamani M, Pilorget C, Soerjomataram I (2021) Estimated number of cancers attributable to occupational exposures in France in 2017: an update using a new method for improved estimates. J Expo Sci Environ Epidemiol 33:125

Niemeier RT, Williams PRD, Rossner A, Clougherty JE, Rice GE (2020) A cumulative risk perspective for occupational health and safety (OHS) professionals. Int J Environ Res Public Health 17:6342

Nieuwenhuijsen M, Paustenbach D, Duarte-Davidson R (2006) New developments in exposure assessment: the impact on the practice of health risk assessment and epidemiological studies. Environ Int 32:996–1009

Pannett B, Coggon D, Acheson ED (1985) A job-exposure matrix for use in population based studies in England and Wales. Br J Ind Med 42:777–783

Pasquiou A, Pelluard F, Manangama G, Brochard P, Audignon S, Sentilhes L, Delva F (2021) Occupational exposure to ultrafine particles and placental histopathological lesions: A retrospective study about 130 cases. Int J Environ Res Public Health 18:12719

Peters S, Vermeulen R, Olsson A, Van Gelder R, Kendzia B, Vincent R, Savary B, Williams N, Woldbæk T, Lavoué J, Cavallo D, Cattaneo A, Mirabelli D, Plato N, Dahmann D, Fevotte J, Pesch B, Brüning T, Straif K, Kromhout H (2012) Development of an exposure measurement database on five lung carcinogens (ExpoSYN) for quantitative retrospective occupational exposure assessment. Ann Occup Hyg 56:70–79

Peters S, Vermeulen R, Portengen L, Olsson A, Kendzia B, Vincent R, Savary B, Lavoué J, Cavallo D, Cattaneo A, Mirabelli D, Plato N, Fevotte J, Pesch B, Brüning T, Straif K, Kromhout H (2016) SYN-JEM: A quantitative job-exposure matrix for five lung carcinogens. Ann Occup Hyg 60:795–811

Peters S, Vienneau D, Sampri A, Turner MC, Castaño-Vinyals G, Bugge M, Vermeulen R (2021) Occupational exposure assessment tools in Europe: A comprehensive inventory overview, vol 66. Ann Work Expo Health, p 671

Plys E, Bovio N, Arveux P, Bergeron Y, Bulliard JL, Elia N, Fournier E, Konzelmann I, Maspoli M, Rapiti Aylward E, Guseva Canu I (2022) Research on occupational diseases in the absence of occupational data: a mixed-method study among cancer registries of Western Switzerland. Swiss Med Wkly 152:w30127

Reed JV, Harcourt AK (1941) The essentials of occupational diseases. Springfield, Thomas, C.C

Remy VFM (2022) Bus technology development over the last sixty years in Switzerland and their impact on driver's health. Ecole Polytechnique fédérale de Lausanne (EPFL), Lausanne, Switzerland

Ribalta C, López-Lilao A, Estupiñá S, Fonseca AS, Tobías A, García-Cobos A, Minguillón MC, Monfort E, Viana M (2019) Health risk assessment from exposure to particles during packing in working environments. Sci Total Environ 671:474–487

Riddell A, Wakeford R, Liu H, O'Hagan J, MacGregor D, Agius R, Wilson C, Peace M, de Vocht F (2019) Building a job-exposure matrix for early plutonium workers at the Sellafield nuclear site, United Kingdom. *J Radiol Prot* 39:620–634

Sauvé JF, Siemiatycki J, Labrèche F, Richardson L, Pintos J, Sylvestre MP, Gérin M, Bégin D, Lacourt A, Kirkham TL, Rémen T, Pasquet R, Goldberg MS, Rousseau MC, Parent MÉ, Lavoué J (2018) Development of and selected performance characteristics of CANJEM, a general population job-exposure matrix based on past expert assessments of exposure. Ann Work Expo Health 62:783–795

Savic N, Gasic B, Vernez D (2017) ART, Stoffenmanager, and TRA: A systematic comparison of exposure estimates using the TREXMO translation System. Ann Work Expo Health 62:72–87

Savic N, Lee EG, Gasic B, Vernez D (2020) TREXMO plus: an advanced self-learning model for occupational exposure assessment. J Expo Sci Environ Epidemiol 30:554–566

Siemiatycki J, Day NE, Fabry J, Cooper JA (1981) Discovering carcinogens in the occupational environment: a novel epidemiologic approach. J Natl Cancer Inst 66:217–225

van de Ven P, Fransman W, Schinkel J, Rubingh C, Warren N, Tielemans E (2010) Stoffenmanager exposure model: company-specific exposure assessments using a Bayesian methodology. J Occup Environ Hyg 7:216–223

Viegas S, Jeddi MZ, Hopf NB, Bessems J, Palmen N, Galea KS, Jones K, Kujath P, Duca R-C, Verhagen H, Santonen T, Pasanen-Kase R (2020) Biomonitoring as an underused exposure assessment tool in occupational safety and health context-challenges and way forward. Int J Environ Res Public Health 17:5884

Zare Jeddi M, Hopf NB, Viegas S, Price AB, Paini A, van Thriel C, Benfenati E, Ndaw S, Bessems J, Behnisch PA, Leng G, Duca RC, Verhagen H, Cubadda F, Brennan L, Ali I, David A, Mustieles V, Fernandez MF, Louro H, Pasanen-Kase R (2021) Towards a systematic use of effect biomarkers in population and occupational biomonitoring. Environ Int 146:106257

Zhivin S, Laurier D, Caër-Lorho S, Acker A, Guseva Canu I (2013) Impact of chemical exposure on cancer mortality in a French cohort of uranium processing workers. Am J Ind Med 56: 1262–1271

Zhivin S, Laurier D, Guseva Canu I (2014) Health effects of occupational exposure to uranium: do physicochemical properties matter? Int J Radiat Biol 90:1104–1113

Zhivin S, Guseva Canu I, Davesne E, Blanchardon E, Garsi JP, Samson E, Niogret C, Zablotska LB, Laurier D (2018) Circulatory disease in French nuclear fuel cycle workers chronically exposed to uranium: a nested case-control study. Occup Environ Med 75:270–276

Biomechanical Hazards at Work and Adverse Health Using Job-Exposure Matrices

13

Johan H. Andersen, Bradley A. Evanoff, and Alexis Descatha

Contents

Introduction	214
Musculoskeletal Disorders	215
Measuring Biomechanical Exposures	215
Job-Exposure Matrices (JEMs)	218
Specific MSDs Related to Workplace Exposures	220
Main Disorders	220
From Biomechanical to Other Determinants	222
Conclusion	222
References	223

Abstract

Occupational risk factors for musculoskeletal disorders (MSDs) are mainly related to the effect of biomechanical exposures on bones, joints, muscles, tendons, ligaments, and nerves that are caused and/or exacerbated by the working conditions. Biomechanical exposures increase risk for MSD based on their

---

J. H. Andersen (✉)
Danish Ramazzini Centre, Department of Occupational Medicine – University Research Clinic, Goedstrup Hospital, Herning, Denmark
e-mail: joande@rm.dk

B. A. Evanoff
Division of General Medical Sciences, Washington University School of Medicine, St. Louis, MO, USA

A. Descatha
Univ Angers, CHU Angers, Univ Rennes, Inserm, EHESP, Irset (Institut de recherche en santé, environnement et travail), UMR_S 1085, SFR ICAT, Ester Team, Angers, France

CHU Angers, Poisoning Control Center-Clinical Data Center, Angers, France

Epidemiology and Prevention, Donald and Barbara Zucker School of Medicine, Hofstra University Northwell Health, New York, NY, USA

intensity (or level), frequency, and duration. Exposures can be estimated through expert judgments, systematic observations, direct measurements, or through use of a job exposure matrixes (JEMs). JEM have strengths that allow to study working history associated with some chronic MSDs. In the last decades some biomechanical JEM have been developed. Some JEM will be detailed as example: two Danish JEMs and JEM Constances. In the future, such JEMs will allow to be used for other disorders and even other field than occupational health (considered work as a confounder) to consider work exposure through the life course perspective.

Keywords

Job-exposure matrix · Public health · Occupational work · Musculoskeletal disorders · Exposure assessment · Cumulative exposures · Life course perspective

Introduction

Musculoskeletal disorders (MSDs) are the leading cause of work-related health conditions and work disability. Occupational risk factors for MSDs are mainly related to the effects of biomechanical exposures from job demands requiring high force, repetitive or sustained exertions, awkward or prolonged postures, and vibration. Over time, these work exposures influence bones, joints, muscles, tendons, ligaments, and nerves, and a variety of MSDs are caused or exacerbated by work-related biomechanical exposures, which increase the risk for MSD based on their intensity (or level), frequency, and duration. Exposures can be estimated through a variety of methods, including expert judgment, direct observation, direct measurement, or through use of a job-exposure matrix (JEM). A major challenge of studying associations between workplace exposures and health status in middle or older age is the difficulty of making valid and reliable estimates of past or cumulative exposures. Most assessment methods can assess only current exposures, and are most relevant to disorders with relatively short latencies. While these exposures can be extrapolated to previous exposures in the same job, they cannot account for different past jobs, or for changes in work activities (and thus exposure) that may have occurred due to symptoms of a musculoskeletal disorder. An important strength of JEMs is that they allow unbiased estimates of past biomechanical exposures across different jobs, and can thus study exposures across the life course and their association with chronic MSDs. In recent decades, several JEMs specific to biomechanical exposures have been developed and applied to past or cumulative exposures, demonstrating associations between past exposures and MSD. We describe the use of several JEMs as examples. Expanding the use of JEMs will allow addition of job biomechanical exposure data to large population registries, to expand our knowledge of workplace physical determinants of musculoskeletal health and other conditions related to physical activity.

Musculoskeletal Disorders

Musculoskeletal disorders (MSDs) are the leading cause of work disability, with the prevalence of MSD symptoms and work disability rising with age. MSDs are nontraumatic conditions such as tendinitis, osteoarthritis, and carpal tunnel syndrome that affect bones, joints, muscles, tendons, ligaments, and nerves. The causation of MSD is often multifactorial, with both nonoccupational and occupational factors influencing etiology and recovery.

Workplace biomechanical exposures increase the risk for MSD based on their intensity (or level), frequency, and duration. Exposures can be estimated by direct measurements of posture or force, by expert judgments, systematic observations, questionnaire responses from workers, or through use of a job-exposure matrix.

Hundreds of studies have shown strong associations between specific workplace biomechanical exposures and MSDs affecting different body regions. For example, good evidence of associations exists hand-arm elevation in the etiology of rotator cuff tendinopathies. Repeated, forceful hand motions, and the duration of time spent in forceful hand tasks, are strongly associated with carpal tunnel syndrome. The incidence of epicondylitis is increased by combined biomechanical exposures (strength, repetition, and/or awkward posture) involving the wrist and elbow. Whole-body vibration, carrying or lifting heavy loads, and working in awkward postures are associated with nonspecific back pain. Hand-arm vibration syndrome is seen in specific populations exposed to vibrating tools. Increased prevalence of hip and knee osteoarthritis is seen in workers whose jobs require carrying loads, frequent kneeling, or squatting.

The majority of studies of MSDs have addressed associations with current job demands, rather than examining cumulative or past exposures. Given the high burden of MSDs among middle-aged and older populations, there is a **strong need for adopting a life course perspective for work-related MSD**, considering cumulative workplace exposures and the effects of aging in order to protect workers and maintain employment among the aging workforces seen in many countries.

Measuring Biomechanical Exposures

Workplace biomechanical exposures include use of force (e.g., force exerted by the forearm muscles when gripping a hand tool), posture (e.g., kneeling work or working with high arms raised), repetitive work (e.g., work with fast repetitive movements), and exposure to hand-arm or whole-body vibrations (e.g., working with vibrating hand tools). There is generally a wide variation between biomechanical exposures in craft work, industrial work, sales, service, health care, and office work. For example, Fig. 1 below shows work with raised arms (more than 60° and more than 90°), repetitive movements of the shoulders (speed of movement), and the force exerted by the shoulder muscles in various job titles in Denmark and Sweden.

In order to assess the extent of work biomechanical exposures, the description of the above types of exposure must include three dimensions: (1) intensity or level (e.g., how many degrees the upper arm is elevated or the force exerted); (2) frequency (e.g.,

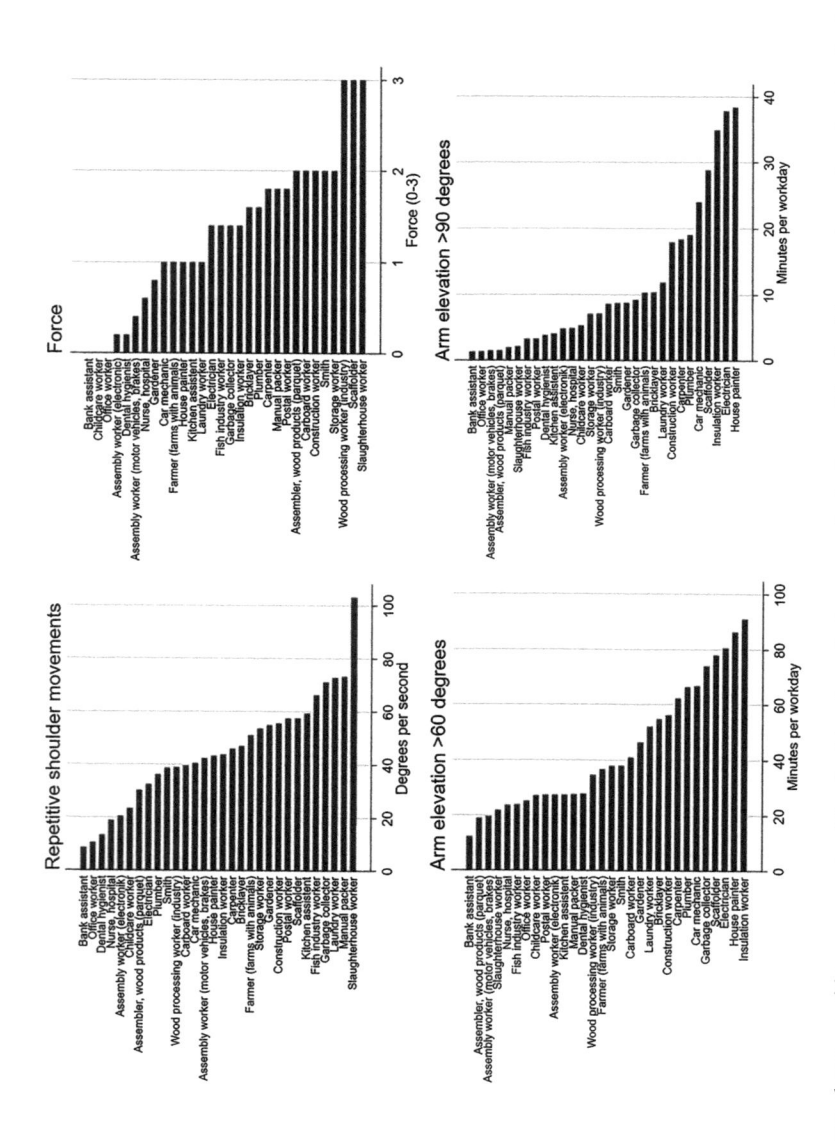

Fig. 1 The figure shows repetitive movements of the shoulders (speed of movement), the force of the shoulder muscles, and work with raised arms (60° and 90°), respectively, in different job titles. The results for work with raised arms and repetitive shoulder movements are based on direct measurements using an inclinometer in Danish and Swedish workers. The force exerted by the shoulder muscles is based on expert assessment by occupational physicians

frequency of movements of the upper arms); and (3) duration (e.g., weekly number of hours with a given task or number of years with a given exposure) (van der Beek and Frings-Dresen 1998). Repetitive work is often perceived as an independent form of biomechanical exposure, although it is actually a description of the frequency of exposure.

These three dimensions of exposure can be combined. The intensity of exposure is the average level of exposure within a specified period of time, i.e., an overall expression of level and variation. "Percentage of working day with heavily stooped back" or "number of mouse clicks per hour" are examples of intensity targets. The cumulative exposure is the product of intensity and duration, i.e., a dose target. Ideally, the entire time window for relevant exposure should be included, but often it is unclear how long the relevant time window is and when it is located in relation to the onset of disease. The length of the time window is presumed to vary from a few days or weeks to several decades, depending on whether the disorder of interest is wrist tendinitis or hip and knee osteoarthritis.

In order to assess the impact of exposures on the development of a given musculoskeletal disorder, the exposure description should be as specific as possible with regard to the relevant anatomical region or structure. Working at a conveyor belt on a poultry slaughterhouse may, for example, involve fixed bending of the neck, repetitive small movement expressions in the shoulder joints, and right-handed force-toned movements of elbows, wrists, and hands. There may also be a difference between the exposures of the right and left arm.

There are a number of methods for quantifying biomechanical exposures, each of which has its advantages and disadvantages. At the individual worker level, exposure estimates can be obtained through (1) self-reporting using questionnaires, interviews, or diaries; (2) making real-time observations of work or analyzing motions on video recordings; and (3) direct measurements using instruments such as inclinometers, electromyography, or force gauges.

Self-reporting of exposures by means of questionnaires or interviews is used in clinical occupational medical records. In interviews, it may be advantageous to start from a list of the patient's jobs and job titles. After that, the working time in each job is divided between the main tasks and, finally, descriptions of the extent (e.g., level, frequency, and duration) of the relevant forms of exposure in each major job task. Workplace visits can increase the quality of the exposure assessment. At group level, epidemiological studies have frequently classified exposures based on job titles and compared more exposed and less exposed job groups that have significant exposure contrast. However, the disadvantage of using job titles is that it can be difficult to assess what exposures are involved and to what extent, and to generalize findings to different job titles that may share similar exposures.

Existing methods for biomechanical exposure assessment all suffer from various limitations. Direct measurement of worker exposures and detailed observational assessments typically yield higher precision than other methods, particularly for estimating the intensity of exposure to postures, movements, and exerted forces, but may misclassify exposures in jobs where exposures vary over a longer time than the period of job observation (Hansson et al. 2001; Mathiassen and Paquet 2010). Direct measurement and observation are expensive and time-consuming, potentially limiting their application to large groups of workers. There is continued rapid improvement and availability of sensors that can be used for direct measurements, including smaller size and lower cost. Future studies will make increasing use of directly measured exposures as this technology continues to improve. Self-reported exposures are easier and less expensive to administer to large populations, and have reasonable accuracy for some exposures. They are less precise than direct measurements or observations, but may more accurately provide the global evaluation of work exposures, particularly for variable jobs (Stock et al. 2005). Importantly, responses by individuals to exposure questionnaires are potentially subject to recall bias or other information biases, particularly if perceptions of exposures may be altered by health status (Viikari-Juntura et al. 1996). Although prospectively obtained individual-level data are considered the best estimates of exposure, these methods are difficult to apply in large cohort studies, and usually cannot be applied to studies of existing data.

Most relevant to life course research, the evaluation of retrospective exposures in general population studies is particularly difficult, and poses a significant obstacle to studying the associations between long-term or past occupational exposures and the development of chronic diseases later in life (Mathiassen and Paquet 2010; Ngabirano et al. 2021). It is often difficult and complicated to evaluate exposures over a wide range of occupations and industries for long periods of time (perhaps decades) to assess exposures that may be relevant to chronic diseases. Few data sources contain both long-term health outcomes data and workplace exposure data; the ability to evaluate the health effects of long-term exposures is thus severely limited (Dembe et al. 2014; Lavoué et al. 2012).

In the absence of individual-level exposure data or historical data, job-exposure matrices (JEMs) are commonly used in occupational epidemiology research to estimate respondents' exposures to chemical and physical risk factors based on job titles, industry information, and population exposure data (Plato and Steineck 1993). A JEM provides a means to convert coded job titles into exposure estimates for epidemiological studies. Although this technique has frequently been used in studies of occupational cancers, using a job-exposure matrix to assign exposures to physical exposures such as posture, repetition, or force is less common. Recognition that JEMs estimating physical exposures have been underutilized has prompted their use in recent studies. In addition to their efficiency, JEMs have additional advantages. Because JEMs make no distinction between diseased and nondiseased subjects, and assign exposures at the group level, their use can decrease information bias between cases and noncases (Kauppinen et al. 1998). Importantly for studying work exposures across the lifespan, JEMs also **allow the estimation of past exposures and calculating cumulative exposures throughout individuals' full working life.**

Job-Exposure Matrices (JEMs)

Job-exposure matrices (JEMs) have been used since the 1980s, and were initially used mainly in studies in need of exposure assessment across many different job groups (refer to chapter "JEM"). A JEM is a cross-tabulation of job groups, e.g., job titles, with average exposure levels for specific exposures. These exposure levels may vary by, e.g., gender, time period, and geographic region. The exposure assessment in a JEM may be based on direct measurements, observations, expert assessments, self-reporting, and combinations thereof (e.g., calibration of expert assessment via direct measurements). JEMs, like other exposure assessment methods, have advantages and disadvantages. Benefits include cost- and time-effective studies, complete objective data, no recall biases, and the ability to apply a JEM to large populations to study less prevalent exposures and rare diseases. However, JEMs can only be used for exposures that vary sufficiently between different job groups. A major limitation is that JEMs do not capture variation between individual workers within the same job. For a JEM to be effective, the variation of exposures within job categories must be smaller than the variation of exposures between job categories.

In Denmark, JEMs have been used in large register studies, where exposure information is often difficult to obtain across the population. A nationwide Danish Occupational Cohort with eXposure data (DOC*X) has recently been established as an open resource to facilitate registry studies of disease and disability associated with occupational exposures (Flachs et al. 2019). The Lower Body JEM, which was originally constructed to study hip and knee osteoarthritis (Rubak et al. 2014), is now available as one of a series of general population JEMs in the DOC*X [www.doc-x.dk/en]. Cumulative lifting estimates based on the JEM have shown strong correlations with self-reported physical work demands throughout working life (Sundstrup et al. 2018). Additionally, various estimates of the occupational exposures based on the Lower Body JEM have shown good predictive validity in cohort studies of inguinal hernia repair (Vad et al. 2017) and surgery for varicose veins (Tabatabaeifar et al. 2015).

The Danish Shoulder job-exposure matrix (Shoulder JEM) has been used to study cumulative occupational shoulder exposures and surgery for subacromial impingement syndrome (SIS) in a series of papers (Dalbøge et al. 2014, 2017, 2020). In these studies it has been shown that mechanical exposures (i.e., arm-elevation $>90°$, repetition $\geq 45°/s$, and force) can be considered independent risk factors for surgery for SIS.

In France, a JEM was created within the CONSTANCES study (JEM Constances), by pooling self-reported work exposure data within a large general population cohort study of working-aged persons representative of the general French population (Evanoff et al. 2019). This JEM has demonstrated strong associations between cumulative work-related exposures across the lifespan and disorders common in later life including Dupuytren's contracture and reduced physical mobility (Fadel et al. 2019; Ngabirano et al. 2021).

In the USA, a number of studies have been performed using the Occupational Information Network (O*NET), a database that provides occupational physical and mental demands for a broad range of jobs. This JEM has been used to describe the association between long-term cumulative occupational exposure and the risk of contracting chronic diseases including arthritis later in life (Dembe et al. 2014) and to demonstrate that past work exposures increased the risk of carpal tunnel syndrome (Dale et al. 2015). Musculoskeletal JEMs have been developed and used in concert with population registries in other countries as well, including Sweden, Finland, and the UK (Lavoué et al. 2012; Yanik et al. 2022).

Specific MSDs Related to Workplace Exposures

In addition to workplace exposure to biomechanical factors, other factors that may play a role in musculoskeletal disorders include psychosocial conditions inside and outside work, and lifestyle factors. The work psychosocial exposures include, for example, job control, job requirements, and social support. Psychosocial exposures are probably more important for the prognosis than they are causally linked to the development of musculoskeletal disorders. Lifestyle factors include, for example, previous fractures, familial predisposition, high body mass index, smoking, physical inactivity, and a variety of medical disorders (including diabetes mellitus). Recent studies on the incidence of musculoskeletal pain across countries and continents have shown large differences with higher incidence in the Western countries, which could not be explained by occupational, individual, social, or economic risk factors. This points to cultural differences in understanding, reporting, and managing musculoskeletal pain. Recognizing that the etiology and prognosis of MSDs are multifactorial, it is still possible to point to modifiable work-specific biomechanical exposures that are associated with different MSDs. The examples below are by no means exhaustive, and include examples of both short-term and longer-term exposures associated with MSDs.

Main Disorders

Rotator Cuff Tendinopathy

There is strong evidence that rotator cuff tendinopathy is associated with workplace biomechanical factors including hand-arm elevation and shoulder load (*Musculoskeletal disorders and workplace factors. A critical review of epidemiologic evidence for work-related musculoskeletal disorders of the neck, upper extremity, and low back*, 1997; van der Molen et al. 2017; van Rijn et al. 2010). There is weaker evidence that forceful hand exertion and hand-arm vibrations are associated with rotator cuff disorders (Sluiter et al. 2001). A previous systematic review defined significant levels of exposure. A force requirement greater than 10% of the maximum voluntary contraction, lifting more than 20 kilos more than 10 times per day, and a high level of hand force (greater than 1 hour per day) were associated with the onset of rotator cuff tendinopathies. Other risk factors included repetitive movements of the shoulder, repetitive motion of the hand or wrist greater than 2 hours per day, hand-arm vibration, working with hands above shoulder level, upper-arm flexion greater or equal to 45° more than 15% of time, duty cycle of forceful exertions more than 9% time, or forceful pinch at any time.

With regard to duration, the incidence of rotator cuff tendinopathies increases with the cumulative duration of exposure over time (Dalbøge et al. 2018). While this study found levels of safe exposure for repetition (median angular velocity lower than 45°/s), it also **found increased risks after 10 years** at low intensities for force (exertion greater or equal to 10% of maximal voluntary activity), and for upper arm elevation (greater than 90° more than 2 min/day).

Lateral and Medial Epicondylitis
There is a large literature showing increased incidence epicondylitis among workers performing hand-intensive tasks. A meta-analysis found a positive association between the incidence of lateral epicondylitis and combined biomechanical exposures (strength, repetition, and/or awkward posture) involving the wrist and/or the elbow, with a meta-odds ratio of 2.6 [1.9–3.5] (Descatha et al. 2016). Handling tools heavier than 1 kg, handling loads over 20 kg at least 10 times per day, and repetitive movements of the hand and wrist more than 2 hours per day were found to be associated with lateral epicondylitis (van Rijn et al. 2008). Medial epicondylitis was associated with handling loads more than 5 kg at least two times per minute for 2 or more hours per day, handling loads more than 20 kg at least ten times per day, high hand grip forces for more than 1 hour per day, repetitive movements for more than 2 hours per day, and working with vibrating tools more than 2 hours per day (Plouvier et al. 2008).

Carpal Tunnel Syndrome
There is strong evidence for an association between the incidence of carpal tunnel syndrome and forceful and repetitive hand exposures, particularly when combined with strong evidence of a dose-response relationship (chapter "Occupational Determinants of Musculoskeletal Disorders"). In detail, hand force requirement of more than 4 kg, repetitiveness at work with a cycle time lower than 10 seconds, or more than 50% of cycle time performing the same movements, and a daily 8-h energy-equivalent frequency-weighted acceleration of 3.9 m/s^2 were related to carpal tunnel syndrome (van Rijn et al. 2009). Recent studies found that low-force repetition alone was not a significant risk factor for CTS, but that peak hand force and the duration or frequency of forceful hand exertion ($\geq$9 N pinch force or $\geq$45 N of power grip) were strongly associated with the incidence of CTS.(Harris-Adamson et al. 2015) Large cohort studies in the USA and in Italy found that incident CTS was strongly associated with exposure values that combine peak hand force with the level of hand activity (Kapellusch et al. 2014; Violante et al. 2016). These and other findings have led to changes in exposure recommendations in the USA (Yung et al. 2019) and in other countries.

Nonspecific Back Pain
A variety of workplace factors have been linked to the incidence of low back pain, one of the most common occupational musculoskeletal disorders, and one that causes significant work absence and disability. Biomechanical factors linked to low back pain include whole-body vibration and vehicle driving (for more than 2 h by day), and awkward postures like prolonged flexion to more than 60° or for more than 5% of the time (Palmer and Bovenzi 2015; Parreira et al. 2018). Prolonged sitting, a postural factor also found during driving, has been described as a risk for low back pain. Heavy lifting and frequent lifting are associated to the incidence of low back pain. A common tool used to evaluate this risk of low back pain is the "lifting equation" created by the American National Institute of Occupational Safety and Health (NIOSH). This equation provides recommended weight limits for specific lifting tasks meant to define the

lifts that most workers could perform without increasing the risk of developing low back pain. In addition to the frequency of lifts and the weight of the object lifted, the calculation includes other factors including the horizontal distance of the hands from the body, the starting height of the hands, the vertical distance the load is lifted, the angle of the load in relation to the body, and the type of hand holds available on the object (Fox et al. 2019). While most studies have focused on recent biomechanical exposures, cumulative exposures to lifting, carrying, and forward bending have also been associated with low back pain (Seidler et al. 2001).

Example of Osteoarthritis of the Knee

Knee osteoarthritis is common and may cause significant disability (39). Older studies found relationships between heavy workplace physical demands and kneeling/squatting and an increased risk of knee osteoarthritis (Felson et al. 1991; Vingård et al. 1991). In more recent studies, there is convergent data among men on increased risks of knee osteoarthritis associated with cumulative carrying of heavy loads and frequent kneeling/squatting, particularly in mining, farming, and construction sectors (Jensen 2008; McWilliams et al. 2011). Carrying loads independent of kneeling/squatting work has more limited evidence, as does frequent stair climbing (Verbeek et al. 2017). These associations are weaker among women (Fouquet et al. 2016).

From Biomechanical to Other Determinants

In addition to biomechanical workplace exposures, there is increasing interest in the role of work organization and workplace psychosocial factors in musculoskeletal disorders. Workplace psychological and psychosocial factors seem to play an important role in subsequent disability and chronicity of disease (Evanoff et al. 2014). Several risk models for MSDs have been proposed in the literature focusing on the biomechanical, psychosocial, and organizational dimensions of work (see chapter "Organizational Factors"). Integrated multidimensional and multilevel conceptual models suggest enlarging the scope of the assessment of risk factors to include: (1) biomechanical factors at the job station level; (2) psychosocial and stress factors at the job levels; (3) organizational factors at work situation and company levels; and (4) socioeconomic factors at the society level.

Conclusion

Workplace biomechanical exposures are a significant contributor to the etiology of MSD. Prevention of disability from MSD requires a global approach incorporating work organization, workplace psychosocial factors, and policies at the employer and societal levels. Much of our knowledge of MSD is based on current or recent working conditions; **adoption of a life course perspective of work and health will improve our understanding of health promotion and disease prevention.**

References

Dalbøge A, Frost P, Andersen JH, Svendsen SW (2014) Cumulative occupational shoulder exposures and surgery for subacromial impingement syndrome: a nationwide Danish cohort study. Occup Environ Med 71:750–756. https://doi.org/10.1136/oemed-2014-102161

Dalbøge A, Frost P, Andersen JH, Svendsen SW (2017) Surgery for subacromial impingement syndrome in relation to occupational exposures, lifestyle factors and diabetes mellitus: a nationwide nested case–control study. Occup Environ Med 74:728–736. https://doi.org/10.1136/oemed-2016-104272

Dalbøge A, Frost P, Andersen JH, Svendsen SW (2018) Surgery for subacromial impingement syndrome in relation to intensities of occupational mechanical exposures across 10-year exposure time windows. Occup Environ Med 75:176–182. https://doi.org/10.1136/oemed-2017-104511

Dalbøge A, Frost P, Andersen JH, Svendsen SW (2020) Exposure–response relationships between cumulative occupational shoulder exposures and different diagnoses related to surgery for subacromial impingement syndrome. Int Arch Occup Environ Health 93:375–380. https://doi.org/10.1007/s00420-019-01485-6

Dale AM, Zeringue A, Harris-Adamson C, Rempel D, Bao S, Thiese MS, Merlino L, Burt S, Kapellusch J, Garg A, Gerr F, Hegmann KT, Eisen EA, Evanoff B (2015) General population job exposure matrix applied to a pooled study of prevalent carpal tunnel syndrome. Am J Epidemiol 181:431–439. https://doi.org/10.1093/aje/kwu286

Dembe AE, Yao X, Wickizer TM, Shoben AB, Dong XS (2014) Using O*NET to estimate the association between work exposures and chronic diseases: estimating work exposures and chronic disease. Am J Ind Med 57:1022–1031. https://doi.org/10.1002/ajim.22342

Descatha A, Albo F, Leclerc A, Carton M, Godeau D, Roquelaure Y, Petit A, Aublet-Cuvelier A (2016) Lateral epicondylitis and physical exposure at work? A review of prospective studies and meta-analysis: work exposure and lateral epicondylitis. Arthritis Care Res 68:1681–1687. https://doi.org/10.1002/acr.22874

Evanoff B, Dale A, Descatha A (2014) A conceptual model of musculoskeletal disorders for occupational health practitioners. Int J Occup Med Environ Health 27. https://doi.org/10.2478/s13382-014-0232-5

Evanoff BA, Yung M, Buckner-Petty S, Andersen JH, Roquelaure Y, Descatha A, Dale AM (2019) The CONSTANCES job exposure matrix based on self-reported exposure to physical risk factors: development and evaluation. Occup Environ Med 76:398–406. https://doi.org/10.1136/oemed-2018-105287

Fadel M, Leclerc A, Evanoff B, Dale A-M, Ngabirano L, Roquelaure Y, Descatha A (2019) Association between occupational exposure and Dupuytren's contracture using a job-exposure matrix and self-reported exposure in the CONSTANCES cohort. Occup Environ Med 76: 845–848. https://doi.org/10.1136/oemed-2019-105912

Felson DT, Hannan MT, Naimark A, Berkeley J, Gordon G, Wilson PW, Anderson J (1991) Occupational physical demands, knee bending, and knee osteoarthritis: results from the Framingham study. J Rheumatol 18:1587–1592

Flachs EM, Petersen SEB, Kolstad HA, Schlünssen V, Svendsen SW, Hansen J, Budtz-Jørgensen E, Andersen JH, Madsen IEH, Bonde JPE (2019) Cohort profile: DOC*X: a nationwide Danish occupational cohort with eXposure data – an open research resource. Int J Epidemiol 48: 1413–1413k. https://doi.org/10.1093/ije/dyz110

Fouquet B, Descatha A, Roulet A, Hérisson C (2016) Arthrose et activités professionnelles, Sauramps Médical. ed, (MPR et pathologies professionnelles)

Fox RR, Lu M-L, Occhipinti E, Jaeger M (2019) Understanding outcome metrics of the revised NIOSH lifting equation. Appl Ergon 81:102897. https://doi.org/10.1016/j.apergo.2019.102897

Hansson GA, Balogh I, Byström JU, Ohlsson K, Nordander C, Asterland P, Sjölander S, Rylander L, Winkel J, Skerfving S, Malmö Shoulder-Neck Study Group (2001) Questionnaire versus direct technical measurements in assessing postures and movements of the head, upper back, arms and hands. Scand J Work Environ Health 27:30–40. https://doi.org/10.5271/sjweh.584

Harris-Adamson C, Eisen EA, Kapellusch J, Garg A, Hegmann KT, Thiese MS, Dale AM, Evanoff B, Burt S, Bao S, Silverstein B, Merlino L, Gerr F, Rempel D (2015) Biomechanical risk factors for carpal tunnel syndrome: a pooled study of 2474 workers. Occup Environ Med 72:33–41. https://doi.org/10.1136/oemed-2014-102378

Jensen LK (2008) Knee osteoarthritis: influence of work involving heavy lifting, kneeling, climbing stairs or ladders, or kneeling/squatting combined with heavy lifting. Occup Environ Med 65: 72–89. https://doi.org/10.1136/oem.2007.032466

Kapellusch JM, Gerr FE, Malloy EJ, Garg A, Harris-Adamson C, Bao SS, Burt SE, Dale AM, Eisen EA, Evanoff BA, Hegmann KT, Silverstein BA, Theise MS, Rempel DM (2014) Exposure–response relationships for the ACGIH threshold limit value for hand-activity level: results from a pooled data study of carpal tunnel syndrome. Scand J Work Environ Health 40: 610–620. https://doi.org/10.5271/sjweh.3456

Kauppinen T, Toikkanen J, Pukkala E (1998) From cross-tabulations to multipurpose exposure information systems: a new job-exposure matrix. Am J Ind Med 33:409–417. https://doi.org/10.1002/(sici)1097-0274(199804)33:4<409::aid-ajim12>3.0.co;2-2

Lavoué J, Pintos J, Van Tongeren M, Kincl L, Richardson L, Kauppinen T, Cardis E, Siemiatycki J (2012) Comparison of exposure estimates in the Finnish job-exposure matrix FINJEM with a JEM derived from expert assessments performed in Montreal. Occup Environ Med 69:465–471. https://doi.org/10.1136/oemed-2011-100154

Mathiassen SE, Paquet V (2010) The ability of limited exposure sampling to detect effects of interventions that reduce the occurrence of pronounced trunk inclination. Appl Ergon 41: 295–304. https://doi.org/10.1016/j.apergo.2009.08.006

McWilliams DF, Leeb BF, Muthuri SG, Doherty M, Zhang W (2011) Occupational risk factors for osteoarthritis of the knee: a meta-analysis. Osteoarthr Cartil 19:829–839. https://doi.org/10.1016/j.joca.2011.02.016

Musculoskeletal disorders and workplace factors. A critical review of epidemiologic evidence for work-related musculoskeletal disorders of the neck, upper extremity, and low back (1997) U.S. Department of Health and Human Services, Public Health Service, Centers for Disease Control and Prevention, National Institute for Occupational Safety and Health. https://doi.org/10.26616/NIOSHPUB97141

Ngabirano L, Fadel M, Leclerc A, Evanoff BA, Dale AM, d'Errico A, Roquelaure Y, Descatha A (2021) Association between physical limitations and working life exposure to carrying heavy loads assessed using a job-exposure matrix: CONSTANCES cohort. Arch Environ Occup Health 76:243–247. https://doi.org/10.1080/19338244.2020.1819184

Palmer KT, Bovenzi M (2015) Rheumatic effects of vibration at work. Best Pract Res Clin Rheumatol 29:424–439. https://doi.org/10.1016/j.berh.2015.05.001

Parreira P, Maher CG, Steffens D, Hancock MJ, Ferreira ML (2018) Risk factors for low back pain and sciatica: an umbrella review. Spine J 18:1715–1721. https://doi.org/10.1016/j.spinee.2018.05.018

Plato N, Steineck G (1993) Methodology and utility of a job-exposure matrix. Am J Ind Med 23: 491–502. https://doi.org/10.1002/ajim.4700230312

Plouvier S, Renahy E, Chastang JF, Bonenfant S, Leclerc A (2008) Biomechanical strains and low back disorders: quantifying the effects of the number of years of exposure on various types of pain. Occup Environ Med 65:268–274. https://doi.org/10.1136/oem.2007.036095

Rubak TS, Svendsen SW, Andersen JH, Haahr JPL, Kryger A, Jensen LD, Frost P (2014) An expert-based job exposure matrix for large scale epidemiologic studies of primary hip and knee osteoarthritis: the lower body JEM. BMC Musculoskelet Disord 15:204. https://doi.org/10.1186/1471-2474-15-204

Seidler A, Bolm-Audorff U, Heiskel H, Henkel N, Roth-Küver B, Kaiser U, Bickeböller R, Willingstorfer WJ, Beck W, Elsner G (2001) The role of cumulative physical work load in lumbar spine disease: risk factors for lumbar osteochondrosis and spondylosis associated with chronic complaints. Occup Environ Med 58:735–746. https://doi.org/10.1136/oem.58.11.735

Sluiter JK, Rest KM, Frings-Dresen MH (2001) Criteria document for evaluating the work-relatedness of upper-extremity musculoskeletal disorders. Scand J Work Environ Health 27 (Suppl 1):1–102

Stock SR, Fernandes R, Delisle A, Vézina N (2005) Reproducibility and validity of workers' self-reports of physical work demands. Scand J Work Environ Health 31:409–437. https://doi.org/10.5271/sjweh.947

Sundstrup E, Hansen ÅM, Mortensen EL, Poulsen OM, Clausen T, Rugulies R, Møller A, Andersen LL (2018) Retrospectively assessed physical work environment during working life and risk of sickness absence and labour market exit among older workers. Occup Environ Med 75:114–123. https://doi.org/10.1136/oemed-2016-104279

Tabatabaeifar S, Frost P, Andersen JH, Jensen LD, Thomsen JF, Svendsen SW (2015) Varicose veins in the lower extremities in relation to occupational mechanical exposures: a longitudinal study. Occup Environ Med 72:330–337. https://doi.org/10.1136/oemed-2014-102495

Vad MV, Frost P, Rosenberg J, Andersen JH, Svendsen SW (2017) Inguinal hernia repair among men in relation to occupational mechanical exposures and lifestyle factors: a longitudinal study. Occup Environ Med 74:769–775. https://doi.org/10.1136/oemed-2016-104160

van der Beek AJ, Frings-Dresen MH (1998) Assessment of mechanical exposure in ergonomic epidemiology. Occup Environ Med 55:291–299. https://doi.org/10.1136/oem.55.5.291

van der Molen HF, Foresti C, Daams JG, Frings-Dresen MHW, Kuijer PPFM (2017) Work-related risk factors for specific shoulder disorders: a systematic review and meta-analysis. Occup Environ Med 74:745–755. https://doi.org/10.1136/oemed-2017-104339

van Rijn RM, Huisstede BMA, Koes BW, Burdorf A (2008) Associations between work-related factors and specific disorders at the elbow: a systematic literature review. Rheumatology 48:528–536. https://doi.org/10.1093/rheumatology/kep013

van Rijn RM, Huisstede BM, Koes BW, Burdorf A (2009) Associations between work-related factors and the carpal tunnel syndrome – a systematic review. Scand J Work Environ Health 35:19–36. https://doi.org/10.5271/sjweh.1306

van Rijn RM, Huisstede BM, Koes BW, Burdorf A (2010) Associations between work-related factors and specific disorders of the shoulder – a systematic review of the literature. Scand J Work Environ Health 36:189–201. https://doi.org/10.5271/sjweh.2895

Verbeek J, Mischke C, Robinson R, Ijaz S, Kuijer P, Kievit A, Ojajärvi A, Neuvonen K (2017) Occupational exposure to knee loading and the risk of osteoarthritis of the knee: a systematic review and a dose-response meta-analysis. Saf Health Work 8:130–142. https://doi.org/10.1016/j.shaw.2017.02.001

Viikari-Juntura E, Rauas S, Martikainen R, Kuosma E, Riihimäki H, Takala EP, Saarenmaa K (1996) Validity of self-reported physical work load in epidemiologic studies on musculoskeletal disorders. Scand J Work Environ Health 22:251–259. https://doi.org/10.5271/sjweh.139

Vingård E, Alfredsson L, Goldie I, Hogstedt C (1991) Occupation and osteoarthrosis of the hip and knee: a register-based cohort study. Int J Epidemiol 20:1025–1031. https://doi.org/10.1093/ije/20.4.1025

Violante FS, Farioli A, Graziosi F, Marinelli F, Curti S, Armstrong TJ, Mattioli S, Bonfiglioli R (2016) Carpal tunnel syndrome and manual work: the OCTOPUS cohort, results of a ten-year longitudinal study. Scand J Work Environ Health 42:280–290. https://doi.org/10.5271/sjweh.3566

Yanik EL, Stevens MJ, Harris EC, Walker-Bone KE, Dale AM, Ma Y, Colditz GA, Evanoff BA (2022) Physical work exposure matrix for use in the UK Biobank. Occup Med (Lond) 72:132–141. https://doi.org/10.1093/occmed/kqab173

Yung M, Dale AM, Kapellusch J, Bao S, Harris-Adamson C, Meyers AR, Hegmann KT, Rempel D, Evanoff BA (2019) Modeling the effect of the 2018 revised ACGIH® hand activity threshold limit value® (TLV) at reducing risk for carpal tunnel syndrome. J Occup Environ Hyg 16:628–633. https://doi.org/10.1080/15459624.2019.1640366

Long Working Hours and Health Effects

14

Marc Fadel, Jian Li, and Grace Sembajwe

Contents

Introduction	228
Adverse Health Effects	231
Evidence from the Literature	231
Focus on Cardiovascular Diseases	234
LWH: From Epidemiology to Public Health	238
LWH As an Indicator for Monitoring Workers' Health	238
LWH As a Target for Prevention Measures	239
Conclusion	240
References	241

Abstract

Decent workplace conditions contribute to positive mental and physical wellness. Due to globalization, demographic changes, and advancements in technology, work has drastically evolved in recent years. People are working longer, and more research studies recognize the adverse health effects of overtime work. The aim of this chapter is to report on the associations between long working hours (LWH) and health, LWH influence on life course, and how LWH can be a potential target for interventions that improve workplace and worker well-being. From increased

---

M. Fadel (✉)
Research Institute for Environmental and Occupational Health (IRSET), UMR_S1085, University of Angers, Angers, France
e-mail: marc.fadel@univ-angers.fr

J. Li
Department of Environmental Health Sciences, Fielding School of Public Health, School of Nursing, University of California, Los Angeles, CA, USA

G. Sembajwe
Department of Occupational Medicine, Epidemiology and Prevention, Donald and Barbara Zucker School of Medicine, Hosftra University Northwell Health, New York, NY, USA

© Springer Nature Switzerland AG 2023
M. Wahrendorf et al. (eds.), *Handbook of Life Course Occupational Health*, Handbook Series in Occupational Health Sciences, https://doi.org/10.1007/978-3-031-30492-7_12

work-related injuries to mental health disorders, there are observed associations between exposure to LWH and many health conditions, including sleep and metabolic disorders. Evidence from multiple systematic reviews and meta-analyses indicates that working 55 or more hours per week results in increased ischemic heart disease and stroke events. The attributable work-related burden of disease, due to LWH exposure, has been carefully estimated, with about 750,000 deaths and 23.3 million disability-adjusted life years from cardiovascular diseases alone, in 2016. Though physiological mechanisms and causal pathways need further exploration in future studies, LWH can be easily measured and used as a single, critical indicator for monitoring adverse working conditions and worker health, especially in resource-challenged settings where collecting precise exposure assessment measures is not feasible. Lastly, LWH may be the appropriate target for interventions at both the individual level, through health promotion, and the organizational level, by advocating for better work environment policies and optimal work hours.

Keywords

Long working hours · Occupational health · Cardiovascular diseases · Mental disorders · Global burden of disease

Introduction

The structure of work life has undergone great changes due to globalization, advancements in technology, and demographic changes (Peckham et al. 2017). This has consequently impacted work time, work conditions, and organization (European Agency for Safety and Health at Work 2021). Globally, the percentage of workers exposed to long working hours (LWH), defined as work-hours ≥ 55 per week, has increased over the last two decades, going from an average of 8.1% (7.8–8.4, 95% uncertainty range) of the relevant population in 2000 to 8.9% (8.6–9.1, 95% uncertainty range) in 2016, with some geographic variations (Pega et al. 2021). In parallel to the increase of LWH exposure, organizational work-hour policies have become more flexible, coinciding with technological advancements that accelerated during the COVID-19 pandemic due to a greater reliance on teleworking alongside an increase in work precariousness or gig work (Kramer and Kramer 2020). Protective workplace polices to curb negative health impacts have been implemented at national and international levels, in accordance with International Labor Organisation (ILO) recommendations (ILO 2018). The ILO created "decent work indicators" to standardize and evaluate, at a glance, labor conditions and their impact on health (ILO 2013). Among the different indicators, work time is of great importance in assessing negative impacts on health. LWH is a growing concern in the medical and public health communities, with a marked increase in research into the adverse effects of LWH on health. Figure 1 illustrates this increase by showing the yearly number of results per 10^6 in PubMed, using the

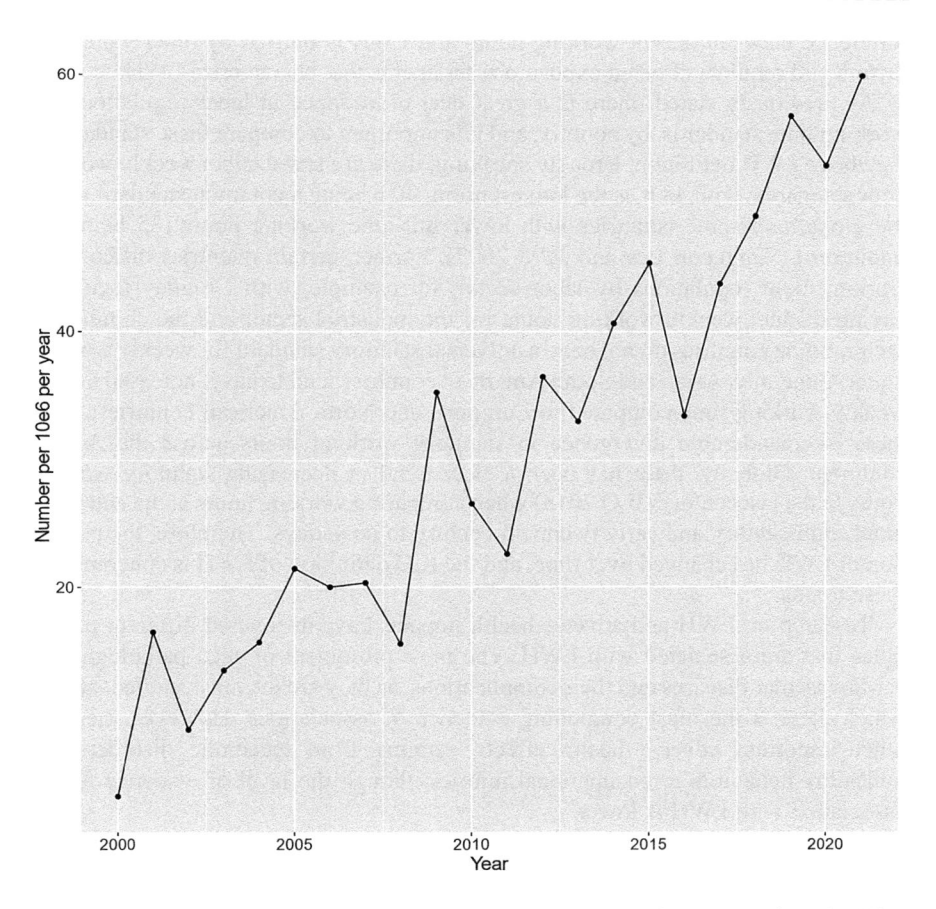

Fig. 1 Number of results for long working hours on PubMed standardized by number of publications per year between 2000 and 2021

search term "long working hours [Title/Abstract]." The number of publications has doubled in the last decade, showing that the topic is of significant interest to public health researchers and practitioners.

In the past decade, joint WHO-ILO research into the burden of disease related to adverse occupational exposure has produced considerably novel findings, including numerous meta-analysis studies and other reports on the disease burden of LWH (Pega et al. 2022).

It is difficult to define and standardize LWH in general terms, given the great variance in labor regulations between countries (Lee et al. 2007). The ILO defines LWH as a weekly work time greater than 48 h (ILO 2018). This definition seems to cover most LWH cases; however, many studies have used 55 weekly worked hours as the limit for LWH because this definition has been shown to be associated with observed negative health impacts (Descatha et al. 2020; Li et al. 2020). Thus, the difference between decent working hours and LWH is blurred by other workplace factors and requires targeted exposure assessments that characterize LWH.

As previously stated, there is a great deal of variance in labor regulation, and working time standards, by country, and it is important to compare these standards to the above LWH definition. Broadly speaking, there are few distinct weekly working hour standards, with 48 h as the longest norm, 40 h being a common standard across the globe, and some countries with lower full-time working hours (35 being the minimum) (Sangheon Lee and JCM 2007). Further, certain countries differentiate working hour regulations by labor sector, for example, with Uruguay regulation having distinct weekly working hours for the industrial sector and the commercial sector. Some countries do not have a universal statutory standard for weekly working hours. Generally, Asian and South American countries tend to have increased normal weekly working time compared to European and North American countries, while there is considerable divergence in statutory working hours across the African continent. Globally, there has been a clear trend in decreasing statutory working hours in the last century (ILO 2018) when comparing working hours at the end of the nineteenth century and early twentieth century to nowadays. Therefore, the perception of LWH has changed over time, and the ILO definition of LWH is coherent with these trends.

Research on LWH and adverse health impacts have uncovered different pathologies that are associated with LWH. The most prominent of such pathologies are cardiovascular diseases and their complications, as they are the most studied, and for which there is the most compelling evidence of associations. However, there are other important adverse health effects, ranging from metabolic disorders and unhealthy behaviors to occupational injuries, though the level of evidence for the association with LWH is lower.

Though the level of association may be moderate compared to other occupational hazard exposures (asbestos, carcinogens, etc.), the impact of such pathologies is significant. In particular, occupational injuries and cardiovascular diseases represent a large expense for individual workers and the workforce (sick leave, decrease in work efficiency, and compensation) as well as high medical costs (hospitalization, surgery) (World Economic Forum 2011). Therefore, there is a strong incentive to investigate prevention measures to offset the LWH impact on cardiovascular health.

The improved understanding of LWH adverse health impacts is tied to technological advances not only in the gathering of statistical data around working conditions (in the general population as well as hospitalized patients), but also an increasing use of database technology and linkage. This has allowed an increasing number of researchers to access relevant stored data and conduct statistical research efficiently (Stevenson 2015). For example, Denmark has built large databases of social and medical information with efficient linkage between them in order to cross-analyze them for large population and cohort studies (Erlangsen and Fedyszyn 2015). The latest advances in statistical research provide novel tools to assess correlation between expositions to relevant factors including LWH, and adverse health effect outcomes. Among these tools, machine learning techniques and

Bayesian models have shown promising results in other fields and could be applied to further LWH research.

This chapter presents an overview of research into the possible adverse health-related impacts of LWH, with a focus on cardiovascular pathologies. This chapter then briefly summarizes the ongoing advances into the research of physiopathological mechanisms that are linked to these LWH-related diseases. Lastly, this chapter discusses how LWH can be studied in an epidemiological framework to evaluate labor conditions at a population level. This understanding in turn is essential to direct public health actions for the prevention of LWH adverse health impacts, with tools ranging from labor condition changes to workplace intervention.

Adverse Health Effects

Evidence from the Literature

There is a large body of research dedicated to adverse health impacts of LWH, which suggest many links to different pathologies. Although there is a great focus on cardiovascular diseases, it is important to outline the other significant pathologies linked to LWH. The evidence reported in the literature linking LWH and these pathologies is generally lower with greater uncertainty as to which physiopathological mechanisms are the root cause. However, this relative lack of conclusive evidence may be due to a greater difficulty in finding appropriate outcomes to measure and to a paucity of studies on these subjects.

First, LWH is correlated with lifestyle factors (such as smoking, physical activity, and diet) that impact health. Intuitively, working for prolonged lengths of time would result in work interference with leisure time, and LWH may disrupt an already precarious balance between work and personal life. Loss of work-life balance due to LWH makes it increasingly difficult for individuals to find time to exercise, get enough sleep, or take actions to implement a balanced diet, all healthy and necessary lifestyle behaviors that are recommended by researchers and public health agencies (Pérez-Martínez et al. 2017). A population-based panel study in Korea found relationship between LWH and several unhealthy lifestyles (Lee et al. 2021), using 4-year longitudinal data from 2011 to 2014 and models with repeated measures of LWH alongside other variables. Workers reported greater alcohol consumption and tobacco intake, and less physical activity and sleep, when they worked more. However, these associations were not linear and varied by job classification (blue-collar workers compared to white-collar workers), work type (doing shiftwork), and gender. Stratified analyses found that blue-collar workers exposed to LWH were more prone to smoking and alcohol drinking and less exercise than white-collar workers. The association between LWH and smoking and alcohol drinking also seemed stronger for women compared to men. Moreover, though the percentage of people working more than 52 hours a week decreased over the 4 years of the study (from 27.8% in 2011 to 21.0% in 2014), adverse health effects were still found, suggesting that, possibly, the effect of LWH may persist over the years.

One particular negative lifestyle behavior is alcohol consumption, for which a systematic review on LWH, from the WHO/ILO Joint Estimates of the Work-related Burden of Disease, found a similar trend, with increased intake by 16.29 g/week (7.93–24.65, 95% CI) for exposure to working more than 55 hours per week compared to 35–40 h (Pachito et al. 2021). The effect on risky drinking and alcohol use disorders remains uncertain, mostly because there are very few studies on this subject.

LWH was also shown to lead to unhealthy weight gain. A meta-analysis found an increased risk of weight gain for both male and female workers exposed to LWH, though most of the studies included were cross-sectional (Zhu et al. 2020). This result was also reported by other authors that focused on cohort studies that followed workers without overweight or obesity (Virtanen et al. 2020). Working for more than 55 hours a week increased the risk of being overweight or obese at follow-up, with an adjusted RR of 1.17 (1.08–1.27) and a significant dose-response association. However, the influence of LWH on eating habits and metabolic disorder is more blurred. Studies have contradictory conclusions on the relation between LWH and metabolic syndrome (Pimenta and Martinez-Gonzalez 2016).

There are several possible factors which may explain the discrepant results. The type of work schedule may have an important role as a meta-analysis found a positive relation between metabolic disorder and shift work but not with LWH (Wang et al. 2021). However, the concomitant exposure of both shift work and LWH is not well known. Another meta-analysis focusing on the relation between LWH and the risk of incident type 2 diabetes found a significant association only in the low socioeconomic status subgroup, with a risk ratio of 1.29 (1.06–1.57, 95% CI) for working more than 55 hours a week compared to standard working hours (Kivimäki et al. 2015b). The authors suggest that residual confounding and mediating factors may explain this result, like chronic stress, eating habits, or sleep deprivation.

On the issue of sleep deprivation, working for prolonged time also has specifically been shown to affect sleep time and sleep habits. Several studies have reported lower sleep time and quality of sleep (Kim and Lee 2015; Yoon et al. 2015; Hori et al. 2020), with insomnia being the main sleep disorder reported. Lack of sleep can lead to increased stress and fatigue and potentially to near-misses and occupational injuries. LWH and sleep-related problems were associated with near-misses and injuries in two studies taking place in different occupational setting, one in healthcare services, and one in an industrial setting (Yamauchi et al. 2019; Anzai et al. 2021). A possible explanation of the physiopathology is that sleep problems could have a mediating effect in the relation between LWH and near-misses/injuries as well as job-related stress or depression to various degrees.

LWH may also have a negative impact on one's mental well-being. The meta-analysis carried out by the WHO/ILO Joint Estimates of Work-related Burden of Disease have qualified the current research available as "inadequate evidence for harmfulness" for the relation between LWH and depression prevalence, incidence, and mortality (Rugulies et al. 2021). Another meta-analysis conducted a few years before highlighted a greater risk of depressive symptoms for people exposed to

LWH, with a stronger association in Asian countries (OR 1.50, 95% CI 1.13–2.01) and a weaker association in European countries (1.11, 95% CI 1.00–1.22) (Virtanen et al. 2018). The differences may be explained by the definition of depression, which can vary greatly between studies from clinical depression to symptoms and mental distress. Work conditions seem to affect the relation between LWH and mental wellbeing; a positive effort-reward imbalance at work may reduce the health risk of LWH (Siegrist 1996). Other mental health outcomes may be related to long working hours like anxiety symptoms or burnout, though the relation may be less precise (Niedhammer et al. 2021). A study in Korea found an increased risk of suicidal thoughts in workers with working time greater than 60 hours per week, with a stronger association in the lower socioeconomic subgroup (Yoon et al. 2015). The authors acknowledge that they did not consider other psychosocial risk factors, like high job demands, low control, or effort-reward imbalance, which can be mediating or confounding factors. Nevertheless, psychosocial risk factors are intertwined and LWH should be considered as one of them as much on a populational scale as on an individual perspective. Indeed, some studies have considered the long-term effects of occupational psychosocial risk factors during midlife on health functioning (Wahrendorf et al. 2012). Questionnaires assessing the demand-control-support model and effort-reward imbalance model were confronted to the mental and physical composite scores of the SF-36 (Short Form Health Survey). The SF-36 survey was passed to the participants almost 10 years after the two questionnaires measuring work stress models, during a period which corresponded to retirement in this study. A positive and significant association between work stress and health functioning was found after considering baseline health, which illustrates the potential long-term effects of psychological risk factors. As discussed above, though LWH can be considered as a psychosocial risk factor and could have health effects beyond retirement, studies will be needed to confirm it.

As mentioned earlier, LWH can lead to potential near-misses and injuries through mediating factors as lack of sleep or job-related stress (Anzai et al. 2021). Broadly, a recent meta-analysis studied the relation between extending work hours and safety incidents (Matre et al. 2021). The study confirmed the higher risk of injuries when working more than 12 hours a day (RR 1.24, 95% CI 1.11–1.40) but also found increased, though not significant, risk of injury for working more than 55 hours a week (RR 1.24, 95% CI 0.98–1.57). Many studies in this systematic review had moderate or high risk of biases, but the results presented are restricted to the studies with moderate or low risk of bias. Yet again, the role of LWH is difficult to isolate, as it is also linked to many other factors like the shift schedule (night or day), the number of consecutive days with extended hours, or commuting time, for example. Garde highlights this issue and recommends more research to better understand the effect of different combination of work hours on occupational injuries and the prolonged exposure to other physical, chemical, or psychosocial hazards (Garde 2021).

Lastly, a multicohort study was conducted on the risk of different types of cancer and in particular colorectal, lung, prostate, and breast cancer (Heikkila et al. 2016). No risk increase was found for overall cancer and specifically for colorectal, lung, and prostate cancer. However, there is a significant association between LWH and incidence of breast cancer among female workers, with a hazard ratio of 1.60 (95% CI 1.12–2.29). Breast cancer is already known to be linked with night work (Gehlert et al. 2020); however, in Heikkila et al. analyses, statistical models were adjusted for nighttime work. Nevertheless, extensive research is still needed to confirm this result, as many potential confounding factors not considered could explain this association, like parity, breastfeeding, or use of hormone therapy replacement. Thus, a cautious interpretation is advised.

From this review of all research into these different pathologies and their possible association with LWH, it is found that the level of evidence for each is quite dissimilar. On the one hand, occupational injury, negative lifestyle choices, weight gain, and sleep deprivation are adverse health impacts that can be confidently linked to LWH, without presuming the causality of this link. On the other hand, mental health impacts and cancer diseases have mixed results or show no correlation in the present state of research, and more research is needed to confidently prove or disprove any link to LWH. This review also shows the heterogeneity of the association, with widely varying effects depending on the highlighted subgroups, for example, blue-collar workers, night-shift workers, or gender-specific workers. Finally, as mentioned previously, LWH interacts with many other factors that are also correlated with adverse health impacts, such as psychosocial factors in the workplace. This not only increases the difficulty in proving a causal link, but also means that these interacting factors can be jointly considered to assess their impacts on the outcome.

Focus on Cardiovascular Diseases

As stated in the introduction, cardiovascular diseases are the primary concern of LWH health impact research. This focus on cardiovascular diseases is rooted in the history of the field, for a number of reasons. First, it echoes the fact that cardiovascular diseases are the most prominent cause of death globally, with around 9 million and 6 million deaths caused by ischemic heart diseases and stroke, respectively, in 2019 (WHO). This is also owed to the ease of measuring the relevant outcomes, such as cases of hospitalization for strokes or myocardial infarctions, where in many countries data is systematically and extensively collected in readily available databases. Furthermore, cardiovascular diseases related to LWH leave a strong impression on the general public, since the consequences often lead to hospitalization and in extreme cases death. For example, in Japan, "karoshi" (Japanese term referring to death by overwork) regularly appear in the media, and more than 60% of such cases are the result of strokes for which legal authorities have ruled in favor of work-related causes (Ke 2012).

Two major diseases are discussed in this section: ischemic heart diseases (IHD) and stroke, whether ischemic or hemorrhagic.

Recently, the WHO/ILO Joint Estimates of the Work-related Burden of Disease has published its conclusion on the effect of exposure to LWH on ischemic heart diseases (Li et al. 2020). This study included 37 studies, among which there were 26 prospective cohorts, from numerous countries in the Americas, Europe, and Western Pacific. Using a rigorous methodology to assess the quality of evidence of each study included, the authors judged the bodies of evidence as "inadequate evidence for harmfulness" for working time exposure between 41–48 hours per week and 49–54 hours per week. On the other hand, working more than 55 hours per week proved to have "sufficient evidence for harmfulness" for both IHD incidence and mortality. Indeed, the relative risk for exposure to LWH compared to the reference group (work time between 35 and 40 hours per week) was of 1.13 (95% CI, 1.02–1.26) for IHD incidence and 1.17 (95% CI, 1.05–1.31) for IHD mortality. Subgroups analyses did not reveal differences for sex or WHO region, but the associations were stronger among workers with low socioeconomic status. There are some limitations to the WHO/ILO meta-analysis. First, the effect estimate is modest, and the authors could not demonstrate a dose-response relationship between LWH and IHD. Nevertheless, even if the effect is modest, the high prevalence of workers exposed to LWH leads inevitably to a considerable mortality and morbidity; all the more, they relate to a working, and thus young, population. Second, though some confounders were considered in the analyses and some pathophysiological mechanisms have been suggested, there was no data on potential mediators and causal pathways to better discriminate both direct and indirect effects. Indeed, as mentioned in this chapter, LWH are associated with unhealthy lifestyles and potentially stressful working conditions which can modify the effect of LWH on IHD.

Stroke is the other major cardiovascular disease that was extensively studied with LWH exposure. The effect of LWH on the risk of stroke is more evident than on IHD. As for stroke, the WHO/ILO Joint Estimates of the Work-related Burden of Disease conducted a thorough systematic review and a meta- analysis on this topic (Descatha et al. 2020). A majority of the studies included were cohort studies (20 out of 22) from eight countries across the Americas, Europe, and Western Pacific. The authors judged the bodies of evidence for stroke incidence as "limited evidence for harmfulness" for exposure to 48–54 h of work per week and as "sufficient evidence for harmfulness" for exposure to more than 55 hours per week. Evidence was deemed inadequate for all categories of exposure for stroke prevalence and mortality. Exposure to weekly work hours greater than 55 was associated with an increased risk of stroke incidence (all types considered) compared to exposure to standard hours (35–40 hours per week) with an RR of 1.35 (95% CI, 1.13–1.61). A weaker association was found for working 48–54 hours per week with an RR of 1.13 (95% CI, 1.00–1.28); however, contrary to the effects of LWH on IHD, a dose-response relation was reported between LWH and stroke incidence. Subgroups analyses did not find any difference between sex, WHO region, age, or socioeconomic status. There were also no differences of the effect of LWH on stroke subtype (ischemic versus hemorrhagic), but only two case-control studies had assessed this association. The results of this study are consistent with previous meta-analyses (Kivimäki et al. 2015a), with newer added work. The main limitation was the limited consideration of potential mediators or confounders, which can have an important part in the indirect effect of LWH on cardiovascular diseases.

The pathophysiological mechanisms underlying the effect of LWH are complex. Multiple potential confounders, effect modifiers, and mediating factors seem to influence the causal pathways, as shown in Fig. 2. LWH can increase the risk of cardiovascular diseases through a direct and an indirect pathway. LWH may directly influence the risk of cardiovascular diseases through chronic stress stimuli. Indeed, chronic stress increases the level of stress hormones, like adrenaline and cortisol, and activates the sympathetic and vagal nervous systems, creating proinflammatory and hypercoagulability setting which is the breeding ground for myocardial infarctions and strokes (Kivimäki and Steptoe 2018). The duration of exposure seems to be an important factor, and longer exposure time seems to be associated with a greater risk of adverse outcomes (Fadel et al. 2019, 2020). The role of higher blood pressure and cardiac arrythmia have also been highlighted, as illustrated by a study that found an increased risk of atrial fibrillation for working more than 55 hours per week compared to standard work hours (Kivimäki et al. 2017). However, mediating factors, which characterize the indirect pathway, may have a prominent role in the

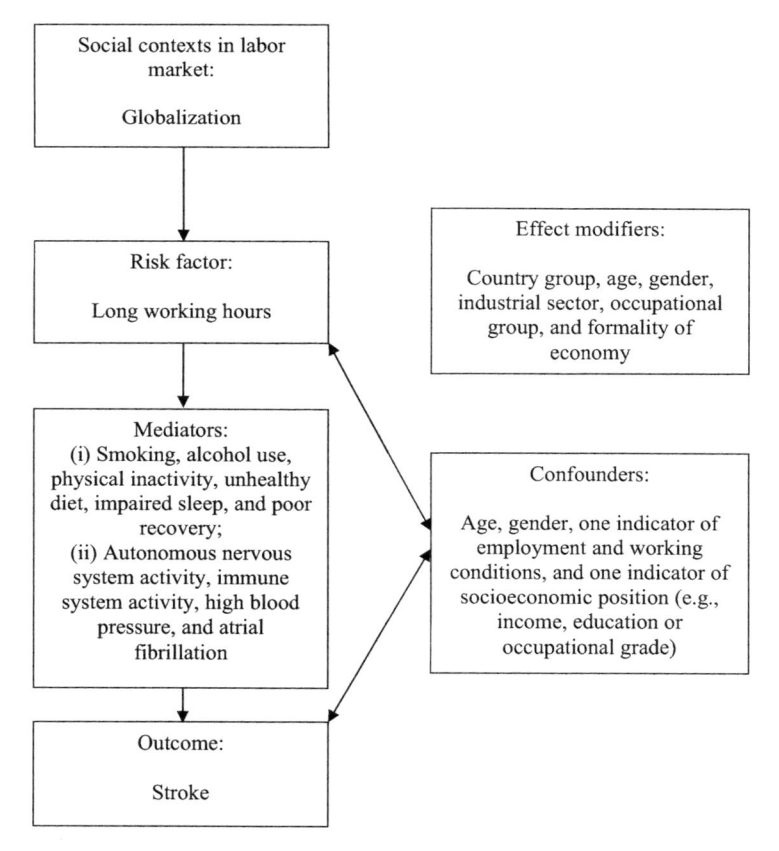

Fig. 2 Logic model of the possible causal relationship between long working hours and stroke. (Figure reproduced with permission from Descatha et al. 2020)

association of LWH and cardiovascular diseases. As mentioned previously, LWH are associated with negative lifestyle behaviors, like smoking, high alcohol consumption, sleep deprivation, and physical inactivity, which are known risk factors of cardiovascular diseases (Taris et al. 2011). Moreover, though chronic stress was discussed previously as a direct effect of LWH, it can also be considered as a mediating effect through working conditions. Job strain, effort reward imbalance, and conflict at work can contribute to stressful working conditions and increase the risk of cardiovascular diseases (Jood et al. 2017; Sara et al. 2018). Lastly, numerous effect modifiers, like socioeconomic status or sex, can influence the relation between LWH and cardiovascular diseases as reported by several previously mentioned studies (Kivimäki et al. 2015a; Li et al. 2020). Some authors have suggested a differential association between LWH and stroke subtype, with a stronger effect of LWH on the risk of hemorrhagic strokes (Hannerz et al. 2018). Given the difference of physiopathology of some outcomes associated with LWH, for example, ischemic stroke and hemorrhagic stroke, we hypothesize that the weight of the direct and indirect pathways may differ, with a greater influence of the indirect effects in ischemic diseases.

In any case, the increasing number of studies finding a link between LWH and cardiovascular diseases must make us think about their health consequences. The two WHO/ILO studies allow us to precisely estimate the burdens of both IHD and stroke attributable to LWH globally. The attributable disease burdens were estimated by applying the population-attributable fractions, calculated from the RR of the meta-analyses and the exposure estimates modeled from survey data, to WHO's Global Health Estimates of total disease burdens (Pega et al. 2021). In 2016, there were 745,194 (705,786–784,601, 95% uncertainty range) deaths and 23.3 million (22.2–24.4, 95% uncertainty range) disability-adjusted life years (DALY) from IHD and stroke attributable to LWH. Though the distribution was roughly equal between IHD and stroke for deaths (respectively, 46.5% and 53.5%), the population-attributable fraction was higher for stroke (6.9% versus 3.7% for IHD), but it increased less between 2000 and 2016 than for IHD (41.5% for IHD versus 19.0% for stroke). Males in South-East Asia carried the most burden. As mentioned earlier, the associations between LWH and cardiovascular diseases are moderate, but the prevalence of exposure to LWH is high. It was estimated that, globally in 2016, 488 million people worked more than 55 hours per week. Exposure varied according to sex (more males), age (early and middle-aged adults), and WHO region (highest proportion of population exposed in Southeast Asia, lowest in Europe). Thus, the burden of disease attributable to LWH is the largest among 19 selected occupational exposures estimated to this day (Pega et al. 2022), including occupational injuries, exposure to particulate matter, gases and fumes, and exposure to asbestos.

Further research is needed to better understand the causal pathways surrounding the effect of LWH on cardiovascular diseases, but new evidence is found regularly. A large multicohort study confirmed the increased mortality by cardiovascular disease for working more than 55 hours per week (Ervasti et al. 2021), and a recent study has highlighted the risk of recurrent coronary events for workers who had a myocardial infarction and who were exposed to LWH after returning to work (Trudel et al.

2021). In Ervasti et al.'s study, sensitivity analyses focusing on two studies which had repeated measure for LWH exposure were carried out, allowing to consider potential changes in working hours during participants' life course. Results were similar, with increased risk of cardiovascular death, injury, musculoskeletal diseases, and bacterial infections, though the increased risk of diabetes was no longer statistically significant. Sensitivity analyses also allowed to study in effect of LWH exposure at maximum follow-up, beyond the age of 65 which is usually the age of retirement. Musculoskeletal diseases and bacterial infection were significantly associated with LWH exposure when considering maximum follow-up, and despite the risk of cardiovascular diseases (including stroke and myocardial infarction) for participants exposed to LWH, the associations were not significant. The authors hypothesized that LWH might act as an acute trigger for cardiovascular diseases for individuals with high risk of cardiac events. However, interpretation of the results is complex because of the multiple risk factors, effect modifiers, and mediation factors involved in the relation between cardiovascular diseases and LWH, with both a possible direct and indirect causal pathway. Nevertheless, increased risks of several diseases were found, suggesting a persistent burden of disease which could affect one's life course beyond the end of the exposure. Thus, all these examples and the consequent toll of LWH illustrate the need of public health policies to prevent further expansion of this threat.

LWH: From Epidemiology to Public Health

LWH As an Indicator for Monitoring Workers' Health

The previous section presented a summary of the research into adverse health impact linked or thought to be linked with LWH. With the body of knowledge into the varied pathologies associated with LWH, it is interesting to discuss how such knowledge may be applied in an epidemiologic framework to assess public health issues and particularly to monitor workers' health.

First, LWH is a useful indicator in health monitoring as it is relatively easy to measure compared to other working condition indicators (Garde 2021), and arguably among all relevant health indicators. It is usually measured through surveys (in population studies) or interview of individual patients. The ILO identifies in a report LWH as an indicator of decent working conditions (ILO 2013).

Other working indicators listed by the ILO such as work stability and security, safe work environment, social dialogue, productive work, or adequate earnings are much more complex and difficult to assess objectively compared to LWH. Unlike LWH, these are qualitative variables which heavily vary and depend on the workplace context. Though they may be more suited for the assessment of working conditions on individual and local levels, they are difficult to implement and require significant investments in large cohort study designs. Furthermore, many countries do not have adequate labor organizations and public health institutions to precisely measure such indicators, whereas LWH can be easily measured for many countries regardless of medical or public infrastructure. Furthermore, the drawback, highlighted in the introduction, of varying LWH definition across countries may be overcome with careful considerations, whereas comparison across countries of complex psychosocial indicators is much more complicated, as these are heavily tied to cultural aspects of work.

Thus, although the pathology mechanisms of LWH and adverse health impacts are not known, LWH is still an efficient indicator, as shown previously for its association to adverse health effects, and a useful proxy to study working conditions at a population level.

LWH As a Target for Prevention Measures

Following the above discussion on LWH as a useful working condition indicator, it is possible to discuss the prevention measures targeting LWH to improve health-related impacts of working conditions. At a population level, these prevention measures are essentially tied to labor regulations, for example, with mandatory maximum worked hours. In fact, working hours are more and more regulated. In Japan, a program aiming to challenge the issue of Karoshi was introduced in 2014 (Yamauchi et al. 2017). Preventive measures were implemented, and overtime work was strictly regulated. The study aimed to estimate the impact of such labor law regulations and preventive measures targeting LWH on the risk of cardiovascular diseases (Lin et al. 2020). The authors revealed that, after the enforcement of the 2014 Act, the incidence rate ratio of overwork-related cardiovascular diseases decreased by 26% cases per year, and that approximatively 40% of this effect could be explained by the reduction of work hours. Similar results were found in South Korea where there is raising concern about LWH (Kim et al. 2019). Knowing the economic and health burden of cardiovascular diseases, the advantages of such policies on people's work retention and life course seem considerable. Recognition of the health consequences of LWH is also critical because it allows to quantify the burden, raise awareness, and compensate victims. Similar results were observed in other countries, for example, in Germany where the legislative reduction of physician's work time was associated with a decrease workplace stress and improved health in psychiatrists (Beschoner et al. 2021). At a local level, work organizations can be adapted to limit working hours in collaboration with employers, workers, and occupational and public health professionals. Several studies analyze the possible impact of workplace-level intervention on different health impacts of LWH, which may suggest possible prevention actions that could be undertaken to improve organization of labor and reduce LWH-related negative health effects. For example, a study conducted in a randomized population of the public sector in Sweden analyzed the impact of reduced working time on sleep and perceived stress (Schiller et al. 2017). Compared to a control group, the intervention group whose working time was decreased by 25% for a period of 18 months (with constant salary) showed increased sleep time, and improved sleep quality. Reduced levels of perceived stress and sleepiness were also observed. In another study conducted in Finnish municipalities, working hour reduction improved work and family life balance, showing the most impact for a labor organization centered around 6-h shifts (Anttila et al. 2005). Through interviews, this experiment also showed possible negative impacts of LWH prevention measures at the workplace level, in particular increase in guilt around having more favorable labor conditions compared to other workers, and a loss of autonomy among the highly educated. Independently from these studies, workplace prevention measures should be carefully implemented so as to avoid workload increase compensating for the reduction in working hours. Such an unintended effect may be difficult to observe in controlled studies but could be more prevalent in nonresearch settings.

Finally, LWH should be considered as an occupational hazard to be monitored at the individual level by occupational health practitioners. Occupational healthcare interviews and appointments represent a good opportunity to raise awareness about the negative health impacts of LWH and overwork, with individualized feedback. LWH are not fully actionable at an individual level, but awareness may promote other healthy lifestyle choices such as exercising, healthy sleep, healthy diet, and limiting negative behaviors (smoking, alcohol consumption). Workers with cardiovascular risk factors may be at greater risk of LWH adverse health effects and should be monitored, and particularly greater care should be given to external cardiovascular risks such as diabetes, high blood pressure, or dyslipidemia. As discussed above, workers that have already suffered from myocardial infarction and who are subject to LWH are at greater risk of recurrent coronary events (Trudel et al. 2021). Thus, return to work after a cardiovascular event that may be partially related to extended working hours is complex and can potentially lead to job loss due to sequalae or recurring events. This example showcases the importance of careful monitoring of at-risk workers in their professional environment.

Conclusion

In conclusion, this chapter has presented a summary of the state of the art of the knowledge about LWH. This relatively new topic in occupational and public health has shown important results on potential LWH adverse health effects, including cardiovascular diseases, worsened lifestyle behaviors, or occupational injuries. Though the measured cardiovascular impact is modest, LWH has become a leading cause of death attributed to work due to the high prevalence of LWH globally. Moreover, LWH can greatly influence the life course because of their effect on health and consequently on professional careers, though much research is still needed on this topic. Despite the lack of comprehensive pathological mechanisms associated with LWH, it remains a useful health indicator for workers, for its simplicity of measurement at population or individual level. Thus, prevention measures targeting LWH are promising tools to tackle negative health impacts of overwork and poor working conditions. However, other psychosocial risk factors in the workplace should not be neglected, as they may be interwound with LWH, and should be included in the assessment and prevention of work-related health issues. Further research in the field is essential to explore pathological mechanisms for proven health impacts, as well as to ascertain LWH association with other possible health impacts (some of which were presented in this chapter).

References

Anttila T, Nätti J, Väisänen M (2005) The experiments of reduced working hours in Finland. Community Work Fam 8:187–209. https://doi.org/10.1080/13668800500049704

Anzai T, Yamauchi T, Ozawa M, Takahashi K (2021) A generalized structural equation model approach to long working hours and near-misses among healthcare professionals in Japan. Int J Environ Res Public Health 18:7154. https://doi.org/10.3390/ijerph18137154

Beschoner P, von Wietersheim J, Jarczok MN et al (2021) Effort-reward-imbalance, burnout, and depression among psychiatrists 2006 and 2016-changes after a legislative intervention. Front Psych 12:641912. https://doi.org/10.3389/fpsyt.2021.641912

Descatha A, Sembajwe G, Pega F et al (2020) The effect of exposure to long working hours on stroke: a systematic review and meta-analysis from the WHO/ILO joint estimates of the work-related burden of disease and injury. Environ Int 142:105746. https://doi.org/10.1016/j.envint.2020.105746

Erlangsen A, Fedyszyn I (2015) Danish nationwide registers for public health and health-related research. Scand J Public Health 43:333–339. https://doi.org/10.1177/1403494815575193

Ervasti J, Pentti J, Nyberg ST et al (2021) Long working hours and risk of 50 health conditions and mortality outcomes: a multicohort study in four European countries. Lancet Reg Health Eur 11:100212. https://doi.org/10.1016/j.lanepe.2021.100212

European Agency for Safety and Health at Work (2021) The digitalisation of work: psychosocial risk factors and work-related musculoskeletal disorders | Safety and health at work EU-OSHA. https://osha.europa.eu/en/publications/digitalisation-work-psychosocial-risk-factors-and-work-related-musculoskeletal-disorders/view. Accessed 21 Mar 2022

Fadel M, Sembajwe G, Gagliardi D et al (2019) Association between reported long working hours and history of stroke in the CONSTANCES cohort. Stroke 50:1879–1882. https://doi.org/10.1161/STROKEAHA.119.025454

Fadel M, Li J, Sembajwe G et al (2020) Cumulative exposure to long working hours and occurrence of ischemic heart disease: evidence from the CONSTANCES cohort at inception. J Am Heart Assoc 9:e015753. https://doi.org/10.1161/JAHA.119.015753

Garde AH (2021) The importance of extended working hours for work-related injuries. Scand J Work Environ Health 47:411–414. https://doi.org/10.5271/sjweh.3981

Gehlert S, Clanton M, On Behalf of the Shift Work and Breast Cancer Strategic Advisory Group null (2020) Shift work and breast cancer. Int J Environ Res Public Health 17:E9544. https://doi.org/10.3390/ijerph17249544

Hannerz H, Albertsen K, Burr H et al (2018) Long working hours and stroke among employees in the general workforce of Denmark. Scand J Public Health 46:368–374. https://doi.org/10.1177/1403494817748264

Heikkila K, Nyberg ST, Madsen IEH et al (2016) Long working hours and cancer risk: a multicohort study. Br J Cancer 114:813–818. https://doi.org/10.1038/bjc.2016.9

Hori D, Sasahara S, Oi Y et al (2020) Relationships between insomnia, long working hours, and long commuting time among public school teachers in Japan: a nationwide cross-sectional diary study. Sleep Med 75:62–72. https://doi.org/10.1016/j.sleep.2019.09.017

ILO (2013) Decent work indicators – concepts and definitions. http://www.ilo.org/integration/resources/pubs/WCMS_229374/lang%2D%2Den/index.htm. Accessed 4 Mar 2022

ILO (2018) Working time and the future of work. http://www.ilo.org/global/topics/future-of-work/publications/research-papers/WCMS_649907/lang%2D%2Den/index.htm. Accessed 12 Mar 2022

Jood K, Karlsson N, Medin J et al (2017) The psychosocial work environment is associated with risk of stroke at working age. Scand J Work Environ Health 43:367–374. https://doi.org/10.5271/sjweh.3636

Ke D-S (2012) Overwork, stroke, and karoshi-death from overwork. Acta Neurol Taiwanica 21:54–59

Kim BH, Lee H-E (2015) The association between working hours and sleep disturbances according to occupation and gender. Chronobiol Int 32:1109–1114. https://doi.org/10.3109/07420528.2015.1064440

Kim I, Koo MJ, Lee H-E et al (2019) Overwork-related disorders and recent improvement of national policy in South Korea. J Occup Health 61:288–296. https://doi.org/10.1002/1348-9585.12060

Kivimäki M, Steptoe A (2018) Effects of stress on the development and progression of cardiovascular disease. Nat Rev Cardiol 15:215–229. https://doi.org/10.1038/nrcardio.2017.189

Kivimäki M, Jokela M, Nyberg ST et al (2015a) Long working hours and risk of coronary heart disease and stroke: a systematic review and meta-analysis of published and unpublished data for 603,838 individuals. Lancet (London, England) 386:1739–1746. https://doi.org/10.1016/S0140-6736(15)60295-1

Kivimäki M, Virtanen M, Kawachi I et al (2015b) Long working hours, socioeconomic status, and the risk of incident type 2 diabetes: a meta-analysis of published and unpublished data from 222 120 individuals. Lancet Diabetes Endocrinol 3:27–34. https://doi.org/10.1016/S2213-8587(14)70178-0

Kivimäki M, Nyberg ST, Batty GD et al (2017) Long working hours as a risk factor for atrial fibrillation: a multi-cohort study. Eur Heart J 38:2621–2628. https://doi.org/10.1093/eurheartj/ehx324

Kramer A, Kramer KZ (2020) The potential impact of the Covid-19 pandemic on occupational status, work from home, and occupational mobility. J Vocat Behav 119:103442. https://doi.org/10.1016/j.jvb.2020.103442

Lee S, McCann D, Messenger JC (2007) Working time around the world

Lee D-W, Jang T-W, Kim H-R, Kang M-Y (2021) The relationship between working hours and lifestyle behaviors: evidence from a population-based panel study in Korea. J Occup Health 63: e12280. https://doi.org/10.1002/1348-9585.12280

Li J, Pega F, Ujita Y et al (2020) The effect of exposure to long working hours on ischaemic heart disease: a systematic review and meta-analysis from the WHO/ILO Joint Estimates of the Work-Related Burden of Disease and Injury. Environ Int 142:105739. https://doi.org/10.1016/j.envint.2020.105739

Lin R-T, Liang Y-W, Takahashi M et al (2020) Effect of implementing an overwork-prevention act on working hours and overwork-related disease: a mediation analysis. J Occup Health 62: e12148. https://doi.org/10.1002/1348-9585.12148

Matre D, Skogstad M, Sterud T et al (2021) Safety incidents associated with extended working hours. A systematic review and meta-analysis. Scand J Work Environ Health 47:415–424. https://doi.org/10.5271/sjweh.3958

Niedhammer I, Bertrais S, Witt K (2021) Psychosocial work exposures and health outcomes: a meta-review of 72 literature reviews with meta-analysis. Scand J Work Environ Health 47:489–508. https://doi.org/10.5271/sjweh.3968

Pachito DV, Pega F, Bakusic J et al (2021) The effect of exposure to long working hours on alcohol consumption, risky drinking and alcohol use disorder: a systematic review and meta-analysis from the WHO/ILO Joint Estimates of the Work-Related Burden of Disease and Injury. Environ Int 146:106205. https://doi.org/10.1016/j.envint.2020.106205

Peckham TK, Baker MG, Camp JE et al (2017) Creating a future for occupational health. Ann Work Expo Health 61:3–15. https://doi.org/10.1093/annweh/wxw011

Pega F, Náfrádi B, Momen NC et al (2021) Global, regional, and national burdens of ischemic heart disease and stroke attributable to exposure to long working hours for 194 countries, 2000-2016: a systematic analysis from the WHO/ILO Joint Estimates of the Work-Related Burden of Disease and Injury. Environ Int 154:106595. https://doi.org/10.1016/j.envint.2021.106595

Pega F, Hamzaoui H, Náfrádi B, Momen NC (2022) Global, regional and national burden of disease attributable to 19 selected occupational risk factors for 183 countries, 2000-2016: a systematic analysis from the WHO/ILO jJoint Estimates of the Work-Related Burden of Disease and Injury. Scand J Work Environ Health 48:158–168. https://doi.org/10.5271/sjweh.4001

Pérez-Martínez P, Mikhailidis DP, Athyros VG et al (2017) Lifestyle recommendations for the prevention and management of metabolic syndrome: an international panel recommendation. Nutr Rev 75:307–326. https://doi.org/10.1093/nutrit/nux014

Pimenta AM, Martinez-Gonzalez MA (2016) The association between long working hours and metabolic syndrome remains elusive. Eur J Pub Health 26:377. https://doi.org/10.1093/eurpub/ckw030

Rugulies R, Sørensen K, Di Tecco C et al (2021) The effect of exposure to long working hours on depression: a systematic review and meta-analysis from the WHO/ILO Joint Estimates of the Work-Related Burden of Disease and Injury. Environ Int 155:106629. https://doi.org/10.1016/j.envint.2021.106629

Sangheon Lee DM, JCM (2007) Working time around the world

Sara JD, Prasad M, Eleid MF et al (2018) Association between work-related stress and coronary heart disease: a review of prospective studies through the job strain, effort-reward balance, and organizational justice models. J Am Heart Assoc 7:e008073. https://doi.org/10.1161/JAHA.117.008073

Schiller H, Lekander M, Rajaleid K et al (2017) The impact of reduced worktime on sleep and perceived stress – a group randomized intervention study using diary data. Scand J Work Environ Health 43:109–116. https://doi.org/10.5271/sjweh.3610

Siegrist J (1996) Adverse health effects of high-effort/low-reward conditions. J Occup Health Psychol 1:27–41. https://doi.org/10.1037//1076-8998.1.1.27

Stevenson F (2015) The use of electronic patient records for medical research: conflicts and contradictions. BMC Health Serv Res 15:124. https://doi.org/10.1186/s12913-015-0783-6

Taris TW, Ybema JF, Beckers DGJ et al (2011) Investigating the associations among overtime work, health behaviors, and health: a longitudinal study among full-time employees. Int J Behav Med 18:352–360. https://doi.org/10.1007/s12529-010-9103-z

Trudel X, Brisson C, Talbot D et al (2021) Long working hours and risk of recurrent coronary events. J Am Coll Cardiol 77:1616–1625. https://doi.org/10.1016/j.jacc.2021.02.012

Virtanen M, Jokela M, Madsen IE et al (2018) Long working hours and depressive symptoms: systematic review and meta-analysis of published studies and unpublished individual participant data. Scand J Work Environ Health 44:239–250. https://doi.org/10.5271/sjweh.3712

Virtanen M, Jokela M, Lallukka T et al (2020) Long working hours and change in body weight: analysis of individual-participant data from 19 cohort studies. Int J Obes 44:1368–1375. https://doi.org/10.1038/s41366-019-0480-3

Wahrendorf M, Sembajwe G, Zins M et al (2012) Long-term effects of psychosocial work stress in midlife on health functioning after labor market exit--results from the GAZEL study. J Gerontol B Psychol Sci Soc Sci 67:471–480. https://doi.org/10.1093/geronb/gbs045

Wang Y, Yu L, Gao Y et al (2021) Association between shift work or long working hours with metabolic syndrome: a systematic review and dose-response meta-analysis of observational studies. Chronobiol Int 38:318–333. https://doi.org/10.1080/07420528.2020.1797763

WHO The top 10 causes of death. https://www.who.int/news-room/fact-sheets/detail/the-top-10-causes-of-death. Accessed 18 Mar 2022

World Economic Forum (2011) The global economic burden of non-communicable diseases. In: World Economic Forum. https://www.weforum.org/reports/global-economic-burden-non-communicable-diseases/. Accessed 21 Mar 2022

Yamauchi T, Yoshikawa T, Takamoto M et al (2017) Overwork-related disorders in Japan: recent trends and development of a national policy to promote preventive measures. Ind Health 55:293–302. https://doi.org/10.2486/indhealth.2016-0198

Yamauchi T, Sasaki T, Takahashi K et al (2019) Long working hours, sleep-related problems, and near-misses/injuries in industrial settings using a nationally representative sample of workers in Japan. PLoS One 14:e0219657. https://doi.org/10.1371/journal.pone.0219657

Yoon J-H, Jung PK, Roh J et al (2015) Relationship between long working hours and suicidal thoughts: Nationwide data from the 4th and 5th Korean National Health and Nutrition Examination Survey. PLoS One 10:e0129142. https://doi.org/10.1371/journal.pone.0129142

Zhu Y, Liu J, Jiang H et al (2020) Are long working hours associated with weight-related outcomes? A meta-analysis of observational studies. Obes Rev 21:e12977. https://doi.org/10.1111/obr.12977

Health Effects of Shift Work and Night Shift Work

15

Pascal Guénel and Damien Léger

Contents

Introduction	246
Definitions of Shift Work and Night Work	247
Shift Work	247
Night Work	248
Prevalence of Night Work Worldwide	248
Physiopathology	248
Circadian Clock and Circadian Desynchronization	249
Melatonin	249
Sleep Disorders and Lifestyle Changes in Shift Workers	250
Assessment of Circadian Disruption in Different Shift Systems	250
Health Outcomes	252
Sleep and Vigilance Disorders	252
Metabolic and Cardiovascular Consequences of Shift Work	254
Cancer	256
Cognitive Disorders and Drowsiness	258
Depression and Anxiety	259
Adverse Pregnancy Outcomes	259
Prevention Strategies and Recommendations	259
Adapting the Night Shift Work Schedule Systems	260
Information-Education and Occupational Medicine	260
Strategic Light/Dark Exposure	260

P. Guénel (✉)
Paris-Saclay University, UVSQ, Gustave Roussy, Inserm, CESP, Team Exposome and Heredity, Inserm, Villejuif, France
e-mail: pascal.guenel@inserm.fr

D. Léger
VIFASOM (ERC 7330 Vigilance Fatigue Sommeil et Santé Publique), Université Paris Cité, Paris, France

APHP, Hôtel-Dieu, Centre du Sommeil et de la Vigilance, Centre de ressources en pathologie professionnelle Sommeil Vigilance et Travail, Paris, France
e-mail: damien.leger@aphp.fr

Opportunistic Napping 261
Physical Activity 261
Meal Timing 261
Conclusion 261
References 262

Abstract

Nowadays, shift work and night work are essential features of work organization. In addition to enabling the continuity of services to the population, such as the production of electricity, health care, transportation, or security, they are also used for the development of new technologies and for productive and commercial activities. The effects of shift work and night shift work have been widely documented in the scientific literature. This chapter describes the effects of night work on the biological circadian rhythms, ranging from sleep disorders to metabolic or cardiovascular diseases and cancer. It also reviews the known or suspected health effects of shift work or night shift work during the working life and provides a few recommendations that may help to reduce its health impact.

Keywords

Night work · Shift work · Circadian rhythm disruption · Melatonin · Sleep disorders · Metabolic diseases · Cardiovascular diseases · Breast cancer · Prostate cancer

Introduction

Until recently, shift and night work were essentially used to secure round-the-clock activities related to the provision of essential basic services to the general population (e.g., light, water, and gas supply; health care; transport; security; and telecommunications), to cope with technological constraints (e.g., power plants, metallurgy, and the chemical industry), and to increase labor productivity and economic profitability of enterprises (e.g., the manufacturing industry) (IARC Working Group 2019). In modern societies, shift and night shift work are essential features of work organization. They permit globalization of the labor market and enhance economic competition by enabling nonstop activities fostered by the development of new technologies (e.g., communication technologies) and productive and commercial strategies (e.g., just-in-time operation and logistics), and the increased exploitation of leisure time (e.g., tourism and entertainment) (Anttila and Oinas 2018).

This chapter summarizes the current knowledge on the health effects of night work and shift work throughout the working life, which have been extensively documented in the scientific literature. First, we will review the definitions of shift work and night work, and will provide an overview of the size of the population affected by this form of work organization. We will then discuss the effects of night/shift work on the biological systems and review the well-established or suspected health outcomes of night work/shift work, before briefly presenting the avenues available for reducing the health impact of staggered work schedules. We will then discuss the effects of night/shift work on biological systems, and the established or suspected health effects, before mentioning a few guidelines for reducing the health impact of night shift work.

Definitions of Shift Work and Night Work

Shift Work

Shift work is defined by the International Labor Organization as *"a method of organization of working time in which workers succeed one another at the workplace so that the establishment can operate longer than the hours of work of individual workers"* (ILO 1990a).

According to the European directives 93/104/EC, 2003/88/EC:

> shift work is any mode of organization of teamwork according to which workers are occupied successively on the same workstations, according to a rhythm, including rotational rhythm. The rhythm may be continuous or discontinuous, requiring workers to perform work at different times over a given period of days or weeks.

In the present "24/7 society" (24 h/day, 7 days/week), shift work may involve various forms of flexible, variable, irregular, and nonstandard working hours, including evening and night work, split shifts, staggered working hours, compressed work weeks, weekend work, on-call work, and on-demand work. There exists a myriad of shift systems that can differ widely according to the following main features (Knauth 1993, 1996, 1998).

There are usually three main recognized categories of shift work:

- Discontinuous shift work where the teams follow one another at the same shift but the work is interrupted at the end of the day and at the end of the week, at least on Sunday.
- Semicontinuous work where the teams follow one another at the same shift over the whole 24 h, but the work is interrupted at the end of the week, at least on Sunday.
- Continuous shift work where the teams follow one another at the same shift 24 h a day, 7 days a week. There is no interruption of activity, neither at the end of the day nor at the end of the week.

In the context of shift work, the teams can be regular, the employees are always assigned to the same work period, but they are most often alternating, the employees successively occupying the different work periods.

More simply, for the US Bureau of Labor statistics: "The term shift work refers to any work schedule that falls outside the hours of 7 am and 6 pm. Shift work can include evening, night, and early morning shifts, as well as fixed or rotating schedules."

Night Work

As defined by the ILO, night work means *"all work which is performed during a period of not less than seven consecutive hours, including the interval from midnight to 5 a.m."*; consequently, *"night worker means an employed person whose work requires performance of a substantial number of hours of night work which exceeds a specified limit"* (ILO 1990a, b).

The European Union (EU) Working Time Directive No. 2003/88/EC (WTD) definition of "night time" is the same as that set by the ILO, and the "night worker" is someone who (a) "during night time, works at least three hours of his daily working time as a normal course" or (b) "is likely during night time to work a certain proportion of his annual working time, as defined at the choice of the Member State concerned" by national legislation or by collective agreements, or agreement between two sides of industry (EU Council 2003).

Prevalence of Night Work Worldwide

In Europe, results from the latest EU Labour Force Survey (Eurostat 2022) covering 28 European countries, indicated that 16.7% of employed men and 9.4% of employed women worked night shifts in 2018. The overall percentage of employed people working nights decreased slightly between the 2009 and 2018 surveys (from 14.9% to 13.3%). The most prevalent types of shift work are alternating or rotating shifts, followed by permanent shifts. "Atypical work," including night work, weekend work (working both Saturday and Sunday), and shift work, is more prevalent among men than women, among the self-employed than the non-self-employed, and during the earliest stage of working life; within Europe, it is most prevalent in the Anglo-Saxon, Central–Eastern, and Southern country clusters (EuroFound 2017). According to the fourth EU Working Conditions Survey (EuroFound 2007), night shift work is used in many work sectors, particularly in: hotels and restaurants (>45% of the workforce); transport and communication (>35%); health care (>30%); public administration and defense (>25%); manufacturing (>20%); and electricity, gas, and water (>20%).

Physiopathology

The circadian system refers to the endogenous timing system that synchronizes physiology and behaviors within 24-h day and night cycles, and enables adapting to daily environmental changes. The nocturnal activities demanded by shift work schedules disrupt the natural sleep-wake cycle and circadian time organization, and expose workers to artificial light at night, an abnormal biological time of light exposure. In addition, night work reduces the 24-h sleep duration, induces poor sleep quality, and causes insomnia. It also leads to a reduction in physical activity, to irregular eating habits, and has deleterious effects on social and family life and on quality of life. These effects contribute to a disruption of physiological circadian rhythms, which varies in magnitude depending on the characteristics of each shift work system.

Circadian Clock and Circadian Desynchronization

In mammals, the circadian system is organized in a hierarchical manner: a master oscillator, the suprachiasmatic nucleus (SCN) of the hypothalamus, regulates multiple downstream peripheral oscillators via hormonal, metabolic, thermal, and neural signals, resulting in a coherent time organization of body processes for optimal performance (Reppert and Weaver 2002; Schibler 2006; Lee et al. 2010). This coordinated network of clocks harmonizes the physiological, psychological, and behavioral functioning of the body, in particular the sleep-wake circadian rhythm. For optimal efficiency, body rhythms must be synchronized. This is accomplished primarily by cyclic time cues provided by the light-dark cycle transmitted to the SCN via retinal and hormonal mechanisms.

At the molecular level, clock mechanisms in the SCN and peripheral organs are similar. Circadian oscillators consist of a network of circadian genes operating in a transcriptional-translational feedback loops that drive ~24-h rhythmic expression patterns of the core clock components (Reppert and Weaver 2002; Schibler 2006; Haus and Smolensky 2013).

Circadian rhythms of individuals synchronized to daytime activity and nighttime sleep must undergo phase adjustment following changes between night and day work schedules. A circadian phase shift brought about by rotating shift work or night work schedules (as well as by rapid trans-meridian displacement by air travel) results in desynchronization at molecular level among cellular oscillators within and between the SCN and peripheral tissues. Phase shift requires several 24-h periods to adjust. With rapid rotating (2–4 day) shift work schedules, or with differing schedules during workdays and free days, phase shift precludes complete phase adjustment due to the slow temporal kinetics of the processes of biological timekeeping and leads to misalignment of internal circadian rhythms.

The external and internal desynchronization of night workers and shift workers constitutes a major functional disturbance of the time organization. Circadian disruption through genetic, epigenetic, metabolic, or hormonal mechanisms, may lead to reduced performance and heightened risk for several medical conditions, e.g., sleep disorder, obesity, metabolic syndrome/type II diabetes, cardiovascular diseases, and cancers (Haus and Smolensky 2006).

Melatonin

One important biochemical signal to synchronize all circadian rhythms and ensure appropriate alignment between internal and external time is the hormone melatonin. In response to signals from the SCN conveyed via the sympathetic chain, melatonin is primarily produced in the pineal gland of the brain and secreted into the general circulation, where it is made available to peripheral tissues. Melatonin is influenced by the SCN and is also a chronobiotic feedback moderator of the oscillatory activity of the SCN, whose neurons express melatonin receptors and are neurophysiologically responsive to melatonin (Kandalepas et al. 2016; Lunn et al. 2017). Nocturnal light exposures directly suppress pineal production of melatonin. In the absence of light at night (LAN), levels of melatonin in blood, cerebral spinal fluid, and saliva are normally low during the day and high during the darkness of night. LAN exposure of sufficient level and duration, appropriate wavelength, and appropriate timing can shift the timing and/or reduce the amplitude of the nighttime melatonin signal, as may happen in night shift workers (Dumont and Paquet 2014; Wei et al. 2020).

The suppression of melatonin by LAN led to the hypothesis that LAN may play a role in the elevated incidence of breast cancer in high-income countries, as increases in incidence of breast cancer have paralleled the expansion of LAN (Haus and Smolensky 2013; Liu et al. 2014). The nighttime circadian melatonin signal in both rats and humans is known to exert an oncostatic role in a variety of cancers (Haus and Smolensky 2013), most particularly in models of human breast cancer tumor growth (Blask 2005, 2011). Human observational studies have also shown higher melatonin levels to be inversely associated with hypertension, type-2 diabetes, and myocardial infarction (McMullan et al. 2013; Strohmaier et al. 2018). Several lines of evidence from experimental studies support that melatonin may have a beneficial effect on glucose metabolism (Peschke et al. 2006) and cardiovascular diseases (Strohmaier et al. 2018), for example, through the ability to neutralize reactive oxygen and nitrogen species, or stimulation of antioxidant enzymes (Zhang and Zhang 2014; Zephy and Ahmad 2015).

Sleep Disorders and Lifestyle Changes in Shift Workers

Shift work may negatively impact health through the consequences of disturbed sleep patterns leading to circadian disruption and melatonin suppression. It may also lead to changes in lifestyle factors like increasing use of tobacco and alcohol, decreased physical activity, and disturbed eating patterns and behavioral risk factors. In a scoping review of longitudinal studies, Crowther et al. (2022) have shown that shift workers have insufficient sleep duration and experience poor sleep quality, in particular recent, inexperienced shift workers. Based on few available informative studies, they also suggest that shift workers may have reduced physical activity and inadequate nutritional intake (i.e., high levels of saturated fat intake). These behaviors (sleep loss, physical activity, and poor nutrition) represent independent risk factors for various health outcomes, including metabolic, cardiovascular, and cancerous diseases, and may also cluster together and interact with each other to induce adverse health effects.

Assessment of Circadian Disruption in Different Shift Systems

To investigate the health effects of shift work in observational studies, it is necessary to assess the degree of circadian rhythm disruption associated with the different shift work systems. This assessment is made difficult in the absence of markers of circadian disruption that can be easily measured in epidemiological studies. In addition, because of the multiplicity of shift work systems in the working populations, heterogeneous definitions of shift work have been used that may explain inconsistencies of study results. In order to assess the major characteristics of non-day shift work and shift schedules that should be assessed in epidemiological studies to evaluate the impact on physiological and circadian rhythms, Stevens et al. (2011) recommended to use a common definition of night work in epidemiological studies and to capture three major domains of shift work: (1) the shift system (start time of shift, number of hours per day, rotating or permanent, speed and direction of a rotating system, regular or irregular); (2) years on a particular non-day shift schedule; and (3) shift intensity (number of night shifts per month/week, time off between successive workdays). These domains are based in part on biological considerations, such as the fact that adaptation to phase shift can occur more quickly after a phase delay than a phase advance. This would suggest that a forward-rotating shift is less disruptive than a backward rotation, though both are presumably more disruptive than a stable shift. In an attempt to follow these recommendations, a study on breast cancer risk among night shifters (Cordina-Duverger et al. 2018) has been conducted by pooling data of epidemiological studies using a harmonized definition of night shift work (i.e., work for at least 3 h between midnight and 5 AM) and using night shift duration, years of shift work, and intensity of night shift work over the work history as exposure metrics. Other studies have assessed exposure to night shift work using objective day-to-day information of working hours based on payroll data (Harma et al. 2015; Vistisen et al. 2017), which is suitable for multidimensional exposure assessment recommended by Stevens et al. (2011). However, detailed information on shiftwork characteristics over the entire work history is generally unavailable in large cohort studies to assess the duration and intensity of circadian disruption among study subjects (Travis et al. 2016).

Evaluating the impact of the different shift system on circadian disruption is not straightforward, as the levels of circadian biomarkers fluctuate with time of day (e.g., core body temperature, sleep-wake cycles, circulating melatonin and its main metabolite 6 sulfatoxy-melatonin, cortisol, and sex hormones) (Lunn et al. 2017). More research is thus needed to assess the circadian disruption associated with the different shift systems. Recently, Zhang et al. (2022) have identified circadian and sleep rhythm markers using on a wearable sensor of activity, sleep, and temperature in night and day shifters. Using such devices may be useful in future epidemiological investigations to assess circadian disruption in shift workers and study the association with health outcomes.

In total, the assessment of exposure to shift work and circadian disruption in epidemiological studies is challenging. The wide variety of shift work systems examined in epidemiological studies and the limitations in exposure assessment methodology should be considered carefully when evaluating the level of evidence for an association between shift work and health.

Health Outcomes

Sleep and Vigilance Disorders

The mismatch between environmental conditions and the sleep-wake cycle caused by night work leads to insomnia, insufficient sleep quantity and quality, and sleepiness.

Effects on Sleep

The quality of sleep is closely related to its synchronization with the internal biological clock. Deep sleep coincides with the period of the night when melatonin levels are highest and internal temperature is lowest, which usually occurs between 1 and 3 am. The daytime sleep of night shift workers induces a desynchronization of the biological clocks and contributes to poor sleep quality. In addition, shift workers have to rest under unfavorable conditions, such as exposure to daylight, high ambient temperature, high noise levels, or family obligations, which also contribute to reduce sleep quality and quantity.

The most common complaints reported by night shift workers include:

- Poor sleep quality such as difficulty falling asleep, frequent awakenings with difficulty going back to sleep, waking up too early compared to the scheduled wake-up time, and feeling unrefreshing sleep. Insomnia is defined by the presence of one or more of these symptoms at least three times per week for at least 1 month with impact such as fatigue, difficulty functioning, irritability, and errors. According to the ICSD-3 classification, insomnia associated with sleepiness is seen as a shift work disease.
- A too short sleeping time: the reduction of sleeping time per 24 h is also commonly reported by night shift workers, because of difficulties in completing the main sleep episode due to adverse environmental conditions. This is further exacerbated by the difficulty of taking naps. Over the long run, insufficient sleep is seen as a cause of various health problems (Kecklund and Axelsson 2016).

Literature reviews have shown a reduction in sleeping time among shift workers, particularly in those with rapid shift rotations (Linton et al. 2015; Kecklund and Axelsson 2016). These work schedules may not only be detrimental to sleep during the work period but also persist after retirement (Tucker et al. 2012). Among 3237 workers included in the VISAT study in France followed-up for 10 years, sleep disorders related to staggered work schedules were more severe around age 42. People who had worked staggered or night shifts during their careers had poorer sleep quality after retirement (Marquié et al. 2015).

Overall, it is estimated that the average sleep time per 24 h in night workers is 1 h shorter than in day workers. The sleep deprivation of night workers caused by short sleeping time and poor sleep quality impacts not only alertness but also several physiological functions. Laboratory studies suggest that sleep deprivation impairs glucose metabolism and is involved in diabetes and obesity. Sleep restriction decreases leptin, a hormone that signals satiety to the brain, and increases orexin, a hormone stimulating the appetite, resulting in an increased consumption of food with high caloric contents (fatty sugary foods) (Knutson 2007). Over the past 10 years, more than 60 epidemiological studies have shown an association between short sleep duration and obesity, hypertension, type 2 diabetes, and other cardiovascular diseases (Knutson 2007; Faraut et al. 2012; Cappuccio and Miller 2017).

Effects on Sleepiness

Sleepiness results from both circadian desynchronization and reduced sleep time. Chronic sleep deprivation and daily reduction of sleep time promote drowsiness in monotonous situations, such as during meetings, while driving, or at the workplace. Sleepiness is considered one of the cardinal symptoms of the "shift work intolerance syndrome" according to the international classification of sleep disorders (2014).

Recently, Krzych et al. (2019) studied sleep complaints and daytime sleepiness in Polish anesthesians, using the Epworth Sleepiness Scale (ESS). Mild- to moderate excessive daytime sleepiness was found in 260 physicians (33.1%) and severe sleepiness in 478 others (60.8%). Sleepiness increased with the number of nights on call and the lower number of days off. Peterson et al. (2019) examined the associations of sleep duration and sleepiness with burnout in a study of 3141 US police officers. They showed that irregular schedules, long shifts (> 11 hours), mandatory overtime, short sleep and sleepiness increased the risk of burnout. Excessive sleepiness was significantly associated with emotional exhaustion. Vanttola et al. (2020) interviewed 2900 hospital employees in Finland about sleep and sleepiness during workdays and rest days and found that night work intolerance syndrome was associated with excessive sleepiness during non-work days.

In order to maintain safety, alertness, and performance during extended work periods and night shifts, one strategy has been to redistribute work time into smaller aliquots spread evenly throughout the 24-h period. These schedules are commonly used in safety-critical industries such as transportation and the maritime industry. Commonly used short cycle work/rest routines or limited wake shift work (LWSW) schedules include 6 hours- on/6 hours-off, 4 hours-on/8 hours-off, and 8 hours-on/ 8 hours-off schedules. These types of shift schedules minimize the number of consecutive hours at work, promote rest opportunities between work bouts, and allow for at least some opportunity for sleep during the night for all workers. Short et al. (2015) conducted a systematic review to determine which LWSW schedules are best to promote sleep, alertness, and performance. The literature supports the utility of LWSW. Findings indicate that LWSW schedules were associated with better sleep and lower sleepiness in the case of (i) shorter time-at-work, (ii) more frequent rest breaks, (iii) shifts began and ended at the same time every 24 h, and (iv) shifts began during the day (as opposed to at night). Overall, the 4 hour-on/8 hour-off schedule best promoted sleep and minimized sleepiness compared to other LWSW schedules.

Risk of Occupational and Traffic Accidents

An obvious consequence of drowsiness and sleepiness at work is an increased risk of accidents and errors, including traffic accidents, while the vast majority of the transportation sector is organized with night shift work schedules. In a review focusing on the safety implications of night shift work and long working hours, Wagstaff examined 43 publications on safety and accidents (Wagstaff and Sigstad Lie 2011). They found that the risk of accidents increased with the number of working hours, and that the risk for a 12 hours workday was about twice the risk for an 8 hours workday. Shift work including nights was also associated with an increased risk of accidents, whereas "pure" night work may provide some protection due to resynchronization of biological clocks to night schedules. There was no clear evidence from the studies reviewed that any age or sex was particularly susceptible to or protected from the effects of working time schedules on the risk of accidents.

In another systematic review that included 29 high-quality studies on occupational injuries and work schedule characteristics, Fischer reported that compared to morning shifts, the risk of work injury increased during night shifts (RR = 1.36 [95%CI = 1.15–1.60] based on 14 studies), while the risk was slightly elevated during afternoon/evening shifts, although nonsignificant (RR = 1.12 [0.76–1.64], $n = 9$ studies) (Fischer et al. 2017). Meta-regressions revealed worker age as a significant effect modifier: adolescent workers ($\leq$20 years) showed a decreased risk on the afternoon/evening shift compared to both morning shifts and adult workers ($p < 0.05$). Compared with the first shift in a block of consecutive shifts, the risk increased for consecutive morning shifts (e.g., fourth consecutive morning shift: RR = 1.09 [0.90–1.32]; $n = 6$ studies) and night shifts (e.g., fourth consecutive night shift: RR = 1.36 [1.14–1.62]; $n = 8$ studies), while the increase in risk for afternoon/evening shifts appeared unsystematic. The risk of injury rose substantially beyond the 9th hour on duty, a trend that was mirrored when looking at shift lengths (e.g., >12 h: RR = 1.34 [1.04–1.51], $n = 3$ studies). Risk decreased for any rest break duration (e.g., 31–60 min: RR = 0.35 [0.29–0.43], $n = 2$ studies).

The impact of sleepiness and night shift work schedules on errors was examined in specific occupations like nurses (Di Muzio et al. 2019), hospital residents (Bolster and Rourke 2015), surgeons (Ahmed et al. 2014), and petroleum industry workers (Fossum et al. 2013). In these situations, as well as in the transportation industry, the lack of vigilance of a single operator may obviously have dramatic consequences on safety, pollution, and public health.

Metabolic and Cardiovascular Consequences of Shift Work

Mechanisms Linking Night Shift Work to Metabolic and Cardiovascular Risk

The circadian system and sleep-wake cycle both contribute to the regulation of metabolism in humans. Glucose metabolism, lipid metabolism, and energy expenditure display endogenous circadian rhythms and are impacted by sleep disturbances (Kervezee et al. 2020). The function of the cardiovascular system is also subject to circadian regulation, as circadian rhythms have been observed in blood pressure, heart rate (Kervezee et al. 2020), as well as in the sympathetic and parasympathetic modulation of the heart (Boudreau et al. 2012). Numerous studies have shown that circadian misalignment and sleep restriction can disrupt the intricate relationships between circadian system and metabolism and independently affects metabolic and cardiovascular processes. For example, experimental studies suggest that decreased diurnal melatonin levels have a detrimental effect on glucose metabolism (Peschke et al. 2006) and cardiovascular diseases (Dominguez-Rodriguez et al. 2010; Sun et al. 2016).

There is evidence that shift work has adverse effects on several risk factors for metabolic and cardiovascular risk factors, including elevated glucose, insulin, and triglyceride levels (Kervezee et al. 2020), as well as resistin, a biomarker of atherosclerosis (Burgueño et al. 2010). In a systematic review comprising 22 longitudinal studies, Proper et al. (2016) found strong evidence of an association between shift work and increased body weight/BMI, risk for overweight, and impaired glucose tolerance. They also concluded to insufficient evidence for the remaining risk factors including cholesterolemia (HDL, LDL), triglycerides, and blood pressure that they refer to a lack of high-methodologic quality studies and inconsistency of findings.

Epidemiologic Evidence of an Association Between Shift Work and Metabolic and Cardiovascular Diseases

Several recent meta-analyses and systematic reviews have combined the various epidemiological studies that addressed the relationship between shift work and metabolic and cardiovascular health.

Metabolic Syndrome

The metabolic syndrome is defined as the simultaneous presence of at least three criteria out of five biological and clinical parameters related to waist circumference, blood pressure, triglyceridemia, cholesterol, and blood glucose. In a recent meta-analysis of 36 studies (30 cross-sectional and 6 cohort or nested case–control studies), Wang et al. (2021) reported a pooled odds ratio of 1.35 (95% CI 0.97–1.46) for metabolic syndrome in shift workers that was slightly higher in women than in men. There was a nonlinear dose-response relationship of metabolic syndrome with the number of years of shift work. In a subgroup analysis restricted to cohorts and nested case–control studies of higher quality, the pooled odds ratio was 2.03 (95% CI 1.31–3.15) (Wang et al. 2014). Overall, there is strong epidemiologic evidence for an association between shift work and the development of metabolic syndrome.

Type 2 Diabetes

Several epidemiologic studies have explored the association between shift work and diabetes. In a meta-analysis including 12 such studies (8 cohorts and 4 cross-sectional studies), the pooled odds ratio indicated a 9% greater risk of diabetes (OR 1.09, 95% CI 1.05–1.12) in ever vs never shift workers. The association was slightly stronger in men than in women, and stronger for rotating shift work compared with other types of shift work (Gan et al. 2015). Cohort studies among female nurses provide the strongest evidence of an association of shift work with diabetes. In the US Nurses Health Studies including more than 190,000 women, a highly significant trend between duration of rotating shift work and diabetes risk was observed, with a hazard ratio of 1.24 (1.43–1.74) in female participants with 20 or more years of rotating shift work compared to those not exposed to shift work, which appeared to be mediated through body weight (Pan et al. 2011). In a more recent analysis of the Nurses' Health Study II, an interaction between diurnal preference (i.e., chronotype) and rotating night shift work in relation to diabetes risk was also suggested (Vetter et al. 2015). Overall, the current epidemiologic literature, as well as mechanistic indications that circadian disruption and/or sleep restriction affect insulin resistance, provides compelling evidence that night shift work may adversely affect the risk of type 2 diabetes (Strohmaier et al. 2018).

Obesity
In a meta-analysis of 28 studies examining the association between shift work and obesity (Sun et al. 2018), the pooled odds ratio of night shift work was 1.23 (1.17–1.29) for risk of obesity/overweight. The risk ratio for cohort studies (1.10 95%CI 0.99–1.21) was slightly lower than the risk for cross-sectional studies (1.26, 95% CI 1.19–1.33). A positive gradient was suggested for the relation between obesity/overweight and frequency and intensity of exposure to night shift work. Interestingly, shift workers had a higher frequency of developing abdominal obesity than other obesity types, and permanent night workers demonstrated a higher risk than rotating shift workers. Although there is substantial evidence that night work is associated with overweight and obesity, prospective cohort studies with a consistent definition of night work and more precise measures of obesity are needed to confirm this association.

Cardiovascular Diseases
Several epidemiological studies of shift work and cardiovascular disease have been conducted. A systematic review and meta-analysis evaluated the literature in 2018 based on 21 epidemiologic studies (15 cohort and 6 case–control studies) (Torquati et al. 2018). The authors reported that the overall risk of any cardiovascular event was 17% higher among shift workers than day workers. The risk of coronary heart disease (CHD) morbidity was 26% higher. In the NHS and NHS II studies the risk of CHD in rotating night shift nurses increased with the number of years of shift work and decreased after quitting shift work (Vetter et al. 2016). Other studies indicated that the association of shift work with CHD (Virkkunen et al. 2006) or ischemic heart disease (Fujino et al. 2006) might be more pronounced among workers with additional risk factors for cardiovascular disease (smoking, obesity, hypertension, etc.) or physical workload. Taken together, these studies provide consistent evidence that shift work increase the risk of cardiovascular-related events, particularly in subgroups of workers at particularly high risk due to the presence of additional risk factors.

Cancer

Mechanisms Linking Night Shift Work to Cancer Risk
Experimental studies have identified several mechanisms by which shift work may lead to cancer. As noted above, the desynchronization of the internal and external

clocks in shift workers constitutes a major functional disturbance that might promote cancers, e.g., through genetic, epigenetic, metabolic, or hormonal mechanisms (Haus and Smolensky 2006). Clock genes are required for the generation and regulation of circadian rhythms. Variations in gene expression could be involved in cancer development through changes in cycle cell control, estrogen signaling system, or response to DNA damage. Exposure to light at night reduces the anti-cancer effects of melatonin, including inhibition of tumor development and reduction in levels of reproductive hormones. Sleep disorders in shift workers may also negatively impact the immune function, which in turn may affect cancer risk. Unhealthy diet and staggered meal times, increased prevalence of smoking, obesity, or lack of physical activity may also mediate an increased risk of cancer among shift workers (Fritschi et al. 2011).

Evaluation from the 2019 IARC Monograph on "Night Shift Work"
In 2019, IARC concluded that night shift work is probably carcinogenic to humans (group 2A) (IARC Working Group 2019). The evaluation of the IARC working group was based in part on a number of informative cohort and case–control studies conducted in specific occupational groups (most predominantly, nurses) exposed to night shift work as well as in the general population, which pointed more particularly to an increased risk of breast and prostate cancer.

The majority of the cohort studies did not find a positive association of breast cancer with duration of night shift work. The nested case–control studies and population-based case–control studies provided support for a positive association. Overall, the discrepancies between studies was attributed to differences in exposure assessment methodology (e.g., over short or long periods of life) or the use of various exposure metrics (e.g., years of night shift vs. number of night shifts per week). Some studies included only older postmenopausal women (IARC Working Group 2019), such that they were not able to determine an effect in younger premenopausal women. According to the IARC working group, the most informative study was a pooled case–control study (Cordina-Duverger et al. 2016) consisting of an harmonized database of 6093 breast cancer cases and 6933 control women, employed in a total of 54,000 jobs, with information on working hours. A common definition of night work was used in this study to assess exposure (work of at least 3 h between midnight and 5 am) following the recommendations of Stevens et al. (2011). An increased risk of breast cancer was found in premenopausal women working at night, especially those working 3 or more nights per week, and those whose night shifts lasted 10 h or more. The risk decreased after cessation of night work, suggesting the risk of breast cancer potentially arising from shift work is reversible.

Studies on cancer of the prostate include several studies in the general population, industrial cohort studies, population-based case–control studies, and one study in airplane cockpit crew. Several of these studies found positive associations between exposure to night shift work and the risk of cancer of the prostate, particularly in association with longer durations of exposure (Stevens et al. 2011); however, other studies reported no, or a very small, increased risk when examining ever versus never exposure to night shift work (Stevens et al. 2011). Although there is suggestive evidence that the risk of cancer of the prostate is positively associated with night shift work, the relatively small number of studies and lack of consistent results with the same exposure metrics, chance, and bias could not be ruled out with reasonable confidence.

Several cohort and case–control studies of night shift work and cancer of the colon and rectum have also been conducted. The majority of the well-designed and informative studies found positive associations between exposure to night shift work and risk of cancer of the colon and rectum, particularly in association with longer durations of exposure. However, the elevated risks observed with longer durations of exposure were moderate in magnitude, and some findings were not consistent between studies. Overall, there s some evidence suggesting that the risk of cancer of the colon and rectum is positively associated with exposure to shift work involving night work, but inconsistencies between studies did not permit definite conclusions.

Thus, positive associations have been observed between night shift work and cancers of the breast, prostate, colon, and rectum. No conclusions could be made for any of the other cancers, because of either the small number of studies, inconsistencies in the findings, or the use of weak methods for assessing exposure to night shift work.

Recent Systematic Reviews and Meta-Analyses
Since the publication of the IARC monograph, several systematic reviews and meta-analysis have been published on cancers of the breast (Hong et al. 2022) and the prostate (Rivera-Izquierdo et al. 2020). The meta-analysis on breast cancer is composed of 33 studies showing that only women who started night work before menopause are at increased risk of breast cancer. Shift work was found to increase the risk of ER, PR, and HER2-positive breast cancers but not triple-negative breast tumors (Hong et al. 2022). The meta-analysis on prostate cancer is composed of 18 studies showing no overall increased risk in shift workers (Rivera-Izquierdo et al. 2020). Systematic reviews and meta-analysis on different cancer sites have also been published with conflicting results (Dun et al. 2020; Wu et al. 2022b), including one that report no overall association with breast cancer (Dun et al. 2020). To date, in the absence of additional large cohort studies with detailed measurements of lifetime night work, these meta-analyses do not alter the main conclusions of the IARC working group based on thorough evaluation of the epidemiological literature.

Cognitive Disorders and Drowsiness

Although there is no convincing evidence of an association with dementia-type cognitive disorders, shift work and night work may affect cognition as assessed by objective tests, such as the PVT (psychomotor vigilance test) (Basner et al. 2018). The impairment of cognitive performance was described in this study as both a slowing of reaction time and an increase in the number of errors. From a pathophysiological point of view, these cognitive impairments are mainly explained by drowsiness, but could also be due to insufficient restorative sleep, the effect of which has been well described on different modes of memory acquisition (Andrillon and Kouider 2016). As a conclusion, night shift work probably affects cognition but not cognitive disorders.

Depression and Anxiety

Mood disorders appear to be closely linked to circadian rhythms. Major depression is often accompanied by exacerbation of diurnal mood variations (Morris et al. 2009) as well as circadian disruption of cortisol secretion and body temperature.

Conversely, several circadian rhythm disorders are often associated with depressive symptoms. Laboratory studies in healthy volunteers have shown that the circadian control of mood is similar to that of alertness (Boivin 2000). The quality of mood varies over the 24-h day: the most negative mood coincides with the minimum of body temperature, whereas the most positive mood coincides with its maximum, which also corresponds to the maximum of the circadian signal of awakening. As with alertness, the combination of these circadian rhythms allows a relatively stable mood to be maintained throughout the waking period. In contrast, a mismatch between the endogenous circadian rhythm and the sleep-wake cycle can lead to a deterioration in mood during the waking period, although it is difficult to distinguish between the effects of sleep deprivation caused by circadian disruption and the direct effect of the circadian misalignment.

Adverse Pregnancy Outcomes

Several studies and meta-analyses on pregnancy outcomes have reported an increased risk of spontaneous abortion and preterm delivery in night and/or shift workers, as well as a probable increased risk of low weight for gestational age (Abeysena et al. 2009; Bonzini et al. 2009; Niedhammer et al. 2009).

It has also been hypothesized that night shift work may affect fertility in both men and women, due to behavioral and biological changes in relation to circadian disruption and sleep loss in night shift workers (Caetano et al. 2021).

Prevention Strategies and Recommendations

Shift work cannot be avoided in jobs such as health care, security, and emergency response, as well as in work settings that require the production of goods and services on a 24/7 basis. In these situations, work schedules should be arranged to minimize the health consequences of circadian misalignment and sleep loss in night and/or rotating shift workers.

Adapting the Night Shift Work Schedule Systems

It is primarily the responsibility of employers, trade unions, and governments to limit as much as possible the use of night shift work to activities that really require 24 h functioning (health, safety, transportation, etc.). Many countries have allowed small food and entertainment businesses in large cities to open all night, 7 days a week, without considering the deleterious effect on health of employees. This is a critical legal issue that needs to be regularly discussed with employers and managers, who have often taken a "world that never sleeps" as their model.

When planning or reorganizing work schedules, the following guidelines should be followed to limit problems related to sleep disorders and circadian disruption

- Rotating shift work should have a forward direction (morning->afternoon-> night) than a backward direction.
- Shift rotations over a period of 3–5 days are less disruptive than rotations over shorter periods of less than 3 days. Fixed night schedules are less disruptive than rotating night shifts.
- Shifts of 8–10 h are more disruptive than shifts of 10–12 h.
- A break of at least 12 h must be taken between shifts.

Information-Education and Occupational Medicine

An important preventive strategy to cope with the health consequences of night shift work is to inform and educate workers about the physiological and medical consequences of his/her work schedules. Every worker engaged in night work or rotating shift work should receive information about the risks and methods of preventing health consequences (Metlaine et al. 2018).

A careful medical examination of night shift workers by occupational doctors or general practitioners is strongly recommended at least once a year (Metlaine et al. 2018). Measurement of the body mass index and blood pressure, sleep diary, and the Epworth sleepiness scale questionnaire are the recommended tools. Specific monitoring of women is also recommended for preventing adverse pregnancy outcomes and breast cancer screening.

Strategic Light/Dark Exposure

One way of minimizing the consequences of circadian misalignment is to promote adaptation to night work through strategic light/dark exposure. Lighting intervention have been proposed in night workers, including lighting in the evening before or in the first part of the night shift followed by reduced lighting in the second part. A recent meta-analysis shows that lighting interventions improved sleepiness. The blue-enriched white light with a color temperature greater than 5000 Kelvin was the most effective in improving sleepiness (Wu et al. 2022a). Another recent systematic review based on five eligible studies concluded that evening light improved sleep quality, sleep duration, and work performance, but no changes in sleepiness were observed (Cyr et al. 2022).

Finally, blue-blocking glasses may be used to reduce sleep onset latency after work. According to a recent review, there was substantial evidence that blue-blocking glasses might be useful (Hester et al. 2021).

Opportunistic Napping

It can be difficult for shift workers to take long consolidated periods of sleep, but multiple short sleep episodes can be similarly recuperative (Roach et al. 2017). Napping is thus one way of minimizing sleep loss in night shift workers. Napping also reduces sleepiness and improve psychomotor vigilance and performance (Li et al. 2019). These naps can be taken at convenient times during breaks between shifts to supplement core sleep episodes. There is no evidence for the optimal duration of naps, either short or long (Patterson et al. 2021). It was shown that naps have a greater impact on those with chronic sleep deprivation (Faraut et al. 2017; Leger et al. 2020).

Physical Activity

The benefits of physical activity on health and fitness are well-known. Physical activity also improves sleep duration and sleep quality. As such, increased physical activity is one avenue through which shift workers might prevent the negative effects of circadian misalignment and sleep loss, especially in sleep deprived subjects (Chennaoui et al. 2015; Sauvet et al. 2020).

Meal Timing

Shift work is often accompanied by changes in eating behaviors. Snacking behaviors are more common among shift workers than among non-shift workers, possibly exacerbating the disruption of metabolic processes and circadian misalignment. Avoiding consuming food during the night should be recommended to shift workers.

Conclusion

Night work and shift work have a significant impact on health, with a variety of effects. The organization of work schedules is an important parameter to be considered in work settings in order to minimize the adverse effects in night/shift workers.

References

Abeysena C, Jayawardana P, Seneviratne RDA (2009) Maternal sleep deprivation is a risk factor for small for gestational age: a cohort study. Aust N Z J Obstet Gynaecol 49:382–387

Ahmed N, Devitt KS, Keshet I, Spicer J, Imrie K, Feldman L et al (2014) A systematic review of the effects of resident duty hour restrictions in surgery: impact on resident wellness, training, and patient outcomes. Ann Surg 259:1041–1053

Andrillon T, Kouider S (2016) Implicit memory for words heard during sleep. Neurosci Conscious 2016:niw014

Anttila T, Oinas T (2018) 24/7 society-the new timing of work? In: Tammelin M (ed) Family, work and well-being: emergence of new issues, pp 63–76

Basner M, Hermosillo E, Nasrini J, McGuire S, Saxena S, Moore TM, Gur RC, Dinge DF (2018) Repeated administration effects on psychomotor vigilance test performance. Sleep 41

Blask DE, Brainard GC, Dauchy RT, Hanifin JP, Davidson LK, Krause JA et al (2005) Melatonin-depleted blood from premenopausal women exposed to light at night stimulates growth of human breast cancer xenografts in nude rats. Cancer Res 65:11174–11184

Blask DE, Hill SM, Dauchy RT, Xiang S, Yuan L, Duplessis T et al (2011) Circadian regulation of molecular, dietary, and metabolic signaling mechanisms of human breast cancer growth by the nocturnal melatonin signal and the consequences of its disruption by light at night. J Pineal Res 51:259–269

Boivin DB (2000) Influence of sleep-wake and circadian rhythm disturbances in psychiatric disorders. J Psychiatry Neurosci 25:446–458

Bolster L, Rourke L (2015) The effect of restricting residents' duty hours on patient safety, resident well-being, and resident education: an updated systematic review. J Grad Med Educ 7:349–363

Bonzini M, Coggon D, Godfrey K, Inskip H, Crozier S, Palmer KT (2009) Occupational physical activities, working hours and outcome of pregnancy: findings from the Southampton women's survey. Occup Environ Med 66:685–690

Boudreau P, Yeh WH, Dumont GA, Boivin DB (2012) A circadian rhythm in heart rate variability contributes to the increased cardiac sympathovagal response to awakening in the morning. Chronobiol Int 29:757–768

Burgueño A, Gemma C, Gianotti TF, Sookoian S, Pirola CJ (2010) Increased levels of resistin in rotating shift workers: a potential mediator of cardiovascular risk associated with circadian misalignment. Atherosclerosis 210:625e629

Caetano G, Bozinovic I, Dupont C, Leger D, Levy R, Sermondade N (2021) Impact of sleep on female and male reproductive functions: a systematic review. Fertil Steril 115:715–731

Cappuccio FP, Miller MA (2017) Sleep and cardio-metabolic disease. Curr Cardiol Rep 19:110

Chennaoui M, Arnal PJ, Sauvet F, Leger D (2015) Sleep and exercise: a reciprocal issue? Sleep Med Rev 20:59–72

Cordina-Duverger E, Koudou Y, Truong T, Arveux P, Kerbrat P, Menegaux F et al (2016) Night work and breast cancer risk defined by human epidermal growth factor receptor-2 (her2) and hormone receptor status: a population-based case-control study in France. Chronobiol Int 33: 783–787

Cordina-Duverger E, Menegaux F, Popa A, Rabstein S, Harth V, Pesch B et al (2018) Night shift work and breast cancer: a pooled analysis of population-based case-control studies with complete work history. Eur J Epidemiol 33:369–379

Crowther ME, Ferguson SA, Reynolds AC (2022) Longitudinal studies of sleep, physical activity and nutritional intake in shift workers: a scoping review. Sleep Med Rev 63:101612

Cyr M, Artenie DZ, Al Bikaii A, Borsook D, Olson JA (2022) The effect of evening light on circadian-related outcomes: a systematic review. Sleep Med Rev 64:101660

Di Muzio M, Dionisi S, Di Simone E, Cianfrocca C, Di Muzio F, Fabbian F et al (2019) Can nurses' shift work jeopardize the patient safety? A systematic review. Eur Rev Med Pharmacol Sci 23: 4507–4519

Dominguez-Rodriguez A, Abreu-Gonzalez P, Sanchez-Sanchez JJ, Kaski JC, Reiter RJ (2010) Melatonin and circadian biology in human cardiovascular disease. J Pineal Res 49:14–22

Dumont M, Paquet J (2014) Progressive decrease of melatonin production over consecutive days of simulated night work. Chronobiol Int 31:1231–1238

Dun A, Zhao X, Jin X, Wei T, Gao X, Wang Y et al (2020) Association between night-shift work and cancer risk: updated systematic review and meta-analysis. Front Oncol 10:1006

EU Council (2003) Directive 2003/88/EC of the European Parliament and of the council of 4 Nov 2003 concerning certain aspects of the organisation of working time. Available: https://eur-lex.europa.eu/legal-content/EN/TXT/PDF/?uri=CELEX:32003L0088&rid=1

EuroFound (2007) Fourth European working conditions survey. Available: https://www.eurofound.europa.eu/publications/report/2007/working-conditions/fourth-european-working-conditions-survey

EuroFound (2017) Working time patterns for sustainable work. Available: https://www.eurofound.europa.eu/publications/report/2017/working-time-patterns-for-sustainable-work

Eurostat (2022) Employed persons working at nights as a percentage of the total employment, by sex, age and professional status (%). Last update: 04 July 2022. Available: https://appsso.eurostat.ec.europa.eu/nui/show.do?dataset=lfsa_ewpnig&lang=en

Faraut B, Touchette E, Gamble H, Royant-Parola S, Safar ME, Varsat B et al (2012) Short sleep duration and increased risk of hypertension: a primary care medicine investigation. J Hypertens 30:1354–1363

Faraut B, Andrillon T, Vecchierini MF, Leger D (2017) Napping: a public health issue. From epidemiological to laboratory studies. Sleep Med Rev 35:85–100

Fischer D, Lombardi DA, Folkard S, Willetts J, Christiani DC (2017) Updating the "risk index": a systematic review and meta-analysis of occupational injuries and work schedule characteristics. Chronobiol Int 34:1423–1438

Fossum IN, Bjorvatn B, Waage S, Pallesen S (2013) Effects of shift and night work in the offshore petroleum industry: a systematic review. Ind Health 51:530–544

Fritschi L, Glass DC, Heyworth JS, Aronson K, Girschik J, Boyle T et al (2011) Hypotheses for mechanisms linking shiftwork and cancer. Med Hypotheses 77:430–436

Fujino Y, Iso H, Tamakoshi A, Inaba Y, Koizumi A, Kubo T et al (2006) A prospective cohort study of shift work and risk of ischemic heart disease in Japanese male workers. Am J Epidemiol 164:128–135

Gan Y, Yang C, Tong X, Sun H, Cong Y, Yin X et al (2015) Shift work and diabetes mellitus: a meta-analysis of observational studies. Occup Environ Med 72:72–78

Harma M, Ropponen A, Hakola T, Koskinen A, Vanttola P, Puttonen S et al (2015) Developing register-based measures for assessment of working time patterns for epidemiologic studies. Scand J Work Environ Health 41:268–279

Haus E, Smolensky M (2006) Biological clocks and shift work: circadian dysregulation and potential long-term effects. Cancer Causes Control 17:489–500

Haus EL, Smolensky MH (2013) Shift work and cancer risk: potential mechanistic roles of circadian disruption, light at night, and sleep deprivation. Sleep Med Rev 17:273–284

Hester L, Dang D, Barker CJ, Heath M, Mesiya S, Tienabeso T et al (2021) Evening wear of blue-blocking glasses for sleep and mood disorders: a systematic review. Chronobiol Int 38:1375–1383

Hong J, He Y, Fu R, Si Y, Xu B, Xu J et al (2022) The relationship between night shift work and breast cancer incidence: a systematic review and meta-analysis of observational studies. Open Med (Wars) 17:712–731

IARC Working Group (2019) Night shift work: IARC monographs volume 124. IARC monographs on the identification of carcinogenic hazards to humans 124

ILO (1990a) International Labour Organization – c171 – night work convention, 1990 (no. 171). Available: https://www.ilo.org/dyn/normlex/en/f?p=NORMLEXPUB:12100:0::NO::P12100_INSTRUMENT_ID:312316

ILO (1990b) R178 – night work recommendation, 1990 (no. 178)

Kandalepas PC, Mitchell JW, Gillette MU (2016) Melatonin signal transduction pathways require e-box-mediated transcription of per1 and per2 to reset the scn clock at dusk. PLoS One 11: e0157824

Kecklund G, Axelsson J (2016) Health consequences of shift work and insufficient sleep. BMJ 355: i5210

Kervezee L, Kosmadopoulos A, Boivin DB (2020) Metabolic and cardiovascular consequences of shift work: the role of circadian disruption and sleep disturbances. Eur J Neurosci 51:396–412

Knauth P (1993) The design of shift systems. Ergonomics 36:15–28

Knauth P (1996) Designing better shift systems. Appl Ergon 27:39–44

Knauth P (1998) Innovative worktime arrangements. Scand J Work Environ Health 24(Suppl 3): 13–17

Knutson KL (2007) Impact of sleep and sleep loss on glucose homeostasis and appetite regulation. Sleep Med Clin 2:187–197

Krzych LJ, Piekielko P, Baca A, Dlugosz A, Liberski P, Jaworski T et al (2019) Sleep quality and daytime sleepiness among polish anaesthesiologists and intensivists. J Crit Care 53:87–90

Lee S, Donehower LA, Herron AJ, Moore DD, Fu L (2010) Disrupting circadian homeostasis of sympathetic signaling promotes tumor development in mice. PLoS One 5:e10995

Leger D, Richard JB, Collin O, Sauvet F, Faraut B (2020) Napping and weekend catchup sleep do not fully compensate for high rates of sleep debt and short sleep at a population level (in a representative nationwide sample of 12,637 adults). Sleep Med 74:278–288

Li H, Shao Y, Xing Z, Li Y, Wang S, Zhang M et al (2019) Napping on night-shifts among nursing staff: a mixed-methods systematic review. J Adv Nurs 75:291–312

Linton SJ, Kecklund G, Franklin KA, Leissner LC, Sivertsen B, Lindberg E et al (2015) The effect of the work environment on future sleep disturbances: a systematic review. Sleep Med Rev 23: 10–19

Liu R, Jacobs DI, Hansen J, Fu A, Stevens RG, Zhu Y (2014) Aberrant methylation of mir-34b is associated with long-term shiftwork: a potential mechanism for increased breast cancer susceptibility. Cancer Causes Control 26:171178

Lunn RM, Blask DE, Coogan AN, Figueiro MG, Gorman MR, Hall JE et al (2017) Health consequences of electric lighting practices in the modern world: a report on the national toxicology program's workshop on shift work at night, artificial light at night, and circadian disruption. Sci Total Environ 607-608:1073–1084

Marquié JC, Tucker P, Folkard S, Gentil C, Ansiau D (2015) Chronic effects of shift work on cognition: findings from the visat longitudinal study. Occup Environ Med 72:258–264

McMullan CJ, Schernhammer ES, Rimm EB, Hu FB, Forman JP (2013) Melatonin secretion and the incidence of type 2 diabetes. JAMA 309:1388–1396

Metlaine A, Leger D, Esquirol Y, et le Groupe consensus chronobiologie et sommeil de la Societe francaise de recherche et medecine du sommeil (SFRMS) (2018) Shift-workers and night-workers' medical watching and prevention: state of art and recommendations. Presse Med 47: 982–990

Morris DW, Trivedi MH, Fava M, Wisniewski SR, Balasubramani GK, Khan AY et al (2009) Diurnal mood variation in outpatients with major depressive disorder. Depress Anxiety 26:851–863

Niedhammer I, O'Mahony D, Daly S, Morrison JJ, Kelleher CC, Lifeways Cross-Generation Cohort Study Steering Group (2009) Occupational predictors of pregnancy outcomes in Irish working women in the lifeways cohort. BJOG 116:943–952

Pan A, Schernhammer ES, Sun Q, Hu FB (2011) Rotating night shift work and risk of type 2 diabetes: two prospective cohort studies in women. PLoS Med 8:e1001141

Patterson PD, Liszka MK, McIlvaine QS, Nong L, Weaver MD, Turner RL et al (2021) Does the evidence support brief (</=30-mins), moderate (31–60-mins), or long duration naps (61+ mins) on the night shift? A systematic review. Sleep Med Rev 59:101509

Peschke E, Frese T, Chankiewitz E, Peschke D, Preiss U, Schneyer U et al (2006) Diabetic goto kakizaki rats as well as type 2 diabetic patients show a decreased diurnal serum melatonin level and an increased pancreatic melatonin-receptor status. J Pineal Res 40:135–143

Peterson SA, Wolkow AP, Lockley SW, O'Brien CS, Qadri S, Sullivan JP et al (2019) Associations between shift work characteristics, shift work schedules, sleep and burnout in North American police officers: a cross-sectional study. BMJ Open 9:e030302

Proper KI, van de Langenberg D, Rodenburg W, Vermeulen RCH, van der Beek AJ, van Steeg H et al (2016) The relationship between shift work and metabolic risk factors: a systematic review of longitudinal studies. Am J Prev Med 50:e147–e157

Reppert SM, Weaver DR (2002) Coordination of circadian timing in mammals. Nature 418:935–941

Rivera-Izquierdo M, Martínez-Ruiz V, Castillo-Ruiz EM, Manzaneda-Navío M, Pérez-Gómez B, Jiménez-Moleón JJ (2020) Shift work and prostate cancer: an updated systematic review and meta-analysis. Int J Environ Res Public Health 17(4):1345

Roach GD, Zhou X, Darwent D, Kosmadopoulos A, Dawson D, Sargent C (2017) Are two halves better than one whole? A comparison of the amount and quality of sleep obtained by healthy adult males living on split and consolidated sleep-wake schedules. Accid Anal Prev 99:428–433

Sauvet F, Arnal PJ, Tardo-Dino PE, Drogou C, Van Beers P, Erblang M et al (2020) Beneficial effects of exercise training on cognitive performances during total sleep deprivation in healthy subjects. Sleep Med 65:26–35

Schibler U (2006) Circadian time keeping: the daily ups and downs of genes, cells, and organisms. Prog Brain Res 153:271–282

Short MA, Agostini A, Lushington K, Dorrian J (2015) A systematic review of the sleep, sleepiness, and performance implications of limited wake shift work schedules. Scand J Work Environ Health 41:425–440

Stevens RG, Hansen J, Costa G, Haus E, Kauppinen T, Aronson KJ et al (2011) Considerations of circadian impact for defining 'shift work' in cancer studies: Iarc working group report. Occup Environ Med 68:154–162

Strohmaier S, Devore EE, Zhang Y, Schernhammer ES (2018) A review of data of findings on night shift work and the development of DM and CVD events: a synthesis of the proposed molecular mechanisms. Curr Diab Rep 18:132

Sun H, Gusdon AM, Qu S (2016) Effects of melatonin on cardiovascular diseases: progress in the past year. Curr Opin Lipidol 27:408–413

Sun M, Feng W, Wang F, Li P, Li Z, Li M et al (2018) Meta-analysis on shift work and risks of specific obesity types. Obes Rev 19:28–40

Torquati L, Mielke GI, Brown WJ, Kolbe-Alexander T (2018) Shift work and the risk of cardiovascular disease. A systematic review and meta-analysis including dose-response relationship. Scand J Work Environ Health 44:229–238

Travis RC, Balkwill A, Fensom GK, Appleby PN, Reeves GK, Wang XS et al (2016) Night shift work and breast cancer incidence: three prospective studies and meta-analysis of published studies. J Natl Cancer Inst 108(12):djw169

Tucker P, Marquie JC, Folkard S, Ansiau D, Esquirol Y (2012) Shiftwork and metabolic dysfunction. Chronobiol Int 29:549–555

Vanttola P, Puttonen S, Karhula K, Oksanen T, M, HA. (2020) Employees with shift work disorder experience excessive sleepiness also on non-work days: a cross-sectional survey linked to working hours register in finnish hospitals. Ind Health 58:366–374

Vetter C, Devore EE, Ramin CA, Speizer FE, Willett WC, Schernhammer ES (2015) Mismatch of sleep and work timing and risk of type 2 diabetes. Diabetes Care 38:1707–1713

Vetter C, Devore EE, Wegrzyn LR, Massa J, Speizer FE, Kawachi I et al (2016) Association between rotating night shift work and risk of coronary heart disease among women. JAMA 315:1726–1734

Virkkunen H, Harma M, Kauppinen T, Tenkanen L (2006) The triad of shift work, occupational noise, and physical workload and risk of coronary heart disease. Occup Environ Med 63:378–386

Vistisen HT, Garde AH, Frydenberg M, Christiansen P, Hansen AM, Andersen J et al (2017) Short-term effects of night shift work on breast cancer risk: a cohort study of payroll data. Scand J Work Environ Health 43:59–67

Wagstaff AS, Sigstad Lie JA (2011) Shift and night work and long working hours – a systematic review of safety implications. Scand J Work Environ Health 37:173–185

Wang F, Zhang L, Zhang Y, Zhang B, He Y, Xie S et al (2014) Meta-analysis on night shift work and risk of metabolic syndrome. Obes Rev 15:709–720

Wang Y, Yu L, Gao Y, Jiang L, Yuan L, Wang P et al (2021) Association between shift work or long working hours with metabolic syndrome: a systematic review and dose-response meta-analysis of observational studies. Chronobiol Int 38:318–333

Wei T, Li C, Heng Y, Gao X, Zhang G, Wang H et al (2020) Association between night-shift work and level of melatonin: systematic review and meta-analysis. Sleep Med 75:502–509

Wu CJ, Huang TY, Ou SF, Shiea JT, Lee BO (2022a) Effects of lighting interventions to improve sleepiness in night-shift workers: a systematic review and meta-analysis. Healthcare (Basel) 10 (8):1390

Wu QJ, Sun H, Wen ZY, Zhang M, Wang HY, He XH et al (2022b) Shift work and health outcomes: an umbrella review of systematic reviews and meta-analyses of epidemiological studies. J Clin Sleep Med 18:653–662

Zephy D, Ahmad J (2015) Type 2 diabetes mellitus: role of melatonin and oxidative stress. Diabetes Metab Syndr 9:127–131

Zhang HM, Zhang Y (2014) Melatonin: a well-documented antioxidant with conditional pro-oxidant actions. J Pineal Res 57:131–146

Zhang Y, Cordina-Duverger E, Komarzynski S, Attari AM, Huang Q, Aristizabal G et al (2022) Digital circadian and sleep health in individual hospital shift workers: a cross sectional telemonitoring study. EBioMedicine 81:104121

Psychosocial Work Environment and Health: Applying Job-Exposure Matrices and Work Organization and Management Practice

16

S. Solovieva and Y. Roquelaure

Contents

Introduction	268
Psychosocial Exposure and JEM	268
Psychosocial Work Environment and Health	268
Subjectivity of Measure as a Major Source of Bias in the Assessment of Psychosocial Exposures	269
Psychosocial Job-Exposure Matrix: Advantages and Disadvantages over Individual Measurements from Questionnaires	270
Use of Psychosocial Job-Exposure Matrices as Exposure Assessment Tool in Epidemiological Studies	272
Work Organization and Management Practice	274
A World of Work in Constant Transformation	274
Occupational Exposures and Economic, Social, Organizational, and Managerial Determinants: An Integrative Approach	275
Organizational and Integrative Model of Occupational Exposures	275
The Organizational Bundle of Determinants of Occupational Exposure as a Lever for Action of Prevention	278
Cross-References	279
References	280

S. Solovieva (✉)
Finnish Institute of Occupational Health, Helsinki, Finland
e-mail: svetlana.solovieva@ttl.fi

Y. Roquelaure
INSERM, EHESP, IRSET (Institut de Recherche en Santé, Environnement et Travail), UMR_S 1085, University of Angers, CHU Angers, Angers, France

University of Rennes, Rennes, France
e-mail: yvroquelaure@chu-angers.fr

© Springer Nature Switzerland AG 2023
M. Wahrendorf et al. (eds.), *Handbook of Life Course Occupational Health*, Handbook Series in Occupational Health Sciences, https://doi.org/10.1007/978-3-031-30492-7_16

Abstract

The importance of psychosocial work environment for workers' health is well recognized. However, a possible causal role of these factors for health is still under debate, mainly due to subjective assessments of psychosocial exposures. The assessment of psychosocial work factors with a job-exposure matrix (JEM), where exposure level is assigned based on the job-specific average of exposure, is not prone to self-reported bias, and may guarantee some degree of objectivity. The aim of this chapter is to overview the evidence on the relationship between the psychosocial work environment and workers' health based on studies that used JEM to assess the psychosocial work environment. The advantages and disadvantages of JEMs in assessment of psychosocial work-related factors are discussed.

The chapter will also discuss the impact of work organization characteristics, management practices, and human resources strategies on the occurrence and prognosis of musculoskeletal disorders. This section may be useful in the context of new forms of work and digitalisation, despite the lack of JEM considering work organisational factors. Work organization characteristics, management practices, and human resources strategies generate domino effects on the conditions under which work is carried out and, consequently, exposure to work-related biomechanical and psychosocial factors. These cascading effects explain why the expected changes in the work organization and management practices following the digitalization of the economy may have major consequences on the risk of musculoskeletal disorders.

Keywords

Job-exposure matrix · Psychosocial · Occupational · Work · Work organization · Management · New forms of work · Digitalization of the economy

Introduction

In the context of growing evidence of the importance of the psychosocial work environment for workers' health, we present in this chapter two important key issues: the assessment of psychosocial exposures through the example of job-exposure matrices, and the complexity of considering multiple levels of organizational determinants within a life course perspective.

Psychosocial Exposure and JEM

Psychosocial Work Environment and Health

The psychosocial work environment is defined by the International Labor Organization (ILO) as "the set of work conditions under which employees perform their activities in organizations" (ILO 1986). This is a very broad concept, related to phenomena both on the workplace and individual level, and reflects the interactions of hazardous job content, work organization, and management with the workers' competencies, skills, and needs (Sauter et al. 1998; Rugulies 2019). The hazardous psychosocial work environment includes those aspects of work at societal (macro), workplace (meso), and individual (micro) levels that have a potential for causing harm to the worker's psychological, physical, and social health and well-being (Rugulies 2019).

Different operationalization models have been used in psychosocial work environment research for the assessment of psychosocial work-related risk factors. The demand–control (job strain) model, introduced by Karasek (1979), and the efforts–rewards imbalance model, introduced by Siegrist (1996), dominate the psychosocial work environment research. According to the job strain model, workers with a combination of high psychosocial job demands and low control over a job (high job strain) have a higher risk of developing an illness as compared to workers with low psychosocial job demands and high job control (low job strain) (Karasek and Theorell 1990). In the late 1980s, a social dimension was added to the job strain model (Johnson and Hall 1988), resulting in the iso-strain model. In the iso-strain model, a job characterized by high demands, low control, and low support (or isolation) is considered to be the most harmful work situation and is labeled as "iso-strain job." According to efforts–rewards imbalance model, a mismatch between workers' perceptions of the effort spent at work and perceptions of the rewards received from work creates an imbalance that can elicit strong negative emotions and stress reactions with adverse long-term effects on health and well-being Siegrist (1996).

Other characteristics of the hazardous psychosocial work conditions, such as work schedules, organizational justice, workplace social capital, workplace bullying, workplace violence, and workplace climate, are more related to the work organization and management characteristics, rather than to the job content (Rugulies 2019).

The contribution of psychosocial working conditions to ill-health has been extensively studied during the past four decades and is well reviewed in the literature (Leka and Jain 2010; Kivimäki et al. 2018; Niedhammer et al. 2021). Longitudinal studies and systematic reviews provide evidence for associations of psychologically stressful work environment with cardiovascular diseases, mental disorders, sleeping problems, diabetes, obesity, musculoskeletal diseases, and cancer (Niedhammer et al. 2021; Santosa et al. 2021). The associations with cardiovascular outcomes are the most consistent, because the heterogeneity of associations is relatively low, and such associations were observed in different study populations, men and women, young and old individuals, as well as in different socioeconomic groups. However, the magnitude of associations seems to be stronger for mental disorders than for cardiovascular diseases. Inconsistency of the associations between psychosocial work environments and the other abovementioned health outcomes across the studies is often acknowledged.

Subjectivity of Measure as a Major Source of Bias in the Assessment of Psychosocial Exposures

Self-administered questionnaires are widely used for the assessment of the psychosocial work environment (Tabanelli et al. 2008). The subjective assessment of psychosocial factors at work has been the largest concern in the debate on the reliability and interpretation of the associations and on the possible causal role of psychosocial work-related factors for ill-health (Theorell and Hasselhorn 2005). Self-reports reflect a subjective worker's perception of the working environment and occupational stress and are therefore susceptible to bias. Workers with health problems are more likely to report certain psychosocial exposures than healthy workers. Such a tendency might lead to a differential misclassification of exposures, which will result either in an overestimation or underestimation of the "true effect" of exposure on the outcome of interest (Blair et al. 2007), particularly in cross-sectional studies, where the exposures and outcome are measured simultaneously. Common source bias increases the likelihood of false positive findings, predominantly in the studies with self-reported health outcomes (Landsbergis et al. 2000; Macleod and Davey Smith 2003).

Psychosocial Job-Exposure Matrix: Advantages and Disadvantages over Individual Measurements from Questionnaires

A job-exposure matrix (JEM) – as an alternative to individual exposure measures – provides more objective, or at least nonsubjective, measures of exposures compared to self-reports. In a JEM for each individual the exposures are not reported by the individual themselves but are estimated from average scores (usually from an independent sample) for occupational groups. The group-level estimation of exposures averages out a large variation of the self-reports across individuals within the occupational groups and thus greatly diminishes the potential impact of self-report bias of the measurement. This is a substantial advantage for studies on psychosocial work-related factors, where it is often impossible to determine, whether the results are genuinely valid or attributable to self-report bias.

Psychosocial exposures may have both short-term and long-term effect on ill-health. Cumulative exposure, as a proxy measure of exposure duration during working life, is used for testing of exposure-time-response associations and provides a more robust answer to the existence of possible causal association between exposure and outcome than the exposure measured at a single time point. Possibility to assess cumulative psychosocial exposures is another major advantage of the JEMs, since self-reported history of occupational exposures are prone to significant recall bias. Moreover, an important advantage of the JEMs for epidemiological studies is related to the possibility of imputing exposure measures in populations with missing exposure information. Furthermore, the JEMs provide exposure estimates irrespective of the study outcome, thus decreasing differential information bias (Kauppinen et al. 1998; Blair et al. 2007).

However, a JEM-based exposure assessment cannot protect against the possibility of a systematic tendency for individuals within an occupational group to collectively over- or underreport their exposures. In general, the JEM can better maintain the between-occupations variation than the within-occupation variation. The loss of individual variation of exposure within an occupation leads to an underestimation of the true strength and a reduced precision of the association between an exposure and outcome of interest. A tendency for an attenuation of observed associations towards "null associations" is one of the major disadvantage of all JEMs. In addition, occupation-level estimates are subject to a high level of sampling error, since the populations used for the construction of the JEM often there are only small numbers of persons per occupation. Furthermore, the measurement error might be exacerbated by an inconsistency between the occupational coding in the JEM and the study population where it is used.

The use of JEMs in epidemiological studies is therefore a trade-off between gains form nonsubjective measures and loss due to measurement error. The performance of a JEM in a study will depend on the magnitude of the measurement error, which might be high for some exposures but acceptable for the others. The JEM will perform better for exposures with large between-occupations variation but relatively small within-occupation variation than for exposures where the within-occupation variation exceeds the between-occupations variation. The usability of JEMs for the assessment of psychosocial exposures is under debate due to the subjective nature of such exposures. It has been argued that even though the aggregated measure is more "objective" than individuals' self-reports, they may still be affected to some extent by broader differences in the composition of different occupations (e.g., type of people in different occupations or difference between occupations with regard to diversity of tasks within the occupations).

While people in one occupation will tend to have similar working conditions, there will still be individual differences in perception and reporting. Moreover, it is necessary to keep in mind that a true variation of working conditions across individuals within the same occupation may exist, particularly when exposures are largely determined by specific tasks. Schwartz et al. conducted a study, where occupational mean scores on control over task situation (decision latitude), psychological workload and physical exertion, derived from the US National Quality of Employment Surveys, were linked to the Health Examination Survey (HES) and the first National Health and Nutrition Examination Survey (NHANES). In the published article, the methodology of the construction of the psychosocial JEM and the validity of the JEM estimates were discussed (Schwartz et al. 1988). According to their findings, the occupational mean estimates captured 45% of the reliable variance of decision latitude and only 7% of the reliable variance of psychological job demands, suggesting that both exposures vary considerably more between the individuals than between the occupations and there might be relatively little between-occupation variance in psychological demands.

In a JEM, some of the between-individuals variation in exposure might be accounted for by the inclusion of additional axes, for example, an industry-axis, such as the activity sector. Furthermore, sex- and age-specific estimates may help to control for part of the exposure heterogeneity. In the French JEM, the proportion of variance in individual scores for psychosocial demands, decision latitude, and social support, explained by occupation alone was increased by 4–7% when economic activity and company size axes were added (Niedhammer et al. 2018).

Use of Psychosocial Job-Exposure Matrices as Exposure Assessment Tool in Epidemiological Studies

The first English-language research article using linkage of occupation-aggregated level of psychosocial job characteristics to the study population with individual-level data on occupation but not psychosocial work-related measures was published in 1982 (Alfredsson et al. 1982). The researchers used this approach to explore associations of demand and control variables with incident myocardial infarction among Swedish men. However, only 10 years later, the term "job exposure matrix" appeared in the title of a research article which presented a methodology for measuring work organization exposure over the lifetime (Johnson and Stewart 1993). This article described the development of a JEM to measure the duration and intensity of psychosocial exposures during the life course. The constructed JEM utilized exposure information from two Surveys of Living Conditions made by Statistics Sweden (1977 and 1979) and included the following psychosocial exposures: work control, psychological job demands, and social support. The JEM metric was exposure score for each job characteristic. In addition to an estimate for each occupation, the JEM included estimates by gender, age (25–44 and 45–74 years), and the duration of time in the specific occupation (1–5, 6–19, and 20+ years).

Up to date, psychosocial JEMs have been constructed using data from Sweden, Denmark, Finland, Norway, France, the USA, the UK, and Australia. The majority of the existing JEMs includes exposures such as job control or decision latitude, psychological job demands, job strain, and social support. Due to a lack of a gold standard, the JEMs cannot be truly validated. Several studies, however, examined the performance of a JEM by testing agreements with self-reports assessment of exposure and analyzed its predictive validity for health outcomes. The JEMs validated against self-reports usually showed a better agreement for job control or decision latitude than for psychosocial job demands. For social support, the correlation between JEM measures and self-reports was the lowest. Several JEMs have been developed during the past decade (Table 1).

The potential usability of psychosocial JEMs in epidemiological studies was tested for several health outcomes, particularly those related to cardiovascular

Table 1 Psychosocial JEMs developed during the past decade

Country	Psychosocial measures
Australia	Job control, job demands and complexity, job insecurity, fairness of pay
Denmark	Quantitative job demands, emotional job demands, decision authority, job insecurity, work-related violence
Finland	Job demands, job control, job strain, monotonous work, social support
France, SUMER JEM	Psychological work demands, decision latitude, job strain, social support, iso-strain
Norway	Psychological demands, decision latitude, monotonous work, supportive leadership
Sweden	Psychological work demands, job control, social support
The Netherlands, GPJEM	Psychological work demands, psychological resources

diseases, but also other outcomes such as mental health, self-rated health, musculoskeletal diseases, and work disability. In general, most of the JEM studies found statistically significant associations (in the expected direction) between job control or decision latitude and health outcomes. However, for psychosocial job demands, the JEM studies showed a tendency towards null associations or even associations in the reverse direction to that predicted by the Karasek model. For example, high job demands, assessed by JEM, were associated with a lower risk of heart disease (Theorell et al. 1998) and anxiety disorders (Wieclaw et al. 2008) and better self-reported health (Niedhammer et al. 2008). The associations between job strain and health have been somewhat inconsistent. Most studies reported no interactive effects of job demands and job control on several health outcomes. It has been suggested that statistically significant JEM-based results provide a strong support for an association between an exposure and a health outcome, while null associations may partly result from study design and loss of statistical power (Schnall et al. 1994). Given the potential strengths and weaknesses of JEMs, it might be useful to compare results of conventional studies with self-reported exposure measures with the results of studies using JEMs.

According to a recent systematic review and meta-analysis of cohort studies on psychosocial work factors and mortality, the risk of all-cause and coronary heart disease mortality in workers with low job control is 1.2 and 1.5 times, respectively, higher compared to workers with high job control (Taouk et al. 2020). No evidence for the associations of job demands, job strain, or social support with mortality was found due to a large heterogeneity across the studies. Of the 45 cohort studies included into the review, 6 studies used a JEM for the assessment of the psychosocial work environment. A statistically significant association of job control or decision latitude with mortality was reported by four JEM studies. In contrast, only one of the five JEM studies with psychological demands found an increased risk of coronary heart disease mortality among employees exposed to high job demands (Nilsen et al. 2016). Two out of three JEM studies observed a high risk of mortality among employees exposed to high job strain. No association was found between social support and mortality (two studies only). Recently, a large French study, which was not included into the systematic review, found that job control, social support, job strain, and iso-strain but not psychological job demands alone were associated with coronary heart disease mortality (Niedhammer et al. 2020). The findings of the study suggest that 5.64% and 6.44% of deaths due to coronary heart diseases among men and women, respectively, could be attributed to job strain.

Two longitudinal studies compared the magnitude and consistency of associations of the current and cumulative JEM-based exposures to low job control and low social support with coronary heart disease mortality (Johnson et al. 1996; Niedhammer et al. 2020). Both studies reported that the current exposure to low job control may be more important than the cumulative. Current and cumulative exposure to low social support increased the risk of coronary heart disease mortality among male and female French employees (Niedhammer et al. 2020), but the risk did not differ between Swedish men with long-term exposure to low or medium social support and those with long-term exposure to high social support (Johnson et al. 1996).

In life course epidemiology, with changing world and organizations, use of a JEM as a source of exposure characterization is a first step to recognize a linkage between psychosocial work environment and heath. In life course occupational epidemiology, the job-exposure matrix can be a useful tool for a "nonsubjective" assessment of psychosocial work environment during entire working life – particularly in large-scale studies with missing exposure information at individual level – and understanding complex interrelationships between psychosocial work environment and heath. However, psychological JEMs have several limitations. Researchers need to critically evaluate, whether the exposure can be reasonably assessed at the occupational group level or whether a further assessment at the workplace, work unit, or at the individual worker level is needed.

Work Organization and Management Practice

A World of Work in Constant Transformation

Very profound economic, technological, organizational, demographic, and social transformations have influenced the world of work for several decades. Such changes in the conditions of production and the performance of work influence, in turn, occupational exposures and the means available to workers to protect themselves. Thus, the growth of the service sector, to the detriment of industry, has changed the structure of occupational exposures in favor of psychosocial and organizational risks, which are new for individuals and prevention bodies (Eurofound 2020). The spread of performance-based management methods and new methods of work organization, increasing the rationalization and flexibility of production and employment processes in industry and services (e.g., lean management and new public policies), has produced an intensification of working conditions characterized by accumulation, for the individuals, of multiple working constraints (physical, biological, psychosocial, and organizational). In recent years, changes have accelerated because of the digitalization of the economy and new forms of communication and production, introducing new economic models (e.g., *the gig* economy) and "privileging" work anywhere and at any time of the day. According to some estimates, by 2030, more than half of the European workforce will face significant professional transitions that will require individuals to acquire new skills (McKinsey Global Institute 2020). New forms of work (e.g., virtual platform work) and work organizations (e.g., algorithmic management) based on artificial intelligence tend to introduce, in industry as in services, a new form of Taylorism, "digital Taylorism," based on a very strict work requirements and close digital monitoring of workers' performance (EU-OSHA 2020; Roquelaure 2021). These algorithmic management and monitoring practices reduce people's room for maneuver and reinforces the intensification of working conditions (Bérastégui 2021).

The Covid-19 pandemic (coronavirus disease 2019) has accelerated the digitalization of the economy as well as the fragmentation of production centers and professional groups, with the spread and development of remote work. In addition to the increase in teleworking, whether compulsory or chosen (Milasi et al. 2020), working conditions have deteriorated sharply, due to an intensification of work combined with a lack of means to carry out this work correctly, and, also, to a weakening of the working collective, for a fraction of the active population (Beatriz et al. 2021).

Occupational Exposures and Economic, Social, Organizational, and Managerial Determinants: An Integrative Approach

Due to its multidimensional nature, work is both (i) a subjective experience, constructing the individual in the context of his work, (ii) an objective experience, producing a result (goods and services), and (iii) a collective experience, source of links between individuals within the company (Gomez 2013). To each of these dimensions of work (subjective, objective, and collective) correspond multiple occupational exposures, ranging from the subjective relationships to work to the material conditions of performance of the working activity (for example, the chemical environment, the weight of the loads handled) and to social relations at work. These multiple occupational exposures can in turn influence the health of the individual throughout his life, with immediate effects due to short- or medium-term exposures (such as occupational accidents), or delayed effects related to long-term and cumulative exposures (such as occupational cancers, occupational disintegration following musculoskeletal disorders).

An integrative approach of occupational exposure is required to embrace the complexity of workplace exposures. The integrative approach to occupational exposures not only makes it possible to integrate simultaneous exposures at a given moment but it also makes it possible to apprehend the evolution of these exposures throughout the professional career of the individual, by introducing a diachronic dimension, evolving over time (Eyles et al. 2019). The *"organizational" and integrative approach to occupational exposures* that we present aims to integrate, from an interdisciplinary perspective, occupational exposures and risks covering a very wide spectrum, ranging from socioeconomic and psychosocial aspects to chemical exposures, from the most generic risks to the most specific risks (Table 2). It proposes, therefore, to broaden the levels of analysis of exposures (whatever they may be) of the individual to the work situation (individual or collective), to the company and its organization, and to the socioeconomic environment (Roquelaure 2018).

Organizational and Integrative Model of Occupational Exposures

The "organizational" approach to the occupational exposures is based on an approach derived from those applied in social epidemiology and ergonomics for the analysis of occupational exposures (Roquelaure 2016). As proposed in the Dahlgren and Whitehead model, established in 1991 (Dahlgren and Whitehead 2021), this approach takes into account all the determinants of exposures, by shifting the levels of analysis of occupational exposures (whatever they may be) from the

Table 2 Main occupational exposure categories. (Based on Bastos 2020)

Exposure classes	Examples of exposure
Socioeconomic	• Industrial restructuring • Precarious employment contract (temporary, seasonal, and contract) • Unemployment
Organizational	• Time constraints • Intensity/pace of work • High demands at work • Autonomy in work • Lack of human and/or material resources • Recent/frequent organizational changes
Psychosocial	• *Job strain* situation • Lack of social support at work • Situation of regular tension with the public • Lack of recognition at work • Verbal or physical aggression from colleagues
Physical	• Biomechanics (carrying heavy loads, repetitive and intense work, painful postures) • Noise (long-term exposure, exposure to peaks in sound intensity, other annoying noises) • Thermal (temperatures <5 °C or >30 °C, wet work, and outdoor work) • Vibrations • Work in a hyperbaric environment • Nonionizing radiations (ultraviolet and infrared) • Ionizing radiations (X-rays, gamma rays, etc.) • Electromagnetic fields
Chemical	• Carcinogenic • Toxic to reproduction • Endocrine disruptors • Skin or respiratory sensitizers • Substances of specific chronic toxicity
Biological	• Implementation of biological agents in the work process (bacteria, viruses, and fungi) • Potential contact via exposure to a human reservoir • Potential contact via exposure to a contaminated environment (water, air, soil, animal, or plant dust)

individual to the work situation (individual or collective), from the individual work situation to the workshop or department, the enterprise and the socioeconomic environment of the enterprise, and from the socioeconomic environment of the company to the society as a whole (Roquelaure 2018). The organizational approach of the occupational exposures is also the result of ergonomics research that has shown that the occupational exposures (biological, chemical, physical, and psychosocial) to which the workers are confronted at the level of their work situation are determined by a bundle of economic, regulatory, technical, organizational, and managerial factors identifiable at the different levels (micro-, meso-, and macroscopic) of the company or administration (NORA Organization of Work Team Members 2002; St-Vincent et al. 2011; Roquelaure 2018).

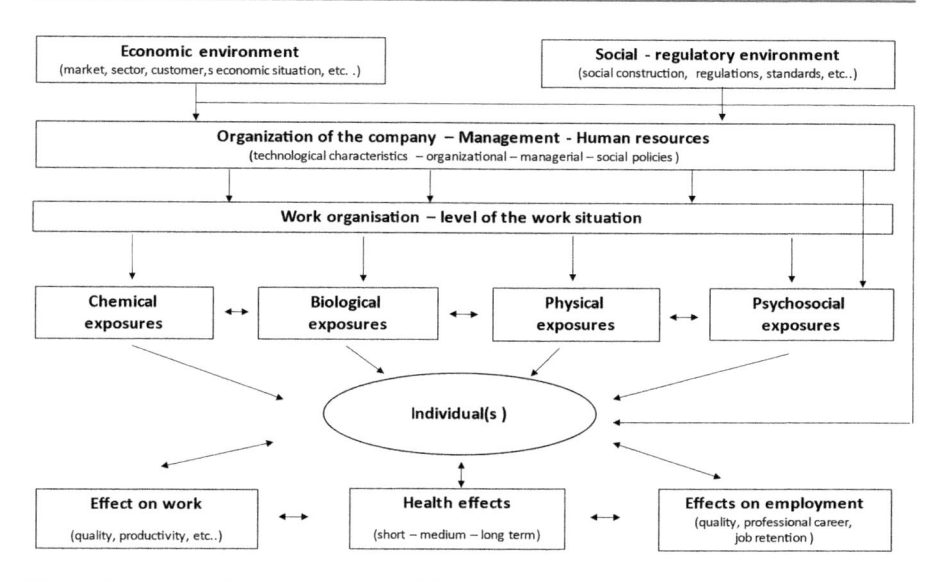

16 Psychosocial Work Environment and Health: Applying Job-Exposure...

Fig. 1 Organizational and integrative model of occupational exposures. Occupational exposures identifiable at the level of work situations are multiple (chemical, biological, physical, and psychosocial). They interact at the individual level to produce effects on health, work, and employment of individuals in the short, medium, and long term. These exposures are part of a bundle of determinants related to the organization of the work at the workplace level, work organization and managerial practices at company (or work unit) level, but also to the economic, social, and regulatory environment of the company

As shown in Fig. 1, the organizational and integrative model of the occupational exposures is a multistage model, including a bundle of determinants ranging from the general context of the company to the individual:

1. *The determinants related to the external context of the company (or macro level)* are macroeconomic (market context, unemployment rate, economic sector, dependence on contractors, technological development, etc.), sociodemographic (such as the ageing of the workforce), political-regulatory (for example, health policy, education, social security, and REACH regulation), and cultural (such as standards and values, the weight of social representation in the sector of activity) of the company.
2. *The determinants related to the internal context of the company (or meso level)* are related to the management methods of the company (or the production unit), the organization of production (technological development, production processes, etc.), the organization of work (the management of work procedures and quality), financial resources, and managerial and human resources practices (social culture, remuneration, career development and social protection policies, the culture of prevention and occupational health and safety, etc.).
3. *The determinants related to the (individual or collective) work situation (or micro level)* are the result of the interactions of higher-order determinants (*macro and meso*), but also of the characteristics of work situations (missions and roles,

organization of the workstation, temporal distribution of tasks, complexity, and autonomy). Thus, management practices influence work-related biomechanical and psychosocial factors by determining the human resources allocated to production activity and the quality of social relations at work.

4. *At the level of the individual (or group of individuals) at work*, all the determinants combine their effects – at the level of the work situation – and determine not only the methods of carrying out the work but also the biological, chemical, physical, and psychosocial constraints that the worker(s) must face. In return, workers mobilize their skills and professional know-how to try to jointly ensure the objectives of production while preserving their health and quality of life at work. Exposures are finally integrated at the level of the individual, whose characteristics may represent either susceptibility factors (genetic factors or health status) or resources (sensory-motor skills, professional knowledge, and know-how, etc.). Individual vulnerabilities and resources are ultimately influenced by exposures, and they thus co-determine the effects on the health of the individual and his long-term maintenance in employment.

The ability to cope with multiple occupational exposures depends on the operational leeway (organizational, spatial, temporal, and collective room for maneuver) offered by the work organization of in the company or that are built by the workers. Thus, the combination of rhythm constraints and rigid procedures, with a strong responsiveness to the customer's request (internal or external), forcing him to work in an emergency – secondary to the establishment of algorithmic management – reduces the possibilities of taking initiatives limiting the worker's ability to regulate his activity in the face of unforeseen events, and, consequently, the deployment of strategies to preserve one's health at work. The preventive nature of the margins of maneuver depends not only on their actual existence (objective and ascertainable) but also on the ability of workers to seize them opportunely in their activity, as shown by ergonomic analyses of work or ergo-toxicology work (Coutarel et al. 2003; Garrigou et al. 2011; St-Vincent et al. 2011).

The Organizational Bundle of Determinants of Occupational Exposure as a Lever for Action of Prevention

The organizational and integrative model of occupational exposures is interesting from an operational point of view in the workplace because it makes it possible to identify and assess health risks in an integrative way to better prevent them at the individual and collective levels. The organizational model of the exposure focuses on the systemic dimension of exposures and on the chain of determinants at the different micro-, meso-, and macroscopic scales of the company, regardless of the sector of activity. It makes it possible to integrate, in the health and safety assessment of work situations, the questioning of the margins of maneuver allowing, in addition to the evaluation of exposures (*defensive approach of health*), to estimate the possibilities offered by the professional environment to the individual to build his or her health through work (*constructive approach of health*). It thus makes it possible to approach health from two angles: that of the exposures that should be *prevented* (i.e., avoiding risks) and that of a construction of the subject that should be promoted (i.e., encouraging actions favorable to health in its broadest sense). The systemic approach to the determinants of the exposome makes it possible to identify the potential levers of action to reduce occupational exposure or increase the resources to deal with it, to put them into debate in the company, and to implement multidimensional, integrated prevention interventions adapted to the work situation, combining, for example, promotion of health at work, eviction of a load handling method or a chemical process, modification of the work organization of or the work process, early detection of damage to health, etc. (Roquelaure 2018).

The organizational and integrative model of occupational exposures assumes that the analysis of exposures integrates an in-depth stage of work analysis that does not focus only on the workstation(s) but explores the company in a systemic way, as a whole, extending the scope of analysis to the network of requirements and constraints in which it is located (customers, suppliers, the population of workers, regulations, local settlement, etc.). However, even if the effects of exposures can be delayed, the integrative dimension should not mask the variability of exposures to multiple stresses in real work situations (as opposed to prescribed work) according to each worker. In the ergonomic sense, exposures are instantaneous and "located" *hic et nunc* (here and now, without delay) because each situation is singular at a moment "t," due to the variability of situations inherent in the complexity of work processes and the variability of individuals.

The organizational and integrative model of occupational exposures is particularly relevant in a period marked by the emergence of new health and safety risks related to technologies, such as technostress, or new ways of organizing work (e.g., teleworking), and increasingly diverse, dispersed, and evolving populations of workers. From an organizational point of view, this concept focuses on the economic (market conditions, organization of the economic sector, etc.), social, regulatory, and political dimensions of the determinants of working conditions in the company and, *ultimately*, occupational exposures and, potentially, occupational health damage.

The model helps to broaden the spectrum of health and safety risk assessment and to promote a comprehensive and integrated approach to the prevention of strenuous work and occupational disorders. The prevention must aim not only to reduce exposure to their biological, chemical, physical, and psychosocial determinants (primary prevention) but also to establish more sustainable and socially responsible modes of production and management (primary prevention) in society.

Cross-References

▶ Biomechanical Hazards at Work and Adverse Health Using Job-Exposure Matrices
▶ Job-Exposure Matrices: Design, Validation, and Limitations

References

Alfredsson L, Karasek RA, Theorell T (1982) Myocardial infarction risk and psychosocial work environment: an analysis of the male Swedish working force. Soc Sci Med 16:463–467

Bastos H (2020) PLAN SANTE AU TRAVAIL 2016–2020 – Amélioration et prise en compte de la polyexposition – Profils homogènes de travailleurs polyexposés [Internet]. Anses. Disponible sur: https://www.anses.fr/fr/system/files/PST3_ProfilTravailleursExposes_Polyexposition.pdf

Beatriz M, Beque M, Coutrot T, Duval M, Erb L, Inan C, Mauroux A, Rosankis É (2021) Quelles conséquences de la crise sanitaire sur les conditions de travail et les risques psychosociaux? Dares Analyses, p 10

Bérastégui P (2021) Exposure to psychosocial risk factors in the gig economy: a systematic review [Internet]. European Trade Union Institute (ETUI), Bruxelles, p 124. Report no. 2021-01. Disponible sur: https://www.etui.org/sites/default/files/2021-02/Exposure%20to%20psychosocial%20risk%20factors%20in%20the%20gig%20economy-a%20systematic%20review-2021.pdf

Blair A, Stewart P, Lubin JH, Forastiere F (2007) Methodological issues regarding confounding and exposure misclassification in epidemiological studies of occupational exposures. Am J Ind Med 50:199–207

Coutarel F, Daniellou F, Dugué B (2003) Interroger l'organisation du travail au regard des marges de manœuvre en conception et en fonctionnement. La rotation est-elle une solution aux TMS?. Pistes [Internet] 5(2). Disponible sur: https://journals.openedition.org/pistes/3328. Cité 25 juill 2015

Dahlgren G, Whitehead M (2021) The Dahlgren-Whitehead model of health determinants: 30 years on and still chasing rainbows. Public Health 199:20–24

EU-OSHA (2020) ESENER 2019: what does it tell us about safety and health in Europe's workplaces? [Internet]. Publications Office of the European Union, Luxembourg. Disponible sur: https://data.europa.eu/doi/10.2802/489857

Eurofound (2020) Working conditions in sectors [Internet]. Publications Office of the European Union, Luxembourg. Disponible sur: https://www.eurofound.europa.eu/sites/default/files/ef_publication/field_ef_document/ef19005en.pdf

Eyles E, Manley D, Jones K (2019) Occupied with classification: which occupational classification scheme better predicts health outcomes? Soc Sci Med 227:56–62

Garrigou A, Baldi I, Le Frious P, Anselm R, Vallier M (2011) Ergonomics contribution to chemical risks prevention: an ergotoxicological investigation of the effectiveness of coverall against plant pest risk in viticulture. Appl Ergon 42(2):321–330

Gomez P (2013) Le travail invisible: Enquête sur une disparition. François Bourin Éditeur, Paris

ILO (1986) Psychosocial factors at work: recognition and control, vol 56. International Labour Office, Geneva, pp 34.32–34.33 (1998). Available from: http://www.iloencyclopaedia.org/part-v/psychosocial-and-organizational-factors/item/9-psychosocial-and-organizational-factors

Johnson JV, Hall EM (1988) Job strain, work place social support, and cardiovascular disease: a cross-sectional study of a random sample of the Swedish working population. Am J Public Health 78:1336–1342

Johnson JV, Stewart WF (1993) Measuring work organization exposure over the life course with a job-exposure matrix. Scand J Work Environ Health 19:21–28

Johnson JV, Stewart W, Hall EM, Fredlund P, Theorell T (1996) Long-term psychosocial work environment and cardiovascular mortality among Swedish men. Am J Public Health 86(3):324–331

Karasek RA (1979) Job demands, job decision latitude, and mental strain: implications for job redesign. Adm Sci Q 24:285–308

Karasek RA, Theorell T (1990) Healthy work, stress, productivity and the reconstruction of working life. Basic Books, New York

Kauppinen T, Toikkanen J, Pukkala E (1998) From cross-tabulations to multipurpose exposure information systems: a new job-exposure matrix. Am J Ind Med 33:409–417

Kivimäki M, Batty GD, Steptoe A, Kawachi I (eds) (2018) The Routledge international handbook of psychosocial epidemiology. Routledge, New York

Landsbergis P, Theorell T, Schwartz J, Greiner BA, Krause N (2000) Measurement of psychosocial workplace exposure variables. Occup Med 15:163–188

Leka S, Jain A (2010) Health impact of psychosocial hazards at work: an overview. World Health Organization, Geneva

Macleod J, Davey Smith G (2003) Psychosocial factors and public health: a suitable case for treatment? J Epidemiol Community Health 57:565–570

McKinsey Global Institute (2020) The future of work in Europe: automation, workforce transitions and the shifting geography of employment [Internet]. Disponible sur: https://www.mckinsey.com/featured-insights/future-of-work/the-future-of-work-in-europe

Milasi E et al (2020) Telework in the EU before and after the COVID-19: where we were, where we head to [Internet]. JRC Science for Policy Brief. Disponible sur: https://ec.europa.eu/jrc/sites/jrcsh/files/jrc120945_policy_brief_-_covid_and_telework_final.pdf

Niedhammer I, Chastang JF, Levy D, David S, Degioanni S, Theorell T (2008) Study of the validity of a job-exposure matrix for psychosocial work factors: results from the national French SUMER survey. Int Arch Occup Environ Health 82(1):87–97

Niedhammer I, Milner A, LaMontagne AD, Chastang JF (2018) Study of the validity of a job-exposure matrix for the job strain model factors: an update and a study of changes over time. Int Arch Occup Environ Health 91(5):523–536

Niedhammer I, Milner A, Geoffroy-Perez B, Coutrot T, LaMontagne AD, Chastang JF (2020) Psychosocial work exposures of the job strain model and cardiovascular mortality in France: results from the STRESSJEM prospective study. Scand J Work Environ Health 46(5):542–551

Niedhammer I, Bertrais S, Witt K (2021) Psychosocial work exposures and health outcomes: a meta-review of 72 literature reviews with meta-analysis. Scand J Work Environ Health 47(7): 489–508

Nilsen C, Andel R, Fritzell J, Kåreholt I (2016) Work-related stress in midlife and all-cause mortality: can sense of coherence modify this association? Eur J Pub Health 26(6):1055–1061

NORA Organization of Work Team Members (2002) The changing organization of work and the safety and health of working people [Internet]. NIOSH Publication report no. 116. NIOSH, Cincinnati. Disponible sur: http://www.cdc.gov/niosh/docs/2002-116/

Roquelaure Y (2016) Promoting a shared representation of workers' activities to improve integrated prevention of work-related musculoskeletal disorders. Saf Health Work 7(2):171–174

Roquelaure Y (2018) Musculoskeletal disorders and psychosocial factors at work. Reports [Internet]. European Trade Union Institute (ETUI). Disponible sur: https://www.etui.org/Publications2/Reports/Musculoskeletal-disorders-and-psychosocial-factors-at-work. Cité 6 févr 2019

Roquelaure Y (2021) New forms of work in the digital era: implications for psychosocial risks and musculoskeletal disorders. Discussion paper [Internet]. EU-OSHA. Disponible sur: https://osha.europa.eu/fr/publications/digitalisation-work-psychosocial-risk-factors-and-work-related-musculoskeletal-disorders/view

Rugulies R (2019) What is a psychosocial work environment? Scand J Work Environ Health 45(1): 1–6

Santosa A, Rosengren A, Ramasundarahettige C et al (2021) Psychosocial risk factors and cardiovascular disease and death in a population-based cohort from 21 low-, middle-, and high-income countries. JAMA Netw Open 4(12):e2138920

Sauter SL, Murphy LR, Hurrell JJ, Levi L (1998) Psychosocial and organizational factors. In: Stellman JM (ed) ILO encyclopedia of occupational health and safety. International Labour Office, Geneva, pp 34.32–34.33 [Internet]. Available from: http://www.iloencyclopaedia.org/part-v/psychosocial-and-organizational-factors/item/9-psychosocial-and-organizational-factors

Schnall PL, Landsbergis PA, Baker D (1994) Job strain and cardiovascular disease. Annu Rev Public Health 15:381–411

Schwartz JE, Pieper CF, Karasek RA (1988) A procedure for linking psychosocial job characteristics data to health surveys. Am J Public Health 78(8):904–909

Siegrist J (1996) Adverse health effects of high-effort/low-reward conditions. J Occup Health Psychol 1(1):27–41. https://doi.org/10.1037/1076-8998.1.1.27

St-Vincent M, Vézina N, Bellemare M, Denis D, Ledoux E, Imbeau D (2011) L'intervention en ergonomie. Éditions MultiMondes, Montréal

Tabanelli MC, Depolo M, Cooke RM, Sarchielli G, Bonfiglioli R, Mattioli S, Violante FS (2008) Available instruments for measurement of psychosocial factors in the work environment. Int Arch Occup Environ Health 82:1–12

Taouk Y, Spittal MJ, LaMontagne AD, Milner AJ (2020) Psychosocial work stressors and risk of all-cause and coronary heart disease mortality: a systematic review and meta-analysis. Scand J Work Environ Health 46(1):19–31

Theorell T, Hasselhorn HM (2005) On cross-sectional questionnaire studies of relationships between psychosocial conditions at work and health – are they reliable? Int Arch Occup Environ Health 78:517–522

Theorell T, Tsutsumi A, Hallquist J, Reuterwall C, Hogstedt C, Fredlund P, Emlund N, Johnson JV (1998) Decision latitude, job strain and myocardial infarction: a study of working men in Stockholm. Am J Public Health 88(3):382–388

Wieclaw J, Agerbo E, Mortensen PB, Burr H, Tuchsen F, Bonde JP (2008) Psychosocial working conditions and the risk of depression and anxiety disorders in the Danish workforce. BMC Public Health 8:280

Occupational Differences in Work-Related Mental Health: A Life Course Analysis of Recent Trends in the European Context

17

Tarani Chandola

Contents

Introduction	284
Work-related Psychosocial Risk Factors Over the Life Course	285
Macrosocial and Economic Trends in the European and UK Contexts That Could Affect Work-Related Mental Health	286
Longitudinal Follow-Up of Work-Related Poor Mental Health Among Workers in Different Occupations	293
Conclusion	297
Cross-References	298
References	298

Abstract

Work-related poor mental health has been increasing in recent years across most European countries. However, the explanations for this increase have not been explored in terms of the life course of workers and the occupations they work in. This chapter examines whether the aging of European workers can explain some of the deteriorating trends in workplace mental health, and whether some occupations are at risk of worsening mental health as workers age. The chapter finds that despite accounting for individual workers' age, sex, and educational levels, workers in occupations that have a high proportion of public contact have had consistently higher rates of work-related poor mental health. However, there was no difference in the recent trends for specific occupations compared to the overall worsening trend in work-related mental health. While the period of the coronavirus pandemic exacerbated this deterioration in work-related mental health, the worsening trend was evident prior to the pandemic. Workers in some occupations in Europe have now faced an accumulation of work-related poor mental health for several years now.

T. Chandola (✉)
Faculty of Social Sciences, University of Hong Kong, Hong Kong SAR, China
e-mail: chandola@hku.hk

© Springer Nature Switzerland AG 2023
M. Wahrendorf et al. (eds.), *Handbook of Life Course Occupational Health*, Handbook Series in Occupational Health Sciences, https://doi.org/10.1007/978-3-031-30492-7_31

Keywords

Age, period, and cohort effects · Psychosocial · Work stress · Longitudinal trends

Introduction

Work-related poor mental health is among common mental health problems (stress, depression, or anxiety) that can be caused or made worse by work. In surveys of people in work, workers are typically asked if they have any health problems that were caused or made worse by work, and then asked to report specific health problems. There has been an increase in work-related poor mental health in recent years in most European countries. The proportion of people employed age 16–64 years old in the EU-27 countries who reported work-related stress, depression, or anxiety increased from 1.2% in 2013 to 1.9% in 2020 (see Fig. 1). In the UK, there has been a similar increase from 1.2% of workers in 2010/2011 to 2% in 2020/2021.

There are a number of potential explanations of this recent increase in work-related poor mental health. This increase could be the result of the global coronavirus pandemic since early 2020. This period effect has resulted in worsening mental health across all population groups, not just among workers. Alternatively, the aging of the workforce could have resulted in an increase in ill-health in the working population, as older workers tend to develop more chronic health conditions. Or else, some occupations may be more at risk of psychosocial ill-health than others and these psychosocial risk factors may have increased in recent years. This chapter will explore these potential explanations for the increasing levels of work-related poor

Fig. 1 Cases of (prevalence) work-related stress, depression, or anxiety per 100,000 workers by broad occupational groups: UK Labor Force Survey 2010–2021

mental health, within the context of the life course of individual workers and the occupational sectors they work in.

Work-related Psychosocial Risk Factors Over the Life Course

A life course approach to work-related stress and psychosocial ill-health explicitly considers the accumulation and duration of work-related psychosocial risk factors and well-being throughout the life course as well as the timing and ordering of exposure to those psychosocial risk factors within a person's life course and their employment trajectories. The timing and recurrences of a persons' exposure to work-related psychosocial risk factors over their working lifetime can have long-lasting impacts on their mental health and well-being (Wahrendorf and Chandola 2016).

Across the adult life course, there is a well-established U-shape pattern between age and subjective well-being or happiness (Blanchflower 2021). In developed and developing countries, the U-shape of the age curve with subjective well-being reaches a nadir at around age 50. The size of the dip in well-being in the late 40s is equivalent to the influence of a major life event like unemployment or marital separation. Most of the analyses on the age association with well-being control for labor market status, although it is noticeable that the nadir occurs during the latter period of the working life course. Moreover, other studies have also observed that work stress has an inverse U-shape association with age, with lower levels of work stress among youngest and oldest worker and higher values in the two middle age categories (Götz et al. 2018). Later in this chapter, we will examine evidence for a similar U-shape pattern of age with work-related mental health.

Changes in work-related psychosocial risk factors over the life course can occur for several reasons, related to a specific individual or their job or the social context in which they work. While there has been considerable evidence on individual and social determinants of work-related psychosocial risk factors (Theorell 2020), there has been less research on the occupational-level determinants, especially within the context of life course research.

In this chapter, we argue that it is important to take a life course perspective when it comes to understanding occupational determinants of work-related poor mental health. This means using longitudinal data that attempts to differentiate between trajectories of work-related poor mental health at the individual and occupational levels, taking into account different life course explanations of those changes, such as age, cohort, and period effects. Some occupations have a higher proportion of older or younger workers, which changes as occupations and industries respond to market and other demands for their services or goods. Moreover, there is a general U-shape association between well-being and age. Changes in workplace mental health could reflect the changed age distribution (and aging) of the workforce. Similarly, period effects may be particularly important for understanding changes, and key events (like the financial crisis or the coronavirus pandemic) could make working in certain occupations more stressful. Moreover, birth cohort effects could have long-lasting life course effects on worker's well-being through the timing of entry into the labor force and the effect of early life adversities on health and well-being in later life.

An individual's working life course is usually conceptualized as a career, although nowadays the idea of a person having a single career of "job for life" within a single occupation or employer is not as common as before (Gregg and Wadsworth 2002). Most of the time, we conceptualize of life course changes in terms of individual worker-level changes such as workers becoming older. What is less conceptualized are occupational-level determinants like the aging workers in particular occupational sectors, or macrolevel trends like deindustrialization and work automation and whether and how these affect an individual's experience of workplace stress and well-being over their working life course.

The key aim of the chapter is to identify which workers are at risk of work-related poor mental health, and whether their trajectories of work psychosocial ill-health vary according to their age, sex, life course, and occupation. The key questions this chapter will attempt to answer are whether workers in specific occupations at particular ages or stages of the life course are more at risk of work-related poor mental health and whether this has changed in recent years. Nearly all the data presented in this chapter come from a European context, so the relevant population for this chapter is the European working population from the early part of the twenty-first century onward.

Macrosocial and Economic Trends in the European and UK Contexts That Could Affect Work-Related Mental Health

This section describes the wider social and economic context of work-related mental health in recent years, which is reviewed in more detail in ▶ Chap. 3, "Transformation of Modern Work, Rise of Atypical Employment, and Health," by Eichhorst and Kalleberg in this volume. In particular, this section will outline some of the common macrosocial, economic, and demographic factors that affect many workers across different countries with evidence drawn from a recent review (Eurofound 2020).

Work Automation

The digitalization of work, which includes increases in work automation, digital processes, and the development of digital platforms, has been a major source of change in working conditions (Eurofound 2018). Work automation uses machines or software to carry out tasks with a high degree of repetition, or some tasks that are too dangerous or that require physical strength and endurance levels beyond an average worker. Automation has been going on for a long time accelerating with the industrial revolution. However, the rate of change brought about by automation in the workplace has increased considerably in recent years (Schwab 2016).

Automation can result in machines working alongside human workers but can also result in job displacement, as some workers are replaced by machines (Arntz et al. 2016). The automation of work results in quicker processing times for work outputs, which can result in time pressure for workers. An extension of work automation is the digitization of work processes, which translates parts of the physical production process into digital information, resulting in the creation of online and digital data, assets, operations, and tools. Digital work also includes the use of sensor and automated devices to collect and monitor data. Digital platforms are virtual networks (an online "platform") that work organizations or individual workers use to procure or transact services in exchange for payment. The use of digital platforms to organize work has increased considerably in the last 10 years.

All of these technological transformations in the workplace can have contradictory impacts on workers, resulting in job creation in some occupations, while destroying jobs in other occupational sectors. The increased use of machines and software in work requires workers to develop related skills. However, many workers lack access to such skills training and development or belong to a generational cohort where such skills were not taught in early life. It is not just routine work that is being replaced by machines. Many complex tasks are becoming increasingly automated, particularly with the introduction of machine learning and algorithms to replace human decision-making. Occupational sectors that are particularly affected by these technological developments include the information and communications technology sector, as well as office work, commerce and sales, transport and logistics, and manufacturing jobs (Frey and Osborne 2017).

Digital work enables some workers to work from home, a very common feature of working conditions during the coronavirus pandemic (Chandola et al. 2020). This has resulted in some workers becoming more independent and being able to organize their work tasks around their other activities (particularly around childcare). However, this increased flexibility could come at a cost as the boundaries between work and family life become less clear, potentially resulting in a poorer work-life balance for some workers and resulting in psychological ill-health (Chandola et al. 2019).

Globalization

Since the 1970s, the organization of work has become increasingly globalized, as economies around the world have become increasingly interdependent. This has resulted in increased competition between companies located in different countries or across multinational contexts. The outsourcing of labor to countries with cheaper labor or production costs has resulted in downward pressures on labor wages in some countries. Such outsourcing could result in a reduction in hazardous work in those countries (while increasing in the countries where such work has been outsourced), but it could also result in greater competition between companies and workers, leading to lower wages, longer working hours, and higher time pressure at work. Globalization has been accompanied by the growth of low-waged service sector in some countries (Huwart and Verdier 2013). This work is often done by labor migrants who lack economic or political capital, and are often in precarious working conditions. Even though some occupational sectors such as education, health, and public administration are shielded to some extent from international competition, there are spillover effects from globalization that could lead to common processes across all occupations such as increasing job complexity and blurring boundaries between work and private life, for example, in relation to the rise of nonstandard employment and work (Eurofound 2020).

Since the financial crisis of 2007–2008, there has been recovery in the European employment rates across nearly all sectors of the economy. However, the period during the coronavirus pandemic has seen a rise in unemployment across many job sectors. It is worth noting that prior to the pandemic, employment rates were consistently rising in some sectors, such as education and health over the period 2008–2019 (Eurofound 2020). However, other occupations within the public sector have witnessed financial cuts resulting in job loss. Employees exposed to workplace downsizing experience higher levels of work demands, role conflict, supervisor aggression, dysfunctional leadership, job insecurity, and employment insecurity, and lower levels of friendship formation, distributive justice, and promotion opportunities (Frone and Blais 2020). It is likely that the twin processes of globalization and the financial crisis of 2007–2008 contributed to the already prevailing trend of an increasing share of employees in Europe working in the service sector, and fewer working in more labor-intensive sectors like manufacturing and construction (Eurofound 2020).

Demographic Change

The aging of the population in the developed world has manifested in an aging workforce. Many countries have increased the age at which workers can retire or are eligible to receive their pensions or related social security programs. As a result, the mean age of workers across nearly all occupations in European countries has increased in the last few years (Eurofound 2017). As aging is associated with the onset of chronic health conditions and impairments, the aging of the workforce has also meant an increasing proportion of older workers with disabilities remaining in work. In some occupational contexts, particularly for large employers, there is scope for older workers to be moved away from tasks that involve physical hazards to other roles with fewer physical risks. However, this is not true across all occupational sectors and types of employers. Moreover, older workers typically have less access to skills development and training opportunities, making them at risk of becoming redundant in the context of other macrotrends in the workplace such as workplace automation. Population aging also has an influence on labor demand in occupational sectors related to health and social care, where there has been an increase in labor demand (Eurofound 2020).

Another key demographic change has been the increasing participation of women in the labor force, typically in some occupational sectors such as in health and social care. Work-related psychosocial risk factors in these caring occupations tend to be different compared to more traditionally male gender occupations like construction, where there are higher physical risks (Eurofound 2020). Women in part-time work are particularly at risk of a "glass ceiling" that prevents them from advancing in their career (Cotter et al. 2001). While policy initiatives on reducing the gender wage gap may have helped to some extent to reduce gender inequalities, there still remain substantial gender segregation at the sector and occupational levels.

Age Differences in Work-Related Mental Health

There is a striking (inverse) U-shape association between age and work-related poor mental health. In the UK, the age groups with the lowest prevalence of work-related stress, depression, or anxiety were workers in the 16–24 and 55 years and older age groups (Fig. 2). Prevalence was highest among workers aged 25–34 years, and slowly declined among older workers. The (inverse) U-shape association between age and work-related poor mental health was mirrored when examining incidence of work-related stress, depression, and anxiety (Fig. 2). A similar pattern was observed at the EU-27 level in 2020 – workers aged 35–54 years old had the highest levels of work-related poor mental health and those aged 15–34 years had the lowest levels (Eurostat 2021).

The U-shape association between age and work-related poor mental health is similar to the U-shape pattern between age and well-being. It is possible that the general association between age and well-being could be driven by a tendency for workers in midlife to develop poorer mental health because of their working conditions. On the other hand, some of the association between work-related poor mental health and age could be driven by the age composition of some occupations. Some jobs such as those engaged in sales-related occupations are comprised of relatively younger workers, while other occupations such as those related to skilled agricultural trades consist of relatively older workers. At the European level, the youngest workforces tend to be found in the commerce, hospitality, and construction sectors, while older employees over the age of 55 years tend to be overrepresented in the sectors of public administration, education, and health (Eurofound 2020).

A higher proportion of older workers in some occupations with greater risk factors for poor mental health could be driving the U-shape pattern between age and work-related poor mental health. Later in this chapter, we will explore whether

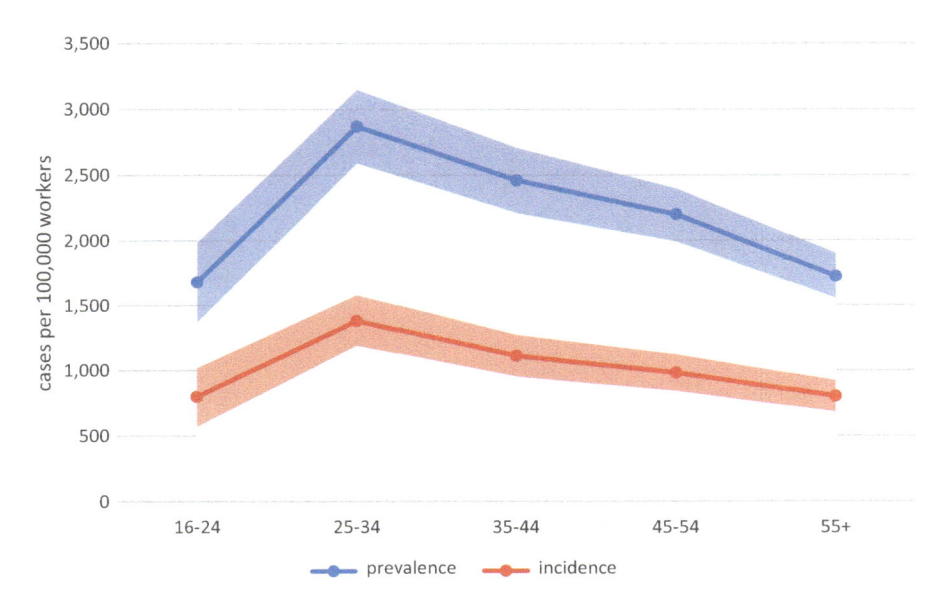

Fig. 2 Prevalence and incidence of work-related stress, depression, or anxiety per 100,000 workers by age-groups: UK Labor Force Survey 2020–2021

the age composition of different occupations has a role in explaining why we observe a U-shape pattern between age and work-related poor mental health.

Period Differences in Work-Related Mental Health

This section examines the period trends in work-related poor mental health in the last 10 years, distinguishing between trends prior to the coronavirus pandemic. It is important to distinguish between the trends of these two periods because mental health during the pandemic has deteriorated to a great extent, either directly or indirectly as a result of the pandemic and related pandemic control policies (Chandola et al. 2020).

Work-related stress, depression, or anxiety is defined as a harmful reaction people have to undue pressures and demands placed on them at work. The prevalence of wok-related stress, anxiety, or depression in the UK increased steadily from 2010–2011 (1170 cases per 100,000 workers) until 2018/2019 (1410 cases per 100,000 workers) and then increased substantially by 2019/2020 (before the coronavirus pandemic), peaking at 2030 cases by 100,000 workers in 2020/2021 – see Fig. 1. This suggests that even before the coronavirus pandemic, there was a steady increase in the prevalence of work-related poor mental health conditions. In relation to incidence (see Fig. 3), the trend prior to 2019/2020 (before the pandemic) was largely flat, between 580 and 710 cases per year. So, the increasing prevalence in work-related ill-health prior to 2019/2020 was not being driven by an increase in incidence, but rather the slower rates of recovery from work-related poor mental health. However, by 2020/2021, the incidence had almost doubled to 1200 cases per 100,000 workers, suggesting that the incidence of work-related poor mental health had increased substantially during the pandemic.

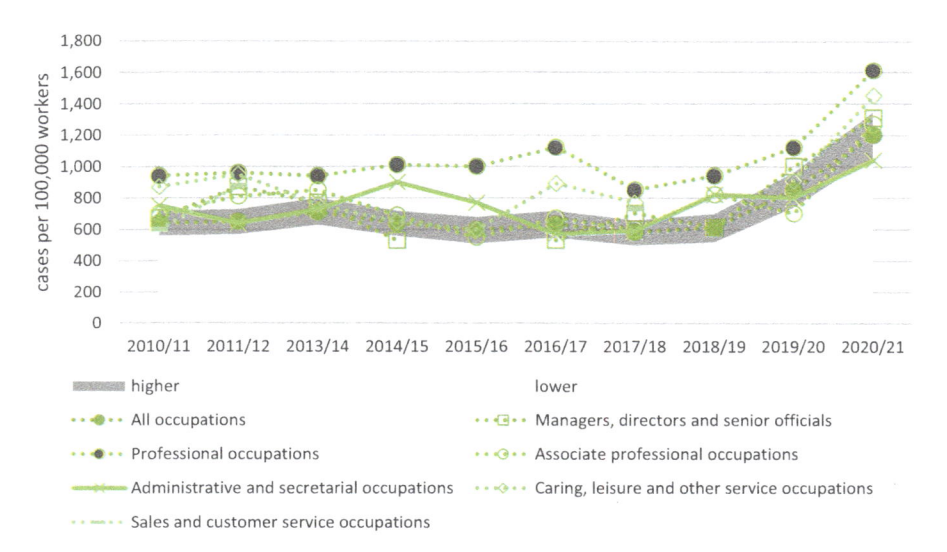

Fig. 3 Incidence of work-related stress, depression, or anxiety per 100,000 workers by broad occupational groups: UK Labor Force Survey 2010–2021

Workers in the occupational sectors of human health and social activities and education (which are mostly in professional occupations) have always had much higher levels of work-related poor mental health in recent years (Eurofound 2020). Moreover, during the pandemic years (2020–2021), the prevalence of poor mental health among associate professional occupations (particularly among business and public service associate professionals), managers, directors, and senior officials, and sales and customer service occupations was much higher than the average levels for that period (Health and Safety Executive 2021). In terms of incidence, the marked increase in work-related poor mental health among workers in caring, leisure, and other service occupations was remarkable. These occupations often involve high levels of public contact or interaction and many are also largely within the public sector (Eurofound 2020). The main work factors cited by respondents as causing work-related stress, depression, or anxiety were workload pressures, including tight deadlines and too much responsibility and a lack of managerial support (Health and Safety Executive 2021).

Looking at the European context, from 2013–2020, there was an increase in the percentage of workers in Europe who reported work-related poor mental health (Eurostat 2021). In 2013, 1.2% of workers aged 16–64 in the EU-27 countries reported work-related stress/depression or anxiety and in 2020, this had increased to 1.9%. This is a similar rise in the prevalence compared to the UK levels of work-related poor mental health.

Cohort Differences in Work-Related Mental Health

There is relatively little evidence on cohort effects on work-related mental health as separate from aging effects. In most studies, age and birth cohort effects on mental health are often conflated. Many of the "baby boomer" generational cohorts are approaching retirement or have already retired. There is some suggestion that people in this cohort have relatively low awareness about protecting their mental well-being (Grant 2013). The abolition of a default retirement age has enabled people from this generation to stay working for a longer period compared to previous generations, and continue earning to supplement pension incomes. Although baby boomers are the best educated generation yet to reach their 60s, they have lower qualifications than succeeding generations. As education is a key life course determinant of health in later life (Chandola et al. 2006), the relatively low levels of education in this cohort may also have an impact on their work-related mental health.

Recent Trends in Risk Factors for Work-Related Poor Mental Health

Prior to the coronavirus pandemic, the predominant cause of work-related stress, depression, or anxiety in the UK was workload, in particular tight deadlines, too much work, or too much pressure or responsibility, accounting for almost half the cases of work-related poor mental health during the period 2009–2012 (Health and Safety Executive 2021). Another key risk factor was the lack of managerial support, followed by bullying, threats, or violence. Data from the UK general practitioner's network were analyzed by precipitating events. The report concluded that workload pressures were the predominant factor, in agreement with the UK Labor Force Survey, with interpersonal relationships at work and changes at work being significant factors as well (Health and Safety Executive 2021). Similar findings were also reported from the European Labor Force Surveys (Eurostat 2021). Time pressure or work overload was the most commonly mentioned risk factor for mental well-being at work, as it was reported by almost one-fifth of employed people in the EU. Dealing with difficult customers, patients, pupils, etc. and job insecurity were the second and third most frequent risk factors for mental well-being that people reported having at work. Health sector employees face high emotional and social demands, such as dealing with angry clients or patients and emotionally disturbing situations.

However, in terms of trends in Europe regarding the risk factors for work-related poor mental health, there is a clear pattern of a downward trajectory at the EU-27 level since 2013–2020 (see Fig. 4). The proportion of all workers reporting time pressure at work decreased from 25% in 2013 to 19.5% in 2020. Similarly, in terms of harassment and bullying or violence and related threats, there was a decline in the prevalence in 2013–2020 from 2.7–0.8% and 2.1–1.1%, respectively. This downward trend in the risk factors for work-related poor mental health is at odds with the upward trend in work-related poor mental health we observe at the EU-27 level as well as in the UK.

This improvement in the risk factors for work-related poor mental health continues the significant improvement in working time quality in Europe from 2005–2015 (Eurofound 2020). There was a significant improvement in work rewards, with jobs becoming more secure, offering better career perspectives and fair pay. Employees over the same period also reported significantly more job control (over methods of work, order of tasks, speed of work, and taking a break when

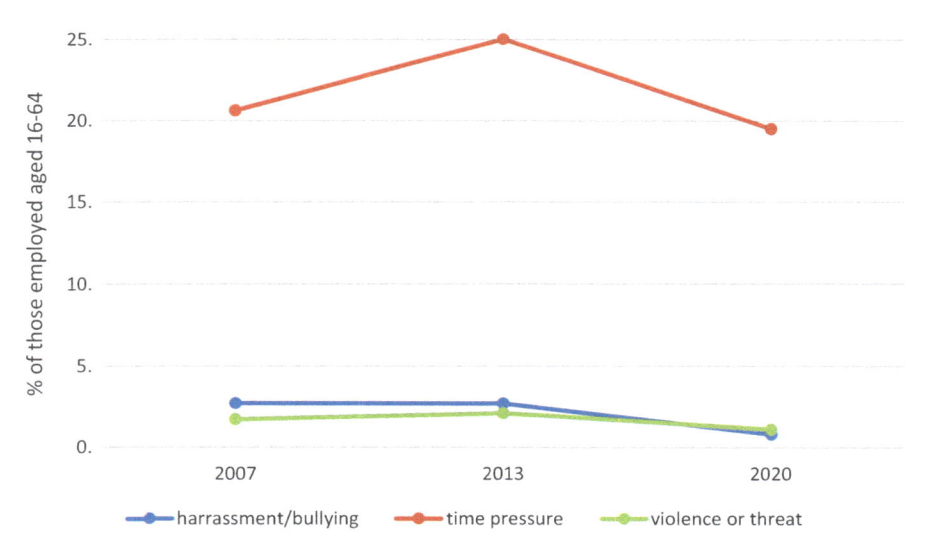

Fig. 4 Prevalence of selected risk factors that can adversely affect the mental well-being of workers aged 15–64 years: European Labor Force Surveys 2007–2020, EU-27 countries

desired). However, work was significantly more emotionally demanding in 2015 compared to 2010. Moreover, in the 15 years prior to 2015, support by supervisors or coworkers had not changed (Eurofound 2020).

In terms of which occupations were most at risk, it was workers in the occupational sector of human health and social work activities that reported the highest levels of work-related risk factors for mental well-being (58.5%), followed by those working for extraterritorial organizations and bodies (52.7%) – although this was an occupational group with low reliability, with workers in the Education sector (50.4%) reporting the third highest levels of work-related risk factors for poor mental health (Eurofound 2020). Work intensity tends to be highest in the education and public administration sectors and poor working time quality tends to be highest in the health sector.

Longitudinal Follow-Up of Work-Related Poor Mental Health Among Workers in Different Occupations

So far in this chapter, we have seen how there are some occupations more at risk of work-related poor mental health. Furthermore, it looks like there is an increasing trend in levels of work-related poor mental health in recent years, even though the trends in some occupational risk factors (like time pressure) seem to be declining.

As all of the evidence examined so far is based on cross-sectional data, we do not know to what extent these observed differences in trends are the result of life course processes. Specifically, we do not know whether they reflect the general pattern of decreasing well-being in midlife, or whether they reflect specific period effects or cohort effects. Moreover, general patterns at the population level could be misleading as that may be ignoring differential patterns at the occupational level. We do not know whether the increase is related to period-related factors or individual life course factors (the age of workers or their birth cohorts). Furthermore, we do not know if some occupations are more at risk of worsening trend in work-related poor mental health over and above the average worsening trend.

Hence there is a need for longitudinal data following up the work-related mental health workers in different occupational sectors using data that is representative of the working population. With longitudinal data, we can take account of the clustering of observations of mental health within workers. What is novel in the analyses that is presented is that the clustering of workers within broad occupational groups is also taken into account, allowing us to examine whether certain occupations are more at risk of work-related poor mental health even after taking into account individual-level factors like their age, sex, and educational levels. Hence, three-level multilevel models (occasions clustered within individuals within occupational groups) are analyzed to examine the life course influences on trajectories of work-related mental health. Period (or occasion) effects are also controlled for in the model.

Understanding Society, the UK Household Longitudinal Study (UKHLS), is a nationally representative household panel study, which began in 2009 recruiting over 60,000 adults in 40,000 households. The survey is conducted every year (wave), following up adult members in each sampled household. To date, there are 11 waves of the data available for researchers (University of Essex 2021). Detailed questions on working conditions (which includes the measure of work-related poor mental health) were asked every 2 years from wave 2 onward. For this chapter, this resulted in data from waves 2 (2010–2011) to wave 10 (2018–2019) being analyzed. The measure of work-related poor mental health was derived from the following six questions: "thinking of the past few weeks, how much of the time has your job made you feel tense/uneasy/worried/depressed/gloomy/miserable?". (Warr 1990) The response categories varied from 1 "never" to 5 "all of the time."

The sample size of the longitudinal sample can be seen in Table 1, which also shows the descriptive statistics of the sample by each occupational group. There were

Table 1 Distribution of age, sex and qualifications by occupational group in the UK Household Longitudinal Study

Occupational group	Mean age (SD)	% Male	% no qualifications	n (unweighted)
Hlth profnl	42.6 (10.8)	41.9%	0.0%	936
Sc/tech prfnl	40.7 (10.4)	80.9%	0.1%	2033
Hlth/socl care assct profnl	43.5 (10.9)	13.6%	0.2%	3276
Educnl profnl	42.2 (10.6)	30.8%	0.2%	3979
Businss/media/public srv profnl	43.8 (11)	52.5%	0.3%	2210
Cult/media/sports occupns	41.9 (12.2)	55.5%	0.6%	1532
Sc/tech assct prfnl	40.4 (11.1)	72.1%	0.6%	1179
Businss/public srv assct profnl	42 (11.4)	48.6%	0.7%	3810
Protect serv occupns	40.1 (9)	71.8%	0.7%	696
Corp mngrs/drctrs	44.4 (9.8)	58.3%	0.9%	6856
Admin occupns	42.5 (11.8)	27.7%	1.0%	5375
Skill metal/electrc trades	42.1 (11.6)	97.9%	1.6%	1725
Sales occupns	37.4 (12.9)	34.3%	1.7%	918
Secrtrl-related occupns	45.5 (11.7)	4.5%	1.8%	1319
Carng/personl serv occupns	42.4 (12.1)	10.1%	2.2%	4809
Leisre/travel-related serv occup	41.7 (14.4)	26.1%	2.4%	947
Othr mngrs	44.7 (11.4)	54.7%	3.5%	2127
Comm/civil enfrcement occupns	37 (14.9)	28.4%	5.6%	2828
Skill construct/building trades	44.3 (12.1)	97.7%	6.1%	1243
Prcess/plnt/mchin operts	46.2 (10.9)	93.8%	7.2%	1671
Custmer serv occupns	43.8 (10.9)	78.8%	7.3%	1492
Skill textile/print/other trades	44.8 (12.1)	52.3%	7.6%	947
Transpt/mchin/drivrs operts	43.5 (13.2)	83.7%	8.7%	1207
Elmntry trdes-rlted occupns	40.6 (14.9)	39.6%	9.7%	3961
Skill agric-related trades	49.2 (12.7)	84.6%	11.3%	514

57,590 observations across waves 2–10, clustered within 25,861 workers across the five waves, which means that each worker was observed an average of 2.2 times over 10 years from 2010/2011. The oldest workers tended to be in the skilled agricultural occupations with a mean age of almost 50 years while the youngest workers tended to be in community and civil enforcement as well as in sales occupations with a mean age of around 37 years. There were marked gender differences in occupations, with very few men in secretarial-related occupations and very few women in the skilled building/construction/electrical trades. Workers in the skilled agricultural occupations also had the highest proportion of workers without any educational qualifications. This is likely to reflect the cohort profile of this group, as a lack of education qualifications was much more common for cohorts born in the UK prior to 1970.

Figure 5 shows the distribution of work-related poor mental health from waves 2–10 by occupational groups. There is a clear pattern of some occupations such as health, education, and social care–associated professionals having higher mean scores on the scale (ranging 1–5 with higher scores indicating poorer mental health), while other occupations such as skilled agricultural trades having lower levels of work-related poor mental health. In some occupations, an increase in poorer mental health can be observed in the last few years, although not all occupations had a similar increasing trajectory of poorer mental health up to 2018/2019.

The results of the three-level multilevel model of work-related poor mental health suggest that there was limited but significant clustering of poor mental health at the

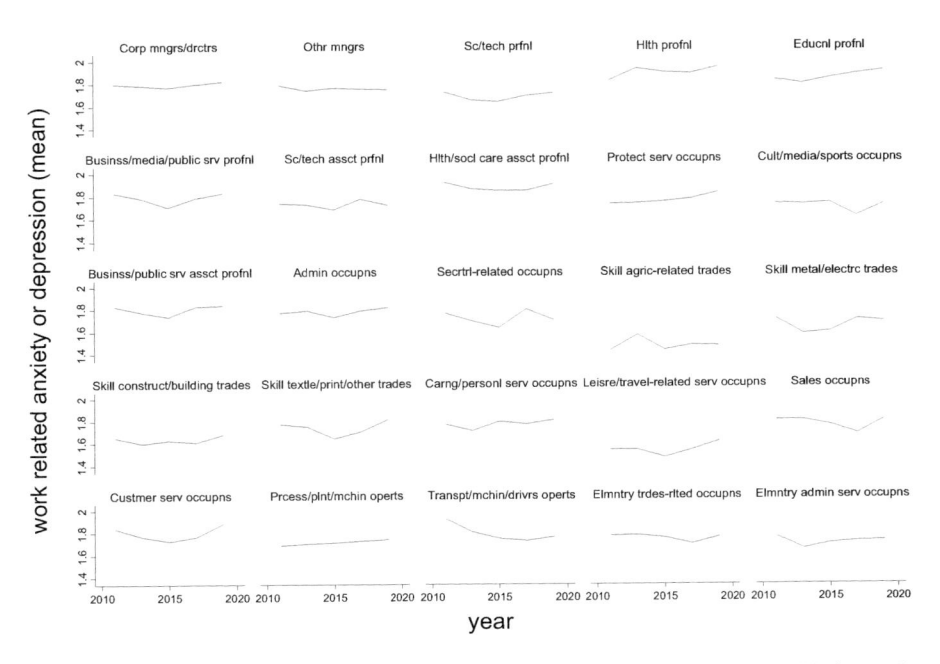

Fig. 5 Mean work-related anxiety or depression (range 1–5) by occupational groups: Understanding Society waves 2 (2010–11) to 10 (2018–19)

occupational level. One percent of the total variance in work-related mental health was attributable to the occupational group level, while 39% was attributable to the individual worker level. After controlling for wave, age, sex, and educational qualifications, the occupation level intraclass correlation reduced to 0.8% but remained significant, suggesting that some occupations still had higher levels of work-related poor mental health even after taking account period, age, sex, and educational effects. These occupations at higher risk of poor mental health are shown in Fig. 6, with education professionals, those working as health and social care associates and in customer service occupations, being particularly at risk of poorer work-related mental health (which ranged from 1–5), around 0.1 units higher than the average for UK workers.

There was strong evidence of a random slope for wave at the individual level which suggests that individual workers' trajectories in work-related poor mental health differed from the average worker across the time. However, there were no significant differences between occupations in relation to the trajectories over time (no random slopes for wave at the occupational level) and there was also no evidence for random slopes/coefficients at the occupational level for any of the other explanatory variables in the model. Random slopes at the occupational level would enable us to identify whether the trajectories in work-related poor mental health for specific occupations differ from the average trajectory. The absence of any random slopes at the occupational level suggests that the period (wave) effects observed in Fig. 7 were similar across all occupations. From 2012/2013 onward, there has been a steady increase in work-related poor mental health so that by 2018/2019, the average levels of work-related poor mental health for all workers was around 0.1 units higher, which was a statistically significant increase in poor mental health.

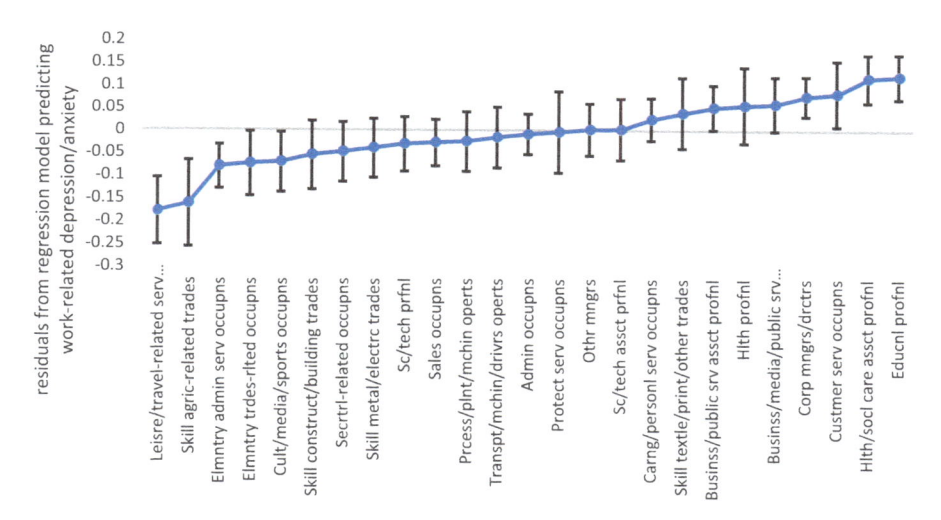

Fig. 6 Occupational-level residuals from three-level multilevel model (occasions within individuals within occupational groups) predicting work-related anxiety or depression: Understanding Society waves 2 (2010–2011) to 10 (2018–2019)

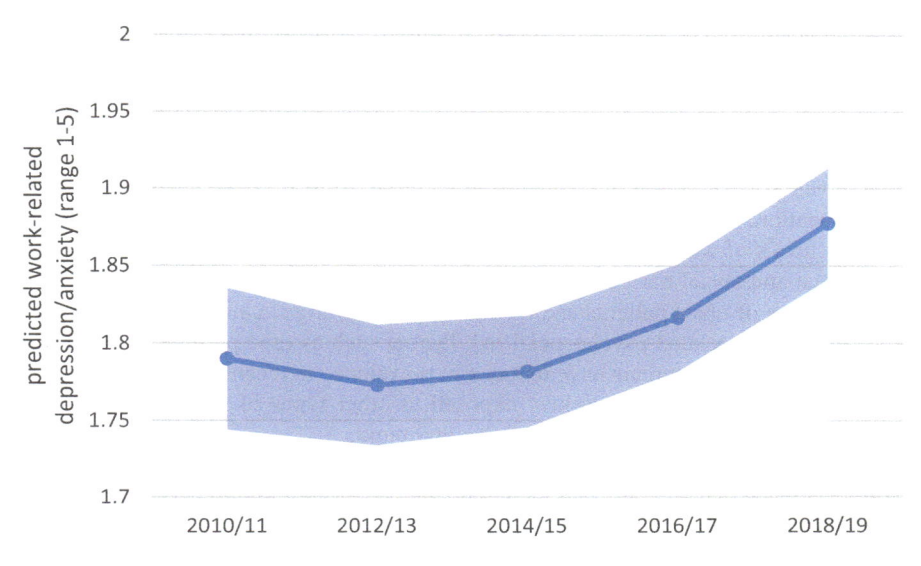

Fig. 7 Predicted work-related depression or anxiety (and 95% confidence intervals) from three-level multilevel model: Understanding Society waves 2 (2010–2011) to 10 (2018–2019)

The possibility of random coefficients for all the explanatory variables in the model at the occupational level was examined, but there were no significant differences between occupations for the overall pattern with age, sex, and education. An inverse U-shape pattern with age was observed, with the nadir of work-related poor mental health around age 40. Women more likely to report poorer mental health, which is a well-established gender difference pattern. As it is statistically impossible to distinguish between age, period, and cohort effects within the same statistical model, the models analyzed assumed that there were no cohort effects. However, the models controlled for educational qualifications which is a proxy for a cohort effect as cohorts born prior to the 1970s were less likely to have any formal educational qualifications. There were no significant differences between educational qualifications. This suggests that cohort differences in work-related mental health may be minimal compared to age and period effects.

Conclusion

There has been an increase in work-related poor mental health since 2010. This was a trend that was apparent in the UK and European contexts before 2020, but the worsening trend in work-related mental health has increased during the pandemic period. While age influenced work-related mental health, with the lowest levels of mental health observed around age 40, the effects of age were similar across occupations. The aging of the workforce did not explain the worsening trends in work-related poor mental health. Similarly, the worsening trend in work-related mental health since 2010 was observed across all occupations – there was no occupation specifically at risk of a worsening trend in recent years.

However, it was also clear that some occupations have remained top of the risk profile for work-related poor mental health and this has not changed in recent years. This has resulted in an accumulation of work-related poor mental health for workers that have remained in the same occupational group for the last 10 years. Workers in the education, health, and social care and customer service occupations had the highest levels of work-related poor mental health which is potentially related to the emotional and social nature of the work, with some workers at risk of dealing with angry clients or upset patients and emotionally disturbing situations. While it is true that some work-related psychosocial risk factors such as time pressure at work and violence and related threats have reduced in prevalence in recent years, there remain a considerable number of workers exposed to other types of risk factors such as dealing with difficult customers, patients, and pupils.

Taking into account life course influences on work-related mental health, we find some evidence that work-related mental health is clustered within occupations, with workers in some occupations consistently at high risk of accumulating poor mental health over their life course. Policies that target the psychosocial risk factors for poor mental health for workers in those occupations are needed to reduce the overall trend in worsening work-related mental health in the European context in the last 12 years.

Cross-References

▶ Gig Work and Health
▶ Methods in Modeling Life Course
▶ Pathways to Retirement and Health Effects
▶ Transformation of Modern Work, Rise of Atypical Employment, and Health

References

Arntz M, Gregory T, Zierahn U (2016) The risk of automation for jobs in OECD countries: a comparative analysis. OECD. https://doi.org/10.1787/5jlz9h56dvq7-en

Blanchflower DG (2021) Is happiness U-shaped everywhere? Age and subjective well-being in 145 countries. J Popul Econ 34(2):575–624. https://doi.org/10.1007/s00148-020-00797-z

Chandola T, Clarke P, Morris JN, Blane D (2006) Pathways between education and health: a causal modelling approach. J R Stat Soc A Stat Soc 169(2):337–359. https://doi.org/10.1111/j.1467-985X.2006.00411.x

Chandola T, Booker CL, Kumari M, Benzeval M (2019) Are flexible work arrangements associated with lower levels of chronic stress-related biomarkers? A study of 6025 employees in the UK household longitudinal study. Sociology 53(4):779–799. https://doi.org/10.1177/0038038519826014

Chandola T, Kumari M, Booker CL, Benzeval M (2020) The mental health impact of COVID-19 and lockdown-related stressors among adults in the UK. Psychol Med:1–10. https://doi.org/10.1017/S0033291720005048

Cotter DA, Hermsen JM, Ovadia S, Vanneman R (2001) The glass ceiling effect. Soc Forces 80(2): 655–681. https://doi.org/10.1353/sof.2001.0091

Eurofound (2017) Working conditions of workers of different ages: European Working Conditions Survey 2015. Publications Office of the European Union. https://www.eurofound.europa.eu/publications/report/2017/working-conditions-of-workers-of-different-ages

Eurofound (2018) Automation, digitisation and platforms: implications for work and employment. Publications Office of the European Union

Eurofound (2020) Working conditions in sectors. Publications Office of the European Union

Eurostat (2021) Self-reported work-related health problems and risk factors – key statistics. https://ec.europa.eu/eurostat/statistics-explained/index.php?title=Self-reported_work-related_health_problems_and_risk_factors_-_key_statistics

Frey CB, Osborne MA (2017) The future of employment: how susceptible are jobs to computerisation? Technol Forecast Soc Chang 114:254–280. https://doi.org/10.1016/j.techfore.2016.08.019

Frone MR, Blais A-R (2020) Organizational downsizing, work conditions, and employee outcomes: identifying targets for workplace intervention among survivors. Int J Environ Res Public Health 17(3):719. https://doi.org/10.3390/ijerph17030719

Götz S, Hoven H, Müller A, Dragano N, Wahrendorf M (2018) Age differences in the association between stressful work and sickness absence among full-time employed workers: evidence from the German socio-economic panel. Int Arch Occup Environ Health 91(4):479–496. https://doi.org/10.1007/s00420-018-1298-3

Grant J (2013) Getting on...with life. Baby boomers, mental health and ageing well: a review. Mental Health Foundation. https://www.mentalhealth.org.uk/publications/getting-life-baby-boomers-mental-health-and-ageing-well-full-report

Gregg P, Wadsworth J (2002) Job tenure in Britain, 1975–2000. Is a job for life or just for Christmas? SSRN scholarly paper ID 313704. Social Science Research Network. https://papers.ssrn.com/abstract=313704

Health & Safety Executive (2021) Work-related stress, anxiety or depression statistics in Great Britain, 2021. Health and Safety Executive. https://www.hse.gov.uk/statistics/causdis/stress.pdf

Huwart J-Y, Verdier L (2013) Economic globalisation: origins and consequences. OECD. https://doi.org/10.1787/9789264111905-en

Schwab K (2016) The fourth industrial revolution (first U.S. edn). Crown Business

Theorell T (ed) (2020) Handbook of socioeconomic determinants of occupational health: from macro-level to micro-level evidence. Springer International Publishing. https://doi.org/10.1007/978-3-030-31438-5

University of Essex, I. F. S. (2021) United Kingdom Household Longitudinal Study Understanding Society: Waves 1-, 2008-Understanding Society: Waves 1–11, 2009–2020 and Harmonised BHPS: Waves 1–18, 1991–2009 (14th edn) [Data set]. UK Data Service. https://doi.org/10.5255/UKDA-SN-6614-15

Wahrendorf M, Chandola T (2016) A life course perspective on work stress and health. In: Work stress and health in a globalized economy. Springer, Cham, pp 43–66

Warr P (1990) The measurement of well-being and other aspects of mental health. J Occup Psychol 63(3):193–210. https://doi.org/10.1111/j.2044-8325.1990.tb00521.x

Part V

Occupational Trajectories and Midlife Health:
Exposure to Irregular and Discontinued Hazards at Work

Adverse Employment Histories: Conceptual Considerations and Selected Health Effects

18

Morten Wahrendorf and Johannes Siegrist

Contents

Introduction	304
Leading Concepts of Psychosocial Work Environments with Relevance to Health	305
Dimensions of Nonstandard Employment with Relevance to Health	307
Selected Health Effects	312
Concluding Remarks	314
Cross-References	315
References	315

Abstract

The world of work and employment underwent profound changes during the past 50 years, with the growth of new forms of employment that differ to traditional standard employment as one of its key features. Research on associations of psychosocial work environments with health produced new knowledge, but its theoretical models were largely focused on standard employment, specifically working conditions of a long-lasting full-time employment that is assumed to define a person's working life. In this chapter, we aim at transferring key stress-theoretical notions of prevailing stress models to entire employment histories by describing six dimensions of emerging trends with relevance to health, and how these can be used to describe entire employment histories. The recurrent experience of threat induced by conditions of unpredictability, instability, and discontinuity of employment histories is a common element underlying these dimensions. Along these lines, we identify three types of adverse employment histories, labeled as "precarious," "discontinuous," and "chronically disadvantaged." In a subsequent

M. Wahrendorf (✉) · J. Siegrist
Centre for Health and Society, Institute of Medical Sociology, Medical Faculty, Heinrich Heine University of Düsseldorf, Düsseldorf, Germany
e-mail: wahrendorf@uni-duesseldorf.de

© Springer Nature Switzerland AG 2023
M. Wahrendorf et al. (eds.), *Handbook of Life Course Occupational Health*, Handbook Series in Occupational Health Sciences, https://doi.org/10.1007/978-3-031-30492-7_28

section, selected empirical findings are displayed, demonstrating associations of adverse employment histories with indicators of health functioning and with allostatic load. The chapter ends with some concluding remarks.

Keywords

Nonstandard employment · Employment histories · Psychosocial work environment · Stress-theoretical models · Life course perspective

Introduction

The past 50 years transformed working lives in the developed countries in profound ways. A shift from the previously dominating industrial workforce to a service-based workforce was already under way when two revolutionary changes occurred. The expansion of computer-based technologies with its accelerated options of information transfer and communication is one such revolutionary change. Within a short time, microelectronic innovations and automation shaped new ways of producing and distributing goods, not least by promoting digitalization and artificial intelligence. In consequence, large parts of the labor market were restructured. This change happened in conjunction with a second far-reaching transformation, the process of economic globalization. This process was initiated by measures of transnational trade liberalization and a deregulation of financial markets, giving rise to a globally operating finance industry and the growth of transnational corporations. Supported by international organizations, in particular the World Bank and the International Monetary Fund, this development enabled the expansion of markets to emerging economies in middle-income countries, resulting in a growing transnational exchange of capital, trade, and labor force. As a consequence, huge numbers of new jobs were created in rapidly developing countries, but, at the same time, labor markets in high-income countries were also affected. Two intimately connected aspects of this development were rather negative and need to be emphasized. First, by shifting jobs at large scale to countries with low labor costs, employment opportunities in developed countries were reduced. At the same time, growing competition increased the economic pressure toward labor cost containment. Employers responded to this pressure by restructuring businesses through downsizing and outsourcing. Overall, work pressure and job insecurity increased in large parts of the work force in Western countries (Gallie 2013; ILO 2017). As a second outcome, related to this transformation, employment relationships were subjected to a far-reaching change. Widely established procedures of offering skilled workers a permanent, stable job with a high level of social protection were gradually replaced by fixed-term contracts, temporary employment, or part-time jobs, giving rise to the growth of nonstandard employment (see ▶ Chap. 3, "Transformation of Modern Work, Rise of Atypical Employment, and Health" of Eichhorst & Kalleberg in this volume). The strategy of flexible contracting was also promoted in response to new technologies and market demands. In the long run, it undermined the power of labor unions in protecting labor rights, and it restricted opportunities of implementing or extending labor and social policies at the national level.

In this context, occupational health research needs to respond to these new developments of work and employment. How were its concepts of analysis and its research approaches affected by these transformations? Importantly, this question mainly concerns those disciplines within occupational health research that address modern working conditions of production, service delivery, and communication, where psycho-mental and socio-emotional challenges are more prevalent than physical hazards, and where mobile, flexible, and insecure jobs affect large parts of the workforce. Sociology, psychology, economic, and business research as well as occupational epidemiology are the main disciplines confronted with this question. In this chapter, we focus our analysis on the psychosocial work environment. We describe theoretical models that laid ground to new knowledge on adverse health effects of stressful psychosocial working conditions. As these models were developed and widely applied during the last quarter of the twentieth century, we ask how they can serve to unravel work-related health risks in the twenty-first century and assess "exposure careers." To this end, six dimensions of nonstandard employment with relevance to health are described, and we propose an integration of key stress-theoretical notions related to these models into the analysis of adverse employment histories. Extending research along these lines also corresponds to a life course perspective (Elder et al. 2003; Kuh and Ben-Shlomo 2004), specifically the idea of considering entire employment histories (instead of exposure at a single time point) in conjunction with health (Wahrendorf and Chandola 2016). In a subsequent section, selected empirical findings are displayed, demonstrating associations of adverse employment histories with elevated risks of stress-related disorders. The chapter ends with some concluding remarks.

Leading Concepts of Psychosocial Work Environments with Relevance to Health

Psychological and sociological research devoted to occupational health generated a range of theoretical constructs to analyze associations of working and employment conditions with health (for an overview, see, e.g.: Cooper and Quick 2017; Cunningham and Black 2021; Theorell 2020). Despite their broad spectrum of approaches, few concepts only were examined with sufficient empirical evidence derived from large-scale observational studies that are based on population-based longitudinal cohort studies. Data analysis of such studies is often considered a gold standard because working conditions are assessed at study onset, and future health outcomes (incident cases) are analyzed as a function of these exposures. Four theoretical models fulfill these criteria rather well. They are briefly described here, and they instruct our further analysis. The models are labeled "demand-control," "effort-reward imbalance," "organizational justice," and "job demands- resources." According to the demand-control model, developed by Robert A. Karasek (Karasek 1979), stressful work results from exposure to job tasks that put high mental demands (e.g., work pressure) on workers while limiting their control of how the task is performed. Piecework is an example of such high-demand/low-control jobs that are frequent among less-skilled workers. If high demands are combined with high control people can develop their skills and experience health-protective effects of autonomy and mastery. This two-dimensional model was extended to include a third dimension, the presence or absence of social support at work (Johnson and Hall 1988). A complementary model, effort-reward imbalance, is concerned with stressful aspects of employment arrangements that are characterized by a discrepancy between high efforts spent at work and low rewards received in return, where rewards include pay, job promotion and security, and esteem (Siegrist 1996). Such arrangements, violating the principle of reciprocity in social change, are frequent in highly competitive jobs and among those with no alternative choice in the labor market. A distinct way of coping with demands, overcommitment, contributes to a sustained experience of imbalance. With the concept of organizational justice, three aspects of fairness in organizational behavior are distinguished. Distributive justice addresses an equitable distribution of resources and rewards between members of a group, while procedural justice is concerned with fair decision-making processes. Relational justice focuses on respectful interpersonal relationships in organizations (Greenberg and Cohen 1982). This established social psychological concept was subsequently applied to occupational health research (Elovainio et al. 2002). The job demands-resources model represents an integrative approach that classifies relevant job characteristics as either demands or resources, assuming that high demands and low resources reduce workers' health. Conversely, high demands and high resources promote work engagement and well-being (Bakker and Demerouti 2017). In this concept, the notion of job-related resources, such as feedback, job control, and social support, was extended to include person-related resources (e.g., resilience and self-efficacy).

Despite some conceptual overlap, these four models represent distinct theoretical approaches toward explaining workers' health. They were all examined in multiple investigations of occupational groups, and in particular in prospective cohort studies. While the job demands-resources concept was mainly analyzed with regard to burnout (Lesener et al. 2019), the other concepts contributed to the explanation of a range of chronic physical and mental disorders, such as depression, cardiovascular disease, metabolic disorders, or musculoskeletal pain. Summary reports of findings are given in three chapters of a recently published handbook of occupational health sciences (Theorell 2020) and in a meta-review of systematic literature reviews and meta-analyses (Niedhammer et al. 2021). The four models share a common feature: They were conceptualized in a time when the standard employment contract still represented the leading paradigm. As described by Eichhorst and Kalleberg in this book, this type of employment is characterized by work performed on a preset schedule, often full-time, within an employer's organization and under the employer's control. It offers job continuity and job promotion prospects, and it protects employees from occupational risks through labor laws and preventive measures. In addition, it provides fundamental social protection in terms of social insurance and pensions. Accordingly, all four models describe job conditions under the assumption of continued performance along a stable employment history. They consider forced job change and job loss as hazards deviating from expected norms and established regulations. In addition, the work settings are conceptualized as steady arrangements localized in organizations where a hierarchically structured workforce performs tasks under control, supported by a distinct organizational culture of leadership and collaboration. Labor laws, trade union impact, and regular bargaining between employers and employees' organizations often contribute to stability and progress.

In fact, in today's world of work and employment, this standard model still represents a significant part of the labor force in economically developed countries. Employees in public sectors, civil servants, and many professional groups in the service and communication sectors as well as in industrial production and distribution benefit from permanent work contracts and extended social security measures. Some longitudinal studies using repeated assessments (either via job exposures matrices or based on self-reports of the scales measuring the theoretical models) provide indirect support of rather stable job conditions (Leineweber et al. 2020; Rigó et al. 2021). In this latter study in Sweden (Leineweber et al. 2020), job stress scores remained unchanged over an observation period of six years in almost 90% of the sample. Yet, given the far-reaching changes of employment policies and working conditions mentioned above, the previously dominant role of standard employment is continuously weakened as the number of fixed-term contracts is rapidly growing, and as new forms of self-employment and independent contracting emerge. The next section discusses key dimensions of nonstandard employment with relevance to health. As mentioned, we propose an integration of key stress-theoretical notions related to these models into the analysis of adverse employment histories.

Dimensions of Nonstandard Employment with Relevance to Health

The following six dimensions of differences between standard and nonstandard employment can be distinguished that may be of importance to (or "critical" for) the health and well-being of working people.

First, the work contract matters. Full-time employment is less frequent in nonstandard conditions than part-time work. An increase in part-time work has been observed in recent time, but only part of this increase is attributable to nonstandard work. New data from OECD indicate that 17% of OECD countries' workforce are part-time employed (see ▶ Chap. 3, "Transformation of Modern Work, Rise of Atypical Employment, and Health" in this volume). However, less than 20% of this share are defined as involuntary part-time. While freely chosen part-time work can be beneficial for health, constraints to involuntary part-time employment, as often experienced in nonstandard work, increase the risk of reduced health (Virtanen et al. 2013). Fixed-term or temporary contracts are highly prevalent in nonstandard employment. They are associated with the recurrent experience of job insecurity, a relevant dimension of occupational health (see below). As a new type of employer-employee relationship, temporary agency work evolved, where workers are employed by an agency, but are performing their work for a distinct firm under contract. Furthermore, self-employment has increased in recent years, but this category contains a diversity of job constellations. A relevant fraction of self-employed people is engaged in atypical work, often in terms of the so-called "gig" economy. Here, freelancers and independent contractors offer their work on demand, mostly in connection with online platforms and modern communication devices, but health effects of this precarious type of employment were not yet analyzed to a sufficient extent (Bérastégui 2021).

Continuity/discontinuity of occupational career is a second dimension with relevance to the health of people involved in atypical employment. Stable, continued full-time employment dominated the work contracts of a skilled labor force in a majority of high-income countries during a period of economic growth following World War II. This trend is continuously weakened at the expense of expanding flexible and unstable employment (Tomlinson et al. 2018).

Type and amount of earnings represent a third dimension. Working in atypical employment is associated with elevated risks of irregular pay, earning instability, low level of pay, and in-work poverty, sometimes forcing people to have a second job. Importantly, besides salary as the standard form of earnings, hourly paid work is becoming more frequent in discontinued work arrangements. A nationally representative survey of employed adults in the USA indicates that over the years 2002–2014 almost 40% were paid on an hourly basis, compared with 60% being paid by regular salary. Hourly paid workers had lower incomes than salaried participants; they experienced higher levels of job insecurity, and they were less often able to influence their work schedules and number of work hours (Lambert et al. 2019). In addition, hourly paid workers indicated significantly greater financial insecurity and household income volatility than salaried works. This insecurity was increased if employees had little control over work schedules and number of work hours (Lambert et al. 2019). The impact of type and amount of earnings on health becomes manifest in material and psychosocial terms. Low-income and in-work poverty reduces healthy living standards, including options of healthy nutrition and time of recovery. Earning instability and unfair pay also elicit worries, anxieties, and frustrated reward expectancies, thus intensifying stressful experience (Falk et al. 2018).

Fourth, work scheduling practices, work time, and workplace are considered a relevant dimension for health in nonstandard employment. This dimension includes long working hours, irregular work hours, forms of shift work, and lack of employee control of work schedule. In several job categories, lack of schedule control goes along with lack of control of workplace assignment, specifically in mobile jobs and in unskilled work. With regard to these dimensions, work contracts in nonstandard employment are usually less specified than contracts in standard employment, due to an increased need for flexibility and recurrent adaptive change in the former type of employment. Fluctuating schedules, low predictability of work hours and timing, and short notice of readiness for action occur frequently within these new forms of employment, and specifically among hourly paid employees and those working in precarious jobs. So far, research on associations of work time and health has been mainly concerned with physiologic consequences of disturbed biorhythms in shift work (Costa 2020), and with excessive activation of stress-axes of the organism due to long working hours (WHO/ILO 2021). A more nuanced analysis of work time experience in atypical employment is an important task of future research in this field.

As a fifth core dimension the job content is of outstanding significance for health. On the one hand, this concerns hazards at work due to exposure to noxious stimuli, physically strenuous work, and elevated risks of accidents. On the other hand, stressful psychosocial work environments, as identified by the theoretical models described above, increase the burden of work-related ill-health and disease. Both kinds of exposures are more prevalent among large parts of people working in nonstandard employment compared to those working in regular jobs. Apart from high-status knowledge workers and other privileged groups, this holds true for atypically employed workers in low-skilled jobs, in hourly paid work, or in fixed-term employment, and for self-employed people engaged in precarious work. Socio-epidemiological investigations consistently documented high levels of health-adverse material and psychosocial working conditions among employees with lower levels of occupational skills, such as manual, blue-collar, or other elementary occupations as well as low-skilled clerical jobs. Health-adverse material work environments include exposure to chemical substances with carcinogenic or mutagenic effects, physical exposures including noise, heat, cold, or radiation, and ergonomic factors, in particular postural constraints, repetitive movements, heavy lifting, or vibrations (Montano 2020). For the two often examined work stress models, job strain and effort-reward imbalance, elevated mean levels of stressful work were documented for low-skilled manual and clerical workers, compared with those with higher skill level. For instance, in a large multiwave cross-country survey of employed people recruited from 29 European countries, social inequality of stressful work according to occupation skill level was observed, with significantly elevated levels among low-skilled workers, persisting over the observation period of ten years (Rigó et al. 2021). Although detailed investigations of differential exposure to material and psychosocial adversity at work among nonstandard employed people are still lacking, available evidence on the social gradient of quality of work supports the notion that atypical employment increases the risk of work-related burden of disease.

Finally, a sixth dimension of nonstandard employment with direct or indirect effects on health relates to social protection at work. Here, employment contracts contain less often measures of health insurance, sick leave compensation, paid holidays, and other forms of welfare benefits. Safety regulations may be less strict, and access to occupational health services may be more restricted among those in irregular or atypical employment. Again, the full set of social protection measures provided by national labor market and social policies in high-income countries during the post-World War II period of economic development was targeted to a full-time, permanently employed, well-trained workforce. Features such as temporary employment, long periods of worklessness, or new risky forms of self-employment were not considered relevant in policy terms. With the expansion of these latter features in current labor markets, an application of labor laws and welfare benefits to these groups of workers is now under development in several countries (see ▶ Chap. 3, "Transformation of Modern Work, Rise of Atypical Employment, and Health" in this volume). Still, continued insecurity about the future of employment and tangible earnings, and exclusion from the full set of social protection measures are key elements of the material and psychosocial situation of large parts of workers in nonstandard employment.

Having described the six dimensions of atypical employment with relevance to health, two general conclusions can be drawn. A first conclusion concerns the extension of occupational conditions that can induce stressful experience among those workers. Compared with people in standard employment, atypically employed workers are more often exposed to a cumulative load of psychosocial adversity. In consequence, stronger coping resources are required to buffer this adversity. Yet, it is unlikely that a majority of those employed in nonstandard work have access to strong material and psychosocial coping resources, given their subordinate occupational positions, their dependency on managers and decision-makers, their limited skill level, and their restricted access to means of organizational influence and power. Rather, in the long run, exposure to a cumulative load of psychosocial adversity may trigger exhaustion and adaptive breakdown among nonstandard workers, thus precipitating the onset of a stress-related disorder. In view of this potential risk, assessing the cumulative load of psychosocial adversity is considered an important measure to define most vulnerable groups of nonstandard employees. Based on this assessment, preventive activities can be developed, targeting these highly susceptible groups. For instance, a summary index composed by indicators of the six dimensions mentioned can be constructed, quantifying the cumulative load. The Employment Precariousness Scale (EPRES) represents a similar approach, assessing the stability of employment, earning opportunities, work schedule and work time control, social protections coverage, as well as training opportunities and options of collective voice (Julià et al. 2017). In a related area of research, dimensions of precarious employment are being studied with respect to health outcomes, but a standardized measurement approach has not yet been established (Bodin et al. 2020; Kreshpaj et al. 2020), as well as its measurement is not applied to entire employment histories and their characteristics, but assesses conditions at one time point.

A second conclusion relates to the need of identifying key stress-theoretical notions underling the six critical dimensions of nonstandard employment. Although such a theoretical analysis has not yet been elaborated to our knowledge, it likely includes the recurrent experience of threat induced by work- and employment-related conditions of unpredictability, instability, and discontinuity. Fear of job loss, forced job change, or career interruption, worries related to earning fluctuations and insecurity, anticipation of in-work poverty, and feelings of helplessness in view of limited social protection in case of a health shock or a forced early exit from paid work are examples of such threats. Furthermore, the satisfaction of essential psychological needs related to the quality of work and employment is threatened in unpredictable and unstable job arrangements. This is best explained in the context of a proposed typology of adverse employment histories aiming to disentangle potential negative effects on health (Wahrendorf et al. 2019). By describing histories and their characteristics over an extended time fame, this approach also aims to grasp the dynamic aspects of modern employment relations described above, specifically the fact that working life is not restricted to one single job. Therefore, working conditions are analyzed in a life course perspective over an extended time frame, without isolating single aspects from larger histories (Aisenbrey and Fasang 2010; Wahrendorf and Chandola 2016; Bernardi et al. 2019). With the increasing availability of retrospectively assessed employment histories as part of life history interviews in current cohort studies (see below for more details), data on exposure duration of each job, number of job changes, interruptions and their causes, and occupational upward or downward mobility over an extended time frame can be assessed and linked to health data. Specifically, in accordance to the conditions described above, the following three types of adverse careers can be studied:

1. Precarious careers (e.g., temporary contracts and repeated job changes)
2. Discontinuous careers (e.g., involuntary interruptions and repeated unemployment)
3. Careers with cumulative disadvantage (e.g., being "locked" in a low-skilled job and lack of job promotion)

In different ways, these types of adverse careers impair or prevent the fulfillment of major psychological needs related to work. A secure sense of social identity is one such need. It is nurtured by the recurrent experience of having a stable job, acting in a core social role, and being member of a socially valued organization offering regular workplaces. Working in a precarious or temporary job, being exposed to an unstable and discontinuous occupational career, and being connected with the organization by weak ties and by lack of social support undermine this sense of social identity. With this fragmentation of the work role, a whole set of expectations and obligations in everyday life is being disturbed or disrupted, evoking feelings of alienation, marginalization, and hopelessness.

As a regular job offers opportunities of skill development, learning, and successful agency, it contributes to the satisfaction of a further psychological need, the need of experiencing autonomy, control, and self-efficacy. Meeting the demands at work by exerting some degree of decision authority and by matching extrinsic obligations with the worker's intrinsic capabilities and preferences are important prerequisites of continued well-being at work. These opportunities are substantially reduced in careers defined by precariousness, discontinuity, and cumulative disadvantage. In many such jobs, tasks are predefined, limiting the working person's influence. With changing demands over time, options of skill development and personal growth are restricted. Lack of control over work schedule and work hours, and a heavy burden of workload, as commonly experienced in disadvantaged jobs, weaken the worker's sense of self-efficacy. As an essential element of the work contract, efforts spent at work by employees are reciprocated by rewards provided by the employer. Fair pay and options of job security and career advancement are explicitly or implicitly included in this type of formal contract that evolved during a period of economic growth and expanding standard employment in high-income countries. This contract contributes to the satisfaction of two additional psychological needs of working persons, a sense of trust and a sense of recognition or appreciation. Experiencing trust is essential in all social relationships involving mutual engagement and obligations. It protects individuals from deception and fraud, and it reinforces the motivation of continued action, as appropriate rewards are anticipated. With the promise of recompense, the work contract is rooted in the evolutionary principle of reciprocity of social exchange. It asserts the employee's rights of being treated in a fair way and recognized for his or her contributions. With the growth of nonstandard employment, work contracts underwent several significant changes. Importantly, permanent job offers were mainly replaced by fixed-term contracts, and job requirements and earnings were less specifically defined, leaving room for flexible arrangements. In temporary agency work, the contractual relationship was dissolved in a tripartite frame, with the risk of offering lack of transparency and arbitrariness, and precarious forms of self-employment were deprived from protective contractual regulations. The consequences of these changes were particularly severe for vulnerable occupational groups as those defined by adverse employment careers. Being constrained to a precarious, discontinued, or chronically disadvantaged career results in a substantial lack of experiencing trust and recognition, of being fairly paid and appreciated, and of experiencing one's work as a secure place and a challenge for personal growth and development.

To summarize, according to a second conclusion drawn from the description of six dimensions of atypical employment with relevance to health, we proposed an integration of some key stress-theoretical notions underling these dimensions into the analysis of employment histories, focusing on the recurrent experience of threat induced by work- and employment-related conditions of unpredictability, instability, and discontinuity over an extended time frame. These stress-theoretical notions were explicated by referring to core psychological needs related to work and employment, such as the need for social identity, the need for autonomy, control and self-efficacy, and the need for trust and appreciation. As the satisfaction of these needs is severely restricted in vulnerable occupational groups, as those defined by precarious, discontinued, and chronically disadvantaged careers, strong negative health effects due to continued stressful experience and related psychobiological stress responses (or a state of "allostatic load" (McEwen 2012; Vineis et al. 2017; Castagné et al. 2018) are expected to result. The next section presents selected results that support these assumptions in relation to several health indicators. They are based on large occupational cohort studies that provide data on adverse employment histories and on health conditions.

Selected Health Effects

To address the above assumption, detailed information on employment histories is needed that can be linked with a set of health indicators in later life. Prospective cohort studies with long observation periods are one data source of interest. But they also have clear limitations because some of the cohorts (especially birth cohort studies) have yet to reach older ages, or because the richness of prospective data (especially the information on employment histories) depends on the number of waves of data collection and the observation period covered. Therefore, established on important methodological developments in the field (for details see: Smith et al. 2021), various ongoing cohort studies currently supplement their data collection with retrospective interviews. These interviews additionally collect life history data, with detailed information on respondent's lives before entering the study. This also covers entire employment histories, including information on number of jobs, the time a person spent in a job, interruptions and theirs causes, details of jobs (e.g., part- or full-time position), occupational upward or downward mobility, as well as details of periods when the respondent was not in paid work. Synthesizing this information provides remarkable opportunities for life courses research allowing an in-depth study of employment sequences (see ▶ Chap. 5, "Sequence Analysis and Its Potential for Occupational Health Studies," of Studer and Cianferoni in this volume), and to link information on previous employment histories with health. The French CONSTANCES project offers an excellent opportunity to do so with retrospective information on employment histories for nearly 200.000 study participants (Goldberg et al. 2017). Other examples are two significant studies of aging in Europe: the English Longitudinal Study of Aging (ELSA) (Steptoe et al. 2013), and the Survey of Health, Aging, and Retirement in Europe (SHARE) (Börsch-Supan et al. 2013). In the following, we focus on selected findings from CONSTANCES.

CONSTANCES is a population-based cohort study, with baseline data between 2012 and 2020 among more than 217,000 participants age 17–67 years. In addition to self-administered questionnaires and medical examination at baseline (including biomarkers and blood samples), the study also collects retrospective information on previous employment histories at baseline. This allows to ascertain specific career characteristics related to precarious, discontinued, and chronically disadvantaged careers (all referring to employment histories between age 25 and 45), and to link these characteristics with health for participants aged 45 or older. As an example, Fig. 1 shows levels of increased depressive symptoms by career characteristics.

For both men and women, we see that the two indicators of precarious careers (i.e., "number of jobs with temporary contract" or "repeated job changes") are clearly linked with increased levels of depressive symptoms. The same holds true for discontinuous careers ("number unemployment periods" and "years out of work") and for careers with cumulative disadvantage (especially continued disadvantaged occupational position, as measured by the mode position between 25 and 45). These findings were confirmed in more refined analyses of the CONSANCES data (for details see: Wahrendorf et al. 2019), where respondents who had a health-related career interruption or retired prior age 45 were excluded from the analyses (plus adjustment for potential confounders), as well as similar associations were found for indicators of physical and cognitive functioning. Another study (combining data of SHARE and ELSA) found similar associations between career characteristics and health functioning across 13 European countries (Wahrendorf et al.

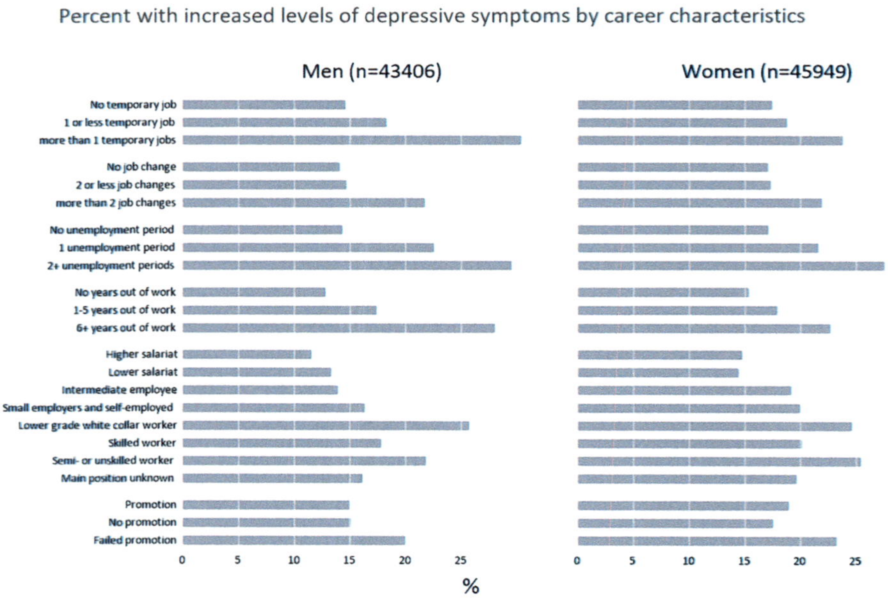

Percent with increased levels of depressive symptoms by career characteristics

Fig. 1 Association between career characteristics and depressive symptoms for men and women. Note: The measure of increased levels of depressive symptoms is based on the Center for Epidemiologic Studies Depression Scale (CES-D), using sex-specific thresholds for elevated depressive symptoms

2021), and additionally suggested consistent associations across countries, with no variations by national labor market policies (i.e., passive or active labor market polices). These two studies provide evidence for a potential psychobiological stress response linking adverse histories work with health – an assumption that was substantiated in another study based on CONSTANCES data (Wahrendorf et al. 2022). Specifically, the study documented that adverse employment histories (especially discontinuous careers and careers with cumulative disadvantage) are related to higher levels of allostatic load (measured with a composite score based on ten biomarkers), and thereby highlighted physiological responses as a mechanism through which chronic stress during working life is linked to poor health.

Concluding Remarks

This chapter demonstrates the necessity to supplement existing occupational health research by shifting the analytical perspective from stable to dynamic work arrangements, considering entire employment trajectories and their properties over an extended time period in a life course perspective. Importantly, the chapter hereby also underlines that this life course perspective needs to be rooted in a conceptual frame that identifies dimensions or aspects of working lives with significance for individual health and well-being. On that basis, the chapter provided some empirical examples of how three types of adverse employment histories – labeled as "precarious," "discontinuous," and "chronically disadvantaged" – are related to indicators of health functioning and allostatic load.

Cross-References

▶ A Life Course Perspective on Work and Mental Health: The Working Lives of Young Adults
▶ Sequence Analysis and Its Potential for Occupational Health Studies
▶ Transformation of Modern Work, Rise of Atypical Employment, and Health

References

Aisenbrey S, Fasang AE (2010) New life for old ideas: the 'Second Wave' of sequence analysis bringing the 'Course' back into the life course. Sociol Methods Res 38(4):652–654. https://doi.org/10.1177/0049124110373134

Bakker AB, Demerouti E (2017) Job demands–resources theory: taking stock and looking forward. J Occup Health Psychol 22(3):273

Bérastégui P (2021) Exposure to psychosocial risk factors in the gig economy: a systematic review. ETUI Research Paper-Report

Bernardi L, Huinink J, Settersten RA Jr (2019) The life course cube: a tool for studying lives. Adv Life Course Res 41:100258

Bodin T, Çağlayan Ç, Garde AH, Gnesi M, Jonsson J, Kiran S et al (2020) Precarious employment in occupational health – an OMEGA-NET working group position paper. Scand J Work Environ Health 46(3):321–329

Börsch-Supan A, Brandt M, Hunkler C, Kneip T, Korbmacher J, Malter F et al (2013) Data resource profile: the survey of health, ageing and retirement in Europe (SHARE). Int J Epidemiol 42(4):992–1001. https://doi.org/10.1093/ije/dyt088

Castagné R, Garès V, Karimi M, Chadeau-Hyam M, Vineis P, Delpierre C et al (2018) Allostatic load and subsequent all-cause mortality: which biological markers drive the relationship? Findings from a UK birth cohort. Eur J Epidemiol 33:441–458. https://doi.org/10.1007/s10654-018-0364-1

Cooper C, Quick JC (2017) The handbook of stress and health: a guide to research and practice. John Wiley & Sons, Chichester

Costa G (2020) Shift work and occupational hazards. In: Theorell T (ed) Handbook of socioeconomic determinants of occupational health: from macro-level to micro-level evidence. Springer International Publishing, Cham, pp 1–18

Cunningham CJ, Black KJ (2021) Essentials of occupational Health Psychology. Routledge, New York

Elder GH, Johnson MK, Crosnoe R (2003) The emergence and development of life course theory. In: Mortimer JT, Shanahan MJ (eds) Handbook of the life course. Kluwer Academic, New York, pp 3–19

Elovainio M, Kivimäki M, Vahtera J (2002) Organizational justice: evidence of a new psychosocial predictor of health. Am J Public Health 92(1):105–108

Falk A, Kosse F, Menrath I, Verde PE, Siegrist J (2018) Unfair pay and health. Manag Sci 64(4):1477–1488

Gallie D (2013) Economic crisis, quality of work and social integration: the European experience: topline results from rounds 2 and 5 of the European social survey (ESS topline results series – 3). Oxford University Press, Oxford

Goldberg M, Carton M, Descatha A, Leclerc A, Roquelaure Y, Santin G et al (2017) CONSTANCES: a general prospective population-based cohort for occupational and environmental epidemiology: cohort profile. Occup Environ Med 74(1):66–71. https://doi.org/10.1136/oemed-2016-103678

Greenberg J, Cohen RL (1982) Why justice? Normative and instrumental interpretations. In: Greenberg J & Cohen RL (eds) Equity and justice in social behavior. Academic Press, London, pp 437–469

ILO (2017) World employment and social outlook – trends 2017. International Labour Organization

Johnson JV, Hall EM (1988) Job strain, work place social support, and cardiovascular disease: a cross-sectional study of random sample of the Swedish Working Population. Am J Public Health 78(10):1336–1342

Julià M, Vanroelen C, Bosmans K, Van Aerden K, Benach J (2017) Precarious employment and quality of employment in relation to health and well-being in Europe. Int J Health Serv 47(3): 389–409

Karasek RA (1979) Job demands, job decision latitude, and mental strain – implications for job redesign. Adm Sci Q 24(2):285–308

Kreshpaj B, Orellana C, Burström B, Davis L, Hemmingsson T, Johansson G et al (2020) What is precarious employment? A systematic review of definitions and operationalizations from quantitative and qualitative studies. Scand J Work Environ Health 46(3):235–247

Kuh D, Ben-Shlomo Y (2004) A life course approach to chronic disease epidemiology, vol 2. Oxford University Press

Lambert SJ, Henly JR, Kim J (2019) Precarious work schedules as a source of economic insecurity and institutional distrust. RSF: The Russell Sage Foundation J Soc Sci 5(4):218–257

Leineweber C, Eib C, Bernhard-Oettel C, Nyberg A (2020) Trajectories of effort-reward imbalance in Swedish workers: differences in demographic and work-related factors and associations with health. Work Stress 34(3):238–258

Lesener T, Gusy B, Wolter C (2019) The job demands-resources model: a meta-analytic review of longitudinal studies. Work Stress 33(1):76–103

McEwen BS (2012) Brain on stress: how the social environment gets under the skin. Proc Natl Acad Sci 109(supplement 2):17180–17185. https://doi.org/10.1073/pnas.1121254109

Montano D (2020) Social distribution of occupational hazards. From Macro-level to Micro-level Evidence, Handbook of Socioeconomic Determinants of Occupational Health, pp 169–189

Niedhammer I, Bertrais S, Witt K (2021) Psychosocial work exposures and health outcomes: a meta-review of 72 literature reviews with meta-analysis. Scand J Work Environ Health 47(7):489

Rigó M, Dragano N, Wahrendorf M, Siegrist J, Lunau T (2021) Work stress on rise? Comparative analysis of trends in work stressors using the European working conditions survey. Int Arch Occup Environ Health 3(94):459–474. https://doi.org/10.1007/s00420-020-01593-8

Siegrist J (1996) Adverse health effects of high-effort/low-reward conditions. J Occup Health Psychol 1:27–41. https://doi.org/10.1037//1076-8998.1.1.27

Smith J, Hu M, Lee H (2021) Chapter 3 – Measuring life course events and life histories. In: Ferraro KF, Carr D (eds) Handbook of aging and the social sciences, 9th edn. Academic Press, San Diego, pp 33–47

Steptoe A, Breeze E, Banks J, Nazroo J (2013) Cohort profile: the English longitudinal study of ageing. Int J Epidemiol:1640–1648. https://doi.org/10.1093/ije/dys168

Theorell T (2020) Handbook of socioeconomic determinants of occupational health. Springer

Tomlinson J, Baird M, Berg P, Cooper R (2018) Flexible careers across the life course: advancing theory, research and practice. Hum Relat 71(1):4–22

Vineis P, Avendano-Pabon M, Barros H, Chadeau-Hyam M, Costa G, Dijmarescu M et al (2017) The biology of inequalities in health: the LIFEPATH project. Longitud Life Course Stud 8(4): 417–449. https://doi.org/10.14301/llcs.v8i4.448

Virtanen M, Nyberg ST, Batty GD, Jokela M, Heikkilä K, Fransson EI et al (2013) Perceived job insecurity as a risk factor for incident coronary heart disease: systematic review and meta-analysis. BMJ 347:f4746

Wahrendorf M, Chandola T (2016) A life course perspective on work stress and health. In: Siegrist J, Wahrendorf M (eds) Work stress and health in a globalized economy: the model of effort-reward imbalance. Springer, Heidelberg, pp 46–66

Wahrendorf M, Hoven H, Goldberg M, Zins M, Siegrist J (2019) Adverse employment histories and health functioning: the CONSTANCES study. Int J Epidemiol 48(2):402–414. https://doi.org/10.1093/ije/dyy235

Wahrendorf M, Hoven H, Deindl C, Lunau T, Zaninotto P (2021) Adverse employment histories, later health functioning and national labor market policies: European findings based on life-history data From SHARE and ELSA. J Gerontol Ser B Psychol Sci Soc Sci 76(Supplement_1): S27–S40. https://doi.org/10.1093/geronb/gbaa049

Wahrendorf M, Chandola T, Goldberg M, Zins M, Hoven H, Siegrist J (2022) Adverse employment histories and allostatic load: associations over the working life. J Epidemiol Community Health 76:374–381

WHO/ILO (2021) WHO/ILO joint estimates of the work-related burden of disease and injury, 2000–2016: global monitoring report. World Health Organization and the International Labour Organization, Geneva

Precarious Work and Health

Gillian Weston and Anne McMunn

Contents

Introduction	320
What Is Precarious Work?	321
Prevalence of Precarious Work	323
Precarious Work Across the Life Course	325
Precarious Work and Models of Work-Related Stress	327
Precarious Work and Mental Health	329
Temporary Work and Mental Health	329
Self-Employment and Mental Health	332
Precarious Work and Sleep	335
Conclusion	336
Cross-References	337
References	337

Abstract

Precarious work is characterized by the absence of the standard employment relationship and by a degree of employment insecurity. It contributes to the flexible workforce which has grown to respond to competition, technical innovation, global crises, and 24/7 business operations. The aim of this chapter is to outline what is known about the associations between this work pattern and health. It focuses on the two main forms, temporary work and self-employment, and two health measures, mental health and sleep, because work-related psychological illness and insufficient sleep contribute to lost working days and work-related accidents. A review of the literature suggests that in comparison to permanent employees, temporary workers, particularly those considered most vulnerable to the labor market, such as casual workers, may experience more psychological distress, whereas self-employed workers have been found to

G. Weston (✉) · A. McMunn
Research Department of Epidemiology and Public Health, University College London, London, UK
e-mail: gillian.weston.14@ucl.ac.uk; a.mcmunn@ucl.ac.uk

experience more stress than employees, but also greater subjective and psychological well-being. Additionally, while job insecurity has been associated with poor sleep quality and sleeping less than and more than the recommended 7–8 h per night, there is no evidence that temporary workers experience poor or insufficient sleep, and only a little evidence that self-employed workers experience poor sleep quality and longer sleep durations than employees. However, this evidence, which is mainly cross-sectional, is somewhat sparse and contradictory, possibly because of the heterogeneity in how researchers measure precarious work, and their tendency mostly to study male workers and those working in specific occupations or workplaces, and to exclude the most precarious types of temporary and self-employed workers.

Keywords

Precarious work · Temporary work · Self-employment · Mental health · Mental well-being · Stress · Depression · Sleep quality · Sleep quantity · Sleep duration

Introduction

It has been asserted that precarious work has been increasing in industrialized countries since the 1970s. Factors including globalization, the 24/7 economy, and technological change, increased market competition and financial crises, and weakened trade unions/collective bargaining has led to a growth in the flexible workforce, downsizing of organizations, and outsourcing of labor. Some workers may have welcomed the expansion of this in the hope that flexibility will facilitate their work-family-life balance. However, while this may be beneficial to some, it poses potential problems in terms of employment relations, job insecurity, a lack of in-work benefits, and long and unsocial working hours.

Poor working conditions can be detrimental to health and well-being with individual, societal, and economic consequences. For example, work-related stress has been associated with depression and poor sleep (Burgard and Ailshire 2009), while an accumulation of sleep loss increases the risk of further mood deterioration, fatigue, and confusion, which in turn can cause human errors and accidents. In Great Britain, according to estimates by the Health and Safety Executive, work-related psychological illness accounted for 17.9 million lost working days in 2019/2020, and 6.3 million working days were lost due to nonfatal injuries in 2018/2019. The World Health Organization (WHO) recently estimated that lost productivity due to depression and anxiety has an annual cost of US$1 trillion to the global economy. While the prevalence of sleep disturbance varies by country, age, and the methods used to assess it, there are estimates that it affects between 7% and 37% of working-age adults in Europe with the Mediterranean and Nordic countries having the lowest rates, and Eastern European the highest rates (Dregan and Armstrong 2011). The global think tank, the RAND Corporation, estimates that insufficient sleep costs up to US$680 billion across five countries (Canada, Germany, Japan, the UK, and the USA).

This chapter will present definitions regarding what it means to work precariously, and evidence of changes in the prevalence of precarious work over time and the life course in Europe and in several other member countries of the Organization for Economic Cooperation and Development (OECD). It will then discuss precarious work in relation to leading models of work-related stress. In light of the economic and societal problem of poor mental health and sleep outlined above, this chapter will also review evidence linking precarious work with mental health and sleep outcomes.

What Is Precarious Work?

There are different concepts and measures of precarious work, though most agree that it is a work pattern characterized by contractual arrangements other than the standard open-ended employment contract, by a degree of insecurity over the duration of employment, and is associated with a lack of social protection and employee benefits. Researchers have considered this by focusing on job attributes like employment rights, conditions, and social protection, or by seeing it in terms of labor market sectors. The market sector approach is the one most commonly adopted by health-related researchers, operationalizing precarious work as temporary work and self-employment, or as subcategories such as fixed-term employment, and usually comparing it to standard employment.

Permanent employment is characterized by the relative security and reciprocal socio-emotional obligations of the long-term open-ended employment contract, and a direct relationship between employer and employee facilitating commitment, training, career prospects, and monetary reward. In contrast, temporary work is typified by flexibility, short-term economic agreements and limited emotional ties with the employer. Assuming a continuum between the two, with permanent employees at one end and the most flexible of temporary work at the other, fixed-term workers, where the worker is hired directly by the employer and a date set for the contract to end, is the closest to permanent employment. Next are agency workers (also known as "despatch workers," "labor hire," and "subcontractors") who have no direct relationship with the hirer and are paid wages by an agency (or despatcher or contractor) from their fee from the hirer. Then there are the casual workers (also known as "bank staff," "on-call," "on-demand," "seasonal," "informal," and "gig worker") who work on a task basis or for a period of hours or weeks. In several European countries including the UK, casual workers who are not guaranteed a minimum number of working hours are often classed as having zero-hour contracts.

There are several categories of self-employment too, with the categories usually related to the motivations for self-employment. Opportunity entrepreneurs are business owners who have previously been employees, are motivated by an idea, opportunity, or desire to be their own boss, tend to start up the business with a partner or family member, and often employ others. In contrast, necessity entrepreneurs often enter self-employment on their own in order to escape or avoid unemployment, or have no better choice of work. Compared to opportunity entrepreneurs, they are often associated with lower levels of education, household income, job tenure, and work autonomy (Stephan 2018). Straddling these two categories are own-account workers – people running their own business but not engaging employees on a continuous basis. Similarly, freelancers and contractors tend not to employ others, however, with their tendency to work on multiple short-term jobs for several different businesses; they occupy an intermediate position between running their own business and being dependent self-employed (Gevaert et al. 2018) and thus their status sometimes overlaps with those of temporary workers. Dependent self-employment is usually associated with necessity entrepreneurship, and is also known as "involuntary," "contingent," and "bogus" self-employment as workers tend to be economically dependent on, and subordinate to, the organization(s) that use their services. Since self-employed workers tend to have fewer legal and social security protection than employees, some workers are deliberately misclassified as self-employed. This enables employers to shift their risks and fiscal obligations to the worker, circumvent labor laws, and deny workers a voice.

Although this unidimensional, market sector approach of operationalizing precarious work as specific work patterns is more prevalent among researchers, multidimensional approaches have been proposed. These range from the relatively simple method of combining factors such as contract type and job insecurity to the use of scales such as the Employment Precariousness Scale (EPRES) (Vives et al. 2020) which measures six dimensions of precariousness – temporariness/employment instability, disempowerment (lack of collective bargaining), vulnerability to unacceptable workplace practices, low/insufficient wages, rights (social security benefit entitlement), and power to exercise workplace rights. However, EPRES was intended for use with workers in salaried employment and fixed-term jobs, but not self-employed workers, nor informal or casual workers. To account for the self-employed and a greater variety of temporary worker, researchers have proposed a new multidimensional approach proposing two methods to operationalize precariousness (Jonsson et al. 2021). The first involves the construction of typologies based on different combinations of work conditions to identify the precarious and non-precarious employment groups in a sample, which can be used to estimate how much of a workforce are precarious and assess their experiences. The typologies take account of different dimensions: employment security (contractual relationships such as employment through an agency, via self-employment or direct employment or a combination of these; contractual temporariness, i.e., stable/unstable; underemployment, i.e., full-time/part-time; and multiple jobs/sectors in a single year), income adequacy (compared to the median of the population), and rights/protection (such as unionization, social protection, regulatory protection, and workplace rights). The second method assesses the degree of precariousness via a summed scale which assigns scores to the dimensions, with zero scores assigned to those dimensions of a job which relate to standard employment (i.e., those directly employed, in stable employment, with a single job/sector, earning 80–119% of median income, and having a 91–100% likelihood of a collective bargaining agreement) and plus or minus scores depending on how much jobs deviate from this.

Prevalence of Precarious Work

Although standard employment is the norm within Europe, the literature often claims that precarious employment has increased in developed countries over the last few decades (Julià et al. 2019; Rönnblad et al. 2019). However, as illustrated in Figs. 1 and 2, the prevalence of precarious employment actually differs by type and country, and fluctuates by year. These figures provide the percentage of temporary and self-employed workers over a 20 year period in countries where precarious work and mental health have been studied. As shown in Fig. 1, in 2020, around 5% of workers in the UK were in temporary employment compared to 25% in Spain and Korea; and while rates have been decreasing in Spain since 2006, there have been

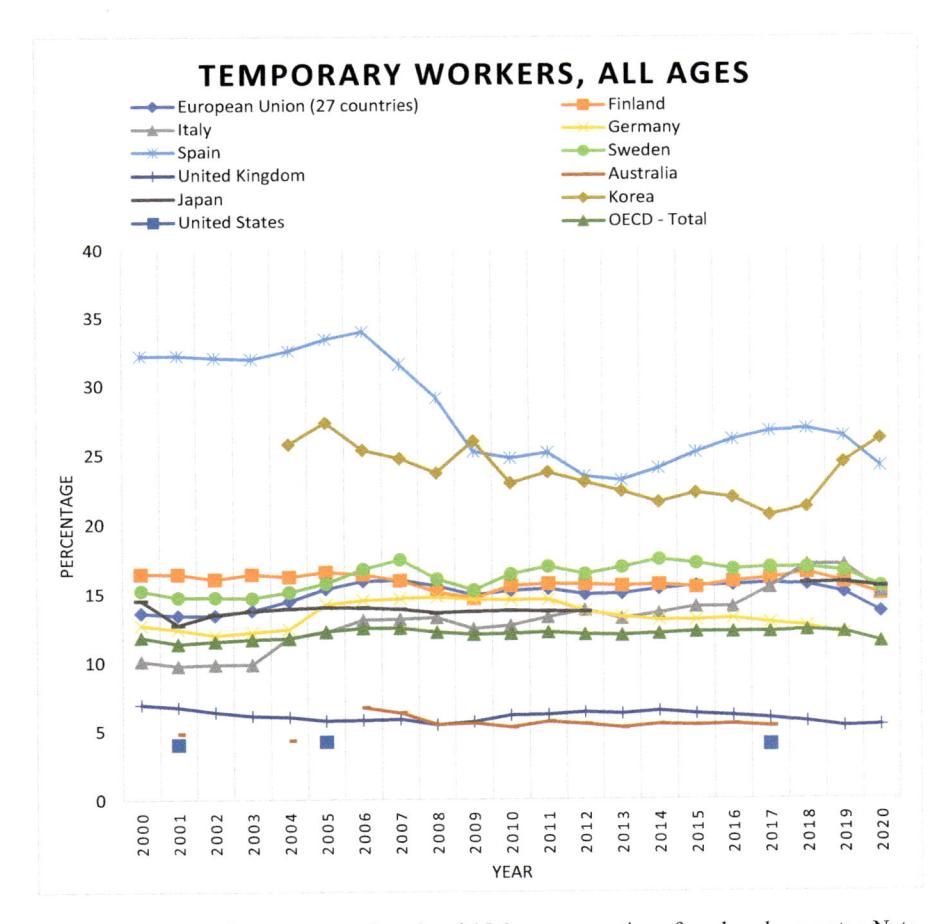

Fig. 1 Percentage of temporary workers (aged 15+) as a proportion of workers by country. Note, data was not collected every year for Australia, Korea, Japan, and the USA. (Source: OECD (2021) Temporary employment (indicator): Labor Market Statistics: Employment by permanency of the job: incidence: OECD https://data.oecd.org/emp/temporary-employment.htm#indicator-chart)

recent increases in Korea, and since 2004, also in Italy. In Europe and the OECD countries overall, growth has been relatively flat for the last 15 years. However, as the data is based on Labor Force Surveys, the figures may not capture all forms of temporary work, such as those of a casual nature.

Figure 2 shows that nearly a quarter of workers in Italy and Korea are self-employed, compared to around 6% in the USA, and that in recent years self-employment has been declining in most countries, though Finland experienced growth between 2002 and 2015. No data were provided for the OECD countries overall, nor for the UK. Nonetheless, data from the UK's Office for National Statistics (ONS) suggests that between 2001 and 2017, self-employment grew from 12% to over 15% in the UK. Furthermore, the largest percentage growth in

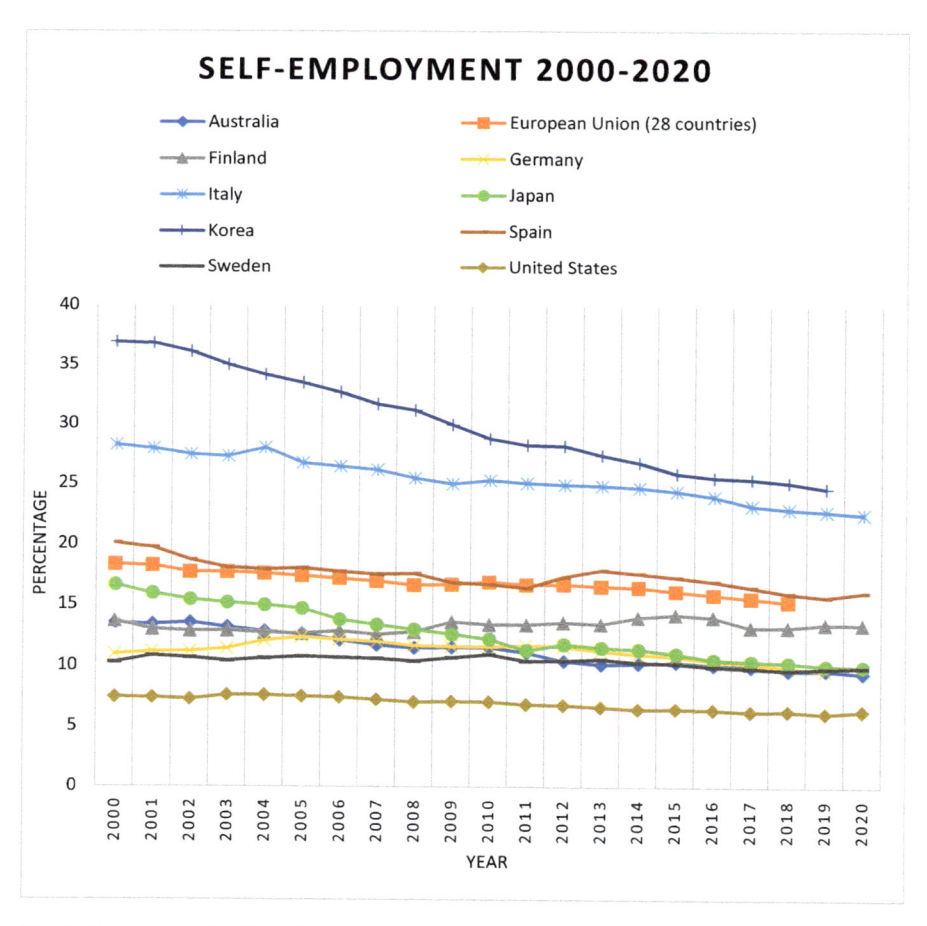

Fig. 2 Percentage of self-employed workers as a proportion of workers by country. Note, data was not collected for the OECD, nor the UK. (Source: OECD (2021) Self-employment rate (indicator). Labor Force Statistics: Summary tables: https://data.oecd.org/emp/self-employment-rate.htm#indicator-chart)

self-employment in the UK was from women – which increased by 45.3% in the 10 years to November 2019, compared to an 18.4% increase for men in the same period. Data from the USA's Bureau of Labor Statistics estimated that self-employment declined from 12.1% in 1994 to 10.1% in 2015. In Europe, in 2020 Eurofound estimated that for the majority, self-employment is voluntary, especially for those employing others, but that around 24% are self-employed because they lack alternatives to work. Self-employment rates tend to be higher among people with disabilities or health conditions compared to the general population. These individuals often feel forced to enter self-employment, often as sole traders, when other employment is inaccessible to their needs. However, due to a lack of practical and financial support, their business failure rates tend to be high.

Precarious Work Across the Life Course

Over the life course, workforce participation is shaped by a series of transitions, such as from school to work, and from work to retirement. Varying by sequence and significance, and differing somewhat by sex (due to gender norms and work-family opportunities/constraints), these transitions can run parallel to, or be interrupted by, the transitions of family formation, education and training, elder care, and events such as illness and economic issues. Nonetheless, we often think of these transitions in terms of linear patterns and relate them to age.

For young people transitioning into work, temporary jobs can act as a stepping stone and/or enable them to earn money while they remain in education. Indeed, according to Eurofound, the majority of 15- to 24-year-olds in temporary jobs had chosen the temporary work or did it because it was part of training or a probationary period. Accordingly, the literature suggests that young, rather than older adults, are the most likely to take up temporary work and a third of workers under 30 are in temporary employment in Europe. Figure 3 shows the trends for temporary working among 15- to 24-year-olds between 2000 and 2020, generally suggesting an increase for the first 17 years followed by a small decline. It also shows that Spain and Italy have the highest proportions at over 60% each, and Australia, the lowest at less than 6%.

In contrast to temporary workers, self-employment is skewed toward older workers. This is illustrated in Fig. 4 which shows self-employment as a share of total employment by age group for a select number of countries and Europe as a whole. The lowest proportions are among the 15- to 24-year-olds, their share ranges from 1.5% in Germany to 8.3% in Italy. The highest proportions are among the oldest workers, with prevalence highest in Italy and Spain. High prevalence among the 65's and older may be a way of extending their working lives. Nonetheless, there tends to be an age-related inverted u-shaped pattern to self-employment, if we consider the proportions of all people only in self-employment rather than work. This is demonstrated by the UK's ONS data from 2019 where 45- to 54-year-olds were the most likely to be self-employed (26.5%), followed by 55- to 64-year-olds (22.2%) and 35- to 44-year olds (21.8%), then 25- to 34-year-olds (15.9%), whereas 65+ year olds (9.6%) and 16- to 24-year-olds (4.0%) were least likely. Somewhat

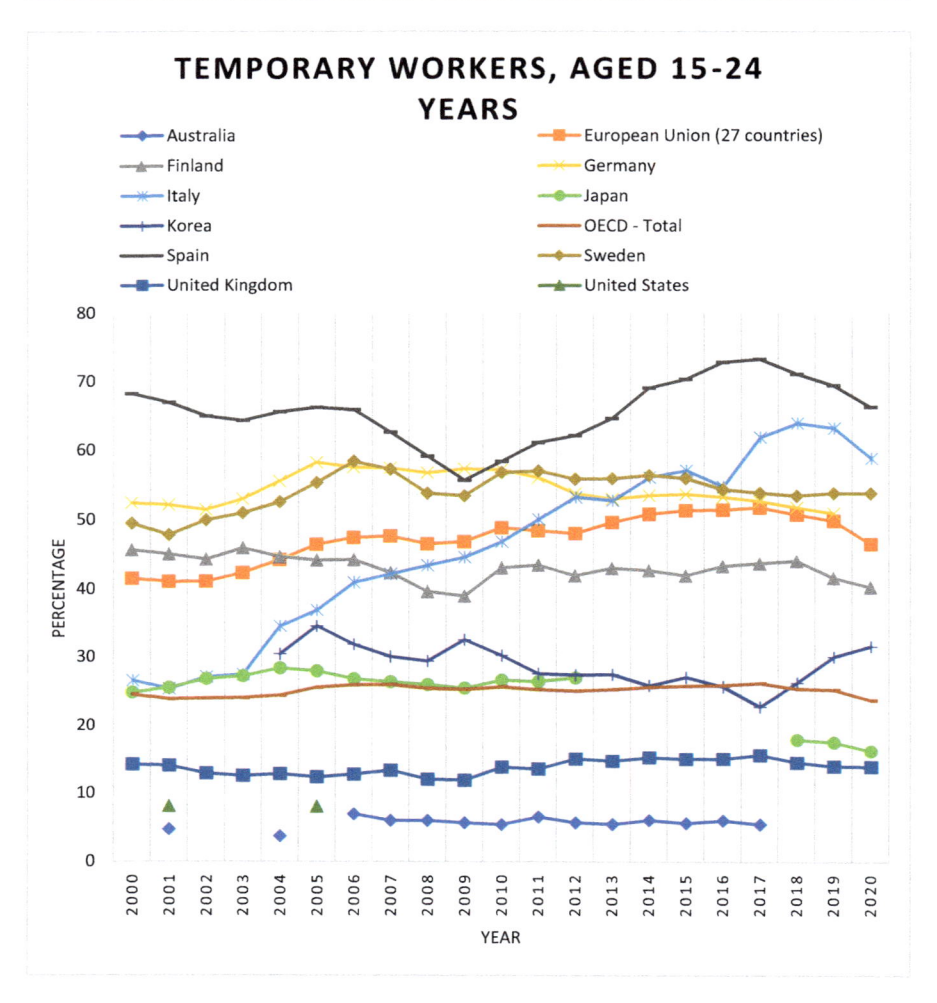

Fig. 3 Percentage of temporary workers aged 15–24 as a proportion of young workers by country. Note, data was not collected every year for Australia, Korea, Japan, and the USA. (Source: OECD (2021) Temporary employment (indicator): Labor Market Statistics: Employment by permanency of the job: incidence: OECD https://data.oecd.org/emp/temporary-employment.htm#indicator-chart)

corresponding to these age groups, but also reflecting work-family transitions, the following pattern was observed for household types in the UK: couples with nondependent/no children were the most likely to be self-employed (35.9%), followed by couples with at least one child aged under 16 (32.7%) and then lone persons with nondependent/no children (13.7%). Lone parents with dependent children aged 16–18 were the least likely to be self-employed (0.4%). Nonetheless, there was a similar pattern for people in employment, so both patterns reflect the household types of working people in the UK.

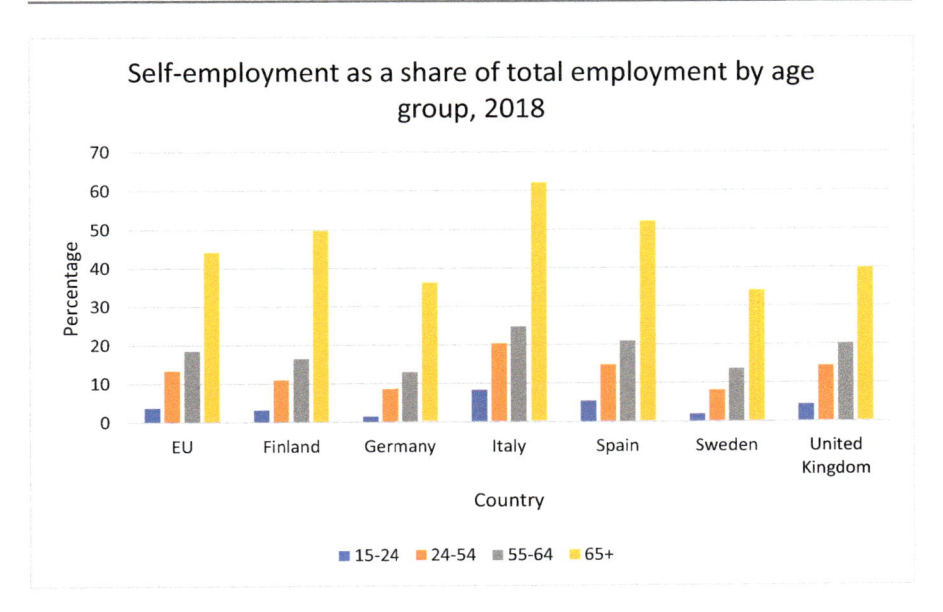

Fig. 4 Percentage of self-employment as a share of total employment in Europe, 2018. (Source: EU-LFS (January 18, 2021), Self-employment (%), by age, 2018: Labour market change: Trends and policy approaches towards flexibilisation)

Precarious Work and Models of Work-Related Stress

Poor work characteristics predict common mental health disorders and stress and related cognitive brooding increase physiological arousal and hinder sleep (Burgard and Ailshire 2009). Several models of work-related stress may help in our understanding of the potential health risks which may be posed by precarious work. The effort-reward imbalance (ERI) model posits that a lack of reciprocity between effort and reward leads to emotional distress (Siegrist 1996). The job-demands-control (JDC) model suggests that mental strain occurs if job demands exceed job control (Karasek 1979), and an expansion of this model suggests that the effects of this are exacerbated when the high strain is combined with low social support. A further model, the job-demands-resources model, describes how high strain and low motivation develop when job demands are high and job resources are limited, and conversely work engagement occurs when job demands are perceived as low or motivationally challenging and resources are high (Bakker and Demerouti 2007). It is important to note that the development of the JDC and ERI models was based on the work role of paid employees. For example, in the ERI, three components comprise the notion of reward for employees – financial (e.g., income), status (e.g., career progression and job security), and socio-emotional (esteem or recognition). However, compared to standard open-ended paid employment, precarious work tends to be less well paid, and is perceived as being more insecure with fewer opportunities for career progression. Therefore, rather than status or financial rewards, their rewards are more likely to be of a socio-emotional nature, and especially in the case of self-employment may also involve nonpecuniary factors such as job satisfaction. It follows that the extant questionnaires on ERI may be inapplicable to weigh the effort involved in precarious work against the socio-emotional rewards alone. Nonetheless, it may be assumed that a mismatch between the efforts (both extrinsic efforts, such as work demands, and intrinsic cognitive-motivational efforts, such as securing contracts, meeting the needs of clients/temporary employers, and devotion to work) against the socio-emotional rewards (such as the status of being one's own boss, or employing others/having a job as opposed to being unemployed) would have a negative effect on precarious workers' health. The recent adaptation of the ERI to measure unpaid housework (labor which usually derives no financial or status rewards) is welcomed. It is hoped similarly, these work-stress models and related questionnaires are revised to reflect work precarity. In the meantime, the models provide a helpful framework by which to develop some understanding of the potential stressors relating to precarious work. Despite these limitations, these widely used models are discussed below in relation to precarious work.

Precarious workers may be exposed to numerous "bad job" characteristics including vulnerability to inadequate income, fewer social benefits and regulatory protections, risks from the uncertainty of work continuation, unpredictable or intensive working hours, and limited training or development opportunities (Julià et al. 2019). Specifically temporary workers may perceive low levels of autonomy and high job insecurity and experience deficiencies in income, benefits, training, and career progression (Kachi et al. 2014). Self-employed workers tend to earn less than employees, but have higher work demands, longer working hours (Hagqvist et al. 2019), lack social support, and experience loneliness and work-family conflict (Stephan 2018). Thus, precarious workers may experience insufficient rewards, high job demands, and poor job resources, and while the self-employed tend to have low levels of support, temporary workers tend to have low levels of control.

However, these work patterns may provide benefits too. Temporary work may provide a valued social position compared to unemployment, and opportunities to try out different jobs, increase employability, and facilitate career development, while also providing social contact with others, goal-oriented motivation, and income. Relative to permanent employees, temporary workers may have less psychological attachment to the job and fewer thoughts about work after-hours and less psychological distress than permanent staff who may feel burdened with increased workloads and responsibilities.

Relative to employees, the self-employed tend to have more autonomy and decision latitude over their jobs (Nikolova 2019), have more psychological capital and job satisfaction, and find their job content is rewarding (Binder and Coad 2016). They may also perceive long working hours as a challenge rather than a threat or a sign of their business success (Hessels et al. 2017).

Precarious Work and Mental Health

Studies of temporary work have generally focused on the negative associations with mental health, and those of self-employment on the positive associations.

Temporary Work and Mental Health

The evidence of an association between temporary work and mental health is varied. Many of the studies are cross-sectional in design utilizing data which measures exposures and outcomes at the same time. Though this design is useful for comparing the differences between subjects who are exposed to temporary work and those who are unexposed to it, causal inferences cannot be made from the results. For example, they can tell if there is an association between temporary work and mental health, but not if temporary work leads to poor mental health or vice versa. Nonetheless, based on cross-sectional studies, temporary work has been associated with psychological distress (Waenerlund et al. 2011b), and poorer psychological well-being (Julià et al. 2019). However, studies have also found no differences in the mental health of temporary workers compared to permanent workers (LaMontagne et al. 2014), nor in their subjective well-being (SWB) (Ciairano et al. 2010).

Although it may be difficult to study temporary workers longitudinally because these workers are least likely to be captured by surveys (Rönnblad et al. 2019), several longitudinal studies have been conducted. Most provide evidence of an association between temporary work and psychological distress (Dawson et al. 2015; Canivet et al. 2016), depressive symptoms (Jang et al. 2015; Kim et al. 2016), depressive disorder-related sickness absence, and antidepressant use (Inoue et al. 2011). However, some found no evidence of poorer mental health among temporary workers (Virtanen et al. 2011); and while a meta-analysis of longitudinal studies found evidence of an effect for temporary work on psychological health, the authors deemed this evidence was of low quality (Rönnblad et al. 2019).

Of the studies which found associations between temporary work and mental health, the strength of the associations varies. The odds of poor mental health tended to be between 1.2 and 1.9 times higher for temporary workers than permanent workers, and they tended to be higher (OR 1.6–2.1) in studies which also accounted for job insecurity. In comparison, a Finnish study found that the unemployed had between 1.5 and 4.8 times poorer mental health than permanent workers, depending on the level of income (e.g., benefits/compensation) and gender of the unemployed (Virtanen et al. 2003).

It has been argued that the unidimensional approach, using temporary employment alone as the measure of precarious employment, may lead to an underestimation of the associations between precarious employment and health outcomes (Vives et al. 2020). However, while a handful of studies, which accounted for at least one other dimension of precariousness in addition to temporary work, found an association with poorer mental health outcomes (Canivet et al. 2016; Ferrante et al. 2019; Vives et al. 2020), one found mental distress only among job-insecure permanent full-time workers (Bernhard-Oettel et al. 2005). Nonetheless, a meta-analysis concluded that the strongest associations with poor mental health were found when temporary jobs were combined with other precarious factors (Rönnblad et al. 2019).

In addition to the influence of precarious conditions additional to work pattern type, factors such as psychological work conditions may contribute to the outcomes. For example, in addition to job insecurity, distress among temporary workers can be due to poor promotion prospects, whereas among permanent workers it can be due to effort-reward imbalances (Inoue et al. 2011). There are also suggestions that psychological work conditions may be better for fixed term rather than permanent and other temporary workers (Benavides et al. 2000), which may help explain the findings of a scoping review which concluded that 60% of studies showed no association between fixed-term working and poor mental health (Hünefeld and Köper 2016).

As noted earlier, other temporary workers include casual, on-call, seasonal, or informal temporary workers, but some research excludes them. Of the few studies investigating these non-fixed-term temporary workers, there is evidence that their mental health is poorer than that of other workers (Dawson et al. 2015) and that their psychological distress and risk of psychological symptoms reduced after exiting this work pattern (Reine et al. 2008). However, there is also evidence of no differences in their psychological well-being compared to permanent workers (Julià et al. 2019). Research specifically on gig workers (i.e., those using online platforms for short-term work typically in the service sector) is rare, though a study during the Covid-19 lockdown in France found that bikers in the gig economy had lower stress levels than non-gig workers (Apouey et al. 2020).

Labor market settings may influence outcomes for temporary workers (Rönnblad et al. 2019). Employment regulations may affect perceptions of precariousness, and the proportion of temporary employees, unemployment rates, welfare state regimes, worker demographics, cultural norms, and spending on labor programs may affect psychological morbidity of temporary workers (Kim et al. 2012). For example, the provision of unemployment benefits and health insurance in the Nordic countries may mitigate some of the perceived stressfulness of temporary work, compared to countries, such as the USA, which are less protective of employees' rights. Yet most studies on temporary work have emanated from Sweden and Finland, with mixed results. In contrast, the growing number of studies from East Asia, particularly from South Korea and Japan, mostly provide evidence of poorer mental health among temporary workers. In comparison to the Nordic countries, East Asia has minimal social policies, fewer state welfare provisions, and a greater reliance on family and community to provide assistance (Kim et al. 2012). Furthermore, while employment rates are high in this region, use of temporary contracts is relatively extensive, as is exposure to long weekly work hours.

It might be noted that there is a tendency for researchers to utilize data from occupational settings, such as the public sector, hospitals, care services, manufacturing, call centers, research institutes, and pharmacies, so research findings might only be pertinent to them.

Several studies have used pan-European labor market data, with results providing evidence of nonpermanent workers having lower psychological well-being (Julià et al. 2019) but lower stress (Benavides et al. 2000). Similarly, data analyzed from national population samples tend to show worse mental health among temporary workers in Spain, Italy, Germany, Korea Japan, the USA, and the UK, but not in Australia.

Additionally, some studies conducted their research prior to the global financial crisis of 2007/2008, which adds to the contextual nature of their findings. For example, since the crisis, work demands and job strain declined for many Swedish workers.

Another consideration is whether duration in temporary work influences associations with mental health. There is a little consideration of contract length, whether the contract is just starting or coming to an end, and whether there is any prospect for its extension. Workers' precariousness may be affected where legislation imposes a time limit by which employers have to provide a permanent contract or end a relationship rather than extend or provide another temporary contract. For example, in Sweden, employers cannot hire someone for more than two years (over a five-year period) in consecutive or repeated contracts, so someone nearing the end of their 18 month tenure may be more precarious than someone starting a short contract who may have the chance of extending their tenure. Furthermore, the cumulative effect of temporary work is under-researched, as are the different trajectories which account for changes in employment status such as spells of underemployment (e.g., involuntary part-time hours), unemployment, and economic inactivity, in addition to temporary work over the working life. Of the few studies which have accounted for employment trajectories, one showed that temporary employment was a risk factor for the subsequent development of depressive symptoms among previously mentally healthy workers (Canivet et al. 2016); one found that the higher the degree of exposure to temporary work over a 12-year period, the higher the psychological distress (Waenerlund et al. 2011a); and another demonstrated that young workers with discontinuous work histories mixed with episodes of fixed-term and part-time jobs had elevated symptoms of depression and anxiety (Sirviö et al. 2012).

It has been suggested that only the healthiest individuals obtain and maintain temporary jobs, and that workers who fall ill may transition to unemployment and become lost to work-related research, but in contrast, temporary workers may feel compelled to work while ill and take fewer sickness absences (Virtanen et al. 2005). However, as yet the research on health selection and temporary work is sparse, there is some evidence that poor health may increase selection into temporary work (Dawson et al. 2015) and increase these workers' risk of intermittent employment histories and weak attachments to work (Waenerlund et al. 2011a).

It has been noted that women are more likely to experience psychological distress, and to have temporary jobs (Kim et al. 2012). However, most studies used mixed samples of men and women, usually containing fewer women; and there are examples where research has been conducted exclusively on male workers. A few researchers disaggregated their results, but the findings were inconclusive. Stronger associations were found among men compared to women (Ferrante et al.

2019), among women compared to men (Jang et al. 2015), and one study found an association for women only if they were unmarried breadwinners (Kachi et al. 2014).

Although temporary work is more prevalent among younger people, a review recently noted there was little evidence regarding the mental health effect of it on them (Gray et al. 2021). Research which followed 18- to 34-year-olds in Sweden over a 10-year period found that those with precarious employment in their employment trajectories had poor mental health at follow-up (Canivet et al. 2016).

Self-Employment and Mental Health

The self-employed lack the same employment and social protections as employees, are subject to disadvantages such as income uncertainty and onerous workloads but also experience nonpecuniary advantages such as work autonomy (Nikolaev et al. 2020) and job satisfaction (Warr 2018). Thus some researchers have likened self-employment to an emotional rollercoaster, with the advantages characterizing the peaks, and adversity and obstacles characterizing the valleys (Nikolova 2019). Accordingly, self-employment has been associated with adverse and favorable mental health outcomes.

Much of the evidence linking self-employment and mental health has been cross-sectional, which as noted in section "Temporary Work and Mental Health" cannot make causal inference or rule out reverse causation (Stephan 2018). However, it can be difficult to follow these workers longitudinally as they are subject to low business success and high attrition rates. For example, 20% of sole traders cease trading in their first year and the median age of businesses closing in the UK is approximately three years (Stephan et al. 2015).

Of the cross-sectional studies, there is evidence that, relative to employees, self-employed workers experience more stress (Benavides et al. 2000), and have 1.78 times more depression and anxiety (Won et al. 2019). But there is also evidence that self-employed workers have more SWB (Patel and Wolfe 2020) and greater psychological well-being (PWB) or flourishing (Warr 2018; Nikolaev et al. 2020) than employees.

Similarly, the few longitudinal studies provide a mixed picture, having found that the self-employed have a greater risk of depression and anxiety, but also lower stress (Hessels et al. 2017), and higher SWB (Abreu et al. 2019) than employees. Furthermore, the longer the tenure in self-employment, the greater the life satisfaction (Litsardopoulos et al. 2021).

These equivocal findings might relate to how researchers operationalize self-employment, and whether they take account of other factors. While it is common for researchers to depict the self-employed as a homogenous group, there has been some progress toward investigating the differences between them. A recent study used latent profile analysis to create six profiles of self-employed workers based on whether they employed others, their working hours, income, and subjective socio-economic position (SEP), and found that well-being outcomes differed between the six groups (Bujacz et al. 2019). These profiles and their prevalence were identified as: "unhappy" (15%), "languishing" (34%), "happy" (23%), "satisfied" (6%), "passionate" (12%), and "flourishing" (10%). Those classed as "happy," "passionate," and "flourishing" tended to have above-average to high SEP, and average to high incomes, and considered their incomes to be sufficient compared to those with "unhappy," and "languishing" profiles who tended to have lower SEP and believed their incomes were insufficient. Those who were "satisfied" tended to have similar SEP to those identified as "languishing," but they had higher incomes than the "languishing" group. Those identified as "happy" tended to work the fewest hours, and those with "passionate" and "unhappy" profiles tended to work the longest hours. Those classed as "languishing," "satisfied," and "flourishing" tended to work an average number of hours. Those with "happy" and "flourishing" profiles tended to have the most highly skilled occupations.

Researchers have also divided the self-employed into groups of opportunity and necessity entrepreneurs – the former pursuing self-employment from employment, and the latter to escape unemployment. However, despite the assumption that opportunity entrepreneurs experience greater well-being than necessity ones, the evidence is inconclusive. Although there is evidence that opportunity, but not necessity, entrepreneurs have more SWB than employees (Binder and Coad 2016), there is also evidence that both opportunity and necessity entrepreneurs have higher SWB than employees (Nikolova 2019; Amorós et al. 2020). As noted above, disabled people tend to become self-employed out of necessity. Their fluctuating health conditions, such as periods of pain, fatigue, and/or poor mental health can make work difficult, so their inclusion in studies could bias results where there is a risk of reverse causation. However, rather than assume they were necessity entrepreneurs, two of these studies matched their exposure and reference groups on a range of factors including presence of a disability (Binder and Coad 2016; Nikolova 2019).

Another approach has been to investigate own account workers (sole traders) and self-employed people who employ others (employers). However, the literature is again mixed. A large pan-European study using data from the European Social Survey (ESS) compared self-employed employers, sole traders, employees with supervisory roles, and employees without supervisory roles, and found that self-employed employers had higher SWB than sole traders, but sole traders had higher SWB than the employees without supervisory roles (Johansson Sevä et al. 2016). Another, using UK-only data from the ESS found that while overall the self-employed had better well-being than employees, it was the sole traders who had the highest scores on flourishing and life satisfaction (Warr 2018). Similarly, findings from a large sample of Australian workers and a global study of 61 countries suggested that employers had more stress than sole traders, but both had less stress than employees (Hessels et al. 2017). Of two studies using data from the European Survey on Working Conditions, one also found less stress among the self-employed and that employers had more stress than sole traders (Benavides et al. 2000), but the other found sole traders had worse mental well-being than employers (Gevaert et al. 2018).

There have been too few studies to conclude whether the size of employer might explain these mixed findings. A large-scale study in Korea found that smaller business owners had poorer working conditions, including long working hours, than those with middle to large businesses (Min et al. 2019). In contrast, evidence from a study of Swedish business owners suggested that the larger the business, the greater the time pressures, and these pressures cancelled out the benefits to SWB from increased finances (Fors Connolly et al. 2021).

The literature is also sparse when it comes to understanding the mental health of the most precarious of self-employed workers, such as those working as freelancers and as dependent self-employed. While these types of self-employed worker are frequently excluded from studies, three papers recently investigated them. Two compared them to other self-employed workers. The first found that they had worse mental well-being, suggesting this might be mediated by lower motivation and ability to recognize opportunities (Gevaert et al. 2018). The second found relatively little difference in their SWB, though freelancers had more satisfaction with their job and free time (van der Zwan et al. 2019). The third found that, relative to employees, the dependent self-employed had an increased risk of depression and anxiety (Won et al. 2019). Nonetheless, regardless of the type of self-employment, there is evidence that those wanting to leave it may have lower SWB, elevated stress and mental issues, and possibly lower earnings than those who prefer to stay (Beutell et al. 2019).

Selection effects have been found for self-employment, though the literature is scant and contradictory. There is evidence that those who are optimistic (van der Zwan et al. 2016), relatively healthy, or have high SWB are selected into self-employment (Amorós et al. 2020), but so are individuals with mental health problems (Stephan et al. 2020a).

The social and cultural contexts may influence findings on this topic. It has been asserted that the work-related well-being of self-employed workers may be moderated by societal attitudes to entrepreneurship and this differs by country (Stephan et al. 2020b). Indeed this idea is supported by a recent study from China which found considerable variation in SWB among rural entrepreneurs, with the variations explained by institutional trust (trust in the political and legal system and business infrastructure) and to a lesser extent by family support (Xu et al. 2021). Although some of the literature is based on global and pan-European samples, much has originated in North America where self-employment has been declining. Despite increasing rates of self-employment in the UK, there have been relatively few studies from the UK. Of these, the self-employed have been found to have higher SWB, but only when they live in semirural locations (Abreu et al. 2019). They have also been found to experience a temporary uplift in their mental health when they enter self-employment from employment (Stephan et al. 2020a). However, elevations in elements of their SWB may depend on their type of self-employment (van der Zwan et al. 2019).

It has been suggested that married women tend to enter self-employment for the flexibility to balance work and family commitments, divorced women exit it to find more secure employment, and men enter it for career advancement and wealth creation (Litsardopoulos et al. 2021). Yet, whether this affects the well-being outcomes is underexplored, and there is little research specifically about women entrepreneurs. Most studies comprise both sexes, though they usually contain more men. A few have disaggregated their analyses. One suggested that longer episodes of self-employment had a positive impact on the life satisfaction of women only (Litsardopoulos et al. 2021). Others suggested that self-employed women had higher life satisfaction than employees (Johansson Sevä et al. 2016), and that relative to men, they tended to be satisfied with their income, but be less satisfied with their leisure time, and they experienced increased psychological demands (Carree and Verheul 2012). They were also more likely to work longer total hours than men due to their tendency to combine self-employment with waged employment and/or childcare (Hagqvist et al. 2019). One study found that men, but not women, experienced a temporary uplift in their mental health following entry into self-employment (Stephan et al. 2020a).

Precarious Work and Sleep

Compared to the literature on the relationship between precarious work and mental health, the research into its associations with sleep is in its infancy. There have been no investigations about temporary work and sleep duration, and just three about its association with sleep quality. Of these, two were cross-sectional. The first, a study of workers in the Swedish labor market in 1997 found no difference in sleep difficulties among temporary workers relative to permanent workers, but workers in substitute, project, and on-call temporary jobs were more likely to be fatigued (Aronsson et al. 2002). The second, from the UK's Health and Employment After Fifty (HEAF) study found relative to permanent work, temporary work had little impact on insomnia, however, workers with insecure jobs had 18.4 times higher odds of insomnia than secure workers (Palmer et al. 2017). The only longitudinal study used data from a Swedish school cohort, and found no association between an accumulation of temporary work over a 12-year period and poor sleep quality (Virtanen et al. 2011).

Six studies, all cross-sectional, have investigated self-employment and sleep problems. The HEAF study in the UK found that relative to employees, the self-employed had 10% lower odds of insomnia, whereas the odds of insomnia among the unemployed was 3.1 times higher (Palmer et al. 2017). In contrast, other studies provided evidence of around 20–40% higher odds of poorer sleep quality among the self-employed. Four of these used data from general population samples, two from the USA (Grandner et al. 2010; Wolfe and Patel 2019), and two from Korea (Won et al. 2019; Lee et al. 2020). The fifth utilized a purposive sample of workers in Germany (Kollmann et al. 2019). Furthermore, three of these investigated types of self-employment. The two Korean studies found a greater risk of sleep disorders among the dependent self-employed (i.e., those sometimes called bogus self-employed due to their dependency on an employer) compared to employees. The German study found no differences between experienced and novice entrepreneurs.

Four studies, all cross-sectional, compared sleep duration among the self-employed relative to employees. Two analyzed time-use data. The first found that self-employed workers in Finland slept about 14 min longer per night (Hyytinen and Ruuskanen 2007). The second found that among people aged 30–59 in Japan, relative to employees, self-employed women had a higher prevalence of short sleep duration (less than 5 h/night) but self-employed men had a lower prevalence, possibly because self-employed women worked longer total hours (paid work plus housework and caring responsibilities) (Maeda et al. 2020). The other two studies, both from nationally representative samples in the USA, found that generally, the self-employed slept longer than employees and were less likely to report insufficient sleep (less than 7 h/night), but if they experienced psychological distress associated with self-employment, they were more likely to experience insufficient sleep (Wolfe and Patel 2019).

Since precarious work tends to involve a higher degree of job insecurity than nonprecarious work, it might be useful to note that job insecurity has been associated with sleeping both short (5 h and less) and long (9 h and more) durations (Ferrie et al. 1998), suboptimal sleep quality, insomnia, and restless sleep (Mai et al. 2019). Similarly, as temporary workers may experience episodes of unemployment, it might be noted that the unemployed are also more likely than employees to experience short and long sleep (Blanchflower and Bryson 2021).

It is possible that the inconsistencies in the literature might be, at least partially, attributed to differences in how work patterns are defined and how sleep outcomes are measured. There is a tendency, particularly among time-use studies, to include time in bed as sleeping time, which may lead to wrong conclusions.

Conclusion

While there is evidence that temporary and self-employed workers experience poorer mental health than employees with open-ended employment contracts, there is also evidence that the self-employed experience greater well-being. However, these findings are not unanimous. There is emerging evidence that the self-employed, but not temporary workers, experience poor sleep quality, but there are too few studies to be conclusive. The research on the associations between self-employment and sleep duration is too sparse to draw conclusions, and as yet we know nothing about sleep duration among temporary workers.

There is heterogeneity in precarious work, and despite the development of scales that can measure work precariousness, they are yet to be widely applied. Often researchers study temporary workers as a homogenous group, or mainly focus on the most stable type of temporary work – fixed term. Similarly, the self-employed are frequently grouped together in the study samples, though research is emerging which differentiates between opportunity and necessity entrepreneurs, and employers and sole traders. Relatively little is known about the most precarious types of these work patterns, such as casual and gig workers.

In accordance with the models of work-related stress, and people's work transitions across the life course, temporary work and self-employment can provide benefits as well as disadvantages. This is likely to affect the research outcomes.

Although one study investigated preferences to stay or leave (Beutell et al. 2019), as yet no studies account for volition and compulsion for working in these precarious patterns. Furthermore, few consider gender differences, despite women being more likely than men to have temporary jobs, and despite women's growing participation rates in self-employment. Moreover, despite the prevalence of the work patterns differing by age, generally there is no disaggregation of results by age. In addition, there has been a reliance on studies from just a handful of countries, occupational settings, and particular cohorts. More should be done to understand the contextual differences and diversity of labor market settings and welfare regimes.

Cross-References

▶ A Life Course Perspective on Work and Mental Health: The Working Lives of Young Adults
▶ Adverse Employment Histories: Conceptual Considerations and Selected Health Effects
▶ Gig Work and Health
▶ Occupational Trajectories and Health Inequalities in a Global Perspective
▶ The Impact of New Technologies on the Quality of Work
▶ Transformation of Modern Work, Rise of Atypical Employment, and Health

References

Abreu M, Oner O, Brouwer A, van Leeuwen E (2019) Well-being effects of self-employment: a spatial inquiry. J Bus Ventur 34(4):589–607. https://doi.org/10.1016/j.jbusvent.2018.11.001

Amorós JE, Cristi O, Naudé W (2020) Entrepreneurship and subjective well-being: does the motivation to start-up a firm matter? J Bus Res. https://doi.org/10.1016/j.jbusres.2020.11.044

Apouey B, Roulet A, Solal I, Stabile M (2020) Gig workers during the COVID-19 crisis in France: financial precarity and mental well-being. J Urban Health Bull NY Acad Med 97(6):776–795. https://doi.org/10.1007/s11524-020-00480-4

Aronsson G, Gustafsson K, Dallner M (2002) Work environment and health in different types of temporary jobs. Eur J Work Organ Psychol 11(2):151–175. https://doi.org/10.1080/13594320143000898

Bakker AB, Demerouti E (2007) The job demands-resources model: state of the art. J Manag Psychol 22(3):309–328. https://doi.org/10.1108/02683940710733115

Benavides FG, Benach J, Diez-Roux AV, Roman C (2000) How do types of employment relate to health indicators? Findings from the second European survey on working conditions. J Epidemiol Community Health 54(7):494–501

Bernhard-Oettel C, Sverke M, De Witte H (2005) Comparing three alternative types of employment with permanent full-time work: how do employment contract and perceived job conditions relate to health complaints? Work Stress 19(4):301–318

Beutell N, Alstete J, Schneer J, Hutt C (2019) Intention to leave self-employment: a comparison of business owners and the independently self-employed. Social Science Research Network, Rochester

Binder M, Coad A (2016) How satisfied are the self-employed? A life domain view. J Happiness Stud Dordr 17(4):1409–1433. https://doi.org/10.1007/s10902-015-9650-8

Blanchflower DG, Bryson A (2021) Unemployment and sleep: evidence from the United States and Europe. Econ Hum Biol 43:101042. https://doi.org/10.1016/j.ehb.2021.101042

Bujacz A, Eib C, Toivanen S (2019) Not all are equal: a latent profile analysis of well-being among the self-employed. J Happiness Stud. https://doi.org/10.1007/s10902-019-00147-1

Burgard SA, Ailshire JA (2009) Putting work to bed: stressful experiences on the job and sleep quality. J Health Soc Behav Wash 50(4):476–492

Canivet C, Bodin T, Emmelin M, Toivanen S, Moghaddassi M, Östergren P-O (2016) Precarious employment is a risk factor for poor mental health in young individuals in Sweden: a cohort study with multiple follow-ups. BMC Public Health 16. https://doi.org/10.1186/s12889-016-3358-5

Carree MA, Verheul I (2012) What makes entrepreneurs happy? Determinants of satisfaction among founders. J Happiness Stud 13(2):371–387. https://doi.org/10.1007/s10902-011-9269-3

Ciairano S, Rabaglietti E, Roggero A, Callari TC (2010) Life satisfaction, sense of coherence and job precariousness in Italian young adults. J Adult Dev 17(3):177–189. https://doi.org/10.1007/s10804-010-9099-2

Dawson C, Veliziotis M, Pacheco G, Webber DJ (2015) Is temporary employment a cause or consequence of poor mental health? A panel data analysis. Soc Sci Med 134:50–58. https://doi.org/10.1016/j.socscimed.2015.04.001

Dregan A, Armstrong D (2011) Cross-country variation in sleep disturbance among working and older age groups: an analysis based on the European Social Survey. Int Psychogeriatr 23(9): 1413–1420. https://doi.org/10.1017/S1041610211000664

Ferrante G, Fasanelli F, Gigantesco A, Ferracin E, Contoli B, Costa G, Gargiulo L, Marra M, Masocco M, Minardi V, Violani C, Zengarini N, d'Errico A, Ricceri F (2019) Is the association between precarious employment and mental health mediated by economic difficulties in males? Results from two Italian studies. BMC Public Health 19(1):869. https://doi.org/10.1186/s12889-019-7243-x

Ferrie JE, Shipley MJ, Marmot MG, Stansfeld S, Smith GD (1998) The health effects of major organisational change and job insecurity. Soc Sci Med 46(2):243–254. https://doi.org/10.1016/S0277-9536(97)00158-5

Fors Connolly F, Johansson Sevä I, Gärling T (2021) The bigger the better? Business size and small-business owners' subjective well-being. J Happiness Stud 22(3):1071–1088. https://doi.org/10.1007/s10902-020-00264-2

Gevaert J, Moortel DD, Wilkens M, Vanroelen C (2018) What's up with the self-employed? A cross-national perspective on the self-employed's work-related mental well-being. SSM-Popul Health 4:317–326. https://doi.org/10.1016/j.ssmph.2018.04.001

Grandner MA, Patel NP, Gehrman PR, Xie D, Sha D, Weaver T, Gooneratne N (2010) Who gets the best sleep? Ethnic and socioeconomic factors related to sleep complaints. Sleep Med 11(5):470–478. https://doi.org/10.1016/j.sleep.2009.10.006

Gray B, Grey C, Hookway A, Homolova L, Davies A (2021) Differences in the impact of precarious employment on health across population subgroups: a scoping review. Perspect Public Health 141(1):37–49. https://doi.org/10.1177/1757913920971333

Hagqvist E, Toivanen S, Vinberg S (2019) The gender time gap: time use among self-employed women and men compared to paid employees in Sweden. Time Soc 28(2):680–696. https://doi.org/10.1177/0961463X16683969

Hessels J, Rietveld CA, van der Zwan P (2017) Self-employment and work-related stress: the mediating role of job control and job demand. J Bus Ventur 32(2):178–196. https://doi.org/10.1016/j.jbusvent.2016.10.007

Hünefeld L, Köper B (2016) Fixed-term employment and job insecurity (JI) as risk factors for mental health. A review of international study results. E-J Int Comp Labour Stud 5(3):1–22.

Hyytinen A, Ruuskanen O-P (2007) Time use of the self-employed. Kyklos 60(1):105–122. https://doi.org/10.1111/j.1467-6435.2007.00361.x

Inoue M, Tsurugano S, Yano E (2011) Job stress and mental health of permanent and fixed-term workers measured by effort-reward imbalance model, depressive complaints, and clinic utilization. J Occup Health 53(2):93–101. https://doi.org/10.1539/joh.L10098

Jang S-Y, Jang S-I, Bae H-C, Shin J, Park E-C (2015) Precarious employment and new-onset severe depressive symptoms: a population-based prospective study in South Korea. Scand J Work Environ Health 41(4):329–337

Johansson Sevä I, Vinberg S, Nordenmark M, Strandh M (2016) Subjective well-being among the self-employed in Europe: macroeconomy, gender and immigrant status. Small Bus Econ 46(2): 239–253. https://doi.org/10.1007/s11187-015-9682-9

Jonsson J, Matilla-Santander N, Kreshpaj B, Orellana C, Johansson G, Burström B, Alderling M, Peckham T, Kjellberg K, Selander J, Östergren P-O, Bodin T (2021) Exploring multi-dimensional operationalizations of precarious employment in Swedish register data – a typological approach and a summative score approach. Scand J Work Environ Health 2:117–126. https://doi.org/10.5271/sjweh.3928

Julià M, Belvis F, Vives A, Tarafa G, Benach J (2019) Informal employees in the European Union: working conditions, employment precariousness and health. J Public Health 41(2):e141–e151. https://doi.org/10.1093/pubmed/fdy111

Kachi Y, Otsuka T, Kawada T (2014) Precarious employment and the risk of serious psychological distress: a population-based cohort study in Japan. Scand J Work Environ Health 40(5):465–472

Karasek RA (1979) Job demands, job decision latitude, and mental strain: implications for job redesign. Adm Sci Q 24(2):285–308

Kim I-H, Muntaner C, Vahid Shahidi F, Vives A, Vanroelen C, Benach J (2012) Welfare states, flexible employment, and health: a critical review. Health Policy Amst Neth 104(2):99–127. https://doi.org/10.1016/j.healthpol.2011.11.002

Kim W, Park E-C, Lee T-H, Kim TH (2016) Effect of working hours and precarious employment on depressive symptoms in South Korean employees: a longitudinal study. Occup Env Med 73(12): 816–822. https://doi.org/10.1136/oemed-2016-103553

Kollmann T, Stöckmann C, Kensbock JM (2019) I can't get no sleep – the differential impact of entrepreneurial stressors on work-home interference and insomnia among experienced versus novice entrepreneurs. J Bus Ventur 34(4):692–708. https://doi.org/10.1016/j.jbusvent.2018.08.001

LaMontagne AD, Milner A, Krnjacki L, Kavanagh AM, Blakely TA, Bentley R (2014) Employment arrangements and mental health in a cohort of working Australians: are transitions from permanent to temporary employment associated with changes in mental health? Am J Epidemiol 179(12):1467–1476. https://doi.org/10.1093/aje/kwu093

Lee SH, Kang D, Lee J, Kim U, Ham S, Lee W, Choi W-J, Kang S-K (2020) Multidimensional sleep quality of dependent self-employment workers. Ann Occup Environ Med 32:e6. https://doi.org/10.35371/aoem.2020.32.e6

Litsardopoulos N, Saridakis G, Hand C (2021) Does the accumulation of self-employment experience impact life satisfaction? J Bus Ventur Insights 16:e00259. https://doi.org/10.1016/j.jbvi.2021.e00259

Maeda M, Filomeno R, Kawata Y, Sato T, Maruyama K, Wada H, Ikeda A, Tanigawa T (2020) Association between employment status and short sleep duration among middle-aged Japanese: the survey on time use and leisure activities. Int J Behav Med 27(1):21–29. https://doi.org/10.1007/s12529-019-09807-1

Mai QD, Hill TD, Vila-Henninger L, Grandner MA (2019) Employment insecurity and sleep disturbance: evidence from 31 European countries. J Sleep Res 28(1):e12763. https://doi.org/10.1111/jsr.12763

Min J-Y, Kim H-J, Min K-B (2019) Self-employment's vulnerability to socioeconomic and working conditions: results from the Korean Working Condition Survey (2006–2014). J Glob Health Rep 3:e2019038. https://doi.org/10.29392/joghr.3.e2019038

Nikolaev B, Boudreaux CJ, Wood M (2020) Entrepreneurship and subjective well-being: the mediating role of psychological functioning. Entrep Theory Pract 44(3):557–586. https://doi.org/10.1177/1042258719830314

Nikolova M (2019) Switching to self-employment can be good for your health. J Bus Ventur 34(4):664–691. https://doi.org/10.1016/j.jbusvent.2018.09.001

Palmer KT, D'Angelo S, Harris EC, Linaker C, Sayer AA, Gale CR, Evandrou M, van Staa T, Cooper C, Coggon D, Walker-Bone K (2017) Sleep disturbance and the older worker: findings from the Health and Employment after Fifty study. Scand J Work Environ Health Stockh 43(2):136–145. https://doi.org/10.5271/sjweh.3618

Patel PC, Wolfe MT (2020) Not all paths lead to Rome: self-employment, wellness beliefs, and well-being. J Bus Ventur Insights 14:e00183. https://doi.org/10.1016/j.jbvi.2020.e00183

Reine I, Novo M, Hammarström A (2008) Does transition from an unstable labour market position to permanent employment protect mental health? Results from a 14-year follow-up of school-leavers. BMC Public Health 8(1):159. https://doi.org/10.1186/1471-2458-8-159

Rönnblad T, Grönholm E, Jonsson J, Koranyi I, Orellana C, Kreshpaj B, Chen L, Stockfelt L, Bodin T (2019) Precarious employment and mental health: a systematic review and meta-analysis of longitudinal studies. Scand J Work Environ Health 45(5):429–443. https://doi.org/10.5271/sjweh.3797

Siegrist J (1996) Adverse health effects of high-effort/low-reward conditions. J Occup Health Psychol 1(1):27–41. https://doi.org/10.1037/1076-8998.1.1.27

Sirviö A, Ek E, Jokelainen J, Koiranen M, Järvikoski T, Taanila A (2012) Precariousness and discontinuous work history in association with health. Scand J Public Health 40(4):360–367. https://doi.org/10.1177/1403494812450092

Stephan U (2018) Entrepreneurs' mental health and well-being: a review and research agenda. Acad Manag Perspect 32(3):290–322. https://doi.org/10.5465/amp.2017.0001

Stephan U, Hart M, Mickiewicz T, Cord-Christian D (2015) Understanding motivations for entrepreneurship. BIS research paper no. 212. Department for Business Innovation & Skills, England

Stephan U, Li J, Qu J (2020a) A fresh look at self-employment, stress and health: accounting for self-selection, time and gender. Int J Entrep Behav Res. (ahead-of-print). https://doi.org/10.1108/IJEBR-06-2019-0362

Stephan U, Tavares SM, Carvalho H, Ramalho JJS, Santos SC, van Veldhoven M (2020b) Self-employment and eudaimonic well-being: energized by meaning, enabled by societal legitimacy. J Bus Ventur 35(6):106047. https://doi.org/10.1016/j.jbusvent.2020.106047

van der Zwan P, Thurik R, Verheul I, Hessels J (2016) Factors influencing the entrepreneurial engagement of opportunity and necessity entrepreneurs. Eurasian Bus Rev 6(3):273–295. https://doi.org/10.1007/s40821-016-0065-1

van der Zwan P, Hessels J, Burger M (2019) Happy free willies? Investigating the relationship between freelancing and subjective well-being. Small Bus Econ. https://doi.org/10.1007/s11187-019-00246-6

Virtanen P, Liukkonen V, Vahtera J, Kivimäki M, Koskenvuo M (2003) Health inequalities in the workforce: the labour market core–periphery structure. Int J Epidemiol 32(6):1015–1021. https://doi.org/10.1093/ije/dyg319

Virtanen M, Kivimäki M, Joensuu M, Virtanen P, Elovainio M, Vahtera J (2005) Temporary employment and health: a review. Int J Epidemiol 34(3):610–622. https://doi.org/10.1093/ije/dyi024

Virtanen P, Janlert U, Hammarström A (2011) Exposure to temporary employment and job insecurity: a longitudinal study of the health effects. Occup Environ Med 68(8):570–574. https://doi.org/10.1136/oem.2010.054890

Vives A, Benmarhnia T, González F, Benach J (2020) The importance of using a multi-dimensional scale to capture the various impacts of precarious employment on health: results from a national survey of Chilean workers. PLoS One 15(9):e0238401. https://doi.org/10.1371/journal.pone.0238401

Waenerlund A-K, Gustafsson PE, Virtanen P, Hammarström A (2011a) Is the core-periphery labour market structure related to perceived health? Findings of the Northern Swedish Cohort. BMC Public Health 11(1):956. https://doi.org/10.1186/1471-2458-11-956

Waenerlund A-K, Virtanen P, Hammarström A (2011b) Is temporary employment related to health status? Analysis of the Northern Swedish Cohort. Scand J Public Health 39(5):533–539. https://doi.org/10.1177/1403494810395821

Warr P (2018) Self-employment, personal values, and varieties of happiness–unhappiness. J Occup Health Psychol 23(3):388–401. https://doi.org/10.1037/ocp0000095

Wolfe MT, Patel PC (2019) I will sleep when I am dead? Small Bus Econ, Sleep and self-employment. https://doi.org/10.1007/s11187-019-00166-5

Won G, Park JB, Lee K-J, Ha R, Lee S, Jeong I (2019) The association between dependent self-employment and self-reported depression/anxiety and sleep disorder in South Korea. Ann Occup Environ Med 31. https://doi.org/10.35371/aoem.2019.31.e13

Xu F, He X, Yang X (2021) A multilevel approach linking entrepreneurial contexts to subjective well-being: evidence from rural Chinese entrepreneurs. J Happiness Stud 22(4):1537–1561. https://doi.org/10.1007/s10902-020-00283-z

Gig Work and Health

20

Hua Wei and Martie van Tongeren

Contents

Background: The Rise of the Gig Economy	344
Occupational Risks of Couriers in the Gig Economy	345
A Life Course Perspective	346
Stressors and Responses: Chinese Couriers in a Digital Era	347
Stressors, Responses, and Coping Mechanisms	348
Agility and Vulnerability: The UK Logistics Sector During the COVID-19 Pandemic	349
Conclusion	352
Cross-References	352
References	353

Abstract

The gig economy has grown rapidly, introducing new employment modes and platform-based algorithmic management. It has attracted large numbers of workers across the globe into jobs such as self-employed couriers. In developing countries, they are mainly young migrant workers with relatively low education background. The quality of work and employment at this stage of their life is important as it may shape their occupational trajectory and affect health and well-being for the rest of their lives and their families. Understanding the potential risks to health from gig work, both short term as well as in later life, is an emerging field of research. This chapter aims to describe the risks faced by couriers, including work stressors, safety issues, and those posed by the COVID-19 pandemic. Individual and organizational responses and risk mitigation measures will also be discussed. The chapter draws upon an extensive review of existing literature published in the English and Chinese languages as well as early findings of our own research in China and the UK. Currently, occupational

H. Wei (✉) · M. van Tongeren
Division of Population Health, Health Services Research & Primary Care, School of Health Sciences, University of Manchester, Manchester, UK
e-mail: hua.wei@manchester.ac.uk

© Springer Nature Switzerland AG 2023
M. Wahrendorf et al. (eds.), *Handbook of Life Course Occupational Health*, Handbook Series in Occupational Health Sciences, https://doi.org/10.1007/978-3-031-30492-7_6

health and safety in the gig economy is an under-regulated domain. These new employment modes need urgent attention as they have the potential for impacting workers' health and well-being. It is important to develop and implement protective measures and build a safe work environment for couriers and other occupatioans that are mostly affected by the rise of the gig economy.

Keywords

Young couriers · Gig economy · Work stress · China · COVID-19

Background: The Rise of the Gig Economy

It is estimated that there are about 1.1 billion on-demand gig workers worldwide and this population is growing fast (https://www.forbes.com/sites/forbesbusinesscouncil/2021/08/12/will-the-gig-economy-become-the-new-working-class-norm/?sh=4a19164eaee6). The term gig economy has been loosely used to describe many new forms of work arrangements, under which the demand and supply of service is matched online or via mobile apps, including "crowdwork" and "work-on-demand via apps" (De Stefano 2016). The gig economy thrives in both developing and developed countries. In 2021, about 0.83 billion people participated in China's sharing economy, of which 84 million were service providers (mainly platform-based workers), a 7.7% year-on-year growth (SIC 2021). In the UK, 14.7% of the working population in 2021 has done platform work (i.e., Deliveroo, Upwork, Care.com, and Uber) at least once a week, compared to 5.8% in 2016 and 11.8% in 2019 (Spencer and Huws 2021). The US Quality of Work and Economic Life Study (A-QWELS) found in 2020 that 28% of the respondents reported some engagement in platform work in the previous month and about 9% were dependent on this work (Glavin and Schieman 2021).

Within the gig economy, digital labor platforms support a wide variety of tasks which can be further categorized as Internet based and location based (ILO 2021). Internet-based tasks (including freelancing hosted on platforms such as PeoplePerHour and Upwork) and microtasking (popular providers such as Amazon Mechanical Turk and Clickworker) are performed online or remotely. Location-based tasks such as delivery (e.g., Deliveroo and Meituan) or taxi services (e.g., Uber and Didi) are carried out by the workers in person in specified geographical locations (Berg et al. 2018). Of these tasks, delivery and taxi jobs have been growing at the fastest pace in the past few years. Taking Meituan, for example, the largest takeaway food delivery platform in China, 2.95 million workers are reported to receive income from the platform in the first half of 2020, a 16.4% year-on-year growth (SIC 2021). In the UK, the proportion of the working population carrying out delivery/driving gig work grew dramatically from 1.9% in 2016 to 8.9% in 2021 (Spencer and Huws 2021). While two-digit growth rate may be the norm for the Chinese economy, it is unusual for the developed countries (Huws et al. 2017). In the same period from 2016–2021, for example, the UK's total employment grew only 2% (ONS 2022).

Occupational Risks of Couriers in the Gig Economy

Courier jobs have traditionally been characterized as high demand, fast paced, and having low control with a lack of support, resulting in high prevalence of work stress and job burnout (Shoman et al. 2021; Kristensen et al. 2005; Bakker and Demerouti 2017). A recent systematic review included 15 studies – primarily involving young males between 20 and 40 years old – found that the prevalence of occupational stress (OS) in couriers ranged from 7–90% (median = 40%) (Wei et al. 2021). They also found that job burnout among these couriers ranged from 20–73% (median = 33%) (Wei et al. 2021). This is comparable to traditional professions with high rates of burnout – such as physicians, a profession for which a systematic review found burnout prevalence ranging from 0–80.5% (Rotenstein et al. 2018). This review also highlighted that design features of platform technology, including methods intended to intensify work, stimulate performance, and tighten managerial controls, such as gamification and customer rating–linked pay, were under-researched risk factors for platform-based couriers.

The rapid expansion of the gig economy has facilitated the development of global e-commerce that has made services and goods more accessible and affordable to consumers. However, the development has also intensified work stress for couriers. The state of overwork is closely associated with Karoshi (sudden death due to overwork) and measures the accumulated effects of long working hours or working overtime continuously for an extended period (Kosugoh et al. 1992). Karoshi has been commonly studied in far-east countries, such as China, Japan, and Korea, as a medical and sociomedical term, because a culture of hardworking and a strong belief that hard work is the only way out of poverty played a key role. Nevertheless, it has been recognized that continuous overwork under excessive stress can cause a range of health problems such as cerebrovascular and cardiovascular diseases, mental ill-health, and death (Kubo et al. 2021; Shan et al. 2017). To investigate overwork and associated risk of Karoshi among Chinese couriers, Lin et al. conducted large-scale surveys in China among takeaway food couriers. They found that 77.7% of respondents (n = 1114) were at high or very high risk of overwork, with only 7.9% considered to be risk free (Lin and Li 2021). The situation was similarly severe among parcel couriers (n = 1214), where the researchers found that 78.7% were at high or very high risk of overwork and only 3.7% were risk free (Lin and Li 2018). The participants reported working nearly 11 h per day on average with more than 50% working 10+ h, on the basis of working 6 days a week. Overwork is a known risk factor associated with a range of stress responses including "irritability," "fatigue," "anxiety," "depression," and "somatic responses" (Kikuchi et al. 2020) and could contribute to Karoshi even without a history of cardiovascular or cerebrovascular diseases (Miao et al. 2020; Shan et al. 2017).

Road safety is another major occupational risk faced with couriers in the gig economy. Intensified work stress could lead to reckless driving behaviors and cognitive failures (Nahrgang et al. 2011; Deligkaris et al. 2014). Wang et al. (2021) conducted a large-scale study that included 600 observations on busy roads and 480 interviews with couriers in Tianjin, China. They reported that in the 600 observations of couriers, the rate of exceeding speed limit was 91.3% and 21.2% used cell phones while riding. In addition, 76.5% of the 480 interviewed had been involved in a traffic crash at least once, of whom 47.4% were injured (Wang et al. 2021).

These results are alarming and demonstrates the urgency to address health and safety concerns in the gig economy and the most impacted jobs.

A Life Course Perspective

Wahrendorf and Chandola (2016) carried out a literature review on the long-term consequences of work stress on health. They found that duration, timing, sequence of stressful work, and employment, as well as risk clustering or accumulation throughout the life course are associated with poor health outcomes in later life, including cardiovascular diseases and mental health problems. Longitudinal data from the Survey of Health, Aging, and Retirement in Europe (SHARE) also showed that the number of years worked in a stressful job (between age 30 and 65) was associated with the level of depressive symptoms during retirement (Börsch-Supan et al. 2013). The research, however, as an aging study cohort, did not include people of younger age. Hence, it is important to consider age-specific vulnerability to work stress as younger workers who are at a critical period of development may be more susceptible to work stressors and poor-quality jobs could contribute to poor health outcomes they experience later in life (Wahrendorf and Chandola 2016).

The life course approach recognizes that all stages of a person's life are not only intricately intertwined with each other, but also connected with the lives of others born in the same period, and with the lives of past and future generations of their families (WHO 2018). Countries that are going through rapid urbanization are adopting gig work and flexible employment uncritically in favor of its short-term economic benefit. The life course lens sheds important light on the health and social impact of these new modes of work. Currently, the majority of the couriers are young males, especially in developing countries. For example, Lin reported that more than 95% of the respondents were male and more than 80% were between 20 and 34 years (Lin and Li 2018, 2021). They do not seem to stay with this occupation for very long. Another survey (N = 600) conducted among couriers who rode electric bikes found that the average occupation length of the respondents was just under 18 months (Wang et al. 2021). Couriers, especially those who become platform-based or have started their career as platform-based workers predominantly come from relatively low socioeconomic background. For example, nearly all the parcel (N = 1214) and takeaway (N = 1114) couriers in Lin's research were migrant workers, and from relative low level of education (college or below) (Lin and Li 2018, 2021). Hence, precarious employment and poor working conditions in the gig economy will likely contribute to widening of the social disparity and health inequality. As the phenomenon is relatively new, strong epidemiological evidence, e.g., large-scale longitudinal cohort studies that follow both platform-based and traditionally employed couriers, is at the time of writing not available. Nevertheless, it is important to take the life course approach for future research as it calls for actions early in the life course, appropriately during life's transition periods, and together as a whole society.

In the remainder of this chapter, our main focus will be on location-based delivery workers and on early findings from two studies of delivery drivers we conducted in the UK and China between April 2020 and Oct 2021. The Chinese study mainly focused on mental health issues. The UK study was an initiative to assess the risk of COVID-19 transmissions and implementation of the risk mitigation measures as demand for home deliveries surged during the pandemic.

Stressors and Responses: Chinese Couriers in a Digital Era

The majority of Chinese couriers are full-time gig workers, meaning that they are dependent on the digital platforms as the sole source of income (Zhou 2020). In the capital city Beijing, nearly 90% of surveyed platform-engaged delivery workers said they relied on it as the only source of income and the majority of them (95%) were doing the job for longer than 8 h every day (Huang et al. 2021). Furthermore, most of them (97%) were migrant workers supporting families who lived in their home towns and could not afford to settle in Beijing (Huang et al. 2021).

Sociological researchers in work, health, and technology have been interested in Chinese couriers since the late 2010s. An emerging body of work has investigated food couriers and similar location-based occupations (taxi drivers, etc.). Although the research interests were stimulated by digital labor platforms and algorithmic management, researchers also reported psychosocial risk factors in this work, including organizational, economic and cultural conditions (Chan 2021; Wu et al. 2019; Sun et al. 2021). For example, the use of economic stimulus for behavioral change and the cultural norm of "customer sovereignty" in the service sectors appeared to be two distinct features. Consumer sovereignty has become the norm in Chinese service sectors. This notion within the sector stems from marketing strategies created by service companies to make customers believe that they are autonomous choice-makers and enjoy relational superiority. This rhetoric (predating the gig economy) has served as a means of managerial control when the managers replaced the bureaucratic control of service quality with constant observation from and management by customers, named as the "extra eyes and ears in the labour process" (Gamble 2007: 9). It can lead to customer abuse when customers become disillusioned about the service standards (Korczynski and Evans 2013). In terms of economic stimulus, researchers repeatedly observed that couriers were fined by platforms for late deliveries, customer complaints, and noncompliance behaviors (including not wearing uniforms or helmets) (Liu and Friedman 2021; Chan 2021; Huang 2022). Positive stimulus, usually monetary rewards were also commonly used to encourage behaviors that complied with managerial goals. Commonly rewarded behaviors were high attendance, high rates of in-time deliveries, and positive customer reviews (Liu and Friedman 2021; Chan 2021). The platforms have further linked customer reviews and complaints with pay and penalties, so that the two features – economic stimulus and customer sovereignty – reinforced each other to deliver even a stronger impact. Platform technology and algorithms may have provided a new and convenient tool for the organizations to tighten the grip; nonetheless, similar controlling mechanisms have been applied to both parcel and food couriers, with or without platforms and apps (Lin and Li 2021; Lin et al. 2018). We therefore investigated both parcel and food couriers under various employment terms, including full-time employed, agency worker, and gig worker. The research purpose was to understand the main stressors among Chinese couriers and potential mitigation measures.

Stressors, Responses, and Coping Mechanisms

Conducted in China, the Chinese study included 14 semistructured interviews with frontline couriers and 5 focus groups with key stakeholders of this sector (Wei et al. 2021). A range of stressors were identified. The overall work environment for Chinese couriers was stressful and demanding, and as one of our interviewees put it, there were "all sorts of triggers for a mental breakdown." Customer attitudes and behavior were the most frequently discussed work stressor. As discussed earlier, the promotion of consumer sovereignty may have led to customer incivility. One of the interviewees described an instance when he did not fulfill an optional request for one customer, and the customer made a false complaint against him, claiming the food was undelivered. Although the courier explained the situation to the platform's customer service and did not get fined in this instance, he stated he felt angry at the customer's grossly unfair treatment. He decided to take the rest of the day off because of his resulting emotional status. The negative impact of customer incivility on service workers has been commonly reported (Gamble 2007; Korczynski and Evans 2013; Sun 2019). We found that interactions with customers could trigger negative as well as positive emotional responses and subsequently, intentions to quit or stay in the career. Some interviewees mentioned how they formed good relationships with fellow couriers and the community they served. One parcel courier had been working for the same area for quite a few years. His site office was at a convenient spot in the community and he and his team felt that they were part of the community. Other interviewees also mentioned rewarding experiences such as being offered hot drinks during cold winters, or a cigarette, or customers' extra help when the courier had difficulty finding the exact address. Positive experiences could boost the workers' mental strength; in the case of one of the interviewees, she described that they helped her focus on the positive side of the job.

In the aforementioned case, the customer service phoned the courier to obtain information about the complaint and decided not to impose any fines. However, other couriers reported a lack of support from the platform and complained about the customer service for always siding with the customer. Courier can be seen as a high-demand job due to time pressure and workload (Bakker and Demerouti 2017; Nahrgang et al. 2011). Perceived organizational support is known to have a moderating effect on the relationship between job demands and job strain, especially those caused by adverse customer behavior (Cheng and Chen 2020; Lin and Li 2021). Hence, strong and adequate organizational support from platform companies could be an effective measure to reduce couriers' work stress, while a lack of support following customer incivility will exacerbate stress.

The interviewees generally used "the system" to refer to the platform technologies which embody a myriad of managerial controls. When the couriers were platform based or app engaged, autonomy mostly existed outside of the system, that is, whether or when to log in and out. Once they logged into the system, the job was highly standardized and scripted. "The system" allocated orders, planned routes, and estimated delivery time. "The system" could track the couriers in real time and analyze feedback from customers. In addition, with all the information and data collected, couriers were rated by their performance whereas the system's logic was not transparent to them. Some interviewees believed that the system subtly discriminated the couriers when allocating orders. They explained how they managed to figure out some of the criteria and adapted their behavior to "curate" their data. For example, if for a few consecutive days they stayed online for adequate lengths of time and hit certain targets of on-time deliveries without incident (customer complaints, bad reviews, etc.), the system was likely to allocate them more orders and short-distance orders. Short-distance orders are generally more profitable orders.

Increasing job control can reduce work stress and improve job engagement (Bakker et al. 2016; van den Heuvel et al. 2015). In the couriers' job, being able to combine orders on a desired route was an essential element of job crafting where they had some decision latitude. However, there were two conditions for achieving such controls. First, workers must be able to understand the system's logic in relation to order allocation, which was not transparent to them. Only workers with high level of digital literacy were able to figure out the system's logic. Second, workers had the ability to deliver multiple orders within an estimated time window and attaining high customer satisfaction. Delivery times for food couriers are normally very short (30–45 min) and they often have to wait for food to be prepared by the restaurants. When delivering multiple orders, road conditions, restaurant delays, and customer not turning up or not picking up phones could all cause delays and hence customer dissatisfaction. Hence, their competence to cope with all of the challenges was another condition to have some job control. Platform systems designed like this indicates organizational injustice, which is another work stressor.

The focus of the Chinese study was on the mental health effects of and especially the impact of gig work. Nevertheless, the COVID-19 pandemic had a significant impact on the logistics sector. Some of the interviewees mentioned that although they had higher risk of infection as continued working during the pandemic, they also felt the importance of their work was recognized by the public and the government. When they delivered food, face masks, and gloves to customers and hospitals, they felt genuinely appreciated.

In early 2020 during the COVID-19 outbreak, we continued this line of research with a focus on the impact of the pandemic on the UK delivery sector and its workers.

Agility and Vulnerability: The UK Logistics Sector During the COVID-19 Pandemic

The novel SARS-CoV-2 virus was first identified in December 2019 in Wuhan, China. It soon developed into a global pandemic and has triggered waves of public health response in an unprecedented manner, including "lockdown" restrictions in many countries that prohibited unnecessary travel and required working from home

(WFH) for all but essential workers. This led to a dramatic increase in demand for home delivery services, including in the UK, which lasted throughout the pandemic. The sudden and dramatic change prompted questions relating to topics surrounding whether the delivery workers were at increased risk of infection, what risk mitigation measures (RMMs) were implemented, and what could be learned during the process.

Linking the UK Office for National Statistics COVID-19 mortality data from 24 January to 28 December 2020 with the census and other health records, a study found several occupations were at increased risk of COVID-19 mortality, particularly those involving contact with patients or the public, such as bus and taxi drivers (Nafilyan et al. 2022). Delivery workers were recognized as essential workers and in regular contact with the public during their work. They had a high contact rate per shift both at their depot (15.0 per shift) and with customers (71.6 per shift), while the mean number of contacts among the general population attending their workplace during the pandemic was between 3 and 10 per day (Bridgen et al., forthcoming). In order to understand what RMMs had been implemented to protect them, two rounds of interviews were carried out in July–August, 2020 and May–June, 2021 (Wei et al. 2022a, b). In total, 11 representatives from 6 logistics companies participated, representing a range of positions in the supply chain, including takeaway food delivery, large and small goods delivery, home appliances delivery and installation, as well as logistics technology providers. The representatives held managerial roles, such as health and safety manager, director of operations, or head of communications. Findings suggested that this sector, similar to other sectors, rapidly introduced measures to reduce risk of transmission for staff and customers. They implemented a wide range of RMMs and continued to adapt to new challenges faced over the pandemic, following government guidance available to them at the time. These included infection and transmission control measures, organizational measures, and broad collaborative activities within the sector, in the UK and globally, and with government departments.

Contact-free delivery was considered the most effective and practical measure in the context of home deliveries and was universally implemented by all the interviewed companies. Companies that delivered large items also temporarily suspended services requiring delivery workers to enter customer's homes, such as installation or delivery to a designated room. Most companies implemented engineering control measures including the installation of physical barriers in warehouses and distribution centers as well as changes to workplace layouts to segregate workers and visitors, or maintaining social distancing among workers. The companies also sent away most of their office staff to work from home to reduce workplace contacts for delivery workers. Throughout the pandemic, the interviewed companies carried out risk assessments continuously, adapted systems of work, and provided information, guidance, and change of practice to both workers and customers. They also set up mechanisms to monitor worker compliance, including internal contact tracing systems, data monitoring, collecting customer or employee feedback, site health and safety audits, remote auditing, i.e., CCTV surveillance, and instructing dedicated staff to monitor compliance behavior in the workplace. They also reported issuing combinations of gloves, face coverings, and hand sanitizers to protect their frontline workers.

Model simulations highlighted some key recommendations. First, for workplaces where deliveries are carried out in pairs (common examples are large-item and white goods deliveries), fixed-pairing of drivers was an important measure to limit the number of high-risk contacts, and hence limit both the number of secondary cases and impact on the business in terms of number of workers in self-isolation. Second, identifying moderate- and high-risk contact scenarios (employees who car share, house share, or work in close proximity) and deploying group isolation of these employees (if one tests positive, all close contacts isolate) was an effective combination. In terms of workplace testing, some companies deployed it reactively when they experienced workplace outbreaks. However, companies also commented that mass testing could be wasteful if adherence rates (either in carrying out tests or reporting the results) were low, so some level of monitoring and enforcing test adherence was likely to be essential for these measures to be effective.

Agility and vulnerability appeared to be key characteristics in the UK logistics sector's entire COVID-19 response process. There was no toolbox or protocols in place for coordinating the logistics sector in the face of a novel pathogen threat of this scale. Government guidance was developed with collective input from the industry as the pandemic unfolded and could not be customized to the level of detail necessary for operations in that short time frame. Hence, the companies filled the gap by developing their own strategies and portfolio of measures that were the most applicable in their situations, with some improvisation. However, this sector's relatively successful response to COVID-19 should not be taken for granted. A range of vulnerabilities were exposed during the prolonged rapid response.

First of all, the majority of parcel and food couriers were self-employed and had no access to sick leave pay. Of the five logistics companies interviewed, one employed drivers directly, three contracted independent drivers, and one engaged couriers via a digital labor platform. Lack of access to sick leave pay is a risk factor for presenteeism (Daniels et al. 2021). In the COVID-19 situation, as many delivery workers would lose income when self-isolating because they did not have access to statutory sick leave pay, it was possible that some would continue to work after testing positive. A survey targeting UK home delivery drivers found that about 5.3% participants reported working while being ill with COVID-19 symptoms or with a member of their household having a suspected or confirmed case of COVID-19, citing financial reasons for continuing to work (Bridgen et al., forthcoming). This highlighted the risk of COVID-19-related presenteeism among delivery workers – particularly those who were self-employed or platform based. Government schemes to support them (e.g., Self-Employment Income Support Scheme) appeared inadequate, and some of the interviewed companies reported providing their own financial support packages to the self-employed couriers when they had to self-isolate due to COVID-19. Such schemes were only provided as ad hoc supporting mechanisms and were gradually withdrawn by the government and organizations.

In the COVID-19 pandemic's case, although the sector responded with extraordinary agility and speed, multiple vulnerabilities were exposed. Most of the temporary measures have gradually receded, including monitoring data on reported cases and isolations, workplace contact tracing, and industry-wide forums. Only contact-free delivery appeared to become a more established practice that we can still observe. COVID-19 or similar respiratory infectious diseases could leave a lifelong impact on one's physical and mental health. Emerging evidence from multiple countries point out that COVID-19 could leave persistent and diverse post-viral symptoms among survivors (Praschan et al. 2021). The ONS reported in May 2022 that about two million people in the UK (3.1% of the population) were experiencing self-reported long COVID (symptoms persisting for more than four weeks after the first suspected COVID-19 infection) (https://www.ons.gov.uk/peoplepopulationandcommunity/healthandsocialcare/conditionsanddiseases/bulletins/prevalenceofongoingsymptomsfollowingcoronaviruscovid19infectionintheuk/1june2022.). It is important that a coherent sectoral strategy is developed to utilize learnings from this pandemic and provide the self-employed couriers adequate protection and support.

Conclusion

Sociological research of work and employment which addresses health and safety (H&S) concerns for gig workers is emerging (Tran and Sokas 2017; Fox et al. 2019; Bajwa et al. 2018; Freni-Sterrantino and Salerno 2021). The rapid global expansion of the gig economy suggests the urgency and scale of the problem. Certain practices of these digital labor platforms could make workers vulnerable to exploitation from algorithmic management, efficiency optimization, and employment precarity (Clarke 2019; Zuboff 2019). Location-based gig workers are at the center of concern. Although their job content has remained the same, the traditional model of work organization has been interrupted by the growing significance of platform technology and new employment modes. It is doubtful as to whether the new model has provided the same level of H&S protection and if newly emerged risk factors associated with gig working are being addressed (BNE 2021; De Stefano 2016).

Currently, occupational health and work safety in the gig economy is an under-regulated domain which requires urgent attention and further research. Workers' health and well-being throughout their working lives depend on interactions between risk and protective measures (WHO 2018). The two case studies have highlighted the mental health risks, safety risks, and the increased risk of a novel infectious disease pandemic, all of which could lead to negative health impacts with life-changing consequences. This occupation has attracted a large number of young males coming from relatively low education backgrounds or socioeconomic statuses, especially in the developing countries. It is particularly important that adequate measures are taken to protect this population and help them build safe and healthy working perceptions and practices from the early stage of their working lives (Ruiz et al. 2019).

Cross-References

▶ Precarious Work and Health
▶ Psychosocial Work Environment and Health: Applying Job-Exposure Matrices and Work Organization and Management Practice

References

Bajwa U, Knorr L, Di Ruggiero E et al (2018) Towards an understanding of workers' experiences in the global gig economy. NA. NA|, April 2018, Toronto|: the University of Toronto Lawrence S. Bloomberg Faculty of Nursing and the Dalla Lana School of Public Health

Bakker AB, Demerouti E (2017) Job demands–resources theory: taking stock and looking forward. J Occup Health Psychol 22(3):273–285

Bakker AB, Rodríguez-Muñoz A, Sanz Vergel AI (2016) Modelling job crafting behaviours: implications for work engagement. Hum Relat 69(1):169–189

Berg J, Furrer M, Harmon E et al (2018) Digital labour platforms and the future of work: Towards decent work in the online world. 30 April 2021. https://braveneweurope.com/gig-economy-project: Brave New Europe

BNE (2021) Gig economy project – digital platform workers in the pandemic crisis: a year of struggle. 2018. International Labour Organization (ILO), Geneva

Börsch-Supan A, Brandt M, Schröder M (2013) Sharelife – one century of life histories in Europe. Adv Life Course Res 18(1):1–4

Chan JW-l (2021) Hunger for profit: how food delivery platforms manage couriers in China. Sociologias 23(57):58–82

Cheng Z-F, Chen X (2020) A study on the influence of improper interaction on couriers' job engagement—the moderating influence of organization support. In: 2020 4th international seminar on education, management and social sciences (ISEMSS 2020). Atlantis Press, pp 1218–1225

Clarke R (2019) Risks inherent in the digital surveillance economy: a research agenda. J Inf Technol 34(1):59–80

Daniels S, Wei H, Han Y et al (2021, 1955) Risk factors associated with respiratory infectious disease-related presenteeism: a rapid review. BMC Public Health 21(1)

De Stefano V (2016) The rise of the just-in-time workforce: on-demand work, crowdwork, and labor protection in the gig-economy. Comp Labor Law Policy J 37(3):471–504

Deligkaris P, Panagopoulou E, Montgomery AJ et al (2014) Job burnout and cognitive functioning: a systematic review. Work Stress 28(2):107–123

Fox D, Webster J, Jones A (2019) Understanding the health and safety implications of the gig economy. Reportno. Report Number|, Date. Place Published|: Institution|

Freni-Sterrantino A, Salerno V (2021) A plea for the need to investigate the health effects of gig-economy. Front Public Health 9:638767–638767

Gamble J (2007) The rhetoric of the consumer and customer control in China. Work Employ Soc 21(1):7–25

Glavin P and Schieman S (2021) Dependency and hardship in the gig economy: the mental health consequences of platform work. Researchgate preprint

Huang H (2022) Riders on the storm: amplified platform Precarity and the impact of COVID-19 on online food-delivery drivers in China. J Contemp China 31(135):351–365

Huang L, Hao Z, Tian Y et al (2021) 新业态从业人员劳动权益保护2020年度调研报告 (2020 annual research report on labour rights protection of new employment forms). Reportno. Report Number|, Date. Place Published|: Institution|

Huws U, Spencer NH, Syrdal DS et al (2017) Work in the European gig economy: research results from the UK, Sweden, Germany, Austria, the Netherlands, Switzerland and Italy. Reportno. Report Number|, Date. Place Published|: Institution|

ILO (2021) World employment and social outlook: the role of digital labour platforms in transforming the world of work. Reportno. Report Number|, Date. Place Published|: Institution|

Kikuchi H, Odagiri Y, Ohya Y et al (2020) Association of overtime work hours with various stress responses in 59,021 Japanese workers: retrospective cross-sectional study. PLoS One 15(3): e0229506

Korczynski M, Evans C (2013) Customer abuse to service workers: an analysis of its social creation within the service economy. Work Employ Soc 27(5):768–784

Kosugoh R, Fujii H, Hirata A (1992) Subjective assessment of workload (1) revision of the cumulative fatigue symptoms index. Journal of Science of Labor. (In Japanese) 68:489–502

Kreshpaj B, Orellana C, Burström B et al (2020) What is precarious employment? A systematic review of definitions and operationalizations from quantitative and qualitative studies. Scand J Work Environ Health 46(3):235–247. https://doi.org/10.5271/sjweh.3875

Kristensen TS, Borritz M, Villadsen E et al (2005) The Copenhagen burnout inventory: a new tool for the assessment of burnout. Work Stress 19(3):192–207

Kubo T, Matsumoto S, Sasaki T et al (2021) Shorter sleep duration is associated with potential risks for overwork-related death among Japanese truck drivers: use of the Karoshi prodromes from worker's compensation cases. Int Arch Occup Environ Health 94(5):991–1001

Lin Y林, Li X李, Li Y李 (2018) 北京市快递员过劳现状及其影响因素——基于1214名快递员的调查 (empirical research on employment and overwork situation of couriers – based on the investigation of 1214 couriers in Beijing). 中国流通经济(China Bus Mark) 32(08):79–88

Lin Y林, Li Y李 (2021) 心理资本、组织支持感在职业紧张与过度劳动关系中的作用——基于北京地区外卖骑手的调查 (the role of psychological capital and organizational support in the relationship between occupational stress and overwork—based on a survey of take-out riders in Beijing). 中国流通经济(China Bus Mark) 35(4):116–126

Liu C, Friedman E (2021) Resistance under the radar: Organization of Work and Collective Action in China's food delivery industry. China J 86:68–89

Miao Q, Li J, Pan YP et al (2020) Three cases of Karoshi without the typical Pathomorphological features of cardiovascular/cerebrovascular disease. Am J Forensic Med Pathol 41(4):305–308

Nafilyan V, Pawelek P, Ayoubkhani D et al (2022) Occupation and COVID-19 mortality in England: a national linked data study of 14.3 million adults. Occup Environ Med 79(7):433–441. https://doi.org/10.1136/oemed-2021-107818

Nahrgang JD, Morgeson FP, Hofmann DA (2011) Safety at work: a meta-analytic investigation of the link between job demands, job resources, burnout, engagement, and safety outcomes. J Appl Psychol 96(1):71–94

ONS (2022) Annual population survey, January – December, 2021. In: Office for National Statistics SSD (ed) Annual population survey. UK Data Service

Praschan N, Josephy-Hernandez S, Kim DD et al (2021) Implications of COVID-19 sequelae for health-care personnel. Lancet Respir Med 9(3):230–231

Rotenstein LS, Torre M, Ramos MA et al (2018) Prevalence of burnout among physicians: a systematic review. JAMA 320(11):1131–1150

Ruiz M, Hu Y, Martikainen P et al (2019) Life course socioeconomic position and incidence of mid–late life depression in China and England: a comparative analysis of CHARLS and ELSA. J Epidemiol Community Health 73(9):817–824

Shan HP, Yang XH, Zhan XL et al (2017) Overwork is a silent killer of Chinese doctors: a review of Karoshi in China 2013–2015. Public Health 147:98–100

Shoman Y, El May E, Marca SC et al (2021) Predictors of occupational burnout: a systematic review. Int J Environ Res Public Health 18(17):9188

SIC (2021) 中国共享经济发展报告 (China's sharing economy development report) 2021. Reportno. Report Number|, Date. Place Published|: Institution|

Spencer NH and Huws U (2021) Platformisation and the pandemic: changes in workers' experiences of platform work in England and Wales, 2016–2021 – Reportno. Report Number|, Date. Place Published|: Institution|

Sun P (2019) Your order, their labor: an exploration of algorithms and laboring on food delivery platforms in China. Chin. J. Commun 12(3):308–323

Sun P, Yujie Chen J, Rani U (2021) From flexible labour to 'sticky labour': a tracking study of Workers in the Food-Delivery Platform Economy of China. Work Employ Soc 2021 (August):09500170211021570

Tran M, Sokas RK (2017) The gig economy and contingent work: an occupational health assessment. J Occup Environ Med 59(4):e63–e66 van den Heuvel M, Demerouti E, Peeters MCW (2015) The job crafting intervention: effects on job resources, self-efficacy, and affective Well-being. J Occup Organ Psychol 88(3):511–532

Wahrendorf M, Chandola T (2016) A life course perspective on work stress and health. *Work stress and health in a globalized economy.* Springer, pp 43–66

Wang Z, Neitzel RL, Zheng W et al (2021) Road safety situation of electric bike riders: a cross-sectional study in courier and take-out food delivery population. Traffic Inj Prev 22(7):564–569

Wei H, Li S, O'Toole T, Li S, O'Toole T, Yu M, Armitage CJ, Chandola T, Whelan P, Xu Y, van Tongeren M (2021) Prevalence of and risk factors for burnout and occupational stress among couriers: a systematic review. https://doi.org/10.1101/2021.11.09.21266103. medRxiv 2021.11.09.21266103

Wei H, Daniels S, Whitfield CA et al (2022a) Agility and sustainability: a qualitative evaluation of COVID-19 non-pharmaceutical interventions in the UK logistics sector. Front Public Health 10

Wei H, Shi H, Kou Y et al (2022b) Customer sovereignty, algorithmic management, economic precarity and networked support: a job demands-resources analysis of stress and response among Chinese couriers. medRxiv

WHO (2018) The life-course approach: from theory to practice: case stories from two small countries in Europe. Reportno. Report Number|, Date. Place Published|: Institution|

Wu Q, Zhang H, Li Z et al (2019) Labor control in the gig economy: evidence from Uber in China. J Ind Relat 61(4):574–596

Zhou I (2020) Digital labour platforms and labour protection in China, ILO working paper no. 11. International Labour Organization (ILO), Geneva

Zuboff S (2019) The age of surveillance capitalism: the fight for a human future at the new frontier of power. PublicAffairs, New York

Gender Differences in Work Participation over the Life Course and Consequences for Socioeconomic and Health Outcomes

21

Anne McMunn

Contents

Introduction	358
Gender Differences in Labor Market Participation Across Working Life	359
Entry to Parenthood As a Gendered Life Course Transition	359
Longer-Term Gender Differences in Labor Market Participation and Uptake of Adult Care	360
Gender and Unpaid Care Work During the COVID-19 Pandemic	360
Socioeconomic Inequalities	360
Country-Level Differences and Policy Drivers of Gender Differences in Labor Market Participation	361
Consequences of Gender Differences in Work Participation: Socioeconomic Outcomes	363
Occupation Downgrading and Positional Power	363
The Gender Pay and Pension Gaps	364
Consequences of Gender Differences in Work Participation: Health and Well-Being Outcomes	364
Self-Reported Health and Quality of Life	365
Mental Health and Well-Being	367
Obesity	367
Metabolic and Inflammatory Markers	368
Cognition	368
Mortality	369
Job Quality	369
Adult Care	369
Single Mothers	370
Conclusion	370
References	371

A. McMunn (✉)
Research Department of Epidemiology and Public Health, University College London, London, UK
e-mail: a.mcmunn@ucl.ac.uk

© Springer Nature Switzerland AG 2023
M. Wahrendorf et al. (eds.), *Handbook of Life Course Occupational Health*, Handbook Series in Occupational Health Sciences, https://doi.org/10.1007/978-3-031-30492-7_21

Abstract

Participation in paid employment, particularly high-quality employment, is linked with a range of economic, social, psychological, and health benefits. Reduced participation – either through periods of nonparticipation or through reduced hours of participation – limits career progression and achievement in terms of pay and conditions, as well as the accumulation of the benefits associated with paid employment. Persistent gender differences in responsibility for unpaid care work within homes and communities mean that women's work life courses remain much more likely than men's to include reduced employment hours and periods of nonemployment in many countries. The aim of this chapter is to review current evidence on gender differences in labor market participation over the life course and the potential consequences of work discontinuities for economic, health, and well-being outcomes, with a particular focus on studies using life course data. The chapter finishes by drawing on international evidence to highlight possible policy solutions for reducing stubborn gender inequalities in access to high-quality employment and equal pay.

Keywords

Gender · Work · Family · Health · Life course

Introduction

Participation in paid employment, particularly high-quality employment, is linked with a range of economic, social, psychological, and health benefits. There are a variety of pathways through which participation in employment fosters positive health: through the ability to independently generate one's own financial resources, access to a wider social network from which to potentially draw support and increased social contact, the imposition of a time structure to the day, and self-esteem derived from participating in a collective purpose, as well as identity and status. Reduced participation – either through periods of nonparticipation or through reduced hours of participation – limits career progression and achievement in terms of pay and conditions, as well as the accumulation of the potential health benefits associated with paid employment.

Gender inequality in employment and occupational attainment has been steadily decreasing for the past half century, although not equally across all countries, and gender inequalities remain across all countries. In addition, women are overrepresented in low-paid, insecure employment – and women of color even more so. Some look to unconscious biases in the work place as a key driver of these persistent gender differences, but persistent gender differences in "unpaid care work" – a term used in this chapter to refer to all of the unpaid services provided within a household to members of that household – are widely recognized as a major driver. While women have increased participation in paid work, similar increases in men's participation in unpaid care work have not followed, despite being highlighted by Hochschild as long ago as 1989 in the seminal *Second Shift* and repeatedly recognized since (e.g., Esping-Anderson 2009).

We will see that gender inequality in labor market participation and attainment persists and is strongly linked with stubborn gender differences in unpaid care work over the life course. These persistent gender differences in paid and unpaid work feed into gender inequality in pay and pensions and have limited women's voices in decision-making processes and positions of power. We will also see that weak labor market attachment over the life course is linked with worse health across a wide range of health outcomes and in many countries.

Gender Differences in Labor Market Participation Across Working Life

Entry to Parenthood As a Gendered Life Course Transition

In almost all high- and middle-income countries, women now achieve higher levels of educational attainment than men, and, for the first time in history, there are more couples in which women have a higher level of education than their male partners. As far back as 2012, half of British women aged 25–34 had achieved tertiary education compared with 46% of men in that age group (OECD 2015).

Thus, men and women in many countries enter the labor market with equal resources in terms of human capital, and the time men and women in couples spend in paid and unpaid care work is similar until the transition to parenthood which appears to trigger a reversion toward a more traditional "separate spheres" division of work, reducing women's paid work time and increasing time spent in childcare, with little impact on the time use of fathers. Thus, gender differences in employment patterns are not so much driven by gender as by the interaction between gender and parenthood. Childless women and men regardless of their parental status are employed at substantially higher levels than mothers in most countries. For example, in the UK, fathers are more likely to work than men without children while the opposite is true for mothers (ONS 2019). The employment rate of fathers is not sensitive to the age or number of children, while that of mothers is highly sensitive to both (ONS 2019). Also, when mothers with young children do work, it is usually part-time (ONS 2019).

Evidence on whether the impact of parenthood on gender divisions of labor may be weakening for more recent generations of parents is mixed. Riederer and Berhmanner (2020) have shown that the parenthood effect on women's employment rates decreased over time in Austria but the employment uptake was part-time, reducing average employment hours overall. In the UK, Zhou and Kan (2019) have shown that the association between traditional divisions of labor and fertility weakened from 2009 onward, and Hoherz and Bryan (2020) have shown that fatherhood led men to reduce their working hours if their partner was employed. However, Harkness et al. (2019) found that less than 20% of all new mothers in the

UK, and 29% of first-time mothers, worked full-time after maternity leave. Among those who were working full-time prior to childbirth, a majority stopped working or moved to part-time work.

Longer-Term Gender Differences in Labor Market Participation and Uptake of Adult Care

There is evidence to suggest that the "reset" in gender relations triggered by entry to parenthood carries on throughout adulthood. Women are more likely to have interrupted careers than men in all countries, although there are large country differences in the extent to which this is true. Nearly half of women in the UK currently work part-time compared with 12% of men (ONS 2021). In addition to childcare, population aging, coupled with more years spent living in poor health, has also led to increases in the need for adult care across countries, with most currently relying on unpaid care provided by families to provide a majority of this care. While gender differences in adult care provision are not as great as for childcare, women are more likely to provide care, to have provided care for longer, and to care more intensively than men, and women's weaker ties to employment over the life course may contribute to their greater likelihood to take up adult care.

Gender and Unpaid Care Work During the COVID-19 Pandemic

The closure of schools and childcare facilities during periods of the pandemic, and vulnerable adults shielding at home, led to an increased unpaid care workload often alongside home working. There was initial speculation that these events might trigger fathers to increase their contribution to unpaid care work, and Shafer et al. (2020) found Canadian parents reported a slightly more equal division of labor in the early months of the pandemic with fathers increasing their participation in housework and childcare. However, evidence from the UK and Ireland has shown that mothers continued to spend more time than fathers in childcare activities during the pandemic (Xue and McMunn 2021; Stevanova et al. 2021). In Ireland, working mothers reported expecting increased childcare during the pandemic to have a negative impact on their career outcomes, while fathers did not have any such expectations (Stevanova et al. 2021). However, a study in Germany found, surprisingly, that having children accelerated mothers' return to prepandemic work hours, but not fathers, which they attribute to fathers' long overtime hours prepandemic (Knize et al. 2021).

Socioeconomic Inequalities

As more women gained educational qualifications, those with tertiary qualifications have tended to maintain continuous employment after becoming mothers (with breaks only for maternity leave) while those with fewer qualifications have tended to take time out of the labor market after entry to parenthood (Harkness et al. 2019). These patterns have led to increasing socioeconomic polarization among families as the advantage of having a university degree is reinforced by an increased likelihood of partnering with a similarly educated spouse and being able to afford stable childcare which further enables strong labor market attachment. On the other hand, those without higher educational qualifications are often unable to afford formal childcare, limiting their job opportunities to those that fit around informal childcare arrangements and/or are geographically close by (Costa Dias et al. 2018). However, these patterns are not universal and may be changing. In Austria, Riederer and Berhmanner (2020) found that maternal employment rates increased most for women with fewer educational qualifications between 1986 and 2016, helping to close the maternal employment gap based on mothers' educational qualifications. The impact of women's education on maternal employment seems to be modified by cultural gender norms with highly educated women undertaking less paid work and more unpaid care work in more traditional cultures. For example, women's increased educational attainment is not being translated into better occupational class, income, or egalitarian divisions of unpaid care work in Spain (Garcia-Roman 2021).

Studies seeking to explain persistent gender inequality in unpaid care work have investigated whether the postparenthood shift toward a more traditional division of labor is weaker for women with higher earnings – both absolute and relative to their partner – but results have been mixed, suggesting gender norms have played a strong role in driving the postparenthood shift to traditional divisions of labor. Several studies have shown that the amount of time new fathers in Australia spent on childcare and paid work did not differ by educational attainment.

Country-Level Differences and Policy Drivers of Gender Differences in Labor Market Participation

Studies of individual or couple-level drivers of gender inequality in unpaid care work focusing on differential bargaining power related to relative incomes and earnings potential or individual- and couple-level attitudes toward gender roles are inevitably influenced by the macrolevel social context. A large body of evidence has investigated the role that country-level policies play in gender divisions of labor. Most have categorized countries into typologies based on a range of policies, but some have focused on specific policies such as parental leave and childcare provision.

There is a long tradition of comparative research into gender equality in paid and unpaid labor, based on welfare regimes either directly or loosely based on Esping-Andersen's welfare regime classification (1990, 2009) of European countries into social democratic, conservative, and liberal, with Mediterranean and former communist categories added subsequently. According to this typology, Nordic social democracies are characterized by widespread government services, income support, and gender equality. In conservative countries, a traditional male breadwinner model is central, reinforced with tax incentives and with fewer outsourcing options for childcare. Both liberal and Mediterranean countries have little government intervention, but with a strong family orientation in the latter. Full-time work for both men and women is central to Eastern European former communist countries, but attitudes to gender equality and parity in unpaid care work lag.

More recently, scholars often use typologies based on family policy rather than broader welfare regimes in which countries are grouped based on their generosity of support for working parents in terms of targeting of financial support, leave entitlement, and childcare provision. Of course, all regime typologies are ideal typical abstractions and countries do not fit perfectly within them. For example, last year Spain (usually considered a familial society with little financial support for leave or childcare) expanded paternity leave to equal maternity leave at 16 weeks with 100% salary replacement. Similarly, Eastern European countries can be divided into those with high degree of familialism (Hungary, Poland, Czech, Slovaidal, Latvia, and Estonia) and those that focus support on women's employment and parental support (Slovenia & Lithuania).

Some studies consider gender divisions in unpaid care work in relation to The Gender Empowerment Measure (GEM) which is based on a country's estimated female-to-male earnings ratio; female parliamentary representation; and women's share of professional and technical workers, legislators, senior officials, and managers.

Overall, regardless of the typology used, countries with generous support for working parents and policies explicitly designed to support gender equality, such as well-paid, dedicated paternity leave and public provision of childcare, as well as countries with high GEM scores, tend to display the highest maternal employment rates, although not always. Also, women continue to do much more unpaid care work than men even in countries with high levels of policy support for gender equality, such as Denmark, and women are more likely to have interrupted careers than men in all countries.

Country differences in support for adult care mirror those for childcare. Many northern European countries provide state support with specific rights and entitlements for carers, while countries in the south tend to rely on family-based care with many other European countries falling somewhere between. Gender inequality in who provides care is greater in countries that rely on a family-based model, and there is some evidence to suggest institutional care is much more effective than home care in supporting adult children to reconcile care with employment. However, looking at employees providing adult care in 33 countries, Bainbridge et al. (2021) found that, contrary to expectation, gender differences in caregiving intensity were greater in more egalitarian countries, with men caring for fewer hours in these countries. The authors speculate that men in these countries may be more preoccupied with childcare than men in other countries and more likely to "outsource" parental care to formal care services which are also more available in more egalitarian countries.

Well-paid parental leave, publicly supported childcare services for very young children, and cultural support for maternal employment appear to be key drivers for reducing the gap in employment participation and working hours between mothers and childless women. Evidence consistently shows that legal job protection and statutory maternity leave are associated with a greater likelihood of women returning to the labor force after childbirth and a reduced gender wage gap; however, the length of leave is important. Long leave (more than 30 weeks), particularly if it is unpaid, may be detrimental to women's employment and the gender pay gap. The importance of father-only leave periods is also increasingly clear, at least in relation to the gender pay gap and fathers' participation in unpaid care work. The introduction of nontransferable paternity leave in Nordic, and increasingly non-Nordic countries such as Spain and Germany, has shown an increase in leave uptake, and fathers who take paternity or parental leave when children are young are more involved in childcare activities and parental relationship quality and mental health. There is also consistent evidence to show that publicly provided or subsidized childcare services boost women's employment outcomes and maternal employment hours, and reduce the motherhood wage and occupational attainment penalty. The impact of parenthood on gender divisions of labor is also reduced in countries with more egalitarian gender norms. Disentangling the effects of cultural norms from country-level family policies is difficult, of course, but cultural norms seem to interact with family policy with egalitarian norms potentially amplifying the association between generous family policies and women's earnings, while the predominance of traditional norms moderate this association.

Consequences of Gender Differences in Work Participation: Socioeconomic Outcomes

Occupation Downgrading and Positional Power

Gender inequality in paid work permeates material as well as time resources, including gender inequality in earnings and promotion over the life course. Historically, mothers, particularly mothers with fewer qualifications, have often returned to more "casual," flexible jobs within the labor market that can be worked around informal childcare arrangements, a process known as "occupational downgrading." This has become less common as legal job protections during maternity leave have come into force, and the current generation of new mothers return to a job with the same occupational status as the one they left. However, there remains, rather, a reduction in the probability of occupational upgrading over time (Harkness et al. 2019). Women's greater likelihood to have interrupted careers leads to difficulties in accumulating as much human capital as men and hindering occupational advancement in many countries. Women are underrepresented in positions of power, for example, making up just under a third of positions of power in politics, business, and public life in the UK, while women of color are simply missing altogether from the highest level of many sectors, and there are just seven female Chief Executives in FTSE 100. Also, women remain disproportionately represented in precarious work characterized by low wages, a lack of benefits and collective representation, and insecurity, such as cleaners and those working in the care and leisure sectors.

Adult care provision also limits access to financial and social resources and leads to labor market exits, reduced working hours, salaries and pension entitlements, and loss of training opportunities and career advancement, although the impact of adult care depends on the type, duration, and intensity of care. Women's greater likelihood of providing care means they are much more likely to experience these job limitations, exacerbating the persistent gender pay gap. In addition, carers who exit employment lose the respite and social support that the work environment provides.

The Gender Pay and Pension Gaps

Women's greater propensity to work part-time in lower paid jobs with fewer progression opportunities, as well as their underrepresentation in the highest paid jobs, contributes to the persistent gender pay gap worldwide. The gender gap in earning power has been shrinking, although progress has stalled in the past 3 years; at the current rate, it will take 257 years to achieve equal pay (Action Aid 2018). In the UK, among all employees gender pay gap increased to 15.4% in 2021 from 14.9% in 2020 but down from 17.4% in 2019 (ONS 2021). Jobs with the same level of skill, responsibility, and working conditions are often paid more in male dominated sectors, such as construction, compared with female-dominated sectors, such as childcare. The gender pay gap exists at all ages, but widens after age 24 (ONS 2021), and gradually widens after childbirth (Costa Dias et al. 2018). Costa Dias et al. (2018) found that accumulated years of differential working hours explain up to two-thirds of the gender pay gap among university graduates 20 years after childbirth, and one-third among those with no higher education. Also, weak labor market attachment from early adulthood has been shown to set women onto trajectories of disadvantage leading to lower socioeconomic attainment in later life in terms of income, wealth, and occupational class (Xue et al. 2020). And women's weaker ties to employment and lower pay accumulate, leading to a gender pension gap as well. The OECD estimates women aged 65+ will earn 26% less pensions income than men across its member countries (OECD 2021).

Consequences of Gender Differences in Work Participation: Health and Well-Being Outcomes

High-quality employment has consistently been linked with better health outcomes. Given that women have had less access to employment than men have over their life courses, we might expect women's exclusion from paid work to manifest in greater morbidity among women than men, and, indeed, while men die younger than women, largely due to riskier jobs and behavior, women worldwide do tend to carry a greater burden of disease, including, but not limited to, psychological distress. However, mothers' initial large-scale entry into the world of work was initially met with concern, particularly in the USA, over the potentially health-damaging effects of trying to combine paid work with family responsibilities, ideas often termed the "Role Overload" or "Role Conflict" hypotheses. However, knowing what we know now about the benefits of participation in paid employment, particularly if it is adequately paid, secure, and stimulating, we might expect this shift to have been health enhancing for women of the time. Indeed, some scholars of the time argued that the multiple roles that these new working mothers occupied might be beneficial by increasing access to health-enhancing factors such as self-esteem, social contact, and financial resources from a greater variety of roles, often labeled the "Role Enhancement" or "Multiple Role" hypothesis. Some early investigators hypothesized a process of role trade-off in which emotional and material resources provided by one role were used to meet the demands of another.

These ideas feel outdated to us now due to their predication on the notion of gendered social roles regarding women as caregivers and men as providers. These days, we might equally ask what the health impact is on men of the felt imperative to increase working hours upon entry to parenthood, and often feeling less able to request the flexible working arrangements required to participate equally in parenting. Yet, while much of the language used in this period is antiquated, the sentiments expressed persist in new forms. These early models can be seen as a precursor to the more recent spillover model which posits that stressful exposures from home or work sometimes spill over from one environment to another leading to role conflict and negative health outcomes.

In terms of the evidence supporting these early hypotheses, many large-scale, often national, social surveys tended to find that women who were participating in all three of these "roles" reported better health than women who were not. However, the vast majority of these studies were cross-sectional in design. The few longitudinal studies to examine social roles at baseline and later health or mortality did not include measures of health earlier in the life course, so were unable to investigate the influence of health prior to social role occupation, and relied on social role measures at one or, at most, two points in time.

In order to understand causal processes related to work, family, and health, in addition to establishing the timing and direction of associations, it is helpful to characterize different states and transitions across an entire life course. For example, it is useful to be able to observe the duration of employment spells, the accumulation of periods of unemployment, or transitions such as parenthood or divorce as potential triggers for employment transitions or health events, which is increasingly enabled by the availability of detailed life course data and the use of sequence analysis, either single- or multichannel (the former using one life course domain, such as employment, and the latter using multiple life course domains simultaneously). This section reviews current evidence which uses a life course perspective to link work trajectories with a variety of health outcomes.

Self-Reported Health and Quality of Life

While many surveys now collect more objective markers of physical health, most early studies relied on people's reports of their own health. These perceptions remain informative and have been shown to significantly predict mortality. Evidence from two British birth cohort studies (born in 1946 and 1958), as well as the National Longitudinal Survey of Youth (NLSY) in the USA, have shown that mothers with weaker ties to paid work (both married and single although much more strongly for single) were significantly more likely to report poor health compared with married mothers working full-time (McDonough et al. 2015; McMunn et al. 2006). Using employment trajectories from the English Longitudinal Study of Ageing (ELSA), Stone et al. (2015) found that mothers who took a break from work and returned full-time were 25% less likely to report poor health than women who maintained full-time employment. The same was found in relation to quality of life in ELSA's sister study in Europe (the Survey of Health and Retirement in Europe, SHARE), but long-term homemakers also reported lower quality of life than those who took time out from work for parenting and returned to full-time employment in SHARE (Wahrendorf 2015).

Work in ELSA was recently updated in an investigation of differences in a latent health index (including self-rated health as well as reported limitations of activities of daily living and observed walking speed) and quality of life trajectories by employment sequences (Di Gessa et al. 2020). Similar to the earlier study in ELSA, women who took medium length breaks from employment (about 8 years on average) and returned to full-time employment ended up with better health and quality of life in retirement compared with women who maintained continuous employment. This study also included men and found that men with weak long-term ties to employment also had worse health and quality of life than men who maintained continuous employment, although the difference between groups decreased somewhat over time. As we will see, these lower levels of reported health among women in continuous employment contradict patterns seen in later-born cohorts. This may partly be due to the fact that a large majority of the women in ELSA formed their families before statutory maternity leave was available in the UK, and once it was available many women continued to be disqualified due to long employment-qualifying periods.

Using employment trajectories between ages 16 and 42, Swedish women with different work trajectories did not differ in general health with one exception: Those who worked part-time for a period around the age of 30, between periods of full-time employment, reported better health in comparison with women who worked full-time followed by entry to part-time employment around the age of 40 (Huang et al. 2007).

Studies in the USA and South Africa have examined self-rated general health in relation to women's work and family transitions in early adulthood (Bennet and Waterhouse 2018; Amato and Kane 2011), and a study in the UK has extended this to investigate associations between transitions in early adulthood and health in later life (Xue et al. 2021). In all of these studies, transitions to early motherhood and nonemployment were associated with worse health outcomes when compared with women who transitioned to full-time employment (combined with motherhood in the South African context), although this association was explained by earlier health selection into employment trajectories in the USA.

Mental Health and Well-Being

There is a long history of studying the impact on mental health of combining employment with married motherhood among women. Longitudinal studies using more than two waves of data have consistently found health benefits of continuous employment for women, and men where men have been included. Four studies have investigated work- or work-family life courses and mental health using sequence analysis. One compared mothers from the USA (using the NLSY) and the UK (using the 1958 British birth cohort) and showed that mothers with weaker ties to paid work (both married and single although much more strongly for single), and divorced women who returned to employment, were more likely to score high on a depression scale in their early 40s compared with married mothers working full-time (McDonough et al. 2015). Similarly, women in the 1946 British birth cohort with weaker ties to paid work over the long-term had significantly lower life satisfaction at age 60 than women who had combined paid work with stable partnership and parenthood, as did both men and women who had not partnered or had children (Lacey et al. 2016c). A comparison across all three of the adult British birth cohort studies showed that later family transitions combined with strong ties to employment were associated with less psychological distress for women born in 1958 and 1970 while early parenthood combined with full-time unpaid care work was linked with greater psychological distress in midlife across all three cohorts (McMunn et al. 2021). Among West Germans born between 1925 and 1955, no associations between employment trajectories and depressive symptoms were found for men, and women who returned to employment full-time, after a period of looking after the family full-time, were more likely to be depressed than women who returned to employment part-time (Engels et al. 2019). The authors attribute this finding to higher levels of single mothers in the group of women who returned to employment full-time. A recent investigation of employment sequences and depressive symptoms in ELSA found no association for men or women (Di Gessa et al. 2020).

Obesity

A few studies have investigated obesity in relation to work and family life courses. An early study showed that women with weak ties to employment in the 1946 British birth cohort were twice as likely than women with stronger long-term ties to employment to be obese at age 53, independent of socioeconomic circumstances, body mass index (BMI) in early life, or number of children (McMunn et al. 2006). This was replicated across all three adult British birth cohort studies which showed that work-family life courses characterized by earlier transitions to parenthood and weaker long-term links to employment were associated with greater increases in BMI across adulthood among both men and women, and this association became stronger across cohorts as these biographies became less normative and less prevalent (Lacey et al. 2017). As in the British birth cohort studies, Hedel et al. (2016) used data from SHARE and its sister study in the USA, the Health and Retirement

Survey (HRS), to compare work-family life course differences in the health of women in Europe and the USA and found that nonworking married mothers were 17% more likely to be obese than working married mothers in the USA, although not Europe. Mooyaart et al. (2019) found a lower likelihood of obesity at age 28 among women who attended higher education and postponed parenthood, while men who married early were more likely to be obese at age 28 in the NLSY.

Metabolic and Inflammatory Markers

"Biomarkers" of metabolic and inflammatory processes are studied not only as objective markers of disease risk, but also to better understand the biological pathways through which stressful social environments may be "embodied" to influence health. These markers have been investigated in relation to work-family life courses among men and women in the 1946 and 1958 British birth cohorts. Six metabolic markers were included in the 1946 cohort at age 53: waist circumference, systolic and diastolic blood pressure, cholesterol, and measures of fat and sugar in the blood (triglycerides and glycated hemoglobin). Men in groups that made later transitions to parenthood had reduced metabolic risk in midlife while women in a group characterized by childlessness had smaller waist circumferences at age 53, but no other differences were seen for women (Lacey et al. 2016a). For women in the 1958 cohort, maintaining long periods out of employment to look after the family was much less common; however, levels of the inflammatory marker fibrinogen were about 5% higher for women in their mid-40s in this later cohort who did take long periods of time out of employment compared with those who combined strong ties to paid work with later transitions to stable family lives. Teen parents also had significantly higher levels of two inflammatory markers – up to 40% higher – independent of childhood health and socioeconomic position, adult socioeconomic position, health behaviors, and BMI (Lacey et al. 2016b). Looking at the metabolic markers in this cohort born in 1958, rather than work-family combinations emerging as important, life courses characterized by earlier transitions into parenthood were associated with significantly increased metabolic risk, regardless of attachment to paid work or marital stability over the life course, and these associations were only partially attenuated by educational qualifications, early life circumstances, and adult mediators, such as social class, health behaviors, and BMI (McMunn et al. 2016).

Cognition

Two studies have investigated cognitive trajectories among women in later life in relation to work-family life courses using HRS in the USA (Mayeda et al. 2020) and SHARE in Europe (Ice et al. 2020). They both find that life courses characterized by continuous employment were associated with the highest levels of cognitive functioning, regardless of partnership or parenting experiences. In the USA, from age 60, the average rate of memory decline was more than 50% greater among women whose work-family life courses did not include employment after childbearing, compared with those who were working mothers (Mayeda et al. 2020). In Europe, partnered mothers who mainly worked part-time had the best cognitive function, with mothers who worked full-time in the middle (Ice et al. 2020), independent of childhood socioeconomic disadvantage and educational status.

Mortality

In the USA, again using multichannel sequence analysis in the HRS to characterize employment, partnership, and parenthood life courses among women, Sabbath et al. (2015a) found patterns in relation to mortality that were very much in line with work on morbidity outcomes. Women whose life courses were characterized by long periods out of employment died significantly younger than women who maintained stronger ties to paid work (Standardized Mortality Ratios of 66.8 for nonworking married mothers and 83.1 for nonworking single mothers compared with 60.4 for working married mothers). The authors adjusted for smoking and BMI, as well as differences in age, income, education, and ethnicity, to account for potential health selection effects, although they were not able to take account of early life health which may have contributed to weaker employment ties. Contrary to this, McKetta et al. (2018) found a 62% higher risk of mortality among never-married women whose life courses were characterized by stronger ties to employment, compared with married later-mothers with strong ties to employment in the USA, suggesting a protective effect of marriage which has been widely shown elsewhere.

Job Quality

The body of work covered in this chapter has focused on work and family states and transitions over the life course, but we know that associations between work and health vary by work characteristics, such as security, pay, hours, and autonomy. We have also seen that women are overrepresented in sectors that are low paid and insecure. However, studies of health in relation to work-family life courses have not incorporated indicators of job quality. One notable exception is Sabbath et al. (2015b) who extended their analysis of mortality in the HRS described above to include measures of job control in the derivation of their work-family life courses. They found mortality rates were highest for single mothers in low-control jobs, and lowest for married mothers who entered family life later and were in high-control jobs.

Adult Care

While the studies above tend to focus on work-family life courses through midlife, generally capturing life stages during which parenthood demands are greatest, there is also a body of evidence linking adult care with poorer psychological and physical health (Pinquart and Sörensen 2003). Evidence from the UK using a large, national study of working aged adults (the UK Household Longitudinal Study, UKHLS) has shown that women aged 45 or younger who provide informal care to an adult have higher levels of adiposity (Lacey et al. 2018a) and metabolic risk factors (Lacey et al. 2018b) as well as psychological symptoms which persisted over time (Lacey et al. 2019). Using instrumental variable techniques in SHARE, Heger (2016) showed caring for a parent to be linked with increased depressive symptoms among daughters in particular, while Brenna and Di Novi (2016) show this association to be concentrated in Southern European countries. One study has used multichannel sequence analysis to characterize work-care (adult and child) trajectories over 15 years in the UKHLS and its precursor the British Household Panel Study (BHPS) and found that psychological distress and self-rated health of people in trajectories characterized by intensive adult caregiving out of employment deteriorated more over time than that of those characterized by long-term full-time employment without young children at home (Carmichael and Ercolani 2016).

Single Mothers

This chapter has focused on couples as research on gender inequality in unpaid care work has tended to focus on divisions of labor within male-female couples. It is important to note, however, that many of the work-family life course studies covered above have found particularly high levels of poor health among single mothers. This builds on a large body of evidence that has documented the poor health of single parents (the vast majority of which are mothers) going back many decades. Most recently a study in the UK showed that levels of distress were particularly high for single working mothers during the pandemic who were juggling employment with childcare or homeschooling (Xue and McMunn 2021).

Conclusion

Adopting a life course approach to the study of employment and health which characterizes the timing and nature of transitions alongside the duration of states such as employment and partnership has been useful for understanding the impact of simultaneous life course processes as they accumulate or shift with age and across generations. This body of work has shown that the duration of exposure to periods of nonemployment for unpaid care work matters, and particularly so where it occurs alongside single parenthood or early transitions to parenthood. It has also enabled researchers to study these processes while taking account of the effects of early health, socioeconomic and family circumstances that may select people into particular employment, family, and health trajectories.

We have seen that women continue to be disadvantaged in terms of labor market participation and outcomes, and evidence suggests this disadvantage is linked with poor health across a range of outcomes and across the life course. So, what are the avenues for change? As we have seen from comparative research, change requires societies to demonstrate that care and family life are valued equally to employment and economic growth. Change requires policies that support equal sharing of unpaid care work and closing the maternal employment gap which will, in turn, foster employment. This means targeting parental leave and flexible working provision at fathers, as well as mothers, and providing subsidized child and adult care. While access to flexible working has been linked with improved work-family outcomes, few fathers adopt flexible working arrangement to assist them in reconciling paid work and childcare. This is because flexibility stigma remains an issue, particularly in male-dominated industries, and the paternal role is largely invisible in workplaces. Displaying work devotion, often through long working hours, continues to be a way of enacting both class and gender identity for many men, and resistance to threats to these identities helps keep workplace norms in place. This means that workplaces must go beyond providing leave or flexibility policies and must also recognize and address workplace norms and bias against those using leave and flexible working policies. The introduction of dedicated father-specific leave is the most likely lever for facilitating uptake and shifting norms.

The EU has been a driving force in improving working parents' ability to share work and care; having reached a policy consensus that increased female labor force participation, a more extensive and efficient use of women's skills and female earnings are central to promoting economic growth. EU countries are required to adopt The EU Directive on Work Life Balance for Parents and Carers by August 2022. This requires countries to provide 2 weeks paid paternity leave, ensure that 2 months of parental leave are nontransferable between parents, and provide 1 week of carers leave to workers per year, as well as the right to request flexible working for carers and those with children up to 8 years of age. In addition, in her State of the Union address, the European Commission President announced her intention to develop a new care strategy to support both formal and informal carers. While ground-breaking it many ways, EU legislation falls short of recognizing caring as a protected characteristic which Mitchell (2020) has argued would increase the value and recognition of care work across the life course. Protected characteristic or not, policies to support gender equality in who provides unpaid care work across the life course have the potential to reduce the gender employment gap with benefits to well-being and financial security into later life.

References

Action Aid (2018) https://www.actionaid.org.uk/our-work/womens-economic-rights/gender-pay-gap

Amato PR, Kane JB (2011) Life-course pathways and the psychosocial adjustment of young adult women. J Marriage Fam 73:279–295. https://doi.org/10.1111/j.1741-3737.2010.00804.x

Bainbridge HTJ, Palm E, Fong MM (2021) Unpaid family caregiving responsibilities, employee job tasks and work-family conflict: a cross-cultural study. Hum Resour Manag J 31:658–674. https://doi.org/10.1111/1748-8583.12333

Bennet R, Waterhouse P (2018) Work and family transitions and the self-rated health of young women in South Africa. Soc Sci Med 203:9–18

Brenna E, Di Novi C (2016) Is caring for older parents detrimental to women's mental health? The role of the European north-south gradient. Rev Econ Househ 14(4):745–778

Carmichael F, Ercolani MG (2016) Unpaid caregiving and paid work over life-courses: different pathways, diverging outcomes. Soc Sci Med 156:1–11. https://doi.org/10.1016/j.socscimed.2016.03.020

Costa Dias M, Joyce R, Parodi F (2018) The gender pay gap in the UK: children and experience in work. Institute for Fiscal Studies, London. https://doi.org/10.1920/wp.ifs.2018.W1802

Di Gessa G, Corna L, Price D, Glaser K (2020) Lifetime employment histories and their relationship with 10-year health trajectories in later life: evidence from England. Eur J Pub Health 30(4): 793–799

Engels M, Weyers S, Moebus S, Jockel K-H, Erbel R, Pesch B, Behrens T, Dragano N, Wahrendorf M (2019) Gendered work-family trajectories and depression at older age. Aging Ment Health 23 (11):1478–1486

Esping-Anderson G (1990) The three worlds of welfare capitalism. Princeton University Press, Princeton

Esping-Anderson G (2009) The incomplete revolution: adapting to women's new roles. Polity Press, Cambridge

Garcia-Roman J (2021) Does women's educational advantage mean a more egalitarian distribution of gender roles? Evidence from dual-earner couples in Spain. J Fam Stud. https://doi.org/10.1080/13229400.2021.1915852

Harkness S, Borkowska M, Pelikh A (2019) Employment pathways and occupational change after childbirth. Government Equalities Office, London

Hedel K, Mejia-Guevara I, Avendano M et al (2016) Work–family trajectories and the higher cardiovascular risk of American women relative to women in 13 European countries. Am J Public Health 106(8):1449–1456. https://doi.org/10.2105/AJPH.2016.303264

Heger D (2016) The mental health of children providing care to their elderly parent. Health Econ 26(12)

Hochschild AR (1989) The second shift: working parents and the revolution at home. Viking Penguin, New York

Hoherz S, Bryan M (2020) Provider or father? British men's work hours and work preferences after the birth of a child. Work Employ Soc 34(2):193–210

Huang Q, El-Khouri BM, Johansson G, Lindroth S, Sverke M (2007) Women's career patterns: a study of Swedish women born in the 1950s. J Occup Organ Psychol 80:387–412. https://doi.org/10.1348/096317906X119738

Ice E, Ang S, Greenberg K, Burgard S (2020) Women's work-family histories and cognitive performance in later life. Am J Epidemiol 189:922–930. https://doi.org/10.1093/aje/kwaa042

Knize V, Tobler L, Christoph B, Fervers L, Jacob M (2021) Workin' moms ain't doing so bad: evidence on the gender gap in working hours at the outset of the COVID-19 pandemic. J Fam Res, Early view:1–32. https://doi.org/10.20377/jfr-714

Lacey R, Kumari M, Sacker A, Stafford M, Kuh D, McMunn A (2016a) Work-family life courses and metabolic markers in the MRC National Survey of Health and Development. PlosOne pone.0161923

Lacey R, Kumari M, Sacker A, Worts D, McDonough P, McMunn A (2016b) Work-family life courses and markers of stress and inflammation in mid-life: evidence from the National Child Development Study. Int J Epidemiol 45(4):1247–1259. https://doi.org/10.1093/ije/dyv205

Lacey R, Stafford M, Sacker A, McMunn A (2016c) Work-family life courses and subjective wellbeing in the MRC National Survey of Health and Development 1946 British birth cohort. J Popul Ageing 9:69–89. https://doi.org/10.1007/s12062-015-9126-y

Lacey R, Sacker A, Bell S, Kumari M, Worts D, McDonough P, Kuh D, McMunn A (2017) Work-family life courses and BMI trajectories in three British birth cohorts. Int J Obes 41:332–339. https://doi.org/10.1038/ijo.2016.197. http://rdcu.be/pIrA

Lacey R, McMunn A, Webb E (2018a) Informal caregiving and markers of adiposity in the UK Household Longitudinal Study. PlosOne. https://doi.org/10.1371/journal.pone.0200777

Lacey R, McMunn A, Webb E (2018b) Providing informal care and metabolic markers in the UK Household Longitudinal Study. Maturitas 109:97–103. https://doi.org/10.1016/j.maturitas.2018.01.002

Lacey R, McMunn A, Webb E (2019) Informal caregiving patterns and trajectories of psychological distress in the UK Household Longitudinal Study. Psychol Med:1–9. https://doi.org/10.1017/S0033291718002222

Mayeda ER, Mobley TM, Weiss RE, Murchland AR, Berkman LF, Sabbath EL (2020) Association of work-family experience with mid- and late-life memory decline in US women. Neurology 95: e3072–e3080. https://doi.org/10.1212/WNL.0000000000010989

McDonough P, Worts D, Booker C, McMunn A, Sacker A (2015) Cumulative disadvantage employment-marriage, and health inequalities among American and British mothers. Adv Life Course Res 25:49–66

McKetta S, Prins SJ, Platt J, Bates LM, Keyes K (2018) Social sequencing to determine patterns in health and work-family trajectories for U.S. women, 1968–2013. SSM – Popul Health 6:301–308. https://doi.org/10.1016/j.ssmph.2018.10.003

McMunn A, Bartley M, Hardy R, Kuh D (2006) Life course social roles and women's health in mid-life: causation or selection? J Epidemiol Community Health 60:484–489. https://doi.org/10.1136/jech.2005.042473

McMunn A, Lacey R, Worts D, McDonough P, Kumari M, Sacker A (2016) Work-family life courses and metabolic markers in mid-life: evidence from the British National Child Development Study. J Epidemiol Community Health 70:481–487. https://doi.org/10.1136/jech-2015-206036

McMunn A, Lacey R, Worts D, Kuh D, McDonough P, Sacker A (2021) Work-family life courses and psychological distress: evidence from three British birth cohort studies. Adv Life Course Res 50. https://doi.org/10.1016/j.alcr.2021.100429

Mitchell G (2020) A right to care: putting care ethics at the heart of UK reconciliation legislation. Ind Law J 49(2):199–230

Mooyaart JE, Liefbroer AC, Billari FC (2019) Becoming obese in young adulthood: the role of career-family pathways in the transition to adulthood for men and women. BMC Public Health 19:1–12. https://doi.org/10.1186/s12889-019-7797-7

OECD (2015) Education at a glance 2015: OECD indicators. OECD Publishing. https://doi.org/10.1787/eag-2015-en

OECD (2021) Towards improved retirement savings outcomes for women. OECD Publishing

Office for National Statistics (2019) Families and the labour market, UK: 2019. https://www.ons.gov.uk/employmentandlabourmarket/peopleinwork/employmentandemployeetypes/articles/familiesandthelabourmarketengland/2019

Office for National Statistics (2021) Gender pay gap in the UK: 2021. https://www.ons.gov.uk/employmentandlabourmarket/peopleinwork/earningsandworkinghours/bulletins/genderpaygapintheuk/2021

Pinquart M, Sörensen S (2003) Differences between caregivers and noncaregivers in psychological health and physical health: a meta-analysis. Psychol Aging 18(2):250–267

Riederer B, Berhmanner C (2020) The part-time revolution: changes in the parenthood effect on women's employment in Austria across the birth cohorts from 1940–1979. Eur Sociol Rev 36 (2):284–302

Sabbath E, Mejia-Guevara I, Glymour MM, Berkman LF (2015a) Use of life course work-family profiles to predict mortality risk among US women. Am J Public Health 105:96–103. https://doi.org/10.2105/AJPH.2014.302471

Sabbath EL, Mejia-Guevara I, Noelke C, Berkman LF (2015b) The long-term mortality impact of combined job strain and family circumstances: a life course analysis of working American mothers. Soc Sci Med 146:111–119

Shafer K, Scheibling C, Milkie MA (2020) The division of domestic labor before an during the COVID-19 pandemic in Canada: stagnation versus shifts in fathers' contributions. Can Rev Sociol 57(4):523–549

Stevanova V, Farrell L, Latu I (2021) Gender and the pandemic: associations between caregiving, working from home, personal and career outcomes for women and men. Curr Psychol. https://doi.org/10.1007/s12144-021-02630-6

Stone J, Evandrou M, Falkingham J, Vlachantoni A (2015) Women's economic activity trajectories over the life course: implications for the self-rated health of women aged 64+ in England. J Epidemiol Community Health 69:873–879

Wahrendorf M (2015) Previous employment histories and quality of life in older ages: sequence analyses using SHARELIFE. Ageing Soc 35(9):1928–1959. https://doi.org/10.1017/S0144686X14000713

Xue B, McMunn A (2021) Gender differences in unpaid care work and psychological distress in the UK Covid-19 lockdown. PLoS One 16(3):e0247959. https://doi.org/10.1371/journal.pone.0247959

Xue B, Tinkler P, Zaninotto P, McMunn A (2020) Girls' transition to adulthood and later life socioeconomic attainment: findings from the English longitudinal study of ageing. Adv Life Course Res 46. https://doi.org/10.1016/j.alcr.2020.100352

Xue B, Tinkler P, McMunn A (2021) The long shadow of youth: girls' transition to adulthood and later life wellbeing: findings from the English longitudinal study of ageing. J Gerontol Soc Sci 76(9):1838–1856

Zhou M, Kan M-Y (2019) A new family equilibrium? Changing dynamics between the gender division of labor and fertility in Great Britain, 1991–2017. Demogr Res 40(50):1455–1500

Part VI

Occupational Trajectories in the Context of Disability and Ageing

Changing Experiences, Needs, and Supports Across the Life Course for Workers Living with Disabilities

22

Arif Jetha and Monique A. M. Gignac

Contents

Introduction	378
Defining Disability	379
Conclusion	392
Cross-References	393
References	393

Abstract

People living with disabilities represent a considerable segment of the labor market. Yet, many face obstacles to finding and sustaining employment. The work experiences of people living with disabilities can be viewed within the context of a life course perspective to highlight the unique challenges and opportunities that can exist during different periods of a person's working life. This chapter examines key barriers and facilitators to employment faced by people with disabilities across the working life course, including the school-to-work transition, advancement within the middle career stages, and preparation to exit the working world at later career phases. Drawing from a biopsychosocial model of disability, the chapter also focuses on the role of the work environment in shaping the employment of people with disabilities and describes the experience of communicating health needs and accessing supports across different life and career phases. This chapter discusses how the constantly evolving nature of work can impact the work environment to which people with disabilities are exposed and describes emerging obstacles to employment participation. Our chapter ends by highlighting important directions for research and practice.

A. Jetha (✉) · M. A. M. Gignac
Institute for Work & Health, Toronto, ON, Canada

Dalla Lana School of Public Health, University of Toronto, Toronto, ON, Canada
e-mail: ajetha@iwh.on.ca; mgignac@iwh.on.ca

© Springer Nature Switzerland AG 2023
M. Wahrendorf et al. (eds.), *Handbook of Life Course Occupational Health*, Handbook Series in Occupational Health Sciences, https://doi.org/10.1007/978-3-031-30492-7_24

Keywords

Disability · Work environment · Biopsychosocial model · Changing nature of work · Disclosure · Job accommodations · Life course · Career stage · Transitions · Aging

Introduction

This chapter examines working with a disability across the life course. It presents data on the experiences of individuals living with a range of physical, cognitive, developmental, mental, or sensory health conditions that can be associated with activity limitations at work. It discusses challenges related to employment over career phases, particularly issues related to gaining and sustaining work. In this chapter, key elements of the work environment that can contribute to or ameliorate disability are outlined. Also discussed is the changing nature of work and the potential for evolving circumstances within the work environment to have a positive or negative impact on the ability of people living with a disability to remain employed across their career. In drawing on a life course perspective, this chapter highlights that no one period of life can be understood without considering earlier experiences, current demands, and future aspirations, goals, and concerns. Persons living with disabilities are not the passive recipients of change but can actively shape and change their own lives and social structures. At the same time, their experiences are embedded in and influenced by the historical, political, and social contexts within which they live (Elder et al. 2003). Key transitions and decision points are often highlighted in life course theory which have been used to better understand the school-to-work transition, advancement within the middle career stages, and preparation to exit the working world at later career phases, which makes life course theory fundamentally about social change (Elder et al. 2003). Drawing from a life course theoretical perspective, this chapter examines how employment experiences, work environments, and broader labor market conditions are shaped by these key transitions.

In this chapter we also discuss the fit between a person and their health, job demands, and the features of the work environment that can contribute to the quality of employment experiences for people living with disabilities. As we describe throughout this chapter, employment is a critical life role. The importance of employment has been underscored in regional and international labor and social policies. Notably, in 2008, the United Nation's Convention on the Rights of Persons with Disabilities (CRPD) was ratified by 177 countries as a human rights instrument to encourage equal participation in different domains of life, including employment (UN General Assembly 2007). The development of the CRPD has mandated that signatory countries develop domestic policies that will ensure full social and physical accessibility and remove all barriers to employment (UN General Assembly 2007). Our chapter is nested within the increasing number of global efforts which aim to make the labor market more inclusive for persons with disabilities and highlights important considerations for research and practice. The chapter presents a snapshot of seminal literature on the employment experiences of people with disabilities but may not capture the full breadth and depth of research in this area.

Defining Disability

Disability is defined as an interaction between a health condition experienced by an individual and personal, social, and environmental factors that can make tasks, activities, and social role participation challenging (World Health Organization 2001). Disability is not an attribute or characteristic of a person but is created by the interaction of diverse factors, including negative attitudes and behaviors like stigma and discrimination, lack of access to social and financial support such as education and training, legislation, and physical and environmental barriers in homes, workplaces, and communities (World Health Organization and The World Bank 2011). In 2011, the *World Report on Disability* estimated that between 15.6% and 19.4% (785–975 million) of the world's population 15 years of age and older lived with a disability with 2.2–3.8% of people (110–190 million individuals) experiencing significant difficulties in functioning with daily activities (World Health Organization and The World Bank 2011). An aging population coupled with a rise in new chronic conditions that may contribute to long-term activity limitations (e.g., long-term impairment cause by COVD-19 infection) (Davis et al. 2021) has meant that the number of people living with disabilities is expected to grow over the next decade (United Nations 2015).

The changing and episodic nature of some disabilities has received more attention in recent years with increased recognition of the dynamic nature of many physical and mental health conditions that can give rise to unpredictable health impairments and activity limitations (World Health Organization 2001; Morris et al. 2019; Gignac et al. 2011; Gignac et al. 2021a, b). In assessing disability, research has recently differentiated continuous activity limitations from recurrent, progressive, and fluctuating limitations. For example, a population-level study found that of 6.2 million Canadians with disabilities, aged 15 years and over, 39% reported relatively stable and continuous limitations (Morris et al. 2019). The remainder of respondents (61%) reported a dynamic disability. Among these individuals, 41% described periods of a month or more with no limitations alternating with stable or improved ability to perform daily activities and were classified as having a recurrent disability. Thirty-seven percent of persons with a dynamic disability reported periods of no disability alternating with worsening limitations over time and were labeled as having a progressive disability, while highly variable patterns of activity limitations were categorized as a fluctuating disability and reported by 22% of persons with a dynamic disability (Morris et al. 2019). The findings underscore that the concept of disability should not be considered as a static state, but rather an ever-changing interface between a person and their work environment.

In addition to their dynamic nature, many conditions that give rise to disability are invisible to others (Clair et al. 2005). That is, signs of a condition may not be readily apparent. People may be unaware that an individual lives with a disabling condition or be unable to gauge changes in the condition until symptoms are severe or more widely manifested. Even if others notice changes in behavior, the cause or reasons may be unclear. As such, there may be misperceptions or stigma about a worker's abilities or motivation (Gignac et al. 2021a, b). Chronic conditions associated with dynamic or invisible disability patterns are often highly prevalent and can include physical and mental health conditions like depression and anxiety, rheumatic diseases, inflammatory bowel disease, multiple sclerosis, migraine, epilepsy, and chronic fatigue syndrome. The invisible nature of many disabilities can create challenges engaging in the labor market and in accessing supports necessary for sustained employment.

Disability and Employment
Employment is a valued role and an important social determinant of health that contributes to an individual's identity, self-esteem, social inclusion, and independence. Income and other benefits generated from paid work enhance resources (e.g., safe housing, food security, and access to health care) and shape pathways to better health and quality of life (Benach et al. 2014; Marmot et al. 2012). Precarious, hazardous, and unsupportive employment has the potential to contribute to poor health and can be a critical driver of the cycle of poverty that can be faced by people living with disabilities (Benach et al. 2014; Ojala and Pyöriä 2019).

People living with disabilities value employment and are motivated to gain and sustain work and make contributions to advancing organizational mandates. However, employment rates among people living with disabilities are highly variable, with consistent findings of lower employment participation, more job insecurity, and more frequent changes to work among persons with disabilities compared to persons not living with a disability (Jetha et al. 2020; Morris et al. 2018; US Department of Labor 2022; World Health Organization and The World Bank 2011). Important to employment and labor market advantage and disadvantage is not only the severity of needs and extent of activity limitations a person may have, but also factors like sex and gender identity, race, culture, and educational attainment (Jetha et al. 2021a; World Health Organization and The World Bank 2011).

At the same time, there is cautious optimism for the future. New clinical treatments, assistive technologies, novel health and employment interventions, and improved management practices of health conditions are enabling more individuals with diverse disabilities to transition into employment and sustain or return to productive work (de Wind et al. 2018; Gignac et al. 2011; Jetha et al. 2019b; OECD 2010; World Health Organization and The World Bank 2011). As we note in later sections of this chapter, the digital transformation of the economy and flexibility in the way work is performed may offer enhanced opportunities for individuals with disabilities to participate in employment and may ameliorate disability at work. At the same time, more research is needed to examine whether technology can also exacerbate workforce inequities and give rise to working conditions that have the potential to disadvantage people living with disabilities (Jetha et al. 2021c).

Although diverse in their etiology, many persons with disabilities experience common challenges related to employment, including in difficulties in acquiring a job and accessing training and skill development opportunities, overcoming negative attitudes and stigma from others, managing periods of disability that can result in reduced performance and absenteeism, making decisions about what, when, and to whom to communicate any needs, and in receiving informal and formal supports and accommodations to sustain employment (Gignac et al. 2011; Jetha et al. 2020, 2021a). These challenges are shaped by life course considerations and make for highly diverse experiences across individuals. These result in a complex picture of disability and employment. For example, younger workers with an invisible, episodic disability may struggle to manage the consequences of a health condition, viewing it as not being age normative and as being more impactful or threatening to future plans than their older counterparts (Gignac et al. 2006). Research finds that younger workers report difficulties managing the attitudes of others who expect them to be healthy, energetic, and strong because of their age and who may interpret work performance challenges as malingering or indicative of poor motivation (Jetha et al. 2015). Younger workers also frequently begin their careers in part-time and short-term jobs which are often precarious (Lewchuk 2017). Obtaining workplace supports can be challenging compared to older workers with longer and more established employment histories.

Some research finds that middle-aged workers report greater depression, stress, and role conflict trying to maintain good health, employment, and family balance compared to older workers (Gignac et al. 2013). These challenges were linked to middle-aged workers' perceptions of greater role demands (e.g., building a career, caring for children and other family members, and financial demands) and greater perceived importance of roles like employment than other age groups (Gignac et al. 2013). Older workers can also experience unique challenges living with an invisible and episodic disability. A qualitative study of older workers found heightened concerns about ageism resulted in older workers expending considerable effort to manage the impressions others had of them, low trust in others to provide support, and perceptions of job insecurity even among those in permanent, relatively stable employment (Gignac et al. 2022). Perceived normative age-related changes in health also may mean that older workers living with limitations that impact their jobs do not perceive themselves as having a disability compared to younger adults with workplace limitations.

The School to Employment Transition and Early Career Experiences
A transition into the working world is viewed as one of the most critical milestones in adult development that contributes to the building of a young person's identity, growth of independence, acquisition and building of job skills, generation of income and employee benefits, and enables a person to be a productive member of society (Jetha et al. 2014, 2015; Scarpetta et al. 2010). Important to note is that the school-to-work transition is variable and does not follow a uniform trajectory. It can consist of numerous and frequent vocational changes or pauses to paid work to build job skills and acquire training, gain life experiences that may enable competitive employment, or manage health and personal needs. Seeking a job and engaging in the job interview process is a significant experience at this time of life, as are changes to

work roles necessary for career advancement. Studies consistently find that challenges at an early career phase can have a scarring effect that contributes to persistent difficulties across the working life course (Scarpetta et al. 2010; Von Wachter 2020).

A considerable amount of research has examined the experiences of youth living with disabilities. Research in industrialized countries find that young people with disabilities place a high value on an education to enable skill development, gain access to jobs that will provide more job security and workplace supports, and cover higher living expenses that may come with a disability or having a health condition (Jetha et al. 2014, 2015, 2021d). The growing cost of education coupled with the costs associated with living with a disability may motivate young adults with disabilities to forgo advanced training opportunities that may impact their labor market competitiveness in the long term. Some young adults with disabilities report taking jobs that are of little interest to them but where they will receive a stable income and job benefits to help manage their disability needs (Jetha et al. 2015, 2021a). This also may mean forfeiting other prevocational roles like postsecondary education, internships, and volunteer opportunities that can be beneficial to finding high-quality and better paying jobs. Being unable to transition into employment or experiencing early challenges in gaining paid work has the potential to impact employment across the life course. It may lead to a greater risk for continued or future unemployment and underemployment, reduced earnings, or deterioration of skills (Jetha et al. 2015; Scarpetta et al. 2010; Von Wachter 2020).

Labor market data, mostly from developed economies, consistently shows that the employment of young people can be disrupted by disability. However, much of this research is narrow in its time frame focusing mostly on entry into the labor market with limited follow-up of study participants as they advance in their careers (Jetha et al. 2019b). As a result, we know little about how early work experiences translate into later career trajectories (see also ▶ Chap. 11, "A Life Course Perspective on Work and Mental Health: The Working Lives of Young Adults," by Veldman et al. in this Handbook). Also, research with young adults has frequently centered on programs and interventions to help improve employment placement and pre-employment skills. It mostly focuses on those living with intellectual and developmental disabilities, autism spectrum disorder, or mental health disabilities (Awsumb 2017; Rosner et al. 2020; Weld-Blundell et al. 2021; Jetha et al. 2019b). Employment intervention evaluation studies show limited effectiveness and small effect sizes (Ma et al. 2020; Rosner et al. 2020; Weld-Blundell et al. 2021). However, one review of the literature found strong evidence for the positive benefits on employment rates of work-related social skills training and moderate evidence for simulation studies and the use of assistive technology and computer applications in studies with young adults living with mostly mental health disabilities (Smith et al. 2017). Among individuals with physical or mental health disabilities, reviews suggest that individualized placement and support interventions demonstrate moderate to strong evidence for a positive impact on employment preparation and work entry (Awsumb 2017). Jetha and colleagues found the evidence was stronger for young adults with physical disabilities compared to those with mental health conditions (Jetha et al. 2019b). A small number of studies have examined the educational modalities used in employment interventions, although this research is expected to grow as technology advances. For example, Munandar and colleagues examined video-based interventions that provide real-time feedback on job interview skills to improve competitiveness in obtaining work among youth and adults with autism spectrum disorder (Munandar et al. 2020). Data were limited but provided some early evidence of the potential for video-based interventions to improve job performance skills (Munandar et al. 2020).

Across intervention and other study designs, researchers have identified several barriers to employment that begin early in the career trajectory of youth living with disabilities. Prior to entering the workforce, research illuminates the challenges that many young adults face in getting and completing an education, as well as the absence of a focus on early employment skills preparation, including counseling and supports to build self-esteem and confidence related to job-seeking activities (Eilenberg et al. 2019; Gmitroski et al. 2018; Haber et al. 2016). Young people with disabilities report challenges associated with leaving more supportive educational environments and entering workplaces where accommodations may be less likely to be formally provided. Studies also highlight gaps in social welfare systems and labor market legislation that fail to meet the unique needs of disabled youth and young adults who are struggling to enter the working world (Awsumb 2017; Perri et al. 2021), as well as the need for more collaboration across health and social service agencies (Awsumb 2017; Gmitroski et al. 2018; Rosner et al. 2020). In addition to education, policy, and service challenges, researchers point to the extended time that it takes many young adults with disabilities to find work and the ongoing challenges in sustaining a job, as employment for youth with disabilities is often in nonstandardized work arrangements (Wei et al. 2018). Once employed, there is little data aimed at understanding how young adults navigate workplace policies related to supports and accommodations or career advancement issues, either early or across their careers (Gmitroski et al. 2018; Jetha et al. 2019b).

Limited research has examined other personal factors important to working with a disability. A small number of studies examining gender similarities and differences report a mix of findings but tend to show that men with disabilities were more likely to be working, reported working more hours, and had better wages compared to women with disabilities (Lindsay et al. 2018a). Racial minority youth and young adults from low-income families on the autism spectrum were found to receive fewer services and were less likely to receive a postsecondary education (Eilenberg et al. 2019). Other research from the USA also found that, despite being eligible for vocational rehabilitation, Black youth, women, and young adults with mental health disabilities experience service gaps which affected their employment (Awsumb 2017).

A life course perspective has been rarely adopted in studies of the transition from school to work and to better understand the early career experiences of young adults with disabilities. Instead, research has focused on this period of life with little examination of ways that educational, training, and work events shape later career experiences and trajectories. Researchers have noted several other study limitations common to this area, including small sample sizes and a reliance primarily on cross-sectional data (Weld-Blundell et al. 2021), a lack of control groups and absence of randomization in intervention studies (Hedley et al. 2017), need for more information about study participants (Hedley et al. 2017), and the limited time focus of vocational programs (often only 6–8 weeks) and follow-up periods for evaluation. Furthermore, while research on youth and young adults with disabilities has examined labor market entry, fewer studies have focused on career advancement and strategies to promote productivity as a young person moves through their career (Jetha et al. 2019b). We bring to light some of these challenges and opportunities in subsequent sections when we discuss experiences of middle- and older-aged adults living with disabilities and their experiences related to sustaining employment.

Work Environments and Disability

A growing number of studies focus on the working experiences of those living with disabilities, as well as the perspectives held by employers and others in the workplace. Much of this research is conducted on samples that consist of individuals spanning a range of ages, especially middle- and older-aged workers. However, the research typically does not address age or life course issues among workers with disabilities as important factors relevant to understanding employment trajectories.

Importantly, studies of the work experiences of people with disabilities highlight that having a job does not guarantee a meaningful or high-quality employment experience. In fact, people with disabilities are more likely to be underemployed or employed in work environments where they are exposed to poor psychosocial work conditions that include less control over job tasks, more stress, more uncertainty about the future of their job (e.g., contract work), and greater unmet accommodation needs (Gignac et al. 2018; Jetha et al. 2021a; LaMontagne et al. 2016; Milner et al. 2019). In studies of people living with disabilities two key issues consistently emerge across age groups. The first is communication and disclosure of a disability and support needs, especially to manage conditions associated with invisible disabilities like mental health conditions, and the second is workplace support and accommodation experiences.

Communication and Disclosure of a Disability and Support Needs

Research shows not only that one's health can impact work, but also that work can impact one's health in positive and negative ways. That is, employment can contribute to psychological health through its impact on one's identity as a productive person and through social interactions. It contributes to physical health through the opportunity for physical activity, and access to benefits and financial resources to manage health needs. At the same time, commuting to and from work, and holding a job with high demands can take a toll on both physical and psychological health (Gignac et al. 2012; Jetha et al. 2015). An ongoing decision that workers with disabilities make is whether to share personal information about their health and disability with others in their workplace, with whom to share information, when to communicate, and what to say. Many workers are concerned about disclosing health and disability information because of negative attitudes that can be held by others, stigma, and potential negative career implications like a loss of promotion opportunities, skills training, or even job loss (Gignac and Cao 2009; Gignac et al. 2021a, b;

Hayward et al. 2018; Lindsay et al. 2018b; Stutterheim et al. 2017). At the same time, there can be positive responses to disclosure of a disability, including more support and access to available accommodations, understanding, and empathy (Stutterheim et al. 2017; Gignac et al. 2021b). Not disclosing can mean that support needs remain unmet and may mean that challenges with a job are interpreted by others as a lack of skills, malingering, or performance problems (Gignac et al. 2021a, b).

Decisions whether to disclose are often related to past experiences, as well as concerns and appraisals about the future and being able to remain employed (Gignac et al. 2007, 2021b). One study of 292 individuals with arthritis found that worries about future problems were rated as more concerning than current needs (Gignac et al. 2007). Moreover, because disability at work is often dynamic with a person's needs, career, and work experiences changing, deciding whether to share information is not a single event (Gignac and Cao 2009). A person living with a disability will make ongoing decisions about sharing information at multiple times during their career. Health needs and treatments may change job demands and limitations at work can alter over time, and the people with whom a worker with a disability interacts and trusts at their job can change. Disclosing needs for support at one time does not mean that an individual will continue to experience difficulties with work tasks or feel they should share aspects of their health at a later stage. Conversely, individuals who have been able to manage their job tasks without sharing information about their health may want or need to share information about their health because support needs change over time or to meet other goals related to educating others and relationship building.

Among the most common reasons for disclosure is a perceived need for support (Brohan et al. 2012; Brouwers et al. 2020; Gignac and Cao 2009; Jetha et al. 2021d). That is, across all ages, individuals with disabilities are more likely to disclose during a crisis or when a health condition is worsening and making it more difficult to perform job tasks. Disclosure is also more common when workers with disabilities perceive their workplace as being potentially supportive of their needs. More research is needed, but the decision not to disclose may be more common among younger and older workers who do not want to be perceived as a problem worker or as a financial burden on an organization (Lindsay et al. 2018b; Gignac et al. 2022).

Sharing Disability Information During the Hiring Process

There is limited evidence examining the sharing of disability information during the hiring process. Studies often focus on human resource (HR) professionals, supervisors, and other workplace representatives involved in hiring. However, this research has typically relied on the developing of hiring scenarios and role-playing studies with participants rating vignettes or videos, or small qualitative studies asking about perceptions and intentions to hire people with disabilities. Longitudinal data on hiring practices and outcomes are lacking. Also missing is an examination of age and life course issues, although some studies have looked at disclosure concerns related to hiring among younger adults (Lindsay et al. 2018b) or older workers, with a hypothesis that many of the same issues communicating disability details occur across ages (Hutton et al. 2012).

A significant reason for not disclosing a potential work limitation is concerns over stigma and potential work reprisals (Brohan et al. 2012; Brouwers et al. 2020; Gignac et al. 2021a, b). To some extent, these concerns may be warranted given research finding that those in hiring roles can have preconceived notions about people with disabilities, especially mental health conditions, that include poor work attendance, performance difficulties, and problems establishing good working relationships with others (Andersson et al. 2015; Baker et al. 2018; Dolce and Bates 2019; Gouvier et al. 2003). Some studies find that those with misconceptions generally have had limited interactions with workers with disabilities (Baker et al. 2018), whereas past positive experiences with hiring people with disabilities were associated with intentions to hire in the future and reports of positive hiring practices (Andersson et al. 2015).

Hiring perceptions, especially negative stereotypes, are important to understand in the context of disclosure advice that employers report they would give to individuals with disabilities who are seeking a job. A small number of qualitative studies have examined workplace disclosure advice during the hiring process. A study of 27 HR professionals, mental health advocates, and employers gave mixed advice (Brouwers et al. 2020). HR professionals believed disclosure of a mental health condition during hiring could reduce a candidate's chances of being hired. They recommended disclosing only if a person knew their condition would impact their productivity. Otherwise, they believed a candidate should build a professional relationship prior to disclosing. Work reintegration professionals in the same study said they would encourage candidates to disclose a mental health condition during hiring as it makes it easier for them to arrange accommodations and could help candidates build a positive relationship with employers (Brouwers et al. 2020). Other qualitative studies have found that, despite wanting an open workplace culture, HR professionals and employers raised concerns about disclosing a disability (Dolce and Bates 2019; Pettersen and Fugletveit 2015). Two experimental studies found that participants rated candidates more favorably when they disclosed some disability information earlier in an interview than at the end of the interview or compared to not disclosing at all (Hebl and Skorinko 2005; Roberts and Macan 2006).

Outcomes of Disclosing Disability Information

Studies of workers with disabilities indicate there is no single correct decision whether to disclose or not, and that outcomes are related to a complex array of factors that include personal characteristics of the worker, characteristics and perceptions of the receiver of information, the nature and extent of support needs, type of job, and other aspects of the work environment, including workplace culture and supportiveness (Brohan et al. 2012; Brouwers et al. 2020; Gignac and Cao 2009; Gignac et al. 2021a, b; Greene 2000; Jetha et al. 2021d). Few studies have examined age similarities and differences. However, one study of 896 workers with physical or mental health conditions causing disability at work examined reasons for disclosing or not disclosing disability information, as well as perceived outcomes of disclosure (Gignac et al. 2021b). The findings indicated that the reasons underpinning disclosure decisions were similar across age groups, as were the perceived outcomes of disclosing or not disclosing. However, older adults were more likely to disclose a disability than younger workers (Gignac et al. 2021b). The reasons for this are unclear but may be related to older workers having more secure employment than younger workers with disabilities, having a longer job tenure where an older worker has built a reputation as a productive worker, and older workers having greater access to workplace benefits to meet their support needs. At the same time, research finds that older workers can face negative stereotypes and ageism about their willingness and ability to learn new skills, especially related to technology, their productivity, and their physical and cognitive capacity (Bal et al. 2011). A study of 69 older workers found that, to manage perceived ageism, older workers were often unwilling to disclose needs related to their health and limitations (Gignac et al. 2022).

Support and Accommodations to Sustain Employment
As we have described throughout this chapter, the work environment poses challenges and opportunities for the employment of persons with disabilities. Providing support and making adaptations to the work environment represents critical part of keeping people with disabilities employed at all phases of their career. Importantly, the workplace is increasing being recognized as a modifiable environment that can be altered to diminish work disability. Many industrialized countries provide duty-to-accommodate legislation that directs employers to provide reasonable support for persons working with disabilities. The United Nation's CRPD further emphasizes this, highlighting the part that policymakers, employers, and society play in removing barriers to employment participation through the provision of job accommodations that can increase inclusion and promote productive and meaningful employment participation (UN General Assembly 2007).

Because of the centrality of work, persons with disabilities expend efforts to protect their jobs. Of interest is that many of the adaptation efforts undertaken by workers to sustain employment occur outside of the workplace. For example, research with middle- and older-aged workers with arthritis found that participants reported efforts to maintain the energy they devoted to their jobs by cutting back on activities like socializing and hobbies and getting help from others with household activities (Gignac 2005). At work, the most common informal coping strategies anticipated problems in advance of their occurrence and avoided them. Examples included better planning of tasks, exercising caution to avoid symptoms like pain, pacing work tasks, and taking short breaks to alternate rest with activity (Gignac 2005). Least common were requests to give up some job demands or getting help from others. By anticipating and avoiding employment difficulties, participants were able to work without drawing attention to their needs, although this wasn't always sustainable in the long term. Many of these anticipatory coping strategies are often learned through experiences gained across the working life course. Those at earlier phases of their careers may have limited understanding and experiences with strategies that can help them to balance work and health demands.

Research also finds that people with disabilities draw on existing policies and practices available to all workers. The most adopted policies are often those that permit flexibility in scheduling, the planning of work tasks, and the location where work is conducted (e.g., work at home). Other policies frequently drawn upon are organizational benefits that pay for medication costs or health care treatment (e.g., rehabilitation costs and mental health therapy), and improve physical environments and their accessibility (e.g., ergonomic workstations and accessible parking). These policies are useful not only to people with disabilities, but also to others, including pregnant workers, workers with acute injuries or illnesses, and workers with child or eldercare responsibilities (Gignac et al. 2015; Gignac et al. 2021a; Hill et al. 2016; Jetha et al. 2021a). They focus attention on universal design, and not on the potential challenges of a particular group.

The range of informal supports and formal workplace accommodations needed are considerable and depend on the nature of the job. Many jobs require some physical demands (e.g., working with one's hands and moving around the workplace), cognitive demands (e.g., paying attention to detail), working with others, and consideration of working conditions (e.g., outdoor work and working around distractions). Support needs also can vary depending on health conditions, although focusing on specific job demands often illuminates that there are similar supports and accommodations that are useful across diverse conditions. For example, individuals with type 1 diabetes who must take injections at work, workers with autism, and workers with anxiety disorders may all benefit from a workstation with more privacy although the reasons for their privacy needs may differ.

Historically, studies examining the role of the work environment in the employment of people living with disabilities have focused mostly on older adults with more established job tenure. However, a growing body of research finds that the types of support needed to enhance the school-to-work transition and early career experiences of young adults are similar to those needed by middle-aged and older adults with disabilities at later phases of their career (Jetha et al. 2019a). Also similar across age groups is the value of workplace supports in helping to sustain work and job productivity (Jetha et al. 2021b, dGignac et al. 2015), with research increasingly pointing to the economic benefits of accommodations that foster the inclusivity of people with disabilities (Tompa et al. 2022).

Despite the positive outcomes associated with various supports and accommodations, many workers with disabilities struggle to have their needs met, which can affect their performance at work and their ability to remain employed. A survey of 1796 Canadian workers found those living with a disability were significantly more likely to report unmet workplace support needs compared to those without a disability (Jetha et al. 2021a). The same study found that women with disabilities were particularly likely to report unmet accommodation needs when compared to men with and without disabilities (Jetha et al. 2021a). Similar findings have been found in another study with women reporting more unmet support needs (Gignac et al. 2018). These studies highlight the importance of applying an intersectional lens that looks not only at disability and age, but other identities (e.g., gender and race), to better understand workplace support and accommodations and their impact on employment.

Challenges in obtaining job support may be especially problematic at the early career phase. As they transition to employment, young adults living with disabilities often work in nonstandard jobs (e.g., part-time work or short-term contracts) in industries with higher physical job demands (e.g., retail sales, food, and beverage). These work conditions may limit formal supports and accommodations. Young adults also may be more apprehensive to request support given the potential for long-term negative repercussions to their career, including being denied a promotion or receiving training opportunities. In comparison, middle- and older-aged workers with a longer tenure within their organization may feel more confidence requesting an accommodation because they are more likely to have an established relationship with their employer. However, research examining age, job tenure, and support remains limited. As noted earlier, there is almost no research examining age and its intersection with other identities, including the experiences of persons of color, immigrants, LGBTQ2+ workers, and workers with low socioeconomic status across the life course. These identities and experiences may add to the challenges of working with a disability across the life course.

Highlighted in the literature are several challenges that people living with disabilities may face to accessing workplace supports. As noted earlier in this chapter, people living with disabilities may struggle with the decision to communicate their support needs and request job accommodations. They may also report apprehension in requesting formal workplace supports to avoid being perceived by others as receiving special treatment or out of fear of losing career development opportunities (Nevala et al. 2015). Employer awareness regarding the legal requirement for reasonable accommodations or an understanding of how to adjust the work environment for people with different disabling conditions may also be lacking.

Another important barrier to accessing workplace support comes from precarious work arrangements and the erosion of standard employment opportunities, which are becoming increasingly common. Precarious work can encompass job insecurity and unpredictable, unprotected, and/or low-paying employment where a person may have limited job control (i.e., high physical or mental job demands coupled with low control or influence over work) and/or regulatory protection (i.e., protection against unfair dismissal or unhealthy working conditions) that is often enforced by labor groups like unions (Lewchuk 2017; Benach et al. 2014). Some recent estimates suggest that up to one-third of people living with disabilities report working precariously. Those employed precariously may have a reduced ability to modify their work or limited access resources that sustain health (e.g., living wages, health insurance, paid sick leave, pension plan, and social support). They also may be more likely to be exposed to workplace hazards when compared to those reporting more secure working conditions (Benach et al. 2014). Although understudied, the impact of precarious work on the employment of people with disabilities can be significant. Research highlights several interrelated factors that can contribute to rising workplace precarity, including broad labor market trends like globalization (e.g., growing numbers of international remote digital workers), recessionary periods, and technological advancement (e.g., automation of work). Additionally, the growth of gig work, digital platform jobs, and increasing numbers of employment vacancies being filled by temporary help agencies may be a driving force that increases precarious work and disproportionately impacts workers with disabilities at all phases of their careers (Vosko 2006).

More research also needs to be conducted at an organizational level to understand the perspectives of those who are expected to provide support to workers with disabilities. Unfortunately, research examining labor arbitration cases in Canada has highlighted that disability in the workplace is often cast as a performance, attendance, or disciplinary issue (Williams-Whitt and Taras 2010). Another study of supervisors, HR professionals, disability managers, and union representatives found employment barriers were commonly related to organizational culture, especially a continued focus on a medical model that emphasizes a health diagnosis rather than environmental and social factors that create disability at work (Gignac et al. 2021a). The study also found that those providing support to workers with disabilities often had misgivings about the abilities of others to provide support (e.g., concerns about supervisor training) and faced difficult challenges in providing support when a worker with a disability did not disclose their needs, but was experiencing difficulties meeting job demands, or a worker denied there were performance problems in the workplace (Gignac et al. 2021a).

Changing Work Environments and the Future of Work and Disability

As noted earlier, the nature of work is changing at a rapid rate and is shaping the employment experiences of people living with disabilities across the working life course (Jetha et al. 2021c). A historical analysis of labor force data in the USA highlights ongoing changes to work, finding that up to two-thirds of occupational titles identified in 2018 did not exist in 1940 (Autor et al. 2020). As new occupations arise, they bring novel physical and psychosocial working demands, job skills and training requirements, and work arrangements and conditions that pose both challenges and opportunities for people living with disabilities at all ages (Jetha et al. 2021c). Scholars highlight that the changing world of work has largely been driven by the digital transformation of the economy and automation of jobs. The current speed at which new technologies are being developed and applied to employment represents a faster pace of change to work compared to past periods of technological change (Schwab 2016) and has contributed to what is sometimes called a hyper-connectivity between people, businesses, digital devices, and data. A comprehensive synthesis of different digital technologies is beyond the scope of this chapter. However, we introduce several key changes that have emerged within the changing nature of work and briefly describe their impact (or potential impact) on employment of people with disabilities. Here again, age and life course issues have not been directly addressed in research. The goal of this final section is to highlight the changing working landscape people with disabilities face, comment on areas where life course issues may be relevant, and to note the need for new research and practice to match the pace of change.

First, the innovation of online collaboration software, virtual reality, and augmented reality has advanced a worker's telepresence and allowed their skills and knowledge to be projected anywhere in the world to perform a range of job tasks (e.g., operating machinery or virtual brainstorming sessions) (Baldwin 2019). The greater ability to work remotely could be beneficial for workers with disabilities of all ages and enhance the flexibility of work (Jetha et al. 2021c). Concerningly, the rise in remote work also increases the likelihood that jobs will be outsourced to a global marketplace of freelancers and further limit the availability of job opportunities for disadvantaged workers within domestic contexts, including people living with disabilities. Research is needed, but the negative impact of outsourcing may be more profoundly felt at early and late career stages. Young workers starting their careers or with fewer job skills may find fewer opportunities for work in their national contexts because of outsourcing. Older workers whose job tenure often cost an organization more in salary may also be particularly vulnerable to outsourcing of work and job loss.

Second, employers are increasingly using digital platforms to parcel out job tasks and to facilitate what are increasingly on-demand, short-term contracts aimed at prospective gig workers instead of hiring full-time employees. Digital platforms often have been applied to occupations with physical demands (e.g., transport, couriering, food delivery, and cleaning), repetitive activities (e.g., data entry and clerical work), and cognitive job tasks where permanent workers are not seen as necessary (e.g., website developers, editors, and graphic designers) (Wood et al. 2019). The use of digital platforms represents a potentially important entry point into the labor market for people with disabilities, especially for those at the early career phase looking to gain work experiences. Gig work also can provide scheduling flexibility for people living with disabilities by enabling them to pick up employment contracts that align with their self-management needs and changes to their health (Harpur and Blanck 2020). Conversely, a growth in gig work has catalyzed the erosion of standard employment opportunities in developed economies and resulted in a rise in unsupportive and precarious forms of employment. Gig workers may have limited access to employment protections and job accommodations that can be essential to the sustained employment of individuals who live with a disability.

Third, the growing discourse on the automation of work notes the increasing use of intelligent machines within workplaces and a redistribution of job tasks from human workers to machines (Acemoglu and Restrepo 2020). The use of machines within workplaces can represent an opportunity for employers to accommodate activity limitations faced by their employees living with different disabilities and to support sustained work productivity. The application of machines within many industries has contributed to the redesign of workplaces in ways that have fostered the creation of new job opportunities that are beneficial to workers who possess technical job skills. However, the automation of work can contribute to job displacement for workers with disabilities. Some research estimates that up to 60% of occupations consist of job tasks of which one-third can be automated (Manyika et al. 2017; Frey and Osborne 2017). It is thought that low-skilled jobs characterized by repetitive tasks, which tend to be occupied by youth and young adults at the early career phase or other vulnerable worker groups, are most likely to be automated when compared to those working in jobs with more cognitive demands.

The advancement and application of artificial intelligence (AI) to automate work is not exclusive to low-skilled jobs. More and more organizations are using machines to solve problems traditionally requiring human intelligence, including detecting patterns, making judgments, or optimizing processes. Studies indicate that the use of AI has meant that occupations that consist of complex and predictive job tasks, which are often held by higher-skilled and highly educated workers in professional settings, could also be automated. The result could be job displacement that may differ from past periods of technological change (Webb 2019) and increased competition for a fewer number of higher-quality jobs. Workers traditionally facing disadvantage could be forced into jobs that are lower paying and that are more likely to involve unpredictable and strenuous manual tasks that are less likely to be performed by machines or displaced altogether (Autor et al. 2020). The implications of these changes on workers of different ages who live with disabilities are not clear.

It is important to highlight that changes to the work environment are not just driven by technological changes but also by sociopolitical (e.g., growth in populist movements), economic (e.g., periods of recession), and environmental shifts (e.g., climate change) (Jetha et al. 2021c). Speculation on these various trends suggests that people living with disabilities may be more likely to find themselves at a position of disadvantage when compared to their peers without a disability and they may lack resources inside and outside of the workplaces to navigate changes the nature and availability of work (Jetha et al. 2021c). Studies examining the intersection between the work environment and employment of people living with disabilities across the working life course will be complex and will need to take a dynamic approach to capture evolving workforce conditions.

Conclusion

People living with disabilities represent a sizable proportion of the labor market. Yet, many people living with disabilities report challenges finding and sustaining high-quality employment. As we describe in this chapter, the challenges and opportunities that people with disabilities can experience may differ according to their life phase and career stage. Youth and young adults with disabilities can face a system of factors that make finding high-quality employment difficult, limit their access to workplace support, and pose barriers to career advancement. Middle- and older-aged adults often experience many competing personal demands that come with being at this stage of life and may fear negative appraisals about their ability to make ongoing contributions to the work environment from others in the workplace related to their age.

This chapter underscores that disability is a biopsychosocial construct that reflects the interrelationship between a health impairment, personal characteristics, and a range of contextual factors. Work environments are a key contextual factor that can shape disability. Workplace policies can often accommodate the needs of people living with disabilities across the age spectrum and can be critical in contributing to long-term employment sustainability and success by increasing the fit between a person and their job. Yet, there is an abundance of evidence that people living with disabilities face challenges accessing informal and formal workplace supports and must make complex decisions related to communicating their needs to others. This includes working in precarious jobs where accommodations and benefits are not likely to be provided. Changing conditions within the workplace caused by technological change and sociopolitical, environmental, and economic driving forces will create new realities for people with disabilities that will require more research and innovations in policies and practice.

Moving forward, it is important for disability and employment scholars to apply a life course perspective toward the understanding of workforce experiences of people living with disabilities. Longitudinal quantitative and qualitative research is needed to understand key transition points within a person's working life and to design relevant policies and programs that reflect the unique experiences at different career phases. Critical to this is that scholars and program developers continue to go beyond a medical model and take a biopsychosocial approach to their research and practices that examines the complexity of the individual and their physical, social, and political environments, including the work environment. In this way, we can understand and design life course–specific programs and policies that are relevant to a changing nature of work.

Cross-References

▶ A Life Course Perspective on Work and Mental Health: The Working Lives of Young Adults

References

Acemoglu D, Restrepo P (2020) Robots and jobs: evidence from US labor markets. J Polit Econ 128 (6):2188–2244. https://doi.org/10.1086/705716

Andersson J, Luthra R, Hurtig P, Tideman M (2015) Employer attitudes toward hiring persons with disabilities: a vignette study in Sweden. J Vocat Rehabil 43(1):41–50. https://doi.org/10.3233/JVR-150753

Autor D, Mindell D, Reynolds E (2020) The work of the future: building better jobs in an age of intelligent machines. MIT Work of the Future, Cambridge, MA

Awsumb JM (2017) Vocational rehabilitation employment outcomes and interagency collaboration for youth with disabilities. Dissertation, University of Illinois at Chicago, ProQuest dissertations publishing

Baker PMA, Linden MA, LaForce SS, Rutledge J et al (2018) Barriers to employment participation of individuals with disabilities: addressing the impact of employer (mis) perception and policy. Am Behav Sci 62(5):657–675. https://doi.org/10.1177/0002764218768868

Bal AC, Reiss AEB, Rudolph CW, Baltes BB (2011) Examining positive and negative perceptions of older workers: a meta-analysis. J Gerontol B Psychol Sci Soc Sci 66(6):687–698. https://doi.org/10.1093/geronb/gbr056

Baldwin R (2019) The globotics upheaval: globalization, robotics, and the future of work. Oxford University Press, Oxford

Benach J, Vives A, Amable M, Vanroelen C et al (2014) Precarious employment: understanding an emerging social determinant of health. Annu Rev Public Health 35:229–253. https://doi.org/10.1146/annurev-publhealth-032013-182500

Brohan E, Henderson C, Wheat K, Malcolm E et al (2012) Systematic review of beliefs, behaviours and influencing factors associated with disclosure of a mental health problem in the workplace. BMC Psychiatry 12(1):11. https://doi.org/10.1186/1471-244X-12-11

Brouwers EPM, Joosen MCW, van Zelst C, Van Weeghel J (2020) To disclose or not to disclose: a multi-stakeholder focus group study on mental health sssues in the work environment. J Occup Rehabil 30(1):84–92. https://doi.org/10.1007/s10926-019-09848-z

Clair JA, Beatty JE, MacLean TL (2005) Out of sight but not out of mind: managing invisible social identities in the workplace. Acad Manag Rev 30(1):78–95. https://doi.org/10.5465/amr.2005.15281431

Davis HE, Assaf GS, McCorkell L, Wei H et al (2021) Characterizing long COVID in an international cohort: 7 months of symptoms and their impact. EClinicalMedicine 38:101019. https://doi.org/10.1016/j.eclinm.2021.101019

de Wind A, van der Noordt M, Deeg DJH, Boot CRL (2018) Working life expectancy in good and poor self-perceived health among Dutch workers aged 55–65 years with a chronic disease over the period 1992–2016. Occup Environ Med 75(11):792–797. https://doi.org/10.1136/oemed-2018-105243

Dolce JN, Bates FM (2019) Hiring and employing individuals with psychiatric disabilities: focus groups with human resource professionals. J Vocat Rehabil 50(1):85–93. https://doi.org/10.3233/JVR-180990

Eilenberg JS, Paff M, Harrison AJ, Long KA (2019) Disparities based on race, ethnicity, and socioeconomic status over the transition to adulthood among adolescents and young adults on the autism spectrum: a systematic review. Curr Psychiatry Rep 21(5):32. https://doi.org/10.1007/s11920-019-1016-1

Elder GH, Johnson MK, Crosnoe R (2003) The emergence and development of life course theory. In: Mortimer JT, Shanahan MJ (eds) Handbook of the life course. Kluwer Academic Publishers, New York, pp 3–19

Frey CB, Osborne MA (2017) The future of employment: how susceptible are jobs to computerisation? Technol Forecast Soc Change 114:254–280. https://doi.org/10.1016/j.techfore.2016.08.019

Gignac MAM (2005) Arthritis and employment: an examination of behavioral coping efforts to manage workplace activity limitations. Arthritis Care Res 53(3):328–336. https://doi.org/10.1002/art.21169

Gignac MAM, Cao X (2009) "should I tell my employer and coworkers I have arthritis?" a longitudinal examination of self-disclosure in the work place. Arthritis Rheum 61(12):1753–1761. https://doi.org/10.1002/art.24889

Gignac MAM, Davis AM, Hawker G, Wright JG et al (2006) "what do you expect? You're just getting older": a comparison of perceived osteoarthritis-related and aging-related health experiences in middle- and older-age adults. Arthritis Rheum 55(6):905–912. https://doi.org/10.1002/art.22338

Gignac MAM, Sutton D, Badley EM (2007) Arthritis symptoms, the work environment, and the future: measuring perceived job strain among employed persons with arthritis. Arthritis Rheum 57(5):738–747. https://doi.org/10.1002/art.22788

Gignac MAM, Cao X, Tang K, Beaton DE (2011) Examination of arthritis-related work place activity limitations and intermittent disability over four-and-a-half years and its relationship to job modifications and outcomes. Arthritis Care Res (Hoboken) 63(7):953–962. https://doi.org/10.1002/acr.20456

Gignac MAM, Backman CL, Kaptein S, Lacaille D et al (2012) Tension at the borders: perceptions of role overload, conflict, strain and facilitation in work, family and health roles among employed individuals with arthritis. Rheumatology (Oxford) 51(2):324–332. https://doi.org/10.1093/rheumatology/ker317

Gignac MAM, Backman CL, Davis AM, Lacaille D et al (2013) Social role participation and the life course in healthy adults and individuals with osteoarthritis: are we overlooking the impact on the middle-aged? Soc Sci Med 81:87–93. https://doi.org/10.1016/j.socscimed.2012.12.013

Gignac MAM, Cao X, McAlpine J (2015) Availability, need for, and use of work accommodations and benefits: are they related to employment outcomes in people with arthritis? Arthritis Care Res (Hoboken) 67(6):855–864. https://doi.org/10.1002/acr.22508

Gignac MAM, Ibrahim S, Smith PM, Kristman V et al (2018) The role of sex, gender, health factors, and job context in workplace accommodation use among men and women with arthritis. Ann Work Expo Health 62(4):490–504. https://doi.org/10.1093/annweh/wxx115

Gignac MAM, Bowring J, Jetha A, Beaton DE et al (2021a) Disclosure, privacy and workplace accommodation of episodic disabilities: organizational perspectives on disability communication-support processes to sustain employment. J Occup Rehabil 31(1):153–165. https://doi.org/10.1007/s10926-020-09901-2

Gignac MAM, Jetha A, Ginis KAM, Ibrahim S (2021b) Does it matter what your reasons are when deciding to disclose (or not disclose) a disability at work? The association of workers' approach and avoidance goals with perceived positive and negative workplace outcomes. J Occup Rehabil 31(3):638–651. https://doi.org/10.1007/s10926-020-09956-1

Gignac MAM, Bowring J, Shahidi FV, Kristman V et al. (2022) Workplace disclosure decisions of older workers wanting to remain employed: a qualitative study of factors considered when contemplating revealing or concealing support needs. Work Aging & Retirement E-Pub Ahead of Press: 1–14. https://academic.oup.com/workar/advance-article/doi/10.1093/workar/waac029/6695122

Gmitroski T, Bradley C, Heinemann L, Liu G et al (2018) Barriers and facilitators to employment for young adults with mental illness: a scoping review. BMJ Open 8(12):e024487. https://doi.org/10.1136/bmjopen-2018-024487

Gouvier WD, Sytsma-Jordan S, Mayville S (2003) Patterns of discrimination in hiring job applicants with disabilities: the role of disability type, job complexity, and public contact. Rehabil Psychol 48(3):175–181. https://doi.org/10.1037/0090-5550.48.3.175

Greene K (2000) Disclosure of chronic illness varies by topic and target: the role of stigma and boundaries in willingness to disclose. In: Petronio S (ed) Balancing the secrets of private disclosures, 1st edn. Psychology Press, New York, pp 123–135

Haber MG, Mazzotti VL, Mustian AL, Rowe DA et al (2016) What works, when, for whom, and with whom: a meta-analytic review of predictors of postsecondary success for students with disabilities. Rev Educ Res 86(1):123–162. https://doi.org/10.3102/0034654315583135

Harpur P, Blanck P (2020) Gig workers with disabilities: opportunities, challenges, and regulatory response. J Occup Rehabil 30(4):511–520. https://doi.org/10.1007/s10926-020-09937-4

Hayward SM, McVilly KR, Stokes MA (2018) Challenges for females with high functioning autism in the workplace: a systematic review. Disabil Rehabil 40(3):249–258. https://doi.org/10.1080/09638288.2016.1254284

Hebl MR, Skorinko JL (2005) Acknowledging one's physical disability in the interview: does "when" make a difference? J Appl Soc Psychol 35(12):2477–2492. https://doi.org/10.1111/j.1559-1816.2005.tb02111.x

Hedley D, Uljarevic M, Cameron L, Halder S et al (2017) Employment programmes and interventions targeting adults with autism spectrum disorder: a systematic review of the literature. Autism 21(8):929–941. https://doi.org/10.1177/1362361316661855

Hill MJ, Maestas N, Mullen KJ (2016) Employer accommodation and labor supply of disabled workers. Labour Econ 41:291–303. https://doi.org/10.1016/j.labeco.2016.05.013

Hutton M, Bohle P, Mc Namara M (2012) Disability and job search among older workers: a narrative review. Int J Disabil Manag 7:27–34. https://doi.org/10.1017/idm.2012.6

Jetha A, Badley E, Beaton D, Fortin PR et al (2014) Transitioning to employment with a rheumatic disease: the role of independence, overprotection, and social support. J Rheumatol 41(12):2386–2394. https://doi.org/10.3899/jrheum.140419

Jetha A, Badley E, Beaton D, Fortin PR et al (2015) Unpacking early work experiences of young adults with rheumatic disease: an examination of absenteeism, job disruptions and productivity loss. Arthritis Care Res (Hoboken) 67(9):1246–1254. https://doi.org/10.1002/acr.22601

Jetha A, Bowring J, Furrie A, Smith F et al (2019a) Supporting the transition into employment: a study of Canadian young adults living with disabilities. J Occup Rehabil 29(1):140–149. https://doi.org/10.1007/s10926-018-9772-z

Jetha A, Shaw R, Sinden AR, Mahood Q et al (2019b) Work-focused interventions that promote the labour market transition of young adults with chronic disabling health conditions: a systematic review. Occup Environ Med 76(3):189–198. https://doi.org/10.1136/oemed-2018-105454

Jetha A, Martin Ginis KA, Ibrahim S, Gignac MAM (2020) The working disadvantaged: the role of age, job tenure and disability in precarious work. BMC Public Health 20(1):1900. https://doi.org/10.1186/s12889-020-09938-1

Jetha A, Gignac MAM, Ibrahim S, Martin Ginis KA (2021a) Disability and sex/gender intersections in unmet workplace support needs: findings from a large Canadian survey of workers. Am J Ind Med 64(2):149–161. https://doi.org/10.1002/ajim.23203

Jetha A, Johnson SR, Gignac MAM (2021b) Unmet workplace support needs and lost productivity of workers with systemic sclerosis: a path analysis study. Arthritis Care Res (Hoboken) 73(3): 423–431. https://doi.org/10.1002/acr.24123

Jetha A, Shamaee A, Bonaccio S, Gignac MAM et al (2021c) Fragmentation in the future of work: a horizon scan examining the impact of the changing nature of work on workers experiencing vulnerability. Am J Ind Med 64(8):649–666. https://doi.org/10.1002/ajim.23262

Jetha A, Tucker L, Backman C, Kristman VL et al (2021d) Rheumatic disease disclosure at the early career phase and its impact on the relationship between workplace supports and presenteeism. Arthritis Care Res (Hoboken) 74:1751. https://doi.org/10.1002/acr.24620

LaMontagne AD, Krnjacki L, Milner A, Butterworth P et al (2016) Psychosocial job quality in a national sample of working Australians: a comparison of persons working with versus without disability. SSM Popul Health 2:175–181. https://doi.org/10.1016/j.ssmph.2016.03.001

Lewchuk W (2017) Precarious jobs: where are they, and how do they affect well-being? Econ Labour Relat Rev 28(3):402–419. https://doi.org/10.1177/1035304617722943

Lindsay S, Cagliostro E, Albarico M, Srikanthan D et al (2018a) A systematic review of the role of gender in securing and maintaining employment among youth and young adults with disabilities. J Occup Rehabil 28(2):232–251. https://doi.org/10.1007/s10926-017-9726-x

Lindsay S, Cagliostro E, Carafa G (2018b) A systematic review of workplace disclosure and accommodation requests among youth and young adults with disabilities. Disabil Rehabil 40 (25):2971–2986. https://doi.org/10.1080/09638288.2017.1363824

Ma Z, Dhir P, Perrier L, Bayley M et al (2020) The impact of vocational interventions on vocational outcomes, quality of life, and community integration in adults with childhood onset disabilities: a systematic review. J Occup Rehabil 30(1):1–21. https://doi.org/10.1007/s10926-019-09854-1

Manyika J, Lund S, Chui M, Bughin J et al. (2017) Jobs lost, jobs gained: workforce transitions in a time of automation. McKinsey Global Institute. https://www.mckinsey.com/~/media/mckinsey/industries/public%20and%20social%20sector/our%20insights/what%20the%20future%20of%20work%20will%20mean%20for%20jobs%20skills%20and%20wages/mgi%20jobs%20lost-jobs%20gained_report_december%202017.pdf

Marmot M, Allen J, Bell R, Bloomer E et al (2012) WHO European review of social determinants of health and the health divide. Lancet 380(9846):1011–1029. https://doi.org/10.1016/S0140-6736(12)61228-8

Milner A, Shields M, King TL, Aitken Z et al (2019) Disabling working environments and mental health: a commentary. Disabil Health J 12(4):537–541. https://doi.org/10.1016/j.dhjo.2019.06.002

Morris S, Fawcett G, Brisebois L, Hughes J (2018) A demographic, employment and income profile of Canadians with disabilities aged 15 years and over, 2017. Canadian survey on disability reports. Statistics Canada, Ottawa. https://www150.statcan.gc.ca/n1/pub/89-654-x/89-654-x2018002-eng.htm. Accessed 29 May 2022

Morris S, Fawcett G, Timoney LR, Hughes J (2019) The dynamics of disability: progressive, recurrent or fluctuating limitations. In: Canadian survey on disability reports, Statistics Canada,

Ottawa. https://www150.statcan.gc.ca/n1/pub/89-654-x/89-654-x2019002-eng.pdf. Accessed 29 May 2022

Munandar VD, Morningstar ME, Carlson SR (2020) A systematic literature review of video-based interventions to improve integrated competitive employment skills among youth and adults with autism spectrum disorder. J Vocat Rehabil 53(1):29–41. https://doi.org/10.3233/jvr-201083

Nevala N, Pehkonen I, Koskela I, Ruusuvuori J et al (2015) Workplace accommodation among persons with disabilities: a systematic review of its effectiveness and barriers or facilitators. J Occup Rehabil 25(2):432–448. https://doi.org/10.1007/s10926-014-9548-z

OECD (2010) Sickness, disability and work: breaking the barriers: a synthesis of findings across OECD countries. OECD Publishing, Paris. https://doi.org/10.1787/9789264088856-en

Ojala S, Pyöriä P (2019) Precarious work and the risk of receiving a disability pension. Scand J Public Health 47(3):293–300. https://doi.org/10.1177/1403494818804106

Perri M, McColl MA, Khan A, Jetha A (2021) Scanning and synthesizing Canadian policies that address the school-to-work transition of youth and young adults with disabilities. Disabil Health J 14(4):101122. https://doi.org/10.1016/j.dhjo.2021.101122

Pettersen KT, Fugletveit R (2015) "Should we talk about it?": a study of the experiences business leaders have of employing people with mental health problems. Work 52(3):635–641. https://doi.org/10.3233/WOR-152125

Roberts LL, Macan TH (2006) Disability disclosure effects on employment interview ratings of applicants with nonvisible disabilities. Rehabil Psychol 51(3):239–246. https://doi.org/10.1037/0090-5550.51.3.239

Rosner T, Grasso A, Scott-Cole L, Villalobos A et al (2020) Scoping review of school-to-work transition for youth with intellectual disabilities: a practice gap. Am J Occup Ther 74(2):7402205020. https://doi.org/10.5014/ajot.2019.035220

Scarpetta S, Sonnet A, Manfredi T (2010) Rising youth unemployment during the crisis: how to prevent negative long-term consequences on a generation? In: OECD social, employment and migration working papers, no. 106. OECD publishing, Paris, pp 1–34. https://doi.org/10.1787/5kmh79zb2mmv-en

Schwab K (2016) The fourth industrial revolution: what it means, how to respond World Economic Forum. https://wwwweforumorg/agenda/2016/01/the-fourth-industrial-revolution-what-it-means-and-how-to-respond/. Accessed 9 June 2020

Smith DL, Atmatzidis K, Capogreco M, Lloyd-Randolfi D et al (2017) Evidence-based interventions for increasing work participation for persons with various disabilities: a systematic review. OTJR (Thorofare N J) 37(Suppl 2):3S–13S. https://doi.org/10.1177/1539449216681276

Stutterheim SE, Brands R, Baas I, Lechner L et al (2017) HIV status disclosure in the workplace: positive and stigmatizing experiences of health care workers living with HIV. J Assoc Nurses AIDS Care 28(6):923–937. https://doi.org/10.1016/j.jana.2017.06.014

Tompa E, Mofidi A, Jetha A, Lahey P et al (2022) Development and implementation of a framework for estimating the economic benefits of an accessible and inclusive society. Equal Divers Incl 41(3):318–339. https://doi.org/10.1108/EDI-07-2020-0186

UN General Assembly (2007) Convention on the rights of persons with disabilities: resolution/adopted by the General Assembly, 24 January 2007, A/RES/61/106. http://www.refworld.org/docid/45f973632.html. Accessed 12 May 2022

United Nations (2015) Ageing and disability. https://www.un.org/development/desa/disabilities/disability-and-ageing.html. Accessed 2 June 2022

US Department of Labor (2022) Persons with a disability: labor force characteristics – 2021. Bureau of Labor Statistics, Washington. www.bls.gov/news.release/pdf/disabl.pdf. Accessed 01 Feb 2022

Von Wachter T (2020) The persistent effects of initial labor market conditions for young adults and their sources. J Econ Perspect 34(4):168–194. https://doi.org/10.1257/jep.34.4.168

Vosko LF (2006) Precarious employment: towards an improved understanding of labour market insecurity. In: Vosko LF (ed) Precarious employment: understanding labour market insecurity in Canada. McGill-Queen's University Press, Montreal and Kingston, pp 3–39

Webb M (2019) The impact of artificial intelligence on the labor market. SSRN. https://doi.org/10.2139/ssrn.3482150

Wei X, Yu JW, Wagner M, Hudson L et al (2018) Job searching, job duration, and job loss among young adults with autism spectrum disorder. J Vocat Rehabil 48(1):1–10. https://doi.org/10.3233/jvr-170922

Weld-Blundell I, Shields M, Devine A, Dickinson H et al (2021) Vocational interventions to improve employment participation of people with psychosocial disability, autism and/or intellectual disability: a systematic review. Int J Environ Res Public Health 18(22):12083. https://doi.org/10.3390/ijerph182212083

Williams-Whitt K, Taras D (2010) Disability and the performance paradox: can social capital bridge the divide? Br J Ind Relat 48(3):534–559. https://doi.org/10.1111/j.1467-8543.2009.00738.x

Wood AJ, Graham M, Lehdonvirta V, Hjorth I (2019) Good gig, bad gig: autonomy and algorithmic control in the global gig economy. Work Employ Soc 33(1):56–75. https://doi.org/10.1177/0950017018785616

World Health Organization (2001) International classification of functioning, disability and health (ICF). World Health Organization, Geneva. https://apps.who.int/iris/bitstream/handle/10665/42407/9241545429.pdf;jsessionid=65F9731533BA9C7FF924601802543EEF?sequence=1. Accessed 29 May 2022

World Health Organization, The World Bank (2011) World report on disability. World Health Organization, Geneva. https://apps.who.int/iris/handle/10665/44575. Accessed 29 May 2022

Working Careers with Common Mental Disorders

23

Gunnel Hensing

Contents

Introduction	400
Common Mental Disorders and Work	400
The Magnitude of CMD	400
The Right to Work	402
CMD in a Life Course Perspective	402
Work Capacity: A Dynamic Phenomenon	403
Mental Health: A Conceptual Framework	404
Exploring the Capacity to Work with Common Mental Disorders	406
Exploring Work Instability in Common Mental Disorders	407
The Sick Leave and Rehabilitation Process in CMD	408
What Employers Can Do	410
Stigma	410
Universal Prevention	411
Early Identification	412
Sickness Absence and Return to Work	412
A Gender Perspective	414
Concluding Remarks	415
Cross-References	416
References	416

Abstract

Most of the 600 billion EURO of the costs of mental illness in the EU relates to low employment rates, reduced productivity, and social security programs. This chapter takes a comprehensive approach to mental health at work from a life course perspective. It explores the concepts "capacity to work" and "work instability" in relation to common mental disorders. Both concepts are dynamic and difficult to

---

G. Hensing (✉)
School of Public Health and Community Medicine, Institute of Medicine, The Sahlgrenska Academy at University of Gothenburg, Gothenburg, Sweden
e-mail: gunnel.hensing@gu.se

© Springer Nature Switzerland AG 2023
M. Wahrendorf et al. (eds.), *Handbook of Life Course Occupational Health*, Handbook Series in Occupational Health Sciences, https://doi.org/10.1007/978-3-031-30492-7_23

grasp and measure for physicians. Studies exploring experiences such as disconnectedness and putting on a working façade among the affected are presented. The sickness absence and rehabilitation process is introduced. Being off sick for longer periods is a severe consequence of CMD due to the risk of more permanent marginalization from work life. This can in particular affect young people early in their work careers. Employers have an important role in initiating universal prevention of detrimental work environment to reduce work-related CMD. The chapter also discusses the importance of reduced stigma around mental illness to facilitate early identification of workers with CMD to prevent sickness absence and support return to work if needed. The complex relation between CMD and work requires a close collaboration between the workplace, appropriate health services, and the worker to avoid prolonged absence and future marginalization. Prevention and early identification of work instability throughout the life course and an increased awareness within occupational health can empower individuals at different stages of their work career to manage CMD and continue to work and function in different social roles.

Keywords

Working careers with common mental disorders · Capacity to work with common mental disorders · Work instability · Mental health at work · Sickness absence with psychiatric disorders · Return to work with common mental disorders

Introduction

Common mental disorders (CMD) such as depression, anxiety, and acute reactions to stress are prevalent across the world (GBD Mental Disorders Collaborators 2022). Most adults with CMD are in work (Ármannsdóttir et al. 2013). Estimates vary depending on how CMD is defined and measured, but approximately 15–20% of the working population is affected with a higher prevalence in women than in men (OECD 2012). Further, a detrimental work environment contributes to the development of CMD (Aronsson et al. 2017; Theorell et al. 2015). Thus, it is unrealistic to research the working life course without considering CMD. Employers and employees alike need to pay attention to the most common group of disorders in working populations. Efforts to prevent work-related CMD are important, as are efforts on how to cope with CMD in the workplace, and as an individual worker. A healthy work life is adapted to the dynamic life courses of the working population with periods of better and worse health. To paraphrase WHO, there is no occupational health without mental health.

Common Mental Disorders and Work

The Magnitude of CMD

It is difficult to estimate the magnitude of common mental disorders. Steel et al. (2014) have contributed by doing a systematic review of psychiatric epidemiological studies using structured diagnostic measures to estimate CMD defined as depressive (including bipolar), anxiety (including stress reactions), and substance use disorders. They account for some challenges in psychiatric epidemiology: a high level of comorbidity, underlying common latent constructs, and some support for effectiveness of transdiagnostic approaches in treatment. These challenges question the assumption of discrete mental disorders. On the other hand, it supports an approach to common mental disorders as a combined concept. Steel et al. (2014) identified 174 surveys published from 1980 to 2013 in peer-reviewed journals. The 12-month global prevalence of criteria-based CMD was 17.6% (95% CI 16.3–18.9%). The lifetime prevalence was 29.2% (25.9–32.6). Women had higher rates of mood and anxiety disorders while men had higher rates of substance use disorders. The prevalence of criteria-based CMD was 17.1% in European high-income countries and 19.0% in English-speaking high-income countries (Steel et al. 2014). Estimates that are more recent based on the EU survey Statistics on Income and Living Conditions (EU-SILC) of psychological distress found an EU average of 11% of the participants reporting distress. The proportion varied from 5% in Ireland to just above 20% in Portugal.

There is a lack of data on how large the proportion of those affected by CMD also have a reduction in work capacity. According to the OECD, the proportion of the population aged 20–64 years who are full-time disability benefits recipients is just above 6% (Hemmings and Prinz 2022). The proportion varies between countries, with Norway having the highest proportion with almost 14%. These data were based on the whole population and not specifically on those with CMD.

The OECD has estimated that mental ill health costs EUR 600 billion in the 28 EU countries (OECD 2018). This is more than 4% of the Gross Domestic Product (GDP) in the EU. Of these costs, lower employment rates and reduced productivity due to mental ill health constitute 1.6% of GDP (EUR 260 billion). Social security programs cost EUR 170 billion (1.2% of GDP) and health care EUR 190 billion (1.3% of GDP). These figures show that mental disorders influence the economy and preventive efforts can be expected to have positive effects not only by reducing the number of persons affected but also by saving money for society, employers, and for the affected person and their family.

Mental disorders affect people around the globe. In many low-income and middle-income countries, there is a severe lack of health care services including appropriate pharmaceuticals. WHO states that almost 50% of the world's population are living in countries with one psychiatrist per 200,000 or more persons (WHO 2021). With this low availability to specialized mental health professionals, even the most severely ill persons will not have access to best available treatment. Furthermore, there are differences between socioeconomic groups. Untreated mental disorders in adults that lead to reduced work participation have economic consequences for themselves and for their family, and this can lead to poverty. It is not surprising that the WHO's action plan for mental health has universal health coverage (UHC) as one of its guiding principles. However, social security compensating income losses is as important as UHC for persons in working ages. Although mental disorders affect work life throughout the world, in this chapter, the focus will be on the situation in Western countries.

The Right to Work

Paid work is necessary to get an income, or to exchange supplies, services, and goods. Working is also important since it gives a structure to the day and in many cases a sense of contribution to the society. In many workplaces, social relations with work mates, customers and clients, and management add to social network resources and personal development. Work is so important that the United Nations has added it to the declaration of human rights. In article 23, it says:

> Everyone has the right to work, to free choice of employment, to just and favourable conditions of work and to protection against unemployment. (United Nations 2022)

A CMD that threatens the individual's possibility to continue working can be devastating in many ways and, in most severe cases, can lead to future marginalization from work life. Despite this, it is only recently that research on mental health at work has increased in numbers, perspectives, and designs.

One approach to research on mental health at work includes work as a cause of CMD. A systematic review found that low control and high demands, low social support, bullying, conflicts at work, precarious employment conditions, and effort-reward imbalance at work were associated with depressive symptoms (Theorell et al. 2015). Another review found that low social support, precarious employment conditions, and effort-reward imbalance were associated with burnout symptoms (Aronsson et al. 2017). These reviews, based on several well-conducted studies, conclude that work may be a cause of depression and burnout symptoms. Few studies exist on anxiety symptoms. The development of CMD-friendly workplaces through preventive interventions is likely to contribute to general health of all employees, and thus be a good investment of time and money.

CMD has multifactorial risk factors, and work is one of many etiologic paths to CMD. Childhood and youth abuse, intimate partner violence, drug use disorders, and traumatic events are examples of risk factors outside work. Even if the cause of CMD is not work related, it will affect work if the disorder affects a person's functions and capacity to work. In most countries, employers have an obligation to adapt work tasks and work environment in the short and long term if needed. The distribution of laws and regulations that protect workers is not equal within a country or between countries. CMD is a global phenomenon, and the right to decent work encompasses all workers.

CMD in a Life Course Perspective

The life course perspective is an approach used by researchers to embrace a more detailed understanding of how health is affected by experiences throughout life. Among researchers, there are slightly different thoughts about how health and life experiences are intertwined.

Life course approach	Working career with CMD example
Negative experiences in sensitive periods have more severe effects on health	*Young person entering first employment is exposed to bullying at work*
Collective negative experiences build up to future effects on health	*The young person was bullied at school as well*
Risk chain – the significance of adverse events is governed by the events that follow	*Experience of bullying at school might not add to ill health for a young person entering a friendly and supportive work environment*

The first job is important to build experience, self-confidence, and competence. An unfortunate start of working life might complicate this development. A risk of chain can be inhibited by a supportive psychosocial work environment while the school bullying might add to the risk for health problem when followed by bullying at work. The risk chain might be extended by absence from work to cope with bullying, and with absence the income might be lower and with those new worries regarding economy.

Sensitive periods have mainly been used to understand development during childhood. However, sensitive periods occur in another sense during the life cycle such as when young people enter working life, pregnancy, and parenthood, and develop chronic diseases, and when aging workers need to do physically demanding work. In fact, the entrance of working life is one of the most sensitive periods. Young persons with mental disorders, including both severe and common disorders, have a higher risk of remaining outside the labor market. Bültmann et al. (2020) not only discuss the importance of this transition for adult health and independence, but also recognize the specific challenges for young persons with mental disorders. de Groot et al. (2022) showed, in a follow-up study from age 11 to 29 years, how work functioning is associated not only by persistently high levels of mental health problems but also by lower and changing levels. The first employment as a sensitive period appears even more important when considering these results.

Work Capacity: A Dynamic Phenomenon

The capacity to work (Another term is work ability which I see as a synonym. Work performance is a related term.) is essential. It defines whether a person can work or not. CMD and associated symptoms can influence the capacity, but how much it influence if a person can work or not depends also on the work situation. There is not a simple or straight line between a CMD diagnosis and the capacity to work. An often-used model is the Person – Environment – Occupation – Model (PEOM) (Law et al. 1996). PEOM suggests that occupational performance is a dynamic interplay between the person, the environment, and the occupation. The model takes a holistic view on the person, who is seen as an active and unique being. The environment is defined broadly including social, economic, physical, cultural, and institutional aspects. Occupation is defined as clusters of activities and tasks. The model is illustrated by three circles, and the surface in the middle is the occupational performance, or in other words, the capacity to work (Fig. 1).

Fig. 1 The person-environment-occupation model by Law et al. (1996)

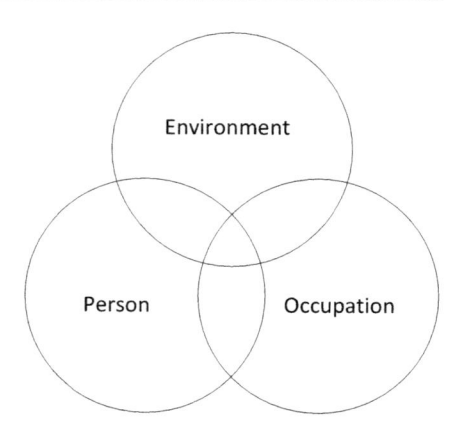

PEOM postulates that the three circles are in a dynamic and transactional relationship. Thus, the capacity to work is not static, and it is not possible to assess the capacity to work without taking the person, the environment, and the occupation into consideration. The transactional relationship means that the person does not only interact with environment and occupation but in fact also is adapted to them as are they to the person. This is interesting in relation to CMD since these kinds of disorders influence the persons themselves. As an example, the optimistic and extrovert colleague changes into a person that withdraws from social situations and avoids contact with others. This changes the dynamic at the workplace and is an example of how interrelated these processes are.

Even physicians have difficulties in assessing work capacity in patients with CMD. In an interview study, Swedish physicians described the assessment as doing a jigsaw puzzle without a master model (Bertilsson et al. 2018). The final assessment was highly individual and composite, and the process repeated itself in new patients. Standardized guidelines did not exist to facilitate the assessment, but with experience, the physicians improved their own ability to do the assessment. In a systematic review, we found 12 mainly qualitative studies that explored how physicians (n = 202) do assessments in patients with CMD (Nordling et al. 2020). A synthesis of findings showed that the assessment is a complex task in which physicians use medical skills, but also to a large extent nonmedical skills. Physicians thought that more knowledge on patient's workplace would enhance their possibility to do appropriate assessments. These findings support the dynamic and transactional nature of work capacity at a daily basis and over the life course.

Mental Health: A Conceptual Framework

Mental health is a broad concept often including both the positive (health) and negative (disorder) dimension. Starting with the positive dimension, the WHO defines mental health as follows:

....a state of well-being in which the individual realizes his or her own abilities, can cope with the normal stresses of life, can work productively and fruitfully, and is able to make a contribution to his or her community. (WHO 2022)

This definition stresses well-being, achievements, and usefulness in society. This focus has been problematized in a paper by Galderisi et al. (2015). They argue that the emphasis on positive emotions and excellence in functioning can lead to a reductionist view on mental health. Further, it ignores structural and contextual factors as reasons for nonproductivity. Galderisi et al. (2015) suggest a new definition focusing more on the whole range of emotions and with a stronger emphasis on societal structures. They also highlight the dynamic aspects of mental health and importance of coping with fluctuations in life:

Mental health is a dynamic state of internal equilibrium which enables individuals to use their abilities in harmony with universal values of society. Basic cognitive and social skills; ability to recognize, express and modulate one's own emotions, as well as empathize with others; flexibility and ability to cope with adverse life events and function in social roles, and harmonious relationship between body and mind represent important components of mental health which contribute, to varying degrees, to the state of internal equilibrium. (Galderisi et al. 2015, p 231)

This definition allows variation in emotions and accepts that also negative emotions such as anger and sadness are appropriate in a dynamic state of mental health. It also points to coping as an important aspect of mental health. According to this definition, mental health at work can involve emotions of happiness and misery, annoyances, minor conflicts, and even more stressful but short-lived situations. Such experiences are expected parts of a modern working life.

With "mental health" as the center, the perspective can turn to supportive factors and resources rather than limitations and demands (Fig. 2).

At the individual level, treatment and coping with symptoms are important to maintain or regain mental health while work adjustments and social support are important at the workplace. Again, irrespective of causes to deteriorating mental health, the workplace has an important role to play in supporting an individual to avoid deteriorating work capacity and sickness absence.

Fig. 2 Mental health and factors that can promote mental health

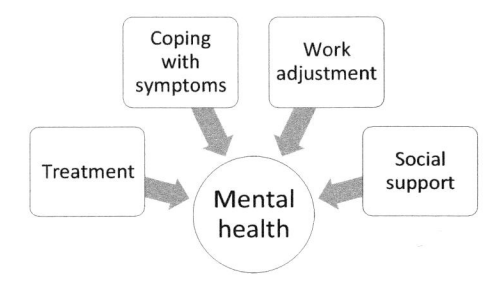

Exploring the Capacity to Work with Common Mental Disorders

The concept work capacity has developed out of legal and administrative purposes. The Swedish sickness insurance, which is a universal and public insurance, stated at its introduction in the early 1950s that medically caused reduction of the capacity to work entitled an individual to benefits. With a growing work force and expectations of compensation for longer periods, the economic costs increased and peaked at the millennium. The requirements for receiving benefits tightened. The insurance scrutinized reduced work capacity, and physicians must certify that the reduction is due to disease, injury, or medical symptoms. As described above, this is difficult in patients with CMD.

To better understand how CMD affects work capacity, Bertilsson et al. (2013) performed a phenomenological study. Phenomenology is a qualitative method that is appropriate and suitable to explore real-life phenomenon, especially when these phenomena are less verbalized and present in a general discourse on a topic. Bertilsson et al. (2013) conclude that work capacity in CMD is an administrative and medical concept, but at the time of the study, there was very little exploration, description, and understanding from the perspective of those affected. Contrary to many studies that explored living with CMD, the researchers found no study exploring working with CMD (Bertilsson et al. 2013). The researchers did focus group interviews with 17 persons with experiences of working with CMD (CMD was in this study defined as depressed and anxious). The questions explored in the focus groups were the following [cited from page 1706 in Bertilsson et al. 2013]:

- *What, in your opinion, characterizes a good capacity to work?*
- *What do you think is part of a good capacity to work?*
- *How is your capacity to work affected by problems such as worry, fatigue, sadness, depression, or anxiety?*
- *What does it mean to you that your capacity to work is affected by problems such as worry, fatigue, sadness, depression, or anxiety?*

Based on the analysis of the discussions in the focus groups, the researchers identified how capacity to work is experienced by persons affected with CMD through nine constituents used to build up the essence of the phenomenon (Fig. 3).

These constituents elaborate the complexity described earlier. They combine experiences of symptoms, behavior, and performance. Noticeable is the loss of "refueling" that probably is taken for granted in periods of mental health. For the participants in the study, the loss of "refueling" meant that experiences of appreciation, meaningfulness, and work satisfaction diminished. It can be assumed that these positive aspects of working could contribute to coping with symptoms at work. When the refueling of energizing experiences disappeared, it became harder to maintain the capacity to work.

The participants described the experiences of putting on a working façade as a way of managing to keep working despite disturbing symptoms. A similar experience recurs in another study focusing on work instability, which theoretically can be described as the process leading up to a reduction of the capacity to work.

Nine constituents build up the essence of capacity to work while depressed and anxious	Surrounded by a continuous work flow with a hypersensitive mind
	Unequipped to handle the demands of time and pace
	Exposed in professional interpersonal encounters
	Putting on a working facade
	The demanding act of being "good enough"
	Deficient work satisfaction and loss of "refueling"
	Trading leisure-time activity with inactivity to manage work
	Disrupting work place order
	The dynamics of alienation

Fig. 3 Nine constituents that together compose the essence of capacity to work

Exploring Work Instability in Common Mental Disorders

Work instability was defined by Gilworth et al. (2006) in a study of patients with traumatic brain injury as a situation at work characterized by a mismatch between the person's capacity and the demands at work. Such a situation calls for increased awareness not only from the employee but also from the manager. A mismatch can be managed by short- or long-term work adjustments or by a consultation with the Occupational Health Services to see if CMD treatment is relevant.

To explore work instability in common mental disorders, Danielsson et al. (2017) did a Grounded Theory study interviewing 27 individuals with own experience of working with CMD (CMD was in this study defined as depression or anxiety diagnoses (n = 22) and low mental well-being (n = 5)) which had not been done before the time of the study. Danielsson et al. (2017) suggest that work instability with CMD is a general process that destabilizes the ordinary work flow, and that the instability can move back and forth to regain flow or toward a situation where work is impossible.

The category identified in the study as the main core conceptualization of work instability reads as follows: Working in dissonance: caught up in a bubble inside the work stream (Danielsson et al. 2017). The category was seen mainly as a social process, and the metaphoric bubble was used to describe the disconnectedness experienced in relation to other persons at work. The "bubble" was a shield that made it possible to continue working, but at the same time, it created a distance. The model visualizes the process (Fig. 4):

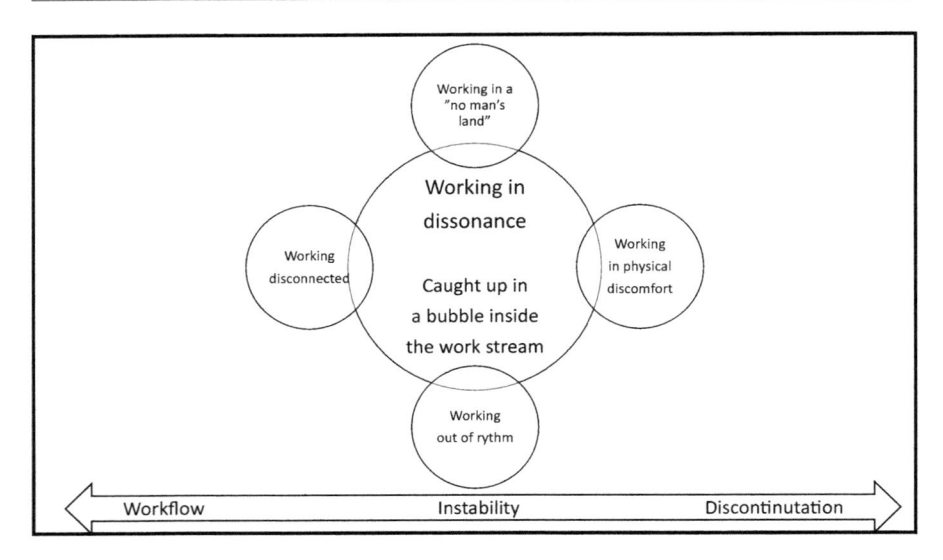

Fig. 4 The process and subprocesses of work instability. (Adapted from Danielsson et al. 2017, page 6)

Four subprocesses compose the social, and main, process of work instability. These four subprocesses reflect temporal-spatial, physical, psychological, and existential aspects of the instability. These subprocesses are interesting findings and elaborate how working in dissonance involved the whole person with mind and body, with disrupted social relations, and with an unusual time and space awareness. The contrast described between the ordinary workflow and the disrupted flow included experiences of changes in the border between inside and outside. Participants described how they tried to protect themselves from sound, light, and social encounters.

Danielsson et al. (2017) discuss their findings in relation to the closely connected concept of work capacity. They suggest that work instability has an advantage of having a more proactive approach already in the name, but also in its focus. The importance of naming and describing experiences in the field of mental health problems at work must not be underestimated. Facilitate communication and management of deteriorated mental health at work. It is worth mentioning that Bertilsson et al. (2013) and Danielsson et al. (2017) find similar experiences of being at work but still isolated from the ordinary life and communication at the workplace. More research is needed, but it is an interesting assumption that this experience might be an important sign of increased risk of not being able to maintain work.

The Sick Leave and Rehabilitation Process in CMD

Work instability and reduced capacity to work (Presenteeism or sickness presence are two concepts that have been used to describe how health problems can influence work. Reduced capacity to work is used to describe a similar situation.) can lead to decreased productivity at work, deteriorated quality of work, and sickness absence. Sickness absence is the most serious outcome for the individual. It has economic and social consequences since the worker is completely cutoff from the workplace. In some cases, sickness absence is the only solution to an unsustainable situation. However, sick leave of an employee tends to lead to individual explanations rather than work-related explanations. In many cases, an adjustment of the work environment or adaptation of the occupation can restore work capacity.

Sickness absence with CMD is common in all age groups. Older workers have a higher risk of longer periods off work, and it is more difficult for older workers to find new jobs. Changes in the work environment such as increased digitalization or corporate changes with owners abroad can be complicated for older workers. They might be less experienced in digital systems than younger workers, and they might not be as fluent in English as is needed for work in global corporates. As mentioned earlier, life course approaches highlight cumulative effects or risk chain effects on future health. This is applicable to sickness absence. Earlier sickness absence is highly predictive of future sickness absence.

Thus, early identification of work instability or reduced capacity to work is important in preventing sickness absence. Also, after the initiation of a sick-leave period, secondary prevention is possible by trying to reduce the number of days off sick. As illustrated by Fig. 5, the Sick leave and Rehabilitation Process consists of several situations that overlap and an individual with deterioration of mental health can move back and forth between the different situations. The employer has a

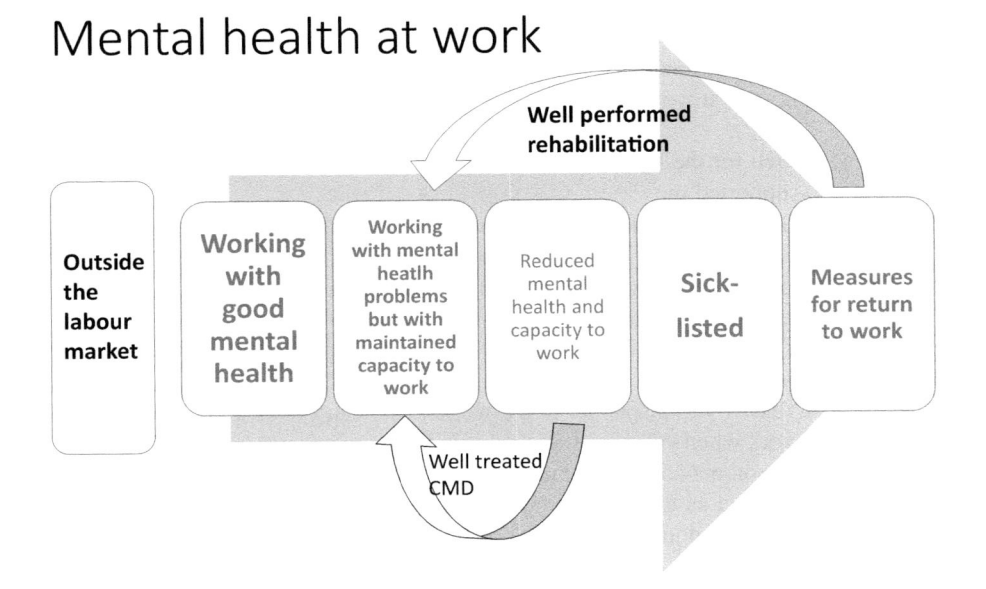

Adapted from a book in Swedish: Return to work, Studentlitteratur 2015

Fig. 5 The sick leave and rehabilitation process

possibility to intervene at any of these situations supported by HR departments and Occupational Health Services (van de Voort et al. 2019). The primary health care services also have a key role in early identification and measures to prevent sickness absence (Holmgren et al. 2019; Hultqvist et al. 2021).

What Employers Can Do

Mental health at work consists of several situations as illustrated in Fig. 5. As we move to the right, the measures become more individualized. However, employers can intervene much earlier in the process to create a CMD-friendly workplace, which will improve the work environment for all workers. A CMD-friendly workplace has the potential to promote mental health and prevent mental disorders.

Stigma

Several studies have identified stigma and insufficient knowledge on mental disorders as problematic. At the individual level, it may delay health care seeking and the possibility of getting treatment (Angermeyer et al. 2017; Olsson et al. 2021). Studies have estimated that in Europe and the USA, 52–74% of persons with mental disorders do not receive treatment (Clement et al. 2015). At the workplace level, stigma and insufficient knowledge may hamper CMD disclosure out of worries for social and economic consequences. In a Swedish focus group study of workers with depression or anxiety disorders, there was some discussion on the different attitudes to CMD disclosure at workplaces:

Person 1: Well for me it has been a prerequisite that my manager has known and supported me.
Person 2: God, what a relief. That's not what it looks like at my workplace. It was the opposite. There you got reduced wage in the end since you were no longer able to work [satisfactorily]. And that of course was a burden in itself, that you knew that you weren't one of the gang.
Person 1: You mean you felt that way when you were sick, that they turned their backs . . .
Person 2: Yeah. I was a spanner in the works. You can't have a good capacity to work when you are ill, so to speak, but things do not improve by the fact that others do not comprehend [the incapacity] either. They probably did as good as they could, but no one ever asked me about anything and then you don't get any feed-back. (Bertilsson et al. 2013, p 1709)

In fact, several studies have found that among the negative public attitudes attached to mental illness, not wanting to work alongside a person with mental illness is one the most common (Rüsch et al. 2005). In general, women, and persons with higher education have less negative attitudes (Holzinger et al. 2012; Mangerini et al. 2020).

Stigma is rooted in social contexts and social relations. This means that it can be influenced and reversed by changes in structures, relations, and knowledge. Rüsch et al. (2005) described stigmatization as a process that develops and reinforces through behaviors such as labeling, stereotyping, prejudice, and discrimination. One way of overcoming stigma is to increase knowledge and change attitudes and norms. In a Swedish study of managers, van de Voort et al. (2019) found that managers who had received training in how to support employees with CMD reported more CMD-related workplace activities (van de Voort et al. 2019). The activities were reviewing work assignments and talking about CMD at the workplace. The study suggests that improved mental health literacy at work can be a first step toward a CMD-friendly workplace. Future research is needed to confirm this hypothesis. Talking about CMD is important, but talking alone without changing the detrimental psychosocial work organization or environment will not lead to a reduction in work-related CMD.

Universal Prevention

Prevention is the effort to avoid negative outcomes while health promotion is the effort to achieve positive outcomes. At work, both these strategies are important. There are three types: universal, selective, and indicative. All three are useful to prevent or manage CMD at work. Universal prevention is directed at all employees irrespective of CMD status. Selective prevention focusses on situations, groups, or persons with increased risk. Indicative prevention targets persons that have developed some type of problem in this case, for example, CMD or work instability. All three types of preventive efforts are important.

Universal improvements in the work organization and work environment are important for all employees. Preventive interventions in Western countries that specifically targeted mental disorders were reviewed on commission from the Swedish Public Health Agency (Hensing et al. 2022). The interventions were universal targeting all employees irrespective of their mental health status. Of 11 identified interventions at the organizational level, 8 had preventive effects on the studied mental health outcome. The interventions consisted of (*i*) structured workplace discussions about psychosocial and/or physical work environment, (*ii*) introduction of new processes (routines at work), (*iii*) fewer working hours with maintained wages, and (*iv*) increased participation. At the individual level, 24 out of 33 studies showed a preventive effect through different types of stress management and through different types of programs for management of life situation and personal development. The drawback of individual interventions is that with staff turnover, the interventions must be repeated continuously. There might also be a positive selection to the interventions and to adherence to the programs. Interventions at the organizational level are less sensitive to selection, and changes made are lasting longer.

Early Identification

In the model presented in Fig. 5, stigma reduction and universal prevention are important to facilitate entrance into the labor market and to maintain working with good mental health. Stigma reduction can also improve early identification of persons at risk for work instability and onset or deterioration of CMD since it facilitates for the employees to contact the manager and ask for support. With better mental health literacy, both affected persons themselves and managers and work mates can improve their capacity to identify symptoms of CMD and to manage these situations.

Early identification can be a sensitive matter at workplaces, and managers can be reluctant to approach an employee with incipient problems. A Swedish study among 3358 managers found that 29% of managers had not met any employee with CMD over the last 2 years while 32% had met one employee and 31% had met two or more employees. Seven percent did not know if they had met an employee with CMD. Most managers are either unaware of CMD among their employees or do not have any employees with CMD. The former is most likely given the high prevalence of CMD in the working population. Research has identified that a common way for managers to get information is by the worker themself disclosing they have mental health problems (Bertilsson et al. 2021). Other ways of identification were through a change in employee work performance or through complaints (Martin et al. 2018).

Managers have a responsibility for a decent and safe work environment. However, managers are also responsible for business development, economy, organizational justice, and adaptation to surrounding society (Ståhl et al. 2014). Each of these responsibilities involves ethical considerations in different ways. Added to this are cultural norms and legal regulations on the involvement of mangers in employees' private life. Thus, early identification can be sensitive, if CMD is a stigmatized topic at the workplace. Again, reducing stigma and increasing mental health literacy and universal prevention are important efforts to facilitate early identification and support to persons affected by CMD and reduced work performance.

Sickness Absence and Return to Work

For the individual, the most severe consequence of CMD-related work instability and reduced capacity to work is sickness absence. Sickness absence occurs when the worker has a reduction in capacity to work due to medical issues. Shorter periods of absence from work are usually unproblematic and can favor treatment and recovery. Prolonged absences can lead to negative consequences such as loss of work-related social networks, difficulties in managing private finances, and changes in life styles, e.g., physical activity. However, the risk of permanent marginalization from work life either through disability pension or through unemployment is by far the most challenging (Alexanderson et al. 2012; Hensing and Wahlström 2004; Kivimäki et al. 2004; OECD 2018).

Sickness Absence with Psychiatric Disorders

Sickness absence with psychiatric disorders has increased in most Western countries (OECD 2018). Comparisons between countries are difficult since sickness absence is dependent on the social security regulations. For example, the Netherlands have a 2-year period during which the employer pays the benefit and has a far-reaching responsibility for vocational rehabilitation to facilitate return to work. If a worker cannot return to their ordinary work or to another employment, social welfare is the next type of social security with much lower levels of economic support. In Denmark, it is common with a 30-day period of full salary from the employer, but individual employment agreements can contract longer periods. An employer in Denmark can fire a person after 120 days of sickness absence. After the first 30 days, the municipality takes over the responsibility and pays sickness benefits for another 5–6 months. At this point, the municipality does an evaluation to assess whether the person is entitled to prolonged sick leave. In Sweden, the sickness insurance legislation states that the employer pays for the first 14 days of a sick leave, and the state takes over the responsibility from day 15. At present, there is no sharp limit in how many days a person can be sick listed. As in most sickness insurances, the sick-listed person must have a sickness certificate. Laws against dismissal due to disease protect workers and reduce the risk of marginalization.

The Swedish Social Insurance Agency has estimated the 12-month cumulative incidence of sickness absence with psychiatric disorders was 2.6% of the labor force in 2018/2019 in women and 1% in men. Sickness absence with psychiatric disorder constitutes approximately 50% of all sick-leave cases in both women and men. Women outnumber men as receivers of sickness benefits and form two-thirds of all sick-listed persons. Common mental disorders form most diagnoses on the certificates. Compared to other diagnoses, the risk of prolonged sickness absence is higher with a psychiatric diagnosis on the certificate, as is the risk of recurrence in a new spell after return to work.

Sickness absence with psychiatric disorders have multifactorial risk factors, and work-related factors are among possible determinants. Duchaine et al. (2020) did a systematic review of psychosocial stressors as defined by three theoretical models common in occupational health research: the effort-reward imbalance model, the job demand-control-support model, and the organizational justice model. They identified 13 studies representing 130,056 individuals. Results from meta-analyses showed that workers exposed to low reward had a higher risk of sickness absence with psychiatric disorders compared to unexposed with a pooled risk ratio (RR) of 1.76 (95% CI 1.49–2.08). Exposure to effort-reward imbalance, job strain, low job control, and high psychological demands had an increased risk of sickness absence compared to workers who were not exposed.

Employer Support in Return to Work

An important task for employers is to reduce the identified risks of sickness absence with psychiatric disorders. However, employers also have a responsibility to support workers that have become sick-listed to facilitate return to work. Sickness absence combines reduced health and reduced capacity to work. In relation to psychiatric disorders, the assessment of how the illness reduces capacity to work is highly individual (Nordling et al. 2020). Even after a reduction of psychiatric symptoms, a reduction in capacity to work can remain. Nieuwenhuijsen et al. (2020) did a systematic review of 45 intervention studies to evaluate the effects of these interventions on sickness absence in persons with depressive disorders. The studies included both clinical and work-related interventions. Despite reviewing 45 studies, the authors conclude that it is difficult to draw firm conclusion due to limited studies on similar interventions and that some studies have few participants. Their conclusion is that combinations of clinical treatment and employer involvement to enable workplace changes most likely will lead to fewer days on sick leave. Examples of workplace changes that can facilitate return to work are changes to the worker's tasks or working hours, supporting a gradual return to work, or supporting the workers to cope with stressful work situations.

Employers can improve support to workers affected by CMD and reduced capacity to work by acknowledging the complexity in balancing individual ability with demands at work including how work is organized in society and in workplaces. As stated in the beginning of this chapter, a healthy work life should adapt to changes in health over a worker's life course. Based on a synthesis of qualitative research on experiences from persons working with CMD, Tengelin (2021) suggests the following points as important for work-related and clinical management of CMD:

Avoid distancing – show empathy and avoid social and emotional distancing.
Pay attention to the risk of individualizing problems – accept that work can be a cause of CMD and develop a mutual understanding of the contribution of both personal- and work-related determinants.
Work against stigmatization and exclusion – CMD is part of any work place, and an openness around mental health problem facilitates for both management and employees.

A Gender Perspective

Women outnumber men as receivers of sickness benefits, and it is therefore important to understand CMD from a gender perspective (Ármannsdóttir et al. 2013). Laaksonen et al. (2010) used a fixed effects model to study sickness absence (irrespective of certification diagnosis) in women and men with similar occupations and at the same workplaces. In that study, the differences in sickness absence were reduced, but some differences remained with a higher absence in women. There is a difference also in sickness absence with psychiatric disorders. The prevalence is higher in women compared to men. Different explanations have been put forward, and the gendered distribution of women and men into different occupations and workplaces is one of the most reasonable (Gonäs et al. 2019). The selection of women into female dominated sectors within health, child and elderly care, and education leads to a different type of exposure at work compared to more male dominated sectors such as technical industries and construction. Employers in female dominated sectors thus have a higher responsibility to perform universal prevention and upgrade their capacity to support workers in the return to work process.

In a study of trends in gender difference in sickness absence (irrespective of certification diagnosis) in eight European countries between 1984 and 2010, Mastekaasa (2014) found increasing differences between women and men in six countries. He tested if these differences could be explained by a higher proportion of mothers with small children in the labor force or by changes in the gender distribution in occupations and industries. However, he could not confirm any of these hypotheses. This study suggests that there are other explanations than the gender segregation of the labor market. Unequal distribution of the unpaid work in families and households has been suggested. A Norwegian study by Østby et al. (2018) could only explain a minor part of the differences between mothers and fathers in sick leave after adjustments for health, work environment, and family difficulties. Research into unpaid work and sickness absence with psychiatric disorders is still undeveloped, and future research should focus on how women and men cope with demands at paid and unpaid work during the years of responsibility for small children.

Concluding Remarks

Common mental disorders are prevalent in the working population. CMD affect persons in all age groups, and a life course perspective is relevant to understand the often-complex relations between CMD and work. Employers need better knowledge on how universal prevention can reduce risk factors in the organization and improve the psychosocial work environment. Applying a life course perspective, young people should be carefully introduced to their first employment, which can be seen as a sensitive period. The careful introduction is particularly important for those with a history of mental health problems. For parents, the period with small children can be a sensitive period with double shifts. Older workers might be vulnerable in relation to new technology and cognitive demands at work. In fact, more research is needed on CMD at work in general but also to a large extent in relation to the challenges in different periods of the life course.

Stigma around mental illness has so far gained less attention in occupational research, but this is mentioned as problematic in interviews with workers affected by CMD. Stigma reduces the openness at work not only for individual workers to seek support but also for managers to discuss mental health at work. Employers also need a structured approach to support employees to prevent sickness absence in the individual case, and to support return to work. Policies aimed at employers and managers are key for promoting a healthier work environment as is adapting the demands to the human resources available. However, the individual worker has also some power to maintain mental health at work by:

- Avoiding compensating psychosocial deficits in the work environment by, for example, repeatedly working overtime or accept working with new digital and other systems without proper introduction

- Pointing out shortcomings in the work environment to their manager, union representatives, or the human resource department
- Participating in discussions at the workplace around what characterizes a good psychosocial work environment and what can be done to reach that goal

Workplaces are arenas for work and health promotion. Much has been done in collaboration between employers and employees to improve ergonomic, chemical, and physical working conditions. Much can be done to improve psychosocial working conditions and to support affected workers to remain in work. Decent work is a source of income, good friendship, and a sense of belonging in society – factors that in different ways contribute to mental health. A CMD-friendly workplace would most likely contribute to the general health of all employees throughout the life course. That is well-invested time and money.

Cross-References

▶ Falling Sick While Working: An Overview of the EU-Level Policy Framework on Returning to Work Following Chronic Disease(s)

References

Alexanderson K, Kivimäki M, Ferrie JE, Westerlund H, Vahtera J, Singh-Manoux A, Melchior M, Zins M, Goldberg M, Head J (2012) Diagnosis-specific sick leave as a long-term predictor of disability pension: a 13-year follow-up of the GAZEL cohort study. 66:155–159. https://doi.org/10.1136/jech.2010.126789

Angermeyer MC, van der Auwera S, Carta MG, Schomerus G (2017) Public attitudes towards psychiatry and psychiatric treatment at the beginning of the 21st century: a systematic review and meta-analysis of population surveys. 16:50–61. https://doi.org/10.1002/wps.20383

Ármannsdóttir B, Mårdby AC, Haukenes I, Hensing G (2013) Cumulative incidence of sickness absence and disease burden among the newly sick-listed, a cross-sectional population-based study. 13:1–10. http://www.biomedcentral.com/1471-2458/13/329

Aronsson G, Theorell T, Grape T, Hammarström A, Hogstedt C, Marteinsdottir I, Skoog I, Träskman-Bendz L, Hall C (2017) A systematic review including meta-analysis of work environment and burnout symptoms. 17:1–13. https://doi.org/10.1186/s12889-015-1954-4

Bertilsson M, Petersson EL, Östlund G, Waern M, Hensing G (2013) Capacity to work while depressed and anxious–a phenomenological study. 35:1705–1711. https://doi.org/10.3109/09638288.2012.751135

Bertilsson M, Maeland S, Löve J, Ahlborg G, Werner EL, Hensing G (2018) The capacity to work puzzle: a qualitative study of physicians' assessments for patients with common mental disorders. 19:1–14. https://doi.org/10.1186/s12875-018-0815-5

Bertilsson M, Klinkhammer S, Staland-Nyman C, de Rijk A (2021) How managers find out about common mental disorders among their employees. 63:975–984. https://doi.org/10.1097/JOM.0000000000002287

Bültmann U, Arends I, Veldman K, McLeod CB, van Zon SKR, Amick III BC (2020) Investigating young adults' mental health and early working life trajectories from a life course perspective: the role of transitions. 74:179–181. https://doi.org/10.1136/jech-2019-213245

Clement S, Schauman O, Graham T, Maggioni F, Evans-Lacko S, Bezborodovs N, Morgan C, Rüsch N, Brown JSL, Thornicroft G (2015) What is the impact of mental health-related stigma on help-seeking? A systematic review of quantitative and qualitative studies. 45:11–27. https://doi.org/10.1017/S0033291714000129

Danielsson L, Bertilsson M, Holmgren K, Hensing G (2017) Working in dissonance: experiences of work instability in workers with common mental disorders. 17:1–11. https://doi.org/10.1186/s12889-017-4388-3

de Groot S, Veldman K, Amick III BC, Bültmann U (2022) Work functioning among young adults: the role of mental health problems from childhood to young adulthood. 79:217–223. https://doi.org/10.1136/oemed-2021-107819

Duchaine CS, Aubé K, Gilbert-Ouimet M, Vézina M, Ndjaboué R, Massamba V, Talbot D, Lavigne-Robichaud M, Trudel X, Bruno Pena-Gralle AP (2020) Psychosocial stressors at work and the risk of sickness absence due to a diagnosed mental disorder: a systematic review and meta-analysis. 77:842–851. https://doi.org/10.1001/jamapsychiatry.2020.0322

Galderisi S, Heinz A, Kastrup M, Beezhold J, Sartorius N (2015) Toward a new definition of mental health. 14:231. https://doi.org/10.1002/wps.20231

GBD Mental Disorders Collaborators (2022) Global, regional, and national burden of 12 mental disorders in 204 countries and territories, 1990–2019: a systematic analysis for the Global Burden of Disease Study 2019. https://doi.org/10.1016/S2215-0366(21)00395-3

Gilworth G, Carey A, Eyres S, Sloan J, Rainford B, Bodenham D, Neumann V, Tennant A (2006) Screening for job loss: development of a work instability scale for traumatic brain injury. 20:835–843. https://doi.org/10.1080/02699050600832221

Gonäs L, Wikman A, Alexanderson K, Gustafsson K (2019) Age, period, and cohort effects for future employment, sickness absence, and disability pension by occupational gender segregation: a population-based study of all employed people in a country (>3 million). 110:584–594. https://doi.org/10.17269/s41997-019-00216-1

Hemmings P, Prinz C (2022) Sickness and disability systems: comparing outcomes and policies in Norway with those in Sweden, The Netherlands and Switzerland no 1601, Feb 2022. https://doi.org/10.1787/c768699b-en

Hensing G, Wahlström R (2004) Chapter 7. Sickness absence and psychiatric disorders. 32:152–180. https://doi.org/10.1080/14034950410021871

Hensing G, Axelsson M, Vaez M, Boström M. To prevent mental illness in working life Results from a mapping literature review on universal interventions in the Workplace (In Swedish: Att förebygga psykisk ohälsa i arbetslivet. En kartläggande litteraturöversikt om universell prevention i arbetslivet.) https://www.folkhalsomyndigheten.se/contentassets/decaa61b169e4d5689acf11662abce/forebygga-psykisk-ohalsa-arbetslivet.pdf. Accessed 30 June 2022

Holmgren K, Hensing G, Bültmann U, Hadzibajramovic E, Larsson MEH (2019) Does early identification of work-related stress, combined with feedback at GP-consultation, prevent sick leave in the following 12 months? A randomized controlled trial in primary health care. 19:1–10. https://doi.org/10.1186/s12889-019-7452-3

Holzinger A, Floris F, Schomerus G, Carta MG, Angermeyer MC (2012) Gender differences in public beliefs and attitudes about mental disorder in western countries: a systematic review of population studies. 21:73–85. https://doi.org/10.1017/S2045796011000552

Hultqvist J, Bjerkeli P, Hensing G, Holmgren K (2021) Does a brief work-stress intervention prevent sick-leave during the following 24 months? A randomized controlled trial in Swedish primary care. 1–10. https://doi.org/10.3233/WOR-205029

Kivimäki M, Forma P, Wikström J, Halmeenmäki T, Pentti J, Elovainio M, Vahtera J (2004) Sickness absence as a risk marker of future disability pension: the 10-town study. 58:710–711. https://doi.org/10.1136/jech.2003.015842

Laaksonen M, Mastekaasa A, Martikainen P, Rahkonen O, Piha K, Lahelma E (2010) Gender differences in sickness absence-the contribution of occupation and workplace. 394–403. https://www.jstor.org/stable/40967875

Law M, Cooper B, Strong S, Stewart D, Rigby P, Letts L (1996) The person-environment-occupation model: a transactive approach to occupational performance. 63:9–23. https://doi.org/10.1177/000841749606300103

Mangerini I, Bertilsson M, de Rijk A, Hensing G (2020) Gender differences in managers' attitudes towards employees with depression: a cross-sectional study in Sweden. 20:1–15. https://doi.org/10.1186/s12889-020-09848-2

Martin A, Woods M, Dawkins S (2018) How managers experience situations involving employee mental ill-health. 11:442–463. https://doi.org/10.1108/IJWHM-09-2017-0069

Mastekaasa A (2014) The gender gap in sickness absence: long-term trends in eight European countries. Eur J Public Health 24:656–662

Nieuwenhuijsen K, Verbeek JH, Neumeyer-Gromen A, Verhoeven A, Bültmann U, Faber B (2020) Interventions to improve return to work in depressed people. Cochrane Database Syst Rev (10). https://doi.org/10.1002/14651858.CD006237

Nordling P, Priebe G, Björkelund C, Hensing G (2020) Assessing work capacity–reviewing the what and how of physicians' clinical practice. 21:1–14. https://doi.org/10.1186/s12875-020-01134-9

OECD (2012) Sick on the job? Myths and realities about mental health and work. http://hdl.voced.edu.au/10707/195540

OECD (2018) Health at a glance: Europe 2018: state of health in the EU cycle. https://doi.org/10.1787/health_glance_eur-2018-en. Accessed 30 June 2022

Olsson S, Hensing G, Burström B, Löve J (2021) Unmet need for mental healthcare in a population sample in Sweden: a cross-sectional study of inequalities based on gender, education, and country of birth. 57:470–481. https://doi.org/10.1007/s10597-020-00668-7

Østby KA, Mykletun A, Nilsen W (2018) Explaining the gender gap in sickness absence. 68:320–26. https://doi.org/10.1093/occmed/kqy062

Rüsch N, Angermeyer MC, Corrigan PW (2005) Mental illness stigma: concepts, consequences, and initiatives to reduce stigma. 20:529–539. https://doi.org/10.1016/j.eurpsy.2005.04.004

Ståhl C, MacEachen E, Lippel K (2014) Ethical perspectives in work disability prevention and return to work: toward a common vocabulary for analyzing stakeholders' actions and interactions. 120:237–250. https://doi.org/10.1007/s10551-013-1661-y

Steel Z, Marnane C, Iranpour C, Chey T, Jackson JW, Patel V, Silove D (2014) The global prevalence of common mental disorders: a systematic review and meta-analysis 1980–2013. 43:476–493. https://doi.org/10.1093/ije/dyu038

Tengelin E in Hensing G, Björk L, Holmgren K (2021) To live with work related mental problems (Att leva med arbetsrelaterade psykiska problem) In: Mental Health at work (Psykisk hälsa i arbetslivet). Lund, Studentlitteratur

Theorell T, Hammarström A, Aronsson G, Träskman Bendz L, Grape T, Hogstedt C, Marteinsdottir I, Skoog I, Hall C (2015) A systematic review including meta-analysis of work environment and depressive symptoms. 15:1–14. https://doi.org/10.1186/s12889-015-1954-4

United Nations (2022) The United Nations' Declaration of Human Rights. https://www.un.org/en/about-us/universal-declaration-of-human-rights. Accessed 14 Feb 2022

van de Voort I, de Rijk A, Hensing G, Bertilsson M (2019) Determinants of managerial preventive actions in relation to common mental disorders at work: a cross-sectional study among Swedish managers. 61:854–862. https://doi.org/10.1097/JOM.0000000000001629

WHO (2021) Comprehensive mental health action plan 2010–2030. World Health Organisation. file:///C:/Users/xhengu/Downloads/9789240031029-eng.pdf. Accessed 2 Feb 2022

WHO (2022) Mental health. World Health Organisation. Accessed 2 Feb 2022. https://www.paho.org/en/topics/mental-health

Adverse Effect of Psychosocial Stressors at Work and Long Working Hours Along the Cardiovascular Continuum

24

Xavier Trudel, Mahée-Gilbert Ouimet, Alain Milot, and Chantal Brisson

Contents

Introduction	420
Psychosocial Stressors at Work and Long Working Hours	421
The Cardiovascular Continuum	423
Psychosocial Stressors at Work and Long Working Hours Along the CV Continuum	424
Blood Pressure	424
Arterial Stiffness	426
Cardiovascular Disease Incidence	426
Cardiovascular Disease Recurrence	427
Sex and Gender Considerations	428
Mechanisms and Interactions with Other Risk Factors	431
Population Attributable Fraction of Cardiovascular Diseases	432
Prevention (Guidelines, Screening, Prediction, and Interventions) from the Individual to the Population and Their Work Environment	433
Psychosocial Stressors at Work in Cardiovascular Prevention Guidelines	433
CVD Risk Prediction	433

X. Trudel (✉) · C. Brisson
Social and Preventive Medicine Department, Université Laval, Québec City, QC, Canada

Population Health and Optimal Health Practices, CHU de Québec Research Center, Québec City, QC, Canada
e-mail: xavier.trudel@crchudequebec.ulaval.ca; chantal.brisson@crchudequebec.ulaval.ca

M.-G. Ouimet
Social and Preventive Medicine Department, Université Laval, Québec City, QC, Canada

Department of Health Science, Université du Québec à Rimouski, Rimouski, QC, Canada
e-mail: mahee_gilbert-ouimet@uqar.ca

A. Milot
Population Health and Optimal Health Practices, CHU de Québec Research Center, Québec City, QC, Canada

Medicine Department, Université Laval, Québec City, QC, Canada
e-mail: alain.milot@fmed.ulaval.ca

© Springer Nature Switzerland AG 2023
M. Wahrendorf et al. (eds.), *Handbook of Life Course Occupational Health*, Handbook Series in Occupational Health Sciences, https://doi.org/10.1007/978-3-031-30492-7_25

Screening 434
Preventive Workplace Interventions 434
Conclusion 435
References 436

Abstract

Cardiovascular diseases (CVD) are the leading cause of morbidity and mortality worldwide. In 2019, CVDs caused an estimated 17.9 million deaths worldwide representing 32% of all global deaths. To improve both primary and secondary CVD prevention, strategies must tackle alterations across all phases of the cardiovascular continuum. This continuum is framed as a chain of events, initiated with risk factors, and progressing to subclinical organ damage, cardiovascular events, and recurrences up to end-stage organ disease and death. Most adults in OECD countries spend over half of their awake time at work, and about 20–25% of them are exposed to psychosocial stressors at work. Work is therefore a major life course component and a promising avenue for prevention. Evidence supports the adverse effect of psychosocial stressors at work and long working hours on cardiovascular manifestations, including high blood pressure, CVD incidence, and CVD recurrence. This chapter presents a synthesis of recent evidence on the adverse effects of these work stressors over the life course, at different stage of the cardiovascular continuum. Considering that important differences between women and men have been observed in these effects, sex and gender considerations will also be presented. The major underlying mechanisms and interactions with other risk factors will be summarized. Finally, the integration of the psychosocial working environment in the most recent guidelines for CVD prevention and in recent legislations will also be discussed. Future directions to improve prevention strategies will be highlighted along with current research priorities.

Keywords

Psychosocial stressors at work · Long working hours · Cardiovascular diseases · Blood pressure · Hypertension · Prevention · Screening · Interventions

Introduction

Cardiovascular diseases (CVD) are the leading cause of morbidity and mortality worldwide (WHO 2011). In 2019, CVDs caused an estimated 17.9 million deaths worldwide representing 32% of all global deaths. High blood pressure (BP) is a major CVD risk factor. It accounts for about 54% of all strokes and 47% of all ischemic heart disease events globally (Lawes et al. 2008). The lifetime risk of developing hypertension among individuals aged 55–65 years and free of hypertension is 90% (Vasan et al. 2002). According to the lowered threshold published in the 2017 ACC/AHA Guideline, nearly half of the working US population aged 45–54 would be hypertensive (Whelton et al. 2017).

Cardiovascular prevention guidelines recommend individual-based approaches to reduce the onset of CVD, including smoking cessation, increased physical activity, and moderate alcohol consumption. However, the CVD burden for healthcare systems and societies keeps increasing around the world (Roth et al. 2020). In order to address the CVD burden, a population-based approach is needed to complement these more traditional individual-based prevention approaches (Carey et al. 2018; Whelton 2015).

Work is a major component of the life course. A majority of adults in countries from the Organization for Economic Co-operation and Development (OECD) spend over half of their awake time at work (Bureau of Labor Statistics 2009; European Foundation for the Improvement of Living and Working Conditions 2006). Workplaces have faced many in-depth transformations in the last decades, mainly characterized by work intensification and job insecurity (Parent-Thirion et al. 2007). Recent European findings suggest that work stress has increased during the same time frame, specifically among workers in lower skilled occupations (Rigo et al. 2021). Globally, the number of people exposed to long working hours (≥ 55 h per week) has increased since 2000 and 479 million workers were exposed in 2016 (Pega et al. 2021). Furthermore, the COVID pandemic has brought about work-life balance challenges along with new work configurations increasing isolation in teleworkers and health risks in workers holding frontline occupations (Faghri et al. 2021). Employers, workers, and public health instances recognize the need to intensify preventive actions to reduce psychosocial stressors at work and long working hours.

Psychosocial Stressors at Work and Long Working Hours

To define psychosocial stressors at work, specific dimensions of the work environment have been identified, for which theoretical models have been developed and for which adverse effects on workers' health have been empirically supported. Using these dimensions reduces the complexity of the psychosocial environment at work and facilitates communication between workers, employers, unions, and other stakeholders. Using specific dimensions also allows to quantify exposure prevalence, increasing opportunities for screening, and surveillance, and facilitating the implementation of prevention measures in workplaces (Vézina et al. 2015).

Two theoretical models have mainly been used to assess psychosocial stressors at work (Fig. 1): the demand-control-support model (Karasek 1979) and the effort-reward imbalance model (Siegrist 1996). In high-income countries, the proportions of working men and women exposed to these combinations of psychosocial stressors at work have been found to be about 20–25% (Brisson et al. 2011). This prevalence tends to be comparable to some major CVD risk factors such as smoking and obesity (around 20–25% in working age groups in Canada).

The demand-control-support model suggests that workers simultaneously experiencing high psychological demands and low job control, called job strain, are more likely to develop stress-related health problems (Karasek 1979).

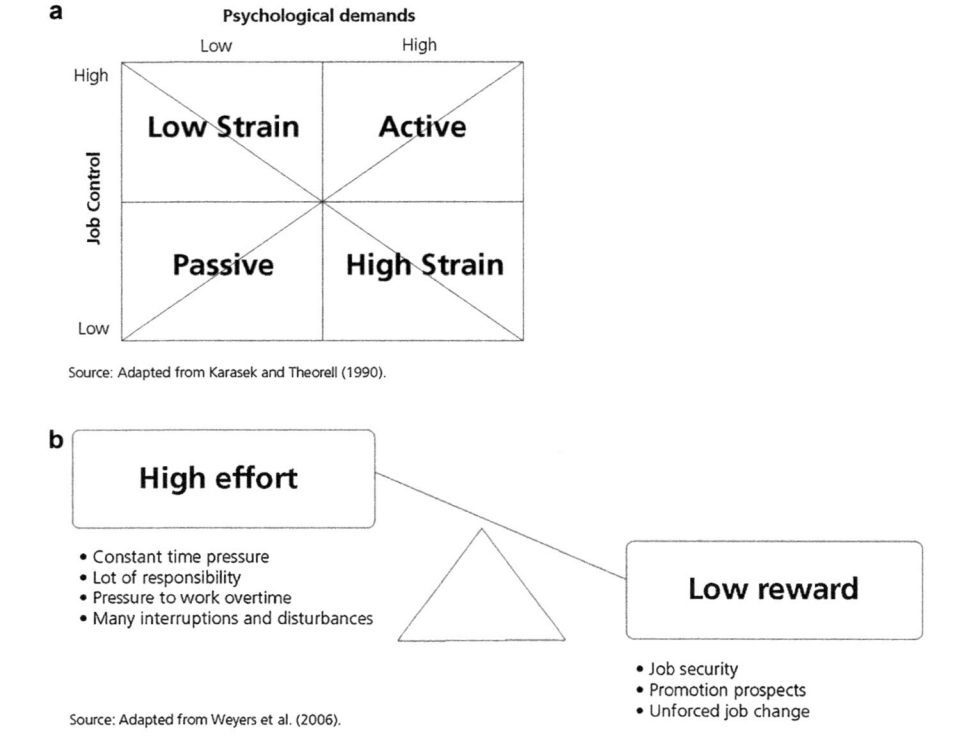

Fig. 1 Psychosocial stressors at work: (**a**) Karasek's demand-control model (©Copyright R. Karasek JCQ Center Global ApS. All rights reserved. www.jcqcenter.com); (**b**) Siegrist's effort-reward imbalance model

Psychological demands refer to an excessive workload, very hard or very fast work, task interruption, intense concentration, and conflicting demands. Job control is a combination of skill discretion and decision authority. Skill discretion refers to the degree to which a worker can develop skills, learn new things, and use creativity at work. Decision authority refers to the extent to which one can take part in decisions, make decisions, and have a say on the job and how the work is accomplished. An extension of this model includes a third component, *low social support*, defined as a lack of help and cooperation from supervisors and coworkers (Johnson and Hall 1988). Supervisor support refers to the availability and supervisor's capacity to support workers. Supervisor support can be operational, informational, and socio-emotional. Coworkers' support refer to cohesion level, team spirit as well as assistance and collaboration while performing given tasks. Low social support may act directly or amplify the effect of job strain.

The effort-reward imbalance (ERI) model proposes that efforts at work (e.g., constant time pressure, many interruptions and disturbances, lot of responsibilities, and pressure to work overtime) should be rewarded in various ways: income (financial reward), respect and esteem (socioemotional reward), and career promotion and job security (status-related reward) (Siegrist 1996). Workers are in a state of detrimental imbalance, e.g., lack of reciprocity, when high efforts are accompanied by low reward, causing a state of emotional distress which can lead to adverse health outcomes.

Long working hours have been commonly defined as working beyond a weekly overtime threshold in a given country. Working more than 40 h per week has been frequently used as the overtime threshold in several countries, including Canada, the USA, China, and Greece. It is also the cut point suggested by the International Labor Organization (ILO) in their Conventions no. 47 adopted in 1935 and still in force.

The Cardiovascular Continuum

The cardiovascular continuum is defined as a sequence, initiated with the presence of CVD risk factors and progressing to subclinical disease, atherosclerosis, cardiovascular events, and CVD mortality (Fig. 2) (Dzau et al. 2006). Evidence supports the adverse effect of psychosocial stressors at work and long working hours on cardiovascular manifestations measured at different stages of the life course. Interventions acting on upstream risk factors, in the early stages of the continuum, may protect against the future development of CVD events (Dzau et al. 2006). Psychosocial stressors at work and long working hours, being frequent and modifiable, could be relevant upstream risk factors to achieve population-based reduction of CVD incidence and complications in working populations.

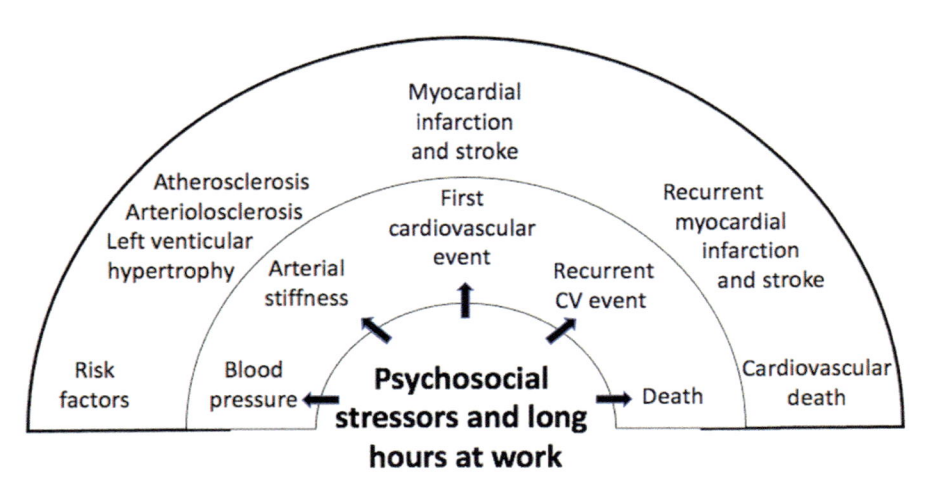

Fig. 2 Psychosocial stressors at work along the cardiovascular continuum. (Adapted from Dzau et al. (2006))

Psychosocial Stressors at Work and Long Working Hours Along the CV Continuum

Blood Pressure

Systematic reviews and meta-analyses have shown that psychosocial stressors at work are associated with BP increases and hypertension prevalence (Gilbert-Ouimet et al. 2014). One main finding from those reviews is the more consistent effect observed in studies using ambulatory BP, e.g., using BP measurement every 15–30 min during the day. The superiority of ambulatory BP over conventional (clinic or casual) BP is well-acknowledged, given its higher precision and validity. Studies using ambulatory measurements have shown BP increases ranging from 1.5 to 11 mmHg among exposed workers. Ambulatory BP can be used in combination with traditional clinic BP to refine the classification of hypertension. Sustained hypertension is defined as BP levels in hypertensive range according to both measurement methods. In contrast, masked hypertension refers to the condition defined by normal clinic BP (less than 140 and less than 90 mmHg) combined with elevated ambulatory BP (at least 135 or at least 85 mmHg). The prevalence of masked hypertension could be up to 30% (Peacock et al. 2014), and the condition has been associated with a similar or even higher cardiovascular risk when compared to sustained hypertension (Banegas et al. 2018).

Psychosocial Stressors at Work and Masked Hypertension

Psychosocial stressors from the work environment may contribute to BP rises during working hours and therefore contribute to the development of masked hypertension. Available evidence supports this hypothesis. In a Canadian cohort composed of 2000 white-collar workers followed for 5 years, exposure to psychosocial stressors at work was associated with a higher prevalence of masked hypertension. A first study from this cohort examined the effect of psychosocial stressors from the demand-control model. In this study, men with job characterized by high demands and high control (active job situations) were about twice more likely to have masked hypertension (Trudel et al. 2010). A second study using the same cohort showed an adverse effect of ERI exposure on masked hypertension prevalence, in both men and women. This association appeared to be mainly driven by the adverse effect of high efforts at work. Therefore, a high workload and its components could be of particular interest. The combined effect of job strain and ERI exposure was also investigated in a US study (Landsbergis et al. 2013a). In this study, workers exposed to both job strain and ERI were twice more likely to have masked hypertension. Other factors from the work environment, including evening, night, and rotating shiftwork, were also associated with the prevalence of masked hypertension suggesting a potential contribution of multiple types of adverse work-related factors (Landsbergis et al. 2013a). To date, no prospective studies have examined whether exposure to psychosocial stressors at work is associated to the development of masked hypertension in working populations. Such prospective studies would be of particular relevance to determine if psychosocial stressors at work are upstream factors that can be acted upon in order to prevent the development of masked hypertension over the course of the working life. A previous study showed that one out of ten workers free of hypertension may develop masked hypertension within a short (3 years) time frame (Trudel et al. 2019). Tackling risk factors before masked hypertension onset could therefore provide significant benefits to reduce the burden associated with this hypertension subtype.

Psychosocial Stressors at Work and Uncontrolled Hypertension
The prevalence of uncontrolled hypertension among treated patients remains high. Indeed, 20–40% of adults receiving a pharmacologic treatment for hypertension have BP values higher than the recommended targets (Gu et al. 2012; McAlister et al. 2011). Two studies using ambulatory BP showed that workers exposed to job strain and ERI had a higher prevalence of uncontrolled hypertension (Trudel et al. 2017; Lavigne-Robichaud et al. 2019). This relationship could be partly explained by lower treatment adherence among workers exposed to these stressors at work. Supporting this hypothesis, one previous US study using secondary data from a randomized controlled trial (RCT) showed that workers exposed to job strain were less adherent to their medication regimen, including for those using renin angiotensin system antagonists and statin (Kearney et al. 2016).

Long Working Hours and Blood Pressure
Evidence about the effect of long working hours on hypertension and high BP have been mixed, with studies reporting an adverse association, no association, or even protective associations. Most studies have used clinic BP and cross-sectional designs to examine this relationship. The introduction of ambulatory BP has allowed to examine whether long working hours are associated with high BP during regular workdays. One previous study conducted among 3547 workers in Canada suggests that long working hours (≥49 h per week) are associated with an increased prevalence of both masked (70%) and sustained hypertension (66%) when compared to standard 35–40 h per week. These associations were observed following control for several sociodemographics, lifestyle-related and CVD risk factors as well as for job strain exposure (Trudel et al. 2020). Furthermore, two recent studies with prospective designs showed that long working hours are associated with midterm BP increases and long-term hypertension incidence. In the first study, women and men working more than 40 h per week had higher BP levels 2.5 years later (Gilbert-Ouimet et al. 2022). This association remained after controlling for job strain and was of greater magnitude among workers with high family responsibilities. In the second study, conducted in China, working at least 56 h per week was associated with an increased risk of hypertension, over a 22-year follow-up (Cheng et al. 2021). Current evidence suggest that long working hours may act as risk factors for BP increases among workers, over and above the contribution of psychosocial stressors at work (Trudel et al. 2020). Strategies that promote work weeks that are not exceeding 40 h per week may be effective in reducing the burden of hypertension.

Arterial Stiffness

Arterial stiffness is an asymptomatic CVD risk factor, which develops in a more advanced stage along the cardiovascular continuum (Fig. 2). It describes the reduced ability of large proximal arteries to dilate and retract. Arterial stiffness can capture the cumulative effect of adverse exposures on vascular aging over the life course. Pulse wave velocity (PWV) is a noninvasive method, recognized as the gold standard method for assessing arterial stiffness. Recent meta-analyses have reported a 15% increased CVD risk for each unit increase in PWV (Vlachopoulos et al. 2010) and an improved CVD risk prediction when combined with traditional CVD risk factors including BP (Ben-Shlomo et al. 2014). To our knowledge, four cross-sectional studies have examined the association between psychosocial stressors at work and arterial stiffness (Nomura et al. 2005; Utsugi et al. 2009; Michikawa et al. 2008; Kaewboonchoo et al. 2018). Three of these studies have reported that exposed workers had increased arterial stiffness, among women (Utsugi et al. 2009) or men (Michikawa et al. 2008; Kaewboonchoo et al. 2018). Previous evidence also suggests an adverse effect of long working hours on arterial stiffness. A study conducted in Japan reported a deleterious effect of overtime work, within a specific subgroup, composed of older workers ($\geq$50 years old) (Hata et al. 2014). Finally, a recent prospective cohort study showed increases in arterial stiffness progression over 5 years among workers exposed to long working hours ($\geq$55 h per week) (Rossnagel et al. 2022). In sum, current evidence supports the adverse effect of work stressors and long worked hours on arterial stiffness. However, no prospective study has examined the effect of these work factors on arterial stiffness progression, using carotid-femoral PWV, recognized as the gold standard assessment. This would strengthen the quality of available evidence. Arterial stiffness progression could be one pathophysiological pathway explaining the effect of psychosocial stressors at work and long working hours on CVD events. Screening for psychosocial stressors and long working hours may help to identify workers more likely to benefit from arterial stiffness assessment in order to detect asymptomatic cardiovascular damage before disease onset.

Cardiovascular Disease Incidence

Systematic reviews and meta-analyses showed that workers exposed to job strain are at increased risk of coronary heart diseases (CHD) (Xu et al. 2015a) and stroke (Huang et al. 2015). In these reviews, excess risk ranged from 20 to 40%. Studies have also supported the pathogenic effect of ERI exposure on CVD incidence with relative risks ranging from 1.2 to 2.5, after accounting for traditional CVD risk factors (Dragano et al. 2017; Kivimaki et al. 2006). There are indications that available measures of effect may underestimate the association between psychosocial stressors at work and CVD incidence (Choi et al. 2015; Taouk et al. 2020). Indeed, methodological limitations could have resulted in risk attenuations. These limitations include the *healthy worker effect*, a well-documented mechanism observed in occupational studies. Furthermore, adjustment for mediating mechanisms (e.g., lifestyle risk factors) could have canceled the intermediate effect occurring through indirect pathways therefore leading to an underestimation of the total effect. Finally, most studies have used stressors from either job strain or ERI, which could have underestimated the effect on CVD risk associated with combined exposure to both types of work stressors. Supporting this hypothesis, a multicohort study conducted in Europe reported a higher CHD risk among workers exposed to both job strain and ERI (41%) when compared to the risk associated with either job strain or ERI (16%) (Dragano et al. 2017). The effect of long working hours on CHD incidence and stroke was recently documented in two systematic reviews and meta-analyses from the WHO/ILO workgroup. In the first meta-analysis, long working hours ($\geq$55 h per week) were associated with an increased risk of dying from ischemic heart diseases (17%), which was mainly observed following a certain follow-up time (8 years) (Li et al. 2020). In the second meta-analysis, long working hours, defined with the same threshold, were associated with an increased risk (35%) of incident stroke over a 20-year follow-up (Descatha et al. 2020). According to the WHO/ILO, long working hours led to 745,000 deaths from ischemic heart diseases and stroke in 2016 (Pega et al. 2021).

Psychosocial stressors and long working hours may also precipitate the development of specific CVD subtypes, including atrial fibrillation (AF). AF is the most common form of arrythmia affecting about one in four men and women over 40 years of age in their lifetime (Lloyd-Jones et al. 2004). AF increases the risk of strokes, heart failure, and other cardiovascular complications (Son et al. 2017). A recent meta-analysis, conducted among three cohort studies, showed that workers exposed to job strain have an increased risk of AF (Fransson et al. 2018). This meta-analysis also examined, within a subsample, the effect of repeated job strain exposure on incident AF. The increased risk was 68% for job strain exposure at a single time and 128% for job strain exposure at both measurement times, highlighting the potential for a risk increase associated with chronic job strain exposure. A recent European multicohort study showed that long working hours are also associated with AF incidence (Kivimaki et al. 2017). There was a 42% risk increase among those working $\geq$55 h per week, after adjusting for age, sex, and socioeconomic status. Interestingly, the magnitude of the observed association was comparable to that of other acknowledged AF risk factors, including hypertension, diabetes, prevalent CHD, and high alcohol intake.

Cardiovascular Disease Recurrence

The adverse effect of psychosocial stressors at work and long working hours on cardiovascular health was also observed at later stages of the continuum and among workers with preexisting cardio-metabolic alterations. A multicohort study conducted in Europe among 102,633 individuals suggests that the contribution of job strain on mortality is mainly observed among men with preexistent cardio-metabolic diseases (Kivimaki et al. 2018). One study was conducted in a

Canadian prospective cohort of 972 men and women returning to work after a first myocardial infarction (MI). This study showed that chronic job strain exposure over 2 years is associated with a twofold risk of recurrent CHD, using a composite outcome consisting of fatal CHD, nonfatal MI, and unstable angina (Aboa-Eboule et al. 2007). These estimates were used in a meta-analysis of five papers derived from four prospective studies, showing a 65% increased risk among workers exposed to psychosocial stressors at work (Li et al. 2015). A recent study, conducted within the same Canadian cohort, showed an association between long working hours and the risk of recurrent CHD events (Trudel et al. 2021a). There was a linear risk increase associated with higher worked hours when compared to the standard 40 h per week. The risk of recurrent CHD increased in magnitude after 4 years of follow-up. This previous study further showed the independent effect of long working hours, after controlling for the adverse effect of job strain exposure. Moreover, the risk was more than two-fold higher among participants who worked long hours while being simultaneously exposed to job strain (Fig. 3). This suggests that workplace strategies targeting both work factors could have a beneficial effect for the secondary prevention of CHD events. Of interest is the magnitude of the observed association. Indeed, the detrimental effect of working long hours after a heart attack was comparable to that of current smoking (67% and 70%, respectively) and was higher when combined with job strain exposure (Trudel et al. 2021a). Therefore, clinicians following post-MI patients should pay attention to their working environment. For example, job strain and long working hours could be assessed as part of routine clinical follow-up of patients who return to work after a heart attack. The effectiveness of workplace interventions to reduce work hours among post-MI on the risk of recurrent CHD events should be evaluated.

Sex and Gender Considerations

There are disparities in CVD incidence and prognosis between women and men, disadvantaging women. Despite these alarming disparities between women and men, research on heart disease mainly focus on men. The WHO is calling for the use of a sex and gender-based approach to better inform practice and prevention (Manandhar et al. 2018). Sex refers to a set of biological attributes. It is primarily associated with physical and physiological features including chromosomes, gene expression, hormone levels and function, and reproductive/sexual anatomy. For example, women's biological attributes place them at a different risk of stroke as men at different periods of their life span. Pregnancy and then menopause increase their risk (Heart & Stroke 2018). Gender "refers to socially constructed roles, behaviors, expressions and identities of girls, women, boys, men, and gender diverse people" (Doyal 2003). Gender evolves in time, as it is culturally based and historically specific (Doyal 2003). It influences "how people perceive themselves and each other, how they act and interact, and the distribution of power and resources in society" (Doyal 2003).

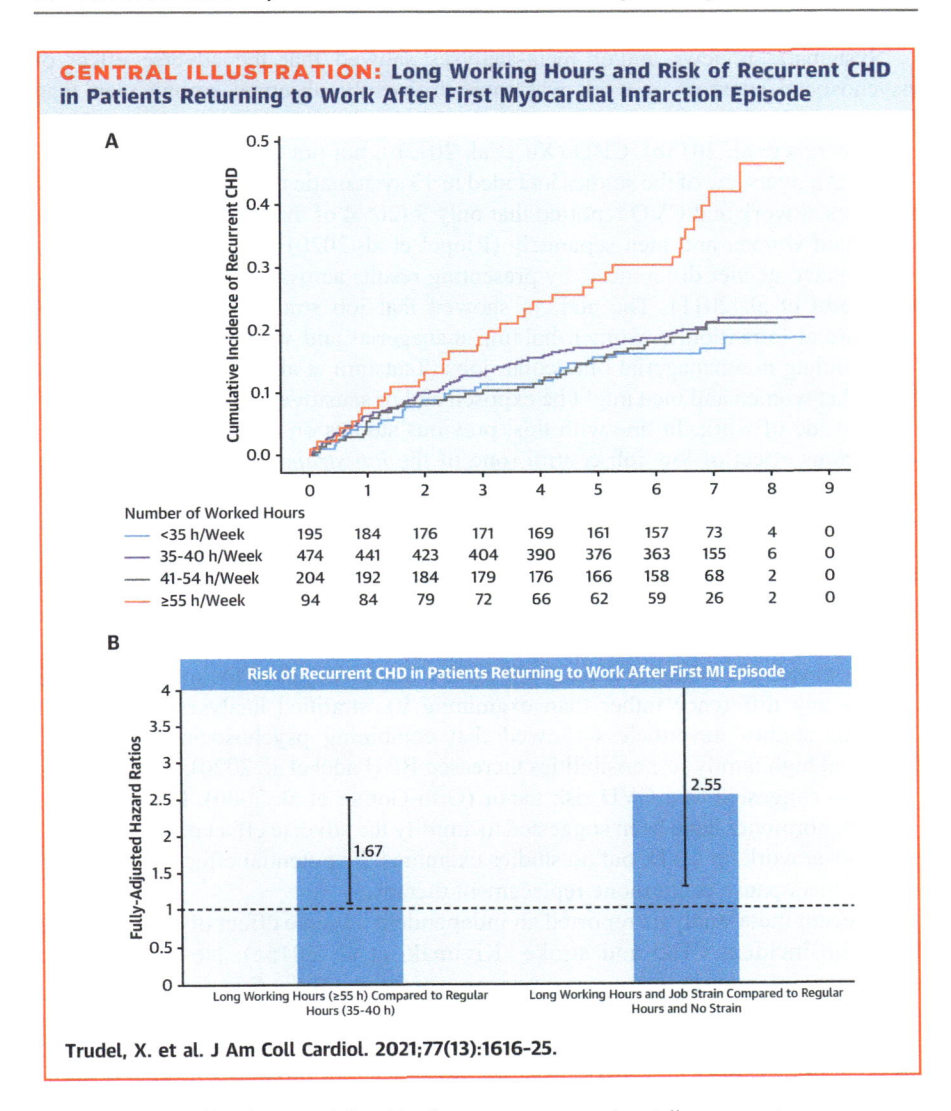

Fig. 3 Long working hours and the risk of recurrent coronary heart disease events

Sex and gender inequalities in the labor market have existed for centuries and arise structurally, disadvantaging women as they tend to be in more precarious labor market positions than men. Women tend to be more frequently exposed to psychosocial stressors at work than men (Brisson et al. 2011). Also, while men working long hours often hold highly skilled and well-paid occupations (Wilkins and Wooden 2014), women working such hours predominate in low paid jobs (Wilkins and Wooden 2014). Considering both paid and unpaid work, employed women are facing stiffer time constraints (Equality EIfG 2015).

Systematic reviews and/or meta-analyses showed that the adverse effect of psychosocial stressors at work was more frequently observed among men than women. This difference was observed for BP level (Gilbert-Ouimet et al. 2014; Landsbergis et al. 2013b), CHD (Xu et al. 2015b), but not for stroke (Huang et al. 2015). An overview of the studies included in 13 systematic reviews on psychosocial stressors at work and CVD reported that only 9 (20%) of the 46 prospective studies examined women and men separately (Riopel et al. 2020). Of these, a single one investigated gender differences, by presenting results across occupational positions (Tsutsumi et al. 2011). The authors showed that job strain elevated the risk of myocardial infraction in women holding managerial and white-collar jobs and in men holding nonmanagerial blue-collar jobs (Tsutsumi et al. 2011). They hypothesized that women and men might be exposed and/or sensitive to different stressors in and outside of work. In line with this, previous studies on hypertension showed a deleterious effect of low job control (one of the *job strain* stressors) in men only (Gilbert-Ouimet et al. 2014). Experts have suggested that women might predominantly favor values such as social utility, solidarity, and social support at work over high levels of control (Kivimaki et al. 2015a). Low social support at work has indeed been associated with higher BP level (Clays et al. 2007) and with depression (Ertel et al. 2008) among women (but not men). However, no studies examined the effect (separate or in combination) of social support at work on CVD across sexes. Another pitfall of available evidence is that, while a few studies adjusted for such sex (which cancels any difference rather than examining it), stratified analyses are lacking. Previous studies nevertheless showed that combining psychosocial stressors at work and high family responsibilities increased BP (Fadel et al. 2020). Marital stress was also suggested as a CVD risk factor (Orth-Gomer et al. 2000). In addition, in women, hormones have been suggested to amplify the adverse effect of psychosocial stressors at work on CVD, but no studies examined the potential effect modification of age, menopause or hormone replacement therapy.

A recent meta-analysis reported an independent adverse effect of long working hours on incident CHD and stroke (Kivimaki et al. 2015a). No sex-stratified results nor interaction tests were however presented. Of the five previous studies on long working hours and CVD including both women and men participants (Fadel et al. 2020; O'Reilly and Rosato 2013; Virtanen et al. 2010; Toker et al. 2012; Netterstrom et al. 2010), three presented sex-stratified results (Fadel et al. 2020; O'Reilly and Rosato 2013; Netterstrom et al. 2010): one study reported an increased risk of CVD death only in men (Fadel et al. 2020), another study showed an increased risk of ischemic heart diseases only in men of low socioeconomic status (O'Reilly and Rosato 2013) while the last reported no association between worked hours and heart disease in both women and men (Netterstrom et al. 2010). Of these studies, none examined whether gender or sex- and gender-related factors contributed to explain the results. Increased consideration of sex and gender differences are needed to improve CVD prevention strategies. Accounting for both sex and gender in public health researches can lead to more effective practices, policies, and programs and thereby save costs for the health care system.

Mechanisms and Interactions with Other Risk Factors

Psychosocial stressors at work increase the neuroendocrine activity of the sympathetic nervous system and the hypothalamic-pituitary-adrenal axis. Moreover, the sympathetic nervous system may activate the renin-angiotensin system. Therefore, in addition with other risk factors, exposure to psychosocial stressors at work can induce endothelial dysfunction, vasoconstriction cellular proliferation, and inflammation that promote arterial stiffness, hypertension, atherosclerosis, and subsequently, cardiovascular events. Long working hours could be associated with sleep deprivation, which has been shown to increase cardiovascular risk (Nagai et al. 2010). It has also been hypothesized that overtime work could imply prolonged exposure to and less time to recover from psychosocial stressors from the work environment (Virtanen et al. 2012).

In addition, workers exposed to psychosocial stressors and long working hours at work might cope with their situation by adopting unhealthy lifestyle behaviors, such as smoking, increased alcohol consumption, poor eating habits, and reduced physical activity, which are all documented CVD risk factors. Lifestyle-related risk factors could therefore act as mediating factors, e.g., factors that are in the causal pathways linking psychosocial stressors at work, long working hours, and cardiovascular outcomes.

Systematic reviews and meta-analyses have documented the adverse effect of psychosocial stressors at work on type 2 diabetes (T2D). These reviews reported that workers exposed to job strain were at increased risk of developing a T2D, especially among women (Pena-Gralle et al. 2022; Li et al. 2021). A recent meta-analysis, conducted by our research team, also reported an increased risk of T2D incidence among workers exposed to ERI (Pena-Gralle et al. 2022). Long working hours were also reported to increase T2D risk, with adverse effects observed among workers of low socioeconomic status (Trudel et al. 2016) and among women (Gilbert-Ouimet et al. 2018).

The effect on obesity and weight gain was also documented (Nyberg et al. 2013). A recent meta-analysis showed no overall association between job strain and the risk of weight gain or obesity. However, an increased risk was reported among workers with increased job strain exposure over the follow-up (Kivimaki et al. 2015b). Weight gain may also contribute to the observed association between psychosocial stressors at work and BP, among initially overweight women (Trudel et al. 2016).

Indirect mechanisms could partly explain the observed associations between psychosocial stressors at work and CVD. However, most studies showed an adverse effect of psychosocial work stressors and long working hours on BP that is robust to statistical adjustment for lifestyle-related CVD risk factors, therefore pointing toward the role of other mechanisms including direct biophysiological mechanisms. Available evidence suggests that acting on these work factors, in addition to other causal CVD risk factors, would provide increased benefits for CVD prevention. Figure 4 presents a simplified conceptual model of the relationships between psychosocial stressors at work, lifestyle-related risk factors, and CVD risk factors (hypertension and T2D) and their adverse effect on CVD incidence.

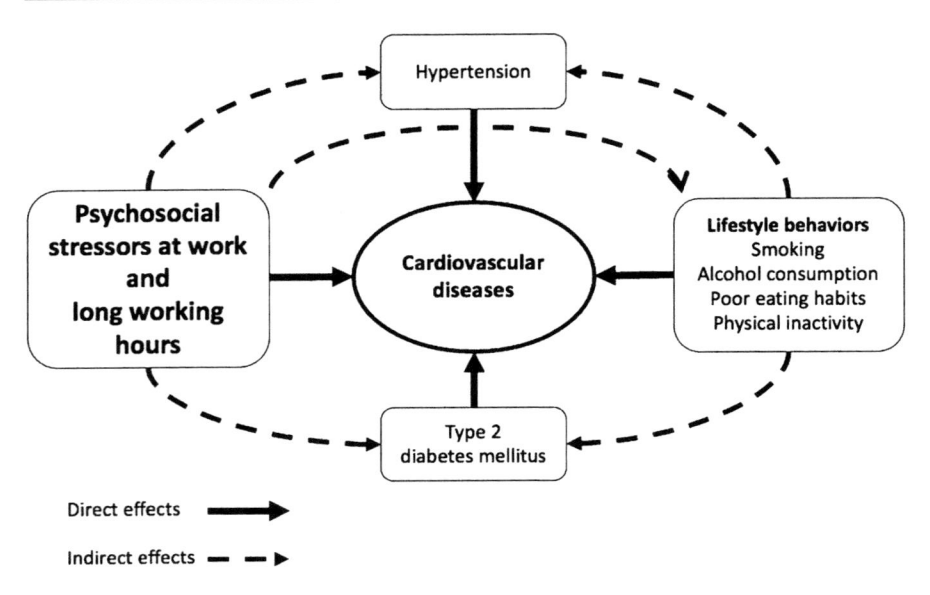

Fig. 4 Simplified conceptual model for the direct and indirect effects of psychosocial stressors at work and long working hours on cardiovascular diseases

Population Attributable Fraction of Cardiovascular Diseases

Population attributable fraction assesses the proportion of diseases cases that would be avoided if a particular exposure was removed. Therefore, population attributable fraction provides useful information about the possible impact of preventive interventions aiming to reduce the prevalence of psychosocial stressors at work and long working hours. The fraction of coronary diseases cases or CVD death attributable to job strain exposure has been estimated to range between 3.4% and 7.7% (Kivimaki et al. 2012; Theorell et al. 2016; Witvliet et al. 2020). The fraction of coronary heart diseases and stroke cases attributable to psychosocial stressors from the ERI model has been estimated to range between 2 and 12%, in Europe (Niedhammer et al. 2014, 2021). Worldwide, long working hours were responsible, in 2016, of 3.7% of death from ischemic diseases and 6.9% of deaths from stroke, according to the most recent estimations provided by the WHO/ILO (Pega et al. 2021). Those studies showed that psychosocial stressors at work and long working hours are important contributors to the burden of CVD in various populations. Applied to worldwide mortality data, and using a unique and conservative estimate (4%), these exposures could be responsible for approximately 716,000 CVD deaths annually (Roth et al. 2020).

Of interest is the comparison between the fraction of CVD cases that is attributable to psychosocial stressors at work to the fraction of CVD cases that is attributable to traditional CVD risk factors, such as smoking and physical inactivity. A large-scale cohort study (PURE), conducted in 21 countries, showed that current smoking was responsible of about 15% of CVD cases in high-income countries while the contribution of physical inactivity was modest (2–4%) (Yusuf et al. 2020). The INTERHEART case-control study suggests that about 36% and 12% of CVD cases are attributable to smoking and physical inactivity, respectively (Yusuf et al. 2004). Unfortunately, psychosocial stressors at work and long working hours were not considered in those large-scale studies. A valid comparison should take into account the fact that psychosocial stressors at work and long working hours could lead to indirect effects through improvement in lifestyle habits (Fig. 3). Furthermore, information on the total fraction of CVD cases that is attributable to psychosocial stressors at work, in combination with other lifestyle-related risk factors, would provide important support for the development of integrated workplace-preventive approaches, targeting both work stressors and lifestyle-related risk factors. Examples and guidelines for such integrative approaches are available (Lamontagne et al. 2007).

Prevention (Guidelines, Screening, Prediction, and Interventions) from the Individual to the Population and Their Work Environment

Psychosocial Stressors at Work in Cardiovascular Prevention Guidelines

Psychosocial stressors at work are poorly considered in current cardiovascular prevention guidelines. Among seven Canadian, American, and European recent guidelines, the European guidelines are the only one mentioning chronic stress at work (Visseren et al. 2021). The most recent American guidelines for hypertension prevention considered psychosocial stress as an individual factor without referring to the environment in which the individual lives (Whelton et al. 2018). The European guidelines are an important step toward the increased recognition of psychosocial stressors at work in CVD prevention in clinical practice (Visseren et al. 2021). In these guidelines, the potential contribution of work stressors, as defined by job strain and ERI, is explicitly mentioned. It is suggested that clinicians could consider them as part of personalized CVD risk estimations and treatment decisions.

CVD Risk Prediction

Little is known on the added benefits of screening for psychosocial stressors at work and long working hours along with traditional risk factors used in CVD risk prediction models. A prospective study conducted in the UK, the Whitehall II study, examined the contribution of long working hours when integrated to the Framingham CVD risk score (Kivimaki et al. 2011). In this study, long working hours increased CVD risk prediction by 4.7% (Kivimaki et al. 2011). The added value of job strain for CVD risk prediction was also examined within the same cohort, but results were inconclusive (Kivimaki et al. 2011). Veronesi et al. (2018) examined the clinical utility of considering lifestyle-related risk factors (smoking, alcohol intake, and sport physical activity) combined with occupational factors (job strain and occupational physical activity) to identify future cardiovascular events among men (Veronesi et al. 2018). The risk model combining these factors showed the same discrimination when compared to a model using blood lipids, BP, smoking, and T2D. Few previous studies have examined the potential benefit for CVD risk prediction resulting from considering job strain or long working hours, and results are mixed. There is a need for future studies to determine whether the consideration of multiple exposures (e.g., job strain, ERI, and long working hours) improve CVD risk prediction. This is of particular relevance given the increased risk of CVD incidence (Dragano et al. 2017) and recurrence (Trudel et al. 2021a) reported among workers exposed to more than one type of exposure. Finally, studies have shown that the 10-year risk can be modest for patients having a substantial remaining lifetime risk (Lloyd-Jones et al. 2006). It is therefore suggested to consider lifetime risk for a better estimation of the burden associated with CVD risk factors, over the life course (Lloyd-Jones 2010). The added value of psychosocial stressors at work and long working hours for the prediction of lifetime CVD risk should be determined.

Screening

Worksite screening is promoted by the American Heart Association (AHA), which considers workplaces as ideal environment to intensify cardiovascular prevention efforts (Arena et al. 2014). The AHA bases its recommendations on the "Simple 7," a number of established CVD risk factors including diet and BP that could be assessed in workplaces. Psychosocial stressors at work and long working hours are however not considered. Since they are upstream factors that could affect both lifestyle and clinical risk factors, an examination of their added benefits is warranted to promote more comprehensive screening initiatives for CVD prevention. The 2021 US Preventive Services Task Force recommendation is to screen all adults for hypertension, with an initial screening performed with clinic BP (Force et al. 2021). A diagnosis of hypertension should then be confirmed using ambulatory BP. This screening method would miss workers with masked hypertension. The lack of consideration for masked hypertension can be explained by the fact that no trials have examined the effect of masked hypertension treatment on CVD morbidity and mortality. Nonetheless, a significant proportion of workers with masked hypertension remains as such over years (Trudel et al. 2013), causing delays in diagnosis and management. Ambulatory BP measurements for workers exposed to psychosocial stressors at work, long working hours, and to other lifestyle-related work factors may reduce those delays and may therefore contribute to improve the prognosis of workers with masked hypertension.

Preventive Workplace Interventions

It is now recognized that psychosocial stressors at work can be reduced with appropriate workplace interventions. The beneficial effect of such interventions on mental health was documented, while few studies have examined the effect of such interventions on cardiovascular health indicators. A study was conducted by our research team to examine the beneficial longitudinal effect of a preventive intervention targeting psychosocial stressors at work on ambulatory BP level and hypertension (Trudel et al. 2021b). The design was a quasi-experimental prepost study with an intervention ($N = 1088$) and a control group ($N = 1068$). Participants were all white-collar workers employed in three public organizations. Postintervention measurements were collected 6 and 36 months after the midpoint of the intervention. The intervention was designed to reduce psychosocial stressors at work by implementing organizational changes and followed a rigorous intervention framework and process. In this study, the differential decrease in BP between the intervention and the control group was 2.0 mmHg for systolic blood pressure and 1.0 mmHg or diastolic BP ($p < 0.01$). The prevalence of hypertension also significantly decreased from 31.0% to 27.5% in the intervention group (p for difference with the control group <0.0001).

It should be noted that even a modest (2 mmHg) reduction in BP has important impact at the population level. Systolic BP decreases of that magnitude would involve about 10% lower stroke mortality and 7% lower mortality from ischemic heart diseases (IHD) or other vascular causes in middle age (Lewington et al. 2002). This reduction is also comparable to that observed in another population-level intervention targeting salt consumption (He et al. 2014). There is a need for additional studies documenting the effect of preventive workplace interventions targeting psychosocial stressors at work on cardiovascular outcomes assessed over the life course. Generally, there is no "one size fits all" solution and no single "pill" to reduce psychosocial stressors at work. For interventions to be feasible and sustainable, they generally need to be developed using a participatory approach, tailored to priorities and context by both workers and managers. Another avenue is to conduct simulation studies, using observational data combined with novel modeling techniques to accelerate knowledge development on intervention effectiveness. These simulations studies can be used to quantify the expected effects resulting from acting upon several exposures simultaneously, using realistic estimates of attainable prevalence reduction. Such studies were successfully used to examine the beneficial effects of hypothetical interventions targeting multiple traditional CVD risk factors on CHD (Taubman et al. 2009) and stroke (Mokhayeri et al. 2019) incidence. Simulation studies could be of relevance to examine the expected effectiveness of multicomponent workplace interventions, targeting multiple work stressors, on the risk of CHD and stroke.

Conclusion

Psychosocial stressors at work are frequent and modifiable CVD risk factors. Their contribution as causal risk factors is supported by available evidence from prospective studies, systematic reviews, and meta-analyses. This contribution was observed at different stages of the cardiovascular continuum, over the life course. Screening for those factors in workplace, and the implementation of preventive strategies to reduce them, could lead to important benefits for worker's cardiovascular health. A better understanding of sex and gender differences is needed to improve the equity and effectiveness of such prevention strategies. Psychosocial stressors at work and long working hours may also be useful for the identification of at-risk individuals who would benefit from CVD risk assessment and from ambulatory BP measurements. At the policy level, preventive action in workplaces can be supported. As an example, public health policies in the province of Quebec (Canada) have integrated a voluntary standard (the Quebec Healthy Enterprise Standard) that includes practices targeting psychosocial stressors at work. Another example is that the current modification of the Quebec Health and Security in workplaces law will soon oblige workplaces of 20 workers or more to assess psychosocial stressors at work and put concrete preventive actions in place to reduce and control these stressors using preventive measures and action plans. The public health and economic burden of CVD may be substantially reduced by the wide-scale adoption of initiatives aiming at reducing psychosocial stressors at work and long working hours.

References

Aboa-Eboule C, Brisson C, Maunsell E, Masse B, Bourbonnais R, Vezina M et al (2007) Job strain and risk of acute recurrent coronary heart disease events. JAMA 298(14):1652–1660. https://doi.org/10.1001/jama.298.14.1652

Arena R, Arnett DK, Terry PE, Li S, Isaac F, Mosca L et al (2014) The role of worksite health screening: a policy statement from the American Heart Association. Circulation 130(8): 719–734. https://doi.org/10.1161/CIR.0000000000000079

Banegas JR, Ruilope LM, de la Sierra A, Vinyoles E, Gorostidi M, de la Cruz JJ et al (2018) Relationship between clinic and ambulatory blood-pressure measurements and mortality. N Engl J Med 378(16):1509–1520. https://doi.org/10.1056/NEJMoa1712231

Ben-Shlomo Y, Spears M, Boustred C, May M, Anderson SG, Benjamin EJ et al (2014) Aortic pulse wave velocity improves cardiovascular event prediction: an individual participant meta-analysis of prospective observational data from 17,635 subjects. J Am Coll Cardiol 63(7): 636–646. https://doi.org/10.1016/j.jacc.2013.09.063

Brisson C, Aboa-Eboulé C, Leroux I, Gilbert-Ouimet M, Vézina M, Bourbonnais R et al (2011) Psychosocial factors at work and heart disease. In: Allan R (ed) Heart and mind: the evolution of cardiac psychology focused on clinical psychology. Amerian Psychological Association, New-York

Bureau of Labor Statistics (2009) Employment, hours, and earnings from the current employment statistics survey (National). http://www.bls.gov. Accessed 18 Mar 2009

Carey RM, Muntner P, Bosworth HB, Whelton PK (2018) Reprint of: prevention and control of hypertension: JACC health promotion series. J Am Coll Cardiol 72(23 Pt B):2996–3011. https://doi.org/10.1016/j.jacc.2018.10.022

Cheng H, Gu X, He Z, Yang Y (2021) Dose-response relationship between working hours and hypertension: a 22-year follow-up study. Medicine (Baltimore) 100(16):e25629. https://doi.org/10.1097/MD.0000000000025629

Choi B, Schnall P, Landsbergis P, Dobson M, Ko S, Gómez-Ortiz V et al (2015) Recommendations for individual participant data meta-analyses on work stressors and health outcomes: comments on IPD-Work Consortium papers. Scand J Work Environ Health 41(3):299–311

Clays E, Leynen F, De Bacquer D, Kornitzer M, Kittel F, Karasek R et al (2007) High job strain and ambulatory blood pressure in middle-aged men and women from the Belgian job stress study. J Occup Environ Med 49(4):360–367

Descatha A, Sembajwe G, Pega F, Ujita Y, Baer M, Boccuni F et al (2020) The effect of exposure to long working hours on stroke: a systematic review and meta-analysis from the WHO/ILO Joint Estimates of the Work-related Burden of Disease and Injury. Environ Int 142:105746. https://doi.org/10.1016/j.envint.2020.105746

Doyal L (2003) Sex and gender: the challenges for epidemiologists. Int J Health Serv 33(3): 569–579. https://doi.org/10.2190/CWK2-U7R6-VCE0-E47P

Dragano N, Siegrist J, Nyberg ST, Lunau T, Fransson EI, Alfredsson L et al (2017) Effort-reward imbalance at work and incident coronary heart disease: a multicohort study of 90,164 individuals. Epidemiology 28(4):619–626. https://doi.org/10.1097/EDE.0000000000000666

Dzau VJ, Antman EM, Black HR, Hayes DL, Manson JE, Plutzky J et al (2006) The cardiovascular disease continuum validated: clinical evidence of improved patient outcomes: part I: pathophysiology and clinical trial evidence (risk factors through stable coronary artery disease). Circulation 114(25):2850–2870. https://doi.org/10.1161/CIRCULATIONAHA.106.655688

Equality EIfG (2015) Gender equality index 2015: measuring gender equality in the European Union 2005–2012. Publications Office of the European Union

Ertel KA, Koenen K, Berkman L (2008) Incorporating home demands into models of job strain: findings from the work, family and health network. J Occup Environ Med 50(11):1244–1252

European Foundation for the Improvement of Living and Working Conditions (2006) Fourth European working conditions survey. Publications of the European Foundation for Improvement of Living and Working Conditions, Dublin

Fadel M, Li J, Sembajwe G, Gagliardi D, Pico F, Ozguler A et al (2020) Cumulative exposure to long working hours and occurrence of ischemic heart disease: evidence from the CONSTANCES cohort at inception. J Am Heart Assoc:e015753. https://doi.org/10.1161/JAHA.119.015753

Faghri PD, Dobson M, Landsbergis P, Schnall PL (2021) COVID-19 pandemic: what has work got to do with it? J Occup Environ Med 63(4):e245–e2e9. https://doi.org/10.1097/JOM.0000000000002154

Force USPST, Krist AH, Davidson KW, Mangione CM, Cabana M, Caughey AB et al (2021) Screening for hypertension in adults: US Preventive Services Task Force reaffirmation recommendation statement. JAMA 325(16):1650–1656. https://doi.org/10.1001/jama.2021.4987

Fransson EI, Nordin M, Magnusson Hanson LL, Westerlund H (2018) Job strain and atrial fibrillation – results from the Swedish Longitudinal Occupational Survey of Health and meta-analysis of three studies. Eur J Prev Cardiol 25(11):1142–1149. https://doi.org/10.1177/2047487318777387

Gilbert-Ouimet M, Trudel X, Brisson C, Milot A, Vezina M (2014) Adverse effects of psychosocial work factors on blood pressure: systematic review of studies on demand-control-support and effort-reward imbalance models. Scand J Work Environ Health 40(2):109–132. https://doi.org/10.5271/sjweh.3390

Gilbert-Ouimet M, Ma H, Glazier R, Brisson C, Mustard C, Smith PM (2018) Adverse effect of long work hours on incident diabetes in 7065 Ontario workers followed for 12 years. BMJ Open Diabetes Res Care 6(1):e000496. https://doi.org/10.1136/bmjdrc-2017-000496

Gilbert-Ouimet M, Trudel X, Talbot D, Vezina M, Milot A, Brisson C (2022) Long working hours associated with elevated ambulatory blood pressure among female and male white-collar workers over a 2.5-year follow-up. J Hum Hypertens 36(2):207–217. https://doi.org/10.1038/s41371-021-00499-3

Gu Q, Burt VL, Dillon CF, Yoon S (2012) Trends in antihypertensive medication use and blood pressure control among United States adults with hypertension: the National Health and Nutrition Examination Survey, 2001 to 2010. Circulation 126(17):2105–2114. https://doi.org/10.1161/CIRCULATIONAHA.112.096156

Hata K, Nakagawa T, Hasegawa M, Kitamura H, Hayashi T, Ogami A (2014) Relationship between overtime work hours and cardio-ankle vascular index (CAVI): a cross-sectional study in Japan. J Occup Health 56(4):271–278. https://doi.org/10.1539/joh.13-0243-oa

He FJ, Pombo-Rodrigues S, Macgregor GA (2014) Salt reduction in England from 2003 to 2011: its relationship to blood pressure, stroke and ischaemic heart disease mortality. BMJ Open 4(4): e004549. https://doi.org/10.1136/bmjopen-2013-004549

Heart & Stroke (2018) Heart report: Ms.Understood, Women's hearts are victims of a system that is ill-equipped to diagnose, treat and support them. Heart & Stroke Foundation. https://www.heartandstroke.ca/-/media/pdf-files/canada/2018-heart-month/hs_2018-heart-report_en.ashx?rev=71bed5e2bcf148b4a0bf5082e50de6c6

Huang Y, Xu S, Hua J, Zhu D, Liu C, Hu Y et al (2015) Association between job strain and risk of incident stroke: a meta-analysis. Neurology 85(19):1648–1654. https://doi.org/10.1212/WNL.0000000000002098

Johnson JV, Hall EM (1988) Job strain, work place social support, and cardiovascular disease: a cross-sectional study of a random sample of the Swedish working population. Am J Public Health 78(10):1336–1342. https://doi.org/10.2105/ajph.78.10.1336

Kaewboonchoo O, Sembajwe G, Li J (2018) Associations between job strain and arterial stiffness: a large survey among Enterprise employees from Thailand. Int J Environ Res Public Health 15(4). https://doi.org/10.3390/ijerph15040659

Karasek R (1979) Job demands, job decision latitude, and mental strain: implications for job redesign. Adm Sci Q 24:285–308

Kearney SM, Aldridge AP, Castle NG, Peterson J, Pringle JL (2016) The association of job strain with medication adherence: is your job affecting your compliance with a prescribed medication regimen? J Occup Environ Med 58(7):707–711. https://doi.org/10.1097/JOM.0000000000000733

Kivimaki M, Virtanen M, Elovainio M, Kouvonen A, Vaananen A, Vahtera J (2006) Work stress in the etiology of coronary heart disease – a meta-analysis. Scand J Work Environ Health 32(6): 431–442

Kivimaki M, Batty GD, Hamer M, Ferrie JE, Vahtera J, Virtanen M et al (2011) Using additional information on working hours to predict coronary heart disease: a cohort study. Ann Intern Med 154(7):457–463. https://doi.org/10.7326/0003-4819-154-7-201104050-00003

Kivimaki M, Nyberg ST, Batty GD, Fransson EI, Heikkila K, Alfredsson L et al (2012) Job strain as a risk factor for coronary heart disease: a collaborative meta-analysis of individual participant data. Lancet 380(9852):1491–1497. https://doi.org/10.1016/S0140-6736(12)60994-5

Kivimaki M, Jokela M, Nyberg ST, Singh-Manoux A, Fransson EI, Alfredsson L et al (2015a) Long working hours and risk of coronary heart disease and stroke: a systematic review and meta-analysis of published and unpublished data for 603,838 individuals. Lancet 386(10005): 1739–1746. https://doi.org/10.1016/S0140-6736(15)60295-1

Kivimaki M, Singh-Manoux A, Nyberg S, Jokela M, Virtanen M (2015b) Job strain and risk of obesity: systematic review and meta-analysis of cohort studies. Int J Obes 39(11):1597–1600. https://doi.org/10.1038/ijo.2015.103

Kivimaki M, Nyberg ST, Batty GD, Kawachi I, Jokela M, Alfredsson L et al (2017) Long working hours as a risk factor for atrial fibrillation: a multi-cohort study. Eur Heart J 38(34):2621–2628. https://doi.org/10.1093/eurheartj/ehx324

Kivimaki M, Pentti J, Ferrie JE, Batty GD, Nyberg ST, Jokela M et al (2018) Work stress and risk of death in men and women with and without cardiometabolic disease: a multicohort study. Lancet Diabetes Endocrinol 6(9):705–713. https://doi.org/10.1016/S2213-8587(18)30140-2

Lamontagne AD, Keegel T, Louie AM, Ostry A, Landsbergis PA (2007) A systematic review of the job-stress intervention evaluation literature, 1990–2005. Int J Occup Environ Health 13(3): 268–280. https://doi.org/10.1179/oeh.2007.13.3.268

Landsbergis PA, Travis A, Schnall PL (2013a) Working conditions and masked hypertension. High Blood Press Cardiovasc Prev 20(2):69–76. https://doi.org/10.1007/s40292-013-0015-2

Landsbergis PA, Dobson M, Koutsouras G, Schnall P (2013b) Job strain and ambulatory blood pressure: a meta-analysis and systematic review. Am J Public Health 103(3):e61–e71. https://doi.org/10.2105/AJPH.2012.301153

Lavigne-Robichaud M, Trudel X, Duchaine CS, Milot A, Gilbert-Ouimet M, Vezina M et al (2019) Job strain and the prevalence of uncontrolled hypertension among white-collar workers. Hypertens Res 42(10):1616–1623. https://doi.org/10.1038/s41440-019-0278-7

Lawes CM, Vander Hoorn S, Rodgers A (2008) Global burden of blood-pressure-related disease, 2001. Lancet 371(9623):1513–1518. https://doi.org/10.1016/S0140-6736(08)60655-8

Lewington S, Clarke R, Qizilbash N, Peto R, Collins R (2002) Age-specific relevance of usual blood pressure to vascular mortality: a meta-analysis of individual data for one million adults in 61 prospective studies. Lancet 360(9349):1903–1913

Li J, Zhang M, Loerbroks A, Angerer P, Siegrist J (2015) Work stress and the risk of recurrent coronary heart disease events: a systematic review and meta-analysis. Int J Occup Med Environ Health 28(1):8–19. https://doi.org/10.2478/s13382-014-0303-7

Li J, Pega F, Ujita Y, Brisson C, Clays E, Descatha A et al (2020) The effect of exposure to long working hours on ischaemic heart disease: a systematic review and meta-analysis from the WHO/ILO joint estimates of the work-related burden of disease and injury. Environ Int 142:105739. https://doi.org/10.1016/j.envint.2020.105739

Li W, Yi G, Chen Z, Dai X, Wu J, Peng Y et al (2021) Is job strain associated with a higher risk of type 2 diabetes mellitus? A systematic review and meta-analysis of prospective cohort studies. Scand J Work Environ Health 47(4):249–257. https://doi.org/10.5271/sjweh.3938

Lloyd-Jones DM (2010) Cardiovascular risk prediction: basic concepts, current status, and future directions. Circulation 121(15):1768–1777. https://doi.org/10.1161/CIRCULATIONAHA.109.849166

Lloyd-Jones DM, Wang TJ, Leip EP, Larson MG, Levy D, Vasan RS et al (2004) Lifetime risk for development of atrial fibrillation: the Framingham Heart Study. Circulation 110(9):1042–1046. https://doi.org/10.1161/01.CIR.0000140263.20897.42

Lloyd-Jones DM, Leip EP, Larson MG, D'Agostino RB, Beiser A, Wilson PW et al (2006) Prediction of lifetime risk for cardiovascular disease by risk factor burden at 50 years of age. Circulation 113(6):791–798. https://doi.org/10.1161/CIRCULATIONAHA.105.548206

Manandhar M, Hawkes S, Buse K, Nosrati E, Magar V (2018) Gender, health and the 2030 agenda for sustainable development. Bull World Health Organ 96:644–653

McAlister FA, Wilkins K, Joffres M, Leenen FH, Fodor G, Gee M et al (2011) Changes in the rates of awareness, treatment and control of hypertension in Canada over the past two decades. CMAJ 183(9):1007–1013. https://doi.org/10.1503/cmaj.101767

Michikawa T, Nishiwaki Y, Nomiyama T, Uemura T, O'Uchi T, Sakurai H et al (2008) Job strain and arteriosclerosis in three different types of arteries among male Japanese factory workers. Scand J Work Environ Health 34(1):48–54. https://doi.org/10.5271/sjweh.1163

Mokhayeri Y, Hashemi-Nazari SS, Khodakarim S, Safiri S, Mansournia N, Mansournia MA et al (2019) Effects of hypothetical interventions on ischemic stroke using parametric G-formula. Stroke 50(11):3286–3288. https://doi.org/10.1161/STROKEAHA.119.025749

Nagai M, Hoshide S, Kario K (2010) Sleep duration as a risk factor for cardiovascular disease- a review of the recent literature. Curr Cardiol Rev 6(1):54–61. https://doi.org/10.2174/157340310790231635

Netterstrom B, Kristensen TS, Jensen G, Schnor P (2010) Is the demand-control model still a useful tool to assess work-related psychosocial risk for ischemic heart disease? Results from 14 year follow up in the Copenhagen City Heart study. Int J Occup Med Environ Health 23(3):217–224. https://doi.org/10.2478/v10001-010-0031-6

Niedhammer I, Sultan-Taieb H, Chastang JF, Vermeylen G, Parent-Thirion A (2014) Fractions of cardiovascular diseases and mental disorders attributable to psychosocial work factors in 31 countries in Europe. Int Arch Occup Environ Health 87(4):403–411. https://doi.org/10.1007/s00420-013-0879-4

Niedhammer I, Sultan-Taieb H, Parent-Thirion A, Chastang JF (2021) Update of the fractions of cardiovascular diseases and mental disorders attributable to psychosocial work factors in Europe. Int Arch Occup Environ Health. https://doi.org/10.1007/s00420-021-01737-4

Nomura K, Nakao M, Karita K, Nishikitani M, Yano E (2005) Association between work-related psychological stress and arterial stiffness measured by brachial-ankle pulse-wave velocity in young Japanese males from an information service company. Scand J Work Environ Health 31(5):352–359

Nyberg ST, Fransson EI, Heikkila K, Alfredsson L, Casini A, Clays E et al (2013) Job strain and cardiovascular disease risk factors: meta-analysis of individual-participant data from 47,000 men and women. PLoS One 8(6):e67323. https://doi.org/10.1371/journal.pone.0067323

O'Reilly D, Rosato M (2013) Worked to death? A census-based longitudinal study of the relationship between the numbers of hours spent working and mortality risk. Int J Epidemiol 42(6): 1820–1830. https://doi.org/10.1093/ije/dyt211

Orth-Gomer K, Wamala SP, Horsten M, Schenck-Gustafsson K, Schneiderman N, Mittleman MA (2000) Marital stress worsens prognosis in women with coronary heart disease: the Stockholm female coronary risk study [in process citation]. JAMA 284(23):3008–3014

Parent-Thirion A, Fernandez Macías E, Hurley J, Vermeylen GG (2007) Fourth European working conditions survey. In: European Foundation for the Improvement of Living and Working Conditions (ed). Office for Official Publications of the European Communities, Luxembourg

Peacock J, Diaz KM, Viera AJ, Schwartz JE, Shimbo D (2014) Unmasking masked hypertension: prevalence, clinical implications, diagnosis, correlates and future directions. J Hum Hypertens 28(9):521–528. https://doi.org/10.1038/jhh.2014.9

Pega F, Nafradi B, Momen NC, Ujita Y, Streicher KN, Pruss-Ustun AM et al (2021) Global, regional, and national burdens of ischemic heart disease and stroke attributable to exposure to long working hours for 194 countries, 2000–2016: a systematic analysis from the WHO/ILO Joint Estimates of the Work-related Burden of Disease and Injury. Environ Int 154:106595. https://doi.org/10.1016/j.envint.2021.106595

Pena-Gralle APB, Talbot D, Duchaine CS, Lavigne-Robichaud M, Trudel X, Aube K et al (2022) Job strain and effort-reward imbalance as risk factors for type 2 diabetes mellitus: a systematic review and meta-analysis of prospective studies. Scand J Work Environ Health 48(1):5–20. https://doi.org/10.5271/sjweh.3987

Rigo M, Dragano N, Wahrendorf M, Siegrist J, Lunau T (2021) Work stress on rise? Comparative analysis of trends in work stressors using the European working conditions survey. Int Arch Occup Environ Health 94(3):459–474. https://doi.org/10.1007/s00420-020-01593-8

Riopel C, Lavigne-Robichaud M, Trudel X, Milot A, Gilbert-Ouimet M, Talbot D et al (2020) Job strain and incident cardiovascular disease: the confounding and mediating effects of lifestyle habits. An overview of systematic reviews. Arch Environ Occup Health:1–8. https://doi.org/10.1080/19338244.2020.1828244

Rossnagel K, Jankowiak S, Liebers F, Schulz A, Wild P, Arnold N et al (2022) Long working hours and risk of cardiovascular outcomes and diabetes type II: five-year follow-up of the Gutenberg Health Study (GHS). Int Arch Occup Environ Health 95(1):303–312. https://doi.org/10.1007/s00420-021-01786-9

Roth GA, Mensah GA, Johnson CO, Addolorato G, Ammirati E, Baddour LM et al (2020) Global burden of cardiovascular diseases and risk factors, 1990–2019: update from the GBD 2019 study. J Am Coll Cardiol 76(25):2982–3021. https://doi.org/10.1016/j.jacc.2020.11.010

Siegrist J (1996) Adverse health effects of high-effort/low-reward conditions. J Occup Health Psychol 1(1):27–41. https://doi.org/10.1037//1076-8998.1.1.27

Son MK, Lim NK, Kim HW, Park HY (2017) Risk of ischemic stroke after atrial fibrillation diagnosis: a national sample cohort. PLoS One 12(6):e0179687. https://doi.org/10.1371/journal.pone.0179687

Taouk Y, Spittal MJ, LaMontagne AD, Milner AJ (2020) Psychosocial work stressors and risk of all-cause and coronary heart disease mortality: a systematic review and meta-analysis. Scand J Work Environ Health 46(1):19–31

Taubman SL, Robins JM, Mittleman MA, Hernan MA (2009) Intervening on risk factors for coronary heart disease: an application of the parametric g-formula. Int J Epidemiol 38(6): 1599–1611. https://doi.org/10.1093/ije/dyp192

Theorell T, Jood K, Jarvholm LS, Vingard E, Perk J, Ostergren PO et al (2016) A systematic review of studies in the contributions of the work environment to ischaemic heart disease development. Eur J Pub Health 26(3):470–477. https://doi.org/10.1093/eurpub/ckw025

Toker S, Melamed S, Berliner S, Zeltser D, Shapira I (2012) Burnout and risk of coronary heart disease: a prospective study of 8838 employees. Psychosom Med 74(8):840–847. https://doi.org/10.1097/PSY.0b013e31826c3174

Trudel X, Brisson C, Milot A (2010) Job strain and masked hypertension. Psychosom Med 72(8): 786–793. https://doi.org/10.1097/PSY.0b013e3181eaf327

Trudel X, Milot A, Brisson C (2013) Persistence and progression of masked hypertension: a 5-year prospective study. Int J Hypertens 2013:836387. https://doi.org/10.1155/2013/836387

Trudel X, Brisson C, Milot A, Masse B, Vezina M (2016) Effort-reward imbalance at work and 5-year changes in blood pressure: the mediating effect of changes in body mass index among 1400 white-collar workers. Int Arch Occup Environ Health 89(8):1229–1238. https://doi.org/10.1007/s00420-016-1159-x

Trudel X, Milot A, Gilbert-Ouimet M, Duchaine C, Guenette L, Dalens V et al (2017) Effort-reward imbalance at work and the prevalence of unsuccessfully treated hypertension among white-collar workers. Am J Epidemiol 186(4):456–462. https://doi.org/10.1093/aje/kwx116

Trudel X, Brisson C, Gilbert-Ouimet M, Duchaine CS, Dalens V, Talbot D et al (2019) Masked hypertension incidence and risk factors in a prospective cohort study. Eur J Prev Cardiol 26(3): 231–237. https://doi.org/10.1177/2047487318802692

Trudel X, Brisson C, Gilbert-Ouimet M, Vezina M, Talbot D, Milot A (2020) Long working hours and the prevalence of masked and sustained hypertension. Hypertension 75(2):532–538. https://doi.org/10.1161/HYPERTENSIONAHA.119.12926

Trudel X, Brisson C, Talbot D, Gilbert-Ouimet M, Milot A (2021a) Long working hours and risk of recurrent coronary events. J Am Coll Cardiol 77(13):1616–1625

Trudel X, Gilbert-Ouimet M, Vezina M, Talbot D, Masse B, Milot A et al (2021b) Effectiveness of a workplace intervention reducing psychosocial stressors at work on blood pressure and hypertension. Occup Environ Med 78(10):738–744. https://doi.org/10.1136/oemed-2020-107293

Tsutsumi A, Kayaba K, Ishikawa S (2011) Impact of occupational stress on stroke across occupational classes and genders. Soc Sci Med 72(10):1652–1658. https://doi.org/10.1016/j.socscimed.2011.03.026

Utsugi M, Saijo Y, Yoshioka E, Sato T, Horikawa N, Gong Y et al (2009) Relationship between two alternative occupational stress models and arterial stiffness: a cross-sectional study among Japanese workers. Int Arch Occup Environ Health 82(2):175–183. https://doi.org/10.1007/s00420-008-0319-z

Vasan RS, Beiser A, Seshadri S, Larson MG, Kannel WB, D'Agostino RB et al (2002) Residual lifetime risk for developing hypertension in middle-aged women and men: the Framingham Heart Study. JAMA 287(8):1003–1010

Veronesi G, Borchini R, Landsbergis P, Iacoviello L, Gianfagna F, Tayoun P et al (2018) Cardiovascular disease prevention at the workplace: assessing the prognostic value of lifestyle risk factors and job-related conditions. Int J Public Health 63(6):723–732. https://doi.org/10.1007/s00038-018-1118-2

Vézina M, Theorell T, Brisson C (2015) Le stress professionel: approche épidémiologique. In: Découverte L (ed) Les risques au travail: pour ne pas perdre sa vie à la gagner

Virtanen M, Ferrie JE, Singh-Manoux A, Shipley MJ, Vahtera J, Marmot MG et al (2010) Overtime work and incident coronary heart disease: the Whitehall II prospective cohort study. Eur Heart J 31(14):1737–1744. https://doi.org/10.1093/eurheartj/ehq124

Virtanen M, Heikkila K, Jokela M, Ferrie JE, Batty GD, Vahtera J et al (2012) Long working hours and coronary heart disease: a systematic review and meta-analysis. Am J Epidemiol 176(7): 586–596. https://doi.org/10.1093/aje/kws139

Visseren FLJ, Mach F, Smulders YM, Carballo D, Koskinas KC, Back M et al (2021) 2021 ESC guidelines on cardiovascular disease prevention in clinical practice. Eur Heart J 42(34): 3227–3337. https://doi.org/10.1093/eurheartj/ehab484

Vlachopoulos C, Aznaouridis K, Stefanadis C (2010) Prediction of cardiovascular events and all-cause mortality with arterial stiffness. A systematic review and meta-analysis. J Am Coll Cardiol 55:1318–1327

Whelton PK (2015) The elusiveness of population-wide high blood pressure control. Annu Rev Public Health 36:109–130. https://doi.org/10.1146/annurev-publhealth-031914-122949

Whelton PK, Carey RM, Aronow WS, Casey DE Jr, Collins KJ, Dennison Himmelfarb C et al (2017) ACC/AHA/AAPA/ABC/ACPM/AGS/APhA/ASH/ASPC/NMA/PCNA guideline for the prevention, detection, evaluation, and management of high blood pressure in adults: a report of the American College of Cardiology/American Heart Association Task Force on Clinical Practice Guidelines. J Am Coll Cardiol 2017. https://doi.org/10.1016/j.jacc.2017.11.006

Whelton PK, Carey RM, Aronow WS, Casey DE Jr, Collins KJ, Dennison Himmelfarb C et al (2018) 2017 ACC/AHA/AAPA/ABC/ACPM/AGS/APhA/ASH/ASPC/NMA/PCNA guideline for the prevention, detection, evaluation, and Management of High Blood Pressure in adults: a report of the American College of Cardiology/American Heart Association Task Force on Clinical Practice Guidelines. J Am Coll Cardiol 71(19):e127–e248. https://doi.org/10.1016/j.jacc.2017.11.006

WHO: Cardiovascular diseases. Fact sheet (2011). http://www.who.int/mediacentre/factsheets/fs317/en/index.html. Accessed 19 July 2011

Wilkins R, Wooden M (2014) Two decades of change: the Australian labour market 1993–2013. Aust Econ Rev 47:417–431

Witvliet MI, Toch-Marquardt M, Eikemo TA, Mackenbach JP (2020) Improving job strain might reduce inequalities in cardiovascular disease mortality in European men. Soc Sci Med 267: 113219. https://doi.org/10.1016/j.socscimed.2020.113219

Xu S, Huang Y, Xiao J, Zhu W, Wang L, Tang H et al (2015a) The association between job strain and coronary heart disease: a meta-analysis of prospective cohort studies. Ann Med 47(6): 512–518

Xu S, Huang Y, Xiao J, Zhu W, Wang L, Tang H et al (2015b) The association between job strain and coronary heart disease: a meta-analysis of prospective cohort studies. Ann Med 47(6): 512–518. https://doi.org/10.3109/07853890.2015.1075658

Yusuf S, Hawken S, Ounpuu S, Dans T, Avezum A, Lanas F et al (2004) Effect of potentially modifiable risk factors associated with myocardial infarction in 52 countries (the INTERHEART study): case-control study. Lancet 364(9438):937–952. https://doi.org/10.1016/S0140-6736(04)17018-9

Yusuf S, Joseph P, Rangarajan S, Islam S, Mente A, Hystad P et al (2020) Modifiable risk factors, cardiovascular disease, and mortality in 155 722 individuals from 21 high-income, middle-income, and low-income countries (PURE): a prospective cohort study. Lancet (London, England) 395(10226):795–808. https://doi.org/10.1016/s0140-6736(19)32008-2

Pathways to Retirement and Health Effects

25

Jenny Head, Maria Fleischmann, and Baowen Xue

Contents

Introduction	444
National Policies and Pathways to Retirement	445
Policies: Availability and Generosity of Pension Benefits and Their Effect on Employment Rates	445
Process of Retirement	448
Predictors of Early Work Exit and Retirement	450
Inequalities in Employment Rates Among Older Workers	451
Working Conditions	453
Poor Health	455
Informal Caregiving	456
The Health Effect of Retirement	456
Theoretical Perspectives on the Health Effect of Retirement	456
Empirical Studies on the Health Effect of Retirement	457
Discussion on the Health Effect of Retirement	460
Conclusion	461
References	462

Abstract

Many governments have successfully introduced policies to raise pension and retirement ages. At the same time, more people take gradual retirement or return to work after retirement. Yet there are inequalities with many people unable to continue working for longer due to disability or poor health. The aim of this

---

J. Head (✉) · B. Xue
Department of Epidemiology and Public Health, University College London, London, UK
e-mail: j.head@ucl.ac.uk; baowen.xue.10@ucl.ac.uk

M. Fleischmann
Rotterdam University of Applied Sciences, Research Center for Innovations in Care, Rotterdam, the Netherlands
e-mail: m.s.fleischmann@hr.nl

© Springer Nature Switzerland AG 2023
M. Wahrendorf et al. (eds.), *Handbook of Life Course Occupational Health*, Handbook Series in Occupational Health Sciences, https://doi.org/10.1007/978-3-031-30492-7_14

chapter is to review how national policies, work environments, and health influence exit from the labor market and to bring together evidence on the health effects of retirement with a focus on evidence from OECD countries. There are three main sections, each covering concepts, theories, methods, and some of the relevant research literature: (1) Pathways to retirement; (2) Predictors of early work exit and retirement; and (3) Effects of retirement on health. Our review of research shows that poor health across the life course and adverse work environments are related to early exit from the labor market. The evidence on the health effects of retirement is more mixed.

Keywords

Retirement · Older workers · Extended working life · Pension policies · Health · Working conditions

Introduction

In many OECD countries, the share of the older population is steadily increasing. The population aged 65 and above constituted 9.3% of the total world population in 2020, whereas it amounted to less than 5% in 1960. The countries with the highest percentage of people aged 65 and above in 2020 were Japan (28%), followed by Italy, Portugal, and Finland (23%) and most other European countries with shares of around 20% (The World Bank 2019). These high percentages are largely caused by demographic ageing, specifically by a combination of increasing life expectancy and consistently low fertility rates. For the availability and generosity of pension benefits, demographic ageing could cause problems in the long run, when the ratio of younger to older people generally, and the ratio of employees to retirees specifically, would decrease (Hofäcker and Radl 2017). A more unfavorable ratio implies that a diminishing number of economically active people would bear the costs of an increasingly large part of society that is not economically active.

In response to the financial challenges of increasing life expectancy and population ageing, many governments have introduced policies to raise retirement ages and extend working lives. In the first part of the chapter, we describe how national policies may affect employment participation and work exit.

Since the mid-1990s, employment rates of the population aged 50 and above have been rising in most OECD countries; however, they still decline from approximately age 50 onwards and a substantial proportion of workers leave the labor market before reaching "normal retirement age." There is ample theoretical and empirical literature indicating that a more favorable working environment can contribute to a prolonged participation in the labor market. In the second part of the chapter, we review how work environment influences exit from employment and contributes to inequalities. In the final part of the chapter, we focus on the health effects of retirement. Based on the life course perspective, we provide insights into how retirement can influence the health and well-being of individuals.

National Policies and Pathways to Retirement

The idea that people should be able to retire at a specific age and gain access to social benefits developed mainly as a response to industrialization, surplus capital, and Protestant ideology at the end of the nineteenth century. Two elements that characterize individuals' retirement will be discussed in the following sections: first, the availability and generosity of pension benefits as defined by national policies in OECD countries and second, the process, rather than the event, of retirement.

Policies: Availability and Generosity of Pension Benefits and Their Effect on Employment Rates

In response to the more unfavorable ratio of employees to retirees, national policies changes were implemented that incentivized postponing labor market exit and restricted access to early retirement. To understand why pension reforms were overdue, we first describe why early retirement possibilities were established in the first place.

Early Retirement Between 1970 and 2000
The origin of early retirement is in the 1970s, when the worldwide oil crisis of 1973 and 1979 put a halt to economic growth. Instead, countries were suddenly facing high unemployment, especially among younger workers, who were less protected against unemployment than more senior workers. To solve this problem, early retirement opportunities were implemented. From workers' perspective, early retirement benefits were financially attractive as they substituted individuals' earnings to very high percentages and provided a unique opportunity to leave the labor market early, mostly around age 60. By using these incentives, older workers would "make way" for labor market entrants and reduce unemployment among younger workers (Hofäcker and Radl 2017). Many advanced economies introduced pathways to leave the labor market early and sustained them over more than three decades. This can be seen in the figure below: The effective retirement age – the average effective age at which older workers withdraw from the labor force – decreased significantly between 1970 and 2000, from age 68.8 to 63.1 for men (dark gray line) and 66.5 to 61.0 for women (light gray line) in OECD countries. This decrease in effective retirement age was mainly accomplished through early retirement benefits. The average normal retirement age – the age at which full social benefits are available for retirees – changed only little in the same time frame and was on average 64.1 years and 62.9 years for men and 62.1 years and 61.3 years for women in 1971 and 2000, respectively (OECD 2019).

From Early to Late Retirement 2000–Ongoing
In the late 1990s, however, in the context of demographic ageing, most advanced economies noted that these generous early retirement benefits were not sustainable in the long run. Therefore, countries changed their policies in the early 2000s. To

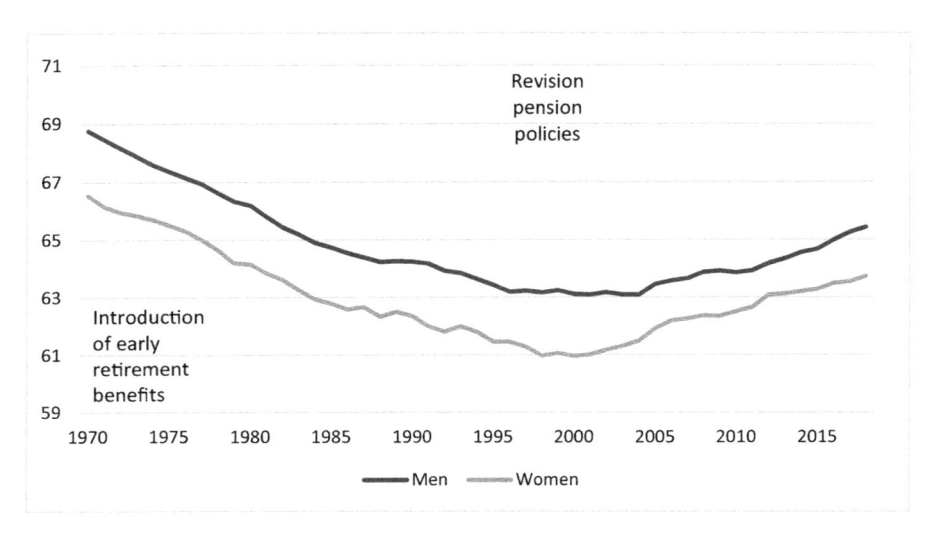

Fig. 1 Average effective age of labor market exit in OECD countries, 1970–2018. (Source: OECD 2019, own depiction https://doi.org/10.1787/888934042048)

encourage higher employment rates of older workers and to increase effective retirement age, pension levels were cut, early retirement pathways were shut, and the age at which individuals received statutory retirement benefits was raised. The success of the reforms is reflected in Fig. 1, which shows that since the early 2000s, both for men and women, the average effective retirement age in OECD countries has been increasing. In 2018, the effective retirement age was 65.4 for men (63.1 in 2000) and 63.7 for women (61.0 in 2000) in OECD countries on average.

Employment Rates and Generosity of Pensions Since the Reforms

After the introduction of policies encouraging a later retirement, the employment rates of older workers increased. Between 2000 and 2018, the employment rate of 55–64 year old persons increased by 17.6 percentage points on average in OECD countries (OECD 2019). In countries of the European Union (with available data) that increase was 21.7 percentage points in the same time frame. Figure 2 shows the employment rates for three age groups in 2018 (OECD 2019), sorted from highest to lowest participation among the age group of 55–64 years. As is visible here, the highest employment rates for those aged 60–64 years (blue dots) are found in Iceland, New Zealand, and Sweden with more than 70% of persons in this age range in employment, and lowest in Belgium, Slovenia, and Luxembourg, where 30% or less of those aged 60–64 years are in employment. On average in OECD countries, the employment rate for this age group amounts to about 50% (49.6%) in 2018, indicating that only every second older worker between 60–64 years is still economically active, despite most countries having a normal retirement age of 65 years or higher.

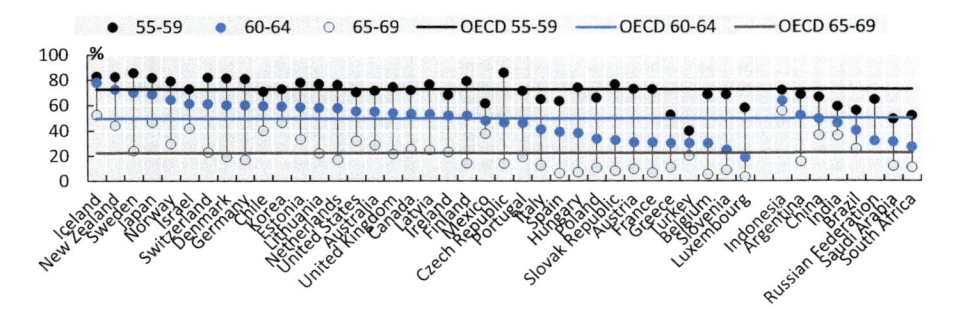

Fig. 2 Employment rates of workers aged 55–59, 60–64, and 65–69 in 2018. (Source: OECD 2019, https://doi.org/10.1787/888934041972)

Figure 2 also provides information on the employment rates of those aged 55–59 years and those aged 65–69 years. Interestingly, the average employment rate in OECD countries of those aged 55–59 years (72.5%) is more than 20 percentage points higher than the one for the subsequent age group. However, the employment rate for the group aged 65–69 years is on average just above 20%. Differences in employment rates of 65–69 year old persons across countries may reflect differences in generosity and availability of (public) pension schemes.

Linking Retirement Age to Life Expectancy

When pension systems were introduced, most people would, if at all, only live for a few years after they received their pension. This has changed tremendously: in 2016–2018, the average life expectancy in EU-27 countries after age 65 was 18.1 years for men and 21.6 years for women (see Fig. 3). This achievement is a challenge for the sustainability of pension systems. In their pension reforms of the late 1990s/early 2000s, many OECD countries have implemented regular reviews or automatic adjustments to normal pension age to take account of changes in life expectancy (OECD 2011). The most direct linkage between retirement and life expectancy – an increase in official retirement age with increasing life expectancy – has been implemented, for example, in the Netherlands, Denmark, Finland, Italy, Slovak Republic, and Portugal (OECD 2018).

However, the focus on linking retirement age to life expectancy ignores the role of health. Healthy life expectancy is considered an important indicator of population health and can provide relevant information regarding the extent to which people might be unable to extend their working lives due to health impediments or their long-term care needs (OECD/European Union 2020). Healthy life expectancy (or healthy life years) "are defined as the number of years spent free of long-term activity limitation" (OECD/European Union 2020). As Fig. 3 below shows for the EU-27 countries, of the 21.6 years women are on average expected to live after age 65, only 10 of these years are spent without a health limitation, while for the majority of years some health limitation exists. For men, the healthy life expectancy after age 65 is just below 10 years on average for the EU-27 countries in 2016–18.

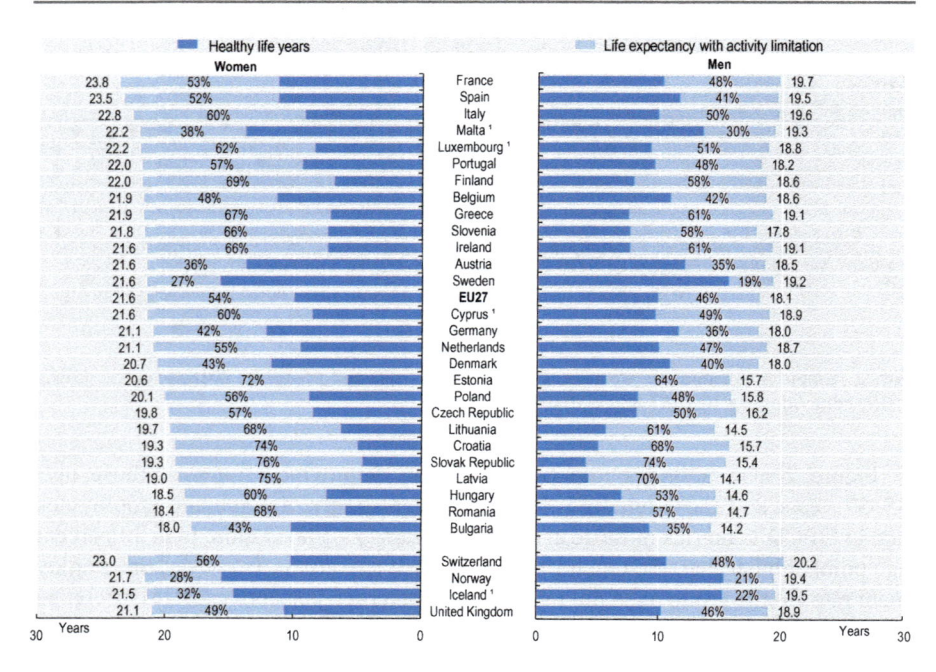

Fig. 3 Life expectancy and healthy life expectancy in 26 OECD countries for men and women (three-year averages 2016–18). (Source: OECD/European Union 2020, https://stat.link/tyhncw)

The benefits of linking retirement ages to life expectancy have been questioned, since this method may exacerbate social inequalities (Alvarez et al. 2021). Previous studies have reported large socio-economic differences in life expectancy and healthy life expectancy: those with higher socio-economic positions could expect to live more years of their older life in good health, compared to people with lower socio-economic positions (Head et al. 2019). Weber and Loichinger (2020) find in their study of European countries that, generally, there is potential to increase the number of years people above age 60 are economically active; however, large differences in this potential between educational groups are reported. Sauerberg (2021) provides an encompassing overview of the healthy life expectancy by educational level in 16 European countries. His study shows that, at age 30, the healthy life expectancy discrepancies between low- and high-educated people amount to 10.4 years on average, and as much as 15 years for Hungarian men. In response to these socio-economic differences, authors have advised policymakers to consider measures that reduce these inequalities in order to extend working lives (Head et al. 2019) and to correct for this heterogeneity in future pension policies (Weber and Loichinger 2020).

Process of Retirement

As the proportion of older persons increases, the need to improve labor market participation of older people aged 50 and over is growing. As shown above, the labor market participation of older workers has already increased, but along with information on *how long* older workers participate, we also need to improve our knowledge of *how* they participate before and around retirement. In the following, we will consider employment patterns before reaching retirement age and the transition from (full-time) employment to (full-time) retirement.

Employment Careers Relate to Retirement
To advance research on retirement and to gain more understanding of factors that might prolong individuals' working lives, a focus on complete employment patterns, rather than single employment experiences, could generate new knowledge. In this context, adopting a life course perspective (Kuh et al. 2003) to the study of retirement has been promoted. Based on the idea of cumulative disadvantages, previous studies show that not only single employment experiences but also complete employment careers are important antecedents for individuals' retirement age and the routes through which they leave the labor market. For example, Hoven et al. (2018) show that people with early-life or mid-life adversities have higher chances than those without adversities of reporting employment pathways characterized by discontinuity or early labor market exit. Wahrendorf et al. (2018) show for England that men with strong labor market attachment throughout their career are most likely to work continuously until retirement. In their paper, they also show that employment experiences are interlinked with family experiences. For example, men with children during mid-adulthood were more likely to report an employment pathway with retirement around age 60, whereas women in this work-family situation were less likely to have such employment pathway. Instead, they were more likely to report part-time work with retirement around age 60 (Wahrendorf et al. 2018).

Transition from Employment to Retirement
Retirement is often regarded as a process from (full-time) employment to (full-time) retirement, rather than a single event (Fisher et al. 2016). Acknowledging that retirement might be a process also implies that retirement does not necessarily mean that a person completely withdraws from the labor market initially – people can remain (partly) active as well and make gradual, rather than abrupt, transitions to retirement (Cahill et al. 2006). Theoretically, this is given shape in the "destandardization" hypothesis, stating that the life course is becoming more destandardized, with nonlinear changes at various ages (Calvo et al. 2018). Applied to retirement, this is reflected in an abundant literature studying, for example, part-time retirement, gradual retirement, bridge employment, and also re-entry into employment after retirement. This literature is acknowledging that retirement is a, not necessarily one-directed, process rather than a single event.

For the United States, Cahill and colleagues show that a majority of workers (40% of men and 42% of women) do not choose to retire abruptly, but rather become involved in bridge jobs after leaving their career job and before retirement. Health is an important antecedent for bridge employment as those with better self-assessed health appear to use bridge jobs more frequently than those with worse health (Cahill et al. 2006). Bridge jobs were also more attractive to workers with either low or high wages, rather than to those in the middle of the wage distribution. Another study on the USA shows that the reversible order of employment and retirement, expressed through un-retirement, is only reported by a small group (Calvo et al. 2018). Rather, pathways such as bridge employment or gradual retirement, where people progress from various forms of work to various forms of retirement, are more frequently observed. Additionally, groups with generally more disadvantageous positions on the labor market, such as women or Blacks, were also found to follow more unconventional pathways to retirement (Calvo et al. 2018).

In Europe, the prevalence of bridge jobs is much lower than in the USA and is estimated to be about 15% (Brunello and Langella 2013). However, such a U-shaped relationship between income and retirement has also been reported in Europe (Radl 2013). For example, using the Survey of Health, Ageing, and Retirement in Europe (SHARE), Radl (2013) finds that workers at both the lower and upper end of the occupational ladder retire latest. He explains this with different mechanisms: workers at the lower end retire later because of their limited access to retirement plans, whereas workers at the higher end retire later mainly because they are sheltered from labor market constraints, such as involuntary unemployment.

Predictors of Early Work Exit and Retirement

Although employment rates of men and women aged 50 and over have been rising since the mid-1990s in most OECD countries, as shown in the previous section, they still begin to decline after the age of 50, and a substantial proportion leave the labor market before reaching state pension age or "normal retirement age."

The push and pull model of retirement is often used when considering potential predictors of early work exit and retirement (Shultz et al. 1998). According to this model, factors may "pull" individuals toward or incentivize retirement, such as generous pension provision or wanting to spend more time on leisure activities. Whereas other factors such as poor health or high unemployment rates may "push" people toward leaving work early. These factors may operate at different levels including national policies, local areas and institutions, and individual characteristics.

At the institutional level, early retirement policies, described in the previous section "Policies: Availability and Generosity of Pension Benefits and their Effect on Employment Rates," can be regarded as pull factors, i.e., economic incentives that "pull" individuals toward retirement (Schils 2008). Institutional push factors are labor market constraints that push individuals out of the labor market, for example, restrictive labor market opportunities such as rising unemployment levels or demographic changes. Institutional pull factors have been reported to be more important than institutional push factors, according to the results of a study in Europe (de Preter et al. 2013).

At the individual level, push and pull factors have been described as relevant factors explaining individuals' timing of retirement. Pull factors have mainly been described as financial and non-financial factors, such as leisure activities, that made retirement appear more attractive than employment (Shultz et al. 1998; de Preter et al. 2013). Individual-level push factors are negative factors that push people out of employment. At the individual level, two of the most important push-factors are poor health and poor working environment. Theories explaining the role of the psychosocial working environment for retirement generally posit that unbalanced working conditions may create job strain, which is unhealthy for individuals. Three theoretical models from this field will be shortly discussed: the job-demands control (support) model and the job demands-resources model, and the effort-reward imbalance model. All these models assume that work is "good" if there is some kind of balance between "positive" and "negative" characteristics of work, and that work entails high stress if that balance is disturbed.

The most widely used model is Karasek's job demands-control model (Karasek 1979). It assumes that job strain is defined by a combination of job demands (e.g., work pace, demands) and job control (e.g., decision latitude, autonomy). The most unfavorable situation, high job strain, emerges from a combination of high job demands and low job control. In contrast, a healthier working environment, with low(er) levels of job strain, exists in jobs where high job demands are buffered by high job control. Johnson and Hall (1988) extended the model to the job demand-control-support model; they suggested that social support of colleagues and supervisors played an important role as well and could diminish adverse effects of high job demands.

One of the more recent models, the job demands-resources model (Bakker and Demerouti 2007) assumes that all psychosocial work characteristics can be categorized as either job demands or job resources. Job demands are effort put in the job and entail costs for the employee, while job resources help employees to achieve goals, reduce job demands, or stimulate personal growth.

Lastly, the effort-reward imbalance model (Siegrist 1996) states that stress reactions and low employee wellbeing emerge from situations where employees encounter situations of high costs and low gains, e.g., due to an imbalance between high efforts (through job demands and motivation) and low rewards (e.g., salary, job security). Most of these theoretical models have successfully been operationalized to be used in standard questionnaires and tools to measure individuals' working conditions.

Several different employment outcomes have been used in research related to extending working lives. Studies have examined predictors of retirement age preferences as these may be formed quite early in working life and may differ from people's expected or intended retirement age, as well as their actual retirement timing. Studies have also investigated factors associated with different routes of exit from paid work, such as disability pension or long-term sick (Carr et al. 2018a) and, more recently, with working life expectancy. Finally, some studies have attempted to distinguish between predictors of voluntary and involuntary retirement/work exit, either by asking a direct question on voluntariness or based on route of exit (e.g., redundancy, disability pension) or difference between preferred and actual retirement timing (Stiemke and Hess 2022).

Inequalities in Employment Rates Among Older Workers

Availability of suitable employment opportunities varies by region within countries and studies have shown associations between local unemployment rates and disability pension (Reime and Claussen 2013). Consistent with this, a study in England and Wales of people aged 40–69 found that higher local unemployment rates were related to a greater likelihood of not being in work 10 years later and that this association was stronger for older people identifying as being sick or disabled rather than being retired (Murray et al. 2016). While there has been a trend toward increasing employment rates among both men and women aged over 50, gender differences persist. For example, Fig. 4 shows that, in 2020, there was a gap in expected duration of working life (working life expectancy) between men and women for all EU countries, with expected duration 4.8 years longer for men than women. As well as gender differences, there are also socioeconomic inequalities in rates of work exit. Employees with low education levels or in low-grade occupations are more likely to exit work, particularly for health-related reasons (long-term sickness or disability retirement) (Carr et al. 2018a).

Negative age stereotypes and age discrimination remain a barrier for many older workers. While ageing populations are driving the extending working lives policy agenda, employment of older workers is often perceived in terms of intergenerational fairness, with older workers pitted against younger workers. These age norms may become internalized in both workers and employers, for example, older workers may feel that they should leave jobs to younger workers – referred to as "a sense of intergenerational unentitlement" (Vickerstaff and van der Horst 2021). A scoping review of research on ageism in relation to employment of older workers found evidence of perceived discrimination but highlighted the need for further research as most studies were cross-sectional (Harris et al. 2018). Studies of attitudes among employers support this, for example, a study in the Netherlands of managers presented with vignettes suggested that age discrimination is an issue (Karpinska et al. 2011). Older people looking for employment perceive that age is

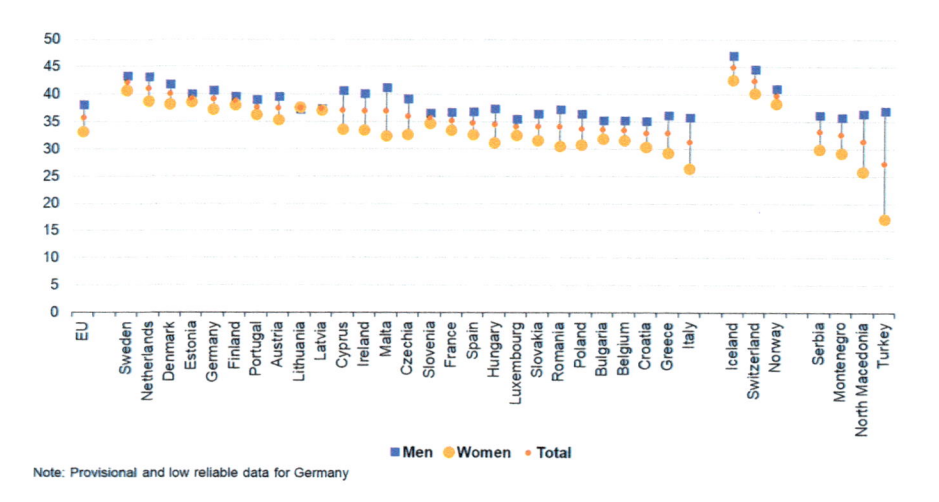

Fig. 4 Expected duration of working life by sex in EU countries, 2020 (Source: Eurostat 2021 (online data code: LFSI_DWL_A) https://ec.europa.eu/eurostat/databrowser/view/lfsi_dwl_a/default/table?lang=en)

one barrier to their success in finding work and some studies show that older workers who are actively seeking work take longer to obtain a new post than their younger counterparts. With the rise of precarious employment, older people who lose their jobs may face barriers to finding suitable alternative employment.

Working Conditions

Previous studies indicate that individuals with negative employment experiences are more prone to retire earlier. Adverse working conditions may be related to early exit from the labor market, either because low quality jobs push people toward retirement or because poor working conditions may make it more difficult for older workers to remain in work, for example, through lack of flexibility or because of high physical demands of the job. Both physical and psychosocial working conditions may be important. There is a substantial body of empirical research showing that adverse working conditions are related to receipt of disability pension or ill-health retirement, particularly from Scandinavian and other countries where register data on receipt of disability pension is available (Knardahl et al. 2017). One systematic review provided evidence that low control, and additionally high job strain – the combination of high demands and low control – predict disability retirement. This systematic review also found some limited evidence that downsizing, organizational change, lack of employee development and supplementary training, repetitive work tasks, and effort-reward imbalance increase the risk of disability pension (Knardahl et al. 2017).

Working conditions throughout the work career may be relevant both because preferences for retirement may be set many years before actual retirement and also because there may be a cumulative effect of long-term adverse working conditions. A systematic review of psychosocial work characteristics in relation to both retirement intentions and actual retirement identified 46 relevant papers and found that employees with high job control and high job satisfaction were more likely to have later retirement intentions (Browne et al. 2018) (Table 1).

In terms of actual exit from paid work, low recognition at work and low decision authority are associated with increased likelihood of exit from paid work, whereas high job satisfaction and high job control are associated with later actual retirement (Browne et al. 2018). These links between adverse working conditions and greater likelihood of early work exit have been observed after taking account of occupational grade and health status. In terms of physical working conditions, one study in Finland used a job exposure matrix approach to classify occupations on the basis of five different physical work characteristics, such as manual handling of heavy loads, and found that employees with a high physical workload had the lowest working life expectancy at age 50 and that this was largely due to early exit for ill-health reasons (Schram et al. 2021).

Working conditions may be related to work exit either directly or indirectly through their link to poor health. Additionally, whether or not people with functional limitations or chronic diseases are able to remain in work may depend on the nature

Table 1 Summary of evidence for association of psychosocial work characteristics with retirement timing. (Source: Browne et al. (2018))

Psychosocial factor (number of papers that include this factor)	Analyses of retirement intentions				Analyses of actual retirement			
	Direction of evidence			Total analyses of retirement intentions	Direction of evidence			Total analyses of actual retirement
	Earlier retirement	Null	Later retirement		Earlier retirement	Null	Later retirement	
Resources (38)	2	12	23	37	1	11	16	28
Demands (30)	8	11	–	19	2	18	2	22
Satisfaction (19)	2	2	12	16	–	5	5	10
Social support (17)	1	5	6	12	1	7	6	14
Organizational resources (6)	–	1	3	4	–	1	1	2
Effort–reward imbalance (5)	–	–	2	2	–	2	1	3
Job insecurity (3)	1	1	–	2	1	1	–	2
Total	14	32	46	92	5	45	31	81

of the work. For example, physically demanding jobs may require a better level of health. Favorable working conditions may also enable people with chronic conditions to remain in employment for longer. For instance, a study in the UK found that favorable working conditions mitigated the effects of some chronic health conditions (Fleischmann et al. 2018).

Conflict between work and family may also be an important factor in decisions to leave work. This can be bidirectional as work responsibilities may interfere with the family, for example, if an extensive workload reduces family time. Or, family responsibilities can interfere with work, for example, if caring for an older relative is incompatible with work meetings. In one study of British civil servants, the extent to which work interfered with family was not associated with any route of work exit in men or women. But men who reported that family interfered with work were less likely to exit work whereas women were more likely to exit work to become a homemaker at a later career stage (Xue et al. 2020a). These different responses to work family conflict may reinforce gender inequality in work participation.

While this research implicating adverse working conditions as one factor leading to early work exit might suggest that workplace adaptations and/or opportunities for training for older workers could do much to promote extended working, particularly for those with chronic disease, functional limitations, or poor health, relatively few empirical studies have studied the extent of provision of workplace adaptations and resulting benefits in terms of employment of older workers.

Poor Health

As state pension ages have increased, this has raised concerns about whether extending working lives is feasible for everyone or whether poor health is a barrier to employment of older workers. Specific health conditions that may affect older workers include depressive disorders, musculoskeletal disorders, respiratory diseases, and cardiovascular diseases and studies have shown that these are associated with higher rates of early exit from the work force. For example, one systematic review found that self-perceived poor health, chronic disease, and poor mental health were all associated with higher rates of disability pension (van Rijn et al. 2014). Even poor health in childhood has been found to influence later employment outcomes, for example, psychological ill-health in childhood reduced the likelihood of working at the age of 55, and this association remained after taking account of adult psychological health (Clark et al. 2017). Similarly, a review of evidence based on longitudinal studies in the UK showed that a range of ill-health measures at three different life stages – childhood, early and middle adulthood, later adulthood (over the age of 50) – were related to later life economic outcomes, including early retirement (Gondek et al. 2018). These included mental health but also chronic conditions, functional limitations, and self-rated health.

Informal Caregiving

In many countries, a large proportion of adult social care is provided informally, and older adults will often be providers of unpaid care to family or friends. At a time when social care budgets are reducing and governments are seeking to extend paid employment, older workers are increasingly expected to provide care for partners or relatives. Informal caregiving may either directly reduce the labor supply or it may indirectly relate to labor market participation through poor health.

While informal caregiving is a socially productive role, the challenges of balancing paid work and caregiving are well known. One conceptual framework used takes an individualistic approach considering individual time allocation and utility such as loss of earnings and job satisfaction. Another framework is based on role theory and conceptualizes this as a conflict between work and family, suggesting that caregiving may be more easily accommodated if people are able to work flexibly.

There are gender differences with women who provide informal care having a higher likelihood of either reducing work hours or leaving the labor market than men (Smith et al. 2020). Onset of caring responsibilities appears to be a key period when people may drop out of the labor market with one study finding that female employees who entered a caregiving role of more than 10 h a week were at increased risk of early exit from paid employment (Carr et al. 2018b).

The Health Effect of Retirement

Theoretical Perspectives on the Health Effect of Retirement

The assumption that retirement may affect health and well-being is based on the idea that retirement is not simply an objective transition marking the passage into later life, but also a subjective developmental and social–psychological transformation that is important for health and well-being. There are several principle theoretical perspectives concerning retirement and health; however, these theories often produce contradictory predictions regarding how retirement may affect physical and psychological health and well-being. For example, role theory highlights the importance of work role and the impact of "role exit" and being "roleless." Role theorists argue that the role loss accompanying retirement can cause psychological distress, which may lead to low levels of well-being in retirement (Riley and Riley 1994). Following social capital theory, retirement might promote health by increasing leisure time and the time that is spent with family and friends and/or through participating in social and volunteer activities. However, retirement may also harm health and well-being if most of an individual's social capital (e.g., social network, social support) is connected to work (Dave et al. 2008). Continuity theory underscores one's ability to continue one's previous lifestyle, and thus, views retirement as an opportunity for individuals to maintain the earlier lifestyle, previous levels of self-esteem, and also longstanding values (Atchley 1989). In this perspective, pre-retirement characteristics and activities could have more impact on later life than retirement itself, and thus, retirement is not viewed as leading to maladjustment or distress. Stage theory suggests a changing pattern of adjustment in retirement across time, which typically starts with the "honeymoon" stage early in the transition to retirement, then some may experience fluctuations in terms of health and well-being before settling into a more predictable and comfortable daily life pattern – "stability" stage (Wang et al. 2011).

The life course perspective integrates these theoretical frameworks and defines retirement as a life course transition, whereby the individual and contextual characteristics before, during, and after retirement can interact to influence the ways in which retirement affects different aspects of health and wellbeing. The life course framework proposed by Moen (Moen 1996) shows how retirement can influence the health and well-being of individuals. It points out that retirement can be either beneficial or detrimental to an individual's health and well-being depending on the current and past personal and environmental situation as well as the timing (whether prior to traditional and legal retirement age or pension age) and that choice of (voluntary/involuntary) retirement and the effects of retirement can change over time depending on the post-retirement environment and activities.

There is a considerable body of literature in epidemiology, sociology, gerontology, and health economics that has studied the impact of retirement on health and wellbeing. Most of the theoretical perspectives described above have been applied and developed our understanding of the effect of retirement on mental health, as the mental health effect of retirement has been most widely studied in the empirical literature. There is also a growing interest in other aspects of health and well-being, such as cognitive function, physical health, cardiovascular health, and general self-assessed health. Overall, the health effect of retirement varies depending on the health outcome examined in different studies.

Empirical Studies on the Health Effect of Retirement

Retirement and Mental Health

Older people, like the wider population, may well experience mental health problems. As they move through different stages of life and their circumstances change, their mental health can change too. There is extensive literature on the impact of retirement on mental health. Mental health has been operationalized in various ways such as well-being, distress, depressive symptoms, and antidepressant use. A systematic review including 22 longitudinal studies found strong evidence that retirement has a beneficial effect on mental health (van der Heide et al. 2013). For instance, a study by Fleischmann et al. (2020) assessed the trajectories of mental health (operationalized by GHQ depression scores) both before and after retirement among British civil servants in the Whitehall II cohort study. It showed that, before retirement, mental health problems were gradually decreasing over time, and then people experienced a steep reduction in mental health problems shortly after retirement before they transited to a stable stage with a relatively low level of mental health problems in the long term (Fig. 5). The improvement in mental health shortly

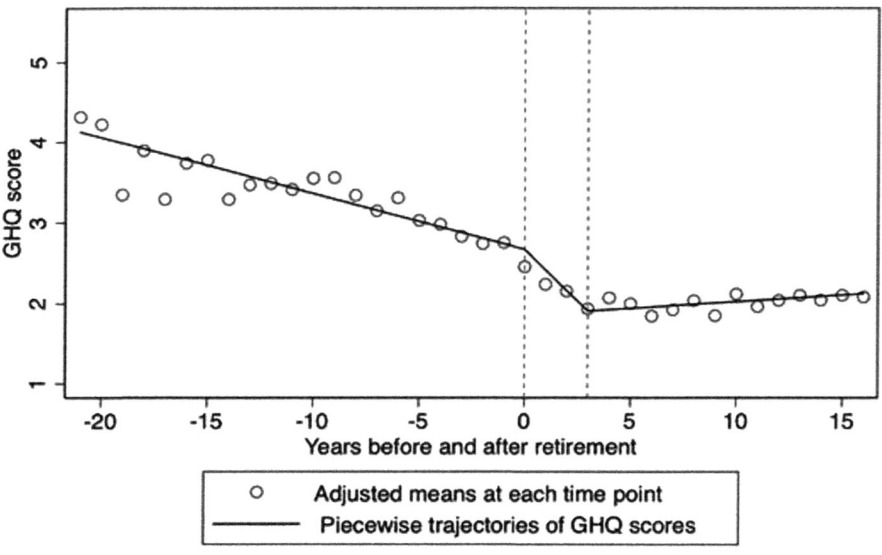

Fig. 5 Development of mental health (General Health Questionnaire [GHQ] score) dependent on retirement. (Source: Fleischmann et al. J Gerontol B Psychol Sci Soc (2020))

after retirement may be linked to a reduction in work-related stress, and this study found that the improvement in mental health was more explicit when retiring from working environments with high psychosocial job demands.

Studies focusing on work-family conflict have found gender differences in retirement experience, such that retirement may come as a relief for men previously experiencing high levels of work demands interfering with family life; however, among women, retirement may not relieve the burdens of family life stressors. Some studies found that socioeconomic status before retirement may modify the mental health effect of retirement (Jokela et al. 2010), but their results contradicted each other in terms of which socioeconomic group benefited more from retirement, and some studies found no differences across socioeconomic groups (Schaap et al. 2018). Studies have suggested that the health effect of retirement may vary by reasons of retirement. Using the same Whitehall II cohort study, Jokela et al. (2010) found that mental health status improved for both statutory retirement (at age 60 for civil servants) and early voluntary retirement. Yet, this group of early voluntary retirees from civil servants may not be the typical retirement story, as many people exit the labor force early due to lost work opportunities and lost choices, and such involuntary early retirement has often been linked with a decline in mental health (Gallo et al. 2006; Voss et al. 2020). In the UK, there is no longer a default retirement age since 2011. A more recent study using the English Longitudinal Study of Ageing (ELSA) found that those who retired or worked past state pension age voluntarily were less likely to report depression in the follow-up than those who either worked or retired without voluntary reasons. This study suggested that mental health in later life hinges less on the timing of retirement and more on whether or not the decision to retire or continue working is voluntary (Xue et al. 2021).

Retirement and Cognition
Cognitive function can decline with age, and cognitive decline is one of the major causes of disability for the older population. In the literature on retirement and cognition, most studies have focused on the effect of retirement on global cognition (i.e., overall ability to function in everyday activities) and memory-related skills (i.e., episodic memory, immediate and delayed recall, working memory, and verbal memory), as global cognition and memory often constitute clinically relevant outcomes. A systematic review of 29 longitudinal studies found that retirement had no negative effects on adults' global cognition and slightly adversely influenced memory (Alvarez-Bueno et al. 2021). Xue et al. (2017) found that declines in verbal memory were 38% faster after retirement compared to before, after taking account of age-related decline, although no change was found in other domains of cognition. In addition, this study found that a higher employment grade was protective against the speed of verbal memory decline while people were still working, but this "protective effect" was lost when individuals retired. Higher-grade jobs often mean more opportunities for the use of skills and variety of work, and this study points to the benefits of cognitively stimulating activities associated with high employment that could benefit older people's memory. However, this study used a sample of civil servants in the UK, whose type of work may be more mentally challenging compared to the general population. Another study using an England representative sample – ELSA – found no difference in trajectories of change in episodic memory before and after retirement (Romero Starke et al. 2019). A more limited number of studies have tested how the timing and choice of retirement could impact cognition, and no clear pattern has emerged.

Retirement and Physical Health
Relatively fewer studies have examined the effect of retirement on physical health, and most of them were conducted in the USA and Europe. A systematic review synthesizing the evidence from 12 longitudinal studies suggested conflicting evidence for retirement having an effect on physical health (van der Heide et al. 2013), with some studies indicating a physical health improvement after retirement, some indicating a decline, and some indicating no effect. There are several reasons that the effects of retirement on physical functioning are likely to vary, and one possible reason is the various measures of physical health across studies, including physical functioning, physical limitation, physical fatigue, having symptoms of an illness, somatic complaints, having a chronic illness, or serious health problems. The effects of retirement on physical functioning are also likely to vary based on job characteristics before retirement. For those working in manual jobs, work might be a key source of exercise and could be protective of physical decline; however, studies that drew comparisons between both blue-collar workers and white-collar workers found

no differences in the effect of retirement on physical health (Seitsamo and Klockars 1997). In terms of socioeconomic status, a systematic review showed that only two out of seven studies found differences across socioeconomic groups, with both suggesting that people retiring from higher socioeconomic occupations benefit more in terms of physical health as opposed to retiring from lower socioeconomic occupations (Schaap et al. 2018). Most studies on physical health did not specify the types of or reasons for retirement, but one study reported that a decline in physical health was found in both voluntary early retirees and statutory retirement from the civil service (Jokela et al. 2010).

Retirement and Other Health and Well-Being Outcomes

Older people are more likely than younger people to suffer from cardiovascular disease, and thus, a lot of previous studies have assessed the link between retirement and cardiovascular disease (CVD) or CVD-related risk factors. A systematic review based on the evidence of 82 longitudinal studies found that the results varied greatly depending on the country (Xue et al. 2020b). For example, empirical studies in the USA often found no significant effect of retirement on CVD, while studies in European countries showed a more consistent detrimental effect of retirement on CVD, indicating that different retirement policies and social-welfare legislations between countries are likely to be one of the factors influencing the health and well-being of individuals after retirement. This review also pointed out that the negative health effects of retirement should be interpreted with caution, as CVD is an important risk factor that can lead to work exit or retirement. Studies designs that did not take account of this selection effect properly will lead to biased results.

Self-reported health (SRH) is another commonly studied outcome in the literature to assess the health effects of retirement. SRH is a subjective reflection of health status. When respondents are asked to rate their general health, they tend to incorporate aspects of both physical and mental health, and thus, some researchers believe SRH may provide a more comprehensive picture of one's overall well-being. But there are also some arguments against using SRH across heterogeneous populations, such as that people may report SRH differently across cultural groups. In terms of the association between retirement and SRH found in the previous studies, results varied greatly with some indicating better SRH after retirement, some suggesting a decrease in SRH after retirement, and some finding no effect (van der Heide et al. 2013).

Discussion on the Health Effect of Retirement

Retirement can influence people's life, health, and well-being in many ways, and the health effect of retirement depends on the type of health outcome studied. Overall, empirical evidence suggests that retirement has a beneficial effect on mental health, but a less consistent effect on other aspects of health and well-being. Moreover, country-level welfare and legislation have a great impact on individuals' timing and choice of retirement and could be possible reasons for explaining inconsistencies across studies. Many other factors, such as the different definitions of retirement or the various ways of measuring health outcomes, may also contribute to the heterogeneity in research findings regarding the health effect of retirement. Another factor, which might be particularly important for assessing the health effect of retirement, is the study design. People who stay in the labor market are generally healthier than retirees – the so-called healthy worker effect. Many studies assessing research on retirement and health may overestimate the detrimental effect of retirement on health due to reverse causality. There is an increasing interest in understanding the "causal effect" of retirement on health and well-being, and several analytic methods, such as instrumental variables (IV) analysis, fixed effect models, propensity score matching, and piecewise models, have been applied in recent literature to reduce the probability of reserve causality (Xue et al. 2017; Kuusi et al. 2020).

In the current literature focusing on the health effect of retirement, retirement has been considered a discrete, one-time labor market exit at expected ages. However, people are increasingly taking different retirement trajectories, such as partially retiring by gradually reducing their working hours or moving in and out of the labor market multiple times. Future studies could assess the impact of different retirement trajectories on health and well-being. Besides, although there are several theoretical arguments, such as role theory, continuity theory, and the social capital model, there is little empirical evidence on the mediating pathway between retirement and health and well-being. The few empirical studies that have examined the mechanisms of the health effects of retirement have found potential mediators to be work-related strain, change in sleep and health behaviors (Eibich 2015). Other potential mediating pathways, such as changes in social relationships and leisure activities, could be further explored. The gender differences in the work-family life course patterns, division of domestic labor, as well as caring responsibilities, could affect the barriers, resources, and opportunities that shape the health and wellbeing of individuals as they move through and beyond retirement. More work needs to be done on gender differences in transitions to retirement and healthy ageing, and this requires us to give more attention to understanding the differential impact of employment and welfare for men and women in different societies.

Conclusion

In the last decades, many countries have shifted away from early retirement, and initiated policies to delay retirement and increase employment participation at older ages. Overall, this has led to an increase in actual retirement ages and employment participation. However, this policy change has also given rise to discussions about the "right" retirement age. Until recently, both life expectancy and healthy life expectancy after age 65 have been increasing and this could point to the possibility to further increase retirement age. However, as this chapter shows, there are inequalities in healthy life expectancy between higher and lower occupational groups or higher and lower educated workers, and also men and women (Head et al. 2019). Future revisions of retirement policies should acknowledge these inequalities and consider them in their policies. Additionally, a large proportion of older people exit paid work several years before state pension age and, although for some this may be for voluntary reasons, this chapter shows that poor health is an important driver of early exit before normal retirement age. Additionally, adverse working conditions are also related to early exit from paid work. Policies to better support people with health conditions to remain in work are needed to avoid exacerbation of existing inequalities. Moreover, our overview of employment pathways before retirement indicates that when and how people retire is not established shortly before retirement. Rather, employment and family patterns earlier in life are relevant for individuals' retirement (Hoven et al. 2018; Wahrendorf et al. 2018). Policy makers should keep this in mind and consider using policies earlier in life to enable individuals to attain stable retirement conditions.

This chapter has focused on retirement and pension policies in OECD countries. Demographic ageing is occurring rapidly in other countries with the fastest growth in numbers of people aged 65 and over projected to take place in Asian and Sub-Saharan African countries (United Nation 2019). In many of these countries, a large proportion of workers do not have access to occupational pensions or social security benefits.

One of the challenges of designing retirement policies and making long-term predictions on pension provision is that they are exposed to unexpected events, such as most recently the global COVID-19 pandemic. This crisis has interrupted the trend of yearly increases in employment rate among people aged 55–64 years (OECD 2021). It appears that there is a trend break: the retired share of the 55–64 year group had been steadily declining since 2010, but has increased again in 2019/2020 (Davis 2021). In many countries, the pandemic has exacerbated pre-existing inequalities, for example, in the USA, employment losses have been substantially larger in occupations and industries with lower pay, and also for Hispanics and non-white workers (Cortes and Forsythe 2020).

Last, the Covid-19 pandemic has caused widespread social and economic upheaval and may threaten the life of retirement for today's retirees and the impact on the health of future retirees is less certain. Continued research on the current and long-term impact of Covid crisis on older population's health and well-being is required.

References

Alvarez J-A, Kallestrup-Lamb M, Kjærgaard S (2021) Linking retirement age to life expectancy does not lessen the demographic implications of unequal lifespans. Insur Math Econ 99:363–375. https://doi.org/10.1016/j.insmatheco.2021.04.010
Alvarez-Bueno C, Cavero-Redondo I, Jimenez-Lopez E et al (2021) Effect of retirement on cognitive function: a systematic review and meta-analysis. Occup Environ Med 78:761–768. https://doi.org/10.1136/OEMED-2020-106892
Atchley R (1989) A continuity theory of normal aging. Gerontologist 29(2):183–190
Bakker AB, Demerouti E (2007) The job demands-resources model: state of the art. J Manag Psychol 22:309–328. https://doi.org/10.1108/02683940710733115/FULL/XML
Browne P, Carr E, Fleischmann M et al (2018) The relationship between workplace psychosocial environment and retirement intentions and actual retirement: a systematic review. Eur J Ageing:1–10. https://doi.org/10.1007/s10433-018-0473-4
Brunello G, Langella M (2013) Bridge jobs in Europe. IZA J Labor Policy 2:11. https://doi.org/10.1186/2193-9004-2-11

Cahill KE, Giandrea MD, Quinn JF (2006) Retirement patterns from career employment. Gerontologist 46:514–523

Calvo E, Madero-Cabib I, Staudinger UM (2018) Retirement sequences of older Americans: moderately destandardized and highly stratified across gender, class, and race. Gerontologist 58:1166–1176. https://doi.org/10.1093/geront/gnx052

Carr E, Fleischmann M, Goldberg M et al (2018a) Occupational and educational inequalities in exit from employment at older ages: evidence from seven prospective cohorts. Occup Environ Med 75:369–377. https://doi.org/10.1136/oemed-2017-104619

Carr E, Murray ET, Zaninotto P et al (2018b) The association between informal caregiving and exit from employment among older workers: prospective findings from the UK household longitudinal study. J Gerontol: Ser B 73:1253–1262. https://doi.org/10.1093/GERONB/GBW156

Clark C, Smuk M, Lain D et al (2017) Impact of childhood and adulthood psychological health on labour force participation and exit in later life. Psychol Med 47:1597–1608. https://doi.org/10.1017/S0033291717000010

Cortes GM, Forsythe E (2020) The heterogeneous labor market impacts of the Covid-19 pandemic. SSRN Electron J. https://doi.org/10.2139/SSRN.3634715

Dave D, Rashad I, Spasojevic J (2008) The effects of retirement on physical and mental health outcomes. Southern Economic Journal 75:497–523. https://doi.org/10.1002/j.2325-8012.2008.tb00916.x

Davis O (2021) Employment and retirement among older workers during the COVID-19 pandemic. Schwartz Center for Economic Policy Analysis (SCEPA), Department of Economics, the New School for Social Research. https://www.economicpolicyresearch.org/images/docs/research/nssr_working_papers/NSSR_WP_062021.pdf

de Preter H, van Looy D, Mortelmans D (2013) Individual and institutional push and pull factors as predictors of retirement timing in Europe: a multilevel analysis. J Aging Stud 27:299–307. https://doi.org/10.1016/J.JAGING.2013.06.003

Eibich P (2015) Understanding the effect of retirement on health: mechanisms and heterogeneity. J Health Econ 43:1–12. https://doi.org/10.1016/j.jhealeco.2015.05.001

Eurostat (2021) Figure from expected duration of working life by country and sex, 2020 (years) https://ec.europa.eu/eurostat/databrowser/view/lfsi_dwl_a/default/table?lang=en

Fisher GG, Chaffee DS, Sonnega A (2016) Retirement timing: a review and recommendations for future research. Work Aging Retire 2:230–261. https://doi.org/10.1093/workar/waw001

Fleischmann M, Carr E, Stansfeld SA et al (2018) Can favourable psychosocial working conditions in midlife moderate the risk of work exit for chronically ill workers? A 20 year follow-up of the Whitehall II study. Occup Environ Med 75:183–190. https://doi.org/10.1136/OEMED-2017-104452

Fleischmann M, Xue B, Head J (2020) Mental health before and after retirement–assessing the relevance of psychosocial working conditions: the Whitehall II prospective study of British civil servants. J Gerontol: Ser B 75:403–413. https://doi.org/10.1093/GERONB/GBZ042

Gallo WT, Bradley EH, Teng HM, Kasl S, v. (2006) The effect of recurrent involuntary job loss on the depressive symptoms of older US workers. Int Arch Occup Environ Health 80:109–116. https://doi.org/10.1007/s00420-006-0108-5

Gondek D, Ning K, Ploubidis GB et al (2018) The impact of health on economic and social outcomes in the United Kingdom: a scoping literature review. PLoS One 13. https://doi.org/10.1371/JOURNAL.PONE.0209659

Harris K, Krygsman S, Waschenko J, Laliberte Rudman D (2018) Ageism and the older worker: a scoping review. Gerontologist 58:e1–e14. https://doi.org/10.1093/GERONT/GNW194

Head J, Chungkham HS, Hyde M et al (2019) Socioeconomic differences in healthy and disease-free life expectancy between ages 50 and 75: a multi-cohort study. Eur J Pub Health 29:267–272. https://doi.org/10.1093/eurpub/cky215

Hofäcker D, Radl J (2017) Retirement transitions in times of institutional change: theoretical concept. In: Hofäcker D, König S, Hess M (eds) Delaying retirement: Progress and challenges of active ageing in Europe, the United States and Japan. Palgrave, Macmillan, pp 1–22

Hoven H, Dragano N, Blane D, Wahrendorf M (2018) Early adversity and late life employment history – a sequence analysis based on SHARE. Work Aging Retire 4:238–250. https://doi.org/10.1093/workar/wax014

Johnson JV, Hall EM (1988) Job strain, work place social support, and cardiovascular disease: a cross-sectional study of random sample of the Swedish Working Population. Am J Public Health 78:1336–1342. https://doi.org/10.2105/AJPH.78.10.1336

Jokela M, Ferrie JE, Gimeno D et al (2010) From midlife to early old age: health trajectories associated with retirement. Epidemiology 21:284–290. https://doi.org/10.1097/EDE.0b013e3181d61f53

Karasek RA (1979) Job demands, job decision latitude, and mental strain: implications for job redesign. Adm Sci Q 24:285–308. https://doi.org/10.2307/2392498

Karpinska K, Henkens K, Schippers J (2011) The recruitment of early retirees: a vignette study of the factors that affect managers' decisions. Ageing Soc 31:570–589. https://doi.org/10.1017/S0144686X10001078

Knardahl S, Johannessen HA, Sterud T et al (2017) The contribution from psychological, social, and organizational work factors to risk of disability retirement: a systematic review with meta-analyses. BMC Public Health 17. https://doi.org/10.1186/S12889-017-4059-4

Kuh D, Ben-Shlomo Y, Lynch J et al (2003) Life course epidemiology. J Epidemiol Community Health 57:778–783. https://doi.org/10.1136/jech.57.10.778

Kuusi T, Martikainen P, Valkonen T (2020) The influence of old-age retirement on health: causal evidence from the Finnish register data. J Econ Ageing 17:100257. https://doi.org/10.1016/J.JEOA.2020.100257

Moen P (1996) A life course perspective on retirement, gender, and well-being. J Occup Health Psychol 1(2):131–144. https://doi.org/10.1037/1076-8998.1.2.131

Murray ET, Head J, Shelton N et al (2016) Local area unemployment, individual health and workforce exit: ONS longitudinal study. Eur J Pub Health 26:463–469. https://doi.org/10.1093/EURPUB/CKW005

OECD (2011) Linking pensions to life expectancy. In: Pensions at a glance 2011: retirement-income systems in OECD and G20 countries. OECD, Paris, pp 81–102. https://doi.org/10.1787/pension_glance-2011-en

OECD (2018) OECD pensions outlook 2018. OECD, Paris. https://doi.org/10.1787/pens_outlook-2018-en

OECD (2019) Pensions at a glance 2019: OECD and G20 indicators. OECD, Paris. https://doi.org/10.1787/b6d3dcfc-en

OECD (2021) Pensions at a glance 2021: OECD and G20 indicators. OECD, Paris. https://doi.org/10.1787/ca401ebd-en

OECD/European Union (2020) Healthy life expectancy at birth and at age 65. In: Health at a glance: Europe 2020: state of health in the EU cycle. OECD, Paris. https://doi.org/10.1787/82129230-en

Radl J (2013) Labour market exit and social stratification in Western Europe: the effects of social class and gender on the timing of retirement. Eur Sociol Rev 29:654–668. https://doi.org/10.1093/esr/jcs045

Reime LJ, Claussen B (2013) Municipal unemployment and municipal typologies as predictors of disability pensioning in Norway: a multilevel analysis. Scand J Public Health 41:158–165. https://doi.org/10.1177/1403494812472004

Riley M, Riley J (1994) Structural lag: past and future. In: Riley MW, Kahn RL, Foner A (eds) Age and structural lag: the mismatch between people's lives and opportunities in work, family, and leisure. Wiley, New York, pp 15–36

Romero Starke K, Seidler A, Hegewald J et al (2019) Retirement and decline in episodic memory: analysis from a prospective study of adults in England. Int J Epidemiol 48:1925–1936. https://doi.org/10.1093/IJE/DYZ135

Sauerberg M (2021) The impact of population's educational composition on healthy life years: an empirical illustration of 16 European countries. SSM-Popul Health 15:100857. https://doi.org/10.1016/j.ssmph.2021.100857

Schaap R, de Wind A, Coenen P et al (2018) The effects of exit from work on health across different socioeconomic groups: a systematic literature review. Soc Sci Med 198:36–45. https://doi.org/10.1016/J.SOCSCIMED.2017.12.015

Schils T (2008) Early retirement in Germany, The Netherlands, and the United Kingdom: a longitudinal analysis of individual factors and institutional regimes. Eur Sociol Rev 24:315–329. https://doi.org/10.1093/ESR/JCN009

Schram JLD, Solovieva S, Leinonen T et al (2021) The influence of occupational class and physical workload on working life expectancy among older employees. Scand J Work Environ Health 47:5–14. https://doi.org/10.5271/sjweh.3919

Seitsamo J, Klockars M (1997) Aging and changes in health. Scand J Work Environ Health 23:27–35. JSTOR

Shultz KS, Morton KR, Weckerle JR (1998) The influence of push and pull factors on voluntary and involuntary early retirees' retirement decision and adjustment. J Vocat Behav 53:45–57. https://doi.org/10.1006/JVBE.1997.1610

Siegrist J (1996) Adverse health effects of high-effort/low-reward conditions. J Occup Health Psychol 1:27–41. https://doi.org/10.1037/1076-8998.1.1.27

Smith PM, Cawley C, Williams A, Mustard C (2020) Male/female differences in the impact of caring for elderly relatives on labor market attachment and hours of work: 1997–2015. J Gerontol Ser B 75:694–704. https://doi.org/10.1093/GERONB/GBZ026

Stiemke P, Hess M (2022) Determinants of (in-)voluntary retirement: a systematic literature review. J Eur Soc Policy 2022:1–11. https://doi.org/10.1177/09589287221089465

The World Bank (2019) Population ages 65 and above (% of population). https://data.worldbank.org/indicator/SP.POP.65UP.TO.ZS?end=2020&most_recent_value_desc=false&start=1960&view=map&year=2020. Accessed 28 Jan 2022

United Nation, Department of Economic and Social Affairs, Population Division (2019) World population ageing 2019: highlights (ST/ESA/SER.A/430)

van der Heide I, van Rijn RM, Robroek SJW et al (2013) Is retirement good for your health? A systematic review of longitudinal studies. BMC Public Health 13:1–11. https://doi.org/10.1186/1471-2458-13-1180/FIGURES/4

van Rijn RM, Robroek SJW, Brouwer S, Burdorf A (2014) Influence of poor health on exit from paid employment: a systematic review. Occup Environ Med 71:295–301. https://doi.org/10.1136/oemed-2013-101591

Vickerstaff S, van der Horst M (2021) The impact of age stereotypes and age norms on employees' retirement choices: a neglected aspect of research on extended working lives. Front Sociol. https://doi.org/10.3389/FSOC.2021.686645

Voss MW, Wadsworth LL, Birmingham W et al (2020) Health effects of late-career unemployment. J Aging Health 32:106–116. https://doi.org/10.1177/0898264318806792

Wahrendorf M, Zaninotto P, Hoven H et al (2018) Late life employment histories and their association with work and family formation during adulthood: a sequence analysis based on ELSA. J Gerontol Ser B 73:1263–1277. https://doi.org/10.1093/geronb/gbx066

Wang M, Henkens K, van Solinge H (2011) Retirement adjustment: a review of theoretical and empirical advancements. Am Psychol 66:204–213

Weber D, Loichinger E (2020) Live longer, retire later? Developments of healthy life expectancies and working life expectancies between age 50–59 and age 60–69 in Europe. Eur J Ageing. https://doi.org/10.1007/s10433-020-00592-5

Xue B, Cadar D, Fleischmann M et al (2017) Effect of retirement on cognitive function: the Whitehall II cohort study. Eur J Epidemiol:1–13. https://doi.org/10.1007/s10654-017-0347-7

Xue B, Fleischmann M, Head J et al (2020a) Work-family conflict and work exit in later career stage. J Gerontol B Psychol Sci Soc Sci 75:716–727. https://doi.org/10.1093/geronb/gby146

Xue B, Head J, McMunn A, Heyn PC (2020b) The impact of retirement on cardiovascular disease and its risk factors: a systematic review of longitudinal studies. Gerontologist 60:e367–e377. https://doi.org/10.1093/GERONT/GNZ062

Xue B, Pai M, Luo M (2021) Working beyond SPA and the trajectories of cognitive and mental health of UK pensioners: do gender, choice, and occupational status matter? Eur J Ageing. https://doi.org/10.1007/S10433-021-00644-4

Part VII

Interventions and Policy Implications

Worksite Health Promotion: Evidence on Effects and Challenges

26

Paula Franklin

Contents

Introduction	470
Workplace Health Promotion (WHP) Definitions and Approaches	471
Workplace Health Promotion and Health/Risk Behaviors	473
Workplace Health Promotion and Mental Health	475
Inequalities in Workplace Health Promotion	477
Workplace Health Promotion and Workforce Retention	478
Precarious Employment and Psychosocial Risks: Major Challenge for Workplace Health Promotion	479
Overview of Legislation and Policies on Work-Related Psychosocial Risks	481
Conclusions	484
Cross-References	488
References	488

Abstract

While workplace health promotion (WHP) carries a promise of supporting better health of the working population over the life course, there are many challenges that limit the approach. This chapter provides an overview of the evidence on WHP effects on physical and mental health and discusses the challenges. The first part of the chapter introduces the concept of WHP. The second part reviews recent evidence on the effectiveness of WHP and outlines key challenges that relate to the implementation of WHP interventions, participation, and evaluation. The role of WHP in worker retention is also addressed. The third part of the chapter places WHP in the broader context of labor market transformations that impact job quality through precarious employment. Precarious employment is linked to adverse health effects, mediated through psychosocial risks (PSR) in the working environment that hinder comprehensive WHP. The final part of the chapter pro-

---

P. Franklin (✉)
European Trade Union Institute (ETUI), Brussels, Belgium
e-mail: pfranklin@etui.org

vides an overview of legislation and policies on work-related psychosocial risks in Europe, and the chapter concludes with a reflection on future considerations for WHP from health equity perspective.

Keywords

Workplace health promotion · Healthy workplaces · Psychosocial risks · Precarious employment · Health inequalities

Introduction

A key element of health promotion is to enable people to increase control over and improve the determinants of their health (WHO 1986). One of the major determinants is work. People spend a considerable time at work over their life course; the expected average duration of working life in the European Union in 2020 was 35.7 years, which is 3.4 years longer than in 2000. For men, the estimated expected duration of working life was 38.0 years and for women 33.2 years (Eurostat 2021). Due to the centrality of work in people's life course trajectories, workplaces are considered as major sites for health promotion. Yet, workplace health promotion (WHP) is relatively rare in policy and practice, as merely 29.5% of EU establishments have measures to promote health (Verra et al. 2019).

WHP started to develop in the 1970s with a narrow focus on risk prevention and on single individual behavior interventions. Since the 1990s, there has been a call towards a more comprehensive approach, also known as "health-promoting workplaces" and "healthy workplaces," that emphasizes the importance of a combined effort of employers, employees, and society to improve the health and well-being of people at work (Rojatz et al. 2017; World Health Organization and Burton 2010).

Practices and interventions in workplace health promotion are heterogeneous, addressing chronic illnesses, mental health, and lifestyles and delivered across different sized enterprises (European Network for Workplace Health Promotion). But while WHP carries a promise of supporting better health of the working population over the life course, research points to several challenges that limit the effectiveness. These concern the WHP implementation, participation, and evaluation.

The broader context of working and employment conditions also impacts the practice of WHP. Over the past decades, global market integration has led to labor market restructuring in most countries around the world and a growth of precarious employment, which poses further challenges to WHP. The instability of precarious work affects peoples' labor market experiences, and studies on social epidemiology have found a clear association between precarious employment and poor health (Rivero et al. 2021). Even within a decent quality working environment, WHP can lead to health inequalities through biases in participant selection and non-context fitting interventions and implementation methods. When the working environment itself has negative impact on the workers – which is the case in precarious employment – the possibilities for WHP to be effective are severely reduced. This creates a dual pathway into increased relative health inequalities between groups of workers; people in lower paying, insecure jobs are less likely to have access to and benefit from WHP and their working environment can be detrimental to health.

This chapter describes first WHP approaches, followed by an evidence review of the effectiveness of and the challenges to WHP interventions on physical and mental health. The evidence is then located within the context of broader trends in working and employment conditions, in particular the increase of precarious employment that has been linked to adverse health effects mediated through psychosocial risk factors (PSR). The final part of the chapter provides an overview of legislation and policies on work-related psychosocial risks in Europe, and the conclusions provide a reflection on future considerations for WHP from the perspective of health equity over the life course.

Workplace Health Promotion (WHP) Definitions and Approaches

The concept of well-being at the workplace has different meanings within and across organizations and countries in Europe. These are influenced by cultural and societal processes and constraints, as well as how the concept has developed locally over time (Guazzi et al. 2014).

The principles of general health promotion developed by WHO in 1984 have been adapted for use in a workplace setting. WHP is directed at the underlying causes of ill health, and it combines diverse methods of approach. It aims at effective worker participation and is not primarily a medical activity but a part of work organization and working conditions (Wynne 1997).

Work organization is about the division of labor, the coordination, and control of work: how work is divided into job tasks, bundling of tasks into jobs and assignments, interdependencies between workers, and how work is coordinated and controlled in order to fulfill the goals of the organization. It encompasses the tasks performed, who performs them, and how they are performed in the process of making a product or providing a service. Work organization thus refers to how work is planned, organized, and managed within companies and to choices on a range of aspects such as work processes, job design, responsibilities, task allocation, work scheduling, work pace, rules and procedures, and decision-making processes (Eurofound 2020a).

The World Health Organization (WHO) uses the concept of "health-promoting workplace" which highlights the importance of a flexible and dynamic balance between an organization and the employees and notes that the development of health-promoting workplaces is a prerequisite for sustainable social and economic development (International Social Security Association website). The European Network for Workplace Health Promotion (ENWHP) definition emphasizes the combined efforts of employers, employees, and society to improve the health and well-being of people at work. This can be achieved by improving work organization and the working environment, promoting active participation, and encouraging personal development.

The definitions above share the notion that *WHP is a comprehensive approach* that involves a combination of improving the work organization and working environment, promoting the participation of workers in healthy activities, enabling healthy choices, and encouraging personal development. Comprehensive workplace health promotion considers mental and physical health (individual factors) as well as the need to make work structures supportive of health-promoting choices (organizational factors) (Jarman et al. 2016). Important success factor for the development and implementation of interventions for disease prevention and health promotion in the workplace is the adoption of a participative approach that engages employees, employers, and management in communication and joint participation (Pieper et al. 2019).

Comprehensive WHP includes interventions targeting both individual and system levels and has been associated with decreases in absenteeism, presenteeism, and financial returns on investment (Jarman et al. 2016). Results from a representative nationwide sample of employers within the social care sector in Sweden found that organizations that had more favorable psychosocial work conditions and workplace health promotion measures had better health and lower sickness absence levels among their employees (Ljungblad et al. 2014). Proper and van Oostrom (2019) systematic review of reviews on the effectiveness of workplace health promotion interventions on physical and mental health outcomes showed that comprehensive multimodal interventions are more effective in the prevention of chronic disease compared to single component interventions. Examples of organizational measures include offering flexible working hours and workplaces, enabling employees to participate in the improvement of their work organization and their work environment, and giving employees opportunities for lifelong learning (Jarman et al. 2016). Individual-level measures concern offering and funding sports courses and events, encouraging healthy eating, offering smoking cessation programs, and supporting mental well-being by, for example, offering counselling (European Network for Workplace Health Promotion).

In practice, a "settings-based approach to health promotion" integrates health promotion into the usual activities of the workplace. The interventions call for an active participation of the workers and enable them to have a say in how the actions are conducted (Magnavita 2018). The second layer of this approach concerns changing the setting itself, to support healthy choices, and the third layer uses social policy to create health-promoting conditions in society at large (Mittelmark 2014).

On the contrary, "non-participatory settings approach" aims at improving health by altering the physical work environment or work organization without involving employees in decisions about what changes should be made or how these should come about. These interventions rely mainly on the opinions of experts and on technical measures, and often resort to industrial hygiene or human resource management methods. Health promotion projects that adopt a "non-settings approach" use the workplace only as an environment in which health-promoting activities could be carried out on workers in order to change their behavior in relation to lifestyle factors such as diet, smoking, and physical activity. Such interventions do not focus on the setting itself (Magnavita 2018).

Workplace Health Promotion and Health/Risk Behaviors

The workplace is an important setting for health promotion during adulthood. WHP on health risk behaviors such as smoking, alcohol, and drug abuse, and health-promoting behaviors, such as physical activity and healthy diet, should consider the situation of specific groups of workers. Working years cover several decades of the life course and different aged people will have different WHP needs, and gender is a well-known factor in health and risk behaviors. Research shows differences in terms of health/risk behaviors and WHP participation between different occupational groups, including at the same workplace (Tsiga et al. 2015; Chiou et al. 2014). There is also a difference by the type of the employer on the prevalence of health promotion measures. Public employers are more likely to have in place measures for health promotion among employees than private employers. Table 1 shows EU-27 average for health promotion in % of establishments in 2019.

Health/risk behavior interventions at workplaces include promotion of healthy food options in canteens, offering nutrition education and counselling, developing workplace policies that restrict alcohol and tobacco, and providing opportunities and incentives for physical activity (including active transport). There is evidence that such interventions can promote mental health, prevent and rehabilitate musculoskeletal disorders, and improve heart health (Mikkelsen et al. 2019).

Concurrently, the evidence on the effectiveness or cost-benefits of individual-level health promotion interventions regarding health and risk behaviors remains inconclusive, with numerous documented challenges and limitations ranging from low participation rate and peer pressure from colleagues to short-lived benefits (Balk-Møller et al. 2017; Freak-Poli et al. 2020).

Wolfenden et al. (2018) systematic review and meta-analysis assessed the effects of strategies for improving the implementation of workplace-based policies or practices targeting diet, physical activity, obesity, tobacco use, and alcohol use. They also assessed the impact of such strategies on employee health behaviors, including dietary intake, physical activity, weight status, and alcohol and tobacco

Table 1 EU-27 average for health promotion in % of establishments (Source: EU-OSHA ESENER Survey 2019)

Health promotion measure	Public (%)	Private (%)
Raising awareness about healthy nutrition	38.0	31.0
Raising awareness about preventing addiction (alcohol, tobacco, and drugs)	38.4	35.6
Promoting sports activities outside working hours	37.8	28.6
Promoting physical exercise at work	32.0	26.0

use, and evaluated their cost-effectiveness. They concluded that the available evidence is sparse and inconsistent, and the low certainty evidence suggests that such strategies may make little or no difference on employee health behavior outcomes. It was also unclear if such strategies are cost-effective or have potential unintended adverse consequences. Lutz et al. (2019) systematic review of cost-effectiveness and cost-benefit of workplace health promotion concluded that the economic value of WHP remains uncertain, due to considerable heterogeneity of interventions.

Two Dutch studies based on individual participant data meta-analysis concluded that workplace health promotion programs were in general not effective; Robroek et al. (2020) assessed the effectiveness of workplace health promotion programs on body mass index (BMI) across socioeconomic groups and found that compared with control conditions, workplace health promotion programs overall showed a statistically nonsignificant decrease in BMI. Coenen et al. (2020) investigated socioeconomic inequalities in effectiveness on healthy behavior of, and compliance to, workplace health promotion programs, and found that except for fruit intake, no effects were found on health behaviors.

Data collected by the European Agency for Safety and Health at Work (EU-OSHA) via their European Survey of Enterprises on New and Emerging Risks (ESENER) survey shows the focus on individual-level interventions. The data on the measures for health promotion among employees include "raising awareness of nutrition," "raising awareness about preventing addiction," "promoting sports activities outside of working hours," and "promoting physical exercise at work." The 2019 data show that the most frequently reported measure (35% of establishments in the EU-28) is raising awareness of the prevention of addiction (smoking, alcohol, and drugs) (Fig. 1), followed by raising awareness of nutrition (29%) (Fig. 2) and the promotion of sports activities outside working hours (28%). By sector, measures for health promotion are more frequently reported by establishments in education, and human health and social work activities (EU-OSHA 2019).

Larger establishments tend to be more likely to offer health promotion for their employees than small or medium ones. Data show that 58.1% of European establishments with 250 or more employees have measures in place to raise awareness about healthy nutrition, in comparison to 42.2% of establishments with 50–249 employees, 32.1% of establishments with 10–49 employees, and 30.1% of

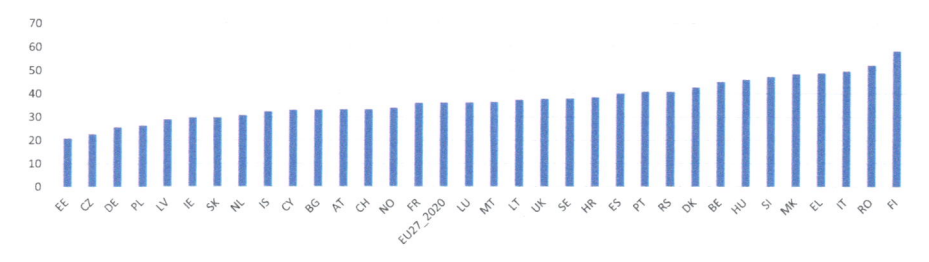

Fig. 1 Establishments raising awareness about preventing addiction, e.g., to smoking, alcohol, or drugs (%) (Source: EU-OSHA ESENER Survey 2019)

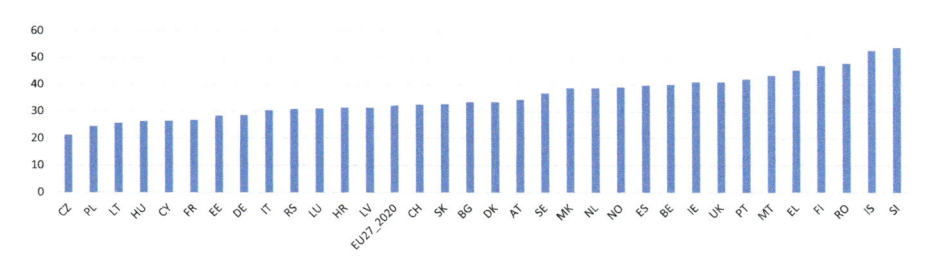

Fig. 2 Establishments raising awareness about healthy nutrition (%). (Source: EU-OSHA ESENER Survey 2019)

establishments with 5–9 employees. The same pattern holds for "raising awareness about preventing addiction," with 65.4% of the largest establishments in the EU (250 or more employees) addressing the harmful use of alcohol, and the use of tobacco and drugs, as opposed to 48.4% of those with 50–249 employees. Thirty-seven percent of establishments with 10–49 employees, and 32.5% of the smallest companies (5–9 employees) have WHP measures that address addiction.

Maes et al. (2012) systematic review on the effectiveness of workplace interventions in Europe promoting healthy eating found limited to moderate evidence for positive effects. The main issue they highlighted was the unmet quality criteria for interventions. The quality of the evaluated interventions was assessed using the criteria of the European Network for Workplace Health Promotion (ENWHP), which includes:

- Prior analysis of the needs of the worksite
- Involvement of all stakeholders
- Improvement of the quality of working life and conditions as well as focusing on the behavior of the individual worker
- Integration of the activities in the management practices and daily working life of the enterprise

Workplace Health Promotion and Mental Health

Although there have been several calls for incorporating multiple levels of analysis in employee health and well-being research, studies examining the interplay between individual, workgroup, organizational, and broader societal factors in relation to employee mental health outcomes remain an exception rather than the norm. At the same time, organizational intervention research and practice also tend to be limited by a single-level focus, omitting potentially important influences (Martin et al. 2016).

Jarman et al. (2016) note that evaluation research on mental health interventions incorporating individual and organizational components is complex and challenging, and as a result such studies are rare; in addition, studies that would evaluate the effects of comprehensive WHP in relation to mental health outcomes are nonexistent. Their cross-sectional survey research into the association between mental health and comprehensive workplace health promotion showed that comprehensive promotion was successful in attracting participation from men with higher average psychological distress and increasing participation among women with poorer mental health scores. However, the participation did not translate into a change in men's mental health and only made a partial contribution to the observed reduction in women's psychological distress over time (Jarman et al. 2016).

Employers increasingly offer mindfulness classes and individual resilience training for workers in response to high intensity work environment that can cause stress. An evaluation study of a mindfulness-based intervention on workers with poor mental health showed significantly lower psychological distress, prolonged fatigue, and perceived stress when the intervention was completed, as compared to a control group. However, there were no promising findings regarding work-related psychosocial risk factors (PSR), such as job strain, job control, or job demands (Huang et al. 2015). This indicates that individual-level interventions are unlikely to lead into sustainable well-being if the stressors remain in the working environment. Similar results have been reported regarding healthcare professionals; a Cochrane systematic review established that for healthcare professionals, there is very low certainty evidence that resilience training may result in lower levels of depression or stress and higher levels of resilience factors at post-intervention (Kunzler et al. 2020), and a systematic review by Robertson et al. (2016) concluded that training and individual interventions must combine personal, social, and workplace features.

The sources of stress in the working environment are called psychosocial risks (PSR). An individual worker does not have an agency to change these, as they stem from the design and management of work, and its social and organizational context. Exposure to PSR can affect a worker's psychological and physical health through a stress-mediated pathway. The sources of psychosocial risks are numerous, including:

1) *Job content*, e.g., conflicting demands, lack of role clarity, lack of training and development opportunities, and lack of workers' influence over the way the job is done.
2) *Work organization and management*, e.g., excessive workloads and work intensity, lack of workers' involvement in making decisions that affect the worker (autonomy), poorly managed organizational changes, ineffective communication, working time arrangements, and poor work-life balance.
3) *The social context of the job*, e.g., lack of support from management or colleagues, psychological and sexual harassment, third-party violence, and job insecurity (EU-OSHA Psychosocial risks and stress at work).

Psychosocial risk factors (PSR) can have immediate health impacts and they can contribute to burden of disease over the life course. Findings from a meta-review of the associations between psychosocial work factors and health outcomes showed that they are significantly associated with cardiovascular diseases and mental disorders (Niedhammer et al. 2021). International Labour Organization (ILO) (2012) guide on integration of health promotion into workplace occupational safety and health (OSH) policies highlights that psychosocial risks (PSR) are among the most important emerging risk in the workplace. Their outcomes affect all countries, all professions, and all workers, having a significant impact on workers' health, absenteeism, and performance.

Despite efforts to direct attention towards changing environmental and organizational factors aimed at improving and protecting workers' health, the majority of WHP activities remain focused at the level of the individual (Guazzi et al. 2014; Pieper et al. 2019). It is observed that companies are more likely to delegate responsibility for employee health and well-being to their staff, and not fully realize the potential of healthy leadership and organizational health promotion (Koinig and Diehl 2021). This is a missed opportunity to use WHP to address mental health morbidity in Europe. In 2013, more than half of workers in the EU (51%) reported that work-related stress was common in their workplace (EU-OSHA 2013), and the Covid-19 pandemic has further exacerbated the situation both for frontline essential workers and teleworkers.

Inequalities in Workplace Health Promotion

Individual-level WHP has been studied in relation to socioeconomic position (SEP). van Heijster et al. (2021) evaluated whether workplace health promotion programs improve self-perceived health of employees with a low socioeconomic position, concluding that compared to control conditions, the programs did not show an overall improvement. van der Put et al. (2020) tested whether three types of WHP mediate or moderate the relation between education and health: healthy menus, sports facilities, and health checks. They found that the use of healthy menus and sports facilities in the workplace can contribute to increasing health inequalities, as lower educated employees were less likely to make use of these. They observed that WHP may relate to health inequalities in two ways: higher educated employees may be more likely to use WHP than lower educated employees and the effect of WHP on health may be stronger for higher educated than for lower educated employees (van der Put et al. 2020). Similar observations were made by Nielsen and Midtsundstad (2021) in Norway, where workplace health intervention success was more likely among white-collar workers (e.g., in public administration) compared to blue-collar workers (e.g., in manufacturing).

WHP can also suffer from issues with the selection of participants; when you already like exercise, it is easier to do more. Further, the extent to which the usual approaches to WHP can be transferred to everyone is limited, and people with cognitive and/or physical impairments are often excluded (EuroHealthNet Magazine 2021). Many workplace health promotion studies use a design in which voluntary participants are compared before and after the intervention or participants are compared to nonparticipants, and in these studies, selection bias, i.e., selection of more favorable participants into the study, impacts the results (Robroek et al. 2021).

Robroek et al. (2021) note that reaching workers with a lower socioeconomic position who typically work in blue-collar occupations and jobs involving difficult work circumstances such as shift work is particularly challenging. A lack of a clear implementation strategy and understanding of the "real life" context and factors of the workers can hinder the uptake of WHP. As poor health, unhealthy behaviors, unemployment, and work disability are more prevalent among workers from low socioeconomic positions, it would be important that WHP reaches these workers (Robroek et al. 2021; Niedhammer et al. 2011). However, review on workplace health promotion showed that researchers substantially more often conduct studies on workplace health promotion among workers from higher compared to lower socioeconomic groups, and low-wage workers have also limited access to and utilization of worksite health promotion programs (van de Ven et al. 2020; Stiehl et al. 2018).

Workplace Health Promotion and Workforce Retention

In Europe, the ageing of workers is one of the most important issues for occupational health and safety, and the ageing of the active population means that health promotion is a necessity rather than a mere option (Magnavita 2018). Many workers leave the labor market well before reaching the official pension age due to health reasons: 20% of workers aged 50+ think they would not be able to do their current job at the age of 60, and around 21% of EU-28 pensioners (50–69 years) indicated that their own health or disability was the main reason to quit working (European Commission 2016). WHP is seen as an important element for supporting workability, preventing early exit from the labor market, retention of workers, and return to work after illness.

EU Member States' approaches to WHP in terms of policies, strategies, and programs for addressing the challenges of an ageing workforce are heterogeneous. Poscia et al. (2016) systematic literature review showed that studies addressing WHP actions for older workers are few and generally of poor quality. Sippli et al. (2021) qualitative study showed that promotion of workability of older workers in a large manufacturing company was counteracted by many challenges, including issues to do with the work environment (physical challenges), the work organization (e.g., tight time allowances and age stereotypes), and the management of the workplace intervention (bad information, feeling of occupational insecurity, and lack of being valued). The findings suggest that the challenges might have been avoided, for example, by considering workers' perspective during the design and the implementation of the intervention. In general, there remains a lack of sufficient evidence regarding the impact of the effectiveness of workplace interventions on workability across age groups (Grimani et al. 2019; Oakman et al. 2018).

At the same time, there is research and collations of case studies that have found that WHP can mitigate the early exits from the labor market (OECD 2020a). Nielsen and Midtsundstad (2021) study of a representative sample of Norwegian establishments suggests that WHP measures prolong working careers for some workers. Gorgenyi-Hegyes et al. (2021) note that corporate benefits from 1 to 2 years of workplace health promotion include increased labor retention and attractiveness.

Fehér and Reich (2020) found that WHP is positively correlated with commitment of the employees with the organization, and attractiveness of the employer or the organization. However, their data did not support the relationship with voluntary quits, meaning that there are limits to the positive effects of WHP, and other factors of the employment relationship may be more important. A study in Germany that surveyed nursing institutions found that every fifth nursing institution reported nurses leaving the occupation for reasons of health. The application of health promotion strategies was considered largely successful in retaining staff, but approaches related to structural prevention, i.e., fostering a healthy working environment (Box 1), were given only little consideration (Boscher et al. 2020).

> **Box 1 An Example of a Healthy Workplace Strategy to Prevent Early Exit from the Labour Market**
> *A Working Environment Strategy for Modern Working Life 2016–2020, Sweden*
> The strategy for modern working life was drawn up in consultation with social partners. The aim of the government's work environment policy is for more people to work longer and not be excluded from working life prematurely as a result of physical, social, or organizational aspects of the work environment. The strategy emphasizes the role of social dialogue for achieving its goals, and sets out concrete measures within prioritized areas, including a sustainable working life and the psychosocial work environment.
>
> Work environment management must take into account people's differing circumstances and contribute to the development of both individuals and operations. Working conditions must also allow those with health problems or disabilities to participate in working life. Preventive efforts need to be strengthened so that workers are able to get support when health problems related to work first emerge, and continued efforts must be made to improve the work environment in mentally and physically taxing jobs (OSH Wiki 2023).

Precarious Employment and Psychosocial Risks: Major Challenge for Workplace Health Promotion

Supportive and good quality working environment is a prerequisite to the comprehensive WHP approach, which is why the context of nontraditional employment relationships pose challenges to WHP. Precarious forms of employment have become an increasingly defining feature of countries' labor markets, and fewer workers are employed in a standard employment relationship with full-time employment, permanent contracts, stable and adequate levels of income, social protection, and high levels of occupational health and safety standards (McNamara et al. 2021). The incidence of nonstandard forms of work has increased in the EU over the past decade, and it is anticipated that the incidence and intensity of precarious employment will continue to increase (Eurofound 2018). Notable examples of precarious work include temporary and contract work as well as the jobs in the "gig" or platform economy. Precarious employment is socially patterned across Europe, with worse conditions being more prevalent in lower socioeconomic groups. Women, young people, low educated people, and migrants are more likely to be engaged in precarious work such as part-time or temporary work, seasonal work, and self-employment (McNamara et al. 2021).

World Health Organization (WHO) healthy workplace framework and model notes that precarious work contracts are a psychosocial risk with major concern for worker health and well-being (World Health Organization and Burton 2010). Precarious employment is linked to many psychosocial risks, as workers in this situation often face unhealthy and hazardous working conditions, employment insecurity, income inadequacy, and lack of rights and protection (Julià et al. 2017; Quinlan 2015; Benach et al. 2014; Méndez Rivero et al. 2021).

In addition to being a determinant of population health and health inequities per se, precarious employment limits the reach and effectiveness of WHP, and the rise of precarious employment marks a new frontier for workplace health promotion (Gunn et al. 2021; Caldbick et al. 2014). The traditional remit of workplace health promotion with a focus on individual workers and their lifestyles is not sufficient to address the structural transformations of labor markets and the impact on workers (Caldbick et al. 2014). WHP should strive for decent labor conditions through coordinated efforts of state, labor, and industry representatives. The evidence shows, however, that WHP often adopts workplace interventions with insufficient attention paid to organizational risks factors stemming from poor working conditions.

WHP is not efficient if the working environment is not conducive to or is detrimental to health. Research shows that worker participation in WHP is lower when they experience stress and are exposed to work-related PSR factors, such as low social support, very fatiguing work, and high physical or emotional demands with low job control (Jørgensen et al. 2016; Sangachin and Cavuoto 2018) Sorensen et al. (2021) tested an intervention to improve the work organization as a means of promoting and protecting the safety, health, and well-being of low-wage food service workers. The workers regularly encounter physically demanding work, job insecurity, uncertainty around work hours, contributing to instability in earnings, repetitive work, and low job decision latitude and autonomy. Despite strong support from corporate senior leadership, there were many barriers in the implementation. These included financial demands that drove work intensity, turnover of managers, and staffing constraints that further increased the workload and pace. Health and social care sectors are another example of a highly demanding working environment within which WHP could support workers' health and well-being. Yet PSR, such as high job insecurity combined with insecurity over working conditions (e.g., work schedule, tasks, and location) hinders the interventions, as the tendency is to heavily rely on flexible deployments such as temporary hirings or agency nurses to meet growing demand for care (Box 2).

Box 2 How Precarious Employment Hinders Workplace Health Promotion (WHP): The Case of Long-Term Care Sector

Poor working conditions in the long-term care sector (LTC) illustrate how psychosocial risks (PSR) cause direct and accumulative health impacts over the life course and limit the possibility to adopt comprehensive health promotion approach.

The long-term care sector includes many low-paid jobs with specific challenges around working conditions. In the European Union, 42% of the long-term care (LTC) workers work part time, double the rate for the entire workforce (19%). Many do so because they cannot find full-time work (30% in nonresidential LTC and 20% in residential LTC). New forms of employment, such as casual work and zero-hours contracts, are common in some countries, contributing to job insecurity in the sector. Workers under this type of contract typically have less access to training, do not always have benefits such as paid annual leave, and have less access to social protection (OECD 2020b).

Four in five (81%) formal LTC workers are female, and migrants and mobile workers form an important part of the LTC workforce. The proportion of workers aged 50 years or older is higher than in other sectors and has increased faster, from 28% in 2009 to 38% in 2019.

The LTC sector suffers from high levels of absenteeism owing to sickness. More than 60% of LTC workers report being exposed to physical risk factors at work, and 46% of LTC workers are exposed to mental well-being risk factors, which generate high psychological stress (OECD 2020b). LTC workers often report that they do not believe they will be able to keep working until the age of 60 (Eurofound 2020b).

Work environment factors are highly correlated with workers' health and well-being, and good work organization is essential to obtain proper effect of health promotion in a workplace. Alas, the possibilities to introduce effective WHP in the context of a work setting with PSR are limited, as the major components – decent working environment and worker participation – are lacking. The paradox is that WHP should in particular reach and support these workers, yet the implementation of interventions would not result in sustainable change as the working environment is detrimental to health. This highlights the importance of adopting the comprehensive WHP approach that involves the improvement of work organization and working environment, as well as enabling healthy choices, and encouraging personal development.

Overview of Legislation and Policies on Work-Related Psychosocial Risks

It is evident that psychosocial working environment impacts workers' health. Therefore, the fragmented legal and policy landscape on prevention of work-related psychosocial risks is a cause for concern. The EU Framework Directive 89/391/

EEC Safety and Health of Workers at Work has a broad scope and covers workers' health and safety in all aspects of work. In addition, there are single Directives that set out the principles and instruments of the Framework Directive with regards to specific hazards at work (e.g., exposure to dangerous substances), single tasks (e.g., manual handling of loads), and different workplaces of elevated risk (e.g., temporary work sites). It also considers specific groups of workers, such as pregnant women and breastfeeding mothers. But there is no direct reference to PSR within the framework (Brück et al. 2021; Cefaliello 2021).

Cefaliello's (2022) comparison of the various ways the EU Member States address PSR at work displays heterogeneity. The legal systems of 15 out of the 26 examined EU countries refer to workers' psychological or mental health (Fig. 3) and 20 of countries have legal provisions on preventing PSR factors (Fig. 4). Fourteen countries make explicit reference to work-related stress and 17 countries to workplace bullying in their laws (Figs. 5 and 6).

Verra et al. (2019) report that overall, 73.1% of EU establishments take preventive measures against direct physical harm, in comparison to 35.4% that take measures to prevent psychosocial risks. Psychosocial risks are often addressed in national policy but not implemented by institutions, and current risk assessment methods are outdated and often lack psychosocial indicators.

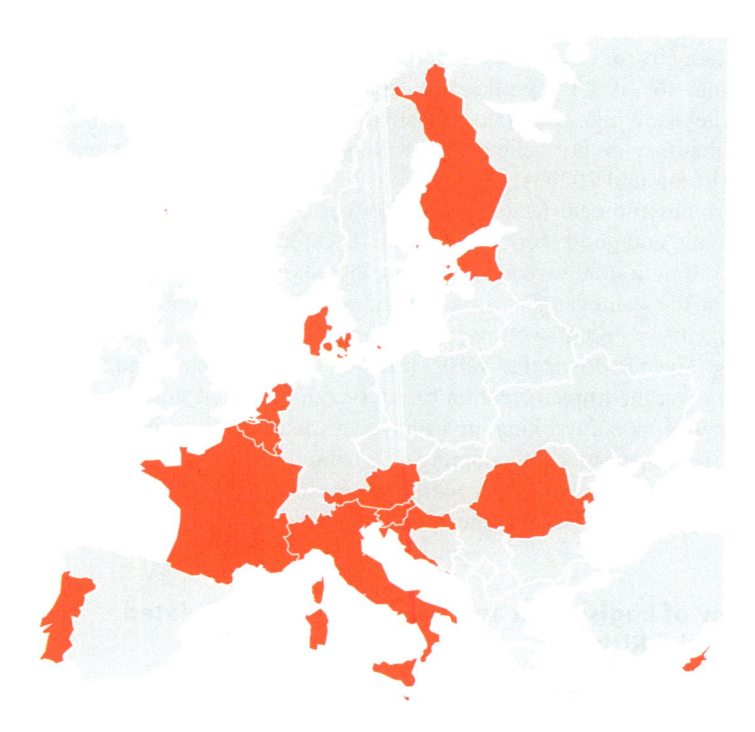

Fig. 3 Legal provisions with mentions of psychological or mental health (Cefaliello 2022). (With permission from the European Trade Union Institute)

Fig. 4 Legal provisions addressing psychosocial risk factors (Cefaliello 2022). (With permission from the European Trade Union Institute)

The implementation of two non-legally binding framework agreements adopted by the European social partners on work-related stress (2004) and bullying and violence at work (2007) has been inconsistent among the Member States. The number of workplaces with action plans to prevent stress varies considerably between countries, from 71.3% in Sweden to 9.3% in Czechia. The EU-27 average is 34.6% (Fig. 7). EU average of workplaces with no procedures in place to deal with bullying or harassment is 53.7%, varying between 89.3% in Hungary and 4.9% in Ireland (Fig. 8).

The uneven legislative provisions of PSR prevention across the Member States is relevant for the implementation and effectiveness of WHP interventions. Data on WHP interventions show a continuing focus on individual-level interventions that target physical health, while system approach with multimodal interventions that address environmental factors, such as work-related psychosocial risks, remain scarce or outside the remit or WHP practitioners.

Comprehensive WHP acknowledges the importance of addressing individual, organizational, and broader health determinants to initiate and support sustainable health results. WHP interventions should improve working conditions by changing the design, organization, and management of work, and research has demonstrated that organizational interventions to increase decision latitude, reduce work intensity,

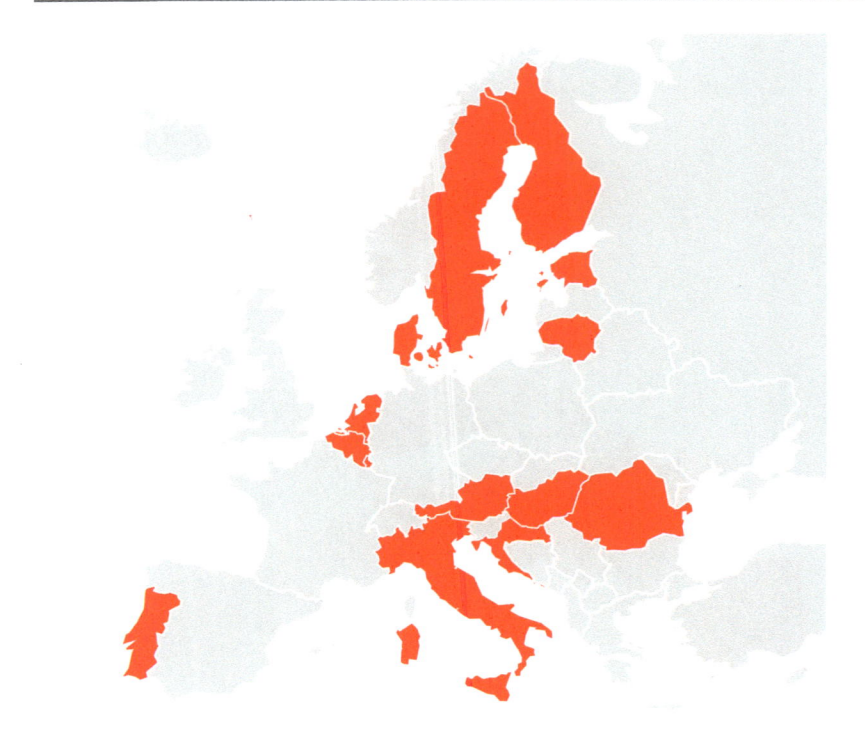

Fig. 5 Legal provisions addressing work-related stress (Cefaliello 2022). (With permission from the European Trade Union Institute)

and support teams, contribute to workers' improved well-being, psychological health, and reduced sickness absence (Sorensen et al. 2021). The issue is not the approach, but the challenges lie in the implementation that can exclude those workers who would most benefit from WHP:

– There is no point in implementing a WHP programme without also offering a safe and healthy working environment. WHP is based on a healthy culture first of all requiring proper risk management.
– Workplace health promotion goes beyond legal requirements. It's based on voluntary action on both sides.
– WHP only can only be successful if it is integrated as a permanent component in all organisational processes. (European Agency for Safety and Health at Work 2010)

Conclusions

Life course perspective into health inequalities highlights that they are the result of the accumulation of social, economic, and psychological advantages and disadvantages over time. Health trajectories are shaped through exposure to social determinants of health, including working and employment conditions, and it is

Fig. 6 Legal provisions addressing workplace bullying (Cefaliello 2022). (With permission from the European Trade Union Institute)

within this context that the workplace health promotion (WHP) holds its promises and faces its trials.

The reviewed research shows no consistent evidence that single, individual-level health interventions would be effective, but WHP should include organizational-level factors as well as adopt a participatory approach. Downstream solutions such as health behavior interventions and upstream solutions that address the sources of PSR factors must be developed in parallel. In the ethos of healthy workplaces, prevention of risk factors should come first, and downstream interventions can only then follow.

Evidence shows that there are several challenges to effective WHP that operate at different levels. There is no health promotion program that fits the workforce of an entire company and evaluating health promotion is challenging. Individual-level interventions continue to reign, yet do not show sustainable positive results. Interventions that address the mental health and well-being of workers should be further

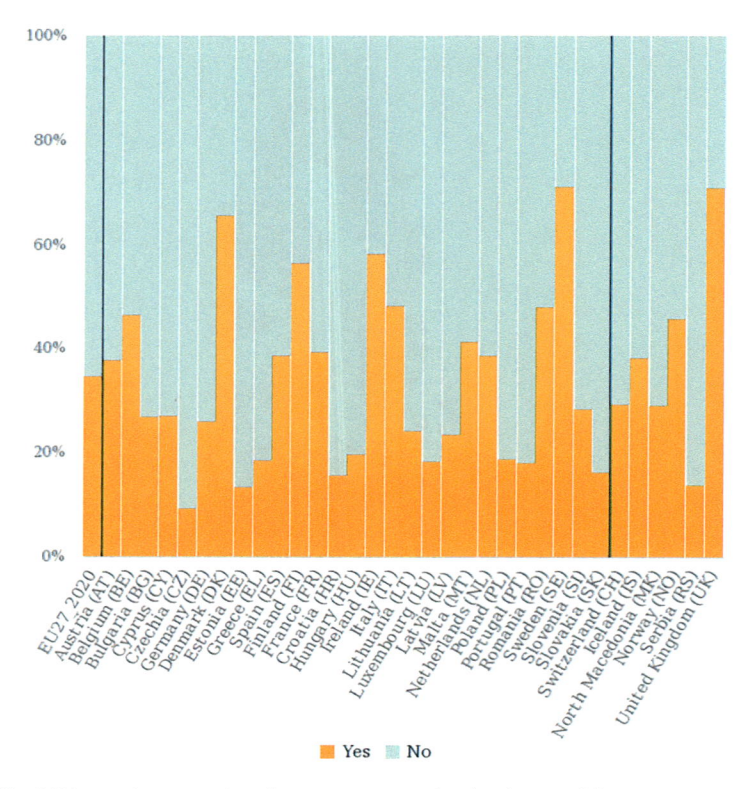

Fig. 7 Establishment has an action plan to prevent work-related stress (%)

developed to address the working environment, including PSR, not only the individual worker. Benefits from WHP on mental health rely on well-designed, multi-component programs that are sustained via an embedded health-promoting workplace culture (Jarman et al. 2016). According to LaMontagne et al. (2014), to realize the greatest population mental health benefits, workplace mental health interventions need to comprehensively (1) protect mental health by reducing work-related risk factors for mental health problems; (2) promote mental health by developing the positive aspects of work as well as worker strengths and positive capacities; and (3) address mental health problems among working people regardless of cause.

Prevention of early exit from the labor market due to poor health is a key policy concern in Europe. WHP should have a prominent role in this context, yet the evidence on the effectiveness to date is mixed. What is apparent is that the same concerns apply to interventions for older workers than other age groups – work organization and working environment are important. In addition, age discrimination and stereotypes should be tackled as part of a comprehensive WHP strategy.

Contextual factors matter, and the increasing prevalence of precarious employment with the related poor working and employment conditions is a major challenge

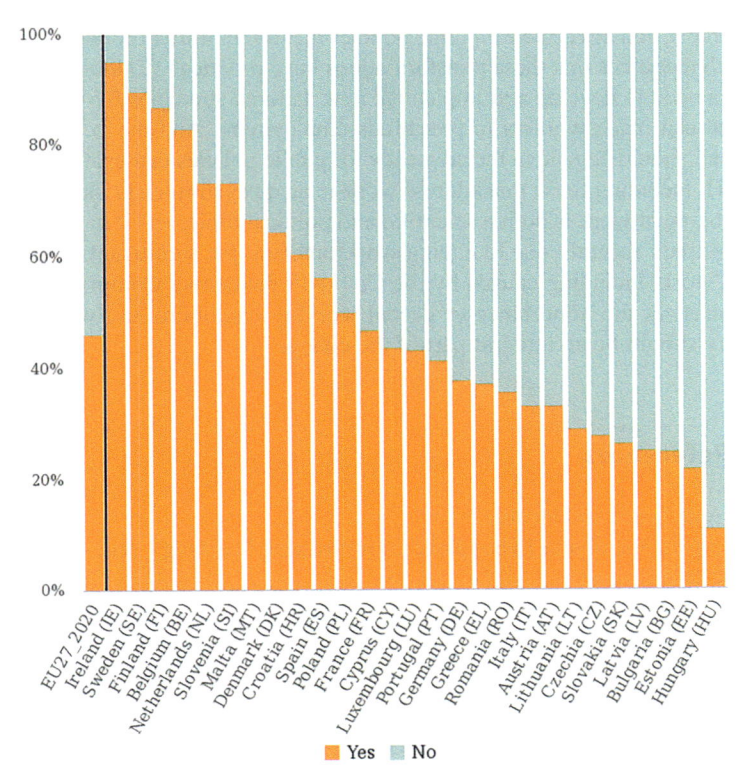

Fig. 8 Establishment has procedures in place to deal with bullying or harassment. (Source: EU-OSHA ESENER Survey 2019)

for WHP. Working environment with PSR factors impacts workers' health and creates limits to WHP. And even within a decent work environment, WHP can drive health inequalities due to the selection of participants. A key issue in WHP is equity – relative health inequalities between groups of workers can increase due to poor working conditions, and WHP should not contribute to this trend but to mitigate it. With the words of Robroek et al. (2021): "*workplace health promotion programs thus far show marginal gains, as the effectiveness and implementation of traditional universal preventative workplace health promotion interventions are still disappointing. A drastic turnaround in occupational health research would be needed for us to have a bright future ahead with better tailoring and delivering interventions to the needs of the target group, in particular for workers with low socioeconomic positions.*"

Precarious employment presents a deeper and more structural determinant of health than what health promoters have traditionally considered (Caldbick et al. 2014). But the challenges posed on WHP can also be considered as prospects for further development of WHP. Workplace health promotion will have to go beyond enabling healthier lifestyle choices, engage critically in the structural transformations of global labor markets, and advocate for public policies that might buffer the social, economic, and health inequities that these transformations have produced (Caldbick et al. 2014). There is a need to develop and implement new, tailored strategies for comprehensive WHP that can reach workers in precarious employment. And the health promotion community should engage in the advocacy for public policies that enable comprehensive WPH, including those that address work-related psychosocial risk factors (PSR).

Well-being at work is both a scientific and political topic, and it has become even more important recently due to ageing workforce and the significant changes in the world of work, including caused by the Covid-19 pandemic. Comprehensive WHP that emphasizes the importance of decent working conditions and workers' health and safety should be an integral part of the change.

Cross-References

▶ Precarious Work and Health
▶ The Role of Social and Labor Policies in Shaping Working Conditions Throughout the Life Course

References

Balk-Møller NC, Larsen TM, Holm L (2017) Experiences from a web- and app-based workplace health promotion intervention among employees in the social and health care sector based on use-data and qualitative interviews. J Med Internet Res 19(10):e350. https://doi.org/10.2196/jmir.7278

Benach J, Vives A, Amable M, Vanroelen C, Tarafa G, Muntaner C (2014) Precarious employment: understanding an emerging social determinant of health. Annu Rev Public Health 35(1):229–253. https://www.annualreviews.org/doi/full/10.1146/annurev-publhealth-032013-182500

Boscher C, Raiber L, Fischer F, Winter MH (2020) Einsatz und Erfolg gesundheitsbezogener Maßnahmen zur Personalbindung in der Pflege: Ergebnisse einer schriftlichen Befragung von Führungskräften aus der Region Bodensee-Oberschwaben [German; The perceived impact of workplace health promotion measures on employee retention in the nursing sector: results of a survey of human resources and management in Southern Germany]. Gesundheitswesen 83(8–9):611–618. https://doi.org/10.1055/a-1173-9555

Brück C, Schmitz-Felten E, Kuhl K (2021) General principles of EU OSH legislation. OSH Wiki. Available at: https://oshwiki.eu/wiki/General_principles_of_EU_OSH_legislation. Accessed 22 Aug 2022

Caldbick S et al (2014) Globalization and the rise of precarious employment: the new frontier for workplace health promotion. Glob Health Promot 21(2):23–31. https://doi.org/10.1177/1757975913514781

Cefaliello A (2021) A legislative patchwork on psychosocial risks in the European Union. In: Contouris N, Jagodzinski R, Theodoropoulou S (eds) Benchmarking working Europe: unequal Europe. European Trade Union Institute (ETUI), Brussels, pp 142–148. Available at: https://www.etui.org/publications/benchmarking-working-europe-2021. Accessed 14 Feb 2022

Cefaliello A (2022, June – forthcoming) National law, collective agreements and jurisprudence concerning work-related psychosocial risks in the European Union. ETUI working paper. ETUI, Brussels

Chiou ST, Chiang JH, Huang N et al (2014) Health behaviors and participation in health promotion activities among hospital staff: which occupational group performs better? BMC Health Serv Res 14:474. https://doi.org/10.1186/1472-6963-14-474

Coenen P, Robroek SJW, van der Beek AJ, Boot CRL, van Lenthe FJ, Burdorf A, Oude Hengel KM (2020) Socioeconomic inequalities in effectiveness of and compliance to workplace health promotion programs: an individual participant data (IPD) meta-analysis. Int J Behav Nutr Phys Act 17(1):112. https://doi.org/10.1186/s12966-020-01002-w

EU-OSHA. Psychosocial risks and stress at work website. https://osha.europa.eu/en/themes/psychosocial-risks-and-stress. Accessed 14 Feb 2022

Eurofound (2018) Precarious work. Available at: https://www.eurofound.europa.eu/observatories/eurwork/industrial-relations-dictionary/precarious-work. Accessed 11 Feb 2022

Eurofound (2020a) Work organisation. https://www.eurofound.europa.eu/topic/work-organisation

Eurofound (2020b) Long-term care workforce: employment and working conditions. Publications Office of the European Union, Luxembourg. Available at: https://www.eurofound.europa.eu/sites/default/files/ef_publication/field_ef_document/ef20028en.pdf. Accessed 14 Feb 2022

EuroHealthNet Magazine (2021) Workplace health promotion for employees with disabilities: introducing "health inclusive". EuroHealthNet Magazine, 18th Edition. https://eurohealthnet-magazine.eu/workplace-health-promotion-for-employees-with-disabilities-introducing-health-inculsive/

European Agency for Safety and Health and Safety at Work (EU-OSHA) (2013) European opinion poll on occupational safety and health, May 2013. Available at: https://osha.europa.eu/en/facts-and-figures/european-opinion-polls-safety-and-health-work. Accessed 14 Feb 2022

European Agency for Safety and Health at Work (EU-OSHA) (2010) Workplace health promotion for employers. "Factsheet" 93. https://osha.europa.eu/en/publications/factsheet-93-workplace-health-promotion-employers

European Agency for Safety and Health at Work (EU-OSHA) (2019) ESENER II summary. Available at: https://osha.europa.eu/sites/default/files/publications/documents/esener-ii-summary-en.PDF. Accessed 11 Feb 2022

European Commission memo, Facts and figures: Healthy Workplaces Campaign for All Ages 2016-17, 15 April 2016. https://ec.europa.eu/commission/presscorner/detail/en/MEMO_16_1421. Accessed 5 May 2023

European Network for Workplace Health Promotion. Good practices in workplace health promotion website. https://www.enwhp.org/?i=portal.en.good-practices. Accessed 11 Feb 2022

Eurostat (2021) Duration of working life – statistics. Available at: https://ec.europa.eu/eurostat/statistics-explained/index.php?title=Duration_of_working_life_-_statistics. Accessed 11 Feb 2022

Fehér J, Reich M (2020) Perceived impacts of company Workplace Health Promotion on employment relationship. Journal of Eastern European and Central Asian Research (JEECAR), 7(3):238–254. https://doi.org/10.15549/jeecar.v7i3.357

Freak-Poli R, Cumpston M, Albarqouni L, Clemes SA, Peeters A (2020) Workplace pedometer interventions for increasing physical activity. Cochrane Database Syst Rev 7(7):CD009209. https://doi.org/10.1002/14651858

Gorgenyi-Hegyes E, Nathan RJ, Fekete-Farkas M (2021) Workplace health promotion, employee wellbeing and loyalty during Covid-19 pandemic – large scale empirical evidence from Hungary. Economies 9(2):55. https://doi.org/10.3390/economies9020055

Grimani A, Aboagye E, Kwak L (2019) The effectiveness of workplace nutrition and physical activity interventions in improving productivity, work performance and workability: a systematic review. BMC Public Health 19:1676. https://doi.org/10.1186/s12889-019-8033-1

Guazzi M, Faggiano P, Mureddu GF, Faden G, Niebauer J, Temporelli PL (2014) Worksite health and wellness in the European Union. Prog Cardiovasc Dis 56(5):508–514. https://doi.org/10.1016/j.pcad.2013.11.003

Gunn V, Håkansta C, Vignola E et al (2021) Initiatives addressing precarious employment and its effects on workers' health and well-being: a protocol for a systematic review. Syst Rev 10:195. https://doi.org/10.1186/s13643-021-01728-z

Huang SL, Li RH, Huang FY, Tang FC (2015) The potential for mindfulness-based intervention in workplace mental health promotion: results of a randomized controlled trial. PLoS One 10(9): e0138089. https://doi.org/10.1371/journal.pone.0138089

International Labour Organization (2012) The SOLVE training package: Integrating health promotion into workplace OSH policies. https://www.ilo.org/safework/info/instr/WCMS_178438/lang--en/index.htm

International Social Security Association (ISSA) website. ISSA guidelines: workplace health promotion. https://ww1.issa.int/guidelines/whp/174864

Jarman L, Martin A, Venn A et al (2016) Does workplace health promotion contribute to job stress reduction? Three-year findings from Partnering Healthy@Work. BMC Public Health 15:1293. https://doi.org/10.1186/s12889-015-2625-1

Jørgensen MB, Villadsen E, Burr H et al (2016) Does employee participation in workplace health promotion depend on the working environment? A cross-sectional study of Danish workers. BMJ Open 6:e010516. https://doi.org/10.1136/bmjopen-2015-010516

Julià M, Vanroelen C, Bosmans K, Van Aerden K, Benach J (2017) Precarious employment and quality of employment in relation to health and well-being in Europe. Int J Health Serv 47(3): 389–409. https://doi.org/10.1177/0020731417707491

Koinig I, Diehl S (2021) Healthy leadership and workplace health promotion as a pre-requisite for organizational health. Int J Environ Res Public Health 18(17):9260. https://doi.org/10.3390/ijerph18179260

Kunzler AM, Helmreich I, Chmitorz A, König J, Binder H, Wessa M, Lieb K (2020) Psychological interventions to foster resilience in healthcare professionals. Cochrane Database Syst Rev 7. https://doi.org/10.1002/14651858.CD012527

LaMontagne AD, Martin A, Page KM et al (2014) Workplace mental health: developing an integrated intervention approach. BMC Psychiatry 14:131. https://doi.org/10.1186/1471-244X-14-131

Ljungblad C, Granström F, Dellve L, Åkerlind I (2014) Workplace health promotion and working conditions as determinants of employee health. Int J Workplace Health Manag 7(2):89–104. https://doi.org/10.1108/IJWHM-02-2013-0003

Lutz N, Taeymans J, Ballmer C, Verhaeghe N, Clarys P, Deliens T (2019) Cost-effectiveness and cost-benefit of worksite health promotion programs in Europe: a systematic review. Eur J Public Health 29(3):540–546. https://doi.org/10.1093/eurpub/cky269

Maes L, Van Cauwenberghe E, Van Lippevelde W, Spittaels H, De Pauw E, Oppert J-M, Van Lenthe FJ, Brug J, De Bourdeaudhuij I (2012) Effectiveness of workplace interventions in Europe promoting healthy eating: a systematic review. Eur J Public Health 22(5):677–683. https://doi.org/10.1093/eurpub/ckr098

Magnavita N (2018) Obstacles and future prospects: considerations on health promotion activities for older workers in Europe. Int J Environ Res Public Health 15(6):1096. https://doi.org/10.3390/ijerph15061096

Martin A, Karanika-Murray M, Biron C, Sanderson K (2016) The psychosocial work environment, employee mental health and organizational interventions: improving research and practice by taking a multilevel approach. Stress Health 32:201–215. https://doi.org/10.1002/smi.2593

McNamara CL, Toch-Marquardt M, Albani V, Eikemo TA, Bambra C (2021) The contribution of employment and working conditions to occupational inequalities in non-communicable diseases in Europe. Eur J Public Health 31(1):181–185. https://doi.org/10.1093/eurpub/ckaa175

Méndez Rivero F, Padrosa E, Utzet M, Benach J, Julià M (2021) Precarious employment, psychosocial risk factors and poor mental health: a cross-sectional mediation analysis. Saf Sci 143. https://doi.org/10.1016/j.ssci.2021.105439

Mikkelsen B, Williams J, Rakovac I, Wickramasinghe K, Hennis A, Shin H-R, Farmer M, Weber M, Berdzuli N, Borges C, Huber M, Breda J (2019) Life course approach to prevention and control of non-communicable diseases. BMJ 364:l257. https://doi.org/10.1136/bmj.l257

Mittelmark MB (2014) Unintended effects in settings-based health promotion. Scand J Public Health 42(15 Suppl):17–24. https://doi.org/10.1177/1403494814545108

Niedhammer I, Bourgkard E, Chau N, Lorhandicap Study Group (2011) Occupational and behavioural factors in the explanation of social inequalities in premature and total mortality: a 12.5-year follow-up in the Lorhandicap study. Eur J Epidemiol 26:1–12. https://doi.org/10.1007/s10654-010-9506-9

Niedhammer I, Bertrais S, Witt K (2021) Psychosocial work exposures and health outcomes: a meta-review of 72 literature reviews with meta-analysis. Scand J Work Environ Health 47(7):489–508. https://doi.org/10.5271/sjweh.3968

Nielsen RA, Midtsundstad TI (2021) Do workplace health-promotion interventions targeting employees with poor health reduce sick-leave probability and disability rates? Scand J Public Health 49(2):219–227. https://doi.org/10.1177/1403494820946543

Oakman J, Neupane S, Proper KI, Kinsman N, Nygård CH (2018) Workplace interventions to improve work ability: a systematic review and meta-analysis of their effectiveness. Scand J Work Environ Health 44(2):134–146

OECD (2020a) Promoting an age-inclusive workforce: living, learning and earning longer. OECD Publishing, Paris. https://doi.org/10.1787/59752153-en

OECD (2020b) Who cares? Attracting and retaining care workers for the elderly. OECD health policy studies. Available at: https://doi.org/10.1787/92c0ef68-en. Accessed 14 Feb 2022

OSH Wiki (2023) National OSH Strategy – Sweden. https://oshwiki.osha.europa.eu/en/themes/national-osh-strategy-sweden

Pieper C, Schröer S, Eilerts AL (2019) Evidence of workplace interventions – a systematic review of systematic reviews. Int J Environ Res Public Health 16(19):3553. https://doi.org/10.3390/ijerph16193553

Poscia A, Moscato U, La Milia DI, Milovanovic S, Stojanovic J, Borghini A, Collamati A, Ricciardi W, Magnavita N (2016) Workplace health promotion for older workers: a systematic literature review. BMC Health Serv Res 16(Suppl 5):329. https://doi.org/10.1186/s12913-016-1518-z

Proper KI, van Oostrom SH (2019) The effectiveness of workplace health promotion interventions on physical and mental health outcomes – a systematic review of reviews. Scand J Work Environ Health 45(6):546–559. https://doi.org/10.5271/sjweh.3833

Quinlan M (2015) The effects of non-standard forms of employment on worker health and safety. Conditions of work and employment series no. 67. International Labour Organization, Inclusive Labour Markets, Labour Relations and Working Conditions Branch. ILO, Geneva. Available at: https://www.ilo.org/wcmsp5/groups/public/%2D%2D-ed_protect/%2D%2D-protrav/%2D%2D-travail/documents/publication/wcms_443266.pdf. Accessed 14 Feb 2022

Robertson HD, Elliott AM, Burton C, Iversen L, Murchie P, Porteous T, Matheson C (2016) Resilience of primary healthcare professionals: a systematic review. Br J Gen Pract 66(647):e423–e433. https://doi.org/10.3399/bjgp16X685261

Robroek SJW, Oude Hengel KM, van der Beek AJ, Boot CRL, van Lenthe FJ, Burdorf A, Coenen P (2020) Socio-economic inequalities in the effectiveness of workplace health promotion programmes on body mass index: an individual participant data meta-analysis. Obes Rev 21(11):e13101. https://doi.org/10.1111/obr.13101

Robroek SJ, Coenen P, Oude Hengel KM (2021) Decades of workplace health promotion research: marginal gains or a bright future ahead. Scand J Work Environ Health 47(8):561–564. https://doi.org/10.5271/sjweh.3995

Rojatz D, Merchant A, Nitsch M (2017) Factors influencing workplace health promotion intervention: a qualitative systematic review. Health Promot Int 32(5):831–839. https://doi.org/10.1093/heapro/daw015

Sangachin MG, Cavuoto LA (2018) Interactive effects of work psychosocial factors on participation in workplace wellness programs. J Workplace Behav Health 33(1):24–42. https://doi.org/10.1080/15555240.2017.1408415

Sippli K, Schmalzried P, Rieger MA et al (2021) Challenges arising for older workers from participating in a workplace intervention addressing work ability: a qualitative study from

Germany. Int Arch Occup Environ Health 94:919–933. https://doi.org/10.1007/s00420-020-01639-x

Sorensen G, Peters SE, Nielsen K et al (2021) Implementation of an organizational intervention to improve low-wage food service workers' safety, health and wellbeing: findings from the Workplace Organizational Health Study. BMC Public Health 21:1869. https://doi.org/10.1186/s12889-021-11937-9

Stiehl E, Shivaprakash N, Thatcher E et al (2018) Worksite health promotion for low-wage workers: a scoping literature review. Am J Health Promot 32(2):359–373. https://doi.org/10.1177/0890117117728607

Tsiga E, Panagopoulou E, Niakas D (2015) Health promotion across occupational groups: one size does not fit all. Occup Med 65(7):552–557. https://doi.org/10.1093/occmed/kqv097

Van de Ven D, Robroek SJW, Burdorf A (2020) Are workplace health promotion programmes effective for all socioeconomic groups? A systematic review. Occup Environ Med 77:589–596. https://doi.org/10.1136/oemed-2019-106311

van der Put AC, Mandemakers JJ, de Wit JBF, van der Lippe T (2020) Worksite health promotion and social inequalities in health. SSM Popul Health 10. https://doi.org/10.1016/j.ssmph.2020.100543

van Heijster H, Boot CRL, Robroek SJW, Oude Hengel K, van Berkel J, de Vet E, Coenen P (2021) The effectiveness of workplace health promotion programs on self-perceived health of employees with a low socioeconomic position: an individual participant data meta-analysis. SSM Popul Health 26(13):100743. https://doi.org/10.1016/j.ssmph.2021.100743

Verra SE, Benzerga A, Jiao B, Ruggeri K (2019) Health promotion at work: a comparison of policy and practice across Europe. Saf Health Work 10(1):21–29. https://doi.org/10.1016/j.shaw.2018.07.003

Wolfenden L, Goldman S, Stacey FG, Grady A, Kingsland M, Williams CM, Wiggers J, Milat A, Rissel C, Bauman A, Farrell MM, Légaré F, Ben Charif A, Zomahoun HTV, Hodder RK, Jones J, Booth D, Parmenter B, Regan T, Yoong SL (2018) Strategies to improve the implementation of workplace-based policies or practices targeting tobacco, alcohol, diet, physical activity and obesity. Cochrane Database Syst Rev 11(11):CD012439. https://doi.org/10.1002/14651858.CD012439.pub2. Accessed 14 Feb 2022

World Health Organization (1986) The Ottawa Charter for health promotion. In World Health Organisation Regional Office for Europe (2017) Strengthening resilience: a priority shared by health 2020 and the sustainable development goals, Copenhagen. Available at: https://www.euro.who.int/__data/assets/pdf_file/0005/351284/resilience-report-20171004-h1635.pdf. Accessed 11 Feb 2022

World Health Organization, Burton J (2010) WHO healthy workplace framework and model: background and supporting literature and practices. World Health Organization. https://apps.who.int/iris/handle/10665/113144

Wynne R (1997) What makes workplace health promotion work? Findings from the European Foundation's Research Program. Paper presented to The European Workplace Health Promotion Network Meeting, Luxembourg, Nov 1997

Falling Sick While Working: An Overview of the EU-Level Policy Framework on Returning to Work Following Chronic Disease(s)

27

Mehtap Akgüç

Contents

Introduction	494
A Snapshot of Demographic and Health Trends in Europe	495
Ageing Population	496
Prevalence of Disabilities and Chronic Diseases	497
Implications of Chronic Health Conditions for Labor Markets	499
The EU-Level Approach to the Return to Work	500
The EU Occupational Health and Safety Framework	500
Disability and Social Inclusion Policies	502
Other Relevant EU-Level Initiatives	504
The Way Ahead on the Return to Work: Further Reflections	505
Cross-References	508
References	508

Abstract

Demographic transitions together with advancements in healthcare have resulted in ageing and longevity of individuals during the life course in many developed countries. However, increased life expectancy has also come along with increased working lives during which the prevalence of disability and sickness – particularly among the elderly, but not only – has also increased. Coupled with ageing, shrinking workforce, and soaring sickness or disability benefits, return to work following long-term illness is, therefore, emerging as an important issue in the occupational health and safety over the life course of individuals. Against this background, this chapter initially provides a lay of the land overviewing the empirical evidence on the nexus of demographic and health challenges in the workplace over the life course in the

---

M. Akgüç (✉)
European Trade Union Institute, Brussels, Belgium

IZA (Institute of Labor Economics), Bonn, Germany
e-mail: makguc@etui.org

© Springer Nature Switzerland AG 2023
M. Wahrendorf et al. (eds.), *Handbook of Life Course Occupational Health*, Handbook Series in Occupational Health Sciences, https://doi.org/10.1007/978-3-031-30492-7_17

EU. Using academic and policy documents, it then provides insights on existing relevant EU-level occupational health and safety framework jointly with related social and labor policies in addressing return to work and work reintegration (or rehabilitation) of individuals experiencing long-term health conditions. While there are important EU-level relevant policy initiatives in the context of return to work, what is often missing is either a comprehensive framework or a tailored approach to the work reintegration following chronic diseases during the occupational life course. Therefore, the chapter critically reviews the potentials as well as shortcomings of the recent policy actions, including the Strategic EU Health and Safety Framework 2021–2027, among others, in dealing with return to work and reintegration of workers. Finally, the chapter reflects on possible policy recommendations on return to work considering different layers of action by various actors ranging from the EU- and national-level stakeholders to companies and workers themselves. It argues that while the Covid-19 pandemic could be seen as a lever to facilitate the return to work, it also has the potential to complicate the situation for individuals with existing chronic health conditions.

Keywords

Return to work · Work reintegration · Chronic diseases · Disability · Ageing · EU-level occupational health and safety policies

Introduction

Demographic transitions together with advancements in healthcare have resulted in ageing and longevity of individuals in many developed countries. While these changes have led to increased life expectancy and quality in some respects, they also pose strains on the sustainability of healthcare and welfare systems faced with soaring disability and sickness benefits or pension payments. On the one hand, this is partly related to ageing as well as increasing incidence of poorer health conditions among the elderly. On the other hand, it is also related – in addition to other contextual and genetic factors – to longer working lives, in which people tend to fall sick more often as they get older while working to earn a living during the occupational life course. Together with the increasing population of elderly, soaring public health expenditures, and the current public health context of the Covid-19 pandemic, the return to work following long-term or chronic illness is, therefore, emerging as an important issue in the health and safety framework over the occupational life course of individuals.

Moreover, the aforementioned societal and public health challenges call for deeper understanding of the issues as well as a policy action to ensure inclusive and prosperous societies and economies. Some of these policy actions include measures to extend working lives by increasing the retirement age while ensuring active and healthy ageing as well as promoting the return to work, reintegration, and retention of individuals who have been absent from work due to long-lasting chronic health conditions. While the geographical focus of the chapter is on Europe, the issues at hand are increasingly observed in many other places as well.

According to the Centers for Disease Control and Prevention (CDC), chronic diseases are "conditions that last one year or more and require ongoing medical attention or limit activities of daily living or both (the dedicated page on chronic diseases of the CDC contains further detail: https://www.cdc.gov/chronicdisease/about/index.htm#:~: text=Chronic%20diseases%20are%20defined%20broadly,disability%20in%20the% 20United%20States)." One of the key features of chronic diseases is their non-communicable characteristic. Examples to chronic diseases include diabetes (metabolic disease characterized by elevated levels of blood sugar), cancer (abnormal cell growing out of control in one or more organs), cardiovascular diseases (such as heart attacks and stroke), chronic respiratory diseases (such as asthma and chronic obstructive pulmonary disease), musculoskeletal disorders (such as lower back pain or neck pain), and mental illnesses (such as depression). As the key subject of this chapter, the return to work could be defined as "a concept encompassing all procedures and initiatives intended to facilitate the workplace integration of persons who experience a reduction in work capacity or capability, whether this is due to invalidity, illness or ageing" (ISSA 2013). In a similar vein, rehabilitation is defined by the World Health Organization (WHO) as the process of "recovering optimal physical, sensory, intellectual, psychological and social functional levels" which jointly includes medical, social, and vocational aspects (EU-OSHA 2016). As Akgüç et al. (2019) has put it, the return to work is "a complex process, unfolding in time, with many stakeholders and factors shaping it."

Against this background, this chapter has several objectives looking at the specific case of the return to work or work reintegration following long-term illness such as chronic diseases during the occupational life course. First, the chapter provides a lay of the land overviewing the empirical evidence on the nexus of demographic and health challenges in the workplace in the European Union (EU) and illustrates the consequences for the labor markets and economy. Secondly, reviewing key academic and policy documents, it provides insights on existing relevant EU-level occupational health and safety framework jointly with related EU-level social and labor policies in addressing the return to work and work reintegration (or rehabilitation) of individuals experiencing long-term health conditions. Thirdly, the chapter then critically reviews the potentials and shortcomings of the overall EU-level policy framework as well as the recent policy actions, including the Strategic EU Health and Safety Framework 2021–2027, among others, in dealing with the return to work and reintegration of workers. Finally, the chapter reflects on the way ahead and proposes some reflections on the return to work considering different layers of action to be taken by various actors ranging from the EU- and national-level stakeholders to company-level practices and workers themselves, as well as a number of other relevant elements to consider in this complex process.

A Snapshot of Demographic and Health Trends in Europe

As a result of various demographic transitions besides others (e.g., green transition or digital transformations), labor markets are facing a number of challenges: on the one hand, workforce is shrinking due to lower birth rates, and this might lead to labor shortages in some regions and sectors as well as a decline in productivity overall due to a decreased talent pool. On the other hand, workforce is getting older with increased prevalence of chronic health conditions over the occupational life course in general, but particularly among elderly, which might impact the capability of older workers as well as the overall functioning of labor markets.

Ageing Population

The recent population projections estimate that at least one-third of the population will be aged 65 or older by 2070, with implied increases for life expectancy (86 for men and 90 for women) in the EU. By 2100, almost all EU countries will have life expectancies between 87 and 90 years (For more details by country and year, see the dedicated Eurostat page on population projections https://ec.europa.eu/eurostat/databrowser/view/PROJ_19NALEXP/default/map?lang=en&category=proj.proj_19n).

Figure 1 displays the projected evolution of population broken down by different age groups for the EU-27. While the overall EU population is expected to decline from 2030 onward, the share of the elderly (aged 65 or above) will increase from its current level of around 20–30% by 2050 as opposed to the share of working age individuals (20–64), which will shrink further in the coming decades making up 52% of the full population by 2050, down from 59% currently.

Another indicator of ageing is the expected number of healthy life years at birth, which has been slightly increasing with the ageing in the EU over the last years. As

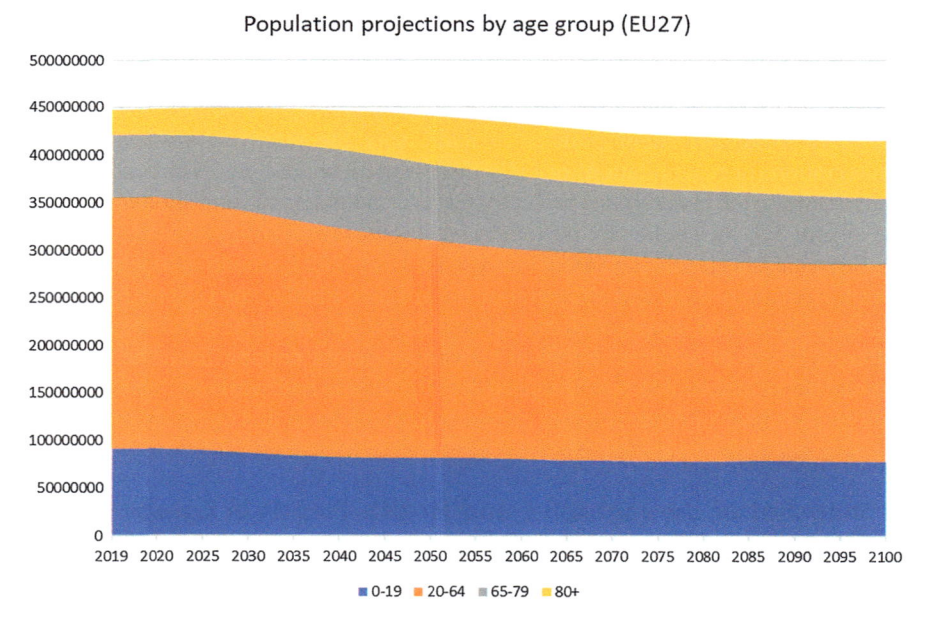

Fig. 1 Population projections by age groups. (Source: Eurostat (proj_19np), 2020)

Healthy life years at birth (EU-27)

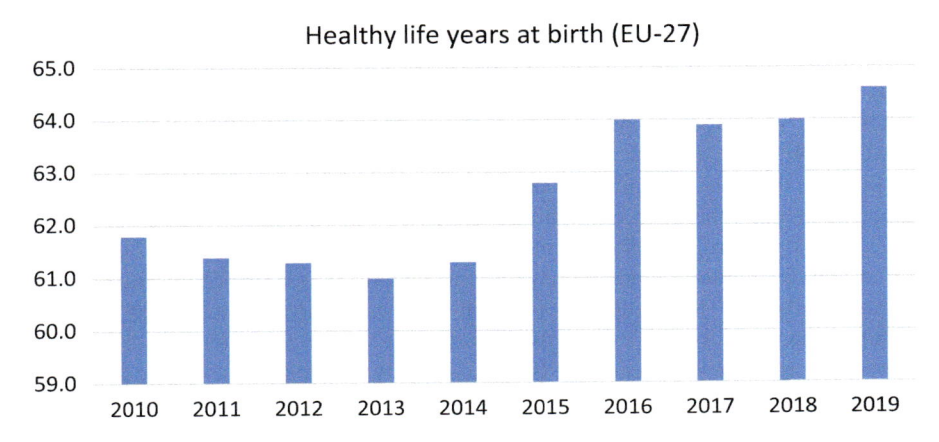

Year	Healthy life years
2010	61.8
2011	61.4
2012	61.3
2013	61.0
2014	61.3
2015	62.8
2016	64.1
2017	63.9
2018	64.1
2019	64.7

Fig. 2 Healthy life years at birth. (Source: Eurostat (hlth_hlye), 2019)

Figure 2 shows, it is about 65 years on average for the EU-27, although there are large variations across countries: it can go up to 73 years in Malta and Sweden compared to 56 years in Estonia and Slovakia or 53 years in Latvia. The crude difference between overall life expectancy and expected healthy life years at birth gives an indication of the lifetime that is spent experiencing health problems or illness, which also seems to vary largely by country.

Meanwhile, fertility rates have been on a declining path in most of the member states, with the EU having an average fertility rate of 1.53 live births per woman in 2019. In this context, most of the EU countries – despite variations across countries – have strictly lower birth rates than the replacement rate of 2.1, which is the fertility rate at which a population exactly replaces itself between the two consecutive generations (without counting migration) (https://ec.europa.eu/eurostat/statistics-explained/index.php?title=Fertility_statistics). Ageing and declining birth rates together not only impact the people and their lifestyles with varying health conditions along the life course or lead to shrinking populations, but they also affect the organization of economic activities immensely as well as sustainability of social security systems, or allocation of public finances more generally.

Prevalence of Disabilities and Chronic Diseases

While the dividing line between having chronic diseases and disability status is often blurred, the two are likely interrelated as the former can be a precursor of the latter (or vice versa). According to recent estimates, about 87 million (nearly one in five) individuals in Europe have some form of disability (http://www.inclusion-europe.eu/european-commission-presents-strategy-for-the-rights-of-persons-with-disabilities-2021-2030/) that can lead to various vulnerabilities in accessing healthcare, education, employment, or social life in general.

The incidence of chronic diseases, which are those of long duration and slow progression with or without a cure, could also cause some form of disability and they tend to increase with age (Eurofound 2019; Akgüç 2021a), as health conditions deteriorate with ageing and increased longevity along the life course. Chronic diseases, among which the most commonly observed ones are cardiovascular and respiratory diseases, musculoskeletal disorders, cancer, diabetes, and mental health issues, constitute the main cause of mortality and (co)morbidity in the EU (Guazzi et al. 2014). According to the recent data from 2020, about 35% of individuals aged 16 or above in Europe report to have a longstanding illness or health problem (for more details, see the dedicated page of Eurostat: https://ec.europa.eu/eurostat/databrowser/view/HLTH_SILC_04/default/table?lang=en&category=hlth.hlth_state.hlth_srcm). While it can be difficult to identify the main cause behind a chronic disease, a multitude of factors such as work environment, genetic predisposition, or other individual factors could be partially or jointly at play (Akgüç 2021a).

Figure 3 displays the prevalence of chronic diseases broken by age group and sex for the EU-27 for 2019. It suggests that prevalence of long-term health problems is positively correlated with the age group. While less than one person in three among the younger individuals (aged between 16 and 34) report to have a chronic condition, over two-thirds of individuals aged 75 or older have long-lasting health problems in the EU-27.

There is also a gender dimension, whereby a striking picture between men and women emerges from Figure 3: women at all age groups are more prone to having chronic health conditions than men. Despite having longer life expectancy than men, various researches point to women often having poorer health (Franklin et al. 2021) and being disproportionately exposed to the incidence of chronic diseases at domestic or professional work due to risks related to biomechanical stress such as repetitive

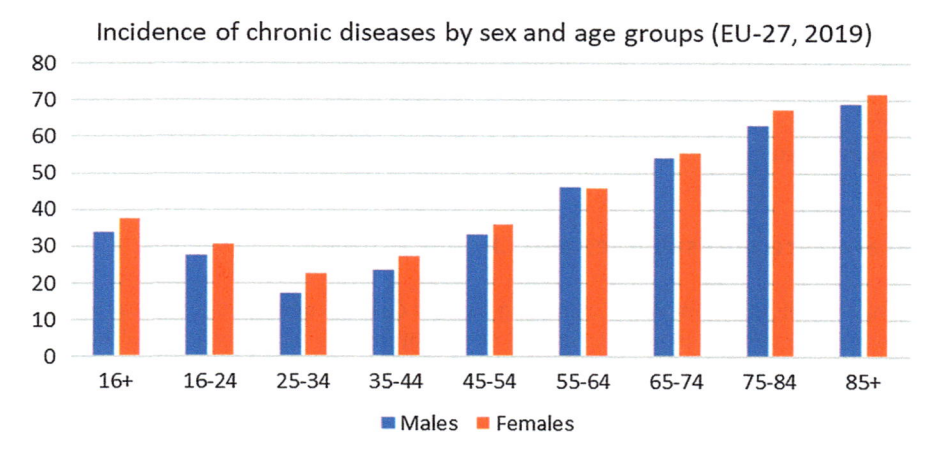

Fig. 3 Prevalence of chronic conditions by sex and age group. (Source: Eurostat (hlth_silc_11), 2019)

work or physical work with little maneuver as well as psychosocial stress (Casse and De Troyer 2021).

Implications of Chronic Health Conditions for Labor Markets

Chronic health problems often imply a significant burden on the health and well-being of the workforce and have considerable implications not only for the individuals themselves, but also for the wider economy and society. In particular, the prevalence of chronic diseases has a number of consequences ranging from the impacts on the experiencing individual's life (and her or his career) to labor markets and the wider economy via the social security and welfare systems responsible of benefits distribution.

First and foremost, chronic disease impacts the individual capacities depending on the type of disease. The disease can lead to chronic pain or physical discomfort and reduced quality of life. Besides, carers of individuals suffering from chronic diseases also see their vulnerabilities and psychosocial risks (e.g., stress and anxiety) go up during the process and can even witness a change in their labor market behavior (e.g., reducing labor supply or dropping out of labor market completely).

From the labor markets perspective, chronic diseases are among the leading causes of absence from work, early retirement, long-term unemployment as well as reduced work capability or disability which might impact productivity over the occupational life course. It can thus have considerable economic consequences for individuals, such as lower pay or rates of labor force participation (Busse et al. 2010) or employment. While there is no specific data identifying the employment gap between individuals with or without chronic diseases, it could be expected to be near the disability employment gap, which has been slightly increasing over the last years and stands between 22% and 25% at the EU level, again with large variations across countries (https://ec.europa.eu/eurostat/databrowser/view/HLTH_DLM200__custom_2121156/default/line?lang=en).

Chronic diseases can also lead to presenteeism at work, which is the situation where a worker is present at work despite continuing chronic conditions causing physical discomfort or pain and which can decrease productivity substantially (Hemp 2004). The issue of presenteeism is less emphasized – perhaps because it is not sufficiently visible and can often go unnoticed – as opposed to absenteeism from work, but both might lead to significant burden in the workplace.

Long-term absences due to illness can also generate organizational complications in the workplace, particularly in small and medium enterprises (SMEs), which are often lacking resources and information to either accommodate the workers with chronic health problems, manage their work rehabilitation process, or replacing the worker with someone else during the absence. More often than not, pending work is redistributed to other colleagues potentially generating negative externality for them.

Finally, the wider implications for the economy can include reduced labor supply and outputs, lower tax revenues, and returns on human capital investments (https://ec.europa.eu/jrc/en/health-knowledge-gateway/societal-impacts/costs). For example, as one of the main causes of work-related death, the direct costs of work-related cancer in terms of healthcare and productivity losses can amount to nearly 4–7 billion euros, while indirect costs can reach nearly 350 billion euros per year (European Commission 2017).

The EU-Level Approach to the Return to Work

Before starting the overview of the existing EU-level policy framework and approaches in the context of the return to work after chronic disease, it is useful to note that since the return to work after a long-term disease is linked to social security and welfare systems as well as specific national social and labor market policies, the EU does not have the competence to intervene directly to design specific return-to-work policies in member states. This subsidiarity principle, nonetheless, the EU can still have a direct or indirect effect in shaping these policies by providing guiding principles, setting minimum standards in occupational health and safety domain, and serving as a platform where member states can exchange good practices (Akgüç and Westhoff 2021). As it will be seen from the analysis in the following, the EU-level approach to the return to work remains fragmented though due the latter's multidisciplinary nature and reflects the diversity of policies and practices in different member states.

The key EU policy areas relevant in the context of the return to work can be largely grouped under (i) occupational health and safety regulations, (ii) social inclusion policies closely tied to labor market integration of disabled individuals, and (iii) other initiatives promoting equal opportunities and work rehabilitation following long-term health conditions. Although not all of these policy frameworks directly address the issue of the return to work following a chronic disease, they contain elements that are relevant and useful in this context. Other common characteristics about the EU-level approach to the return to work are the fragmented nature likely due to the distinction between the EU and national policy competences, the emphasis on soft law measures, and the challenges in transposing EU-level policies to member states for implementation (and enforcement).

The EU Occupational Health and Safety Framework

As one of the key policy competences of the EU, occupational health and safety is one of the most developed aspects of the EU policy on employment and social affairs concerning 164.3 million workers aged 15–64 in the EU (according to Eurostat, using the variable *lfsa_eegan2*, based on the European Labor Force Survey with the following link https://ec.europa.eu/eurostat/databrowser/view/LFSA_EGAN2/default/table?lang=en). In legal terms, the Article 153 of the Treaty of the Functioning of the EU (TFEU) provides the basis of legislation that aims to improve the working environment according to the occupational health and safety framework. From the disability perspective, which might overlap with the extent of the chronic disease as mentioned earlier, the Charter of Fundamental Rights of the EU (https://www.europarl.europa.eu/charter/pdf/text_en.pdf) also states that it "recognises and respects the right of persons with disabilities to benefit from measures designed to ensure their independence, social and occupational integration..." Along these lines, as part of the Lisbon strategy in 2000, member states have acknowledged that the promotion of economic growth and prosperity is closely linked to guaranteeing quality and productivity at work, and achieving the latter is closely tied to improving workplace conditions and complying with the occupational health and safety standards set both at the EU and national levels. Noncompliance with key occupational safety and health requirements usually comes with increased costs due to occupational accidents, illness, or disability. These costs are, in turn, born not only by the workers and enterprises but also have implications for the sustainability of social security systems and public finances.

In this domain, the EU has taken a number of legislative and nonlegislative actions over the last three decades and these actions have been transposed to member states in various forms in order to achieve minimum standards in occupational health and safety in the EU. In particular, the EU has adopted the Framework Directive 89/391/EEC followed by 23 specific directives introducing a number of measures to encourage improvements in the health and safety of workers at work, which altogether constitute the fundamentals of the EU's occupational health and safety legislation (the full list of the EU directives on occupational health and safety can be found in Table 1–1 in European Commission (2015)). This legislative framework aims to provide generalized provisions to improve health and safety in the workplace and also pay attention to sector- and hazard-specific considerations to ensure protective working environments in the EU.

One of the key features of the EU's occupational health and safety framework is that the focus of the measures is on prevention of occupational accidents and diseases (Akgüç and Westhoff 2021). That also implies that the various legislative or nonlegislative provisions do not necessarily contain specific elements addressing the return to work after chronic diseases as the core subject of this chapter. This emphasis on prevention is still relevant in the sense that prevention aims to create work environments to protect workers against various risks and promote measures to prevent occupational accidents or diseases that could lead to chronic diseases.

The return to work has been addressed, although partly, in some EU-level strategies. Already back in 2007, the Community Strategy on Health and Safety at Work envisioned that national- and EU-level policies should aim to create working environments that protect and enable workers to contribute to their jobs until they reach old age (European Commission 2007). The strategy also specifically referred to the return to work of individuals who have had occupational accident, illness, or disability at work. It encouraged member states to incorporate specific measures including financial assistance or training tailored to individual needs into their national strategies to improve the rehabilitation and reintegration of workers excluded from the workplace for a long period of time because of an accident at work, an occupational illness, or a disability. Along the same lines, the previous EU Strategic Framework on Health and Safety 2014–2020 also emphasized the importance of workplace adaptation and work organization according to the needs of ageing workers and proposed measures to promote reintegration and rehabilitation of these workers to avoid their exclusion from the labor markets (European Commission 2014).

More recently, the Strategic Framework on Health and Safety 2021–2027 published by the European Commission (2021b) came at a period in which the key priorities and actions are set to improve the health and safety of the workers in a post-pandemic world faced with green transition and digital transformations, changing world of work and added demographic challenges impacting the future workforce. The new strategic framework acknowledges the increasing prevalence of chronic diseases particularly among the elderly and foresees the presentation of a package that will "include guidance and support for mutual learning on: securing health and safety at work; and on vocational rehabilitation schemes for people suffering from chronic diseases or people who have been victims of accidents" (European Commission 2021b). Moreover, it is mentioned to support awareness raising on common chronic diseases such as musculoskeletal disorders, cancer, and mental health problems, as well as a specific reference to "actively support reintegration, non-discrimination and the adaptation of working conditions of workers who are cancer patients or cancer survivors" (ibid).

Disability and Social Inclusion Policies

Considering labor market reintegration of individuals with chronic disease, while the EU legislation does not specifically target them, this group is implicitly included in various policies that focus on the employment of people with disabilities. It is possible that chronic disease might lead to a limitation of the full capacity – which could be certified by a medical authority – of the worker and can result in certain degree of disability. However, from a legal perspective, it is not always straightforward whether the definition of disability automatically includes the concept of chronic disease, and it appears to depend on the specific case given the diverging rulings by the European Court of Justice in this context (Eurofound 2019). Nevertheless, given that the blurry distinction between chronic disease and disability and the former can lead to the latter (or vice versa), most of the policies on disability is relevant in the context of the return to work after chronic disease.

Meanwhile, the EU approach on this issue is also heavily influenced by the international organizations, such as the United Nations (UN), International Labor Organization (ILO), WHO, and the Organization for the Economic Cooperation and Development (OECD) (EU-OSHA 2016). In this regard, the key elements that have shaped the EU approach is the ILO Convention No. 159 on Vocational Rehabilitation and Employment (Disabled Persons) that is adopted in 1983 as well as the UN Convention on the Rights of Persons with Disabilities (Akgüç and Westhoff 2021). Compared to the ILO Convention, the UN convention uses a broader definition of disability to include "those who have long-term physical, mental, intellectual or sensory impairments which, in interaction with various barriers, may hinder their full and effective participation in society on an equal basis with others" (UN 2006). As regard the return to work and rehabilitation, the most relevant articles of the UN Convention are Articles 26 on Habilitation and Rehabilitation and Article 27 on Work and Employment. These articles altogether provide the general principles of rehabilitation that is recommended to be started as early as possible and coordinated by a multidisciplinary team. The articles of the UN Convention also refer to various measures to prohibit discrimination, improve and adapt the workplace in line with occupational safety and health recommendations to accommodate it to people with disability (reasonable accommodation clause), assist the latter in their return to employment as well as career advancement. The EU has been party to this UN Convention since 2011. This implies that all disability-related EU legislation, policies, and programs must comply with the provisions of the UN Convention within the limits of the subsidiarity principle.

The OECD has also emphasized the participation of disabled individuals in social and economic life in a number of studies and provided an important platform for knowledge and discussion among member countries. These conventions and guiding studies have provided the general framework and principles of rehabilitation and career protection of workers experiencing limiting health conditions, and they have been influential in the relevant EU policies on the return to work overall.

One of the key actions on disability and inclusion that the EU has taken is the Employment Equality Directive (2000/78/EC (https://eur-lex.europa.eu/legal-content/EN/TXT/?uri=celex%3A32000L0078)) which provides a general framework for equal treatment in employment and occupation and covers specifically the case of disabled individuals. Accordingly, the employers are required to undertake "reasonable adjustments to accommodate disabled people" which could also be relevant for work reintegration of workers with chronic disease (Akgüç and Westhoff 2021). Nevertheless, the provisions of the directive do not specifically mention the returning to work of individuals with chronic disease, insofar as the latter does not lead to an explicit disability status or impairment (ibid).

Along these lines, the initial European Disability Strategy (https://eur-lex.europa.eu/LexUriServ/LexUriServ.do?uri=COM%3A2010%3A0636%3AFIN%3Aen%3APDF) in 2010 came with the objective to "empower people with disabilities so that they enjoy their full rights and benefit fully from participating in society and in the European economy." The strategy identified eight areas of action including employment and health. As regard employment, the EU action included supporting and supplementing national efforts to analyze the labor market situation of people with disabilities as well as fighting those "disability benefit cultures and traps that discourage them from entering the labour market" (European Commission 2010; Akgüç and Westhoff 2021). As regard health, the strategy mentioned the promotion of actions "in the field of health and safety at work to reduce risks of disabilities developing during working life and to improve the reintegration of workers with disabilities."

Furthermore, the European Commission's recent Strategy for the Rights of Persons with Disabilities 2021–2030 put particular emphasis on the employment of individuals with disabilities and promotes reasonable accommodation in the workplace taking into account health conditions and disability status of workers. As part of this disability strategy, one of the flagship initiatives – Disability Employment Package that came out in 2022 (https://ec.europa.eu/social/main.jsp?catId=1597& langId=en) – aims to improve labor market outcomes of disabled people by providing further support and guidance to member states in areas such as vocational rehabilitation following chronic disease or accidents. This initiative also reflects the calls by the European Parliament on these issues, as they were raised in a comprehensive resolution on the reintegration or workers recovering from injury and illness into quality employment by the Committee on Employment and Social Affairs of the European Parliament in 2018 (European Parliament 2018). The European Parliament has also been pushing various European institutions to address the lack of clarity on whether chronic diseases could be defined as a form of disability and thus has drawn attention to the specific needs of individuals experiencing chronic diseases in the labor markets.

Other Relevant EU-Level Initiatives

In addition to what was described earlier, other EU-level relevant policy framework and initiatives exist on the return to work in the face of sociodemographic transitions in particular. The most prominent ones include active labor market policies around healthy and active ageing, which aim to provide incentives for activating elderly people while ensuring a better work-life balance. Such policies targeting specific age groups taking into account existing or potential health conditions are essential to boost inclusive growth as well as sustainability of social security systems.

The other broader but relevant initiative is the European Pillar of Social Rights (EPSR) that is proclaimed by the European Parliament, the Council, and the European Commission in 2017 as the social compass for the EU aiming for a social Europe that is fair and inclusive. The EPSR is structured under three broad chapters on (i) equal opportunities and access to the labor market, (ii) fair working conditions, and (iii) social protection and inclusion and consists of 20 corresponding principles (for the detailed list of EPSR principles, see https://ec.europa.eu/info/strategy/priorities-2019-2024/economy-works-people/jobs-growth-and-investment/european-pillar-social-rights/european-pillar-social-rights-20-principles_en). These principles aim to ensure equal opportunities and fair working conditions in the labor markets regardless of gender, age, racial or ethnic origin, disability, or health conditions of citizens and constitute another key EU policy framework in this context.

Last but not least, given the soaring number of cancer patients in Europe – 2.7 million diagnoses versus 1.3 million deaths due to cancer in the EU – the recently published Europe's Beating Cancer is an important step to address the suffering caused by cancer in the EU (https://ec.europa.eu/health/system/files/2022-02/eu_cancer-plan_en_0.pdf). The plan is structured around four action areas where there is an added value of an EU action, including (i) prevention, (ii) early detection, (iii) diagnosis and treatment, and (iv) quality of life of cancer patients and survivors (European Commission 2021a). Constituting one of the key pillars of the

European Health Union, the plan includes a number of initiatives ranging from re-skilling and upskilling programs for cancer survivors to promoting proper management of rehabilitation or return to work of cancer patients with possible funding from the European Social Fund Plus. The European Commission also proposes a detailed mapping of national employment and social protection policies, which an help to identify barriers and challenges for cancer survivors in the workplace. Finally, the increased funding on cancer studies is expected to boost technologies related to prevention and treatment that will also impact the future of cancer disease.

The Way Ahead on the Return to Work: Further Reflections

As described earlier, the existing demographic transitions toward increasingly ageing societies and rising prevalence of chronic diseases imply that more and more people will fall sick during their occupational life course. Given the shrinking workforce and soaring financing of social protection and benefit systems, the reintegration of workers experiencing chronic health conditions emerges to be an important step in addressing demographic and health challenges facing the EU. What is more, the moment to raise awareness and take policy action on the subject of return to work following chronic disease that causes long-term absence from work could not be more appropriate given the recent pandemic context with implications for the labor markets and raised awareness about health issues and prevention in general.

This chapter initially provided an empirical ground to explain why the return to work after chronic disease is emerging to be an important subject in the occupational health and safety over the life course of individuals. It then provided a detailed overview of existing EU-level policy framework through which the return-to-work policies are shaped to address the existing demographic and health challenges. A number of policy considerations and reflections on successful return-to-work policies are discussed briefly in the following. These reflections are mostly based on previous empirical and multidisciplinary research findings which are collected under a dedicated volume (Akgüç 2021b), among others. As the field of returning to work after chronic diseases is still emerging, further research, data collection, and availability of comparable statistics across different countries would increase knowledge on these issues and help better inform policymaking.

First of all, a carefully managed occupational rehabilitation and return-to-work scheme could encourage workers facing chronic diseases or other health complications to remain in the labor market as long as medical circumstances of the worker permits it and there is mutual willingness both by workers and employers. Returning to work after chronic disease could also help workers facing isolation or risk of poverty and support their social integration and professional rehabilitation after a long-term medical absence. Moreover, the evidence reflecting the perspective of the workers suffering from chronic diseases points to the sensitive and private nature of the diagnosis, treatment, and recovery processes, which require a gentle and voluntary approach to the return to work (Akgüç 2021b).

There is also a need to design tailored-made and targeted approaches as every chronic disease (or a combination of several of them) can express itself (themselves) differently across different individuals depending on genetic or environmental factors. Such an approach would be in line with an occupational health approach whereby the return-to-work policies are tailored to specific health conditions or chronic diseases, each of which possibly requiring different treatment and accommodation when reintegrating to work. For example, the work reintegration following musculoskeletal disorders can require different (ergonomic) accommodations in the workplace compared to people with cardiovascular diseases or mental health problems which might result in other types of accommodations. Some recovering workers might need flexible working time to continue their treatment while working as it is the case with cancer or diabetes. This is why a case-by-case management of the return-to-work process paying attention to the type of chronic disease (among other factors) could be more successful than generic and one-size-fits-all approaches. This also necessitates the corporation and coordination of several policy domains including occupational health and safety (e.g., prevention), education and training (e.g., work rehabilitation), social inclusion, and finance (e.g., sickness or disability benefits), to name a few. So far, except the recent disease-specific campaigns such as the Beating Cancer Plan, the EU approach has been tilting more toward a social model of disability, in which most of the action takes place when chronic diseases lead to some form of disability. At the national level, what seems to work pretty well is when the various policy areas (e.g., health, social, welfare, and labor) coordinate together and aim for the most inclusive approach possible (EU-OSHA 2016).

However, the aim for simplicity in the return-to-work procedures is also much welcome (both by workers and employers) because the already complex national legislation and policies as well as diverging company practices coupled with the stress of dealing with a chronic disease can make it hard for workers to navigate successfully through the return-to-work processes (Akgüç 2021b). When it is possible, one-stop-shop information sources could simplify things both for worker and employers in facilitating the return to work (ibid). At the same time, having clear policies by themselves is not sufficient to guarantee a successful return to work. For example, the power imbalances between a worker and manager could mean that the former may not find it easy to negotiate reasonable accommodations for their health condition.

Similar to the tailor-made approach depending on the disease, there are also sectoral specificities that expose workers to different types of risks that might lead to (different) chronic diseases. Because of sectoral risk differences, the return-to-work policies should also take into account the differences across sectors and design prevention and rehabilitation policies accordingly. For example, in some sectors the return to work may not even be possible following the disease because of continuing risk which might make health conditions of the returning worker worse or because of impossibility of assigning the returning worker to other tasks in the company.

As regard stakeholders, a number of them play a key role in the overall process of the return to work. This ranges from the occupational doctors and social security agencies or insurance companies disbursing sickness or disability benefits to line managers at work and patient organizations campaigning for the rights of patients

(Akgüç et al. 2019). Moreover, as the key actors of industrial relations – which broadly refer to the relations and interactions between the industry and labor, whereby the two sides are represented by interest groups, often called social partners – social partners could play an important role in improving working conditions through social dialogue and negotiation on working conditions. For that reason, their role – despite limitations and challenges as detailed in (Akgüç 2021b) – is also relevant in the context of return to work following chronic diseases in guiding their members and navigating them during the complex return-to-work process.

On the employer front, creating a supportive environment, where transparent and careful communication prevails, could facilitate the overall process during which workers might feel more at ease to cope with the returning to work. Avoiding stigma and discrimination through careful management and communication, raising awareness among other colleagues, and focusing on existing capabilities rather than incapacities can generate a positive atmosphere in general.

As regards the recent pandemic, there are at least two opposing effects of it on the return-to-work process (Akgüç 2021a). On the one hand, the Covid-19 has been negatively impacting the individuals already suffering from chronic conditions and make their health further fragile. Moreover, severe disruption in health services during the first phases of the pandemic has also led to delays in early detection or disrupted the treatment of some of the chronic diseases. Both of these elements have possibly led to compromises on the return-to-work process. On the other hand, the increased flexibility in the labor markets through remote working has also allowed for some chronically ill workers to resume or continue their work compared to the relatively more rigid and less common remote work practices prior to the pandemic.

As a final analysis, it is fair to say that the EU-level approach can only go so far in facilitating the return to work given the distinct national competences in social, labor market and health policy domains. There are also a number of sectoral and company-level specificities that challenges to have too generic or broad top-down approaches (Akgüç 2021b). Nevertheless, the existing EU policy framework, strategies, and initiatives provide a useful framework to shape national policies on return to work where the EU has an added value. For example, there are countries (e.g., Austria, Denmark, Finland, Germany, the Netherlands, and Sweden) with inclusive rehabilitation systems and integrated policy framework in which successful return-to-work practices could be observed (EU-OSHA 2016; Akgüç et al. 2019). In that sense, the EU also serves as a platform to exchange such best practices and experiences across member states.

Moreover, the recent EU strategies on health and safety at work referring to – although partly – the rehabilitation of workers experiencing chronic diseases constitute important steps toward inclusive, fair, and healthy workplaces. The EU's Beating Cancer Plan is also promising in which attention is drawn to a particular yet very important and prevalent chronic disease in the EU. However, this is only a limited approach so far. Similar strategies targeting other chronic diseases will also be necessary given the prevalence of various diseases. Finally, delivering on the key principles – such as equal opportunities – of the EPSR or implementing fully the EU occupational health and safety regulation could pave the way for healthy and fair workplaces where the return to work following chronic diseases could be further facilitated.

Cross-References

▶ Changing Experiences, Needs, and Supports Across the Life Course for Workers Living with Disabilities
▶ Two Pathways Between Occupation and Health

References

Akgüç M (2021a) Returning to work after chronic illness: elevating the role of the social partners. In: Akgüç M (ed) Continuing at work, long-term illness, return to work schemes and the role of industrial relations. ETUI, Brussels. https://www.etui.org/publications/continuing-work

Akgüç M (2021b) Return to work after chronic illness and the way ahead. In: Akgüç M (ed) Continuing at work, long-term illness, return to work schemes and the role of industrial relations. ETUI, Brussels. https://www.etui.org/publications/continuing-work

Akgüç M, Kahancová M, Popa A (2019) Working paper presenting a literature review on return to work policies and the role that industrial relations play in facilitating return to work at the EU, national and sub-national levels, REWIR project no. VS/2019/0075. Central European Labour Studies Institute, Bratislava. https://celsi.sk/en/projects/detail/64/

Akgüç M, Westhoff L (2021) The EU-level policy framework and stakeholder perspectives on returning to work after chronic illness. In: Akgüç M (ed) continuing at work long-term illness, return to work schemes and the role of industrial relations. ETUI, Brussels

Busse R, Blümel M, Schneller-Kreinsen D, Zentner A (2010) Tackling chronic disease in Europe: strategies, interventions and challenges, Observatory Studies Series. European Observatory on Health Systems and Policies, Copenhagen

Casse C, De Troyer M (eds) (2021) Gender, working conditions and health, what has changed? Report 143. ETUI, Brussels

EU-OSHA (2016) Rehabilitation and return to work: analysis report on EU and member states policies, strategies and programmes. Publications Office of the European Union, Luxembourg

Eurofound (2019) How to respond to chronic health problems in the workplace? Publications Office of the European Union, Luxembourg

European Commission (2007) Communication from the commission to the European Parliament, the council, the European economic and social committee and the Committee of the Regions – improving quality and productivity at work: community strategy 2007–2012 on health and safety at work, COM (2007) 62 final, 21 February 2007

European Commission (2010) Communication from the commission to the European Parliament, the council, the European economic and social committee and the Committee of the Regions – European disability strategy 2010–2020: a renewed commitment to a barrier-free Europe, COM (2010) 636 final, 15 November 2010

European Commission (2014) Communication from the commission to the European Parliament, the council, the European economic and social committee and the Committee of the Regions – an EU strategic framework on health and safety at work 2014–2020, COM (2014) 332 final, 6 June 2014

European Commission (2015) Evaluation of the practical implementation of the EU Occupational Safety and Health (OSH) directives in EU member states. https://ec.europa.eu/social/BlobServlet?docId=16897&langId=en

European Commission (2017) Communication from the commission to the European Parliament, the council, the European economic and social committee and the Committee of the Regions – safer and healthier work for all – modernisation of the EU occupational safety and health legislation and policy, COM (2017) 12 final, 10 January 2017

European Commission (2021a) Communication from the commission to the European Parliament and the council – Europe's beating cancer plan, COM (2021) 44 final, 3 February 2021

European Commission (2021b) Communication from the commission to the European Parliament, the council, the European economic and social committee and the Committee of the Regions – EU strategic framework on health and safety at work 2021–2027: occupational safety and health in a changing world of work, COM (2021) 323 final, 28 June 2021

European Parliament (2018) On pathways for the reintegration of workers recovering from injury and illness into quality employment, committee on employment and social affairs. Report A8–0208/2018, 12 June 2018

Franklin P, Bambra C, Albani V (2021) Gender equality and health in the EU. Publications Office of the European Union, Luxembourg

Guazzi M, Faggiano P, Mureddu GF, Faden G, Niebauer J, Temporelli PL (2014) Worksite health and wellness in the European Union. Prog Cardiovasc Dis 56(5):508–514

Hemp P (2004) Presenteeism at work – but out of it. Harvard Business Review 2004(October):1–10

ISSA (2013) Guidelines on return to work and reintegration. International Social Security Association, Geneva

UN (2006) Convention on the rights of persons with disabilities. https://www.un.org/development/desa/disabilities/convention-on-the-rights-of-persons-with-disabilities/convention-on-the-rights-of-persons-with-disabilities-2.html

The Role of Social and Labor Policies in Shaping Working Conditions Throughout the Life Course

28

Mariann Rigó and Thorsten Lunau

Contents

Introduction	512
Theoretical Background	513
National Labor Policies (Definition and Mechanisms)	513
Conceptual Framework	515
Empirical Evidence	516
Cross-Country Evidence	516
Longitudinal Evidence	519
Trend Studies	520
Conclusion	521
Cross-References	522
References	522

Abstract

Our contribution highlights the role of the political context, specifically distinct social and labor market policies in shaping individuals' working lives, and thereby their health. For this, we summarize the most recent evidence about the impacts of active and passive labor market policies on working lives, as well we discuss the potential causal relationships between macrolevel policies and work-related individual outcomes together with first estimates quantifying the impact of policies. We do this by showing trends of work stressors in different countries with different set of macropolicies. Labor and social policies are often designed to improve the situation of individuals with disadvantaged working conditions. As such, they

---

M. Rigó (✉)
Institute of Medical Sociology, Centre for Health and Society, Medical Faculty and University Hospital Düsseldorf, Heinrich-Heine-University, Düsseldorf, Germany
e-mail: Mariann.Rigo@hhu.de

T. Lunau
Institut für Sozialforschung und Sozialwirtschaft (iso) e.V., Saarbrücken, Germany

© Springer Nature Switzerland AG 2023
M. Wahrendorf et al. (eds.), *Handbook of Life Course Occupational Health*, Handbook Series in Occupational Health Sciences, https://doi.org/10.1007/978-3-031-30492-7_10

can have an impact on the employment and health trajectories of these individuals with indirect effects on health. Our contribution, thereby, pays particular attention on the impacts of macrolevel policies on socially disadvantaged population groups.

Keywords

ALMP · PLMP · Psychosocial working conditions · Effort-reward imbalance · Job strain · Socioeconomic inequalities · Low skilled

Introduction

The negative health-related effects of adverse psychosocial working conditions have been extensively documented in the occupational health research. Poor working conditions have been shown to be associated with higher risk for several diseases such as depressive disorders (Rugulies et al. 2017), coronary heart disease (Dragano et al. 2017), and cardiovascular disease (Kivimäki and Kawachi 2015). Importantly, this link has been shown for a broad array of different work stressors, including single indicators of work stress (Kim and Knesebeck 2016) and those based on more comprehensive theoretical work stress models (Madsen et al. 2017), or studies that investigate whole employment histories in conjunction with health (Wahrendorf et al. 2019). In addition to the adverse health impacts, work stress was found to be associated with higher rate of sickness absence (Götz et al. 2018; Mortensen et al. 2017) and a premature career break (Hintsa et al. 2015; Mäcken 2019). As such, psychosocial working conditions throughout working lives are important determinants of individuals' employment and health trajectories.

The global sociopolitical developments of the last decades such as globalization, job polarization, or digitization had profound impact on working conditions (see also ▶ Chap. 3, "Transformation of Modern Work, Rise of Atypical Employment, and Health"). New forms of work organizations appeared where the service sector gained more and more importance. Employees in a growing number of jobs were facing higher job insecurity due to the growing share of temporary contracts. Flexibility in terms of time and location brought about new opportunities to improve resources in the form of higher level of control and more autonomy. On the other hand, a variety of hidden dangers permeated, for instance, the difficulty of balancing between work and private life or handling the less predictable and more complex jobs (Jensen et al. 2019; Eurofound 2013). These changes led, in general, to higher level of work stress in European countries (Rigó et al. 2021). Given the persuasive evidence on the unfavorable impacts of work stress and the global developments leading to higher level of work stress, there is growing interest in identifying promising entry points for successful interventions to counteract the impact of global developments, thereby providing individuals a shelter from market forces and improve their health and maintain their employability.

The way how psychosocial working conditions are perceived is shaped by individual, meso-, and macrolevel factors. A conceptual framework about the interrelations between the individual, meso-, macrolevels, and their relation to psychosocial working conditions is outlined in a previous publication (Lunau et al. 2020b). The current book chapter focuses on possible interventions at the macrolevel, specifically on the role of national labor policies. Previous research has shown that labor market policies, social security systems, and continued educational programs contribute toward a healthier workforce and buffer the effects of stressful work environments (Dragano et al. 2011; Lunau et al. 2015; Wahrendorf and Siegrist 2014). In this chapter, we synthesize the available empirical evidence on the health-related impacts of the two main types of labor market programs: active and passive labor market policies. The book chapter places special emphasis on individuals with disadvantageous socioeconomic position as labor market policies may differently affect them (Lundberg 2009). Indeed, an important aim of labor market policies is to decrease social inequalities by improving the situation of the most disadvantaged ones.

Theoretical Background

National Labor Policies (Definition and Mechanisms)

Labor market policies (LMPs) are governmental programs, which aim to reduce unemployment and provide financial compensation for individuals in case of job joss. Two main groups of LMPs are active (ALMP) and passive (PLMP) labor market programs.

ALMPs aim to integrate unemployed people into the labor market and create employment possibilities. Most often used examples of ALMPs are job search assistance, job training, and subsidized public or subsidized private employment. These programs can improve the working conditions indirectly through a variety of mechanisms. *Job search assistance*, by providing training and counseling for individuals seeking for a job, improves job match, thus the likelihood that individuals get into jobs being appropriate to their skills and expectations (Lunau et al. 2020a). As we can expect that individuals in better matched jobs will experience lower levels of work stress, this would lead to an improvement of working conditions. Furthermore, job search assistance can also enhance mental health by improving participants' self-confidence and self-efficacy (Puig-Barrachina et al. 2019; Crépon and van den Berg 2016). Individuals with higher self-esteem are more likely to obtain gainful regular employment, as well as they are more likely to find better matched jobs, which again leads to an improvement of their working conditions.

Job training empowers individuals to expand and refresh their skills and improve their knowledge over the life course. As digitalization processes advance, a variety of skills and occupations become obsolete. Therefore, for individuals in such jobs further training might be crucial to enhance their room for maneuver to stay employed. Full-time job training has also been found to improve participants' mental well-being by equipping them with the psychosocial needs, which are usually met by employment (Puig-Barrachina et al. 2019). Individuals in better mental well-being are expected to be more successful in finding a suitable job tailored for their qualifications. Therefore, training possibilities constitute an important policy instrument to lessen the adverse financial consequences of layoffs.

Programs of *subsidized public employment* create jobs for the unemployed by ensuring temporary job opportunities for them. We expect that such programs improve individuals' situation by offering temporarily financial security, social interactions, and daily routine during a period when otherwise they would have likely been unemployed (Puig-Barrachina et al. 2019). *Subsidized private employment* programs on the other hand provide financial incentives to hire certain workers (e.g., unemployed, young workers, and women) or to set up start-up firms. These programs are often used by employers to screen applicants (who are often long-term unemployed) and to test their skills during the subsidy phase (Brown 2015). Participants can also improve their human capital, and enhance on-the-job skills, which makes them more attractive to the employers and improves the likelihood of staying in employment also after the subsidy phase (Brown 2015). These processes indirectly improve the job match, thereby result in lower level of work stress. Therefore, we expect again that these programs not only decrease unemployment but also improve the working conditions, thereby reduce work stress.

Among the single ALMP measures, previous empirical results pointed out the beneficial impacts of job search assistance most often. Puig-Barrachina et al. (2019) and Crépon and van den Berg (2016) emphasized their favorable health-related impacts (e.g., better mental health, higher job satisfaction, and higher motivation), while Card et al. (2010) highlighted their beneficial labor market effects. Training programs seemed to be effective only in the longer run, while subsidized public sector employment programs were found to be the least successful (Card et al. 2010). The positive impacts of subsidized public sector employment programs were usually temporary, and reemployment chances after the program have often not improved (Card et al. 2010). The study by Haapanala (2022) found that "soft ALMP" strategies focusing on upskilling and public sector employment have more advantageous impact resulting in lower involuntary part-time employment compared to "hard ALMP" instruments encouraging the rapid reemployment of participants by threating them with the withdrawal of unemployment benefit.

PLMP measures are also called as protective measures. Examples of PLMP measures are unemployment benefits, unemployment assistance, disability benefits, and investments into early retirement. Their aim is to provide protection for individuals in case of job instability, job insecurity, to ensure financial support in case of job loss or to offer financial compensation for disabled people. By reducing the costs associated with unemployment, PLMP measures allow individuals to quit jobs with stressful working conditions and to spend more time searching for a suitable job and avoid taking a job with disadvantageous working conditions (Lunau et al. 2020a). Therefore, PLMP measures play an important role in reducing the adverse financial consequences of layoffs and unemployment. It has been extensively documented in previous literature that the threat of job insecurity affects workers' mental health (Llosa et al. 2018). Therefore, LMP measures can be directly enhancing workers' health by dampening their feelings of job insecurity.

Conceptual Framework

When synthetizing the literature on the health-related impacts of national labor policies, two main research line gets crystallized. First, macroeconomic policies have been shown to have a direct impact on the average level of work stress within the country. This line of research focuses on the association between country-specific indicators (e.g., country groups, as well as macroeconomic indicators) and the average level of work stress in the country. Some papers take a further step, and besides focusing on the average level of work stress, the distribution of work stress by socioeconomic position is also examined. The usual hypothesis is that countries with well-developed labor market policies experience, on average, lower level of work stress as well as smaller socioeconomic inequalities in work stress. Second, national labor policies can modify the association between work stress and health. Papers pursuing this research question examine whether it is statistically justified if interactions between macroeconomic policy indicators and work stress are added to a model where the association between health and work stress is assessed. The usual assumption is that national labor policies buffer the adverse health impacts of work stress. Thus, a less pronounced association between health and work stress is hypothesized in countries with more developed labor market policies.

Macroeconomic policies can be operationalized in a variety of ways. One possibility is to group countries into welfare regimes. Most papers rely on the typology by Esping-Andersen (1990) differentiating between Liberal, Conservative, and Scandinavian welfare state regimes. This has been recently complemented with the group of Southern European and Eastern European countries (Bambra and Eikemo 2009). However, as the typology of welfare regimes incorporates a variety of interrelated labor and social policies along the dimensions of decommodification and defamiliarization, papers using this typology do not provide clear-cut conclusions on the impact and effectiveness of specific labor market policies. Another possibility to operationalize macroeconomic policies is to use specific macroeconomic indicators such as investments into single items of ALMP, total investments into ALMP/PLMP, old age employment rate, or participation in further education among adults. Though the last two items do not explicitly capture ALMP investments, they tell us about the extent and quality of implementation of ALMP measures by quantifying their outcomes in terms of employment or training participation.

Work stress is most often operationalized by using work stress constructs of the demand-control model (Karasek and Theorell 1990) and the effort-reward imbalance model (Siegrist 1996). The demand-control model asserts that work stress is the result of high psychological demands combined with a lack of control. As a complementary approach, the effort-reward imbalance model rests on the principle of social reciprocity and argues that high effort coupled with low rewards in terms of money, esteem, or social status can be perceived as failed reciprocity and can evoke strong negative emotions and stress reactions. While job security is one component of the reward dimension, a growing number of empirical papers focuses on this single item. Therefore, our synthesis will also devote attention to job insecurity being a single indicator of psychosocial working conditions.

Health outcomes are often operationalized using measures of depressive symptoms such as CES-D (Radloff 1977) or EURO-D (Prince et al. 1999).

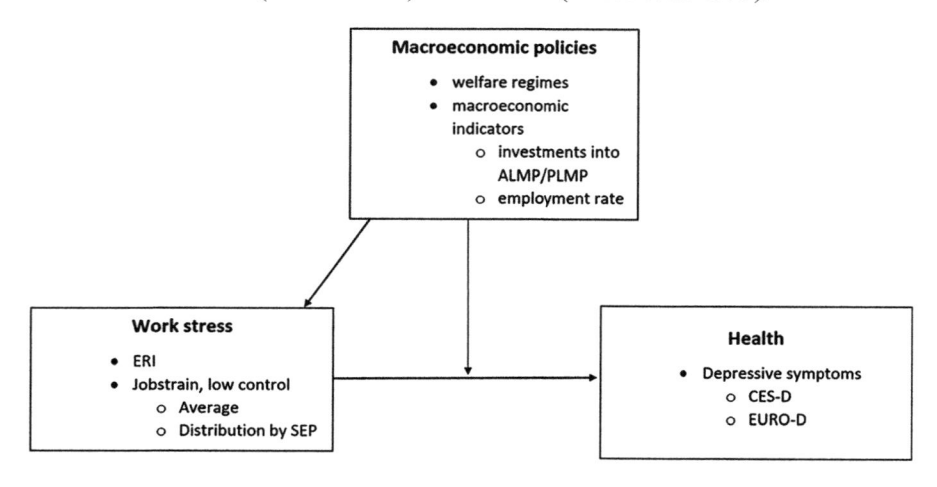

```
                    ┌─────────────────────────────┐
                    │   Macroeconomic policies    │
                    │  • welfare regimes          │
                    │  • macroeconomic            │
                    │    indicators               │
                    │      o investments into     │
                    │        ALMP/PLMP            │
                    │      o employment rate      │
                    └─────────────────────────────┘
                           │           
                           ▼           
┌──────────────────────────┐         ┌──────────────────────────┐
│  Work stress             │         │  Health                  │
│  • ERI                   │────────▶│  • Depressive symptoms   │
│  • Jobstrain, low control│         │      o CES-D             │
│      o Average           │         │      o EURO-D            │
│      o Distribution by SEP│        │                          │
└──────────────────────────┘         └──────────────────────────┘
```

Empirical Evidence

Cross-Country Evidence

Existing studies document a significant relationship between countries' average level of work stress and their macroeconomic political context. The findings show important differences by geographical area, as well as by indicators of national labor market policies. Psychosocial working conditions are perceived, on average, as the least favorable in Southern and Eastern European countries and most favorable in the Scandinavian countries (Lunau et al. 2013; Dragano et al. 2011; Wahrendorf and Siegrist 2014). Socioeconomic differences in work stress are also found to be more pronounced in Eastern European countries compared to Northern Europe (Lunau et al. 2015). Recent publications shift their focus from the welfare and geographical typologies toward more quantifiable measures of labor market policies. They show first evidence that investments into LMP measures are associated with better psychosocial working conditions (Wahrendorf and Siegrist 2014; Lunau et al. 2015), and ALMP measures (in general and single items) seem to be more effective in terms of enhancing working conditions compared to passive measures (Wahrendorf and Siegrist 2014). Furthermore, differences in socioeconomic position in work stress were found to be smaller in countries with higher investments into LMP measures (Lunau et al. 2015).

Siegrist and Wahrendorf (2011) found that policies promoting further qualification among adults, subsidized employment, and rehabilitation services are associated, on average, with better psychosocial working conditions in those countries. The results by Dragano et al. (2011) documented a negative association between work stress (ERI, low control) and the macroeconomic indicators of old age employment rate and investments into further adult education, and a positive association in case of long-term unemployment. As boosting the employment of disadvantaged groups or incentivizing further education is among the explicit goals of ALMP investments, these findings may indicate a positive association between ALMP investments and psychosocial working conditions. Lunau et al. (2015) examined the role of integrative policies captured by investments into ALMP in general and lifelong learning possibilities compared to the role of protective policies captured by investments into PLMP in general and the replacement rate showing the expected net income after job loss with respect to the net income before job loss. Their results point to a slightly stronger association between integrative policies and average work stress levels than in case of protective policies. Similarly, integrative policies seemed to be slightly more successful in decreasing socioeconomic inequalities in work stress compared to protective policies. Note, however, that the associations were also significant in case of protective policies.

Wahrendorf and Siegrist (2014) examined the association between psychosocial working conditions throughout the working lives and macroeconomic policies using two indices developed by OECD capturing the compensating and integrating nature of labor market policies. While the compensation index measures the availability and generosity of benefits provided in case of disability, the integration index captures how successful labor market programs are in reintegrating individuals in case of disability. Besides documenting the highest prevalence of stressful working careers in Eastern and Southern countries, the paper provides evidence on the significant negative association between the integration index and mean levels of stressful work. This was, however, not the case for the compensation index.

The above papers relied on datasets including older workers (e.g., SHARE and ELSA). While these datasets have important advantages to analyze the research question (e.g., large sample size by country, rich variables to operationalize work stress, and retrospective data), their generalizability is limited as they are based on a specific cohort of older workers. Among them, the sample selection bias due to the healthy worker effect may be even stronger than in the general population of employees. Some recent publications use international datasets including employees from all age groups such as the European Working Conditions Survey (EWCS), the European Social Survey (ESS), or the International Social Survey Program (ISSP). One example is the publication by Lunau et al. (2020a) who found that in countries with higher investments into ALMP and PLMP (as % of GDP), the perceived levels of reward and control were also higher. One strength of the paper is its large sample: the estimations are based on the 2005, 2010, and 2015 waves of the European Working Conditions Surveys (EWCS) encompassing 27 countries and a representative sample of employed individuals. Though country-level differences in the composite indicators of ERI and job strain were not found to be associated with country-level differences in ALMP/PLMP investments, significant associations were found for the subdimensions of control and reward. Specifically, in countries with higher investments into ALMP or PLMP measures, higher level of control was reported. In case of reward, the association was only significant in case of ALMP investments. These results partly contrast to previous findings where a significant association between ERI/job strain and LMP investments were found (Wahrendorf and Siegrist 2014; Lunau et al. 2015). Note, however, that an important difference compared to these studies is the inclusion of GDP among the controls by Lunau et al. (2020a). Therefore, one explanation can be the high correlation between ALMP and GDP implying that the macrolevel effects cannot be disentangled. Another difference can be due to the different operationalization of the work stressors and the different sample size in terms of employees and countries.

Focusing on the single indicator of job insecurity, the available empirical evidence investigates the following labor market characteristics most often: the generosity of unemployment benefits, investments into ALMP measures, and the strength of employment protection legislations. The results indicate that generous unemployment benefits are positively associated with job security perceptions (Anderson and Pontusson 2007; Hipp 2016; Clark and Postel-Vinay 2009). Thereby in countries with substantial unemployment benefits, the anxiety of loosing the job is less pronounced than in countries where workers are less protected. However, the findings regarding the strengths of the dismissal protection are inconclusive: while Anderson and Pontusson (2007) documented a positive association, Erlinghagen (2008) found insignificant, and Chung and van Oorschot (2011) and Clark and Postel-Vinay (2009) showed a negative association. An important argument against strong dismissal protection regulations is that though they improve job security, at the same time they may hamper the reemployment chances of particularly disadvantaged groups (Chung and Mau 2014).

Macroeconomic factors, besides directly impacting the average level of work stress throughout the working lives, may also modify the strength of the association between work stress and individual health. Therefore, another line of research analyzes if certain macroeconomic policies act as a moderator between work stress and employees' mental health. Related to this line, Lunau et al. (2013) found that the relationship between effort-reward imbalance and depressive symptoms differs between countries having different national labor and social policies. Specifically, the authors detected protective effects related to certain national labor and social policies such as: (1) higher investments into ALMP in general; (2) higher investments into rehabilitation services; and (3) higher income support for the unemployed. Furthermore, the association between ERI and mental health was also less pronounced in countries characterized with low income inequality (measured by the Gini coefficient). The work by Dragano et al. (2011) found that the association between work-related stress (ERI, low control) and health operationalized by depressive symptoms is less pronounced in countries with Scandinavian welfare regimes compared to Liberal, Conservative, or Southern states.

Differences by Socioeconomic Position

Previous empirical research extensively documented the social gradient between socioeconomic position (SEP) and stressful working careers, pointing out that individuals with lower SEP are exposed to higher work stress in terms of ERI (particular for the reward dimension), job strain, and control (Lunau et al. 2015;

Brunner et al. 2004). Note, however, that the results concerning effort and demand do not necessarily follow a social gradient as high-skilled workers often face higher demands. This is, however, compensated by higher control or rewards leading to lower ERI or job strain in their case (Rigó et al. 2022). This holds true using various definitions of SEP. For instance, Lunau et al. (2015) using a sample of older employees (2010/2011 waves of SHARE and ELSA) covering 16 European countries provided robust evidence on the association between lower level of education and higher levels of work stress captured by low control and effort-reward imbalance.

Against this background, it is an important research question whether certain macroeconomic policies can reduce socioeconomic differences in stressful working careers. This question was addressed by Lunau et al. (2015) focusing on the roles of integrative (amount of ALMP investments and investments into lifelong learning) and protective (amount of PLMP investments and replacement rate) policies. The authors found stronger supportive evidence for integrative policies in reducing educational differences in work stress compared to protective policies.

Longitudinal Evidence

An important limitation of studies using cross-sectional data is that the estimated results can only be interpreted as associations. Therefore, using such analysis technique causal conclusions on the impacts of labor market policies cannot be drawn limiting their relevance for policy interventions. For that purpose, longitudinal data is needed. In order to establish a causal link between investments into LMP and country mean levels of work stress, repeated country-level data at several time points is needed. Such country-level panel data offers the opportunity to link within-country changes in LMP investments to within-country changes in work stress, thereby providing a causal interpretation. Examples of country-level panel datasets suitable for such analysis are the EWCS or the European Social Survey (ESS). These datasets are appropriate both for cross-sectional and longitudinal analysis: each wave includes a cross-section of individuals and provides country-level aggregates. This ensures its country-level panel feature when merging all the available waves. The pioneering work of Fairbrother (2014) discussed how to use such datasets for the analysis of both cross-sectional and longitudinal implications. The key step of the statistical method is the decomposition of the macroeconomic variable into two terms. One of them is the within-country average during the studied time period, while the other one includes the country-time-specific deviations from this mean variable. While the first term captures the between-country variation, thereby measures the association between the average level of spending and the average level of work stress, the second term links within-country changes in LMP to within-country changes in work stress, thereby allowing for a causal interpretation.

Longitudinal evidence on the impact of national labor policies is scarce. Lunau et al. (2020a) provide the first analysis linking within-country changes in ALMP/PLMP investment to changes in the perceived level of work stress following the method of Fairbrother (2014). The paper found evidence that an increase in ALMP investments lead to a decrease in ERI. The result was primarily driven by an increase in rewards. The same relationship was not found in case of control. A possible explanation could be that ALMP investments may be more linked to the components of reward (job security and income satisfaction) than to the components of control. However, the finding that the link between ERI and ALMP investments was significant even in the within dimension and even after adding all the control variables provides a strong case for a causal interpretation, thereby an argumentation for investing more in such policy instruments to improve the psychosocial working conditions over the working careers.

Two additional studies could be added to the synthesis of longitudinal evidence, both of them examining job insecurity. The study by Lübke and Erlinghagen (2014) fits into the previous line of research and examines the role of ALMP measures. The authors found that past changes in ALMP are negatively linked to the level of job insecurity. Kohlrausch and Rasner (2014) take a different approach and a German individual-level panel survey (GSOEP). They analyze the impact of workplace training. Their findings show that it is positively linked to job security taking into account individual fixed effects. Due to the richness of the dataset, they also analyze whether the impact of workplace training differs by employees' educational background. The results indicate that the low skilled benefit the most from such workplace training programs. The results hold even after controlling for individual fixed effects. These results provide a strong case arguing for the beneficial impacts of training programs, which have the potential to improve the skill set, self-esteem, and labor market position of those with precarious working conditions.

Trend Studies

Trend studies analyze the prevalence of work stress over a specific time interval. By providing estimates in several consecutive time points, these studies offer an insight into how global developments affected psychosocial working conditions. When focusing on separate groups of countries with distinct labor market policies, these analyses complement longitudinal studies. They can show whether certain macroeconomic policy instruments were successful in sheltering individuals from market forces.

An exhaustive analysis of short-term trends in psychosocial working conditions is provided by Malard et al. (2013) analyzing changes in psychosocial working conditions in two consecutive waves (from 2005–2010) of the EWCS on a sample of 30 European countries. The authors pointed out that countries had heterogeneous experiences. While Poland and Czech Republic enjoyed positive changes, Ireland, Croatia, France, and Latvia underwent a deterioration in working conditions. In general, low-skilled employees were more likely to be affected by negative changes than higher-skilled ones. A further analysis of country-specific characteristics that could be linked to changes in working conditions is, however, not included in the chapter.

Long-term trends in psychosocial working conditions in general have been analyzed in a previous publication of our research group (Rigó et al. 2021). Similar to Malard et al. (2013), the analysis relies on the EWCS. However, it includes the longest possible time span of 20 years and 15 countries being surveyed in each wave. Using the survey items, which were available in each wave, the shorter version of job strain could be constructed as outcome variable. The chapter found evidence that job strain was rising from 1995–2005, and it was stagnating between 2005 and 2015. A heterogeneity analysis by occupational background revealed further that low-skilled employees experienced the largest deterioration in working conditions.

A further publication of our research group took a next step and examined how the long-term trend in working conditions differed by countries' investments into labor market programs, and within country groups by skill level (Rigó et al. 2022). The article provided evidence that the highest increase in job strain took place in countries with the lowest investments into LMP measures. Furthermore, within those countries, the low skilled were especially severely hit. While low-skilled experienced a 14% increase in job strain from 1995–2015 in low-LMP countries, the same occupational group in middle- and high-LMP countries saw a small and insignificant movement in work stress.

Conclusion

National labor policies are important tools to improve the psychosocial working conditions over working lives, thereby they play key role in influencing individuals' employment and health trajectories. Previous studies indicate that psychosocial working conditions tend to be better in countries with well-developed labor policies indicated by higher investments into ALMP and PLMP programs. Recently, there has been a shift from compensating toward integrating measures, which is in line with recent empirical research pointing to the higher effectiveness of integrative measures to enhance psychosocial working conditions compared to compensating measures. Furthermore, investing in LMP measures were found to be effective not only in terms of decreasing the average level of work stress, but also to decrease the socioeconomic inequalities in work stress. This is an important finding which indicates that certain groups benefit more from such investments. Indeed, the explicit aim of ALMP measures is to integrate disadvantaged individuals into the labor market. Therefore, their effectiveness can be best evaluated in analyses focusing on groups of employees with unfavorable socioeconomic background.

Longitudinal studies provide the strongest case for the effectiveness of LMP measures. The available empirical evidence utilizing the longitudinal nature of some available datasets is, however, rather thin. The first results point to the effectiveness of ALMP investments to improve psychosocial working conditions in general. Further research would be necessary to study if the impacts differ by groups of workers (e.g., by age, SEP), or to analyze different indicators of psychosocial working conditions such as single items or work-life conflict. Importantly, future research could also address the effectiveness of less aggregated items of LMP measures, and their impacts on different social groups.

Cross-References

▶ Transformation of Modern Work, Rise of Atypical Employment, and Health

References

Anderson CJ, Pontusson J (2007) Workers, worries and welfare states: social protection and job insecurity in 15 OECD countries. Eur J Polit Res 46(2):211–235. https://doi.org/10.1111/j.1475-6765.2007.00692.x

Bambra C, Eikemo TA (2009) Welfare state regimes, unemployment and health: a comparative study of the relationship between unemployment and self-reported health in 23 European countries. J Epidemiol Community Health 63(2):92–98. https://doi.org/10.1136/jech.2008.077354

Brown A (2015) Can hiring subsidies benefit the unemployed? izawol. https://doi.org/10.15185/izawol.163

Brunner EJ, Kivimaki M, Siegrist J, Theorell T, Luukkonen R, Riihimaki H et al (2004) Is the effect of work stress on cardiovascular mortality confounded by socioeconomic factors in the Valmet study? J Epidemiol Community Health 58(12):1019–1020

Card D, Kluve J, Weber A (2010) Active labour market policy evaluations: a meta-analysis. Econ J 120(548):F452–F477. https://doi.org/10.1111/j.1468-0297.2010.02387.x

Chung H, Mau S (2014) Subjective insecurity and the role of institutions. J Eur Soc Policy 24(4): 303–318. https://doi.org/10.1177/0958928714538214

Chung H, van Oorschot W (2011) Institutions versus market forces: explaining the employment insecurity of European individuals during (the beginning of) the financial crisis. J Eur Soc Policy 21(4):287–301. https://doi.org/10.1177/0958928711412224

Clark AE, Postel-Vinay F (2009) Job security and job protection. Oxf Econ Pap 61(2):207–239

Crépon B, van den Berg GJ (2016) Active labor market policies. Annu Rev Econ 8(1):521–546. https://doi.org/10.1146/annurev-economics-080614-115738

Dragano N, Siegrist J, Wahrendorf M (2011) Welfare regimes, labour policies and unhealthy psychosocial working conditions: a comparative study with 9917 older employees from 12 European countries. J Epidemiol Community Health 65(9):793–799. https://doi.org/10.1136/jech.2009.098541

Dragano N, Siegrist J, Nyberg ST, Lunau T, Fransson EI, Alfredsson L et al (2017) Effort-reward imbalance at work and incident coronary heart disease. a multi-cohort study of 90,164 individuals. In Epidemiology 28(4):619–626. https://doi.org/10.1097/EDE.0000000000 000666

Erlinghagen M (2008) Self-perceived job insecurity and social context: a multi-level analysis of 17 European countries. Eur Sociol Rev 24(2):183–197. https://doi.org/10.1093/esr/jcm042

Esping-Andersen G (1990) The three worlds of welfare capitalism. Polity Press, Cambridge

Eurofound (2013) Employment polarisation and job quality in the crisis: European Jobs Monitor 2013. Eurofound, Dublin. Available online at https://www.eurofound.europa.eu/sites/default/files/ef_publication/field_ef_document/ef1304en.pdf

Fairbrother M (2014) Two multilevel modeling techniques for analyzing comparative longitudinal survey datasets. In PSRM 2(01):119–140. https://doi.org/10.1017/psrm.2013.24

Götz S, Hoven H, Müller A, Dragano N, Wahrendorf M (2018) Age differences in the association between stressful work and sickness absence among full-time employed workers: evidence from the German socio-economic panel. In Int Arch Occup Environ Health 91(4):479–496. https://doi.org/10.1007/s00420-018-1298-3

Haapanala H (2022) Carrots or sticks? A multilevel analysis of active labour market policies and non-standard employment in Europe. In Social Policy & Administration 56(3):360–377. https://doi.org/10.1111/spol.12770

Hintsa T, Kouvonen A, McCann M, Jokela M, Elovainio M, Demakakos P (2015) Higher effort-reward imbalance and lower job control predict exit from the labour market at the age of 61 years or younger: evidence from the English Longitudinal Study of Ageing. In J Epidemiol Community Health 69(6):543–549. https://doi.org/10.1136/jech-2014-205148

Hipp L (2016) Insecure times? Workers' perceived job and labor market security in 23 OECD countries. Soc Sci Res 60:1–14. https://doi.org/10.1016/j.ssresearch.2016.04.004

Jensen TL, Nielsen J, Christiansen AG (2019) Job polarisation has increased inequality across Western Europe. In FEPS Policy Brief.

Karasek R, Theorell T (1990) Healthy work. Stress, productivity, and the reconstruction of working life. Basic Books, New York

Kim TJ, von dem Knesebeck O (2016) Perceived job insecurity, unemployment and depressive symptoms: a systematic review and meta-analysis of prospective observational studies. International archives of occupational and environmental health 89(4):561–573. https://doi.org/10.1007/s00420-015-1107-1

Kivimäki M, Kawachi I (2015) Work stress as a risk factor for cardiovascular disease. Current Cardiology Reports 17(9):630. https://doi.org/10.1007/s11886-015-0630-8

Kohlrausch B, Rasner A (2014) Workplace training in Germany and its impact on subjective job security: short- or long-term returns? J Eur Soc Policy 24(4):337–350. https://doi.org/10.1177/0958928714538216

Llosa JA, Menéndez-Espina S, Agulló-Tomás E, Rodríguez-Suárez J (2018) Job insecurity and mental health: a meta-analytical review of the consequences of precarious work in clinical disorders. Anales de Psicología 34(2):211–223.

Lübke C, Erlinghagen M (2014) Self-perceived job insecurity across Europe over time. Does changing context matter? In. J Eur Soc Policy 24(4):319–336. https://doi.org/10.1177/0958928714538215

Lunau T, Wahrendorf M, Dragano N, Siegrist J (2013) Work stress and depressive symptoms in older employees: impact of national labour and social policies. BMC Public Health 13(1):1086

Lunau T, Siegrist J, Dragano N, Wahrendorf M (2015) The association between education and work stress: does the policy context matter? PLoS ONE 10(3):e0121573. https://doi.org/10.1371/journal.pone.0121573

Lunau T, Rigó M, Dragano N (2020a) From national labor and social policies to individual work stressors. Multilevel concepts, evidence, and challenges. In: Theorell T (ed) Handbook of socioeconomic determinants of occupational health. Handbook series in occupational health sciences

Lunau T, Wahrendorf M, Dragano N, Siegrist J, van der Wel KA, Rigó M (2020b) Associations between change in labour market policies and work stressors: a comparative longitudinal survey data analysis from 27 European countries. BMC Public Health 20(1):1377. https://doi.org/10.1186/s12889-020-09364-3

Lundberg O (2009) How do welfare policies contribute to the reduction of health inequalities? Eurohealth 15(3):24–27

Mäcken J (2019) Work stress among older employees in Germany: effects on health and retirement age. In PLoS ONE 14(2):e0211487. https://doi.org/10.1371/journal.pone.0211487

Madsen IEH, Nyberg ST, Magnusson Hanson LL, Ferrie JE, Ahola K, Alfredsson L (2017) Job strain as a risk factor for clinical depression: systematic review and meta-analysis with additional individual participant data. In Psychological medicine 47(8):1342–1356. https://doi.org/10.1017/S003329171600355X

Malard L, Chastang J-F, Schutte S, Parent-Thirion A, Vermeylen G, Niedhammer I (2013) Changes in psychosocial work exposures among employees between 2005 and 2010 in 30 countries in Europe. J Occup Environ Med 55(10):1135–1141. https://doi.org/10.1097/JOM.0b013e3182a3eb90

Mortensen J, Dich N, Lange T, Alexanderson K, Goldberg M, Head J et al (2017) Job strain and informal caregiving as predictors of long-term sickness absence: a longitudinal multi-cohort study. In Scand J Work Environ Health 43(1):5–14. https://doi.org/10.5271/sjweh.3587

Prince MJ, Reischies F, Beekman AT, Fuhrer R, Jonker C, Kivela SL et al (1999) Development of the EURO-D scale – a European, Union initiative to compare symptoms of depression in 14 European centres. Br J Psychiatry 174:330–338. https://doi.org/10.1192/bjp.174.4.330

Puig-Barrachina V, Giró P, Artazcoz L, Bartoll X, Cortés-Franch I, Fernández A et al (2019) The impact of active labour market policies on health outcomes: a scoping review. Eur J Public Health 30:36. https://doi.org/10.1093/eurpub/ckz026

Radloff LS (1977) The CES-D scale. Appl Psychol Meas 1(3):385–401. https://doi.org/10.1177/014662167700100306

Rigó M, Dragano N, Wahrendorf M, Siegrist J, Lunau T (2021) Work stress on rise? Comparative analysis of trends in work stressors using the European working conditions survey. Int Arch Occup Environ Health 94(3):459–474. https://doi.org/10.1007/s00420-020-01593-8

Rigó M, Dragano N, Wahrendorf M, Siegrist J, Lunau T (2022) Long-term trends in psychosocial working conditions in Europe-the role of labor market policies. Eur J Public Health 32(3):384–391. https://doi.org/10.1093/eurpub/ckac038

Rugulies R, Aust B, Madsen IE (2017) Effort-reward imbalance at work and risk of depressive disorders. A systematic review and meta-analysis of prospective cohort studies. In Scand J Work Environ Health 43(4):294–306. https://doi.org/10.5271/sjweh.3632

Siegrist J (1996) Adverse health effects of high-effort/low-reward conditions. J Occup Health Psychol 1(1):27–41

Siegrist J, Wahrendorf M (2011) Quality of work, health and early retirement: European comparisons. In: Börsch-Supan A, Brandt M, Hank K, Schröder M (eds) The individual and the welfare state, vol 19. Springer Berlin Heidelberg, Berlin, Heidelberg, pp 169–177

Wahrendorf M, Siegrist J (2014) Proximal and distal determinants of stressful work: framework and analysis of retrospective European data. BMC Public Health 14:849. https://doi.org/10.1186/1471-2458-14-849

Wahrendorf M, Hoven H, Goldberg M, Zins M, Siegrist J (2019) Adverse employment histories and health functioning: the CONSTANCES study. Int J Epidemiol 48(2):402–414. https://doi.org/10.1093/ije/dyy235

Part VIII

Future Perspectives

Occupational Trajectories and Health Inequalities in a Global Perspective

29

Johannes Siegrist and Michael Marmot

Contents

Introduction	528
Social Inequalities in Access to the Labor Market and Young Adults' Health	530
Adverse Working Conditions During Midlife and Their Effects on Health	532
The Contribution of Work Toward Explaining Social Inequalities in Health	536
Implications for Policy	538
Cross-References	540
References	541

Abstract

Continued paid work is an important prerequisite of material and psychosocial well-being during adult life. In economically advanced societies large parts of working-age populations are formally employed, whereas worklessness and informal, unprotected employment conditions prevail in a majority of less-developed countries. Still, substantial social inequalities of quality of work and employment persist in the former countries, exposing workers in lower socioeconomic positions to more disadvantaged, less healthy jobs. In this chapter, this observation is substantiated by research findings applied to two stages of occupational careers, the stage of entrance into the labor market in young adulthood and the stage in midlife when large parts of workers have achieved their main occupational position. Here, social gradients of adverse material and psychosocial work environments and their impact on workers' physical and mental health are

---

J. Siegrist (✉)
Centre for Health and Society, Institute of Medical Sociology, Medical Faculty, Heinrich Heine University of Düsseldorf, Düsseldorf, Germany
e-mail: siegrist@uni-duesseldorf.de

M. Marmot
Institute of Health Equity, University College London, London, UK
e-mail: m.marmot@ucl.ac.uk

© Springer Nature Switzerland AG 2023
M. Wahrendorf et al. (eds.), *Handbook of Life Course Occupational Health*, Handbook Series in Occupational Health Sciences, https://doi.org/10.1007/978-3-031-30492-7_29

demonstrated. In a subsequent section, we ask to what extent adverse work and employment conditions contribute to the explanation of social inequalities in health in working populations, referring to findings from mediation and moderation analyses. In view of limited current evidence of this contribution, a more elaborated conceptual approach to the analysis of advantaged and disadvantaged occupational trajectories is proposed. The chapter ends with a short discussion of policy implications of this new knowledge. There are at least two compelling reasons to extend these implications to a global scale; first, the far-reaching impact of economic globalization and, second, the involvement of occupational health in two globally emerging concerns, the recent worldwide pandemic of COVID-19 and the climate crisis of global warming. As working populations are affected by these challenges all over the world, common and inclusive strategies need to be developed to promote and ensure decent and healthy work.

Keywords

Quality of work · Social inequalities · Occupational trajectories · Burden of disease

Introduction

In economically advanced societies, continued participation of adult people in the labor market is considered a core societal aim. It offers a regular income and basic social protection, it provides opportunities of skill development and personal growth, and it confers social status and social identity. Access to paid work and occupational career opportunities largely depend on educational qualification and level of skills. Developing these capabilities is a central task of primary socialization and education during childhood and young adulthood. Thus, work is shaping the life course, directly or indirectly, to a substantial degree. However, while the notion of a life course shaped by continued formal participation in the labor market represents a societal norm, it only partially describes the social reality. Even in economically most advanced countries, tangible parts of the adult population are excluded from paid work, either voluntarily or involuntarily, or their occupational trajectories are characterized by extended periods of interruption, including unemployment. Moreover, a growing proportion of people working in qualified jobs is facing job instability and job insecurity. In part, this is due to the fact that full-time permanent employment relationships are increasingly replaced by temporary jobs and other forms of nonstandard employment (see above; ▶ Chap. 13, "Biomechanical Hazards at Work and Adverse Health Using Job-Exposure Matrices"). In addition, economic competition and pressure on return-on-investment urge employers to implement restructuring strategies, such as off-shoring, downsizing, and outsourcing, resulting in layoffs and forced occupational mobility. These processes are exacerbated, and their consequences are magnified, by macroeconomic shocks and crises, and by technological innovations with far-reaching impact on employment. As a result of these developments, the notion of continuous employment as a dominant pattern of the adult life course before retirement has lost its supremacy.

Importantly, this dominant pattern is even less obvious among employed populations with lower levels of skills and occupational standing. Here, threats to employment continuity, risks of worklessness, and exposure to poor quality of work and employment are highly prevalent, and the same holds true for their adverse effects on individual life, including health and well-being (OECD 2021; see below). If we extend this perspective to economically less developed countries, adult life courses are often determined by the absence, rather than the presence of continuous employment. For instance, considering the distribution of informal workers across the world, more than 90% belong to low- and middle-income countries (ILO 2017). Informal work is characterized by a lack of protection by labor laws, including regular employment contracts ensuring continued pay, social security, and health insurance. In these countries, options of entering the labor market are restricted, and risks of long-term unemployment are high. As an example, in Northern Africa, over 25% of young adults in 2017 were neither employed, nor educated, nor in training (NEETs), with many more young women than men (ILO 2017). In general, in less developed countries, access to paid work is scarce, sporadic, poorly paid, and risky in terms of safety and health. This situation worsened rather dramatically following the outbreak of the COVID-19 pandemic in 2020. According to a recent international report, this was most obvious in lower-middle-income countries, where, in addition to the direct burden of morbidity and mortality due to the infection, a sharp drop of employment rates and a rapid increase of out-of-work and in-work poverty were observed, with disproportionally negative impact on women's employment and youth employment (ILO 2022). As mentioned, lack of formal employment and exposure to poor work at best are shaping life trajectories in large parts of adult populations in economically less-developed countries. This pattern differs rather substantially from the one observed in advanced societies.

As this chapter sets out to analyze social inequalities of work and health in a life course perspective, empirical evidence is required from research on occupational trajectories of employed populations. Preferably, this research contains longitudinal data on work and employment as well as on health. Given these restrictions, there is no surprise that the main body of scientific evidence is derived from social-epidemiological studies conducted in economically advanced societies, and mainly from European countries and Northern America. Therefore, the content of the next three parts of the chapter is largely based on information derived from these countries. These parts deal with two relevant stages of occupational trajectories. First, we consider the stage of entrance into the labor market in young adulthood. What is known about social inequalities in access to paid work? And what are the health consequences of exclusion from this main opportunity? In a more extended second part a stage in midlife is addressed when large parts of workers have achieved their main occupational position. Here, we are interested in the social distribution of specific material and psychosocial working conditions related to this position, and we ask how exposure to these conditions affects the health of working people. Subsequently, the challenging problem of attributing the social gradient of morbidity and mortality, at least in part, to adverse work and employment conditions is addressed (Marmot 2004; Mackenbach 2019). Answers to this question are of interest not only to science, but equally so to policy. The final part of the chapter contains a short discussion of policy implications of available scientific knowledge. Here, we extend the scope beyond economically advanced countries to address challenges of global concern.

Social Inequalities in Access to the Labor Market and Young Adults' Health

Macrolevel determinants of labor markets include the stage of economic development, technological advances, political, social, and ecological crises, and the demographic composition of workforces. Irrespective of their extension and quality, labor markets face the challenge of replacing older generations of workers by younger ones. To this end, an appropriate quantity and quality of incoming new workers needs to be available, and an acceptable balance between supply and demand should be reached through appropriate recruitment procedures. Here, educational qualification and skill level are the most important selection criteria. In all advanced societies, albeit to a different extent, we observe social inequalities of occupational attainment among young adults. On average across all OECD countries, 58% of the 25- to 34-year-old adults without completion of upper-secondary education are employed, compared to 85% among those with tertiary attainment. The unemployment rate of the former versus the latter group is twice as high. Although this rate is highest during the first two years after graduation, it is still high one to two years later. For instance, among 25- to 34-year-old adults with upper-secondary (but not tertiary) educational attainment, the unemployment rate dropped rather modestly from 21% to 14% (OECD 2021). Thus, educational attainment is a critical determinant of access to the labor market in young adulthood. In addition, it affects the quality of available jobs and the level of earnings. Technological progress is widening the social disparities among new generations entering the labor market. To date, it is already obvious that many routine jobs that can easily be automated will disappear, not only among blue-collar manufacturing jobs, but also in medium-skilled white-collar occupations, while jobs requiring intense knowledge, social skills, and adaptive coping abilities are expanding (Eichhorst 2020). To acquire these latter qualifications, tertiary education and/or continued vocational training are essential prerequisites. Initiatives of combining apprenticeships with continued education are a promising strategy to increase labor market participation of young adults. Even after labor market entry, job continuity and career promotion largely depend on recurrent and timely adjustment and updating of skills along occupational trajectories.

Unexpected macrosocietal shocks have profoundly aggravated social inequalities in access to paid work among young adults. The global financial crisis of 2008–2009 is one such shock. It caused a sharp increase in youth employment, in particular in Southern Europe, where the percentage of 15- to 24-year-olds defined by NEET approached a level comparable to the one reported from Northern Africa. In 2011, across the European Union, some 7.5 million young people in this age groups were classified as NEETs, and this number was augmented by an additional 6.5 million young adults in the age group 25–29 years. This massive exclusion of young adults from paid work results in substantial costs in terms of individual health and well-being, societal functioning, and economic growth (Eichhorst et al. 2013). Although job opportunities improved in recent years in these regions, expanding employment was mainly characterized by a growth of part-time jobs, temporary employment, fixed-term contingent work, or independent contracting, reducing the availability of full-time, permanent, well-protected jobs (Eurofound 2021). The COVID-19 pandemic starting in 2020 is a further macrosocietal shock. During its first wave, it caused a sudden increase in unemployment rates. As an example, in the USA, this rate rose from 3.5% in February 2020 to 14.7% in April the same year (OECD 2021). In many countries, job retention schemes mitigated these effects to some extent, and trends of recovery were observed. However, the pandemic's afflictions to education and job opportunities, as well as to the health and well-being of young adults, go far beyond elevated unemployment risks (Barfood et al. 2021).

Against these developments we ask what are the consequences of these socially unequal opportunities of entering the labor market for young adults' health and well-being? To date, there is considerable evidence that the experience of unemployment at the age of expected labor market entry increases the risk of incident mental disorder, mainly depression. Findings from observational studies in several Southern European countries hit by the global financial crisis of 2008–2009 support this claim (Van Hal 2015). However, a causal link underlying this association is still under debate as personal vulnerability factors of youth unemployment may interfere with this conclusion. In a recent review of 14 studies exploring the links between social deprivation in early life and disadvantaged labor market entry, a strong, consistent impact of social disadvantage in early life on poor employment opportunities later on was demonstrated (Wahrendorf and Demakakos 2020). Conditions of early social deprivation included father's low socioeconomic position, adverse childhood experiences, lack of parental support during school, and broken family relationships. In addition to its negative effect on employment opportunities, socioeconomic disadvantage in early life reduced young adults' mental and physical health. Moreover, impaired health during childhood contributed to the explanation of poor occupational standing in early adulthood. These observations support the notion of a bidirectional association between difficulties of entering paid work and mental health, with a considerable impact of childhood adversity (Duncan et al. 2017).

On balance, there are more studies available that document socioeconomic, psychological, and health-related determinants of youth unemployment than investigations that explore the health consequences of experienced unemployment at entry or early stage of employment careers. An early study based on the 1958 British birth cohort examined the risk of depressive or anxiety disorder following the year of manifest unemployment among young men aged 24–33 years. Based on diagnoses from medical consultations, this study revealed a relative risk of poor mental health that was twice as high among unemployed compared to the remaining young men.

This significantly elevated risk was confirmed after adjusting for preexisting mental health problems as well as adverse health behaviors and disadvantaged socioeconomic conditions (Montgomery et al. 1999). Similar findings are available from some developing economies, although derived from less convincing, cross-sectional study designs and based on a less vigorous definition of unemployment. As a consistent result, the prevalence rate of depression among young unemployed adults was found to be more than twice as high as the rate observed among older unemployed populations. While among the latter the prevalence rate was 13–14% according to a systematic review (Paul and Moser 2009), rates were 30.9% in Ethiopia (Mokona et al. 2020), 39.5% in South Korea (Lim et al. 2018), and 49.3% in Bangladesh (Rafi et al. 2019). The study from Ethiopia is particularly instructive as it included a large community-based sample and collected a comprehensive set of additional sociological and psychological data. Multivariate analysis revealed that male sex, long duration of unemployment, poor social support, low self-esteem, and alcohol use were factors most strongly related to depression within this sample (Mokona et al. 2020).

Preventing young adults from starting paid work and dismissing them from an early job are highly stressful experiences as they disrupt status acquisition, reduce their chances of future labor market participation, and their options of developing personal autonomy and financial independence. Unfortunately, developing despair and mental distress under these conditions is a frequent outcome. Although youth unemployment is not restricted to less skilled, less educated groups, these outcomes are more severe among these latter, given their lack of material and psychosocial resources to tackle this threat (Edwards 2008). Therefore, the recommendation from the Independent Inquiry into Inequalities in Health proposed in the UK in 1998 is still universally valid: "We recommend policies which improve the opportunities for work and which ameliorate the health consequences of unemployment. Specifically, we recommend ... further investment in high-quality training for young and long-term unemployed people" (Marmot 2004, p. 268).

Adverse Working Conditions During Midlife and Their Effects on Health

With a major shift from an industrial to a postindustrial, service and information-based economy, the nature of work and employment underwent far-reaching changes. At the level of employment sectors, tertiary occupations and professions were expanding, at the expense of industrial and agricultural occupations. With this shift, physically strenuous workplaces with exposure to noxious physical, chemical, and biological hazards were reduced, whereas more jobs were characterized by mental and socioemotional demands. At the level of employment relations, technological developments promoted flexible work arrangements, including mobile and home-based work. And more importantly, as a result of economic globalization, the standard employment relationship with its full-time, continued work contracts eroded, whereas different forms of nonstandard employment became more prevalent, reducing job stability and security (Kalleberg 2009).

How did these changes affect the quality of work and employment and their distribution across the social hierarchy of employed populations? Despite a reduced industrial workforce, exposure to physically adverse working conditions is still prevalent to a considerable extent. According to a European-wide survey, between 10% and 20% of employed men and women are confronted with posture-related, ambient, biological, or chemical hazards at their workplace (Eurofound 2021). The distribution of exposure follows a pronounced social gradient, with people working in less-skilled, manual, blue-collar, or other elementary occupations being more often exposed than those with higher occupational standing. This was documented for chemical substances with carcinogenic or mutagenic effects (Montano 2020), physical exposures including noise, heat, cold, or radiation (Toch et al. 2014), and ergonomic factors, in particular postural constraints, repetitive movements, heavy lifting, or vibrations (Montano 2014). However, with the shift from an industrial to a service and communication–oriented economy, nonmaterial, psychosocial work environments became more prominent. The identification of these latter conditions through scientific research provides a challenging task, due to their complexity and variability. In essence, psychosocial work environments with relevance to health and well-being include those employment conditions, organizational and interpersonal factors that affect workers' mental and physical health via sensory input, cognitions, emotions, and their physiological consequences. Work intensity, conflicting demands, repetitive tasks, job insecurity, or interpersonal tensions with superiors and colleagues are examples of such environments. Exposure to these environments matters for health to the extent that they threaten important human needs. These needs include, among others, a sense of security, trust and belonging, and recurrent experiences self-efficacy and self-esteem (Siegrist and Marmot 2004). Threats to these needs by lack of autonomy and control, job instability, poor rewards, or social isolation evoke strong negative emotions and pronounced physiological stress reactions with adverse long-term consequences for health. With the help of a theoretical model, critical aspects of stressful psychosocial work environments can be delineated at a level of generalization that allows for their identification in a wide range of occupations.

Whereas several such theoretical models were developed and tested (for review Theorell 2020), two concepts received special attention in occupational and epidemiological research dealing with occupational health and its social determinants, the models termed "demand-control" and "effort-reward imbalance." The former model posits that jobs characterized by high (mainly psychological) demands and by low job task control or decision authority exert noxious effects on health. Effects of this combination, termed "job strain," on health are even more pronounced if no social support at work is available (Karasek and Theorell 1990). The latter model focuses on contractual features at work where high effort is often not met by adequate rewards in terms of pay, promotion, job security, and esteem. A recurrent imbalance between high "cost" and low "gain" compromises workers' coping abilities, triggering adaptive emotional and physiological breakdown (Siegrist 1996; Siegrist and

Wahrendorf 2016). It is therefore of interest to know whether the exposure to these types of stressful work environments follows the known social gradient as well. The findings of studies exploring this question are not always consistent, but they repeatedly confirm the social gradient for the models' core dimensions of "low control" and "low reward," respectively (Dragano and Wahrendorf 2016). A recent analysis based on a comprehensive dataset supports the notion of a social gradient of the two theoretical models, as displayed in Fig. 1. Based on several waves of the European Working Conditions Survey conducted between 1995 and 2015 in 15 countries, the prevalence of job strain and effort-reward imbalance, assessed by appropriate proxy measures, was analyzed according to four occupational categories (high- vs. low-skilled manual; high- vs. low-skilled clerical occupations) (Rigó et al. 2021). Predicted values of work stressors by occupational group are shown in Fig. 1, derived from three-way multilevel regression analysis (with employees nested in country-years, which are in turn nested in countries). The upper part of the figure relates to the job strain model, covering data from all five waves, while the lower part concerns the effort-reward imbalance model, with available data from three waves from 2005 to 2015. Overall, highest levels of stressful work are obvious in non-skilled manual occupations, and lowest levels in high-skilled occupations.

Due to a rapidly growing field of epidemiologic research dealing with these models, a well-developed body of knowledge on their effects on health and well-

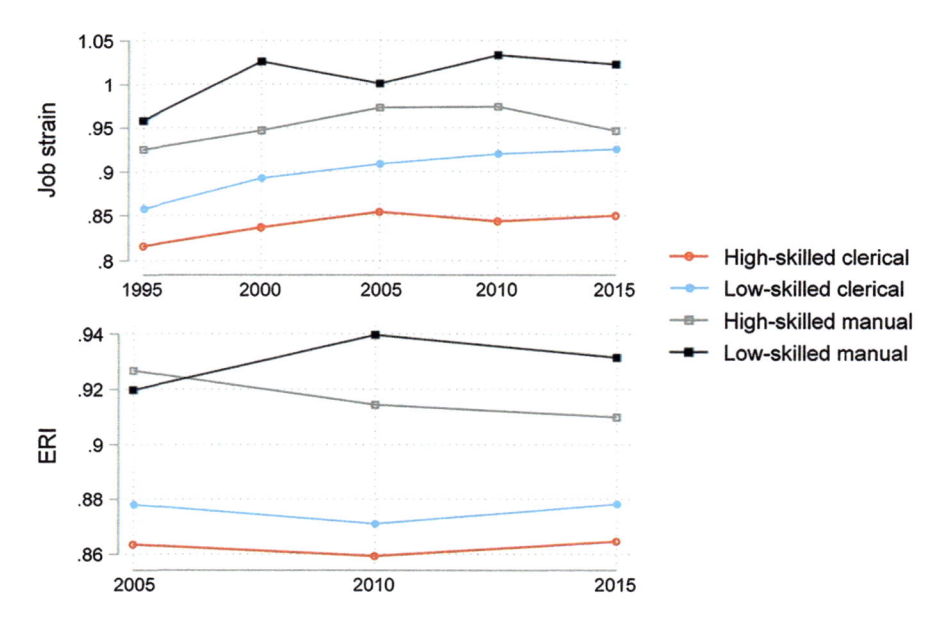

Fig. 1 Results of three-way multilevel regression analysis: Mean level of work stress (job strain, upper part; 1995–2015; N = 74,959; effort-reward imbalance (ERI), lower part; 2005–2015; N = 45,329) according to occupational grade (four groups). Source: Rigó et al. 2021 (extracts from Figure 1, p. 469, and from Figure 2, p. 470). This is an open access article distributed under the terms of the Creative Commons CC BY license, http://creativecommons.org/licenses/by/4.0/.

being is available. A meta-review of a variety of systematic literature reviews of these studies offers a preliminary summary of evidence (Niedhammer et al. 2021). It documents relatively strongest support for associations of stressful psychosocial work with depressive disorders and ischemic heart disease. For instance, for job strain, significantly elevated odds ratios of depressive disorders varied across studies between 1.22 and 1.77, and those of ischemic heart disease varied between 1.17 and 1.45. Related odds ratios of depression were elevated by 60–70% for effort-reward imbalance, and by 18–58% in case of ischemic heart disease (Niedhammer et al. 2021). To a lesser extent, these associations were observed for a variety of other health outcomes, in particular type 2 diabetes (Pena-Gralle et al. 2021), musculoskeletal disorders (Taibi et al. 2021), hypertension (Gilbert-Ouimet et al. 2013), and reduced health functioning (Niedhammer et al. 2021). Health outcomes with immediate negative effects on the economy are long-term sick leave and disability pension due to a chronic disorder. For both conditions associations with the two work stress models were reported (Head et al. 2007; Robroek et al. 2013). More specifically, in an influential Finnish study, the risk of disability pension from depressive disorders was 4.7 times as high among employees who were simultaneously exposed to job strain, effort-reward imbalance, and organizational injustice compared to those without these exposures (Juvani et al. 2018). Finally, few studies assessed mortality risks of stressful work. In an early report, cardiovascular mortality was substantially increased in a blue-collar cohort exposed to job strain and effort-reward imbalance at work (Kivimäki et al. 2002). A more recent, more extensive multicohort study found less consistent results. Among men, within the subgroup of participants with prevalent cardiometabolic disease, a significantly elevated risk of total mortality was observed for job strain, but not for effort-reward imbalance. In contrast, in the majority sample without prevalent cardiometabolic disease, this significant effect was restricted to effort-reward imbalance. For women, no respective associations were apparent (Kivimäki et al. 2018).

Of notice, positive health effects are also reported from studies that measure a health-protective psychosocial work environment. Active, cognitively stimulating work, as defined by high demand and high control, is one such measure. As an example, a longitudinal analysis of data from seven cohort studies revealed a significantly reduced hazard ratio of dementia among older people who were previously exposed to cognitively stimulating active work, compared to those exposed to passive, stressful work. Moreover, this protective effect was strongest among those with high education (Kivimäki et al. 2021). However, the vast majority of epidemiologic investigations emphasize the work-related burden of disease rather than the work-related resources toward improved health.

Taken together, there is solid evidence of elevated risks of several highly prevalent chronic diseases and disorders due to exposure to a stressful psychosocial work environment, as measured by the two theoretical models or their single components. In a majority of cases, these disorders were shown to be more prevalent among lower socioeconomic population groups (Mackenbach 2019). As a higher prevalence of stressful working conditions was also documented (see above), it is of interest to know whether, and to what extent, these psychosocial working conditions and additional adversity at work can explain the documented social inequalities in morbidity and mortality of working-age populations.

The Contribution of Work Toward Explaining Social Inequalities in Health

In statistical terms, the question of whether work factors contribute to the explanation of social inequalities in health is answered by information derived from mediation analysis. This approach requires that the following three associations are statistically significant: first, the relation between socioeconomic position (SEP) and the health outcome; second, the relation between SEP and the mediator (the stressful work environment); and, third, the association between the mediator and the health outcome. Moreover, in temporal sequence, SEP must precede the occurrence of the mediator, and both factors must precede the onset of the health condition under study. If these requirements are met, mediation analysis compares the estimate of a direct effect of SEP on disease risk with the estimate of an indirect effect mediated by an adverse psychosocial work environment. In a conventional approach (most often applied in respective research), two consecutive models are analyzed, with a first model focusing on the direct effect of SEP on health and a second model estimating the indirect effect after adjustment for the first effect. If a substantial reduction of the first effect results from the second model, this observation is interpreted as evidence of a mediating role of the explanatory construct. In this case, adverse working conditions to some extent contribute to the explanation of higher disease risks among occupational groups with low SEP. A number of studies performed this type of analysis, demonstrating a sizeable contribution of material and psychosocial adversity at work toward explaining the social gradient of morbidity and mortality (Hoven and Siegrist 2013). For instance, in a study of mortality differences between the two groups of manual workers and managers in France, an elevated mortality hazard ratio of 1.88 among manual workers, compared to the one of managers, was reduced to 1.22 after adjusting for adverse material and psychosocial work stressors, such as job insecurity, as well as biomechanical and physical hazards (Niedhammer et al. 2011). In this case, working conditions "explained" about two-thirds of the social difference in mortality risk. In terms of policy implications, results of mediation analysis are important as they instruct interventions that aim at reducing social inequalities in health.

Yet, more recently, this conventional method of mediation analysis was criticized on methodological grounds. It was argued that unobserved confounders may interfere with the three-way associations under study as they can act on the predictor, the mediator, and the outcome, thus causing biased results. Moreover, the so-called "effect heterogeneity" was not addressed in this approach, meaning that the strength of an effect of the mediator on health can vary between socioeconomic groups. Therefore, new statistical approaches based on a counterfactual model were proposed to resolve these problems (VanderWeele 2015). It is currently premature to judge whether results based on a counterfactual model invalidate the evidence available from conventional mediation analysis. However, the problem of effect heterogeneity has already been studied by traditional moderation analysis, applying interaction terms between SEP, mediator, and health outcome. A variable is considered a moderator if it affects the strength of the association between an independent variable (e.g., SEP) and a health outcome. In this regard, moderation analysis is again relevant in policy terms as it may identify a vulnerable subgroup within a population that deserves high priority in resource allocation. Sociological theory predicts that people with a low socioeconomic position, living and working in deprived contexts, are more susceptible to the health effects of social stressors than those in more privileged positions, most likely due to their lack of resources needed to mitigate adverse effects (Mirowsky and Ross 1986). This accumulation of disadvantage may aggravate health effects, as indicated in a synergy exceeds additive effects (see example below).

Although fewer investigations tested the moderation hypothesis of health inequalities, if compared to tests of the mediation hypothesis, several studies lend support to this notion. To mention just one example, the joint effect of low SEP and stressful work, as measured by effort-reward imbalance, on the risk of experiencing insomnia was explored among several thousand middle-aged employed men in Japan. These men were stratified according to their occupational position into three groups with high, medium, and low status. It was hypothesized that the effect of stressful work on insomnia was strongest among the low-status group. Taking the highest of three occupational groups that scored low on work stress as reference (odds ratio [OR] = 1.0), the OR for insomnia in this occupational group scoring high on work stress (upper tertile) was 3.94. In comparison, in the lowest occupational group with low level of work stress the respective OR was 1.31, but in the low occupation group with high work stress the OR of insomnia was 9.43. A statistically significant synergy index indicated that this combination exceeded the additive effects, thus supporting the hypothesis (Yoshioka et al. 2013).

To summarize, despite some promising examples, the success of current research efforts to attribute the social gradient of health in working populations, at least in part, to adverse material and psychosocial working conditions is restricted. Both statistical approaches of mediation and moderation analysis suffer from methodological weaknesses. In addition, the requirement of large sample sizes to conduct moderation analysis in terms of multiplicative interaction prevented an extensive test of this approach. Finally, the quantitative contribution of work toward explaining social inequalities in health was relatively modest in several studies that estimated the difference between direct and indirect effects in mediation analysis. What does this mean for future research on this topic?

At the conceptual level, it seems important to apply the life course perspective in a more elaborated way when dealing with the explanation of health inequalities. In this contribution, the two stages of access to labor market and midlife exposure to work were considered separate processes rather than being analyzed as parts of long-term trajectories with successive cumulative advantage and disadvantage. With this latter approach, a more pronounced breadth of inequalities of occupational careers becomes apparent, reaching from the low end of a precarious low skill arrangement without promotion prospects and job stability to the high end of a socioeconomically and emotionally privileged, upwardly mobile "flourishing" career. Across this spectrum of occupational trajectories, distinct clusters can be identified that mirror differences in relative deprivation. Along these lines, a recent approach to study whole employment histories in relation to unequal health is of interest. Using retrospectively assessed occupational trajectories, information on risk accumulation, exposure duration, interruptions, and mobility processes was collected in a stress-theoretical framework (Wahrendorf et al. 2019). More specifically, three types of critical occupational trajectories were identified that were assumed to predict poor health: (1) precarious careers (e.g., temporary contracts and repeated job changes); (2) discontinuous careers (e.g., involuntary interruptions and temporary unemployment); and (3) careers with cumulative disadvantage (e.g., being "locked" in a hazardous low-skill job). In a next step, associations of these types of critical occupational trajectories (experienced between the ages of 25 and 45 years) with distinct measures of health (collected at later age, i.e., between 45 and 60 years) were analyzed in a large cohort study. Results demonstrated similar significant relations of single indicators of the three types of employment histories with measures of physical and mental health functioning among men and women (Wahrendorf et al. 2019). In a consecutive analysis of the same cohort, these adverse employment histories were partly associated with a composite score of allostatic load (Wahrendorf et al. 2022). In both analyses, strongest associations were observed in case of cumulative disadvantage.

It is still premature to judge the potential contribution of this extended frame of analysis to the explanation of health inequalities. Even if further research along these lines is needed the solid evidence base of adverse health effects of stressful psychosocial working conditions during midlife, as documented above with reference to the job strain and the effort-reward imbalance models, calls for preventive activities, in particular, as working populations with lower socioeconomic positions are most often exposed to these conditions.

Implications for Policy

In this chapter, a major part of scientific information supporting the main argument has been derived from research in advanced societies. There are at least two compelling reasons to extend the policy implications of this knowledge beyond these societies. First, with the extension of economic globalization, the workforce of several rapidly developing countries in the Global "South" is being profoundly transformed by a shift from agricultural and industrial sectors to an expanding service sector. As a result, the structural features of work organization and employment relations observed in advanced societies are becoming increasingly common in these countries, and the same holds true for a substantial impact of transnational corporations and worldwide operating financial markets on national economies. There is reason to believe that the main scientific findings on working conditions and health inequalities reported above are valid for rapidly developing countries as well, as documented by emerging research on occupational health in some of these regions, such as China and Latin America (Siegrist and Wahrendorf 2016). However, overall, quality of work and employment in these and related regions is still substantially worse, given the continued high proportion of informal workers exposed to precarious, unsafe, and unhealthy work (Hyde et al. 2020; Muntaner et al. 2020). A recent joint WHO-ILO report assessing the global burden of deaths attributable to main occupational risk factors (long working hours, exposure to particulate matters, gases and fumes, asbestos, and injuries) confirmed a disproportionally high impact on the low-skilled workforce in the Global "South" (WHO/ILO 2021). Therefore, these regions deserve highest priority if policy measures, like the ones proposed below, are being implemented. Taking a broader perspective and based on reports from WHO commissions, several far-reaching recommendations of policies toward reducing health inequalities were developed in two important world regions, the Americas (Commission of PAHO 2019) and the Eastern Mediterranean Region (WHO 2021).

The second compelling reason of extending the policy perspective beyond economically advanced countries relates to the involvement of occupational health in globally emerging concerns, i.e., the recent worldwide pandemic of COVID-19 (Barfood et al. 2021), the climate crisis of global warming (Thiery et al. 2021), and the related threats to economic and societal progress (United Nations 2015). Working populations are affected by these challenges all over the world, independent of their economic and social standing. Thus, common and inclusive strategies need to be developed to ensure decent and healthy work. Being aware of an urgent need of action, several relevant international organizations, scientific expert groups, and influential stakeholders have proposed policy recommendations that aim at integrating sustainable climate, decent working and employment conditions, and more equitably health across populations. These recommendations include long-term goals of developing a more resilient, decarbonized, circular economy, combined with a fair distribution of economic resources, and a substantial improvement of working and living conditions that reduce health inequalities.

Long-term goals need to be supported by medium- and short-term goals. For instance, in order to improve health-promoting quality of work and employment with sustainable effects across the life course of workers and across future generations, hazardous work and employment arrangements deserve systematic monitoring and surveillance, followed by improved prevention through well-resourced occupational health and safety services, implementation of national and international regulations, and structural worksite health promotion programs. Based on the scientific evidence reported above, these latter programs strengthen health and well-being of workers through targeted organizational developments. Several intervention studies based on the theoretical models mentioned documented beneficial effects on mental and cardiovascular health by improving job control and occupational rewards, strengthening social support at work, and reducing the duration and intensity of work demands (Brisson et al. 2020). While promising, these interventions so far were realized in white-collar occupations rather than among blue-collar or precariously employed workers with highest needs of support. A recent report proposed synergy effects of health-promoting worksite programs and investments into sustainable environments, e.g., by reducing working time, shortening the working week and reducing commuting, and by extending homework and reconciling work with nonwork demands (Munro et al. 2020).

Given the intimate links between the microenvironment of enterprises and the macroenvironment of influential labor-market developments and economic forces, a different type of preventive measures must be addressed, i.e., national labor and social policies. These policies represent essential elements of modern welfare states offering basic safety and protection against major threats, such as unemployment, occupational injury, work-related disability, need for medical care, and poverty at old age. Moreover, through active labor market policies, they integrate unemployed people into the labor market, and they qualify the less educated workforce by offering extended training programs. While these policies aim at improving work participation and quality of work, they also exert positive effects on workers' well-being (Lunau et al. 2020). If targeting specific vulnerable groups, they contribute to a reduction of social inequalities. At the level of the European Union, the Youth Employment Initiative is one respective example. It was developed to reduce youth unemployment and NEET by providing financial resources to member states with poorly developed labor markets. As part of the endorsed European Social Funds Plus program, Youth Guarantee schemes are offered to workless people under the age of 30, promoting their integration through apprenticeships, vocational education and training, and employer incentives. A preliminary evaluation confirms an increased employability of these target groups (European Union 2020). Strengthening national labor, as well as health and social policies, and providing the resources needed to mitigate the deleterious effects of the COVID-19 pandemic are aims of global importance. Obviously, substantial policy efforts will be required to reduce the developmental gaps between more and less advanced societies. Prioritizing investments into sustainable work and employment represents one approach to this end.

Cross-References

- ▶ A Life Course Perspective on Work and Mental Health: The Working Lives of Young Adults
- ▶ Adverse Effect of Psychosocial Stressors at Work and Long Working Hours Along the Cardiovascular Continuum
- ▶ Gig Work and Health
- ▶ Pathways to Retirement and Health Effects
- ▶ Precarious Work and Health
- ▶ Psychosocial Work Environment and Health: Applying Job-Exposure Matrices and Work Organization and Management Practice
- ▶ Transformation of Modern Work, Rise of Atypical Employment, and Health

References

Barfood A, Coutts A, Salai G (2021) Youth employment in times of Covid. ILO, Geneva

Brisson C, Aubé K, Gilbert-Ouimet M, Duchaine CS, Trudel X, Vézina M (2020) Organizational-level interventions and occupational health. In: Theorell T (ed) Handbook of socioeconomic determinants of occupational health, pp 505–536. Springer Nature Switzerland

Commission of the Pan American Health Organization on Equity and Health Inequalities in the Americas (2019) Just societies: health equity and dignified lives. Report of the Commission of the Pan American Health Organization on Equity and Health Inequalities in America. PAHO, Washington DC

Duncan GJ, Magnuson K, Votruba-Drzal E (2017) Moving beyond correlations in assessing the consequences of poverty. Ann Rev Psychol, 68:413–434

Dragano N, Wahrendorf M (2016) A social inequalities perspective on effort-reward imbalance at work. In: Siegrist J, Wahrendorf M (eds) Work stress and health in a globalized economy: the model of effort-reward imbalance. Springer International Publications, Cham, pp 67–85

Edwards R (2008) Who is hurt by procyclical mortality? Soc Sci Med 67(12):2051–2058

Eichhorst W (2020) The changing nature of work and employment in developed countries. In: Bültmann U, Siegrist J (eds) Handbook of disability, work and health. Springer Nature, Cham, pp 17–32

Eichhorst W, Hint H, Rinne U (2013) Youth unemployment in Europe: what to do about it? IZA policy paper no. 65. Institute for the Study of labor (IZA), Bonn

Eurofound (2021) Covid-19: implications for employment and working life. Publications Office of the European Union, Luxembourg. https://www.eurofound.europa.eu/publications/report/2021/covid-19-implications-for-employment-and-working-life. Accessed 4 May 2022

European Commission (2020) Commission staff working document evaluation. Evaluation of the ESF and YEI Support to Youth Employment. European Commission SWD, Brussels. 24 Sept 2022

Gilbert-Ouimet M, Trudel X, Brisson C, Milot A, Vézina M (2013) Adverse effects of psychosocial work factors on blood pressure: systematic review of studies on demand-control and effort-reward imbalance models. Scand J Work Environ Health 40:109–132

Head J, Kivimäki M, Siegrist J et al (2007) Effort-reward imbalance and relational injustice at work predict sickness absence: the Whitehall II study. J Pychosom Res 63:433–440

Hoven H, Siegrist J (2013) Work characteristics, socioeconomic position and health: a systematic review of mediation and moderation effects in prospective studies. Occup Environ Med 70(9): 663–669

Hyde M, George S, Kumar V (2020) Trends in work and employment in rapidly developing countries. In: Bültmann U, Siegrist J (eds) Handbook of disability, work and health. Springer Nature, Cham, pp 33–52

International Labour Organization (2017) World employment and social outlook – trends 2017. ILO, Geneva

International Labour Organization (2022) World employment and social outlook – trends 2022. ILO, Geneva

Juvani A, Oksanen T, Vitanen M, Salo P, Pentti J, Kivimäki M, Vahtera J (2018) Clustering of job strain, effort-reward imbalance, and organizational injustice and the risk of work disability: a cohort study. Scand J Work Environ Health 44(5):485–495

Kalleberg AL (2009) Precarious work, insecure workers: employment relations in transition. Am Sociol Rev 74(1):1–22

Karasek RA, Theorell T (1990) Healthy work. Basic Books, New York

Kivimäki M, Leino-Arias P, Lukkonen R, Riihimäi H, Vahtera J, Kirjonen J (2002) Work stress and risk of cardiovascular mortality: prospective cohort study of industrial employees. BMJ 325: 857–860

Kivimäki M, Pentti J, Ferrie JE et al (2018) Work stress and risk of death in men and women with and without cardiometabolic disease: a multicohort study. Lancet Diabetes Endocrinol 6:705–713

Kivimäki M, Walker KA, Pentti J, Nyberg S, Mars N, Vahtera J et al (2021) Cognitive stimulation in the workplace, plasma proteins, and risk of dementia: three analyses of population cohort studies. BMJ 374:n1804

Lim AY, Lee S-H, Jeon Y, Yoo R, Jung H-Y (2018) Job-seeking stress, mental health problems, and the role of perceived social support in university graduates in Korea. J Korean Med Sci 33(19): e149

Lunau T, Rigo M, Dragano N (2020) From national labour and social policies to individual work stressors. In: Theorell T (ed) Handbook of socioeconomic determinants of occupational health. Springer Nature, Cham, pp 131–148

Mackenbach JP (2019) Health inequalities. Oxford University Press, Oxford

Marmot M (2004) The status syndrome, vol 1. Bloomsbury, London, p 150

Mirowsky J, Ross CE (1986) Social patterns of distress. Ann Rev Sociol 12:23–45

Mokona H, Kalkidan Y, Getinet A (2020) Youth unemployment and mental health: prevalence and associate factors of depression among unemployed young adults in Gedeo zone, Southern Ethiopia. Int J Mental Health Syst 14:61

Montano D (2014) Upper body and lower limbs musculoskeletal symptoms and health inequalities in Europe: an analysis of cross-sectional data. BMC Musculoskel Disord 15:285

Montano D (2020) Social distribution of occupational hazards. In: Theorell T (ed) Handbook of socioeconomic determinants of occupational health. Springer Nature, Cham, pp 169–189

Montgomery SM, Cook DG, Bartley MJ, Wadsworth ME (1999) Unemployment predates symptoms of depression and anxiety resulting in medical consultation in young men. Int J Epidemiol 29(1):95–100

Munro A, Boyce T, Marmot M (2020) Sustainable health equity: achieving a net-zero UK, vol 4. Institute of Health Equity, London, p e551

Muntaner C, Ng E, Gunn V, Shahidi FV, Vives A, Mahabir DF, Chung H (2020) Precarious employment conditions, exploitation, and health in two global regions: Latin America and the Caribbean and East Asia. In: Theorell T (ed) Handbook of socioeconomic determinants of occupational health. Springer Nature, Cham, pp 13–35

Niedhammer I, Bertais S, Witt K (2021) Psychosocial work exposures and health outcomes: a meta-review of 72 literature reviews with meta-analysis. Scand J Work Environ Health 47(7):489–508

Niedhammer I, Bourgkard E, Chau N, The Lorhandicap Study Group (2011) Occupational and behavioural factors in the explanation of social inequalities in premature and total mortality: a 12.5-year follow-up in the Lorhandicap study. Eur J Epidemiol 26(1):1–12

OECD (2021) Education at a glance 2021. OECD, Paris

Paul KI, Moser K (2009) Unemployment impairs mental health: meta-analyses. J Vocat Behav 74(3):264–282

Pena-Gralle APB, Talbot D, Duchaine CS, Lavigne-Robichaud M, Trudel X, Aubé K, Gralle M, Gilbert-Ouimet M, Milot A, Brisson C (2021) Job strain and effort-reward imbalance as risk factors for type 2 diabetes mellitus: a systematic review and meta-analysis of prospective studies. Scand J Work Environ Health 47(4):249–257

Rafi M, Mamun MA, Hsan K, Hossain M, Gozal D (2019) Psychological implications of unemployment among Bangladesh civil service job seekers. Front Psych 10:578

Rigó M, Dragano N, Wahrendorf M, Siegrist J, Lunau T (2021) Work stress on rise? Comparative analysis of trends in work stressors using the European working conditions survey. Int Arch Occup Environ Health 94(3):459–474

Robroek SJ, Schuring M, Croezen S et al (2013) Poor health, unhealthy behaviors and unfavourable work characteristics influence pathways of exit from paid employment among older workers- a four-year follow-up study. Scand J Work Environ Health 39(2):125–133

Siegrist J (1996) Adverse health effects of high effort-low reward conditions at work. J Occup Health Psychol 1(1):27–43

Siegrist J, Marmot M (2004) Health inequalities and the psychosocial environment – two scientific challenges. Soc Sci Med 58(8):1463–1473

Siegrist J, Wahrendorf M (eds) (2016) Work stress and health in a globalized economy: the model of effort-reward imbalance. Springer International Publications, Cham

Taibi Y, Metzler YA, Bellingrath S, Müller A (2021) A systematic overview on the risk effects of psychosocial work characteristics on musculoskeletal disorders, absenteeism and workplace accidents. Appl Ergon 95:103434

Theorell T (ed) (2020) Handbook of socioeconomic determinants of occupational health. Springer Nature, Cham

Thiery W, Lange S, Rogely J, Schleussner CF, Gudmundsson L, Seneviratne SI et al (2021) Intergenerational inequities in exposure to climate extremes. Science 374(6564):158–160

Toch M, Bambra C, Lunau T, van der Wel K, Witvliet M, Dragano N et al (2014) All part of the job? The contribution of the psychosocial and physical work environment to health inequalities in Europe and the European health divide. Int J Health Serv 44(2):285–305

United Nations (2015) Transforming our world: the 2030 agenda for sustainable development, New York

Van Hal G (2015) The true cost of the economic crisis on psychological well-being: a review. Psychol Res Behav Manag 8:17–25

VanderWeele T (2015) Explanation in causal inference: methods for mediation and interaction. Oxford University Press, Oxford, p dyw277

Wahrendorf M, Chandola T, Goldberg M, Zins M, Hoven H, Siegrist J (2022) Adverse employment histories and allostatic load: associations over the working life. J Epidemiol Community Health 76:374–381

Wahrendorf M, Demakakos P (2020) Childhood determinants of occupational health at older ages. In: Theorell T (ed) Handbook of socioeconomic determinants of occupational health. Springer Nature, Cham, pp 321–338

Wahrendorf M, Hoven H, Goldberg M, Zins M, Siegrist J (2019) Adverse employment histories and health functioning: the CONSTANCES study. Int J Epidemiol 48:402–414

WHO (2021) Build back fairer: achieving health equity in the eastern Mediterranean region. Executive summary. Commission on Social Determinants of Health. WHO Regional Office for the Eastern Mediterranean, Cairo

WHO/ILO (2021) WHO/ILO joint estimates of the work-related burden of disease and injury, 2000–2016. WHO, ILO, Geneva

Yoshioka E, Saijo Y, Kita T, Staoh H, Kawaharada M, Kishi R (2013) Effect of the interaction between employment level and psychosocial work environment on insomnia in male Japanese public service workers. Int J Behav Med 20(3):355–364

Conceptual and Methodological Directions of Occupational Life Course Research

30

Alexis Descatha, Tarani Chandola, and Morten Wahrendorf

Contents

Introduction	546
Objective	546
From Perspective	546
...To Challenges	551
Through Possible Rupture like COVID-19 Pandemic	553
To the Future Using Prospective Modeling?	555
Cross-References	556
References	557

Abstract

This chapter is not a conclusion but an outline of possible future directions and summary of current challenges of life course epidemiology in the field of occupational health. Thereby, it aims to integrate the introduction and the chapters of the book that each mention possible future directions and current challenges in the field. Challenges include the need for integrative approaches that take into account the transformation of the working world, the increase in inequalities, and the need for

---

A. Descatha (✉)
Univ Angers, CHU Angers, Univ Rennes, Inserm, EHESP, Irset (Institut de recherche en santé, environnement et travail), UMR_S 1085, SFR ICAT, Ester Team, Angers, France

CHU Angers, Poisoning Control Center-Clinical Data Center, Angers, France

Epidemiology and Prevention, Donald and Barbara Zucker School of Medicine, Hofstra University Northwell Health, New York, NY, USA
e-mail: alexis.descatha@inserm.fr

T. Chandola
Faculty of Social Sciences, University of Hong Kong, Hong Kong SAR, China

M. Wahrendorf
Centre for Health and Society, Institute of Medical Sociology, Medical Faculty, Heinrich Heine University of Düsseldorf, Düsseldorf, Germany

© Springer Nature Switzerland AG 2023
M. Wahrendorf et al. (eds.), *Handbook of Life Course Occupational Health*, Handbook Series in Occupational Health Sciences, https://doi.org/10.1007/978-3-031-30492-7_30

developing appropriate methodological tools. Beside addressing these challenges, core questions that remain are how can life course occupational health epidemiology develop predictions of the near future, help in prioritizing prevention actions, and quantify the effect of this prevention. Finally, the chapter uses the pandemic as an example of an event with the potential to rupture or accelerate certain transformations.

Keywords

Transformation · Integration · Prediction · Prospective · Future · Inequalities · Policies

Introduction

To conclude such valuable book written by specialists with different backgrounds, gathered in a synthesis around life course epidemiology, is not an easy task. Indeed, it is not possible nor even suitable to propose a "conclusion of conclusions." This would necessarily mean a brutal reduction of each chapter. Nevertheless, drawing a common perspective might be attempted with a projection of important challenges for the conceptual and methodological direction in the field of life course epidemiology in occupational health. The pandemic is also important to consider, specifically, what it represents for the researcher. This can be a major rupture, a minor event with relatively little impact on occupational health in the future, or even an acceleration of trajectories that started a few years before. This question, approached through research published before and after the pandemic, will allow us to discuss the way of considering this event for the past but especially for the future of life course epidemiology in occupational health.

Objective

After reviewing the key perspectives from each chapter of the book, we will attempt a synthesis of the underlying concepts that are highlighted by life course occupational health, before discussing the pandemic effect and how to use such life course approaches in future occupational health research.

From Perspective...

Some emerging themes around the Covid pandemic, the need for longitudinal data, as well as expertise in the field and around the world were highlighted in the introduction (▶ Chap. 1, "Introduction"), which reviewed the challenges of life course epidemiology in occupational health research (▶ Chap. 29, "Occupational Trajectories and Health Inequalities in a Global Perspective").

Mixing approaches has been suggested in many chapters: understanding the complexity of pathways between occupation and health around occupation-specific hazard and social class, and how this increased during pandemic period, is illustrated by an interesting practical case (▶ Chap. 2, "Two Pathways Between Occupation and Health"). The exposome represents a way to summarily integrate the individual and their life course. The broad scope of the original exposome concept is a continuation of the refinement of tools and methods to capture the broadest possible array of environmental exposures and to analyze occupational health as a multilevel phenomenon (▶ Chap. 8, "Integration of Occupational Exposure into the Exposome"). As the authors concluded, there can be no skepticism or over-enthusiasm: the road will still be long to operationalize the notion of occupational exposome, but this is the way to follow while still respecting ethical principles. It also means the classical occupational factors are considered: emerging hazards and new occupational settings. For example, research on **chemical exposures** at work needs to consider all possible exposure routes (▶ Chap. 12, "Chemical Hazards at Work and Occupational Diseases Using Job-Exposure Matrices"). Inhalation exposure has been the traditional focus for most epidemiological investigations but there is now growing awareness of the importance of the dermal and ingested routes of contact and internalization of chemicals, consistent with the exposome paradigm. The increasing use of exposure biomonitoring and biomarkers discovery and validation thanks to the omics approaches and in silico studies is certainly a future consideration in chemical exposure and risk assessment in addition to job-exposure matrices. In addition to the use of **job-exposure matrices** for studies specifically assessing associations between workplace exposure and related disorders, it is increasingly clear that public health risk factor models should include all relevant factors in the "**exposome**," including workplace factors (▶ Chap. 6, "Job-Exposure Matrices: Design, Validation, and Limitations"). Workplace **biomechanical** exposures are also a significant contributor to the etiology of musculoskeletal disorders. Prevention of disability from musculoskeletal disorders requires an integrated approach incorporating work organization, workplace psychosocial factors, and policies at the employer and societal levels (▶ Chap. 13, "Biomechanical Hazards at Work and Adverse Health Using Job-Exposure Matrices"). Much of our knowledge of musculoskeletal disorders is based on current or recent working conditions; adoption of a life course perspective of work and health will improve our understanding of health promotion and disease prevention. **Work organization characteristics, management practices, and human resources strategies** generate domino effects on the conditions under which work is carried out and, consequently, exposure to work-related biomechanical and psychosocial factors using job-exposure matrices (▶ Chap. 16, "Psychosocial Work Environment and Health: Applying Job-Exposure Matrices and Work Organization and Management Practice"). Emerging risks associated with specific work conditions such as long working hours have adverse health effects, including cardiovascular diseases, worsened lifestyle behaviors, or occupational injuries (▶ Chap. 14, "Long Working Hours and Health Effects"). Though the measured cardiovascular impact is modest, long working hours have become a leading cause of death attributed to work. Possible pathways include shift work and night work that are essential features of work organization. In addition to enabling the continuity of services to the population such as the production of electricity, health care, transportation, or security, they are also used for the development of new technologies, as well as productive and commercial activities (▶ Chap. 15, "Health Effects of Shift Work and Night Shift Work"). The effects of shift work and night shift work have been widely documented in the scientific literature. In addition to such factors, psychosocial stressors at work are also frequent and modifiable cardiovascular risk factors. Screening for those factors in workplace, and the implementation of preventive strategies to reduce them could lead to important benefits for worker's cardiovascular health. A better understanding of sex and gender differences is needed to improve the equity and effectiveness of such prevention strategies (▶ Chap. 24, "Adverse Effect of Psychosocial Stressors at Work and Long Working Hours Along the Cardiovascular Continuum"). Furthermore, the underlying biological mechanisms remains scarce. So far, biomarkers of work-related stress and burnout have been used to identify the biological stress response. Recently, epigenetics has emerged as the key mechanism by which environment and genetics interact, making it an appealing target biomarker for stress-related phenotypes such as burnout. In the chapter (▶ Chap. 10, "Genetics, Epigenetics, and Mental Health at Work"), an overview of current knowledge on (epi)genetic mechanisms linked to work-related stress and burnout is discussed along with their potential contribution to our understanding of these phenomena. Moreover, the authors try to elucidate the potential translational contribution of (epi)genetics and its significance for clinical practice and life course research.

Transformation is the second concept. The **world of work and employment underwent profound changes** during the past 50 years, with the growth of new forms of employment that differ to traditional standard employment as one of its key features (▶ Chap. 18, "Adverse Employment Histories: Conceptual Considerations and Selected Health Effects"). **In this context,** Wahrendorf and Siegrist illustrated how key stress-theoretical notions of prevailing stress models can be used to identify adverse conditions of entire employment histories by describing six dimensions of emerging trends with relevance to health (work contract, continuity/discontinuity of occupational career, type and amount of earnings, job content, work scheduling practices, and social protection at work). The authors, on this basis, identify three types of adverse employment histories, labeled as "precarious," "discontinuous," and "chronically disadvantaged." **Technological innovation leads to a major transformation** and comes with great opportunities to improve job quality and the work situation of employees, but at the same time possesses serious threats to several aspects of job quality and to individual worker outcomes (▶ Chap. 4, "The Impact of New Technologies on the Quality of Work"). Indeed, the impact of digitalization on job quality and the sustainability of employment is ambiguous and largely depends on factors lying outside a strict notion of technology: It depends on how organizations, managers, workers, and worker representatives introduce new technologies and on the specific context of the worker. The increase **of atypical or nonstandard employment has transformed** both the structure and the functioning of postindustrial labor markets (▶ Chap. 3, "Transformation of Modern Work, Rise of

Atypical Employment, and Health"). From a policy perspective, differences across countries in the incidence of nonstandard work and inequalities in job quality, in transitions to regular employment, or in health risks point to a prominent role of institutions in governing the labor market and in mitigating the impacts of precarious work and inequality within employment systems. The **COVID-19 pandemic was asymmetrical with regard to occupations**, with particularly strong contagion risks in jobs that required personal proximity and interaction with person. This also very visible for some disorders such as mental problems. Indeed, work-related **poor mental health has grown since 2010 for some occupations**, with a trend that was apparent in the UK and European contexts before 2020, but the worsening trend in work-related mental health has increased during the pandemic period (▶ Chap. 17, "Occupational Differences in Work-Related Mental Health: A Life Course Analysis of Recent Trends in the European Context"). While age influenced work-related mental health, with the lowest levels of mental health observed around age 40, the effects of age were similar across occupations. The aging of the workforce did not explain the worsening trends in work-related poor mental health. Similarly, the worsening trend in work-related mental health since 2010 was observed across all occupations – there was no occupation specifically at risk of a worsening trend in recent years. There is evidence that temporary and self-employed workers experience **poorer mental health** than employees with open-ended employment contracts; however, there is also evidence that the self-employed experience greater well-being (▶ Chap. 19, "Precarious Work and Health"). In accordance with the models of work-related stress, and people's work transitions across the life course, temporary work and self-employment can provide benefits as well as disadvantages. This is likely to affect health outcomes and is a challenge for understanding the contextual differences and diversity of labor market settings and welfare regimes. The **gig economy has grown rapidly**, introducing new employment modes and platform-based algorithmic management (▶ Chap. 20, "Gig Work and Health"). It has attracted large numbers of often young workers across the globe into jobs such as self-employed couriers, increased by Covid-19 period. In the last decades, many countries **have shifted away from early retirement**, and initiated policies to delay retirement and increase employment participation at older ages. Overall, this has led to an increase in actual retirement ages and employment participation (▶ Chap. 25, "Pathways to Retirement and Health Effects"). However, this policy change has also given rise to discussions about the "right" retirement age. Nevertheless, the authors highlighted there are inequalities in healthy life expectancy between higher and lower occupational groups or higher and lower educated workers, and also men and women. Future revisions of retirement **policies should acknowledge these inequalities** and consider them in their policies. Additionally, a large proportion of older people exit paid work several years before state pension age and, although for some this may be for voluntary reasons, this chapter shows that poor health is an important driver of early exit before normal retirement age. Additionally, adverse working conditions are also related to early exit from paid work. Last, the Covid-19 pandemic has caused widespread social and economic upheaval and may threaten the life of retirement for today's retirees and the impact on the health of future retirees is less certain. Return to work after chronic disease is emerging to be an important subject in the occupational health and safety over the life course of individuals (▶ Chap. 27, "Falling Sick While Working: An Overview of the EU-Level Policy Framework on Returning to Work Following Chronic Disease(s)"). As the field of returning to work after chronic diseases is still emerging, further research, data collection, and availability of comparable statistics across different countries would increase knowledge on these issues and help better inform policymaking. The nature of work is changing at a rapid rate and is shaping the employment experiences of **people living with disabilities across the working life course**. As new occupations arise, they bring novel physical and psychosocial working demands, job skills and training requirements, and work arrangements and conditions that pose both challenges and opportunities for people living with disabilities at all ages (▶ Chap. 22, "Changing Experiences, Needs, and Supports Across the Life Course for Workers Living with Disabilities"). Workers' health and well-being throughout their working lives depend on interactions between risk and protective measures, and **such transformations need adequate evaluation and research**. While workplace health promotion carries a promise of supporting better health of the working population over the life course, there are many challenges that limit the approach (▶ Chap. 26, "Worksite Health Promotion: Evidence on Effects and Challenges"). Precarious employment is linked to adverse health effects, mediated through psychosocial risks of the working environment that hinder comprehensive workplace health promotion. Comprehensive work health promotion that emphasizes the importance of decent working conditions and workers' health and safety **should be an integral part of the change**. Common mental disorders affect persons in all age groups and a life course perspective is relevant to understand the often-complex relations between **common mental disorders and work** (▶ Chap. 23, "Working Careers with Common Mental Disorders"). Employers need better knowledge on how universal prevention can reduce risk factors in the organization and improve the psychosocial work environment. **Applying a life course perspective,** young people should be carefully introduced to their first employment, which can be seen as a sensitive period. The careful introduction is particularly important for those with a history of mental health problems. Persistent **gender differences** in responsibility for unpaid care work within homes and communities (▶ Chap. 21, "Gender Differences in Work Participation over the Life Course and Consequences for Socioeconomic and Health Outcomes"). It means that women's work life courses remain much more likely than men's to include reduced employment hours and periods of nonemployment in many countries, though possible policy solutions exist for reducing stubborn gender inequalities in access to high-quality employment and equal pay. A life course perspective highlights the importance of prior life experiences such as **where individuals grew up, who they grew up with, and their education and health status prior to working**. This chapter explains and emphasizes the importance of applying a life course perspective to the working lives of young adults (▶ Chap. 11, "A Life Course Perspective on Work and Mental Health: The Working Lives of Young Adults").

The last important concept is the development of **appropriate tools to evaluate** life course epidemiology. Data are central and **large-scale massive cohort data** in occupational health research has both advantages and challenges (▶ Chap. 7, "Challenges of Large Cohort and Massive Data in Occupational Health"). The combination of different study types, with different strengths and limitations, and collaboration between research groups across countries, certainly contributes to increased knowledge in occupation and health. Recent efforts have sought to develop new theoretical frameworks, concepts, and definitions in occupational health and to inventory numerous existing cohort studies and combine their data, to ultimately lead to more definitive studies in disease etiology. Statistical modeling might be challenging (▶ Chap. 9, "Methods in Modeling Life Course"). From purely descriptive methods requiring few or no hypotheses, some models needs to formally formulate life course hypotheses. With them come several statistical methods to measure how well they hold up against real-life data. Along the way, many difficulties such as missing data, heterogeneous data sources, or hypothesis hierarchy are discussed with tools and approaches available to handle them. One example is the sequence analysis framework that takes some key aspects into account by considering the previous trajectory as a whole unit of analysis (▶ Chap. 5, "Sequence Analysis and Its Potential for Occupational Health Studies"). It offers tools to describe and visualize these trajectories, but also to summarize the information by building a typology of the trajectories. Tools are also applied to labor and social policies, since national labor policies are important tools to improve the psychosocial working conditions, thereby they play key role in influencing individuals' employment and health trajectories (▶ Chap. 28, "The Role of Social and Labor Policies in Shaping Working Conditions Throughout the Life Course").

...To Challenges

We can distil the various challenges in life course occupational health around several axes: the importance of **integrated life course approaches** in a **world in transformation** with globalization and digitalization, the importance of considering specificities of different **populations** with their inherent **inequalities**, and the use of **improved tools**.

Figure 1 attempts to represent the different challenges of the epidemiological life course through a traditional life course epidemiological model. Indeed, this model as applied to occupational health initially developed the idea of longitudinal follow-up during and after the working life trajectory, punctuated by events that are considered as risk factors for adverse outcomes later on in life, especially those that have high risk effects (Fig. 1a).

We might add the different challenges that have been highlighted in the book to this model. First, the integrative approaches that we need to consider: events and effects must not be differentiated per se, because effects are themselves events potentially related to work, as well the effects may become an event in themselves as well. For instance, some working conditions might be associated with obesity or alcohol consumption, which in turn concur with changes in working conditions and might

Fig. 1 Challenges. NB: All of these aspect needs specific tools

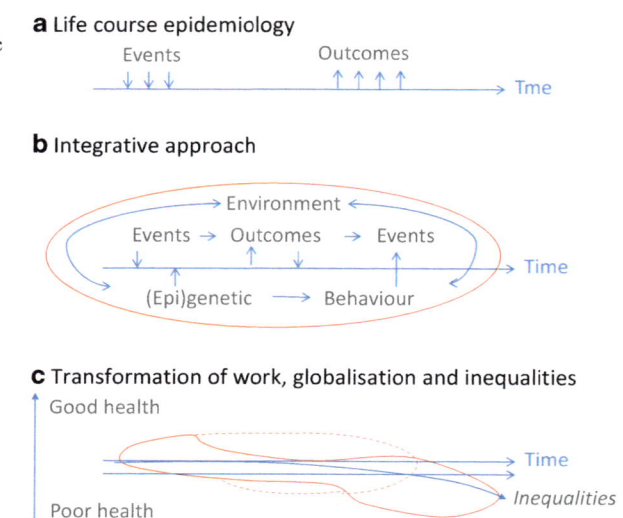

a Life course epidemiology

Events   Outcomes
↓ ↓ ↓   ↑ ↑ ↑ ↑ ────────→ Tme

b Integrative approach

          → Environment ←
    Events → Outcomes → Events
      ↓   ↑   ↓   ────→ Time
    (Epi)genetic ──→ Behaviour

c Transformation of work, globalisation and inequalities

Good health
                                            ────→ Time
                                            ↘ Inequalities
Poor health

be related to other health effects. Furthermore, these events not only explain each other but interact at different levels of the individual, collective, supra-collective, and societal levels. Indeed, some health determinants will have indirect effects on health through other determinants. For example, psychosocial factors will modify biomechanical factors which will be related to musculoskeletal pain (▶ Chap. 16, "Psychosocial Work Environment and Health: Applying Job-Exposure Matrices and Work Organization and Management Practice"). This integration of the different exposures that constitutes the environment that interacts with genetic, epigenetic, behavioral effects, and events is the concept of exposome (Fig. 1b).

Third, social and occupational change must also be taken into account, since the work environment is changing. The working world has changed in the last 20 years and will probably continue evolving in the next 20 years with greater digitalization of the world. However, this transformation is not only temporal but also spatial, with globalization affecting all countries and connecting workers across economies and societies. Furthermore, these aspects might also explain possible changes in the trajectory of some individuals, at different age through time, although not necessarily all individuals. While the transformation of the work environment has modified the average trajectory of occupational health for all workers, but its effects are particularly marked for subgroups of workers characterized by disadvantage, gender, and precariousness over the life course (Fig. 1c).

In each of the Fig. 1a, b, and c, we emphasized the importance of the developing tools that enable the collection of high-quality data on the different aspects life course epidemiology, integrating thus the exposome to different moments and places allowing us to consider the whole of life trajectory across different time periods. In addition to these data, mathematical and computer models, as well as statistical and conceptual models are absolutely essential to allow an understanding and correct predictions of current and future trajectories of occupational health.

Through Possible Rupture like COVID-19 Pandemic

Even if it is not possible with certainty to know the precise effect of the Covid-19 pandemic for now, it is interesting to use it as a potential breakthrough element in the consideration of occupational life course epidemiology. Indeed, the statistical modeling that has been detailed throughout the chapters of the book may be deeply modified by major societal events that were not anticipated.

In order to study the possibilities of the interactions between occupational trajectories and the pandemic, we have chosen a particular approach. We have voluntarily avoided making a synthesis by conducting a systematic review on the effects of the pandemic in relation to what has been published or what has been published in the last few months, given the difficulty of the absence of hindsight. We have preferred to take a pragmatic approach, looking for a synthesis that has been published a few years ago on the prospective in the broad field of occupational health and to analyze only the aspects related to the trajectories by comparing them with recent research done after the Covid-19 pandemic. This approach is subjective and limited to certain types of research but offers the advantage of not being biased by the per-pandemic evaluation.

We are going to precede this analysis with extreme and caricatural hypotheses on the effects of the pandemic on the trajectories: In the Fig. 2, we specify the three scenarios retained a priori. The first scenario is that of a rupture with brutal modification during the period of the pandemic (Fig. 2a). The opposite hypothesis is a stable episode without modification on any of the trajectories except a possible slowing down but without modification of the events and the effects at the level of the population (Fig. 2c). The figure of 2b illustrates an intermediate between the scenarios often summarized as accelerator of changes: The pandemic increases the trajectory without modifying the slope of the trajectory in a brutal way (compared to Fig. 2a).

A publication dating from 2017 by five American authors was chosen as a work of foresight prior to the pandemic. The publication was a synthesis of an event organized on the University of Washington to describe potential consequences on different communications and reading. (Peckham et al. 2017) The authors summarized in a table the challenges and emerging risks and trends for the health of workers in the future: They identified several types of significant transformation – changes in work organization, demographics with aging, diversity, and a presence of more and more important of people with disabilities, globalization, and interactions between work and nonwork factors. To these elements are added the effects of climate change, changes in worker groups and unions associated with a modification of funding and policies (particularly true in the USA but applicable to other environments), emerging technologies and capacities related to massive data, as well as the contribution of increased health inequalities. All these elements, supported by references and reflections raised during the symposium, were put forward as hypotheses for change such as the democratization of occupational health issues

Fig. 2 Possible pandemic effect (red box)

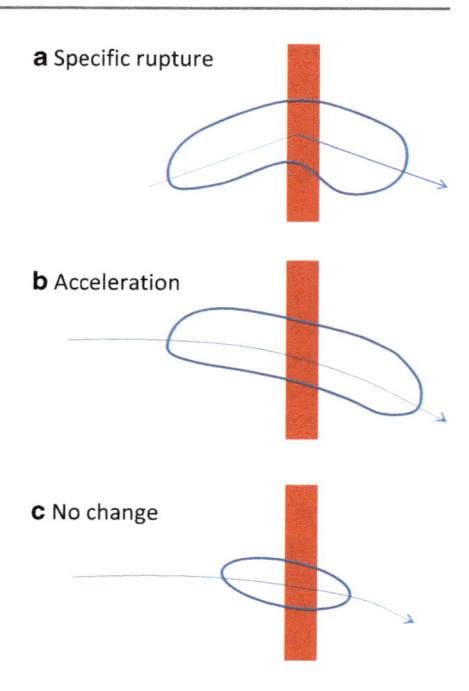

a Specific rupture

b Acceleration

c No change

(multidisciplinary approaches, the involvement of local politicians as well as citizen structures, industry, etc.) to broaden research and improve training by integrating richer concepts on risk exposures, the effect of work on quality of life, impact of new technologies and globalization issues, and finally to allow for the improvement and development of expertise in occupational health.

A synthesis has recently been published on the effects of work on the health of the workers after the pandemic.(Peters et al. 2022) The figure of the document summarizes the social, economic, and political environments during the Covid-19 pandemic and their effects on the health of the workers and working conditions. This figure continues the conceptual framework that was written in 2021 by one of the authors (Sorensen et al. 2021). We notice key factors that are discussed include globalization, improvement of the technologies, inequalities, public and sanitary policies, integrated approaches to working conditions, as well as the effect of worker characteristics on their health, security, and well-being. The comparison of these two documents written before and during the pandemic illustrates the great similarity between life course occupational health factors before the Covid-19 pandemic and now. Nevertheless, different details in the publications are worth being noted. The impacts at the level of the society during the pandemic include increasing heterogeneity according to the work sectors: some essential jobs were prioritized during the pandemic (e.g., health) from other job sectors (e.g., tourism). The changes in social and public policies were very heterogeneous depending on the country and on its economy, and some questions have increased, such as of the balance between work and outside-work life due to the rise of telework and with the consequent increases in certain inequalities (precariousness, gender, etc.). When we compare other sources of work determinants of certain pathologies, we also notice similar patterns, where general work exposomes were similar in 2016 and in 2022 (Roquelaure 2016; Roquelaure et al. 2022). Furthermore, new pathologies like Covid or even long-Covid have challenged workers in health and social care. This highlights the importance of not neglecting these patients in care, rehabilitation, and work (Descatha 2020; Sim 2020; Burdorf et al. 2021; Godeau et al. 2021). An interesting point is the evolution of research after Covid. After an exponentially increasing number of articles at the beginning of the pandemic, there are currently comparatively less research publications on other topic occupational health as observed in the many calls for tenders, reviews on research in this field of occupational health.

All of these different elements suggest that the pandemic represents an acceleration of certain changes rather than a rupture (or even a stable state). Prospective modeling needs to be carried out in the future to confirm or refute the facts of the pandemic on work and health trajectories in the field of occupational health.

To the Future Using Prospective Modeling?

One of the future challenges in life course occupational health is the ability to predict trends, based on the complexity of life course epidemiology approaches. These predictions are not only needed in the long term but also in the short- to medium-term periods. Indeed, if researchers and practitioners in this field could develop tools to overcome the challenges to life course occupational health posed throughout this book, it may be possible to make projections into the future based on these models (Fig. 3, with some subjects showed as example as arrows). Their purpose is not to look

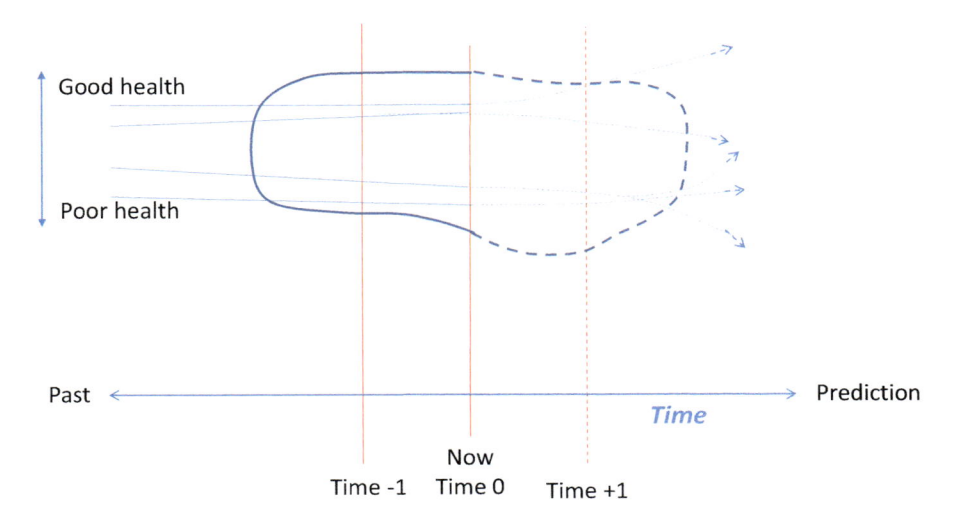

Fig. 3 Application of life course in the future prospective modeling

into the future in several decades, but to study on a time window that is neither too short (a few months) nor too long (a few decades), to examine the possibilities of modeling and to test the adequacy of the model as presented as a perspective in the tools. The possible advantage of these models is not in the analysis of their details, but on the prediction of valid global trends in the near future. This will enable us to provide answers on the major effects of the pandemic on occupational health, which may include negative and positive effects.

This life course approach will necessarily become more complex as it requires the integration of different complementary approaches, social transformations such as globalization or digitalization of our world, while enabling us to evaluate preventive actions that build from a passive understanding to an active prevention approach.

Cross-References

- ▶ A Life Course Perspective on Work and Mental Health: The Working Lives of Young Adults
- ▶ Adverse Effect of Psychosocial Stressors at Work and Long Working Hours Along the Cardiovascular Continuum
- ▶ Adverse Employment Histories: Conceptual Considerations and Selected Health Effects
- ▶ Biomechanical Hazards at Work and Adverse Health Using Job-Exposure Matrices
- ▶ Challenges of Large Cohort and Massive Data in Occupational Health
- ▶ Chemical Hazards at Work and Occupational Diseases Using Job-Exposure Matrices
- ▶ Falling Sick While Working: An Overview of the EU-Level Policy Framework on Returning to Work Following Chronic Disease(s)
- ▶ Genetics, Epigenetics, and Mental Health at Work
- ▶ Gig Work and Health
- ▶ Health Effects of Shift Work and Night Shift Work
- ▶ Integration of Occupational Exposure into the Exposome
- ▶ Introduction
- ▶ Long Working Hours and Health Effects
- ▶ Methods in Modeling Life Course
- ▶ Occupational Differences in Work-Related Mental Health: A Life Course Analysis of Recent Trends in the European Context
- ▶ Occupational Trajectories and Health Inequalities in a Global Perspective
- ▶ Pathways to Retirement and Health Effects
- ▶ Precarious Work and Health
- ▶ Psychosocial Work Environment and Health: Applying Job-Exposure Matrices and Work Organization and Management Practice
- ▶ Sequence Analysis and Its Potential for Occupational Health Studies
- ▶ The Impact of New Technologies on the Quality of Work

- ▶ The Role of Social and Labor Policies in Shaping Working Conditions Throughout the Life Course
- ▶ Transformation of Modern Work, Rise of Atypical Employment, and Health
- ▶ Two Pathways Between Occupation and Health
- ▶ Working Careers with Common Mental Disorders
- ▶ Worksite Health Promotion: Evidence on Effects and Challenges

References

Burdorf A, Porru F, Rugulies R (2021) The COVID-19 pandemic: one year later – an occupational perspective. Scand J Work Environ Health 47(4):245–247

Descatha A (2020) COVID-19: tribute to health care warriors, to their occupational health units, and to their strategists. Arch MalProf Env 3:171–172

Godeau D, Petit A, Richard I, Roquelaure Y, Descatha A (2021) Return-to-work, disabilities and occupational health in the age of COVID-19. Scand J Work Environ Health 47:408–409

Peckham TK, Baker MG, Camp JE, Kaufman JD, Seixas NS (2017) Creating a Future for Occupational Health. Ann Work Expo Health 61(1):3–15

Peters SE, Dennerlein JT, Wagner GR, Sorensen G (2022) Work and worker health in the post-pandemic world: a public health perspective. Lancet Public Health févr 7(2):e188–e194

Roquelaure Y (2016) Promoting a shared representation of workers' activities to improve integrated prevention of work-related musculoskeletal disorders. Saf Health Work 7(2):171–174

Roquelaure Y, Luce D, Descatha A, Bonvallot N, Porro B, Coutarel F (2022) Occupational exposome: an organisational model. Med Sci MS 38(3):288–293

Sim MR (2020) The COVID-19 pandemic: major risks to healthcare and other workers on the front line. Occup Environ Med 77(5):281–282

Sorensen G, Dennerlein JT, Peters SE, Sabbath EL, Kelly EL, Wagner GR (2021) The future of research on work, safety, health and wellbeing: a guiding conceptual framework. Soc Sci Med 1982 269:113593

Index

A
Accelerator of changes, 553
Accidents, 320
Accumulation, 5, 22, 61, 74, 138, 285
Active labor market program (ALMP), 513, 515, 517, 518, 520
Active prevention, 556
Adaptive strategies, 10
Adrenocorticotropic hormone (ACTH), 160
Adverse employment histories, 5
Adverse working conditions, 455, 532–536
Age, 284–286, 288–291, 293, 295–297
Age discrimination, 452
Ageing, 8, 284, 379, 478, 496–498, 502, 505
Agency workers, 321
Age-related inverted u-shaped pattern, 325
Agility, 351
Ambulatory BP, 424
American Heart Association (AHA), 434
Analytic methods, 461
Anti-depressant, 329
Appropriate tools, 551
Arterial stiffness, 426
Artificial intelligence (AI), 44, 45, 391
A sense of intergenerational unentitlement, 452
Atrial fibrillation (AF), 427
Atypical employment, 30
Automation, 286
Autonomic nervous system (ANS), 159

B
Bank staff, 321
Bayesian relevant life course exposure model, 146
Big data, 46
Bioinformatics, 130
Biologically effective dose, 197, 199
Biomarkers, 123

Biomechanical exposures, 214
  direct measurement of worker exposures, 217
  duration, 217
  force, 215
  frequency, 215
  hand-arm/whole-body vibrations, 215
  intensity/level, 215
  limitations, 217
  posture, 215
  repetitive work, 215
  self-reporting of exposures, 217
Biopsychosocial model, 392, 393
Blood pressure (BP), 420, 424
  ambulatory BP, 424
  long working hours and blood pressure, 425
  psychosocial stressors at work and masked hypertension, 424–425
  psychosocial stressors at work and uncontrolled hypertension, 425
Brain-derived neurotrophic factor (BDNF), 161, 164, 165, 167, 169, 170
Breast cancer, 250, 251, 257, 258, 260
British JEM, 201
Burden of disease, 229, 535
Burnout, 158, 161, 164–170

C
Canadian JEM (CANJEM), 201
Cancer, 233
  IARC, 257
  meta-analyses, 258
  night shift work, 257, 258
  studies, 257, 258
  systematic reviews, 258
Cancer registries, 100
5-carboxycytosine (5-caC), 163
Cardiovascular continuum, 423

Cardiovascular disease (CVD), 230, 234–238, 249, 256, 460
  arterial stiffness, 426
  causes, 420
  incidence, 426–427
  prevention guidelines, 421, 431
  risk factors, 421
  risk of recurrent CHD, 427–428
  sex and gender considerations, 428–430
Career advancement, 334
Career stage, 378
Careers with cumulative disadvantage, 313
Career trajectories, 382
Carpal tunnel syndrome, 221
Casual inference, 147–151
Casual workers, 321
Causality, 132
Causal models, 149
Cause of Death Registries, 100
Centre for Epidemiologic Studies Depression Scale (CES-D), 314
Challenges, 551
Change scores, 143
Changing nature of work, 378, 390, 393
Chemical hazards, 200, 201
China, 345, 347–349
Chinese couriers, 347–349
Chronically disadvantaged career, 312, 313, 315
Chronic diseases, 495, 497–499
Chronic stress, 236
Chronogram, 67
Circadian rhythm disruption, 250
Circadian system, 248
Climate crisis, 539
Cluster analysis, 70–71
Cluster quality, 70
Cognition, 368, 459
Cognitive function, 459
Cognitively stimulating work, 535
Cohort differences, 291
Cohort studies
  AGRICOH consortium, 105
  birth cohort studies, 106
  concepts and definitions, 110
  consortia, 103
  crop-exposure matrices, 105
  effects, 126–127, 285
  exposure measurement error, 105, 106
  INWORKS, 104
  IPD-Work consortium, 103, 104
  multi-center worker cohorts, 106
  participation rates, 106

population distribution, 109
pre-defined meta-analyses, 103
publication bias, 103
PUMA cohorts, 104
Common mental disorders
  capacity to work, 403–404
  in life course perspective, 402–403
  magnitude, 400–401
  right to work, 402
  sick-leave and rehabilitation process in, 408–409
  sickness absence and return to work, 412–415
  work instability, 407–408
Common mental disorders and work, 550
Communication, 246, 384
Complexity, 406
Comprehensive WHP, 472, 475, 479, 481, 483, 486, 488
CONSTANCES study, 313, 314
Consumer sovereignty, 347
Contact-free delivery, 350
Contextual, 7–8
Continuity/discontinuity of occupational career, 308
Contract type, 322
Contribution of work, 537
Convention on the Rights of Persons with Disabilities (CRPD), 378
Copenhagen Burnout Inventory (CBI), 111
Coronary heart disease (CHD), 256, 426–428, 430, 435
Corporate restructuring, 61, 65, 71
Corticotrophin-releasing hormone (CRH), 159
Corticotrophin-releasing hormone receptor 1 (CRHR1), 165
Cortisol, 160
Cotton T-shirt, 24
Counterfactual mediation, 150
Counterfactual model, 536
Couriers, 345, 347–349
Covariates, 72–73
COVID-19 pandemic, 11, 22–23, 158, 168, 274, 347, 349–352, 421, 462, 477, 488, 531, 539, 540, 549, 553
Coworkers support, 422
CpG8, 166
Critical period model, 60
Crowdsourcing, 131
Cultural and Psychosocial Influences on Disability (CUPID), 106
Culture, 7–8
Cumulative advantage and disadvantage, 537
Cumulative exposures, 214, 217, 218, 222

Index

D
Dangerous work, 46
Danish Occupational Cohort with eXposure data (DOC*X), 87, 219
Danish Shoulder job exposure matrix, 219
Data Aggregation Through Anonymous Summary-statistics from Harmonised Individual-levEL Databases (DataSHIELD), 114
Databases, 97
Data harmonization, 97, 114
Data Protection Impact Assessment (DPIA), 102
Decent and safe work environment, 412
Decent labor conditions, 480
Decision authority, 422
Decreased productivity, 409
Degree of precariousness, 322
Demand-control model, 269, 515, 533
Demand-control-support model, 421
Demographic changes, 288
Dependent self-employment, 322
Depression, 320, 531
Depressive symptoms, 313, 314, 329
Despatch workers, 321
Destandardization hypothesis, 449
Digitalization
  artificial intelligence (AI), 45
  Big data, 46
  of economy, 274
  information and communication technologies (ICT), 44
  information of things (IoT), 45
  of production, 44
  robotic process automation (RPA), 45
  of work, 44
Digital labor, 48, 50, 344, 391
Digital work, 287
Directed acyclic graph, 139, 148
Direct measures, 82
Disability
  communication and disclosure of, 384
  definition, 379
  and employment, 380–381
  future of work and, 390–392
  during hiring process, 385
  outcomes of disclosing disability information, 386
  prevalence of, 497–499
  and social inclusion policies, 502–504
  support and accommodations to sustain employment, 387
  support needs, 385
  transition, 381–384
  work environments, 384
Disability-adjusted life years, 237
Disability pension, 451
Disclosure, 384–385
Discontinuous careers, 311, 313
Dispersion models, 129
Dissimilarity measure, 69
Distance measure, 64, 69
DNA methylation, 163–170
Dose, 197, 202, 204
Dose-response relationship, 197, 202, 203
Duration, 217
Dynamic disability, 379

E
Early career experiences, 382, 383, 388, 391
Early identification, 409
Early retirement (1970-2000), 445, 549
Early work exit, 450, 453, 455
Eco-exposome, 124–125
Economic globalization, 532
Educational qualification, 530
Effect heterogeneity, 536
Effort-reward imbalance (ERI), 327, 422, 451, 453, 515, 517–520, 533
Embedded liberalism, 32
Emerging risks, 204–205
Employment, 48, 380–381
  contracts, 321, 336
  histories, 331
  interventions, 380, 382, 383
  rates, 446, 447
  regulations, 330
  relationships, 528
  security, 322
  status, 98
  trajectories, 331
Employment Precariousness Scale (EPRES), 310, 322
Employment quality
  representation and voice, 50–51
  terms of employment, 48
  work, pay and other rewards, 48
  working times, 49
  work-life balance, 49
Employment relations, 28, 320
  nonstandard, 29–30
  SER, 28
English Longitudinal Study of Ageing (ELSA), 313, 366, 458, 459

Enterprise level, 101
Environmental exposure, 122, 133
Environmental stressors, 125
Epicondylitis, 221
Epidemiological studies, 255, 256
Epidemiology, 123, 126, 127
Epigenetic age acceleration (EAA), 168
Epigenetics, 162
 DNA methylation, 163
 histone modifications, 163
 microRNAs, 163
 for work-related stress and burnout, 164, 165, 167, 169
Epworth Sleepiness Scale (ESS), 253
Ethical principles, 133
EU Framework Directive 89/391/EEC Safety and Health of Workers at Work, 482
EU-level occupational health and safety framework, 500
European Agency for Safety and Health at Work (EU-OSHA), 474
European birth cohorts, 107
European Community Respiratory Health Survey (ECRHS), 106
European Human Exposome Network (EHEN), 113
European Network for Workplace Health Promotion (ENWHP), 471, 475
European Pillar of Social Rights (EPSR), 504
European Prospective Investigation into Cancer and nutrition study (EPIC), 112
European Social Funds Plus program, 540
European Social Survey (ESS), 333
European Survey of Enterprises on New and Emerging Risks (ESENER) survey, 474
European Survey on Working Conditions, 333
European Union (EU), 248
European Union level policy initiatives, 6
Existential aspect, 408
Expert assessment, 82, 84
Exposome Project for Health and Occupational Research (EPHOR), 113
Exposome, 89, 547
 agnostic, 112
 algorithmic transformations, 114
 challenges, 112
 concept, 111
 eco-exposome, 124–125
 environmental exposures, 112
 infrastructure, 114
 job coding, 114
 life course, 112
 occupational exposure, 112–114
 occupational risk factors, 112

 origins, 123
 working life, 113
 xeno-metabolomics, 123–124
Exposome-wide association study (EWAS), 112
Exposure assessment, 201, 202, 204, 206, 217–219
Extended working life, 452
Extend working lives, 444
External exposure, 197

F
Family life courses, 367
Favorable working conditions, 455
Fight or flight response, 159
Financial crisis of 2007-08, 288
Financial independence, 532
Findable, accessible, interoperable, reusable (FAIR), 108
Finland experienced growth, 324
Fixed-term
 contracts, 32
 employment, 321
 temporary contracts, 307
 workers, 321
Flexible work arrangements, 532
Flourishing, 332
Force, 215
Freelancers, 322, 334
Frequency, 83, 215
Full-time employment, 307, 308
Fundamental cause theory, 34
Future occupational health research, 546, 547, 549, 553, 555

G
Gender, 358–370
 differences, 337, 550
 distribution in occupations and industries, 415
 perspective, 414
Gender empowerment measure (GEM), 362
Genetics, 161
Geocoded data, 128
Geographic information systems (GISs), 128–129
Geostatistical methods, 129
Gig economy, 8, 33–34, 344, 352, 480, 549
 occupational risks of couriers, 345–346
Gig workers, 321, 391
Global approach, 222
Global financial crisis, 530
Globalization, 206, 287

Global positioning systems (GPSs), 128
Glucocorticoid receptor (GR), 160
Grounded theory, 407
Growth curve models, 64, 144
Growth mixture model, 144
Growth trajectories, 141–145

H
Hand-arm/whole-body vibrations, 215
Health, 34–37
    mental, 367
    self-reported, 365
Health and Employment After Fifty (HEAF) study, 335
Health effect of retirement
    empirical studies, 457–460
    mediating pathways, 461
    research findings, 461
    retirement trajectories, 461
    theoretical arguments, 456–457, 461
Health Examination Survey (HES), 271
Health inequalities, 470, 471, 477, 484, 487, 538, 539
Health outcomes
    cognitive disorders, 258
    depression, 259
    metabolic/cardiovascular risk, 254–256
    occupational injuries, 253, 254
    pregnancy outcomes, 259
    sleep, 252, 253
    sleepiness, 253
    traffic accidents, 253, 254
Health-promoting workplace, 470, 471, 474
Health/risk behaviors, 473
Health selection, 331
Healthy ageing, 111
Healthy life expectancy, 447
Healthy worker effect, 426
Healthy workplaces, 470, 485
Hippocampal neurogenesis, 161
Hiring process, 385
Histones, 163
Holistic methods, 64
Human resources strategies, 547
Hypertension, 420, 425, 430, 434, 435, 535
Hypothalamic pituitary adrenal (HPA) axis, 159

I
Income levels, 48
Index plots, 66
Individual-level push factors, 450

Individual-Participant Data Meta-Analysis in Working Populations (IPD-Work), 103, 104
Industry, 98
Inequalities, 537, 549, 550, 555
Informal caregiving, 456
Information and Communication Technologies (ICT), 44, 45, 47, 48, 50
Inherent inequalities, 551
Insomnia, 335, 537
Instrumental variables (IV) analysis, 461
Integrated life course approaches, 551
Integration, 552, 556
Intensity, 83, 215
Internal chemical exposome, 122
International Classification of Diseases (ICD), 114
International Consortium of Agricultural Cohort Studies (AGRICOH), 105
International Labor Organization (ILO), 98, 268
International Nuclear Workers Study (INWORKS), 104
International or National Standard Classification, 82
International Standard Classification of Occupations (ISCO), 98, 114
Internet of Things (IoT), 45
Interventions, 434, 435
Intraclass correlation coefficients (ICC), 85
Intrinsic cognitive-motivational efforts, 328
Intrinsic quality of work
    health and safety at work, 46
    skill requirements, 47
Invisible disability, 380
Ischemic heart diseases (IHD), 435, 535
Iso-strain job, 269

J
JEM Constances, 87, 219
Job accommodations, 387, 389, 391
Job content, 309
Job demand-control-support model, 451
Job-demands-control (JDC), 327
Job demands-resources model, 327, 451
Job Exposure Matrices (JEMs), 3, 4, 99, 214, 218–220, 268, 270–274, 547
    based on existing exposure data, 84
    Constances, 87
    definition, 79
    design of, 82–84
    DOC*X, 87
    expert assessment based, 84
    generic JEMs, 200–201

Job Exposure Matrices (JEMs) (cont.)
  limitations, 88–89
  literature review, 80–81
  Matgéné, 86
  mixed approaches, 84
  O*NET, 86
  objectives of, 80
  in public health research and practice, 89–90
  specific JEM for, 202–204
  SYN-JEM, 85
  validation, 85
Job insecurity, 320, 322, 336, 380, 381, 389, 480, 518, 520
Job intensity, 73
Job quality, 42–44, 46, 51–53
  employment quality (see Employment quality)
  health and safety at work, 47
  intrinsic work quality (see Intrinsic quality of work)
  life course, 51
Job satisfaction, 332
Job strain, 518, 521, 533

K
Knee osteoarthritis, 222

L
Labor regulation, 230, 239
Labor Force Survey, 248, 324
Labor market, 176, 177, 180, 184–188, 337, 378, 380, 382–384, 389, 391, 392
Labor retention, 478
Large cohort studies, 96
Large-scale massive cohort data, 551
Large-scale registry data
  accessing, 102
  approximate, 97
  business/enterprise data, 101
  complete study populations, 102
  covariates, 101
  crosswalks, 99
  crude data, 102
  large sample size, 102
  misclassified (non-differentially), 102
  occupational exposures, 98, 99
  outcome data, 100
  population, 97
  potential confounders, 101
  rare exposures and outcomes, 102
  residual confounding, 102
  strengths and limitations, 102
  studies, 97
  unmeasured confounding, 101
Latent growth curve model, 144
Lateral epicondylitis, 221
Less developed countries, 529
Life course, 51, 123, 378, 381–383, 385, 387, 389, 390, 392, 393, 457, 528, 529, 537, 539
  approach, 7
  concepts, 182–184, 187
  epidemiology, 147–151, 181
  hypotheses, 145–147
  mechanisms, 187, 188
  paradigm, 60
  perspective, 177, 183, 184, 215, 222, 305, 314, 346, 457, 547, 550
  principles, 181–183, 187
  research, 183, 187, 188
  theoretical models, 187
  transition, 359–360
Life expectancy, 444, 447–448, 452, 453, 461
Lifestyle, 101, 220, 431
LIFETRAIL research programme, 22
Light at night (LAN), 250
Limited wake shift work (LWSW), 253
Linked lives, 10
Longitudinal follow up, 293–297
Longitudinal method, 61, 67
Long non-coding RNA, 164
Long-term care (LTC) workers, 481
Long-term goals, 539
Long-term sick, 451
Long working hours (LWH)
  adverse health effects, 231–238
  as an indicator for monitoring workers' health, 238–239
  cardiovascular diseases, 234–238
  definition, 228
  lifestyle factors, 231
  mental well-being, 232
  pathologies, 230
  as target for prevention measures, 239–240
Lost productivity, 320
Low back pain, 221
Low-skilled employees, 520
Low social support, 422

M
Management, 269, 274, 277–279
Marginalization, 412
Masked hypertension, 424, 425, 434

Index

Matgéné, 86
Mat-O-Covid, 87
Medial epicondylitis, 221
Mediating factors, 233, 236
Mediation analysis, 536
Melatonin, 249, 250
Mental distress, 233
Mental health, 180, 183, 187, 404–405, 455, 457, 458, 460, 473, 475–477
  literacy, 411
  at work, 402, 405, 410, 415
Mental health problems, 178
  identification and management, 183
  internalizing and externalizing, 184
  levels, 186
  timing and duration, 184, 185
  trajectories, 185, 186
  young adults, 176
Mental ill health costs, 401
Mental well-being, 232, 333
Messenger RNAs (mRNA), 164
Meta-analysis, 330
Metabolic diseases, 255
Metabolomics, 123
Methodology, 151
Methylation of the DNA, 163
MicroRNAs (miRNAs), 163
Migrant workers, 111
Mineralocorticoid receptor (MR), 160
Minimum number of measures, 84
Missing data, 148
Missingness at random (MAR), 148
Mixed approaches, 84, 547
Mixed models, 143
Modelling, 129
Moderation analysis, 537
Modern societies, 246
Multidimensional and multilevel conceptual models, 222
Multilevel models, 143, 296, 297
Multimedia models, 129
Multimodal interventions, 483
Multinomial regression, 73
Musculoskeletal disorders (MSDs), 214, 215, 220, 222, 535
Myocardial infarctions, 234

N

National Health and Nutrition Examination Survey (NHANES), 271
National health registers, 100
National Institute of Occupational Safety and Health (NIOSH), 221
National labor and social policies, 540
National population registers, 97
Nature of work, 176
Necessity entrepreneurs, 321
Negative public attitudes, 410
Neison Defence, 19
Neither in Employment, Education, nor Training (NEET), 185, 186
Nerve growth factor-inducible protein A (NGFI-A) binding site, 166
Network on the Coordination and Harmonisation of European Occupational Cohorts (OMEGA-NET), 97, 108
Neurobiology of stress, 159–161
New exposure settings, 206
New forms of work, 274
Night work/shift work, 9
  categories, 247
  definitions, 247, 248
  domains, 251
  education, 260
  health effects, 246
  meal timing, 261
  occupational medicine, 260
  opportunistic napping, 261
  physical activity, 261
  physiopathology (*see* Physiopathology)
  prevalence, 248
  schedule systems, 253, 260
  strategic light/dark exposure, 260
  working hours, 247
Non-coding RNAs, 163
Non-dependent/no children, 326
Non-fatal injuries, 320
Non-participatory settings approach, 472
Non-pecuniary factors, 328
Non-precarious employment groups, 322
Non-skilled manual occupations, 534
Non-specific back pain, 221–222
Nonstandard employment, 29–30, 304, 305, 307–312, 533
Nonstandard work, 29–31, 35
Nordic countries, 98, 100
Nordic Occupational Cancer Study (NOCCA), 99
Normal retirement age, 444, 450
Novel technologies, 111
NR3C1 methylation, 166
Nuclear industry, 202
Nuclear Receptor Subfamily 3 Group C Member 1 (NR3C1), 166
Null associations, 271

O

O*NET, 86
Obesity, 256, 367
Objective job characteristics, 43
Occupation, 98
Occupational cohorts, 97, 126–127
   concepts and definitions, 110, 111
   exposure assessment tools, 109, 110
   harmonization, 107
   inventory of cohort studies, 108
   meta-data, 108
   occupational burnout, 110
   OMEGA-NET, 108
   theoretical framework, 110, 111
   work participation, 111
Organizational and integrative model, 279
Occupational databases, 130
Occupational exposome, 4
Occupational exposures, 270, 271, 274–279
Occupational health, 74, 122, 126, 127, 133, 477
Occupational Information Network (O*NET), 219
Occupational injuries, 232
Occupational practitioner, 90
Occupational risk factors, 214
Occupational settings, 330
Occupational trajectories, 528–530, 538
Occupation exposure assessment, 196–199
OLdenburg Burnout Inventory (OLBI), 111
Older population, 444, 459
Older workers
   effective retirement age, 445
   employment opportunities, inequalities, 451–453
   employment rates, 446
   incentives, 445
   labor market participation, 449
   poor health, 455
   poor working conditions, 453
   social care budgets, 456
   workplace adaptations/opportunities, 455
Omics, 111, 124, 130
On job titles, 79
Opportunity entrepreneurs, 321
Optimal matching, 69
Organization for Economic Co-operation and Development (OECD), 176, 188, 321
Organizational approach, 275
Own-account workers, 322
Oxytocin, 161

P

Parallel Coordinates Plot, 67
Parenthood, 359
Passive labor market program (PLMP), 514, 517, 519
Path analysis, 142
Pathway model, 74
Patient or hospital discharge registries, 100
Patient-Reported Outcome Measures (PROMs), 111
Pension benefits, 444–448
Pension policies, 448, 462
Period and cohort effects, 297
Period differences, 290, 291
Period effect, 284
Permanent employment, 321
Personal autonomy, 532
Personal breathing zone (PBZ), 196
Personal identification number, 97
Personal sensors, 128
Person–Environment–Occupation–Model (PEOM), 403
Perspective, 546
Phenomenology, 406
Physical aspect, 408
Physical exposures, 533
Physical functioning, 459
Physical health, 457, 459
Physical working conditions, 453
Physiologically based pharmacokinetic (PBPK), 130
Physiopathology
   circadian rhythms, 249
   circadian system, 248, 249
   desynchronization, 249
   melatonin, 249
   SCN (*see* Suprachiasmatic nucleus (SCN))
   shift system, circadian disruption, 251
   sleep disorders, 250
Policies, 547, 549, 551, 553, 554
Pooled Uranium Miner Analysis (PUMA) cohorts, 104
Poor health, 443, 450, 451, 453, 455, 456, 462
Poor mental health, 549
Population at risk, 97
Population subgroups, 114
Positive health effects, 535
Posture, 215
Precarious careers, 308–313, 315
Precarious employment, 111, 470, 471, 480, 481, 486–488

Precarious work, 35, 389
  concepts and measures, 321
  flexible workforce, 320
  heterogeneity, 336
  in industrialized countries, 320
  life course, 325
  market sector approach, 322
  mental health, 329–335
  multidimensional approach, 322
  prevalence, 321, 323–325
  self-employment, 321
  sleep, 335–336
  temporary work, 321
  workers, 328
  working conditions, 287
  work-related stress models, 327–328
Predict, 555
Prediction, 553, 555, 556
Pre-employment skills, 382
Pre-retirement characteristics and
    activities, 456
Prescribed drug registries, 101
Prevention
  CVD risk prediction, 433–434
  preventive workplace interventions,
    434–435
  psychosocial stressors at work in
    cardiovascular prevention guidelines,
    433
  of risk factors, 485
Principle of agency, 181
Principle of life-span development, 181
Principle of linked lives, 182
Principle of time and place, 181
Principle of timing, 182
Process time, 65
Productive and commercial strategies, 246
Profile regression mixture (PRM), 112
Prospective modelling, 555
Prostate cancer, 257, 258
Proteomics, 123
Psychological aspect, 408
Psychological demands, 335, 422
Psychological distress, 329, 331, 336
Psychological health, 329
Psychological wellbeing (PWB), 329–332
Psychological work conditions, 330
Psychomotor Vigilance Test (PVT), 258
Psychosocial conditions, 220
Psychosocial ill health, 284–286, 288, 298
Psychosocial risk factors (PSR), 233, 471, 476,
    477, 480–483, 485, 487, 488
Psychosocial stressors, 9, 413, 422, 423

Psychosocial work environment, 305, 307, 309,
    472, 512, 515, 516, 520, 533
  characteristics, 453
  and health, 268–269
  job exposure matrix (JEM), 270–274
  occupational exposures, 274–279
  subjective assessment, 269
Public health, 89–90, 238
Pull factors, 450
Pulse wave velocity (PWV), 426

Q
Quality of work, 529
Quality of working life, 43, 44
Quantitative exposure score, 199

R
Radioactive chemicals, 202–204
Random-effect models, 143
Recent trends, 291–293
Recommendation, 532
Recovery, 63
Reduced health functioning, 535
Registers, 97
Registry-based studies, 96, 97, 102, 114
Regulatory non-coding RNAs, 163
Relevant life course exposure, 146
Reliability and validity, 85
Remote sensing, 129
Renin-angiotensin system, 431
Repetitive work, 215, 217
Representation and voice, 50
Research initiatives, 90
Resilient trajectory, 62
Respiratory Health in Northern Europe, Spain,
    and Australia (RHINESSA), 106
Restrictive labor market opportunities, 450
Retirement
  age preferences predictors, 451
  causal effect, 461
  cognition, 459
  early retirement, 445, 446, 450, 455, 458,
    461
  employment careers, 449
  and life expectancy, 447
  mental health, 457–459
  national policies, 445
  physical health, 459–460
  retirement ages, 443, 444, 448, 461
  transition, 449, 450
Retirement policies, 462

Return to work, 413
  after chronic diseases, 505
  EU-level approach, 500–505
  occupational rehabilitation, 505
Risk assessment, 128, 129, 132
Risk mitigation measures (RMMs), 350
Road safety, 345
Robotic Process Automation (RPA), 45
Robots, 45
Role conflict hypothesis, 365
Role loss, 456
Role overload hypothesis, 365
Rotator cuff tendinopathy, 220–221
Routine biased technological change hypothesis, 43
Rupture, 553
Rural entrepreneurs, 334

S
Screening, 426, 433–435
Self-employed workers, 322, 324, 328
Self-employment, 325, 327
  cross-sectional studies, 332
  disadvantages, 332
  entrepreneurs, 333
  ESS, 333
  homogenous group, 332
  languishing group, 333
  longitudinal studies, 332
  and mental health, 332
  positive impact, 335
  precarious work, 334
  prevalence, 332
  selection effects, 334
  SWB, 332, 334
  wellbeing, 332
Self-reported health (SRH), 460
Self-reporting of exposures, 217
Sensitive period model, 74
Sequence analysis, 64–65, 74, 139–141
Sequence of developmental changes, 3
Serotonin (5-hydroxytryptamine or 5-HT), 161, 165, 166
Settings-based approach, 472
Shift work, 9
Short-interfering RNAs, 164
Short sleep, 336
Sickness absence, 329, 409
Sickness absence with psychiatric disorders, 413
Sickness insurance, 406
Single nucleotide polymorphism (SNP), 161
Single working mothers, 370
Skill discretion, 422
Skill requirements, 47
Skills biased technological change hypothesis, 43
Sleep, 320
  disorders, 250, 252, 253, 257, 335
  disturbance, 320
  duration, 335
  problems, 335
  quality, 335
Social benefits registries, 101
Social capital theory, 456
Social class, 21–22
Social determinants of health, 124, 484
Social gradient, 533
Social inequalities, 529–532, 536–538
Social partners, 483
Social policies, 10
Social protection, 43, 50
Social protection at work, 309
Social security, 413
Socio-economic background characteristics, 52
Socioeconomic inequalities, 361, 452, 474, 515, 517
Socioeconomic occupations, 460
Socio economic position (SEP), 147, 332, 477, 531, 536, 537
Socioeconomic status, 237
Sole-traders, 325, 333
Solute Carrier Family 6 Member 4 (SLC6A4) gene, 166
Specification of gender, 83
Specific health conditions, 455
Stable, 553
Stage theory, 457
Standard employment, 321
Standard employment relationship (SER), 28
Standardized incidence ratios (SIRs), 105
Standardized mortality ratios (SMRs), 105
Standard labor contracts, 44
Standard open-ended paid employment, 327
State sequences, 65
Statistical methods, 139
Status, 23
Stigma, 410
Strength, repetition and/or awkward posture, 215
Stress, 61, 62, 284, 289, 290, 331, 333, 476
Stressful work, 534
Stressors, 348, 349
Stress-theoretical models, 305, 307, 310, 312
Strokes, 234

Structural equation modelling, 142
Subacromial impingement syndrome (SIS), 219
Subcontractors, 321
Subjective wellbeing (SWB), 285, 329
Supervisor support, 422
Support needs, 385–389
Suprachiasmatic nucleus (SCN), 249
Survey of Health, Ageing and Retirement in Europe (SHARE), 313, 346, 450
Sustained hypertension, 424
Swedish business, 334
Sympathetic nervous system, 431
SYN-JEM, 85
Systematic review, 459
Systematized Nomenclature of Medicine Clinical Terms (SNOMED-CT), 111

T
Targeted organizational developments, 539
Technical fragmentation, 19
Technological constraints, 246
Technological innovation, 548
Technology, 42–47, 49–53
Telomeres, 168
Temporality, 123, 126
Temporal-spatial aspect, 408
Temporary agency work (TAW), 31
Temporary employment, 325, 326
Temporary work and mental health, 328
    associations, 329, 331
    cross-sectional studies, 329
    employment status, 331
    longitudinal studies, 329
    pan-European labor market data, 331
    psychological distress, 331
    unidimensional approach, 329
    workers, 328, 330
    work pattern type, 330
    younger people, 332
Time, 65
Timing of life events, 8–9
Toxicokinetics, 127
TRacking Adolescents' Individual Lives Survey (TRAILS), 184
Trajectories, 3, 60, 64, 140, 183
Trajectories of work-related poor mental health, 285
Transcriptomics, 123
Transformation, 548
Transitions, 5–6, 64, 183, 378, 380–383, 388, 393
Trends in work-related mental health, 286–293
Turning points, 6

Type 2 diabetes (T2D), 255, 256, 431, 535
Type and amount of earnings, 308
Typology, 64, 67–71
Tyrosine hydroxylase (TH), 168

U
UK Household Longitudinal Study (UKHLS), 293
UK logistics sector, 349–352
UK Office for National Statistics (ONS), 324, 350
Unbalanced working conditions, 451
Unconventional pathways, 450
Underemployment, 322, 330
    benefits, 330
    rate, 530
Unpaid care work, 360
USA's Bureau of Labor Statistics, 325
U-shaped relationship, 450

V
Victim-blaming, 18
Visualization, 61, 66, 67, 74
Vocational training, 530
Vulnerability, 62, 63, 68, 124, 127, 351

W
Welfare regimes, 515, 518
Wellbeing, 367, 476, 488
WHO commissions, 539
Work, 268–270, 272–279, 363–364, 421
    automation, 286, 287
    autonomy, 332
    capacity, 404
    contract, 307, 308, 311, 312
    environment, 378, 379, 384, 386–389, 392
Worker
    empowerment, 50
    participation, 481
    precariousness, 331
    right to privacy, 50
Work exposures, 214
Work-family conflict, 455, 458
Workforce participation, 325
Working careers with CMD, 403
Working conditions, 238
    cumulative effect, 453
    empirical research, 453
    favorable, 455
    health and wellbeing, 320
    individuals, 451

Working conditions (cont.)
  occupational grade and health status, 453
  poor health, 453
  retirement, 453
  systematic review, 453
  unbalanced, 451
Working Conditions Survey, 248
Working environment, 479
Working façade, 406
Working from home (WFH), 350
Working life expectancy, 451
Working times, 49
Work instability, 407–408
Work intensification, 47
Work-life balance, 49, 50
Work organization, 239, 269, 272, 274, 277–279, 471, 472, 476, 478, 480, 481, 486
Workplace biomechanical exposures, 215
Workplace health promotion (WHP), 10
  definition, 472
  and health/risk behaviors, 473–475
  inequalities, 477
  legislation and policies on work-related psychosocial risks, 481, 482, 484
  and mental health, 475–477
  precarious employment, 480
  psychosocial risk factors (PSR), 480
  and workforce retention, 478
Workplace interventions, 434, 475
Work reintegration, 495, 503, 506
Work-related mental health, 8
  age differences, 288
  cohort differences, 291
  demographic changes, 288
  globalization, 287
  longitudinal follow up, 293–297
  period differences, 290
  recent trends in risk factors for, 291, 293
  work automation, 286
Work-related musculoskeletal disorders, 111
Work-related poor mental health, 284
Work-related psychological illness, 320
Work-related stress, 320, 327, 328, 336
  BDNF (epi)genetic regulation, 167, 168
  biological research, 158
  clinical practice, 169
  epigenetics, 164
  future perspectives, 169, 170
  HPA axis (epi)genetic regulation, 165
Work-related wellbeing, 334
Work safety, 352
Work scheduling practices, 308

Worksite screening, 434
Worksome, 4, 122
  biological matrices and analytical methodologies, exposure biomarkers with, 127–128
  causality challenges, 132
  conceptual and societal challenges, 131
  conceptual framework, 126
  exposure modelling, 129–130
  geographic information technologies, 128–129
  multidisciplinary consortia, 130–131
  occupational cohorts, 126–127
  occupational databases, 130
  omics and bioinformatics, 130
  online questionnaire, smartphones, 128
  personal-sensing technologies, 128
  technical challenges, 131–132
Work stress, 285, 345, 346, 348, 349, 421, 512–518

X
Xeno-metabolomics, 123–124

Y
Young adults
  accumulation, 183, 184
  contextual factor, 178, 188
  critical period, 182
  earlier life experiences, 176
  education and employment, 179
  emerging adulthood, 178
  intersectional research, 188
  labor market trajectories, 184
  life course perspective, 177, 180, 181
  mental health, 176, 180–182, 185, 187, 188
  overeducation, 179
  sensitive period, 182, 183
  trajectories, 177, 182, 185
  transitional period, 178
  transitions, 176, 177, 182, 186, 188
  work, 180
  working lives, 177, 179, 188
  world of work, 178, 179
Youth Guarantee schemes, 540
Youth unemployment, 531

Z
Zero-hour contracts, 321
Z-scores, 141

9783031304910